PAYMENTS AND CREDITS

EIGHTH EDITION

by

WILLIAM D. WARREN
Connell Professor of Law Emeritus
University of California, Los Angeles

STEVEN D. WALT
Percy Brown Jr. Professor of Law
University of Virginia School of Law

FOUNDATION PRESS
2011

THOMSON REUTERS

1 New York Plaza, 34th Floor
New York, NY 10004
Phone Toll Free 1–877–888–1330
Fax 646–424–5201
foundation–press.com
Printed in the United States of America

ISBN 978–1–59941–746–2

Mat #40880705

PREFACE

The Eighth Edition traces the dramatic shift from paper checks and notes to plastic debit and credit cards, ACH electronic payments and other electronic payments through imaging technology. Major federal statutes and regulations considered are the Check 21 Act, the Credit Card Act of 2009, and the 2010 revisions on debit cards under Regulation DD. Also discussed are the amendments of the ACH regulations that led to widespread check conversion in which paper checks merely commenced funds transfers carried out electronically. The increased federalization of bank-customer relations is discussed in detail.

We gather from the reaction of teachers to our book that most prefer to teach from a mix of cases and problems, and the Eighth Edition takes this approach throughout. We are grateful to Arthur G. Spence, Associate General Counsel of City National Bank of Los Angeles, and to the Bank for allowing us to use several of the Bank's forms. The cooperation of Mr. Spence and others at the Bank in sharing their experience with law students through the use of their forms has been outstanding.

We are deeply grateful to Tal Grietzer for his skill and dedication in preparing the camera-ready manuscript for publication. We also thank Robin Shofner, UCLA Class of 2011, and Dylan Raife, UCLA Class of 2012, for their skilled editorial assistance and research.

William D. Warren
Steven D. Walt

August 2010

ACKNOWLEDGMENTS

We gratefully acknowledge the permission extended to reprint excerpts from the following works:

The American Law Institute has given permission to reprint the following materials:

Restatement (Third) of Property (Mortgages) § 5.5 (1996). Copyright © 1997 by the American Law Institute.

City National Bank. All forms in this book are reprinted with permission of City National Bank, a national banking association, of Los Angeles, California.

Grant Gilmore, Formalism and the Law of Negotiable Instruments, 13 Creighton Law Review 441, 446–450 (1979). Copyright © 1979 Creighton University School of Law. Reprinted from the Creighton Law Review by permission.

Albert J. Rosenthal, Negotiability–Who Needs It?, 71 Colum. L. Rev. 375, 382–385 (1971). Copyright © 1971 by the Directors of the Columbia Law Review Association, Inc. All Rights Reserved. This article originally appeared at 71 Colum. L. Rev. 375 (1971). Reprinted with permission.

SUMMARY OF CONTENTS

TABLE OF CONTENTS

Chapter 3.

Chapter 4.

Chapter 5.

TABLE OF CASES

Principal cases are in **bold** type. Non-principal cases are in roman type. References are to Pages to this 2010 Edition.

Payments and Credits

CHAPTER 1

NEGOTIABILITY AND HOLDERS IN DUE COURSE

A. INTRODUCTION

We introduce the materials on payments and credits by a treatment in this chapter of two traditional doctrines unique to negotiable instruments. We will refer to these as the merger doctrine (the instrument reifies the obligation to pay; the holder of the instrument is entitled to payment) and the holder-in-due-course doctrine (the holder of an instrument may take free of claims and defenses on the instrument). As we shall see, the holder-in-due-course doctrine, conceived long ago under different social and economic conditions, has been under attack for years by courts, legislatures and commentators. The policy justification for this harsh doctrine is so questionable that there was debate on whether what now remains of the doctrine should be retained in Revised Article 3. However, under the drafting-by-consensus regime that prevails in the writing of uniform state laws, the doctrine was retained. In recent years the merger doctrine has come under criticism for the results it yields in securitization transactions. We will inquire throughout this chapter whether the decision to retain these doctrines in Revised Article 3 was sound. Whatever the merit of these rules they are still with us and an understanding of them is essential to those planning and executing payment and credit transactions, and we deal with them in some detail in this chapter. Since adoption of Revised Articles 3 and 4 has been widespread, citation of the provisions of these articles in the text of the following chapters will usually not be prefaced by "revised." Citation of the provisions of the pre-revision statutes will be prefaced by "former."

The law of negotiable instruments is based in large part on common law doctrines developed primarily in the last half of the eighteenth century and the first half of the nineteenth century. This law was codified in Great Britain in 1882 in the Bills of Exchange Act and in 1896 in the United States in the

Uniform Negotiable Instruments Law, usually referred to as the NIL. In 1952 the American Law Institute and the National Conference of Commissioners on Uniform State Laws promulgated the Uniform Commercial Code. Article 3 of the Code eventually displaced the NIL as the primary statute governing negotiable instruments. Article 4 of the Code complements Article 3 with respect to collection of negotiable instruments by banks and also governs the bank-customer relationship with respect to some matters relating to instruments. In 1990 Revised Article 3 was promulgated to take the place of the original Article 3. At the same time conforming amendments to Articles 1 and 4 were promulgated. Revised Article 3 and the conforming amendments to Articles 1 and 4 have been enacted in all but one state. In 2002 several amendments to these Articles were promulgated. Revised Article 3 is not a radical departure from the earlier statute; the principal concepts of traditional negotiable instruments law have been preserved. But Revised Article 3 differs from former Article 3 with respect to a number of important substantive areas.

B. Concept of Negotiability

1. Historical Origin

Professor Grant Gilmore sketches the background of negotiable instruments law in the following quotation from his article "Formalism and the Law of Negotiable Instruments," 13 Creighton L. Rev. 441, 446–450 (1979):

> Our law of negotiable instruments dates from the late eighteenth century.... Lord Mansfield and his colleagues in the late eighteenth century were faced with radically new problems for which they devised radically new solutions.
>
> The radically new problems all stemmed from the industrial revolution and the vastly increased number of commercial transactions which it spawned. When goods were shipped, they had to be paid for. The idea that the payments could be made in metallic currency, chronically in short supply, was ludicrous. The primitive banking system could not cope with the situation: the bank check which—a hundred years later—became the universal payment device was unknown. In effect the merchants and the bankers invented their own paper currency. The form which they used was an old one: the so-called bill of exchange which was an order issued by one person (the drawer) to a second person (the drawee) directing the drawee to pay a specified sum of money at a specified time to a third person (the holder). Frequently these bills, drawn by sellers on buyers, represented the purchase price of goods sold. In a more sophisticated and

somewhat later variant a mercantile banking house issued what came to be called a letter of credit to a customer. The letter authorized the customer to draw on the bankers for the purchase price of goods which he intended to buy: Through the first half of the nineteenth century Yankees trading out of Boston, armed with their letters of credit which were frequently issued by English houses, roamed the Far East assembling their precious and fabulously profitable cargoes of silks and teas and spices, paying for them with drafts on London. For half a century these bills or drafts were an indispensable supplement to the official currencies and were indeed used as currency: the bills which showed up in litigation had, as the case reports tell us, passed from hand to hand in a long series of transactions. And a draft on a ranking London house was a much safer as well as a much more convenient thing to have than a bag-full of clipped Maria Theresa dollars. These bills moved in a world-wide market, typically ending up in the possession of people who knew nothing about the transaction which had given rise to the bill, had no way of finding out anything about the transaction and, in any case, had not the slightest interest in it.

Against that background, the courts, English and American, put together, in not much more than half a century, the law of negotiable instruments almost exactly as we know it today. Indeed anyone who has mastered the current American formulation of the subject in Article 3 of the Uniform Commercial Code will have a startling sense of *deja vu*—I suppose this is *deja vu* in reverse—if he then goes back to the mid-nineteenth century treatises: time seems to have been suspended, nothing has changed, the late twentieth century law of negotiable instruments is still a law for clipper ships and their exotic cargoes from the Indies. The *deja vu* is false, a sort of floating mirage—but I will return to that later.

In putting together their law of negotiable instruments, the courts assumed that the new mercantile currency was a good thing whose use should be encouraged. Two quite simple ideas became the foundation pieces for the whole structure. One was the good faith purchase idea. The stranger who purchased the bill in the market was entitled to do so without inquiry into the facts of the underlying transaction or of previous transfers of the bill and without being affected by them: if he bought the bill for value, in good faith and in the ordinary course of business, he held it free both of underlying contract defenses and of outstanding equities of ownership. The other idea which, the first time you run into it, sounds like nonsense—the legal mind at its worst—was even more basic to the structure and indeed was what gave the completed edifice its pure and almost unearthly beauty. That was the idea that the piece of paper on which the bill was written or printed should be treated as if it—the piece of paper—was itself the claim or debt which it evidenced. This idea came to be

> known as the doctrine of merger—the debt was merged in the instrument. At one stroke it drastically simplified the law of negotiable instruments, to the benefit of both purchasers and the people required to pay the instruments. Under merger theory the only way of transferring the debt represented by the bill was by physical delivery of the bill itself to the transferee. The courts also worked out an elaborate set of rules on when the transferor was required to endorse, as well as deliver, the bill and on what liabilities to subsequent parties he assumed by endorsing. When these formalities—delivery and endorsement—had been accomplished—but not until then—the transfer became a negotiation and the transferee a holder. Only the holder—the person physically in possession of the bill under a proper chain of endorsements—was entitled to demand payment of the bill from the party required to pay it; only payment to such a holder discharged the bill as well as the underlying obligation. Merger theory was also of immense importance from the point of view of the paying party: not only did he know whom he was supposed to pay—the holder—but, under another aspect of the theory, he was entitled to pay (and get his discharge) even if he knew, to state an extreme case, that the holder he paid had acquired the bill by fraud or trickery from a previous holder. Parties with claims adverse to the holder were required to fight their own battles; they could not involve the payor by serving notice on him not to pay.

See also James S. Rogers, The Early History of the Law of Bills and Notes (Cambridge University Press 1995).

A 21st century business or consumer lawyer is wise to consider the doctrine of negotiability to be a legal landmine. In the next two chapters, we will learn how to protect your clients from it. In Professor Gilmore's sketch on the background of negotiability, we learn that it emerged centuries ago as a substitute for money. There surely is no shortage of money in circulation now, but when the law of payments was restated in 1990 in UCC Articles 3 and 4, the ancient doctrine of negotiability survived—limited somewhat but still around. And, as we will see, causing a lot of trouble.

We need a few preliminary working definitions in order to communicate.

A "note," often referred to as a "promissory note," is *promise* to pay another person, a "payee" (3–104(e)). This is a two-party transaction. A note is a negotiable instrument if it complies with the requirements of 3–104(a) (unconditional promise to pay money to a bearer or order, etc.).

A "draft" is an *order* by a "drawer" (3–103(a)(5)) to a "drawee" (3–103(a)(4)) to pay a payee(3–104(e)). This is a three-party transaction. A "check" is the most common form of a draft. 3–104(f). The person signing the check is the drawer and the bank on which the check is drawn is the drawee.

In most cases a "holder" is the possessor of an instrument that is either payable to that person or indorsed to that person. But the possessor of a bearer instrument is also a holder. This is a very important definition because we will be dealing with the rights of holders in due course, and a person must be a holder before it can be a holder in due course. 1–201(b)(21).

2. MERGER DOCTRINE

a. NEGOTIATION AND TRANSFER

(1) NEGOTIATION

The merger doctrine described by Professor Gilmore determines two important issues: (i) who can enforce the instrument against the obligor, and (ii) whom does the obligor pay to be discharged on the instrument. We discuss the first of these issues in this section on "Negotiation and Transfer," and the second in the next section on "Discharge."

The basic rule on enforcement is stated in 3–301:

> "[P]erson entitled to enforce" an instrument means (i) the holder of the instrument, (ii) a nonholder in possession of the instrument who has the rights of a holder, or (iii) a person not in possession of the instrument who is entitled to enforce the instrument pursuant to Section 3–309 [lost instrument] or 3–418(d) [dishonored instrument]. A person may be a person entitled to enforce the instrument even though the person is not the owner of the instrument or is in wrongful possession of the instrument.

This provision implements the merger doctrine as described by Professor Gilmore by stating that, with minor exceptions, the right to enforce an instrument belongs to the holder of the instrument. The following elementary cases illustrate 3–301 and some basic concepts and terminology regarding negotiation and transfer of instruments.

> Case #1. John signs a note and delivers it to Rachel. The note reads as follows:
>
> I promise to pay $1,000 on April 1, 2011 to the bearer of this note.
>
> The note is "issued" by John, the "maker," when it is delivered to Rachel. 3–105(a) and 3–103(a)(5). The note is "payable to bearer." 3–109(a). When Rachel receives possession, she becomes the bearer of the note as well as its holder. 1–201(5) and (20). Normally, Rachel is also the owner of the note. But the right of Rachel to receive or enforce payment is based on the fact that Rachel is the holder of the note, not on Rachel's ownership. 3–301.

Suppose Rachel loses the note and it is found by Peter who takes possession of it. By obtaining possession Peter does not become the owner of the note, but he becomes the holder of the note and thereby obtains the right to enforce it. 3–301. The transfer of possession which resulted in Peter's becoming a holder is described in 3–201(a) as "negotiation" of the note. Typically, negotiation is the result of a voluntary transfer of possession, but 3–201(a) applies to any transfer of possession, voluntary or involuntary.

Case #2. John signs a note and delivers it to Rachel. The note reads as follows:

I promise to pay $1,000 on April 1, 2011 to the order of Rachel.

In this case the note is not payable to bearer. Rather, it is "payable to order" because it is "payable to the order of an identified person." 3–109(b). Upon delivery of the note to Rachel, she becomes its holder because she has possession and she is the person identified in the note as its payee. 1–201(b)(21). In Case #1 we saw that a finder or thief can obtain the right to enforce a note payable to bearer simply by obtaining possession of it. That rule does not apply if an instrument is payable to an identified person. Negotiation of such an instrument also requires transfer of possession, but an indorsement by the holder is necessary as well. 3–201(b). (Note the UCC spelling, or misspelling, of "indorse.") Thus, the note payable to Rachel cannot be negotiated unless she indorses it; no one else can become its holder until then.

Suppose Rachel does not lose the note. Instead, she sells it to Peter for cash and delivers the note to him. In this case no negotiation to Peter occurs unless Rachel indorses the note. Indorsement is defined in 3–204(a) and can be made for several purposes. The most important purpose is to negotiate the instrument. An indorsement is normally made on the reverse side of the instrument and can consist of a signature alone or a signature accompanied by other words. An indorsement by Rachel consisting of her signature preceded by the words "Pay to Peter" identifies a person to whom it makes the note payable and is called a "special indorsement." 3–205(a). An indorsement by Rachel consisting solely of her signature does not identify a person to whom the note is payable and is called a "blank indorsement." 3–205(b). The effect of a blank indorsement is to make the note payable to bearer. 3–205(b) and 3–109(c). If either indorsement is made, Peter becomes the holder when he obtains possession of the note (1–201(b)(21)(A)) and may enforce the note as holder. If Rachel indorses in blank, Peter can negotiate the note to somebody else either by delivery alone or by delivery plus Peter's indorsement. 3–205(b) and 3–109(c). If Rachel indorses specially, Peter must indorse the note in order to negotiate it and may indorse either specially or in blank. 3–205(a).

By way of a reality check, we will see that the fact that a finder or a thief may be the correct person to sue on a note doesn't necessarily mean that this person will recover. If the maker can prove that the instrument was lost or stolen, she has a valid defense under 3–305(c) unless the person suing on the note can prove holder-in-due-course status. 3–302.

(2) TRANSFER

Although the right to enforce an instrument is normally obtained as a result of negotiation, the right to enforce an instrument can also be obtained in some transactions in which negotiation does not occur. Suppose Rachel delivers the note in Case #2 to Peter without indorsing it. What rights does Peter obtain? Because Rachel's purpose in delivering the note is to give Peter the right to enforce it, Rachel has "transferred" the note to Peter. 3–203(a). Transfer means that there has been a conveyance by the transferor to the transferee of the transferor's right to enforce the instrument. This transfer can occur only by "delivery," a voluntary transfer of possession (1–201(b)(15)), plus an intent by the transferor to give to the transferee the right to enforce. Since the note was not indorsed by Rachel, Peter cannot enforce the note in his own right as holder and cannot negotiate the note to somebody else. But as a result of the transfer from Rachel, Peter obtains Rachel's right as holder to enforce the note. 3–203(b). This result is commonly referred to as the "shelter doctrine." Armed with that right and possession of the note, Peter becomes a person entitled to enforce the note under clause (ii) of the first sentence of 3–301. In addition, Peter, as a buyer of the note for value, obtains a specifically enforceable right to have Rachel indorse the note so that Peter can become its holder. 3–203(c).

If, by transfer, Peter acquires Rachel's right as holder to enforce the note, why is it important whether Peter, in enforcing the note, is asserting his own right as holder or a right to enforce derived from Rachel's right as holder? The answer is burden of proof under 3–308, as illustrated in Problem 1 below. Read Comments 2 through 4 to 3–203 as well as 3–308(b) and the first two paragraphs of Comment 2 to 3–308.

PROBLEMS

1. Mark signed a note and delivered it to Patricia for value; she, in turn, delivered it to Teresa for value. The note reads as follows:

I promise to pay $1,000 to the order of Patricia on November 1, 2011.

Mark defaulted on the note and Teresa brought an action to enforce the note against him. In his pleadings, Mark did not deny the authenticity of his signature or raise any defense to his liability on the note. Teresa introduced the note into evidence and rested. Mark sought a directed verdict. Is he entitled to one under 3–203, 3–301 and 3–308 if the following facts obtained:

a. When Patricia delivered the note to Teresa she indorsed the instrument?

b. When Patricia delivered the note to Teresa she intended to pass ownership to Teresa but failed to indorse the instrument?

James J. White and Robert S. Summers, Uniform Commercial Code § 16 (5th ed. 2000).

2. Pete fraudulently induced Maria to issue a note to him. The note reads as follows:

I promise to pay $1,000 to the order of Pete on July 1, 2011.

In May 2011, Pete indorsed and delivered the note to Helen who gave value, was acting in good faith and had no notice of any claims or defenses on the instrument. In June, Maria discovered that she had been defrauded, notified Helen of the fraud, and stated her intention to refuse payment of the note. Helen, a busy executive, had no interest in incurring the litigation expenses needed to enforce the note, and, in August 2011, out of sympathy, gave the note, without indorsement, to her former husband, David, now an impecunious law student and desperate for money. She told him the circumstances surrounding the note and said that if he could recover anything on the note he could keep the recovery "for old-time's sake." May David recover on the note from Maria free of her defense of fraud? 3–203(b). What policy is furthered by Article 3 in this case? Comment 2 to 3–203.

b. DISCHARGE

A corollary to the merger doctrine that the right to enforce an instrument is the exclusive right of the holder is that the person obliged to pay the instrument discharges the obligation only by paying the holder. Until 2002, Revised Article 3 reflected this corollary in 3–602. The obligor who pays the holder is assured that nobody else can obtain a right to enforce the instrument if the obligor obtains surrender of the instrument from the holder at the time of payment. 3–501(a) and (b)(2). But there is also a corollary to the discharge rule: payment to a person who is not the holder might not result in discharge. This result raised the issue that caused the real property finance industry to vigorously challenge the traditional discharge rule.

PROBLEM

Debtor bought a home from Seller in part with money that she borrowed from Bank. In order to secure her $100,000 obligation, evidenced by a negotiable promissory note, she granted Bank a mortgage on the property. The agreement was that payments on the note would be made to Bank each month. Bank immediately negotiated the note and assigned the mortgage to Assignee. Neither Bank nor Assignee notified Debtor about the assignment. Bank deliberately withheld notice for the purpose of defrauding Debtor by continuing to receive Debtor's payments after the assignment. After a number of payments were made to Bank, Assignee notified Debtor that she was in default and that unless she cured her default Assignee would initiate foreclosure proceedings. Bank has "suspended payments" (closed) and its owners have absconded. Should Debtor receive credit for the payments made to Bank after it had negotiated the note and assigned the mortgage to Assignee? What result under 3–602(a) before the 2002 amendment? How could Debtor have protected herself in this case? Should she have demanded to see her note each month before making her payment?

The traditional doctrine of former 3–602 that payment had to be made to the holder to achieve discharge was disapproved in Restatement (Third) of Property (Mortgages) § 5.5 (1996). It states:

> § 5.5 Effect of Performance to the Transferor After Transfer of an Obligation Secured by a Mortgage
>
> [A]fter transfer of an obligation secured by a mortgage, performance of the obligation to the transferor is effective against the transferee if rendered before the obligor receives notice of the transfer.

The effect of former 3–602 was to impose the burden on the mortgagor to be sure that payments go to the note holder or its agent. This may be appropriate in commercial cases, but the Restatement view has much to commend it in cases involving mortgages on residential real estate. In these cases, as the Restatement commentary points out, it is unrealistic to require that consumer mortgagors ascertain the identity of the holder of their notes, either in the case of periodic payments or even for the final payment, given the practice in the industry of notifying the mortgagor at the time of payoff that the note and mortgage will be returned a month or six weeks later. Imposing the burden on the transferee of the mortgage note to notify the mortgagor of the transfer in these cases seems fair.

After a decade of debate, the Permanent Editorial Board, charged with oversight of the UCC, promulgated in 2002 an amended version of 3–602, set out below, which revokes the traditional rule that only payments to a holder discharge instruments. This change is a broad rejection of the discharge rule that prevailed for hundreds of years: it is not restricted to real estate, and applies to commercial as well as consumer transactions.

Section 3–602.

(a) Subject to subsection (e), an instrument is paid to the extent payment is made by or on behalf of a party obliged to pay the instrument, and to a person entitled to enforce the instrument.

(b) Subject to subsection (e), a note is paid to the extent payment is made by or on behalf of a party obliged to pay the note to a person that formerly was entitled to enforce the note only if at the time of the payment the party obliged to pay has not received adequate notification that the note has been transferred and that the payment is to be made to the transferee. A notification is adequate only if it is signed by the transferor or the transferee; reasonably identifies the transferred note; and provides an address at which payments subsequently are to be made. Upon request, a transferee shall seasonably furnish reasonable proof that the note has been transferred. Unless the transferee complies with the request, a payment to the person that formerly was entitled to enforce the note is effective for purposes of subsection (c) even if the party obliged to pay the note has received a notification under this paragraph.

(c) Subject to subsection (e), to the extent of payment under subsections (a) and (b), the obligation of the party obliged to pay the instrument is discharged even though payment is made with knowledge of a claim to the instrument under Section 3–306 by another person.

(d) Subject to subsection (e), a transferee, or any party that has acquired rights in the instrument directly or indirectly from a transferee, including any such party that has rights as a holder in due course, is deemed to have notice of any payment that is made under subsection (b) after the date that the note is transferred to the transferee but before the party obliged to pay the note receives adequate notification of the transfer.

The traditional rule worked well if the transferor and transferee were honest parties. When they were not, obligors, particularly consumer obligors could be damaged. Does the new rule adequately protect obligors against dishonest parties? See the Problem below.

PROBLEM

Maker issued a note payable to the order of Payee, which Payee indorsed and delivered to Transferee. The note was payable in 60 monthly installments.

(a) Neither Payee nor Transferee notified Maker of the transfer and Maker made six payments to Payee after the transfer before discovering that Payee no longer held the note. Must Transferee credit Maker for the amount of the six payments made to Payee? If so, is Payee liable to Transferee for the payments under this statute?

(b) Payee did not notify Maker of the transfer but Transferee gave adequate notification to Maker. Maker, a financially unsophisticated person, was not familiar with Transferee, and, since she had heard nothing from Payee, was suspicious about sending any money to Transferee. Maker first phoned, then wrote Payee asking what she should do. Payee, a crook, told Maker to continue making payments to it because it was Transferee's agent for collection. Must Transferee credit Maker for the payments made to Payee after its notice to Maker?

3. Merger Doctrine and Securitization

While the UCC Permanent Editorial Board and Restatement of Property drafters argued for years about whom to pay in cases in which a mortgage has been assigned—an issue which caused very little trouble owing to the self-interest of assignees in seeing that debtors were promptly notified about transfers—a revolution in real property finance was occurring that raised a more basic issue about the merger doctrine: who can enforce a negotiable real property mortgage note that has been securitized?

Until the 1970s, banks making home loans usually held those loans, evidenced by a negotiable note and a mortgage document, in the bank's own portfolio, receiving monthly payments until the loan was paid off, in, say, 20 years. New loans had to be funded from the bank's deposit accounts. But rising demand for home mortgage credit forced banks to seek other sources for credit. The practice of securitization was devised to give real property lenders the liquidity that they sought. Briefly stated, in a home mortgage securitization, loans to real property buyers held by the the bank that made the loans (originating bank) are sold in batches to an entity, the sponsor, which pools the loans and transfers them to a trust. Fractional interests in the loans in the trust are then sold to investors as securities (usually bonds). The proceeds from these sales are used to pay the originating banks for the loans sold, funds which these banks can then lend to new customers. The cash flow from the mortgages in the trust goes to the investors holding the securities as periodic payments. This process transforms static bank loans into tradeable asset-based securities. An essential party to a securitization transaction is the servicer, which collects the payments from the mortgage debtors and monitors the assets on behalf of the trust. This party must deal with defaulting debtors. The servicer may be the originator bank. Among the major mortgage servicers are J.P. Morgan Chase, Wells Fargo and Bank of America. Securitization started with real property mortgages but rapidly spread to other enterprises that produce a stable cash flow: automobile financing, bank credit cards, collateralized debt obligations, student loans and the like. The practice started in the United States but is now international in scope. In this brief introduction, we ignore the bankruptcy and corporate finance aspects of securitization as being unrelated to the merger issues regarding negotiable instruments.

The following opinion demonstrates the difficulties of applying negotiable instruments doctrine in a case involving securitization of home loans.

In re Hwang

United States Bankruptcy Court, Central District, California, 2008.
396 B.R. 757.

■ SAMUEL L. BUFFORD, BANKRUPTCY JUDGE

[Eds. Mortgageit made a loan to Hwang to enable him to purchase real property. Debtor executed a negotiable promissory note for the amount of the loan payable to Mortgageit and secured by a trust deed (a form of mortgage) on the property. Mortgageit sold the note, duly indorsed, to IndyMac, which sold the rights under the note to Freddie Mac, but retained possession of the note. Presumably Freddie Mac sponsored a securitization pool and sold the rights in the note to the pooling trust, which issued securities to investors. Hwang defaulted on his payments and IndyMac, acting as the servicer, moved in the bankruptcy court for relief from the automatic stay that was triggered by Debtor's filing in Chapter 7 bankruptcy so that it could foreclose on the trust deed under state law. IndyMac came to court in possession of the original promissory note properly indorsed and asserted its rights as holder of the note under 3-301. In a path-breaking decision, the court denied the motion for relief from the stay. In effect, the court said that the holder of a properly indorsed negotiable note should not be able lift the stay preparatory to enforcing it by foreclosure unless certain other parties joined.]

III. DISCUSSION

IndyMac argues that it is entitled to enforce the note because it possesses the note and the note shows it as transferee and no indorsement transferring it to any other party....

A motion for relief from the automatic stay must satisfy both substantive and procedural requirements. The substantive requirements are provided by [Bankruptcy Code] § 362(d). The procedural requirements are imposed by the United States Constitution (due process) and the Federal Rules of Bankruptcy Procedure (which mostly incorporate the Federal Rules of Civil Procedure). The applicable rules here are the "real party in interest" rule and the "required joinder" rule.

The court finds that IndyMac is entitled to enforce the note, notwithstanding the sale to Freddie Mac. However, in coming to federal court, IndyMac must comply with the applicable procedures in this court. Two of these rules, the real party in interest rule and the required joinder rule, each requires IndyMac to join the present owner of the note in this motion for relief from stay, which it has refused to do.

A. Right to Enforce the Note

Since a party (such as IndyMac in this case) that seeks relief under § 362(d) does so in order to enforce rights that have been stayed by § 362(a), it is necessary to consider who is entitled to enforce the note under the substantive law that governs those rights. Thus, for a relief from stay motion based on a promissory note, the court must look to the substantive law that governs promissory notes.

Bankruptcy law does not provide for the enforcement of promissory notes generally. In the absence of bankruptcy law, the legal obligations of the parties are determined by the applicable non-bankruptcy law, which is usually state law.

In the United States, the law of promissory notes is not unified at the federal level. Instead, each state has its own law on promissory notes. However, every state has adopted a version of the UCC to govern negotiable promissory notes.

1. Relevant Law of Negotiable Instruments

The substantive California law that governs negotiable instruments is UCC Article 3. A negotiable instrument (or more briefly, an "instrument") typically takes one of two forms: a promissory note (designated as a "note"), or a draft (such as a check). This case involves a note secured by a deed of trust.

An instrument (including a secured note) may only be enforced by the "holder" of the note *See* UCC § 3-301(a). For an instrument payable to an identified person (such as the note in this case), there are two requirements for a person to qualify as a holder: (a) the person must be in possession of the instrument, and (b) the instrument must be payable to that person. *See* UCC § 1-201(21) ("holder").

> The payee of an instrument may negotiate it by indorsing it and delivering it to another person, who then becomes its holder (and entitled to enforce it)....
>
> A fundamental feature of negotiable instruments is that they are transferred by the delivery of possession, not by contract or assignment. The transfer of an instrument "vests in the transferee any right of the transferor to enforce the instrument...." UCC § 3-203(b). Thus, the right to enforce a negotiable instrument is only transferable by delivery of the instrument itself. UCC § 3-203.

The transfer of a negotiable instrument has an additional requirement: the transferor must indorse the instrument to make it payable to the transferee. UCC § 3-205(a). Alternatively, the transferor may indorse the instrument in blank, and thereby make it enforceable by anyone in its possession (much like paper currency). *See* UCC § 3-205(b)....

2. Who May Enforce the Note in this Case

IndyMac contends, and the court assumes without deciding, that the note here at issue is a negotiable instrument.... Thus IndyMac must be the holder of the note to entitle it to enforce the note (including bringing this relief from stay motion)....

In this case, the note is payable to IndyMac (pursuant to its negotiation from Mortgageit to IndyMac), and IndyMac had possession of the note at the time that the motion was filed. Under these facts, IndyMac qualifies as the holder of the note.

3. Sale of the Note to Freddie Mac

In this case IndyMac sold the note to Freddie Mac, which in turn most likely sold it again as part of a securitization transaction. Insofar as the record before the court discloses, the owner of the note today is unknown.

In this case, IndyMac has not delivered the note to Freddie Mac (or its successor): IndyMac still possesses the note. In addition, the note bears no indication of a transfer: it still shows IndyMac as the payee (pursuant to the indorsement from Mortgageit). In consequence, IndyMac remains the holder of the note and is entitled to enforce it under UCC § 3-301(a): the right to enforce the note has not yet passed to Freddie Mac or its successor owner of the note....

The foregoing makes it clear that no successor to IndyMac presently has a right to enforce the note, because IndyMac still has possession of the note.

This raises the question of who, if anybody, is presently entitled to enforce the note in these circumstances....

In the court's view the holder of a note is entitled to enforce it, notwithstanding sale of the note to another party, until the note is delivered to the purchaser (after indorsement, if appropriate). This assures that, notwithstanding the sale of the note and the failure to deliver the note pursuant to the sale, a holder exists that may enforce the note against the obligor. Thus, the court holds that, notwithstanding the sale of the note, IndyMac remains the holder of the note and is entitled to enforce it.

The debtor is not at risk in making payments on the note to IndyMac instead of the owner of the note. UCC § 3-602 provides that any payment to a "person entitled to enforce the instrument" must be credited against the note, even if the debtor knows that a different party is claiming ownership of or an interest in the note.

B. Real Party in Interest

IndyMac's substantive right to enforce the note, as the holder, does not dispose of the motion before the court. In coming to federal court to enforce this right, IndyMac must comply with the applicable procedures of federal court. Two such procedures stand in the way of granting the motion for relief from stay in this case. The first procedural problem arises from the real party in interest rule.

Rule 17 of the Federal Rules of Civil Procedure provides: "An action must be prosecuted in the name of the real party in interest." The purpose of this rule is to require that an action be brought "in the name of the party who possesses the substantive right being asserted under the applicable law...."6A WRIGHT, MILLER & KANE, FEDERAL PRACTICE AND PROCEDURE: CIVIL 2d § 1541 (1990) ("WRIGHT")....

1. Real Party in Interest After Securitization

If a loan has been securitized, the real party in interest is the trustee of the securitization trust, not the servicing agent. *See LaSalle Bank N.A. v. Nomura Asset Capital Corp.,* 180 F.Supp.2d 465, 469-71 (S.D.N.Y.2001) ("*LaSalle-Nomura*"); *accord, LaSalle Bank N.A. v. Lehman Bros. Holdings, Inc.,* 237 F.Supp.2d 618, 631-34 (D.Md.2002) (" *LaSalle-Lehman* "). This rule does not turn on who is in possession of the note....

In this case, although it is most likely that the note here at issue has been included in a securitization, IndyMac has refused to provide any information about the present owner of the note, to join the owner as a moving party, or to provide copies of any of the relevant contracts. Because IndyMac has not provided the relevant documents, the court cannot determine the identity of the real party in interest.

If the note is part of a securitization, the burden of joining the owner of the note is not substantial. A securitization typically involves the creation of a trust, the appointment of a trustee, a transfer to the trust of some ten thousand secured real estate notes (such as the one involved in this case) and the sale of interests in the trust to a substantial number of investors. *See generally,* Katherine Porter, *Misbehavior and Mistake in Bankruptcy Mortgage Claims,* 87 TEX. L.REV. 121, 126-28 (2008). The trustee of the trust is authorized, pursuant to trust law, to act on behalf of the trust. Thus only the trustee, and not the investors, should be joined as the owner of the note at issue. Indeed, this is exactly what happened in both *LaSalle-Nomura* and *LaSalle-Lehman*....

The court concludes that the real party in interest has not joined in the motion before the court. Indeed, neither the court nor IndyMac even knows who the real party in interest is. Pursuant to Rule 17(a)(3), the court must give IndyMac a reasonable amount of time to accomplish this joinder. Despite two continuances (totaling more than two months) to accomplish this joinder, IndyMac has refused to join the owner of the note in this motion. Thus, the motion must be denied on these grounds

...

C. Required Joinder of Parties

Rule 17 is not the end of the procedural difficulties before the court. Movant must also comply with the joinder requirements of Rule 19 by bringing before the court every person with an interest in the note.

Rule 17 must be interpreted together with Rule 19, which requires the joinder of parties in appropriate circumstances. *See* 6A WRIGHT § 1543. IndyMac fails to satisfy the required joinder of parties rule in this case....

There is no precise formula for determining whether a particular non-party must be joined under Rule 19(a). The application of the rule turns on the facts of the individual case in light of the general policies of (a) avoiding multiple litigation, (b) providing the parties with complete and effective relief in a single action, and (c) protecting the absent persons from the possible prejudicial effect of deciding the case without them. 7 WRIGHT § 1604.

IndyMac gives no explanation for its failure to join the owner of the note in this motion. The likely reason is that IndyMac does not know who the owner is, and thus cannot have any authority to join the owner voluntarily. If IndyMac were the duly authorized loan servicer for the owner, the servicing agreement would presumably authorize IndyMac to join the owner of the note in this motion, and the problem would disappear. If the servicing agreement did not grant this authority, IndyMac should have obtained authority from the owner to join the owner as a movant in this case....

.... As stated above, the court has given IndyMac more than two months to join the owner of the note, and IndyMac has failed and refused to do so.

IV. CONCLUSION

In conclusion, the court finds upon reconsideration that IndyMac is entitled to enforce the secured note here at issue. However, it must satisfy the procedural requirements of federal law in seeking relief from the automatic stay for this purpose. These requirements include joining the owner of the note on two separate grounds: it is the real party in interest under Rule 17, and it is a required party under Rule 19.

Because IndyMac has failed and refused to join the owner of the secured note, the motion for relief from stay is denied.

NOTES

1. Kenneth E. Scott and John B. Taylor, Why Toxic Assets Are So Hard to Clean Up, Wall St. J., July 20, 2009, at A13, describes what probably happened to Mr. Hwang's mortgage rights: "The bulk of toxic assets are based on residential mortage-backed securities (RMBS), in which thousands of mortgages were gathered into mortgage pools. The returns on these pools were then sliced into a hierarchy of 'tranches' that were sold to investors as separate classes of securities. The most senior tranches, rated AAA, received the lowest returns, and then they went down the line to lower ratings and finally to the unrated 'equity' tranches at the bottom. But the process didn't stop there. Some tranches from one mortgage pool were combined with tranches from other mortgage pools...." Who owns Mr. Hwang's mortgage? IndyMac

probably purchased large pools of mortgage loans on an ongoing basis and, in turn, sold them to different sponsors to be securitized. Without documentation enabling title to be traced, IndyMac would have a hard time finding the owner of Mr. Hwang's mortage loan. IndyMac's failure to join the owner of Hwang's note in its motion suggests that it was unable to identify the owner.

2. Is the decision in *Hwang* just judicial backlash against sloppy documentation on the part of the securitization industry that has been so evident in subprime securitizations? Courts have become impatient with loan servicers attempting to enforce mortgage loans without being able to produce a duly negotiated note. See In re Foreclosure Cases, 2007 WL 3232430 (N.D. Ohio Oct. 31, 2007). Or is something bigger going on in this case? Does it show that in the securitization context, the use of paper negotiable promissory notes that must be stored, delivered and presented for payment in enforcement cases is a relic of a bygone age? In *Hwang*, Judge Bufford acknowledged the time-honored rule stated in 3-301 that, under the merger doctrine, the holder is the party to enforce the instrument. However, Federal Rules of Civil Procedure Rules 17 and 19 together require the holder of the note to join parties with interests in it. Judge Bufford speaks of the trust investors as "owners" of the note who are the real parties in interest and must be represented in enforcement of securitized notes. He appears to require the owners to join even if they have authorized the holder of the note to enforce it on their behalf.

Maybe Judge Bufford is on to something. Under the merger doctrine, ownership is not in issue; the possessor of the negotiable note duly indorsed has all the enforcement rights. But when rights in a $100,000 loan are held in a securitization trust and spread all over the world in fractionalized units, the merger doctrine makes no sense. Modern contract law is vastly superior to 18th century negotiable instruments doctrines in dealing with the exigencies of securitization. The existence of paper negotiable instruments gathering dust in the trustee's Document Custody file a thousand of miles away is just a troublesome irrelevance. Ruth Simon, Loan Proposal Shifts Risk on to Lenders, Wall St. J., July 15, 2009, at C9, discusses proposed industry guidelines aimed at restoring credibility to the mortgage securitization market that "collapsed in the wake of rising delinquencies and foreclosures from poor underwriting practices and fraud" in 2008. A number of contractual provisions concerning warranties and representations were discussed; no mention was made of negotiable instruments. Are electronic "instruments" the answer to the securitization puzzle? For a discussion of alternatives to the current merger doctrine, see Neil B. Cohen, The Calamitous Law of Notes, 68 Ohio St. L.J. 161, 182 (2007).

3. There has been a market response to the huge increase in the trading of mortgages driven by securitization. Mortgage Electronic Registration System (MERS) Corporation is a private corporation that manages the MERS system for tracking the transfer of ownership and servicing of mortgages electronically. Under the system, participating lenders list MERS as the mortgagee in the official records maintained at registry of deeds offices. This enables lenders and their transferees to sell their mortgages without having to record the sale in the registry of deeds. Instead, MERS records the sales electronically in its system. Avoiding multiple recordations in official registries produces savings (and avoids errors) that are significant when profit margins on home loans sold in the secondary market are thin. Participating lenders deal separately with the promissory notes associated with their mortgage loans. Membership in MERS includes Fannie Mae, Freddie Mac, Ginnie Mae and the Federal Home Loan Bank, and accounts for about one half of domestic mortgages. The typical loan document lists MERS as the nominee of the mortgage lender. Litigation has focused on whether, as a nominee, MERS has an interest in the mortgage entitling it to foreclose or receive notice in the mortgagor's foreclosure. See, e.g., Landmark Nat'l Bank v. Kesler, 216 P.3d 158 (Kan. 2009); Jackson v. MERS, 770 N.W.2d 487 (Minn. 2009). See Barkley Clark & Barbara Clark, The Law of Bank Deposits, Collections and Credit Cards, ¶¶ 1.08[10][a][iv] and 2.09[2] (2009).

C. Formal Requisites of Negotiable Instruments

Mechanical Tests. The consequences of the use of negotiable instruments vary greatly from those of ordinary contracts. What kinds of contracts qualify for the special treatment accorded negotiable instruments? Under Article 3, as under the common law, form follows function.

Merger theory and the ability of a good faith purchaser for value to take free of claims and defenses with respect to the instrument were based on a separation of the right to payment represented by the instrument from the underlying transaction giving rise to the instrument. But merger theory assumed that the terms of the instrument were not inconsistent with separation from the underlying transaction, and that the terms of the right to receive payment could be determined simply by examination of the instrument itself. Thus, the consequences of negotiability were applied by the common law courts only if the instrument met certain criteria that satisfied these assumptions. The definition of negotiable instrument is found in Article 3 in 3–104(a), and this definition differs only slightly from the requisites for negotiability stated in the NIL and the original Article 3.

The definition of "negotiable instrument" in 3–104 defines the scope of Article 3. 3–102(a). The most important elements of that definition can be briefly described. Only an "order" or "promise" can qualify as a negotiable instrument. "Order" is defined in 3–103(a)(6) as a written instruction to pay money signed by the person giving the instruction. "Promise" is defined in 3–103(a)(9) as a written undertaking to pay money signed by the person undertaking to pay. Thus, a negotiable instrument is always a signed writing that promises or orders payment of money. Negotiable instruments fall into two categories: drafts and notes. An instrument is a draft if it is an order and is a note if it is a promise. 3–104(e). Checks are the most common examples of drafts. 3–104(f). Certificates of deposit are considered to be notes. 3–104(j). Representative simple Note Forms are set out at the end of this chapter. More complex Forms are found in Appendix III.

Because the rules applicable to negotiable instruments and the rules applicable to ordinary contracts can produce dramatically different results in some cases, it is imperative that both the person issuing a promise or order to pay money and the person to whom the promise or order is issued be able to know in advance whether Article 3 or ordinary contract law will apply. The various requirements of 3–104(a) are designed to provide mechanical tests to allow that determination to be made. One particularly important requirement is that the order or promise be "payable to bearer or to order," a term explained in 3–109. Thus, a technical and wholly formal distinction is made between a promise to pay "to John Doe" and a promise to pay "to the order of John Doe." The second promise may be a negotiable instrument if it otherwise qualifies under 3–104. The first promise cannot be a negotiable instrument. Because of this distinction, the issuer of a promissory note payable to an identified person can easily avoid the consequences of negotiability by avoiding use of the words of negotiability: "to order" or "to bearer," sometimes called the "magic words." Another device for avoiding the effects of Article 3 is provided by 3–104(d). These devices for excluding an order or promise from Article 3 are discussed in Comments 2 and 3 to 3–104.

Certainty of Obligation. Three of the requisites of a negotiable instrument relate to the certainty of the obligation to pay. First, the order or promise to pay must be "unconditional," a term explained in 3–106. An examination of that provision discloses that some promises or orders that are in fact conditional are deemed to be unconditional while others that are in fact unconditional are deemed to be conditional for the purposes of 3–104(a). The Comment to 3–106 is a guide to the rather arbitrary distinctions and refinements of 3–106. Second, the order or promise must be payable on demand or at a definite time, a requirement explained in 3–108. Third, the order or promise must be to pay a "fixed amount of money, with or without interest or other charges described in the promise or order." 3–104(a). The quoted language differs from 3–104(1)(b) of the original Article 3, which used the phrase "sum certain in money." In Taylor v. Roeder, 360 S.E.2d 191 (Va. 1987), the court shook up the real property finance world when it held that under the original Article 3, a note payable with interest at "three percent (3.00%) over Chase Manhattan Prime to be adjusted monthly" was not negotiable because it was not a promise to pay "a sum certain in money." The court applied a "four-corners rule" under which the obligation represented by the note had to be ascertainable by an examination of the note itself without reference to outside sources. The dissent pointed out that the rate could easily be established by a telephone call or from published lists. Adjustable rate mortgage notes (ARMS) are hugely popular today. How are they dealt with by Revised Article 3–112(b)?

> (b) Interest may be stated in an instrument as a fixed or variable amount of money or it may be expressed as a fixed or variable rate or rates. The amount or rate of interest may be stated or described in the instrument in any manner and may require reference to information not contained in the instrument. If an instrument provides for interest, but the amount of interest payable cannot be ascertained from the description, interest is payable at the judgment rate in effect at the place of payment of the instrument and at the time the interest first accrues.

Bright Line Test. Since the scope of Article 3 (3–102(a)) is determined by the definition of negotiable instrument in 3–104, it is not surprising that this definition was the subject of a great deal of debate in the drafting of Revised Article 3. There were a number of proposals either to restrict or enlarge the kinds of instruments to which the harsh doctrine of negotiability would apply by changing the definition of negotiable instrument. At one extreme was the view that the concept of negotiability was no longer needed; let the parties contract for whatever terms they can agree on for credit and payment instruments. A recurring suggestion for reform was to discard the "magic words"—"order" and "bearer"—as prerequisites of negotiability. Then too, a number of proposals were made to junk the traditional formal requirements of negotiability in favor of a functional test along the lines of that suggested in Fred H. Miller & Alvin C. Harrell, The Law of Modern Payment Systems 2.01, at [2][c] (2003):

> (1) [A]ny writing to be a negotiable instrument within this article must be
>
> (a) signed by the maker or drawer;
>
> (b) for the payment, or evidence a right to the payment, of money; and
>
> (c) of a type which in the ordinary course of business is transferred by delivery with any necessary endorsement or assignment.

This is similar to the definition of "instrument" in 9–102(a)(47).

After five years of discussion, the Drafting Committee decided to retain the traditional, somewhat mechanical tests similar to those developed at common law and codified in both the NIL and the 1962 version of Article 3. The strongest reason for this was the elusive quest for a "bright line." Comment 2 to 3–104 explains:

> Total exclusion from Article 3 of other promises or orders that are not payable to bearer or order serves a useful purpose. It provides a simple

device to clearly exclude a writing that does not fit the pattern of typical negotiable instruments and which is not intended to be a negotiable instrument. If a writing could be an instrument despite the absence of "to order" or "to bearer" language and a dispute arises with respect to the writing, it might be argued that the writing is a negotiable instrument because the other requirements of subsection (a) are somehow met. Even if the argument is eventually found to be without merit it can be used as a litigation ploy. Words making a promise or order payable to bearer or to order are the most distinguishing feature of a negotiable instrument and such words are frequently referred to as "words of negotiability." Article 3 is not meant to apply to contracts for the sale of goods or services or the sale or lease of real property or similar writings that may contain a promise to pay money. The use of words of negotiability in such contracts would be an aberration. Absence of the words precludes any argument that such contracts might be negotiable instruments.

Checks. Why then is a check that says "Pay to Payee" a negotiable instrument under 3–104(c) while a promissory note with this language is not? The reason for this distinction is that, as we shall see, banks deal with the billions of checks issued each year almost entirely on an automated basis. They pay checks drawn on them largely on the basis of machine-readable information encoded on the bottom of the check. Virtually all checks are printed with the words "Pay to the order of." If a drawer scratches out the word "order," the depositary and drawee banks have no feasible way of detecting that they are taking a nonnegotiable instrument. Section 3–104(c) largely relieves them of the burden of having to look at the face of each check to know whether it is negotiable. Comment 2 to 3–104.

Warning Legend? The justification for retaining the "words of negotiability"—"bearer" or "order"—stated above is that they describe a bright line test for negotiability. Certainly most creditors know what these words mean, but is this true of most debtors? There is nothing about this 18th century formalism that would indicate to an unsophisticated debtor that its inclusion means a debtor who is defrauded by a payee is, nevertheless, liable to a good faith purchaser of the instrument. This is a harsh consequence to visit upon a debtor who has no way of learning what these words mean short of consulting a lawyer. During the Drafting Committee discussions, a strong view was pressed that if the doctrine of negotiability was to be retained (and not all were in favor of doing so), then any note that purported to be negotiable should bear a legend warning of the consequences of negotiability. Such a provision was carried in a number of drafts until late in the drafting process. When it was finally dropped in the last year of the project, the justification for doing so was that business debtors should be held to know what business documents mean and, as we have seen, the doctrine of negotiability has been severely circumscribed in consumer transactions.

D. Holder in Due Course: Freedom from Claims and Defenses

The most dramatic aspect of negotiability is the holder-in-due-course rule. The Restatement (Second) of Contracts § 336(1) (1981) provides that the assignment of a contract gives the assignee rights against the obligor "only to the extent that the obligor is under a duty to the assignor." And § 336(2) provides that the right of an assignee is subject to any defense or claim that the obligor had against the assignor. In other words, when the obligee of an ordinary contract assigns the contract, the assignee gets only the rights of the obligee. Why has a different rule prevailed for negotiable instruments for centuries? Under Article 3, a holder in due course (3–302) takes free of some defenses of the obligor (3–305(b)) as well as claims of ownership (3–306). As a counselor, you cannot assume that either your business or consumer clients understand what a negotiable instrument is, much less how much trouble they can get into by becoming a party to one in any of several different capacities. The holder-in-due-course rule is counter-intuitive and difficult to justify to an irate client that has been victimized by it. We see it in action in a contemporary setting in the following Problem.

PROBLEM

Mark is one of 20 limited partners of a limited partnership (LP) in which Parker is the general partner. At the inception of the partnership, each limited partner contributed $100,000 in cash and gave Parker a negotiable promissory note for another $50,000, payable on demand. The understanding was that Parker would hold these notes until LP needed more funds and then would request each limited partner to contribute $50,000 more. Upon receipt of the money from each partner, Parker would return the note to the partner. The notes were made payable to the order of LP, and Parker had express authority to receive and indorse all instruments made payable to LP. Without informing the limited partners of his intentions, which were entirely fraudulent, Parker indorsed the notes of all the limited partners to Bank and delivered them to Bank, which knew nothing of Parker's fraud and purchased the notes for 85% of the face value of each note. Parker took the money and ran. Mark calls you when Bank demands payment of his note. He heatedly informed Bank that Parker had no authority to do what he did and that Bank was at fault in dealing with a crook, therefore Bank should take the loss. Bank disagreed, explaining that before it bought the notes it had diligently inquired into the creditworthiness of the general and limited partners.

(a) On which party does the UCC impose the loss, Mark or Bank? What is the policy basis for this result? Why wouldn't the rules of Restatement § 336(1) and (2) serve as well in this case? Bank could assess the risk involved with respect to Parker's fraud and adjust the price it will pay for the notes accordingly. It discounted the notes by 15%, doubtless to deal with the risk that the makers and LP may not be able or willing to pay the note. If it feared fraud, it could price this risk as well. Critics of negotiability contend that modern contract law can deal adequately with transfers of promissory notes and that the doctrine of holding-in-due-course is no longer needed. These arguments were made before the Drafting Committee of the 1990 revision and were summarily rejected.

(b) How does Mark discover whether he is dealing with a negotiable note? See 3–104(a) (formalities). If by any chance you didn't know about these formal requirements before you took this course, why is Mark expected to know about them under the UCC? Should negotiable instruments bear legends warning of the consequences of negotiability? See our discussion of formalities later.

We will first examine the claims and defenses that holders in due course take free of, and then we will go into detail on the issue of who qualifies as a holder in due course.

1. Claims of Ownership

Lord Mansfield created the doctrine that a good faith purchaser for value takes better rights than its assignor in two seminal 18th century cases involving claims of ownership: Miller v. Race, (1758) 97 Eng. Rep. 398 (K.B.), and Rhodes v. Peacock, (1781) 99 Eng. Rep. 402 (K.B.). In the latter case, he said: "The holder of a bill of exchange [a draft], or promissory note, is not to be considered in the light of an assignee of the payee. An assignee must take the thing assigned, subject to all the equity to which the original party was subject. If this rule applied to bills and promissory notes, it would stop their currency. The law is settled, that a holder, coming fairly by a bill or note has nothing to do with the transaction between the original parties...." The doctrine was later applied to defenses.

Lord Mansfield's doctrine on claims of ownership is found in 3–306. Defenses and claims of recoupment arise between the original parties to the instrument, e.g., between the maker of a note and the payee. Claims of ownership arise between the owner of the instrument and subsequent transferees, e.g., between the payee and a subsequent takers of the instrument. The Comment to 3–306 construes "claims" broadly, so that claims to the instrument includes a lien or a possessory right in it. Thus, 3–306's rule applies to these interests in the instrument as well.

PROBLEM

In October 2009, for valuable consideration, Maurice made and delivered a negotiable promissory note to Patricia for $25,000, payable in annual installments of $5,000, at 10% interest. The first payment was due in October 2010. Patricia, a member of the Ohio National Guard, was called for active duty in January 2011, and requested that Alice, a family friend, hold the note and collect the payments until Patricia returned from abroad. In order to allow Alice to make the collections, Patricia indorsed the note to Alice by writing "Pay to Alice" on the back of the note. Alice was down on her luck and, in breach of her agreement with Patricia, wrongfully indorsed and delivered the note to Harry in February 2010, who paid 85% of the face amount of the note to Alice. When Patricia returned from duty in 2011, she learned of Alice's wrongdoing, and sued Harry to retake possession of the note and to recover the $5,000 payment that Harry had collected from Maurice in October 2010. If Harry is a holder in due course, does he take free of Patricia's claim of ownership with respect to the note? With respect to the $5,000? See 3–306 and its Comment.

2. Ordinary Defenses

The extent to which a holder takes free of defenses is governed by 3–305(a) and (b). Subsection (a) states that the right to enforce an instrument is subject to defenses described in paragraphs (1) and (2) of that subsection and claims in recoupment described in paragraph (3). Subsection (b) of 3–305 is a limitation on subsection (a). The right of a holder in due course to enforce an instrument is subject to the defenses stated in subsection (a)(1)—the so-called "real defenses"—but is not subject to the "ordinary" defenses stated in subsection (a)(2) or claims in recoupment described in subsection (a)(3).

Section 3–305(a)(2) refers to defenses that are specifically stated in other sections of Article 3. Those defenses and the sections in which they are found are listed in the first paragraph of Comment 2 to 3–305. Subsection (a)(2) also refers to the common law defenses applicable to simple contracts which are not enumerated. The principal common law defenses are fraud, misrepresentation, and mistake in the issuance of the instrument.

3. Real Defenses

Section 3–305(a)(1) lists the defenses that may be asserted against even a holder in due course. These defenses are discussed in Comment 1 to 3–305. With the exception of the defense of discharge in bankruptcy, all of the real defenses refer to an instrument that is made unenforceable in order to carry out some public policy of the state not related to the law of negotiable instruments (illegality), or to an instrument that does not represent a contract of the person who signed the instrument (infancy, duress, fraud in the factum).

4. Claims in Recoupment

Restatement (Second) of Contracts § 336(2) (1981) states: "The right of an assignee is subject to any defense or claim of the obligor which accrues before the obligor receives notification of the assignment, but not to defenses or claims which accrue thereafter...." Suppose A promises to pay $1,000 to B in return for a promise by B to deliver goods to A. B assigns to C the right of B to receive $1,000 from A. A receives no notification of the assignment. If A's promise to pay B was induced by B's fraud or if B failed to deliver the goods as promised, A has a defense to the obligation to pay B. The defense can be asserted against C, the assignee. Change the facts. Suppose there was no fraud by B and B tendered the goods to A, who accepted them. A has no defense to the obligation to pay for the goods. But suppose A has a claim against B to receive $600. If C demands payment of $1,000 from A, A can assert the $600 claim as a reduction of the amount owing to C from $1,000 to $400.

If A's promise to pay is a negotiable instrument and the instrument is negotiated to C, 3–305 rather than the Restatement governs the rights of A and C. Subsection (a)(2) of 3–305 applies to the defense of fraud or failure to deliver the goods. Subsection (a)(3) applies to A's $600 claim against B if A's claim arose from the transaction that gave rise to the instrument and is therefore a claim in recoupment. Furthermore, the rights of C depend upon whether C is a holder in due course. 3–305(b). Claims in recoupment are discussed in Comment 3 to 3–305.

E. Requirements for Holder in Due Course

Section 3–302. Holder in Due Course

(a) "[H]older in due course" means the holder of an instrument if:

> (1) the instrument when issued or negotiated to the holder does not bear such apparent evidence of forgery or alteration or is not otherwise so irregular or incomplete as to call into question its authenticity; and
>
> (2) the holder took the instrument (i) for value, (ii) in good faith, (iii) without notice that the instrument is overdue or has been dishonored or that there is an uncured default with respect to payment of another instrument issued as part of the same series, (iv) without notice that the instrument contains an unauthorized signature or has been altered, (v) without notice of any claim to the instrument described in Section 3–306, and (vi) without notice that any party has a defense or claim in recoupment described in Section 3–305(a).

1. GOOD FAITH AND NOTICE

To qualify as a holder in due course under 3–302, a holder must, among other requirements, have taken the instrument in good faith and without notice of any defense against or claim to it on the part of any person. The meaning of good faith as applied to negotiable instruments has varied over the years. The definition of "good faith" in former Article 3 was purely subjective: "honesty in fact." In Revised Article 3, the definition was changed to "honesty in fact and observance of reasonable commercial standards of fair dealing." This definition is now found in 1–201(b)(20) and applies to all Articles except Article 5. There is no definition of "fair dealing." Section 3–302(a)(2) continues the previous Article 3 requirement that the instrument be taken both in good faith and without notice of claims or defenses. "Notice" is defined in 1–202(a):

> (a) [A] person has "notice" of a fact if the person
>
> (1) has actual knowledge of it:
>
> (2) has received a notice or notification of it; or
>
> (3) from all the facts and circumstances known to the person at the time in question, has reason to know that it exists.

Clearly, there are aspects of both subjectivity and objectivity in the standards Article 3 requires for holder-in-due-course status. We include two opinions in this section. The first, *Kaw Valley*, decided under the former statute, is one of the few decisions in which a court discusses the difference between good faith and notice. It involves a very common transaction, inventory financing. The second, *Maine Family Federal*, is one of the first cases to consider the meaning of "fair dealing" in the amended definition of good faith in Revised Article 3. It is a much discussed opinion.

Kaw Valley State Bank & Trust Co. v. Riddle

Supreme Court of Kansas, 1976.
549 P.2d 927.

■ FROMME, JUSTICE.

This action was brought by The Kaw Valley State Bank and Trust Company (hereinafter referred to as Kaw Valley) to recover judgment against John H. Riddle d/b/a Riddle Contracting Company (hereafter referred to as Riddle) on two notes and to determine the priority of conflicting security agreements. The two notes were covered by separate security agreements and were given to purchase construction equipment. The Planters State Bank and Trust Company (hereinafter referred to as Planters) held a note and security interest on the same and other construction equipment acquired by Riddle. Kaw Valley had acquired the two notes and the security agreements by assignment from Co–Mac, Inc. (hereinafter referred to as Co–Mac), a dealer, from whom Riddle purchased the construction equipment.

In a trial to the court Kaw Valley was found not to be a holder in due course of one of the notes. Its claim on said note, totaling $21,904.64, was successfully defended on the grounds of failure of consideration. It was stipulated at the trial that none of the construction equipment for which the note was given had ever been delivered by Co–Mac. Kaw Valley has appealed.

....

Prior to the transactions in question Riddle had purchased construction equipment and machinery from the dealer, Co–Mac. A number of these purchases had been on credit and discounted to Kaw Valley by Co–Mac. Including the Riddle transactions, Kaw Valley had purchased over 250 notes and security agreements from Co–Mac during the prior ten year period. All were guaranteed by Co–Mac and by its president personally.

In May, 1971, Riddle negotiated for the purchase of a model 6–c Caterpillar tractor, a dozer and a used 944 Caterpillar wheel tractor with a two yard bucket. Riddle was advised that this machinery could be delivered but it would first be necessary for Co–Mac to have a signed note and security agreement to complete the transaction. An installment note, security agreement and acceptance of delivery of the machinery was mailed to Riddle. These were signed and returned to Co–Mac. Ten days later, the machinery not having been delivered, Riddle called Co–Mac and inquired about purchasing a D–8 Caterpillar and a #80 Caterpillar scraper in place of the first machinery ordered. Co–Mac agreed to destroy the May 11, 1971 papers and sell this larger machinery to Riddle in place of that previously ordered.

The sale of this substitute machinery was completed and the machinery was delivered after the execution of an additional note and security agreement. However, the May 11, 1971 papers were not destroyed. The note had been discounted and assigned to Kaw Valley prior to the sale of the substitute machinery. Thereafter Co–Mac, who was in financial trouble, made regular payments on the first note to Kaw Valley. The note was thus kept current by Co–Mac and Riddle had no knowledge of the continued existence of that note. The 6–c Caterpillar tractor, dozer and the used 944 Caterpillar wheel tractor were never delivered to Riddle. Riddle received no consideration for the May 11, 1971 note and no lien attached under the security agreement because the machinery never came into possession of Riddle. (See UCC § 9–204.) The debtor never had rights in any of the collateral.

On February 24, 1972, representatives of Riddle, Co–Mac and Kaw Valley met for the purpose of consolidating the indebtedness of Riddle on machinery notes held by Kaw Valley and guaranteed by Co–Mac. Riddle was behind in some of his payments and wanted to consolidate the notes and reduce his monthly payments to $4,500.00. Kaw Valley disclosed eight past due machinery notes, each representing separate purchase transactions by Riddle. Riddle objected to one of these notes dated July 16, 1971, because the machinery purchased under this particular transaction had been previously returned to Co–Mac.

It was agreed by Kaw Valley that Riddle did not owe for this machinery because of the previous settlement between Co–Mac and Riddle. Kaw Valley cancelled the $5,000.00 balance shown to be due from Riddle.

Thereupon a renewal note and security agreement for $44,557.70 dated February 24, 1972, was drawn consolidating and renewing the seven remaining notes. Riddle then asked Kaw Valley if this was all that it owed the bank and he was assured that it was. The renewal note was then executed by Riddle.

It was not until March 12, 1972, that Riddle was advised by Kaw Valley that it held the note and security agreement dated May 11, 1971, which Riddle believed had been destroyed by Co–Mac. This was within a week after a receiver had been appointed to take over Co–Mac's business affairs. Riddle explained the machinery had never been delivered and Co–Mac promised to destroy the papers. No demand for payment of the May 11, 1971 note was made on Riddle until this action was filed.

Prior to the time this action was filed, Riddle executed a note and granted a security agreement in all of its machinery and equipment to Planters. This included the machinery covered in the previous consolidation transaction of February 24, 1972, with Kaw Valley and Co–Mac.

Subsequently Kaw Valley obtained possession of the machinery covered by the February 24 transaction by court order. Thereupon by agreement in writing between Kaw Valley, Planters and Riddle an immediate sale of the collateral covered in the February 24 transaction was held. By the terms of this agreement the first $22,200.00 in proceeds was to be paid to Kaw Valley in full satisfaction of the note of February 24, 1972. The money received from the sale in excess of this amount was to be paid to the Merchants National Bank to hold as escrow agent, awaiting a determination of entitlement by the court.

At the time of the trial the $22,200.00 had been received by Kaw Valley and the balance of the proceeds of the agreed sale amounting to $25,371.15 was in the hands of the escrow agent.

In the court's memorandum of decision filed November 19, 1974, the court found:

> "That the proceeds remaining in plaintiff's possession from the agreed equipment sale are $25,371.15. The plaintiff claims $21,904.64 of same is due on the transaction of May 11, 1971. The parties agree that the excess of $3,466.51 should be paid to defendant Planters State Bank to apply on its August 28, 1972 claim;"

On December 20, 1974, the court entered the following pay-out order:

"TO THE CLERK OF THE DISTRICT COURT:

"Now on this 20th day of December 1974, you are ordered to pay to The Planters State Bank and Trust Company the sum of $3,466.51 now in your hands, having been paid by the Kaw Valley State Bank and Trust Company, pursuant to the Journal Entry of Judgment entered herein on November 19, 1974."

Although it does not appear who initiated the order, the $3,466.51 was paid to and accepted by Planters leaving the disputed proceeds of the sale ($21,904.64) in the hands of either the escrow agent or the court.

....

The primary point on appeal questions the holding of the trial court that Kaw Valley was not a holder in due course of the note and security agreement dated May 11, 1971.

UCC § 3–306 provides that unless a holder of an instrument is a holder in due course he takes the instrument subject to the defenses of want or failure of consideration, nonperformance of any condition precedent, nondelivery or delivery for a special purpose. It was undisputed in this case that Riddle received no consideration after executing the note. The machinery was never delivered and he was assured by Co–Mac that the papers would be destroyed. The parties so stipulated. If Kaw Valley was not a holder in due course the proven defense was a bar to recovery by Kaw Valley.

UCC § 3–302 states that a holder in due course is a holder who takes the instrument (1) for value, (2) in good faith and (3) without notice of any defense against it. It was not disputed and the court found that Kaw Valley took the note for value so the first requirement was satisfied. The other requirements were subject to dispute. The trial court concluded:

> "Kaw Valley State Bank and Trust Company is not a holder in due course of the note and security agreement, dated May 11, 1971 for the

reason that it did not establish in all respects that it took said instruments in good faith and without notice of any defense against or claimed to it on the part of John H. Riddle, and Kaw Valley State Bank and Trust Company therefor took said instruments subject to the defense of failure of consideration. (Citations omitted.)"

So we are confronted with the question of what is required for a holder to take an instrument "in good faith" and "without notice of defense." We will consider the two parts of the question in the order mentioned.

"Good faith" is defined in UCC § 1–201(19) as "honesty in fact in the conduct or transaction concerned." The first draft of the Uniform Commercial Code (U.C.C.) as proposed required not only that the actions of a holder be honest in fact but in addition it required the actions to conform to *reasonable commercial standards.* This would have permitted the courts to inquire as to whether a particular commercial standard was in fact reasonable. (See Uniform Commercial Code, Proposed Final Draft [1950], § 1–201, 18, p. 30.) However, when the final draft was approved the test of reasonable commercial standards was excised thus indicating that a more rigid standard must be applied for determining "good faith."....

From the history of the Uniform Commercial Code it would appear that "good faith" requires no actual knowledge of or participation in any material infirmity in the original transaction.

The second part of our question concerns the requirement of the U.C.C. that a holder in due course take the instrument without notice of any defense to the instrument. UCC § 1–201(25) provides:

"A person has 'notice' of a fact when

"(a) he has actual knowledge of it; or

"(b) he has received a notice or notification of it; or

"(c) from all the facts and circumstances known to him at the time in question he has reason to know that it exists. A person 'knows' or has 'knowledge' of a fact when he has actual knowledge of it. 'Discover' or 'learn' or a word or phrase of similar import refers to knowledge rather than to reason to know. The time and circumstances under which a notice or notification may cease to be effective are not determined by this act."

As is apparent from reading the above statute the standard enunciated is not limited to the rigid standard of actual knowledge of the defense. Reason to know appears to be premised on the use of reasonable commercial practices. Since "good faith" and "no notice of defense" are both required of a holder to claim the status of a holder-in-due course it would appear that the two standards are not in conflict even though the standards of conduct may be different.

There is little or no evidence in the present case to indicate that Kaw Valley acted dishonestly or "not in good faith" when it purchased the note of May 11, 1971. However, as to "notice of defense" the court found from all the facts and circumstances known to Kaw Valley at the time in question it had reason to know a defense existed. The court found:

> "During the period 1960 to May, 1971, plaintiff purchased from Co–Mac over 250 notes and secured transactions and held at any given time between $100,000.00 and $250,000.00 of such obligations. All of which were guaranteed by Co–Mac and personally guaranteed by D. J. Wickern, its president. Conant Wait personally handled most if not all of such transactions for plaintiff. Mr. Wait was aware that Co–Mac was making warranties and representation as to fitness to some purchasers of new and used equipment. Mr. Wait further knew that some transactions were in fact not as they would appear to be in that the money from Kaw Valley would be used by Co–Mac to buy the equipment that was the subject matter of the sale. Further, that delivery to the customer of said purchased equipment was sometimes delayed 60 to 90 days for repairing and/or overhauling of same. The plaintiff obviously on many transactions was relying on Co–Mac to insure payment of the obligations and contacted Co–Mac to collect delinquent payments. Some transactions involved delivery of coupon books to Co–Mac rather than the debtor so Co–Mac could bill service and parts charges along with the secured debt. Co–Mac collected payments directly from debtors in various transactions and paid plaintiff. Plaintiff did not concern itself with known irregularities in the transactions as it clearly was relying on Co–Mac;
>
> "The coupon book on the May 11, 1971 transaction was not sent to defendant Riddle; no payments on same were made by defendant Riddle; the payments were made by Co–Mac until January 25, 1972; prior to early March, 1972, defendant Riddle did not know plaintiff had the May 11, 1971 secured transaction; knowledge of said transaction came to defendant Riddle on March 12, 1972 when Mr. Wait contacted defendant Riddle's manager; that Co–Mac had shortly before been placed in receivership; that no demand for any payment on said transaction was made by plaintiff to defendant Riddle until September 1972."

To further support its holding that Kaw Valley had reason to know that the defense existed the court found that when Kaw Valley, Co–Mac and Riddle met on February 24, 1972, to consolidate all of Riddle's past due notes Kaw Valley recognized Co–Mac's authority to act for it. Co–Mac had accepted return of the machinery on one of the eight transactions and Kaw Valley recognized its authority as their agent to do so and cancelled the $5,000.00 balance remaining due on the note held by the bank.

The cases dealing with the question of "reason to know a defense exists" seem to fall into four categories.

The first includes those cases where it is established the holder had information from the transferor or the obligor which disclosed the existence of a defense. In those cases it is clear if the holder takes an instrument having received prior or contemporaneous notice of a defense he is not a holder-in-due course. (Billingsley v. Mackay, 382 F.2d 290 (5th Cir. 1967). Our present case does not fall in that category for there is no evidence that Co–Mac or Riddle informed Kaw Valley that the machinery had not been delivered when the note was negotiated.

The second group of cases are those in which the defense appears in an accompanying document delivered to the holder with the note. For example, when a security agreement is executed concurrently with a note evidencing an indebtedness incurred for machinery to be delivered in the future. In such case the instrument may under certain circumstances disclose a defense to the note, such as nondelivery of the machinery purchased. (See also Commerce Trust Company v. Denson, 437 S.W.2d 94 [Mo. App. 1968], and HIMC Investment Co. v. Siciliano, 103 N.J. Super. 27, 246 A.2d 502, for other examples.) Our present case does not fall in this category because Riddle had signed a written delivery acceptance which was handed to Kaw Valley along with the note and security agreement.

A third group of cases are those in which information appears in the written instrument indicating the existence of a defense, such as when the note on its face shows that the due date has passed or the note bears visible evidence of alteration and forgery or the note is clearly incomplete. (See E. F. Corporation v. Smith, 496 F.2d 826 [10th Cir. 1974]; Srochi v. Kamensky, 118 Ga. App. 182, 162 S.E.2d 889; and Winter & Hirsch, Inc. v. Passarelli, 122 Ill. App.2d 372, 259 N.E.2d 312.) In our present case the instrument assigned bore nothing unusual on its face and appeared complete and proper in all respects.

In the fourth category of cases it has been held that the holder of a negotiable instrument may be prevented from assuming holder in due course status because of knowledge of the business practices of his transferor or when he is so closely aligned with the transferor that transferor may be considered an agent of the holder and the transferee is charged with the actions and knowledge of the transferor.

Under our former negotiable instruments law containing provisions similar to the U.C.C. this court refused to accord holder in due course status to a machinery company receiving notes from one of its dealers because of its knowledge of the business practices of the dealer and the company's participation and alignment with the dealer who transferred the note. (International Harvester Co. v. Watkins, 127 Kan. 50, Sly. ¶ 3, 272 P. 139, 61 A.L.R. 687.)

In Unico v. Owen, 50 N.J. 101, 232 A.2d 405, the New Jersey court refused to accord holder in due course status to a financing partnership which was closely connected with the transferor and had been organized to finance the commercial paper obtained by the transferor and others. The financing partnership had a voice in setting the policies and standards to be followed by the transferor. Under such circumstances the court found that the holder must be considered a participant in the transaction and subject to defenses available against the payee-transferor. In United States Finance Company v. Jones, 285 Ala. 105, 229 So.2d 495, it was held that a finance company purchasing a note from a payee for fifty percent of its face value did not establish holder in due course status and must be held subject to defenses inherent in the original transaction. Other jurisdictions have followed the rationale of Unico. See American Plan Corp. v. Woods, 16 Ohio App.2d 1, 240 N.E.2d 886, where the holder supplied forms to the payee, established financing charges and investigated the credit of the maker of the note; Calvert Credit Corporation v. Williams, 244 A.2d 494 (D.C.App.1968), where the holder exerted total control over payee's financial affairs; and Jones v. Approved Bancredit Corp., 256 A.2d 739 (Del.1969), where ownership and management of the holder and payee were connected.

In the present case Kaw Valley had worked closely with Co–Mac in over 250 financing transactions over a period of ten years. It knew that some of these transactions were not for valuable consideration at the time the paper was delivered since the bank's money was to be used in purchasing the machinery or equipment represented in the instruments as already in possession of the maker of the note. Kaw Valley had been advised that delivery to Co–Mac's customers was sometimes delayed from 60 to 90 days. Kaw Valley continued to rely on Co–Mac to assure payment of the obligations and contacted it to collect delinquent payments. Some of these transactions, including the one in question, involved the use of coupon books to be used by the debtor in making payment on the notes. In the present case Kaw Valley did not notify Riddle that it was the holder of the note. It delivered Riddle's coupon book to Co–Mac as if it were the obligor or was authorized as its collection agent for this transaction.

Throughout the period from May 11, 1971, to February 25, 1972, Kaw Valley received and credited the monthly payments knowing that payments were being made by Co–Mac and not by Riddle. Then when Riddle's loans were consolidated, the May 11, 1971 transaction was not included by Kaw Valley, either by oversight or by intention, as an obligation of Riddle. Co–Mac occupied a close relationship with Kaw Valley and with its knowledge and consent acted as its agent in collecting payments on notes held by Kaw Valley. The working relationship existing between Kaw Valley and Co–Mac was further demonstrated on February 24, 1972, when the $5,000.00 balance due on one of Riddle's notes was cancelled when it was shown that the machinery for which the note was given had previously been returned to Co–Mac with the understanding that no further payments were due.

UCC § 3–307(3) provides:

> "After it is shown that a defense exists a person claiming the rights of a holder in due course has the burden of establishing that he or some person under whom he claims is in all respects a holder in due course."

In the present case the court found that the appellant, Kaw Valley, had not sustained its burden of proving that it was a holder in due course. Under the evidence in this case the holder failed to advise the maker of the note of its acquisition of the note and security agreement. It placed the payment coupon book in the hands of Co–Mac and received all monthly payments from them. A close working relationship existed between the two companies and Co–Mac was clothed with authority to collect and forward all payments due on the transaction. Agency and authority was further shown to exist by authorizing return of machinery to Co–Mac and terminating balances due on purchase money paper. We cannot say under the facts and circumstances known and participated in by Kaw Valley in this transaction it did not at the time in question have reason to know that the defense existed. This was a question of fact to be determined by the trier of fact which if supported by substantial competent evidence must stand.

....

The judgment is affirmed.

NOTE

Is the court telling us that the doctrine of holder-in-due-course performs no legitimate function in inventory and sales financing?

Maine Family Federal Credit Union v. Sun Life Assurance Co.

Supreme Judicial Court of Maine, 1999.
727 A.2d 335.

■ SAUFLEY, J.

We are called upon here to address the concept of "holder in due course" as defined by recent amendments to the negotiable instruments provisions of the Maine Uniform Commercial Code. We conclude that, pursuant to those amendments, the Superior Court (Cumberland County, Calkins, J.) did not err when it entered a judgment based on the jury's finding that the Maine Family Federal Credit Union was not a holder in due course....

I. FACTS

Daniel, Joel, and Claire Guerrette are the adult children of Elden Guerrette, who died on September 24, 1995. Before his death, Elden had purchased a life insurance policy from Sun Life Assurance Company of Canada, through Sun Life's agent, Steven Hall, and had named his children as his beneficiaries. Upon his death, Sun Life issued three checks, each in the amount of $40,759.35, to each of Elden's children.[1] The checks were drawn on Sun Life's account at Chase Manhattan Bank in Syracuse, New York.[2] The checks were given to Hall for delivery to the Guerrettes.

The parties have stipulated that Hall and an associate, Paul Richard, then fraudulently induced the Guerrettes to indorse the checks in blank and to transfer them to Hall and Richard, purportedly to be invested in "HER, Inc.," a corporation formed by Hall and Richard.[3] Hall took the checks from the Guerrettes and turned them over to Richard, who deposited them in his account at the Credit Union on October 26, 1995.[4] The Credit Union immediately made the funds available to Richard.

The Guerrettes quickly regretted having negotiated their checks to Hall and Richard, and they contacted Sun Life the next day to request that Sun Life stop payment on the checks. Sun Life immediately ordered Chase Manhattan to stop payment on the checks.[5] Thus, when the checks were

---

[1] " 'Issue' means the first delivery of an instrument by the maker or drawer, whether to a holder or nonholder, for the purpose of giving rights on the instrument to any person." § 3–105(a).

[2] Accordingly, Sun Life was the drawer of the checks. " 'Drawer' means a person who signs or is identified in a draft as a person ordering payment." § 3–103(a)(3). Chase Manhattan was the "drawee." " 'Drawee' means a person ordered in a draft to make payment." § 3–103(a)(2). More specifically, Chase Manhattan was also the "payor bank." " 'Payor bank' means a bank that is the drawee of a draft." § 4–105(3).

[3] " 'Indorsement' means a signature, other than that of a signer as maker, drawer or acceptor, that alone or accompanied by other words is made on an instrument for the purpose of: (a) Negotiating the instrument; (b) Restricting payment of the instrument; or (c) Incurring indorser's liability on the instrument." § 3–204(a).

[4] Maine Family Federal Credit Union is a "federally chartered credit union," regulated by the National Credit Union Administration. See 12 U.S.C.A. § 1752a (Law.Co-op.1996). It qualifies as an "insured credit union" under the Federal Credit Union Act, 12 U.S.C.A. §§ 1751–1795k (Law. Co-op.1996 and Supp.1998), and is therefore subject to the provisions of Regulation CC. 12 C.F.R. § 229 (1998).

By accepting the checks for deposit, Maine Family Federal Credit Union became the "depositary bank." Under Maine law, " '[d]epositary bank' means the first bank to take an item ... unless the item is presented for immediate payment over the counter." § 4–105(2).

[5] "A customer ... may stop payment of any item drawn on the customer's account ... by an order to the bank describing the item or account with reasonable certainty received at a time and in a manner that affords the bank a reasonable opportunity to act on it before any action by the bank with respect to the item...." § 4–403(a). Thus, Sun Life, as the customer of Chase Manhattan Bank, had the right to order Chase Manhattan to stop payment on the three checks deposited by Paul Richard at the Maine Family Federal Credit Union.

ultimately presented to Chase Manhattan for payment, Chase refused to pay the checks, and they were returned to the Credit Union.

The Credit Union received notice that the checks had been dishonored on November 3, 1995, the sixth business day following their deposit.[6] By that time, however, Richard had withdrawn from his account all of the funds represented by the three checks. The Credit Union was able to recover almost $80,000 from Richard, but there remained an unpaid balance of $42,366.56, the amount now in controversy.

The Credit Union filed a complaint against Sun Life alleging that Sun Life was liable as drawer of the instruments, and that Sun Life had been unjustly enriched at the Credit Union's expense....

The Credit Union moved for summary judgment. The Superior Court held, as a matter of law, that Daniel Guerrette had raised a "claim of a property or possessory right in the instrument or its proceeds," § 3–306, and therefore that Sun Life was entitled to assert that claim as a "defense" against the Credit Union. See § 3–305(c). The court found, however, that a genuine issue of material fact remained as to whether the Credit Union had acted in "good faith" when it gave value for the checks—a fact relevant to determining whether the Credit Union was a holder in due course. See § 3–302(a)(2)(ii). Accordingly, the court denied the Credit Union's motion for summary judgment, and the matter proceeded to trial.

At trial, the only issue presented to the jury was whether the Credit Union had acted in "good faith" when it gave value for the checks, thus entitling it to holder in due course status.[10] At the close of evidence, the Credit Union made a motion for a judgment as a matter of law, which the Superior Court denied. The jury found that the Credit Union had not acted in good faith and therefore was not a holder in due course. Therefore, the Superior Court entered judgment in favor of Sun Life...against the Credit Union. The court denied the Credit Union's renewed motion for judgment as a matter of law and motion to amend the judgment, and the Credit Union filed this appeal.

II. OBLIGATIONS OF THE PARTIES

At the heart of the controversy in this case is the allocation of responsibility for the loss of the unpaid $42,366.56, given the fact that Paul Richard and

---

[6] "Notice of dishonor may be given by any person and by any commercially reasonable means, including an oral, written or electronic communication, and is sufficient if it reasonably identifies the instrument and indicates that the instrument has been dishonored or has not been paid or accepted." § 3–503(b).

[10] The parties stipulated to the fact that Daniel, Joel, and Claire were defrauded by Hall and Richard, and Paul Richard consented to the entry of judgment against him in the amount of $42,366.56 on the Credit Union's cross-claim against him. In addition, the parties stipulated that the Credit Union had incurred damages in the amount of $42,366.56. The parties' cooperation in crafting the stipulations appropriately allowed the court and the jury to focus on the only issue in dispute.

Steven Hall, the real wrongdoers, appear to be unable to pay. Maine, like the other forty-nine states, has adopted the Uniform Commercial Code. Under the Maine U.C.C., Articles 3 and 4 deal with "Negotiable Instruments" and "Bank Deposits and Collections...." It is these statutes that govern the parties' dispute.

Pursuant to Article 4 of the Maine U.C.C., the Credit Union, as a depositary bank, is a "holder" of the instruments, see § 4–205(1),[12] making it a "person entitled to enforce" the instrument under § 3–301(i). Upon producing an instrument containing the valid signature of a party liable on the instrument, a person entitled to enforce the instrument is entitled to payment, unless the party liable proves a defense or claim in recoupment, see § 3–308(b), or a possessory claim to the instrument itself. See § 3–306.

Because their signatures appear on the backs of the checks, Daniel, Joel, and Claire are "indorsers" of the checks. See § 3–204(a), (b). As indorsers, they are obligated to pay the amounts due on each dishonored instrument "[a]ccording to the terms of [each] instrument at the time it was indorsed." § 3–415(a)(i). This obligation is owed "to a person entitled to enforce the instrument or to a subsequent indorser who paid the instrument under this section." § 3–415(a).

As drawer of the checks, Sun Life is obligated to pay each dishonored instrument "[a]ccording to its terms at the time it was issued." § 3–414(b)(i). Again, this obligation is owed to a person entitled to enforce the instrument or to an indorser who paid the draft under § 3–415. See § 3–414(b). Chase Manhattan, as drawee of these checks, was not obligated to accept them for payment, see § 3–408, and therefore has not been made a party to this action.

Unless the Credit Union is a holder in due course, its right to enforce the obligations of the drawer and indorsers of the instruments is subject to a variety of defenses, including all those defenses available "if the person entitled to enforce the instrument[s] were enforcing a right to payment under a simple contract." See § 3–305(a)(2). In addition, its right to enforce is subject to any claims in recoupment, see § 3–305(a)(3), or claims to the instruments themselves. See § 3–306. If, however, the Credit Union establishes that it is a "holder in due course," it is subject to only those few defenses listed in § 3–305(a)(1). See § 3–305(b). None of those specific defenses is applicable here. Thus, the Credit Union argues that because it is entitled as a matter of law to

[12] § 4–205(1) provides that a depositary bank becomes a holder of an item if the item was deposited by a customer who was also a holder. The Credit Union's customer, Paul Richard, became a holder of the checks when Daniel, Joel, and Claire indorsed them in blank and transferred them to Richard and Hall. See § 3–201(a) (" 'Negotiation' means a transfer of possession, whether voluntary or involuntary, of an instrument by a person other than the issuer to a person who thereby becomes its holder."); § 3–202(a)(ii) ("Negotiation is effective even if obtained ... [b]y fraud.").

holder in due course status, it is entitled to enforce the instruments against the Guerrettes and Sun Life.

III. HOLDER IN DUE COURSE

A. Burden of Proof and Standard of Review

A holder in due course is a holder who takes an instrument in good faith, for value, and without notice of any claims or defenses. See § 3–302(a)....

The Credit Union argues that the court erred in failing to find, as a matter of law, that it was a holder in due course.... The question before us, therefore, is whether any reasonable view of the evidence, along with any justifiable inferences therefrom, can possibly support the jury's conclusion that the Credit Union did not act in good faith and therefore was not a holder in due course. Alternatively stated, the question is whether the evidence compelled a finding that the Credit Union was a holder in due course. If there is any rational basis for the jury's verdict, we must affirm the judgment.

B. Good Faith

We therefore turn to the definition of "good faith" contained in Article 3 of the Maine U.C.C. In 1990, the National Conference of Commissioners on Uniform State Law recommended substantial changes in the U.C.C. The Maine Legislature responded to those recommendations in 1993 by repealing the entirety of Article 3 and enacting a new version [of Article 3], which contains a new definition of "good faith." While the previous version of the good faith definition only required holder to prove that it acted with "honesty in fact," the new definition provides:

> "Good faith" means honesty in fact *and the observance of reasonable commercial standards of fair dealing.*

§ 3–103(a)(4) (emphasis added). Because the tests are presented in the conjunctive, a holder must now satisfy both a subjective and an objective test of "good faith."

1. Honesty in fact

Prior to the changes adopted by the Legislature in 1993, the holder in due course doctrine turned on a subjective standard of good faith and was often referred to as the "pure heart and empty head" standard. See M.B.W. Sinclair, Codification of Negotiable Instruments Law: A Tale of Reiterated Anachronism, 21 U. TOL. L. REV. 625, 654 (1990); see also Seinfeld v. Commercial Bank & Trust Co., 405 So.2d 1039, 1042 (Fla.Dist.Ct.App.1981) (noting that the U.C.C. "seem[s] to protect the objectively stupid so long as he is subjectively pure at heart"). That standard merely required a holder to take an instrument with "honesty in fact" to become a holder in due course.

Courts interpreting this language have routinely declared banks to be holders in due course, notwithstanding the failures of these banks to investigate or hold otherwise negotiable instruments, when they took the instruments with no knowledge of any defects, defenses, or stop payment orders. See, e.g., UAW–CIO Local #31 Credit Union v. Royal Ins. Co., 594 S.W.2d 276, 279 (Mo.1980) (en banc); Bank of New York v. Asati, Inc., 15 U.C.C. Rep. Serv.2d (CBC) 521, 1991 WL 322989 (N.Y.Sup.Ct. July 8, 1991). This approach has been understood to promote the negotiability of instruments, particularly checks, in the stream of commerce. Rejecting a contrary approach, one court put it bluntly:

> The requirement urged by defendant would bring the banking system to a grinding halt. A stop payment order issued by the drawer to the drawee which is unknown to the paying-collecting bank cannot fasten upon the paying bank any legal disability; particularly it cannot reduce the status of the collecting bank to a mere assignee of the instrument or a holder of a non-negotiable instrument, or a mere holder of a negotiable instrument.

Mellon Bank, N.A. v. Donegal Mutual Ins. Co., 29 U.C.C. Rep. Serv. (CBC) 912, 1980 WL 98414 (Pa. Ct. C.P. Alleghany County, Jan. 8, 1980).

Although courts were often urged to engraft an objective reasonableness standard onto the concept of "honesty in fact," most refused to do so. Their refusals recognized that: "[T]he check is the major method for transfer of funds in commercial practice. The maker, payee, and endorsers of a check naturally expect it will be rapidly negotiated and collected.... The wheels of commerce would grind to a halt [if an objective standard were adopted]." Bowling Green, Inc. v. State St. Bank & Trust, 425 F.2d 81, 85 (1st Cir.1970).

Moreover, under the purely subjective standard, a bank was not expected to require the presence of offsetting collected funds in the customers' account in order to give value on newly deposited checks: "A bank's permitting its customers to draw against uncollected funds does not negate its good faith." Asati, Inc., 15 U.C.C. Rep. Serv.2d at 521....

Application of the "honesty in fact" standard to the Credit Union's conduct here demonstrates these principles at work. It is undisputed that the Credit Union had no knowledge that Richard obtained the Sun Life checks by fraud. Nor was the Credit Union aware that a stop payment order had been placed on the Sun Life checks. The Credit Union expeditiously gave value on the checks, having no knowledge that they would be dishonored. In essence the Credit Union acted as banks have, for years, been allowed to act without risk to holder in due course status. The Credit Union acted with honesty in fact.

Thus, had the matter at bar been decided before the Legislature's addition of the objective component of "good faith," there can be little question that the Credit Union would have been determined to have been a holder in due course. Because it took the instruments without notice of any possible dishonor, defect, fraud, or illegality, it could have given value immediately and yet have been assured of holder in due course status.... Today, however, something more than mere subjective good faith is required of a holder in due course.

2. Reasonable commercial standards of fair dealing

We turn then to the objective prong of the good faith analysis. The addition of the language requiring the holder to prove conduct meeting "reasonable commercial standards of fair dealing" signals a significant change in the definition of a holder in due course.[19] While there has been little time for the development of a body of law interpreting this new objective requirement, there can be no mistaking the fact that a holder may no longer act with a pure heart and an empty head and still obtain holder in due course status.[20] The pure heart of the holder must now be accompanied by reasoning that assures conduct comporting with reasonable commercial standards of fair dealing.

The addition of the objective element represents not so much a new concept in the doctrinal development of holder in due course status, but rather a return, in part, to an earlier approach to the doctrine. See JAMES J. WHITE & ROBERT S. SUMMERS, UNIFORM COMMERCIAL CODE § 14–6, at 628–29 (3d ed. 1988) (discussing the objective test of good faith in England, first applied by the King's Bench in Gill v. Cubitt, 3 B & C 466, 107 Eng.Rep. 806 (K.B. 1824)). The concept of an objective component of good faith has been part of the discussion regarding the holder in due course doctrine since the first enactment of the U.C.C. See id. (noting that "[t]he good faith requirement has been the source of a continuing and ancient dispute"). The early drafters debated the need and wisdom of including such an objective component and ultimately determined *not* to include it in the definition of good faith because of its potential for freezing commercial practices.... The "new" element of good faith requiring the holder to act according to reasonable commercial standards of fair dealing is actually a more narrow version of the "reasonable person" standard considered and rejected by the drafters of the 1962 Code.

The new objective standard, however, is not a model of drafting clarity. Although use of the word "reasonable" in the objective portion of the good faith test may evoke concepts of negligence, the drafters attempted to distinguish the concept of "fair" dealing from concepts of "careful" dealing:

---

[19] "The new definition of good faith *substantially affects* ... the requirements for holder in due course status." Hawkland and Lawrence UCC Series § 3–103:05 (Rev. Art. 3) (emphasis added).

[20] The objective requirement, however, has generated a number of articles and commentaries on the reason, meaning, and anticipated interpretations of the changes. See, e.g., Patricia L. Heatherman, Comment, Good Faith in Revised Article 3 of the Uniform Commercial Code: Any Change? Should There Be? 29 WILLAMETTE L. REV. 567 (1993); Kerry Lynn Macintosh, Liberty, Trade, and the Uniform Commercial Code, When Should Default Rules be Based on Business Practices? 38 WM. and MARY L. REV. 1465, 1466 (1997).

> Although fair dealing is a broad term that must be defined in context, it is clear that it is concerned with the fairness of conduct rather than the care with which an act is performed. Failure to exercise ordinary care in conducting a transaction is an entirely different concept than failure to deal fairly in conducting the transaction.

U.C.C. § 3–103 cmt. 4 (1991).

Unfortunately, the ease with which the distinction between "fair dealing" and "careful dealing" was set forth in the comments to the U.C.C. revisions belies the difficulty in applying these concepts to the facts of any particular case, or in conveying them to a jury. The difficulty is exacerbated by the lack of definition of the term "fair dealing" in the U.C.C.[21] The most obvious question arising from the use of the term "fair" is: fairness to whom? Transactions involving negotiable instruments have traditionally required the detailed level of control and definition of roles set out in the U.C.C. precisely because there are so many parties who may be involved in a single transaction. If a holder is required to act "fairly," regarding all parties, it must engage in an almost impossible balancing of rights and interests. Accordingly, the drafters limited the requirement of fair dealing to conduct that is reasonable in the commercial context of the transaction at issue. In other words, the holder must act in a way that is fair according to commercial standards that are themselves reasonable.

The factfinder must therefore determine, first, whether the conduct of the holder comported with industry or "commercial" standards applicable to the transaction and, second, whether those standards were reasonable standards intended to result in fair dealing. Each of those determinations must be made in the context of the specific transaction at hand. If the factfinder's conclusion on each point is "yes," the holder will be determined to have acted in good faith even if, in the individual transaction at issue, the result appears unreasonable. Thus, a holder may be accorded holder in due course status where it acts pursuant to those reasonable commercial standards of fair dealing—even if it is negligent—but may lose that status, even where it complies with commercial standards, if those standards are not reasonably related to achieving fair dealing.

Therefore the jury's task here was to decide whether the Credit Union observed the banking industries' commercial standards relating to the giving of value on uncollected funds, and, if so, whether those standards are reasonably designed to result in fair dealing.

The evidence produced by the Credit Union in support of its position that it acted in accordance with objective good faith included the following: The

[21] One commentator has suggested that fair dealing refers to "playing by the rules." See Heatherman, supra, at 585. Yet "the rules" ordinarily define the parameters of reasonable conduct, a concept which sounds much like a negligence analysis.

Credit Union's internal policy was to make provisional credit available immediately upon the deposit of a check by one of its members. In certain circumstances—where the check was for a large amount and where it was drawn on an out-of-state bank—its policy allowed for a hold to be placed on the uncollected funds for up to nine days. The Credit Union's general written policy on this issue was reviewed annually—and had always been approved—by the National Credit Union Administration, the federal agency charged with the duty of regulating federal credit unions. See 12 U.S.C.A. § 1752a (Law. Co-op. 1996). In addition, the policy complied with applicable banking laws, including Regulation CC. See 12 C.F.R. §§ 229.12(c), 229.13(b) (1998).

The Credit Union also presented evidence that neither Regulation CC nor the Credit Union's internal policy *required* it to hold the checks or to investigate the genesis of checks before extending provisional credit. It asserted that it acted exactly as its policy and the law allowed when it immediately extended provisional credit on these checks, despite the fact that they were drawn for relatively large amounts on an out-of-state bank.[22] Finally, the Credit Union presented expert testimony that most credit unions in Maine follow similar policies.

In urging the jury to find that the Credit Union had not acted in good faith, Sun Life and the Guerrettes argued that the Credit Union's conduct did not comport with reasonable commercial standards of fair dealing when it allowed its member access to provisional credit on checks totalling over $120,000 drawn on an out-of-state bank without either: (1) further investigation to assure that the deposited checks would be paid by the bank upon which they were drawn, or (2) holding the instruments to allow any irregularities to come to light.

The applicable federal regulations provide the outside limit on the Credit Union's ability to hold the checks. Although the limit on allowable holds established by law is evidence to be considered by the jury, it does not itself establish reasonable commercial standard of fair dealing. The factfinder must consider all of the facts relevant to the transaction. The amount of the checks and the location of the payor bank, however, are relevant facts that a bank, observing reasonable commercial standards of fair dealing, takes into account when deciding whether to place such a hold on the account. The jury was entitled to consider that, under Regulation CC, when a check in an amount greater than $5,000 is deposited, or when a check is payable by a nonlocal bank, a credit union is permitted to withhold provisional credit for longer periods of time than it is allowed in other circumstances. See 12 C.F.R. § 229.13(b), (h) (1998). Therefore, the size of the check and the location of the

[22] The Credit Union could also have withheld provisional credit under the law and its own internal policy if there were other reasons to doubt the validity of the checks. See 12 C.F.R. § 229.13(e) (1998).

payor bank are, under the objective standard of good faith, factors which a jury may also consider when deciding whether a depositary bank is a holder in due course.

The Credit Union's President admitted the risks inherent in the Credit Union's policy and admitted that it would not have been difficult to place a hold on these funds for the few days that it would normally take for the payor bank to pay the checks. He conceded that the amount of the checks were relatively large, that they were drawn on an out-of-state bank, and that these circumstances "could have" presented the Credit Union with cause to place a hold on the account. He also testified to his understanding that some commercial banks followed a policy of holding nonlocal checks for three business days before giving provisional credit.[23] Moreover, the Credit Union had no written policy explicitly guiding its staff regarding the placing of a hold on uncollected funds. Rather, the decision on whether to place a temporary hold on an account was left to the "comfort level" of the teller accepting the deposit. There was no dispute that the amount of the three checks far exceeded the $5,000 threshold for a discretionary hold established by the Credit Union's own policy.

On these facts the jury could rationally have concluded that the reasonable commercial standard of fair dealing would require the placing of a hold on the uncollected funds for a reasonable period of time and that, in giving value under these circumstances, the Credit Union did not act according to commercial standards that were reasonably structured to result in fair dealing.

We recognize that the Legislature's addition of an objective standard of conduct in this area of law may well have the effect of slowing the "wheels of commerce."[24] As one commentator noted:

> Historically, it was always argued that if negotiable instruments were to be usefully negotiable a subsequent holder should not have to investigate the transaction giving rise to the paper. The paramount necessity of negotiability has dominated thinking and legislation on negotiable instruments law. Drafts and promissory notes, it has been believed, must be able to change hands freely, without investigation beyond the face of the instrument, and with no greater requirement than the indorsement of the holder.

---

[23] There was evidence that, on the second business day after he deposited the checks, Paul Richard notified the Credit Union that there may have been a problem with his deposit.

[24] The new definition of "good faith" has been forecasted by some to bring possible "undesirable changes" to the law of negotiable instruments. See Henry J. Bailey, New 1990 Uniform Commercial Code: Article 3, Negotiable Instruments, and Article 4, Bank Deposits and Collections, 29 WILLAMETTE L. REV. 409, 415 (1993).

Sinclair, supra, at 630 (footnotes omitted). Notwithstanding society's oft-cited need for certainty and speed in commercial transactions, however, the Legislature necessarily must have concluded that the addition of the objective requirement to the definition of "good faith" serves an important goal. The paramount necessity of unquestioned negotiability has given way, at least in part, to the desire for reasonable commercial fairness in negotiable transactions....

NOTES

1. Is the court's interpretation of "fair dealing" consistent with Comment 4 to 3–103? As we will see later, the purpose of Regulation CC is to enable depositors to withdraw funds from their bank accounts more rapidly. However, it permits depositary banks to place holds on checks in specified cases to protect the banks. In this case, the credit union could have placed a 9-day hold on the check, but Reg. CC does not require that banks place maximum holds on checks, and we will find that in most cases banks allow their depositors to withdraw the proceeds of checks much more quickly as a convenience. If a check is dishonored and the drawer later raises defenses on the check, banks have been able to recover from the drawer as holders in due course.

In *Maine Family Federal*, everything on the face of the checks paid by the credit union (CU) was regular ("in order," as bankers say). They were drawn by a large insurance company, Sun Life, on one of the largest banks in the world at that time, Chase, and were payable to the beneficiaries of an insurance policy in satisfaction of legitimate claims. The payees properly indorsed the checks and they were deposited by a customer of CU, Paul Richard, into his account. There was no basis for CU to have the slightest suspicion about the transaction. The fraud giving rise to the beneficiaries' claim of ownership arose entirely from activities about which CU knew nothing. CU got into trouble when it accommodated the wishes of its customer by allowing him to draw on the checks on the date of deposit. The strongest argument Sun Life had was that CU acted imprudently because these were checks of substantial amounts. But large checks from insurance companies are not unusual, and the fact that they were drawn on an out-of-state bank in no way makes them appear unreliable; this would probably be normal for insurance checks. How this arguably imprudent conduct led the court to hold that the jury could have rationally concluded that CU did not act according to commercial standards of fair dealing is a stretch. CU dealt only with its customer, Richard, and whether its accommodation to him constituted dealing unfairly is highly problematic.

What effect will *Maine Family Federal* have on the practice of granting early withdrawal privileges to bank customers that has proved so popular? If this case is followed, where will courts draw the line on the size of checks that can be paid out by the depositary bank promptly? Will every payment by a depositary bank on an uncollected check be subject to scrutiny on fair-dealing grounds. The Clarks, in Clarks' Bank Deposits and Payments Monthly, Vol.7, No.10 (April 1999), describe the Maine decision as "dead wrong." But some cases purport to have adopted its analysis. See, e.g., Any Kind Checks Cashed, Inc. v. Talcott, 830 So.2d 160 (Fla. Dist. Ct. App. 2002). Others do not. See, e.g., Wachovia Bank, N.A. v. Federal Reserve Bank of Richmond, 338 F.3d 318, 323 (4th Cir.2003) ("To determine whether Wachovia acted in conformity with reasonable commercial standards of fair dealing, we consider the fairness of Wachovia's actions, rather than any negligence on its part.... [There must be] evidence in the record indicating that Wachovia acted in an unfair or dishonest manner, rather than in a negligent manner."); State Bank of the Lakes v. Kansas Bankers Surety Co., 328 F.3d 906, 909 (7th Cir.2003) (["'G]ood faith' is in a different phylum from 'due care'.... Article 3 of the UCC, which contains a definition of 'good faith'...links commercial reasonableness to 'fair dealing.' Avoidance of advantage-taking, which this section is getting at, differs from due care.")

2. The fair-dealing prong of good faith was enshrined in American contract law by Restatement (Second) Contracts § 205 (1981), which provides: "Every contract imposes upon each party a duty of good faith and fair dealing in its performance and its enforcement." Comments b and d draw an important distinction in the application of fair dealing between good faith purchase cases and those involving the performance of contracts. They explain that in determining whether one is a good faith purchaser, the focus is on the honesty of the purchaser but in cases of performance of contracts, fair dealing may require more than honesty. Thus, in performing a contract, one party may not take unfair advantage of another. Since the principal use of the good faith definition in Article 3 involves whether the taker of an instrument is, in effect, a good faith purchaser, should Article 3 have omitted the fair-dealing prong of the good faith definition? Cf. Comment 3 to 5–102, in which the drafters explain why they rejected the fair-dealing prong of the good faith definition with respect to letters of credit.

2. Overdue or Irregular Instruments

PROBLEM

In payment of goods, Maker signed a negotiable note in the amount of $10,000 and mailed it to Payee. The note should have been payable in the amount of $20,000. Payee noticed the discrepancy and called Maker's attention to it. Maker told Payee to change the $10,000 to $20,000. Payee did so by erasing and typing over. The alteration was crudely done and very obvious. Payee then sold the note to Holder. Holder noticed the alteration but accepted Payee's truthful explanation of the circumstances under which it was made. When Holder demanded payment Maker refused, stating that Payee failed to deliver the goods for which the note was given. Assuming that Maker had a valid defense against Payee under 3–305(a)(2) relating to Payee's failure to perform the contract, is Holder subject to the defense? Suppose Holder, before completing the transaction, had called Maker and Maker had verified that the $20,000 figure was correct. How does this affect your answer? See 3–302(a)(1) and Comment 1 to 3–302.

Section 3–302(a) incorporates two traditional rules: holder-in-due-course status cannot be attained if the instrument is taken with notice that it is overdue or if the instrument is so irregular or incomplete as to call into question its authenticity. These doctrines are rooted in the law of good faith and may be viewed as special applications of the suspicious circumstances rule of Gill v. Cubitt, (1824) 3 B & C 466 (K.B.) But for a long time they have enjoyed independent status, and NIL § 52 adopted them as separate requirements for holder-in-due-course status in addition to the good faith requirement.

Under the common law view, the fact that an instrument was overdue or irregular or incomplete was notice that something was wrong. But the fact that an instrument is overdue does not point to any particular defense or claim or, for that matter, to the existence of any defense or claim at all. Most notes are probably overdue because the makers can't pay them. Most checks that are still out more than 90 days (3–304(a)(2)) have not been collected because the holder hasn't deposited them. In the range of possibilities raised in the mind of one purchasing an overdue instrument, it is doubtful that the likelihood of a defense rises very high or that the possibility of a claim of ownership by a prior party is considered at all. The fact that an instrument bears an obvious alteration does warn a taker of the possibility of a fraudulent alteration but not of defenses or claims wholly unrelated to the alteration.

Why shouldn't a purchaser who is willing to pay good money for an overdue or irregular or incomplete instrument be entitled to holder-in-due-course-status? Perhaps the question is better phrased in terms of why such a purchaser should be accorded that status. The answer to these questions may depend upon whether one looks upon holder-in-due-course status to be the norm or whether it should be seen as something unusual to be given only when a clear commercial benefit is achieved. If negotiability is a doctrine to promote the free flow of instruments, what social or economic gain is achieved by encouraging the currency of stale, irregular or incomplete instruments?

3. HOLDER IN DUE COURSE IN CONSUMER TRANSACTIONS

a. INTRODUCTION

In Universal CIT Credit Corp. v. Ingel, 196 N.E.2d 847 (Mass. 1964), we see the ruthless effect of the holder-in-due-course doctrine in consumer transactions. In that case the Ingels bought aluminum siding from Allied Aluminum (AA) and signed a negotiable promissory note for $1890 to be repaid in 60 monthly installments. After the note was negotiated to CIT for value, difficulties regarding the quality of the siding and alleged misrepresentations regarding the product arose, and the Ingels stopped making payments. When CIT sued, the Ingels tried to introduce (i) a Better Business Bureau credit report concerning AA (procured for them by a disaffected former branch manager of CIT) disclosing that it had a reputation for high pressure sales methods and the use of false and misleading statements, (ii) an eat-your-carrots letter from CIT to the Ingels, and (iii) Mrs. Ingel's testimony regarding her negotiations with AA that she believed showed fraud on the part of AA. The trial court excluded this evidence and granted summary judgment to CIT. The case went up on the evidentury exclusion issue and was affirmed. The letter of CIT's collection agent to Mr. Ingel, quoted below, is the classic statement of the holder-in-due-course view, as though it had been preserved in amber.

> Dear Sir.
>
> We are sorry to learn that the Aluminum Siding on which we hold your promissory note, is giving you cause for complaint. Our part in the transactions consisted of extending the credit which you desired, and arranging to accept prepayment of the advance on terms convenient to you. We did not perform any of the work, and any questions in connection with materials and workmanship should be adjusted with the dealer from whom you made your purchase. Therefore, we have passed your report along to Allied Aluminum and we are confident that everything reasonably possible will be done to correct any faulty conditions which may exist.
>
> In the meantime, we shall appreciate your continuing to make payments on your note as they fall due so that your account may be kept in current condition.
>
> Very truly yours,

CIT says that it merely provides the financing and has nothing to do with the underlying sales transaction, however fraudulent or unconscionable it may be. The basis for this statement is CIT's assumption that it is a holder in due course.

Determining holder-in-due-course status allocates the loss of the payee-dealer's insolvency. If the payee-dealer is still solvent and operating its business when the consumer's defense arises, the consumer can throw the defective product loss back on the payee-dealer. If the financer has to take the loss, it can throw the loss back on a solvent payee-dealer. It is when the payee-dealer cannot absorb the loss because of insolvency that courts must determine where to allocate the loss as between the consumer debtor and the financer. In consumer cases, the financer is in a much better position to monitor the solvency of its customer, the payee-dealer, than is the consumer. If the financer is willing to continue financing the operations of a company like AA in this case, it can adjust the price it pays for AA's paper. If a shady operator like AA can find no one to buy its paper at an acceptable price, so much the better. If financers cannot hide behind the holder-in-due-course doctrine, the market is self-correcting: good operators get financing; bad operators are driven out of business.

This 1964 case is the most recent authoritative opinion that we can find holding a consumer financer to be a holder in due course in a sales transaction. So far as we can tell, since that date all courts have found some basis for denying financers that status. For a heated indictment of the holder-in-due-course doctrine in a consumer case by the Supreme Court of New Jersey, see Unico v. Owen, 232 A.2d 405 (N.J. 1967).

b. THE LEGISLATIVE RESPONSE

The drafters of original Article 3, working in the early 1950s, could not agree on whether to have a consumer exception to the holder-in-due-course rule. The solution to the issue, eventually agreed upon in the Uniform Consumer Credit Code (UCCC) (1964-1974), discussed below, after years of debate, was not widely enacted. However, by the time Revised Article 3 was drafted in the late 1980s, there was a large body of state statutory and case law restricting the use of the holder-in-due-course doctrine in consumer transactions, and the drafting committee finally settled on 3–302(g), which has the effect of subordinating Article 3 to that law, and not only to existing law but to similar law that may evolve in the future. See Comment 7 to 3–302.

(1) CONSUMER CREDIT SALES

(A) STATE LAW

By the early 1960s the handwriting was on the wall with respect to the judicial enforceability of notes against consumers who had valid defenses. One way or another, courts allowed consumers to assert their defenses. Indeed, many creditors had long since given up the use of negotiable instruments and contract clauses cutting off defenses upon assignment. Nevertheless, the issue of negotiability occupied more time and caused more rancor in the drafting of the UCCC than any other issue. Creditor representatives saw negotiability as an issue of freedom of contract and wanted the UCCC to turn back the clock. To consumer advocates, negotiability was a symbol of creditor overreaching; they saw the UCCC as the instrumentality for finally driving a stake through the heart of negotiability in consumer cases. As we see below, the consumers won, but not before years of wrangling and equivocation. While these bitter debates were going on as late as the early 1970s, consumer credit was being revolutionized by the growth of the bank credit card which, in all but larger consumer purchases, replaced promissory notes and rendered the negotiability issue largely irrelevant in consumer cases.

Consumer credit sales are regulated in most states by statute. Most states have taken the position that the holder-in-due-course doctrine should be abrogated with respect to notes given by buyers to sellers of consumer goods or services. One approach was to prohibit creditors from taking negotiable notes from buyers and to invalidate waiver of defenses clauses in the installment sale contract. The UCCC took this approach in Section 3.307. Section 3.404 followed up by making assignees of negotiable notes issued in violation of the statue subject to the buyer's claims and defenses.

(B) FEDERAL LAW

The difficulties in gaining widespread enactment of the UCCC—only 11 jurisdictions enacted it—made clear that uniformity in the consumer credit field must come from the federal government. Unfortunately it came from the Federal Trade Commission rather than from Congress. The FTC "Holder Rule" (16 C.F.R. § 433.2—Preservation of Consumers' Claims and Defenses) is designed to negate the holder-in-due-course doctrine in sales of consumer goods or services. The rules also apply to leases of consumer goods. References to "seller" also include a lessor. Any "consumer credit contract," a term that includes a promissory note arising out of such a sale or lease, must contain a bold-faced notice stating in effect that any holder of the contract is subject to all claims and defenses that the debtor has against the seller of the goods or services. Since the FTC has no jurisdiction over banks, it cannot bar issuance of negotiable instruments as the UCCC does, but must rely on the notice approach, which has limitations. The FTC notice follows.

NOTICE

ANY HOLDER OF THIS CONSUMER CREDIT CONTRACT IS SUBJECT TO ALL CLAIMS AND DEFENSES WHICH THE DEBTOR COULD ASSERT AGAINST THE SELLER OF THE GOODS OR SERVICES OBTAINED PURSUANT HERETO OR WITH THE PROCEEDS HEREOF. RECOVERY HEREUNDER BY THE DEBTOR SHALL NOT EXCEED AMOUNTS PAID BY THE DEBTOR HEREUNDER.

The effect of the notice is to cause any assignee of the note or sales contract to take subject to the buyer's claims and defenses against the seller. Failure by a seller to include the notice is an unfair or deceptive act or practice under Section 5 of the Federal Trade Commission Act. Under that Act, the seller is subject to a civil suit by the FTC in which the court may "grant such relief as the court finds necessary to redress injury to consumers...resulting from the rule violation.... Such relief may include, but shall not be limited to, rescission or reformation of contracts, the refund of money or return of property, the payment of damages, and public notification respecting the rule violation...except that nothing in this subsection is intended to authorize the imposition of any exemplary or punitive damages." 15 U.S.C. § 57b(b). Under Revised Article 3, a promissory note bearing the FTC notice can be a negotiable instrument if it otherwise complies with 3–104(a) but there cannot be a holder in due course of the note. 3–106(d) and Comment 3 to 3–106.

(2) NEW SUBSECTION 3–305(e)

As we have seen the FTC, owing to lack of jurisdiction, cannot prohibit banks from buying negotiable consumer notes, but under the Holder Rule if a contract containing the requisite FTC notice is assigned to a financer, the assignee is bound by the terms of the notice and cannot take free of claims and defenses. But can the Holder Rule apply when the consumer note omits the notice? Commentators conclude that compliance with the Holder Rule by lenders in including the notice on the notes that they supply to dealers has been poor. Clarks' Secured Transactions Monthly, Vol. 18, No. 5, p. 2 (July 2002). One of the reasons for this is uncertainty over whether the lender in question qualifies as a purchase-money lender under the FTC rule.

Gonzalez v. Old Kent Mortgage Co., 2000 WL 1469313 (E.D. Pa. 2002), an obscure, unreported decision, addressed the effect of omitting the notice and came up with the novel concept of virtual notice. Citing no authority, the court concluded that it must treat a case in which the consumer contract did not contain the legend *as though it did*. The court laconically justified its legerdemain by saying, "[i]t would turn the law on its head to allow [the bank] to avoid the consequences of this language by its own failure...to include the Holder Rule Notice on the loan documents." The decision has been followed by other cases, and when the issue of omitted notice came before the Permanent Editorial Board group drafting the 2002 amendments, the following provision was added to 3-305:

> (e) In a consumer transaction, if law other than this article requires that an instrument include a statement to the effect that the rights of a holder or transferee are subject to a claim or defense that the issuer could assert against the original payee, and the instrument does not include such a statement:
>
> (1) the instrument has the same effect as if the instrument included such a statement;

(2) the issuer may assert against the holder or transferee all claims and defenses that would have been available if the instrument included such a statement; and

(3) the extent to which claims may be asserted against the holder or transferee is determined as if the instrument included such a statement.

See Comment 6 to 3–305.

4. TRANSACTIONS WITH FIDUCIARIES

a. WHY SECTION 3-307?

Under 3–306, a holder in due course of an instrument takes free of "a claim of a property or possessory right in the instrument or its proceeds." For example, a claim to the instrument or its proceeds may arise if a fiduciary, in breach of fiduciary duty, negotiates the instrument for value. The negotiation of the instrument may be the means used by the fiduciary to misappropriate funds of the person to whom the fiduciary duty is owed. The claim of that person falls within the language of 3–306. Under 3–302(a)(2), the person to whom the instrument is negotiated cannot be a holder in due course if the instrument was taken with notice of the claim. Section 3–307, added in 1990, sets a higher standard for holder-in-due-course status for cases in which the misdeeds of a fiduciary (agent, trustee, partner, corporate officer or director, etc.) are the basis for a claim on the part of the represented party (principal, beneficiary, partnership, corporation, etc.) against the taker of a negotiable instrument for breach of fiduciary duty.

Thus, under 3-307, a careless employer who hires an embezzler that engages in check fraud cannot recover the amount embezzled from the careless bank that accepted the fraudulent checks unless the bank actually knew that employee was breaching its fiduciary duty. There is no contributory fault provision in 3-307 as there is in some provisions relating to forged signatures, e.g., 3-404, 3-405, and 3-406, that we will study. Why does 3-307 make it more difficult for the represented party (the employer) to recover from the taker of negotiable instruments (the bank) in cases of breach of fiduciary duty? How does 3-307 relate to holding in due course under 3-306? The following opinion addresses these fundamental issues.

Jelmoli Holding v. Raymond James Financial Services

United States Court of Appeals, First Circuit, 2006.
470 F.3d 14.

■ BEFORE BOUDIN, CHIEF JUDGE.

Jelmoli Holding, Inc. ("Jelmoli"), employed William Potts to handle the liquidation of various Jelmoli assets and the investment of the funds realized. Potts had worked for Jelmoli in various capacities from 1990 onward in a Massachusetts office, but Jelmoli's parent company was based in Switzerland. Jelmoli allowed Potts not only to sign checks on behalf of the company but also left him with the responsibility of verifying that the account in the United States was properly maintained.

Potts had a brokerage account on his own behalf with the Raymond James brokerage firm. The Raymond James broker handling Potts' account was Craig Robinson, based in Raymond James' office in Texas. Potts was permitted to trade "on margin" (effectively paying a percentage for stocks purchased and borrowing the balance from Raymond James). In the stock market decline of 2000, the value of Potts' investments fell and, as Robinson knew, Potts began having difficulty meeting calls for additional cash to maintain the required margin between stock value and balance owed.

In April 2000, Potts for the first time delivered to Robinson checks drawn on a Jelmoli bank account and, when Robinson questioned him, Potts explained that he owned Jelmoli and could use the checks as he pleased. Between April and December 2000, Potts gave Raymond James checks totaling $1.5 million for Potts' personal account, both to cover his loans and to acquire additional stock.

In December 2000, Potts confessed to Jelmoli that he had been embezzling the funds. By the time Jelmoli (some months later) notified Raymond James of the fraud, Potts had removed all the funds from his Raymond James account. Thereafter, Jelmoli filed suit against Raymond James in the federal district court in Massachusetts to recover over $1.3 million taken by Potts and deposited in Potts' brokerage account. Jelmoli's two theories for recovery (a third one was voluntarily dismissed) were money had and received and unjust enrichment.[2]

In addition to denying that it had been unjustly enriched, Raymond James asserted that it had a statutory defense as a holder in due course. By motion, Raymond James also sought to limit Jelmoli's possible recovery to the amount

---

[2] Money had and received is based on money, or its equivalent, which in "equity and good conscience" should be returned to the claimant and is often styled as money that should be returned "where one is unjustly enriched at another's expense." *Rabinowitz v. People's Nat'l Bank,* 235 Mass. 102, 126 N.E. 289, 290 (1920). Unjust enrichment is an equitable claim with the same elements save that it is not limited to enrichment by money, or its equivalent. *Trust Co. of Ga. v. S and W Cafeteria,* 97 Ga.App. 268, 103 S.E.2d 63, 73 (1958).

(just over $105,000) that Raymond James had earned in commissions, fees, and interest on Potts' account in 2000. The district court denied the motion, and the case went to the jury on instructions disputed by Raymond James.

The jury found that Raymond James was a holder in due course for a small number of the checks received from Potts, but it found that Raymond James was otherwise liable to Jelmoli for $1.1 million. Raymond James now appeals. Its primary claims are that it was entitled to judgment limiting recovery to the commissions, interest, and fees and, independently, that it deserves a new trial on any amount arguably due to Jelmoli because of misinstruction on the holder in due course doctrine. On both issues our review is *de novo*.

We begin with the holder in due course issue. The Uniform Commercial Code ("UCC") provides that a holder in due course of a negotiable instrument takes it free and clear of claims that might otherwise be made with respect to it. § 3-306. Thus, if Raymond James were to prevail on that defense, it would defeat Jelmoli's claims entirely as to any check to which it applied, without regard to the terms of the two related common law claims or concern about whether Raymond James was enriched.

So far as pertinent, a holder in due course is one who "took the instrument (i) for value, (ii) in good faith, ... [and] (v) without notice of any claim [by another] to the instrument." § 3-302(a)(2). And notice, as defined by the UCC, can ordinarily be proved by either actual knowledge (here, that Potts was violating his fiduciary duty) or knowledge of facts and circumstances that would lead a reasonable person to so conclude. § 1-201(25).

A more specific companion provision, addressed specifically to "notice of breach of fiduciary duty," lays down a set of special rules where the claim rests upon such a breach:

> *If* (i) an instrument is taken from a fiduciary for payment or collection or for value, (ii) *the taker has knowledge of the fiduciary status of the fiduciary,* and (iii) the represented person makes a claim to the instrument or its proceeds on the basis that the transaction of the fiduciary is a breach of fiduciary duty, *the following rules apply:*
>
> ... (4) If an instrument is issued by the represented person or the fiduciary as such, to the taker as payee, the taker has notice of the breach of fiduciary duty if the instrument is (i) taken in payment of ... a debt known by the taker to be the personal debt of the fiduciary, (ii) taken in a transaction known by the taker to be for the personal benefit of the fiduciary, or (iii) deposited to an account other than an account of the fiduciary, as such, or an account of the represented person.

§ 3-307(b) (emphasis added).

In this case, the conditions of subsection (4) were satisfied: the check was issued by the represented person and taken for Potts' apparent benefit and for deposit in his account. But both by its terms and the underlying logic, section 3-307(b) imputes notice of the breach only if "the taker has knowledge of the fiduciary status of the fiduciary." In its instructions, the district court refused to limit "notice" to a case where such knowledge was proved.

Instead, over objection by Raymond James, the district judge instructed the jury that Jelmoli could defeat holder in due course status for Raymond James as follows:

> Next, the defendants must prove by a preponderance of the evidence that they did not have notice of Jelmoli's claim to each of the checks. In this context, the defendants had notice of Jelmoli's claim if they had actual knowledge of the claim or if the defendants had received notice or notification of the claim or if from all the facts and circumstances known to the defendants at the time in question they had reason to know that the claim existed....
>
> ... Now, special rules apply if the defendants as to any Jelmoli check they received had actual knowledge of the fiduciary status of Potts. If the defendants had actual knowledge of the fiduciary status of Potts, they had notice of his breach of that fiduciary duty and notice of Jelmoli's claim to that check if they, one, took the check in payment of or as security for a debt known by the defendants to be the personal debt of Potts; or, two, took that check in a transaction known by the defendants to be for the personal benefits of Potts; or, three, deposited the check to an account other than an account of Jelmoli or an account of Potts as fiduciary of Jelmoli.

On appeal, Raymond James argues that (contrary to the instructions just quoted) the "special rules" of section 3-307 are the exclusive way of establishing notice where the claim rests upon breach of fiduciary duty. Jelmoli urges (and the district court agreed) that section 3-307 is merely one way (and not the only way) to defeat holder in due course status in the breach of fiduciary duty context. Section 3-307 is by its terms available to block holder in due course status where the taker has knowledge of the beneficiary's fiduciary status. According to Jelmoli, even if section 3-307 is unavailable, a "reason to know" of the competing claim (otherwise proved) will suffice to defeat holder in due course status even if actual knowledge does not exist.

On bare language alone, Jelmoli may have an edge because section 3-302 permits "notice" to defeat holder in due course status; and section 3-307, while it imputes notice (under specified conditions) based on knowledge of fiduciary status, does not say expressly that this is the only way that notice of a claim can be established. But the statute alone is far from clear and the commentary to section 3-307 appears to address this very question and squarely to support Raymond James:

> This section states rules for determining when a person who has taken an instrument from a fiduciary has notice of a breach of fiduciary duty.... Section 3-307 is intended to clarify the law by stating rules that *comprehensively* cover the issue of when the taker of an instrument has notice of a breach of a fiduciary duty and thus notice of a claim to the instrument or its proceeds.
>
> ....
>
> .... The requirement that the taker have knowledge rather than notice is meant to limit Section 3-307 to relatively uncommon cases in which the person who deals with the fiduciary knows all of the relevant facts: the fiduciary status and that the proceeds of the instrument are being used for the personal debt or benefit of the fiduciary.... Mere notice of these facts is not enough to put the taker on notice of the breach of fiduciary duty and does not give rise to any duty of investigation by the taker.

§ 3-307, cmts. 1-2 (emphasis added).

None of the various cases cited to us is conclusive, and policy arguments cut both ways: the district court was concerned that requiring knowledge (as opposed to notice) of fiduciary status would encourage the taker to shut its eyes to clues; but the holder in due course defense was designed to facilitate transactions and encourage the acceptance of negotiable instruments. White and Summers, *Uniform Commercial Code* § 17-1, at 150 (4th ed.1995); Miller, *Hawkland's Uniform Commercial Code Series* § 3-302:1 (West 2006).

Further, as Hawkland states, under section 3-307"[m]isuse of the proceeds by the fiduciary is treated as the responsibility of the represented person, who ... chose the fiduciary." Miller, *supra,* § 3-307:5. On this view, section 3-307 carves out narrow exceptions—*e.g.,* where there is actual knowledge that one known to be a fiduciary is profiting—but mere inquiry notice of fiduciary status is not enough.

Although it is perhaps a close call, on balance we think Raymond James' reading of the statute is correct. The language could be read either way; but comments 1 and 2 appear directly to support Raymond James' position that section 3-307 is meant exclusively to control where the claim is one of breach of fiduciary duty. So read, it is not enough for the plaintiff to show that the conditions of subsection (4) are satisfied, as they are in this case. The plaintiff must also show knowledge by the taker, and not just warning clues, that the person tendering the check is a fiduciary....

Accordingly, the judgment of the district court is *vacated* and the case *remanded* for further proceedings consistent with this decision. The parties should consider settling the case, avoiding not only uncertainty but also what they would spend on lawyers' fees in a new trial followed by another appeal. Each side shall bear its own costs on this appeal.

NOTE

A question that has puzzled courts and commentators is the nature of the cause of action a represented person has under 3-307 to get its money back from the taker in breach of fiduciary duty cases. The Uniform Fiduciary Act affirmatively granted the represented party a cause of action for breach of fiduciary duty against takers in such cases. Section 3-307 does not; it speaks only to the taker's status as a holder in due course. This omission appears to leave to the courts the issue of the represented party's remedy in 3-307 cases. In *Jelmoli,* the court looked to the non-UCC law of Massachusetts and chose unjust enrichment as the appropriate remedy. James J. White and Robert S. Summers, Uniform Commercial Code § 16-5 (5th ed. 2000), exhaustively analyzes the question of remedy; it finds none in Article 3 and expresses some preference for common law conversion.

In Travelers Casual & Surety Co. v. Northwestern Mutual Life Insurance Co., 480 F.3d 499 (7th Cir.2007), Volwood's chief financial officer, Zahner, embezzled by writing checks on Volwood's bank account payable to Merrill Lynch for deposit in his personal account. Volwood's assignee, Travelers, sued Merrill Lynch on the ground that it was negligent and had violated its fiduciary duty to Volwood under 3-307. Chief Judge Posner's only statement about Travelers' cause of action is: "The claim is that Merrill Lynch was negligent, and worse, violated its fiduciary duty to Volwood, by allowing Zahner to deposit a check issued by Volwood to Merrill Lynch in Zahner's personal account. Section 3-307 of the Uniform Commercial Code, in force in California, makes any taker of a negotiable instrument (such as a check)—and thus Merrill Lynch—liable to the drawer of the instrument if the taker knows that the instrument is signed by a fiduciary of the drawer (an agent, as Zahner clearly was) yet it is deposited in the fiduciary's personal account rather than in the principal's account."

The court seems to be saying that Traveler's cause of action was that Merrill Lynch "violated its fiduciary duty to Volwood." This could be interpreted as holding that 3-307 contains its own affirmative cause of action, and that there is no need to look elsewhere for a cause of action. This would be a stretch, given the focus of the statute on holding in due course, but Chief Judge Posner has never been known for timidity, and this view would simplify litigation under 3-307 without changing the balance prescribed by the statute between the represented person and the taker. See Barkley Clark's comments on this issue in Clarks' Bank Deposits and Payments Monthly, Vol. 16, No. 3 (Aug. 2007).

b. NOTICE OF BREACH OF FIDUCIARY DUTY

PROBLEM

Fiscus is the guardian ad litem for a minor child, Welty, who has won a judgment for $25,000 in a personal injury case. A check for this amount was issued payable to the order of "Fred Fiscus, Guardian ad Litem for Roy Welty." In which of the following cases does Bank have notice of a breach of fiduciary duty on the part of Fiscus under 3–307(b)?

Case #1. When Fiscus indorsed the check and delivered it to Bank, he requested that it be applied in partial payment of his overdue loan obligation to Bank. Bank followed his directions.

Case #2. When Fiscus indorsed the check and delivered it to Bank, he completed a deposit slip directing that the check be credited to his personal account. His direction was carried out. It was on this issue, that pre-revision cases were divided. The different views are set out in Smith v. Olympic Bank, below, and Matter of Knox, discussed in the Note following the *Smith* opinion. Which view is adopted by 3–307(b)(2)? Why?

Case #3. Fiscus delivered the check to Bank, indorsed "Fred Fiscus, Guardian ad Litem for Roy Welty," and deposited it in a guardianship account that he had opened in Bank for Welty earlier. A month later, Fiscus drew a check on the guardianship account, purporting to act in his fiduciary capacity, payable to the order of "Fred Fiscus." He deposited the check in his personal account in Bank and later misappropriated the proceeds of the check for his personal benefit.

Smith v. Olympic Bank

Supreme Court of Washington, 1985.
693 P.2d 92.

■ DORE, JUSTICE.

We hold that, where a bank allows a check that is made payable to a guardian to be deposited in a guardian's personal account instead of a guardianship account, the bank is not a holder in due course under the Uniform Commercial Code (UCC) because it has notice that the guardian is breaching his fiduciary duty.

Charles Alcombrack was appointed guardian for his son Chad Stephen Alcombrack who was then 7 years old and the beneficiary of his grandfather's life insurance policy. The insurance company issued a check for $30,588.39 made payable to "Charles Alcombrack, Guardian of the Estate of Chad Stephen Alcombrack a Minor". The attorney for the son's estate directed the father to take the check, along with the letters of guardianship issued to the father, to the bank and open up a guardianship savings and checking account. The father, however, did not follow the attorney's instructions. Instead, he took the check, without the letters of guardianship, to the bank and opened a personal checking and a personal savings account. The following was printed on the back of the check:

> By endorsement of this check the payee acknowledges receipt of the amount thereof in full settlement of all claims resulting from the death of Roy Alcombrack, certificate holder under Group Life Policy No. 9,745,632
>
> /s/ Charles Alcombrack
>
> Guardian of the Estate of Chad Stephen Alcombrack, a minor

Despite the above written notice that the check was payable to the father in his guardianship capacity, the bank allowed the father to place the entire amount in newly opened personal accounts. On the same day that the father opened his accounts, the attorney for the guardian called a trust officer from Olympic Bank and inquired as to the fees the bank charged for maintaining guardianship accounts. Responding to the attorney's questions, the trust officer wrote the attorney, specifically mentioning the "Estate of Chad Alcombrack".[1]

The father, and later his new wife, used all but $320.60 of the trust money for their own personal benefit. Bank records disclosed how the estate money was withdrawn: five withdrawals were made to cash or into the father's checking account (total—approximately $16,000); one withdrawal paid off an unsecured personal loan made by the bank to the father (approximately $3,000); seven debits to the account were made by the bank exercising its right of offset to make payments on or pay off personal loans by the bank to the father (total—approximately $12,500).

After the depletion of the son's estate, J. David Smith was appointed successor guardian. He received a judgment against the father and instituted this suit against the bank. The trial court granted summary judgment in favor of the bank. The Court of Appeals reversed and remanded, holding that the

---

[1] The following is the letter sent by the trust officer to the guardian's attorney:

"October 30, 1975

"Mr. Charles A. Schaaf, Attorney

"Reference: Estate of Chad Alcombrack

"Dear Mr. Schaaf:

"This is a follow up to our telephone conversation of October 28, 1975. The information you requested on the performance of our common trust funds will be available in about four weeks. October 31st is the end of our fiscal year. If this is not too long for you to wait, please let me know and I will send you a copy of our annual report.

"Our fee for handling a Guardianship account is, eight tenths (8/10) of one percent (1%), minimum of $350.00 per year."

trial court should determine the factual issue whether the bank was a holder in due course.

Olympic Bank claims that it is a holder in due course (HIDC) and, as such, is not subject to the claims of the petitioner. In order to qualify as a HIDC, the bank must meet five requirements. It must be (1) a holder (2) of a negotiable instrument, (3) that took the instrument for value (4) in good faith and (5) without notice that it was overdue, dishonored, or of any defense or claim to it on the part of any person.... We need not decide whether the bank met the first four conditions as we hold that the bank took the check with notice of an adverse claim to the instrument and, therefore, is not a holder in due course. Consequently, the bank is liable to the petitioner.[4]

A purchaser has notice of an adverse claim when "he has knowledge that a fiduciary has negotiated the instrument in payment of or as security for his own debt or in any transaction for his own benefit or otherwise in breach of duty." UCC 3–304(2). Thus, the issue raised by this case is whether the bank had knowledge that the guardian was breaching his fiduciary duty when it allowed him to deposit a check, made payable to him in his guardianship capacity, into his personal accounts. As to this issue, Von Gohren v. Pacific Nat'l Bank, 8 Wash.App. 245, 505 P.2d 467 (1973) is persuasive and controlling. In *Von Gohren*, it was held that a bank had notice that an employee was breaching her fiduciary duty when it allowed her to deposit third-party checks payable to her employer in her personal account. The bank was put on notice despite the fact that the employer had authorized the employee to draw checks against his account and also to endorse checks made payable to him and deposit such checks into his account. The court held that notice need not always consist of actual knowledge of a breach of a fiduciary duty, but can be predicated upon reasonable commercial standards. The court concluded by stating:

> It is our view that since defendant had notice of the claim by virtue of UCC § 3–304(2), and since it is undisputed that defendant did nothing to investigate Mrs. Martin's authority to negotiate checks payable to her employer, we must hold as a matter of law it did not act in accordance with reasonable commercial standards.

Von Gohren, at 255, 505 P.2d 467. The same conclusion is mandated in the present case.

---

[4] UCC § 3–306 sets forth the liabilities of one who accepts a check and who is not a holder in due course.

"Unless he has the rights of a holder in due course any person takes the instrument subject to

"(a) all valid claims to it on the part of any person; and

"(b) all defenses of any party which would be available in an action on a simple contract; ..."

Here, the bank knew it was dealing with guardianship funds. The check was payable to the father as guardian and not to him personally. The father endorsed it in his guardianship capacity. The bank received a call from the guardian's attorney inquiring about the fee the bank charged for guardianship accounts, and a trust officer for the bank replied in a letter referring to the "Estate of Chad Alcombrack".

Reasonable commercial practices dictate that when the bank knew that the funds were deposited in a personal account instead of a guardianship account, it also knew that the father was breaching his fiduciary duty. The funds lost the protection they would have received in a guardianship account when they were placed in a personal account. If the funds had been placed in a guardianship account, the bank would not have been allowed to exercise its set-off rights which amounted to approximately $12,500.... Nor would it have been permitted to accept a check, drawn on the guardianship account, from the father in satisfaction of the father's unsecured personal loan in the amount of approximately $3,000. Nor could the father, or bank, have authorized his new wife to write checks against the guardianship account without court approval.... A fiduciary has a duty to ensure that trust funds are protected.... Here, the father breached his duty.

While this is the first time, under the Uniform Commercial Code, that we have held a bank liable for allowing a guardian to deposit trust funds in a personal account, we have held a bank liable in a pre-Code case for allowing a trustee to breach his fiduciary duty.... In addition, other jurisdictions have held banks liable under similar circumstances using the Code...and without using the Code.... The policy reasons for holding a bank liable are compelling—especially in the situation presented in this case. The ward has no control of his own estate. He must rely on his guardian and on the bank for the safekeeping of his money. In order to protect the ward, the guardian and bank must be held to a high standard of care. For the guardian, this means that he must deposit guardian funds in a guardianship account. For the bank, it means that when it receives a check made payable to an individual as a guardian, it must make sure that the check is placed in a guardianship account. This will not place an undue burden on either banks or guardians and will have the beneficial effect of protecting the ward.

NOTE

In Matter of Knox, 477 N.E.2d 448 (N.Y. 1985), a pre-Revision case, the court rejected 9–307(b)'s imputation of notice when a bank allowed a guardian to deposit a check payable to him as guardian in his personal account. Knox involved a father who was guardian of the property of a minor son. Robert, the son, was injured when he was four years old. An action brought on behalf of Robert for damages was settled and a check was issued to the father as guardian of the property of the son. The check was negotiated to a bank and $11,000 of the proceeds of the check was deposited in the personal account of the father in the bank. The amount deposited in the account was eventually spent in the purchase of a house for the family and for other family expenses. The family included three other children besides Robert and the parents. The family was impoverished and the father stated that the money was spent to "give Robert as well as the rest [of the family] the same kind of normal life that any family enjoys." Eventually an action was brought against the father by a guardian ad litem appointed for Robert to recover the funds that had been misappropriated by the father. The bank was joined in the action and the trial court entered judgment against both. The bank appealed and the Appellate Division reversed the judgment against the bank. In affirming the Appellate Division, the Court of Appeals, one judge dissenting, stated:

> In Bradford Trust Co. v. Citibank, 458 N.E.2d 820, we held that "there is no requirement that a check payable to a fiduciary be deposited to a fiduciary account, and the fact that the instrument was not so deposited may not, without more, be relied upon as establishing a wrongful payment on the part of the depositary bank".... Our decision was grounded upon the Uniform Commercial Code which provides that "[a]n instrument made payable to a named person with the addition of words describing him...as [a] fiduciary for a specified person or purpose is payable to the payee and may be negotiated, discharged or enforced by him" (Uniform Commercial Code § 3–117[b]), and that mere knowledge that the "person negotiating the instrument is or was a fiduciary" does not of itself give the purchaser of a negotiable instrument notice of any claims or defenses (Uniform Commercial Code § 3–304[4][e]). The conduct with which [the bank] is charged—having negotiated a check payable to [the father] in a fiduciary capacity without requiring deposit of the check in a fiduciary account—is thus permissible.
>
> In general, a bank may assume that a person acting as a fiduciary will apply entrusted funds to the proper purposes and will adhere to the conditions of the appointment.... A bank is not in the normal course required to conduct an investigation to protect funds from possible misappropriation by a fiduciary, unless there are facts—not here present—indicating misappropriation.... In this event, a bank may be liable for participation in the diversion, either by itself acquiring a benefit, or by notice or knowledge that a diversion is intended or being executed.... No facts are before this court suggesting that [the bank] had notice that [the father] intended to, or did in fact, use the settlement proceeds for improper purposes. Consequently, [the bank] cannot be charged with the misappropriation.

Section 3–307(b)(2)(iii) has been controversial. Some states did not enact it, e.g., Alabama, and others that enacted it repealed it a few years later, e.g., Missouri.

NOTE: UNIFORM FIDUCIARIES ACT

When the National Conference approved the final draft of Revised Article 3, the Commissioners did so knowing that 3–307 took positions contrary to those of another uniform act, the Uniform Fiduciaries Act, that had been promulgated by the National Conference in the 1920s and adopted in about half of the states. The inconsistency between the two acts was before the court in County of Macon v. Edgcomb, 654 N.E.2d 598 (Ill. App. Ct. 1995), in which a county treasurer, Edgcomb, embezzled over $400,000 in county funds by stealing checks made to the county, endorsing them and depositing them in his personal account in Bank. Under UFA § 9, Bank had no liability in the absence of knowledge of the breach of fiduciary obligation or bad faith, but under 3–307(b)(2) Bank would be liable. Conceding that when choosing between conflicting statutes the more recent enactment will prevail as the later expression of legislative intent, the court applied the UFA to the case because Revised Article 3 was not in effect at the time of the embezzlement and amendatory acts should be construed as prospective unless the act indicates otherwise. In Bradley v. First National Bank of Walker, 711 N.W.2d 121 (Minn. Ct. App. 2006), the court held that the UCC preempted the UFA on the length of the statute of limitations. The National Conference has issued an "Addendum to Revised Article 3, Notes to Legislative Counsel....2. If Revised Article 3 is adopted in your state and the Uniform Fiduciaries Act is also in effect in your state, you may want to consider amending Uniform Fiduciaries Act § 9 to conform to Section 3–307(b)(2)(iii) and (4)(iii). See Official Comment 3 to Section 3–307."

5. VALUE

a. INTRODUCTION

If Thief steals a negotiable instrument from Owner and sells it to unsuspecting Holder, it may make sense to give Holder rights in the instrument at the expense of Owner. One or the other must bear a loss. Although each is equally innocent, the negotiability doctrine tips the scales in favor of Holder in order to carry out a policy objective of encouraging free commerce in instruments. But if Holder has paid nothing for the instrument, denial of the right to defeat Owner's title results in no loss to Holder except missing out on a windfall. Thus, if Thief makes a gift of the instrument to Holder it seems unfair to allow Holder to profit at the expense of Owner. Since it is not necessary to impose a loss on Owner in order to carry out the objective of encouraging free commerce in instruments, Holder loses. Section 3–302(a)(2)(i) provides that only a holder who takes the instrument for value can be a holder in due course. Taking for value is defined in 3–303(a). Although the requirement of taking for value can be explained in part by distinguishing between loss and windfall, this distinction is not always clearly apparent in the cases covered by 3–303(a). The elementary problems that follow illustrate some cases covered by that section. In each problem, and the cases that follow, you might ask yourself whether the holder-in-due-course doctrine is necessary to protect some interest of the holder or whether the doctrine simply confers on the holder a windfall. If there is a windfall, is the result justified by commercial necessity? You might also ask whether, if the doctrine did not exist, the taking of the instrument in the particular transaction would have been discouraged.

PROBLEMS

In each of the following problems make these assumptions: Maker gave to Payee a negotiable note in the amount of $1,000 payable on a stated date. Maker's issuance of the note was induced by Payee's fraudulent promise to deliver goods that were never delivered. In each case, Payee, prior to the due date, negotiated the note to Holder who had no notice of the fraud. On the due date, Holder demanded payment of Maker who refused and asserted the defenses of fraud and failure of consideration.

1. Payee negotiates the note to Holder in consideration of Holder's agreement to perform services for Payee. Before Holder is obligated to begin performance of the promised services the note falls due. Was there consideration for the transfer of the note from Payee to Holder? 3–303(b). Was the note taken for value by Holder? 3–303(a)(1).

2. Payee negotiates the note to Holder who pays $900 cash for the note. Is Maker's defense good against Holder? What provision in 3–303(a) applies to this case? If Maker is liable, how much can Holder recover? 3–302(a)(2). Suppose Holder paid $600 cash for the note and promised to pay an additional $300 cash in 60 days. After paying the $600, Holder learned of the fraud and paid no more. How much can Holder recover? See O. P. Ganjo, Inc. v. Tri–Urban Realty Co., 261 A.2d 722 (N.J. Super. Ct. Law Div. 1969). Comment 6, Case #5, to 3–302(d).

3. Payee was indebted to Holder on a loan past due. Holder demanded payment but Payee was unable to pay. In order to forestall legal action by Holder, Payee negotiated Maker's note to Holder as collateral for payment of Payee's loan. When the note became due, Payee was still unable to repay the loan. Holder thereupon demanded payment of the note by Maker. Is Maker's defense good against Holder? 3–303(a)(3).

b. RIGHTS OF DEPOSITARY BANK IN DEPOSITED CHECK

The material in this section examines one of the most common applications of the holder-in-due-course doctrine: when does a bank in which a check is deposited become a holder in due course of that check? Does it give value as soon as the depositor is given a provisional credit in the deposit account, or only when it pays out the proceeds of the check to the depositor? The answer to this question influences the bank's decisions on when to allow its depositors to draw on recently deposited checks. If the bank is a holder in due course, it takes free of any defenses between the drawer and the payee of the check, and if it is unable to recover from the depositor for money paid out on a check that the drawee bank refuses to pay, it can count on the liability of the drawer. As we explain below, Article 4 has its own rules for determining when a depositary or other collecting bank has given value for a check. These rules are stated in 4–210 and 4–211, and they complement 3–303; they do not displace it.

Checks are usually deposited by the payee in the payee's bank. That bank of first deposit is a "depositary bank." 4–105(2). The payee's bank is also referred to as a "collecting bank" if the check is not drawn on the payee's bank. 4–105(5). The depositary bank normally credits the account of the depositor for the amount of the check and forwards the check to the drawee for payment. The drawee is referred to in 4–105(3) as the "payor bank." The depositary bank is considered to be acting as the agent of the depositor in obtaining payment of the deposited check. 4–201. The credit to the depositor's account is normally provisional in nature. When the check is paid by the payor bank, this provisional credit becomes final, i.e., the credit represents a debt owed by the depositary bank to the depositor, 4–215(d). If the check is not paid by the payor bank, the depositary bank has the right to "charge back," i.e., cancel the provisional credit. 4–214(a).

Frequently, the depositary bank will also be a creditor of the depositor because of a past transaction such as a loan. If a debt owing by the depositor to the depositary bank is past due, the depositary bank may exercise a common law right to set off against the debt any amounts which the bank owes the depositor. For example, if the depositor owes the depositary bank \$1,000 on a past-due loan and there is an \$800 final credit balance in the depositor's checking account, the depositary bank may simply wipe out the \$800 balance by applying it to reduce the \$1,000 loan balance.[1] In addition to this right of setoff a depositary bank has a closely-related common law right known as a banker's lien. See Restatement, (First) of Security § 62 (1941).

For example, if the depositor owes the depositary bank \$1,000 on a past-due loan and deposits a check to the depositor's account in the regular

[1] The bank's right of setoff may be limited by statute. For example, Calif. Financial Code § 864 limits setoffs with respect to certain consumer-type installment debt owed to the bank.

course of business, the depositary bank has a lien in the check as security for the $1,000 debt. Although the bank acts as agent for the depositor when it forwards the check to the payor for payment, it also has a property interest in the check represented by the lien. Thus, the depositary bank can collect the check and apply the proceeds to the debt owed by the depositor. Since the taking of an instrument for an antecedent debt is value, the depositary bank could attain the rights of a holder in due course. These two related but separate common law rights—setoff and banker's lien—are preserved under 1–103. Comment 1 to 4–210. The two common law rights are frequently confused. It is not uncommon for a court to refer to the banker's lien as a right of setoff or to refer to the right of setoff as a banker's lien. When a depositary bank is asserting a right in an uncollected check it is relying on a lien. A setoff can occur only if there are mutual debts. There can be no present right of setoff with respect to an uncollected check because until collected the check does not represent a debt of the depositary bank to the depositor. Restatement, (First) of Security § 62 (1941).

Depositary banks may acquire rights as holders in due course under other provisions of the UCC. Suppose there is no debt owing by the depositor when the check is deposited. Whether the depositary bank has given value for the check is determined under 4–211, which states that the bank has given value to the extent it has a security interest in the check. Section 4–210 states rules for determining when a security interest arises. This security interest is in addition to the bank's common law banker's lien. Comment 1 to 4–210. By virtue of 4–210 the depositary bank has a security interest under subsection (a)(1) if the check is deposited and the resulting credit is withdrawn, under subsection (a)(2) if the check is deposited and the depositor is given the right to withdraw the credit, and under (a)(3) if the bank makes a loan or cash payment based on the check. In these cases the bank is treated as though it were a lender to the depositor taking as security a security interest in the check. In the case in which the depositor is not allowed to withdraw the funds, the bank does not have a security interest and is not a holder in due course. It has committed no funds and is fully protected by its ability to charge back the depositor's account in the event the check is not paid by the payor bank.

In most cases the depositor has an existing credit balance in the account when a deposit is made and there may be a series of deposits and withdrawals from the account. In those cases, whether credit for a particular check has been withdrawn cannot be determined except by applying some mechanical tracing rule. Such a rule is provided by the last sentence of 4–210(b), which states that "credits first given are first withdrawn." This rule is usually referred to as the first-in-first-out or FIFO rule.

PROBLEM

The table shows debits and credits made to Depositor's checking account in Depositary Bank. Withdrawals were made by payment by Depositary Bank of checks drawn by Depositor on the account. Deposits were made either in cash or by third-party checks payable to Depositor as indicated.

Date		Credit	Debit	Balance
Nov. 1	Existing balance			4,000
Nov. 2	Deposit by check	5,000		9,000
Nov. 3	Withdrawal		4,000	5,000
Nov. 4	Deposit in cash	6,000		11,000
Nov. 5	Withdrawal		5,000	6,000
Nov. 6	Received notice of dishonor of check deposited on Nov. 2			
Nov. 7 (A.M.)	Withdrawal		3,000	3,000
Nov. 7 (P.M.)	Charge-back of Nov.2 credit		5,000	-2,000

The check deposited on November 2 was not paid by the payor bank because the drawer had stopped payment. 4–403(a). Depositary Bank received notice of dishonor of the check on November 6. Depositor is insolvent. Depositary Bank brings an action against the drawer of the November 2 check to recover the amount of the check. 3–414(b). The drawer defends by asserting that no consideration was given for the check. 3–303(b). Assume that Depositary Bank is a holder in due course if it gave value for the check. Did Depositary Bank give value? 4–210(a)(1) and (b). Is the result in this Problem consistent with the case discussed in Comment 2 to 3–303? That case is governed by 3–303(1)(a), under which the unperformed promise of performance is not value. The rationale is that until performance is made the promisor will not suffer any out-of-pocket loss and dishonor of the check excuses performance by the promisor. In this Problem, is holder-in-due-course status necessary to protect Depositary Bank against an out-of-pocket loss when Depositary Bank received notice of dishonor on November 6? 4–214(a).

Section 4–210(a)(1) refers not only to cases in which a credit has been withdrawn, but also to cases in which the credit has been "applied." The latter term refers to cases in which the credit has been used by the bank to pay an obligation to itself or to make a payment to a third party.

NOTE

The following exerpt is from Albert J. Rosenthal, "Negotiability—Who Needs It?," 71 Colum. L. Rev. 375, 382–385 (1971), on the negotiability of checks. Bankers disagree with Professor Rosenthal's view on the importance of holder-in-due-course status as to checks.

To begin with, negotiability normally plays almost no part with respect to checks. While some checks are cashed at a grocery store or across the counter at a bank, the overwhelming majority of checks are deposited by the payee for collection at his own bank, which, acting merely as the depositor's agent for that purpose, sends the check through banking channels to the drawee bank where it is presented for payment. If paid, the check is so marked and is ultimately returned to the drawer along with his monthly statement; if the check is dishonored, a slip setting forth the reason is attached to it and goes with it back through banking channels to the payee.

There is no holder in due course (except perhaps the payee himself) of such a check since, even though such other requirements as good faith and lack of notice may be met, the bank would not have given value for the check. Any dispute between drawer and payee will, therefore, simply be between themselves, with no one else in a position to assert special rights.

Let us now modify the case of a relatively poor buyer purchasing a refrigerator on installments, and substitute a middle-class consumer paying for it with his personal check. If the refrigerator fails to work properly, if its defect is immediately apparent, if the buyer's attempts to get redress from the seller prove unavailing, and if the buyer moves with sufficient alacrity, he can often stop payment on his check before it has cleared through his own bank. The buyer and seller will then be in a position themselves to resolve their dispute on the merits, with the buyer having the tactical advantage that the seller will have to bring suit in order to collect if the matter cannot be resolved without litigation.

Suppose, however, the bank in which the seller-payee deposits the check allows him to draw against it before it has been collected. This is not standard practice, but it does occur with some frequency. When the check is presented to the drawee bank for payment, it is dishonored because of the stop payment order. This time, however, the depositary bank is given the status of holder in due course "to the extent to which credit for the item has been withdrawn or applied," or "if it makes an advance on or against the item." To this extent, the drawer cannot assert against the bank the defense that the sale of the refrigerator was fraudulent. Although the stop payment order is effective, its utility to the drawer is defeated, since he is liable to the depositary bank....

If the depositary bank were to grant credit to the payee by allowing withdrawals before collection, and if it were to do this in reliance upon its knowledge of the *drawer's* financial standing or reputation, there might be good reason to protect the depositary bank in this fashion. Typically, however the depositary bank pays no attention to the identity of the drawer; in fact, it does not even know whether the drawer's signature is genuine. It will often allow or refuse to allow withdrawals against the check before collection solely on the basis of its relations with and knowledge of the creditworthiness of its own customer, the payee. If payment is stopped, and the depositary bank cannot recover its advances by charging the amount back against the payee's account, but is permitted to hold the drawer liable, the bank receives a windfall: in such cases, it picks up the liability of the drawer, which by hypothesis it had not counted upon when it made its decision to allow withdrawals before collection.

The fact that the depositary bank would not normally be relying upon the drawer's credit may be seen in the improbable combination of circumstances that have to coincide for the drawer's liability to matter. First, the bank's customer, the payee, must have allowed his account to drop to the point at which some of his withdrawals cannot be charged against other funds in the account but must be regarded as advances against the uncollected check. Second, the payee must be insolvent, or at least his assets must not be readily amenable to collection. Third, the drawer has to be solvent and available, and his signature genuine. Fourth, the check must be dishonored. Finally, for the doctrine to make any ultimate difference, the drawer must have a legitimate defense on the check that is good against the payee, but is not of a type that can be asserted against a holder in due course. Only if all of these elements coincide is the bank's position improved by virtue of its becoming a holder in due course. It must therefore be a rare case indeed in which the bank's decision to extend credit before the check is collected can be regarded as having been made in reliance upon its ability to cut off the defenses of the drawer. Neither banks specifically, nor commerce in general, seem to need the rule declaring the bank to be a holder in due course. Where the bank relies entirely on the identity and credit of the payee in allowing withdrawals, it should shock no one's conscience if the bank were limited to the payee as a source of reimbursement.

FORM. PROMISSORY NOTE–FIXED MATURITY

For value received, the undersigned, * ("Borrower"), promises to pay to the order of City National Bank, a national banking association ("CNB"), at its office in this city, in lawful money of the United States of America and in immediately available funds, the principal sum of * Dollars ($*), with interest thereon from the date of disbursement at the rate of * percent (*%) per year (computed on the basis of a 360–day year, actual days elapsed).

Interest accrued on this Note shall be payable on the * day of each *, commencing *, *. The minimum interest charge for the term of this Note shall in no event be less than One Hundred Dollars ($100.00).

Principal and any interest remaining unpaid shall be payable in full on *, *.

The occurrence of any of the following with respect to any Borrower or any guarantor of this Note or any general partner of such Borrower or guarantor, shall constitute an "Event of Default" hereunder:

1. The failure to make any payment of principal or interest when due under this Note;
2. The filing of a petition by or against any of such parties under any provisions of the *Bankruptcy Code*;
3. The appointment of a receiver or an assignee for the benefit of creditors;
4. The commencement of dissolution or liquidation proceedings or the disqualification of any such parties which is a corporation, partnership, joint venture or any other type of entity;
5. The death or incapacity of any of such parties who is an individual;
6. Any financial statement provided by any of such parties to CNB is false or misleading;
7. Any default in the payment or performance of any obligation, or any default under any provisions of any contract or instrument pursuant to which any of such parties has incurred any obligation for borrowed money, any purchase obligation or any other liability of any kind to any person or entity, including CNB;
8. Any sale or transfer of all or a substantial or material part of the assets of any of such parties other than in the ordinary course of business; or
9. Any violation, breach or default under any letter agreement, guaranty, security agreement, deed of trust or any other contract or instrument executed in connection with this Note or securing this Note.

Upon the occurrence of any Event of Default, the holder of this Note, at the holder's option, may declare all sums of principal and interest outstanding hereunder to be immediately due and payable without presentment, demand, protest or notice of dishonor all of which are expressly waived by each Borrower. Each Borrower agrees to pay all costs and expenses, including reasonable attorneys' fees, expended or incurred by the holder (or allocable to the holder's in-house counsel) in connection with the enforcement of this Note or the collection of any sums due hereunder and irrespective of whether suit is filed. Any principal or interest not paid when due hereunder shall thereafter bear additional interest from its due date at a rate of five percent (5.0%) per year higher than the interest rate as determined and computed above, and continuing thereafter until paid.

Should more than one person or entity execute this Note as a Borrower, the obligations of each such Borrower shall be joint and several.

This Note and all matters relating thereto, shall be governed by the laws of the State of California.

*, a

* corporation

BY: __________

ITS: __________

FORM. DEMAND NOTE

On demand, or if no demand is made, then on *, *, for value received, the undersigned * ("Borrower"), promises to pay to the order of City National Bank, a national banking association ("CNB"), at its Office in this city, in lawful money of the United States of America and in immediately available funds, the principal sum of * Dollars ($*), plus interest thereon at a rate computed on the basis of a 360–day year, actual days elapsed, equal to the "Prime Rate" of CNB as it exists from time to time, plus * percent (*%) per year. "Prime Rate" shall mean the rate most recently announced by CNB at its principal office in Beverly Hills as its "Prime Rate." Any change in the Prime Rate shall become effective on the same business day on which the Prime Rate shall change, without prior notice to Borrower.

Interest accrued on this Note shall be payable on the * day of each *, commencing *, *. The minimum interest charge for the term of this Note shall in no event be less than One Hundred Dollars ($100.00).

In the event the interest is not paid as it becomes due, or in the event there occurs any material default in the payment or performance of any obligation owing by any Borrower to CNB, then the holder of this Note, at the holder's option, may declare all sums of principal and interest outstanding hereunder to be immediately due and payable without presentment, demand, protest or notice of dishonor all of which are expressly waived by each Borrower. If principal or interest is not paid on the agreed or accelerated date of maturity, then the interest rate provided for under this Note shall, at CNB's option, and without notice, be increased to an amount 5.0% per year higher than the interest rate as determined and computed above, effective from the day following the time that such payment of principal or interest became overdue and continuing thereafter until paid.

Each Borrower agrees to pay all costs and expenses, including reasonable attorneys' fees, expended or incurred by CNB (or allocable to CNB's in-house counsel) in connection with the enforcement of this Note or the collection of any sums due hereunder and irrespective of whether suit is filed.

Should more than one person or entity execute this Note as a Borrower, the obligations of each such Borrower shall be joint and several.

This Note and all matters relating thereto shall be governed by the laws of the State of California.

*, a

* corporation

By: _______

Its: _______

CHAPTER 2

LIABILITY OF PARTIES TO NEGOTIABLE INSTRUMENTS

A. LIABILITY OF MAKER

An understanding of the liability of the parties to negotiable instruments is essential to counseling clients in planning transactions as well at the litigation stage. The obligations of the parties are set out in four sections: the obligation of a maker in 3–412, of an acceptor in 3–413, of a drawer in 3–414, and of an indorser in 3–415.

The person primarily obliged to pay a promissory note is the maker, who has expressly agreed to do so. The relevant statutory provisions are: 3–103(a)(5), which defines "maker" as "a person who signs or is identified in a note as a person undertaking to pay;" 3–412, which states, "[t]he issuer of a note…is obliged to pay the instrument (i) according to its terms at the time it was issued…;" and 3–105(a), which defines "issue" as "the first delivery of an instrument by the maker or drawer, whether to a holder or nonholder, for the purpose of giving rights on the instrument to any person."

PROBLEM

New Movies Incorporated (NMI) produces films. It has rounded up 20 wealthy backers for a new motion picture, each of whom has agreed to contribute $1 million to the project. Now NMI wishes to obtain some bank financing before signing the talent for the film. In order to do this, NMI has persuaded all the backers to sign a single negotiable promissory note payable to NMI for $20 million that NMI can show banks and others to induce them to commit to the picture. Before production commenced, some of the backers wished to withdraw because of the economic recession. In order to keep them committed, NMI warned the backers that any signer of the note can be sued for the full amount of the note. Your client, a wealthy plastic surgeon, is one of the backers. She calls you and asks (1) whether NMI is correct in asserting that she can be sued for the full $20 million, and (2) if NMI is correct, what rights does she have against the other signers? What do you tell her (besides telling her to call you *before* she signs her name, not *after*)? See 3–412 and 3–116(a) and (b).

B. Drawers, Drawees and Acceptors

How do you answer the Problems below on the basis of the discussion in the text following these Problems? We use ordinary bank checks to illustrate the issues treated in this section.

PROBLEMS

Drawer signed and delivered a check for $1,000 to Payee in payment for goods purchased. The check was drawn on Drawee bank where Drawer maintains a deposit account.

1. When Payee presented the check to Drawee for payment, Drawee dishonored the check because Drawer had stopped payment on the check owing to its dissatisfaction with the goods delivered.

(a) Is Drawee liable on the check to Payee?

(b) Is Drawer liable on the check to Payee?

2. When Payee presented the check to Drawee for payment, Drawee dishonored the check even though no stop payment order had been received and Drawer had sufficient funds in its account to pay the check.

(a) Is Drawee liable on the check to Payee?

(b) Is Drawee liable to Drawer?

3. When Payee presented the check to Drawee for acceptance, Drawee certified the check. Later Payee presented the certified check to Drawee for payment. Drawee dishonored the check because after it had certified the check it received a stop order from Drawer.

(a) Is Drawee liable to Payee?

(b) Is Drawer liable to Payee?

4. When Payee presented the check to Drawee for acceptance, Drawee refused to certify the check even though Drawer had sufficient funds in its account to cover the check. Is Drawee liable to Payee if Payee can show that when it presented the check to Drawee for payment ten days later, the check was dishonored because there were no longer funds in the account to pay the check?

When a drawer orders a drawee to pay an amount of money to the payee, nobody has expressly agreed to make the payment. A draft normally arises out of a pre-existing creditor-debtor relationship between the drawer and the drawee. For example, a seller ships goods to a buyer who is located in a distant market. The contract of sale provides for payment of the price of the goods by a draft drawn by the seller on the buyer or the buyer's bank acting on behalf of the buyer. The seller draws a draft ordering the drawee to pay to the order of a named payee a sum of money equal to the price of the goods. The named payee may be the seller's bank which buys the draft from the seller for the face amount less a discount to compensate the bank for its services. In that case, the draft is delivered to the bank, which then becomes its holder. The draft is then "presented" to the drawee for payment. "Presentment" is defined in 3–501(a). In this case, presentment is simply a demand made on the drawee to pay. Subsection (b) of 3–501 states rules regarding the place, time, and manner of presentment. In our example, presentment might be made by the bank named as payee of the draft, but often the draft will be negotiated to another bank located near the buyer and that bank will present the draft to the drawee for payment. When the draft is paid, the buyer has discharged the obligation to the seller to pay the price of the goods.

The most common example of a draft is the ordinary check which is a draft drawn on a bank and payable on demand. 3–104(f). Payment of checks is also normally based on a creditor-debtor relationship. A check is drawn by a customer of a bank who has a checking account in the bank; the credit balance in the account represents a debt of the bank to the customer. When the bank pays the check, the bank's debt to the customer is reduced by the amount of the check.

Since the drawee of a draft has made no promise in the instrument to pay the payee or other holder, the holder has no action on the instrument against the drawee to enforce payment. 3–408. Sometimes the drawee will obligate itself, by a letter of credit or other separate contract, to pay a draft. In that case, failure by the drawee to pay the draft may result in liability to the holder for breach of the letter of credit, but there is no liability based on an obligation created by the draft. In the absence of a separate contract of the drawee such as a letter of credit, payment by the drawee will normally depend upon the drawee's obligation to the drawer arising from an express or implied contract between them. For example, in opening a checking account for a customer, the bank incurs an obligation to the customer to pay properly payable checks drawn on the account. Failure to pay a properly payable check may result in liability to the customer for wrongful dishonor (4–402), but the holder of the check has no cause of action against the drawee bank. Before codification of negotiable instruments law by the NIL in the late 19th century, a minority of states took the view that a check created a direct liability on the part of the drawee bank to the holder. The theory was that a check amounted to an equitable assignment of the drawer's funds on deposit, but NIL § 189 took the majority view that the check is not itself an assignment. Article 3 follows the NIL in that respect.

Although a draft, by its stated terms, is simply an order of the drawer to the drawee to pay, it is also an obligation of the drawer to pay the draft if the draft is dishonored. 3–414(b). "Dishonor" occurs if the drawee fails to make timely payment when the draft is presented for payment. Dishonor of ordinary checks and drafts is defined in 3–502(b) and (e). The drawer of a draft other than a check can avoid liability under 3–414(b) if the signature of the drawer is accompanied by words that disclaim liability such as "without recourse." 3–414(e). Disclaimer of the drawer's liability is normally limited to documentary drafts. Comment 5 to 3–414. With respect to checks, disclaimer is not effective. 3–414(e). A relatively unimportant limitation on drawer's liability is provided by 3–414(f). This provision is explained in Comment 6 to 3–414.

Section 3–408 states that "the drawee is not liable on the instrument until the drawee accepts it." Section 3–409(a) defines "acceptance" as "the drawee's signed agreement to pay a draft as presented." The acceptance "must be written on the draft and may consist of the drawee's signature alone." A drawee that accepts a draft is known as the "acceptor" and is obliged to the holder to pay the draft. 3–413(a). To understand the concept of acceptance better, it is appropriate to distinguish between two types of drafts. The most common type of draft is the demand draft or "sight draft." It contemplates that the amount of the draft will be paid by the drawee upon presentation or "on sight." A draft that does not specify a time of payment is payable on demand. 3–108(a). A check is the most common example of a demand draft. Another type of draft, called a "time draft," does not contemplate immediate payment by the drawee. For example, suppose the draft reads as follows: "Pay $1,000 to the order of Jane Doe sixty days after presentment of this draft." Here, two steps are contemplated. Jane Doe, or some subsequent holder, will initially present the draft to the drawee to start the running of the 60 days, and when that period of time has passed, a second presentment will be made for payment. The first presentment is known as a "presentment for acceptance." Its purpose is to allow the holder to know whether the drawee is agreeable to honoring the draft. Agreement of the drawee is manifested by acceptance, i.e., the drawee's signing of the draft with or without the addition of the word "accepted" or other words indicating an intention to accept. The date of acceptance is normally included but is not required. 3–409(a) and (c). The drawee's acceptance is equivalent to a promise to pay the amount of the draft to the holder. Thus, the obligation of an acceptor is like that of the maker of a note.

Another example of an accepted draft is the certified check. If the payee of an ordinary check wants assurance of payment, one way of getting it is to insist that the drawer obtain the acceptance of the drawee bank before the check is taken by the payee. This is done by the drawee bank's signing the check in much the same way as described in the case of a time draft. But the terminology differs. The bank's signature is called "certification" but it is identical to acceptance. 3–409(d). Certification is normally obtained by the drawer before delivery of the check to the payee, but in unusual cases, the holder of an uncertified check may prefer to obtain the drawee bank's agreement to pay rather than payment itself. This can be done by asking the drawee bank to certify the check. The drawee of a check may certify it as a courtesy to the drawer or to the holder, but is not obliged to do so. Nor is refusal to certify a dishonor of the check. 3–409(d). Because certification of a check is treated by the bank as the equivalent of payment insofar as the drawer is concerned, the account of the drawer will be debited in the amount of the check at the time of certification. The effect of certification is to transform the check, which originally represented an order to pay by the drawer, into a promise of the drawee to pay the amount of the check to its holder. This transformation is reflected in 3–414(c), which states that acceptance of a draft by a bank discharges the drawer's obligation to pay the draft.

PROBLEM

Seller contracted to sell real property to Buyer for $150,000 cash to be paid on the settlement date by a certified check. Buyer arrived at the settlement with an uncertified check drawn on her funds in Drawee Bank. When Seller refused to take the check, Buyer induced Seller to call Drawee Bank and inquire about the balance of her account. An authorized person at the bank assured Seller that there were funds in the account sufficient to cover the check. "But," Seller countered, "will there be funds there when the check is presented?" The bank representative replied in the affirmative, and when asked to confirm this in writing, sent an immediate fax to Seller stating: "This letter is to verify that the funds are available in Buyer's account. There is a hold on the funds for the check that was given to you." When Seller presented the check for payment, Drawee Bank dishonored on the ground of insufficient funds in the account. The bank representative had mistakenly misstated the balance of the account. Is Drawee Bank liable to Seller on the check? The facts are based on those in Harrington v. MacNab, 163 F.Supp.2d 583 (D.Md. 2001). See also Call v. Ellenville Nat'l Bank, 774 N.Y.2d 76 (N.Y. App. Div. 2004) (bank not bound by oral representation that check had "cleared.")

C. LIABILITY OF INDORSER

In the previous chapter, we examined the function of an indorsement in the negotiation of an instrument. Indorsement also has the additional function of causing the indorser to incur liability on the instrument. The obligation of the indorser, stated in 3–415(a), is to pay the instrument if the instrument is dishonored, but indorser's liability may be avoided by appropriate words accompanying the signature that disclaim liability. The most commonly used words indicating disclaimer are "without recourse." 3–415(b). An indorsement containing such language is called a "qualified indorsement." As we see in Problem 2 below, indorser's liability can be an unpleasant surprise to holders who believe that they are indorsing merely to transfer the instrument.

PROBLEMS

1. Employer sent Peter his paycheck in the amount of $5,000, drawn on Bank One. Peter indorsed the check in blank and deposited it in his depositary bank, Bank Two. Bank Two gave Peter immediate credit for the check in his account, and Peter withdrew the amount of the credit before Bank Two learned that Bank One had dishonored the check because Employer had previously withdrawn all of the money from the account. Employer went out of business, costing Peter his job. Immediately after learning of Bank One's dishonor, Bank Two conveyed the information to an impecunious Peter and demanded $5,000 from him. (i) If Bank Two chooses not to proceed against insolvent Employer on the check, is Peter personally liable to Bank Two for $5,000? (ii) Would Peter have to pay if Bank One waited two months before it demanded payment? 3-503(a), (c). (iii) If Peter has to pay, may he enforce the check against Employer? 3–414(b).

2. Seller sold residential real property to Buyer for the price of $100,000. Buyer was able to borrow $75,000 from a bank, secured by a first mortgage on the property. But Buyer didn't have enough cash to come up with the remaining $25,000. In order to make the sale, Seller agreed to take a second mortgage on the property from Buyer that secured a negotiable promissory note, payable in installments over ten years, in the amount of $20,000 made by Buyer to Seller. Buyer paid Seller the remaining $5,000 balance in cash. In State A, where the land was located, there is a secondary market for second mortgage notes, and Investor was willing to pay Seller $15,000 in cash for the note. Seller indorsed in blank the note to Investor and assigned the mortgage. Buyer defaulted on the payments on the $20,000 note, but under State A's real property anti-deficiency law Buyer is not personally liable on a purchase-money note. Thus, Investor had no right to sue Buyer on the note, so it brought suit against Seller as an indorser. Is Seller liable to Investor on the

note even though the maker, Buyer, was not liable? Had Seller talked to you before indorsing the note, what advice would you have given him? See 3–415(b).

DRAFTS

The obligation of the indorser to pay an instrument arises upon its dishonor. With respect to unaccepted drafts, dishonor usually requires presentment for payment and a failure of the drawee to pay. 3–502(b)(1) through (3). With respect to some time drafts, dishonor requires presentment for acceptance and failure of the drawee to accept. 3–502(b)(4). In some cases, dishonor can occur without presentment. 3–502(e) and 3–504(a).

The obligation of an indorser of an unaccepted draft is subject to discharge in two situations. First, if the draft is a check and collection of the check is not initiated within 30 days of the indorsement, the indorser is discharged. 3–415(e). Second, discharge can occur as the result of a failure to give timely notice of dishonor to the indorser. 3–415(c) and 3–503(a). The manner and time for giving notice are stated in 3–503(b) and (c). Notice of dishonor need not be given if it is excused. 3–504(b). Delay in giving notice may also be excused in some cases. 3–504(c).

Indorser's liability with respect to checks has very limited importance because most checks are deposited by the payee with a depositary bank for collection. The depositary bank gives the depositor provisional credit for the check. Under 4–214(a), if the check is dishonored, the depositary bank may revoke the credit or otherwise obtain refund from the depositor. Normally, the depositary bank will use this remedy rather than the remedy provided by 3–415(a).

If a draft is accepted by a bank after the draft is indorsed, the indorser is discharged. 3–415(d). The rule is similar to 3–414(c) with respect to the liability of a drawer. Thus, with respect to an accepted draft, an indorser has liability under 3–415(a) only if the indorsement is made after the acceptance or if the acceptor is not a bank. Rules with respect to dishonor of accepted drafts are stated in 3–502(d).

NOTES

Dishonor of a note payable at a definite time does not normally require presentment unless the note is payable at or through a bank. 3–502(a)(2) and (3). In the case of notes that do not require presentment, indorser's liability under 3–415(a) arises automatically if the note is not paid when due. If a note is payable on demand, is payable at or through a bank, or the terms of the note require presentment, dishonor requires presentment and a failure to pay by the maker. But the requirements in 3–502(a) with respect to presentment can be waived. 3–504(a). Notice of dishonor required by 3–503(a) also can be waived, and waiver of presentment is also waiver of notice of dishonor. 3–504(b). Since most promissory note forms contain a clause waiving presentment and notice of dishonor, these formalities have little importance with respect to indorser liability in note cases. See the Promissory Note and Demand Note forms at the end of the previous chapter.

D. LIABILITY OF TRANSFEROR

Answer the following Problem on the basis of the discussion in the text following the Problem.

PROBLEM

Maker signed and delivered a promissory note for $1,000 payable to the order of Payee one year after date. Shortly after receiving the note, Payee, who had fraudulently induced Maker to issue the note, indorsed the note "without recourse" and sold it to Holder for $600. When Holder presented the note to Maker for payment, Maker refused to pay because she had learned that Payee had defrauded her. Does Holder have rights against Payee? See 3–415(b) and 3–416(a)(4). Comment 5 to 3–416.

If goods are sold, the law gives to the buyer the benefit of certain warranties of the seller that are implied by reason of the sale and which apply unless they are disclaimed in the contract between the parties. For example, the seller warrants that the buyer is receiving good title to the goods and, if the seller is a merchant, that the goods are fit for the ordinary purposes for which such goods are used. 2–312(1) and 2–314. If an instrument is sold, the law gives to the buyer the benefit of implied warranties that are comparable to sale of goods warranties, but which are expressed in terms appropriate to what the buyer is buying—a right to receive payment from the person obliged to pay the instrument. These warranties are known as "transfer warranties" and are stated in 3–416(a).

Two of the transfer warranties relate to the authenticity of the instrument: the transferor warrants that all signatures are authentic and authorized, and the instrument has not been altered. 3–416(a)(2) and (3). The other three warranties relate to the enforceability of the instrument. Under 3–416(a)(1), there is a warranty that the transferor is a person entitled to enforce the instrument. If the transferor is a person entitled to enforce the instrument, transfer will give the transferee that right. 3–203(b). The 3–416(a)(1) warranty, in practice, serves as a warranty that there are no unauthorized or missing indorsements that prevent the transferor from giving to the transferee the right to enforce the instrument. Under 3–416(a)(4), there is a warranty that the right to enforce the instrument is not subject to defenses that can be asserted against the transferor. Finally, there is a warranty that the transferor has no knowledge of bankruptcy or other insolvency proceedings initiated against the person obliged to pay the instrument. 3–416(a)(5).

The transfer warranties are of very limited importance because in most cases the transferor is also an indorser and, as such, guarantees payment of the instrument. 3–415(a). In those cases, the transfer warranties are redundant because the guarantee of payment gives greater rights to the transferee than do the warranties. Thus, the transfer warranties are important only in cases in which the transfer is made without indorsement or there is an indorsement without recourse. If the payee of a note indorsed the note without recourse, the transferee is assured of receiving an authentic and enforceable instrument but takes the risk that the maker will be unwilling or unable to pay the note.

E. Cashier's Checks and Teller's Checks

In this section we give detailed treatment to the rights of parties under cashier's checks and teller's checks. Our objective is to help you deal with one of the contemporary dilemmas facing business lawyers: how to take payment when the deal closes. Since the obligor side is not likely to lug sacks of money to the closing, the obligee should obtain agreement in advance on how payment is to be made. The ordinary uncertificated check leaves the payee vulnerable on several grounds: the drawer may stop payment on the check, thereby placing the burden on the payee to come after the drawer for payment; the drawer may have no money in its account in the bank; or, in rare cases, the bank on which payment is drawn may suspend payments before the check is paid because of insolvency, leaving the payee with a claim against the bank not covered by deposit insurance because the bank has no liability on the check (3–408) and therefore the payee has no "deposit" insured by the Federal Deposit Insurance Act. 12 U.S.C. § 1813(*l*) ("deposit"). On the other hand, we will see that no one can stop payment under 4–403 on a cashier's check; the payee can be sure that a cashier's check will not be returned marked "not sufficient funds;" and, even if the bank fails, the holder of the check is protected, at least to the extent of $250,000 by federal deposit insurance. 12 U.S.C. § 1813(*l*)(4). So why is it that in some cases even when the parties are across the street from each other, the obligee will insist on a wire transfer, which we will study in a later chapter, instead of a cashier's check? But first we have more to learn about cashier's checks.

1. Use in Payment of Obligations

In some transactions, a creditor is unwilling to take the personal check of the debtor in payment of the obligation owed to the creditor. Instead, the creditor may insist on delivery by the debtor of the obligation of a bank as payment. The debtor can comply by delivering a cashier's check, a teller's check, or a check of the debtor that has been certified by the drawee. We have already discussed the certified check. Some banks have discontinued the practice of certifying checks. Cashier's checks and teller's checks have become the principal means of allowing a debtor to pay a debt with a bank obligation.

A cashier's check is a rather strange instrument. It is always issued by a bank and is in the form of an ordinary check, except that the drawer and the drawee are the same bank. Thus, Bank A orders itself to pay a sum of money to the payee stated in the instrument. One can justly argue that an order to oneself to pay money is fundamentally different from an order by one person to another person to pay money. The liability of the "issuer" (3–105(c)) of a cashier's check is not stated in 3–414(b), which applies to drawers of drafts (3–414(a)), but in 3–412, and is identical to the obligation of the maker of a note. However, 3–104(f) follows the universal banking practice of referring to a cashier's check as a check. This practice is also reflected in legislation other than Articles 3 and 4. Section 3–103(a)(8) defines "order" as a "written instruction to pay money" and artificially states that the "instruction may be addressed to any person, including the person giving the instruction." Thus, a cashier's check is an order and, under 3–104(e) and (f), is a draft and a check. The purpose of the artificiality in the definition of "order" was to allow references to drafts and checks in Article 3 to include cashier's checks.

A teller's check, like a cashier's check, is always issued by a bank. The difference between the two is that a cashier's check is drawn on the issuing bank while a teller's check typically is drawn on another bank. In some cases a teller's check is drawn on a nonbank but is payable at or through a bank. 3–104(h). A typical use of teller's checks is the practice of credit unions or small banks of maintaining deposits in regional or city banks from which to make payments. The issuer of a teller's check is obliged to pay the check as drawer of the check. 3–414(b). If a teller's check is issued by Bank A and the check is drawn on Bank B, presentment for payment of the check is made to Bank B, the drawee. As in the case of the drawee of an ordinary check, Bank B as drawee of a teller's check has no obligation to the payee to pay the check. 3–408. If the check is dishonored, the remedy of the payee is against Bank A. Thus, a teller's check represents an obligation of the bank that issues the check, not of the bank on which it is drawn.

One of the aspects in which cashier's checks differ from ordinary checks is the effect of taking a check on the underlying obligation for which the check was given. Section 3–310(b)(1) provides that if an uncertified check is taken for an obligation, the obligation is suspended "until dishonor of the check or until it is paid or certified." If the check clears, the obligation is discharged; if it is dishonored, the payee has a choice whether to take action against the drawer on the check or on the underlying obligation. Usually, there is no advantage to the payee in being able to pursue the drawer on the underlying transaction, but in a few instances there may be. However, if the obligee takes a cashier's check for an obligation, the obligation is discharged (3–310(a)) and the payee is restricted to its rights on the check against the issuing bank. See Fifth Third Bank v. Jones, 168 P.3d 1 (Colo. Ct. App. 2007). As we explained above, if the bank has failed, the holder is insured by federal deposit insurance.

PROBLEM

Seller contracted to sell goods to Buyer with payment by cashier's check to be made at the time of delivery. Buyer purchased a cashier's check in the amount of $10,000 from Bank made payable to Seller. Bank delivered the check to Buyer who held it pending Seller's performance. Before delivering the cashier's check to Seller, Buyer learned that Seller did not intend to comply with the contract. Buyer asked Bank to return the money that it paid to Bank to issue the check, but Bank delayed in doing so. Is Buyer, the remitter, a person entitled to enforce the instrument under 3–301? The prevailing view in case law is that since a remitter is not a party to an instrument, it cannot enforce the instrument under 3–301. The authorities are marshaled in Perrino v. Salem, Inc., 243 B.R. 550 (D. Me. 1999), which states that although Article 3 does not directly address the issue in the text, Comment 1 to 3–312 expressly says that a remitter is not a person entitled to enforce a check. How do you reconcile this Comment with the 2002 addition to the Comment to 3–301? What is the statutory basis for this language?

2. PAYMENT WITH NOTICE OF ADVERSE CLAIM

a. RIGHT TO STOP PAYMENT

The right of a buyer, who has paid a seller with a cashier's check or a teller's check and has either been defrauded or has received defective goods, to stop payment on the check are considered in the following Problems and the text following the Problems.

PROBLEMS

1. Seller agreed to sell goods to Buyer but insisted on immediate payment by means of a cashier's check or teller's check. Buyer had an account in Bank A. At the request of Buyer, Bank A issued a cashier's check payable to the order of Seller and delivered it to Buyer. Bank A debited the account of Buyer in the amount of the cashier's check. Buyer delivered the check to Seller, but Seller failed to deliver the promised goods stating that they would be delivered as soon as they became available. Buyer, fearing fraud on the part of Seller, stated that Seller had promised immediate delivery and demanded return of the check but Seller refused. Buyer ordered Bank A to stop payment on the check. Since the funds to pay for the cashier's check were withdrawn from Buyer's account, must Bank A comply with Buyer's stop payment order under 4–403(a)?

2. Assume the same facts as in Problem 1 except that at the request of Buyer, Bank A issued a teller's check drawn on Bank B payable to the order of Seller. Bank A debited the account of Buyer in the amount of the teller's check. Buyer delivered the check to Seller. Buyer ordered Bank B to stop payment of the check. Must Bank B comply with Buyer's stop payment order under 4–403(a)? What is Bank A's liability on the check?

Suppose a buyer pays for goods by delivering the buyer's uncertified personal check to the seller. Shortly after the goods are delivered, the buyer examines them and decides that they are unsatisfactory. The buyer seeks to return the goods to the seller and obtain return of the check. The seller denies that the goods are defective and refuses to return the buyer's check. Or, suppose there is a fraudulent sale; the seller took the buyer's check after promising to deliver the goods, but the seller had no intention of carrying out the promise. No goods were ever delivered to the buyer. In either of these two cases the best remedy of the buyer is to prevent the drawee of the check from paying the check. Without that remedy, the buyer has the burden of bringing an action against the seller. If the buyer can prevent payment of the check, it is the seller who has the burden of bringing an action. The buyer can prevent payment of an uncertified check of the buyer if the buyer can act very quickly. The check issued by the buyer to the seller functions as an order by the buyer to the buyer's bank to pay money to the seller. Section 4–403 allows the buyer to countermand that order by what is referred to as a "stop-payment order," which is simply an instruction to the bank not to pay the check. A stop-payment order may be given orally or in writing and must describe the check with reasonable certainty so that the bank can identify the check. The bank is obliged to carry out the order if it is received in time to allow the bank a reasonable opportunity to act on the order before the check is paid. 4–403(a). Failure to carry out the order can give rise to an action for damages. 4–403(c).

The remedy provided by 4–403 is not available, however, if the buyer pays for the goods with a certified check, cashier's check, or teller's check. Section 4–403 applies only to an "item (check) drawn on the customer's (buyer's) account." What are the rights of the buyer under 4–403 if a certified check is delivered to the seller? A certified check, in form, is drawn on the customer's account, but it is not treated that way under 4–403(a). The right of a customer to stop payment of a check is conditioned upon receipt by the bank of a stop-payment order "before any action by the bank with respect to the item described in Section 4–303." One of the actions referred to in 4–303 is payment of the check. 4–303(a)(2). Another is certification. 4–303(a)(1). So far as the rights and obligations of the drawer are concerned, certification of a check is treated as the equivalent of payment. When the check is certified it is treated as an obligation of the certifying bank rather than an item drawn on the drawer's account. Thus, if the buyer delivers a certified check to the seller, no right to stop payment of the check ever arises.

If the buyer delivered a cashier's check or teller's check to the seller, the analysis under 4–403 is somewhat different. A cashier's check or teller's check is not drawn on the buyer's account even though the buyer may have bought the check from the buyer's bank which obtained payment for it by debiting the buyer's account. Section 4–403 allows the buyer to stop payment of a check of the buyer, but does not allow the buyer to stop payment of a check issued by the buyer's bank. Comment 4 to 4–403. Section 4–403 does not apply at all to a cashier's check because the obligation of the issuer is the same as the obligation of the issuer of a note. 3–412. There is no instruction by one person to another that can be countermanded. Section 4–403 does apply to a teller's check. The issuer of a teller's check is like the drawer of an ordinary check. The bank issuing the teller's check draws the check on the account of the issuer in the drawee bank. The issuer is a customer of the drawee bank. § 4–104(a)(5). Thus, under 4–403, the issuer of the teller's check has a right to stop payment by the drawee bank. But that right belongs only to the issuer of the check; the buyer has no right to stop payment.

b. ISSUING BANK DELAYS PAYMENT

Cashier's checks are usually issued by banks at the request of customers of the bank. Some customers may be big institutions that provide a large volume of business for the bank. If such a valued customer of an issuing bank wishes to have payment stopped on a cashier's check, a patient explanation by the bank of why it cannot stop payment on the check under the law may not satisfy the customer. "Just do it," the angry customer says as he slams down the receiver. The following Problem addresses this issue and Revised Article 3's solution.

PROBLEM

Seller agreed to sell goods to Buyer but insisted on immediate payment by means of a cashier's check before it would deliver the goods. Buyer had an account in Bank, and, at the request of Buyer, Bank issued a cashier's check payable to the order of Seller and delivered it to Buyer. Buyer delivered the check to Seller who promised shipment of the goods the following day. Overnight, Buyer developed a common commercial affliction known as "buyer's remorse" and pleaded with Seller to call the deal off and return the check. When Seller proved unreasonable, Buyer demanded that Bank not pay the check ("Just do it!"), promising to reimburse it for any litigation expenses if Seller pressed its claim. Buyer assured Bank that Seller probably didn't want a lawsuit and would just drop the whole matter. Assuming that Buyer is a very good customer of Bank, would you advise Bank that, in view of 3–411, Bank should hold out for an indemnification agreement from Buyer before paying? See 3–411(b) and Comment 2 to 3–411. See MidAmerica Bank, FSB v. Charter One Bank, FSB, 905 N.E.2d 839 (Ill. 2009).

3. Issuing Bank's Right to Raise Own Claims or Defenses

In our inquiry into the question whether you would advise a client to accept a cashier's check in payment, we have seen that the person obtaining a cashier's check has no right to stop payment on the check under 4–403. The issuing bank also cannot assert defenses of others (3–305(c)) unless they are impleaded by the issuer in the holder's action against it (3-305(c)). This leaves a third issue to be resolved: can the issuing bank raise its own claims or defenses when a cashier's check is presented to it for payment? Before enactment of Revised Article 3, there was a split of authority in the cases, as well as a lively disagreement among commentators, on the matter. The initial article on the subject was Lary Lawrence, Making Cashier's Checks and Other Bank Checks Cost–Effective: A Plea for Revision of Articles 3 and 4 of the Uniform Commercial Code, 64 Minn. L. Rev. 275 (1980), which advocated making cashier's checks "cash equivalents" by prohibiting issuing banks from raising any defenses to payment even against non-holders in due course. Flatiron Linen, Inc. v. First American State Bank, 23 P.3d 1209 (Colo. 2001), stated the policy basis for the cashier's-check-as-cash view: "The commercial world treats cashier's checks as the equivalent of cash. People accept cashier's checks as a substitute for cash because the bank, not an individual, stands behind it. By issuing a cashier's check, the bank becomes the guarantor of the value of the check and pledges its resources to the payment of the amount represented upon presentation. 'To allow the bank to stop payment on such an instrument would be inconsistent with the representation it makes in issuing the check. Such a rule would undermine the public confidence in the bank and its checks and thereby deprive the cashier's check of the essential incident which makes it useful.'" Id. at 1213. No mention was made of 3-411.

The cash equivalent theory found no support in Revised Article 3, and 3–411(c) allows the "obligated bank" to refuse payment with impunity if it "asserts a claim or defense of the bank that it has reasonable grounds to believe is available against the person entitled to enforce the instrument." The court in Transcontinental Holding LTD v. First Banks, Inc., 299 S.W.3d 629 (Mo. Ct. App. 2009), allowed the obligated bank to raise its own defense of failure of consideration. But in MidAmerica Bank, FSB v. Charter One Bank, FSB, 905 N.E.2d 839 (Ill. 2009), the drawee's refusal to pay its cashier's check based solely on its customer's request to stop payment was wrongful.

The following Problem probes the meaning of 3-411(c).

PROBLEM

Rolando requested that Bank One issue a cashier's check for $10,000, which he intended to use to pay for goods that Parsons agreed to sell Rolando. Rolando paid for the cashier's check by giving Bank One an ordinary check for $10,000 drawn on his account in Bank Two. At Rolando's request, Bank One made the check payable to Rolando, who indorsed and delivered it to Parsons, who then delivered the goods to Rolando. When Parsons presented the cashier's check to Bank One for payment, it dishonored the check because Rolando's check was returned by Bank Two for insufficient funds. Bank One refused to pay the cashier's check on the ground that it had been fraudulently induced to issue the check and was protected from expenses or consequential damages by 3–411(c)(ii). Does Bank One have "reasonable grounds to believe" that the defense is "available" against Parsons even though it knew that Parsons might be able to prove that he is a holder in due course? See State Bank & Trust v. First State Bank of Texas, 242 F.3d 390 (10th Cir.2000).

4. LOST INSTRUMENTS

a. LOST INSTRUMENTS UNDER SECTION 3–309

We have seen that the person obliged to pay an instrument can obtain discharge by paying the holder even if some other person has a claim to the instrument. The discharge can be asserted against anyone other than a person with rights of a holder in due course who took the instrument without notice of the discharge. 3–601(b). If the instrument is surrendered when payment is made, there is no risk that the instrument will be negotiated to a holder in due course. But we have also seen that in some cases the person entitled to enforce the instrument is not in possession of the instrument. 3–301. Although payment to a person entitled to enforce who does not have possession results in discharge (3–602(a)), there is the possibility that the instrument is in existence and has or will come into the possession of a holder in due course. Section 3–309 deals with enforcement of lost instruments. Suppose the payee indorses the instrument in blank and then loses it. The payee can enforce the instrument, but 3–309(b) requires the court to find that the person required to pay the instrument is "adequately protected against loss that might occur by reason of a claim by another person to enforce the instrument." The predecessor of 3–309 was 3–804 of former Article 3, which provided that "[t]he court may require security indemnifying the defendant against loss by reason of further claims on the instrument." The quoted language in 3–804 was not uniformly adopted. Some states, including New York, as we see in *Diaz* below, changed the language in their versions of former Article 3.

The 2002 amendment to 3–309 is illustrated by the following Problem.

PROBLEM

Maker borrowed $100,000 from Bank and evidenced its loan by a promissory note payable to the order of Bank. When Bank failed, the Federal Deposit Insurance Corporation (FDIC) acquired the note when it became receiver for Bank. FDIC sold the note in a batch of several hundred notes to Pooler, which planned to securitize the notes and issue bonds backed by the note pool. Later, FDIC disclosed to Pooler that it had lost the original of the note before the sale and that possession of the note had never been delivered to Pooler. Pooler now brings suit against Maker on the note under 3–309 as a lost note. Maker defended on the ground that Pooler never had possession of the note and could not have lost it. What does Pooler have to prove to recover under 3–309? The facts are suggested by those in Dennis Joslin Co., LLC v. Robinson Broadcasting Corp., 977 F.Supp. 491 (D.D.C. 1997).

NOTE

In the contemporary world in which notes are pooled and sold in bulk to others for securitization, it is likely that the assignee's first step upon learning that it didn't receive the note would be to proceed against the assignor under warranties contained in the assignment to assure the assignee that it received all the notes described in the assignment documents. Since in large portfolio purchases "due diligence" may not extend to examining each file for a note, the transferee should bargain for a blanket warranty that protects it if a note is missing by requiring the transferor to repurchase the rights to missing notes. The transfer warranty of 3–416 does not apply because the note was not delivered under 3–203(a).

b. LOST CASHIER'S, TELLER'S OR CERTIFIED CHECKS UNDER SECTION 3–312

Although 3–309 and its predecessor, former 3–804, apply to any instrument, most lost instrument problems arise with respect to cashier's checks, teller's checks, and certified checks. Section 3–312, which has no predecessor, applies only to these bank obligations and can be used as an alternative to 3–309. But in some cases a person with rights under 3–312 does not have rights under 3–309 because the person is not a person entitled to enforce the instrument. In that category are remitters of cashier's checks or teller's checks and drawers of certified checks who cannot enforce the lost check, but who can use 3–312 to obtain refund from the bank that issued or certified the check. See Comment 1 to 3–312. Cf. Comment to 3–301.

Diaz, which follows, was decided under the New York version of 3–804 of the original Article 3. It involved loss of a certified check by the payee of the check. Section 3–312 was a direct response to the hardship suffered by people in the position of Ms. Diaz in the following case.

Diaz v. Manufacturers Hanover Trust Co.

New York Supreme Court, Queens County, Special Term, 1977.
92 Misc.2d 802, 401 N.Y.S.2d 952.

■ MARTIN RODELL, JUSTICE.

The petitioner moves by order to show cause to require the respondent Manufacturers Hanover Trust Company to pay the sum of $37,000 or in the alternative to require the respondent Al Newman to issue a new negotiable instrument to her in the same amount.

The facts are uncontroverted. The petitioner posted the sum of $37,000 as security for a bond in behalf of a defendant in a criminal proceeding. Said security was posted with the respondent Newman, a licensed bail bondsman.

The aforementioned criminal action was concluded on July 20, 1977. Subsequently, the petitioner made demand upon the respondent Newman for the sum of $37,000, which she had heretofore posted with him. On August 4, 1977 the respondent Newman dutifully delivered to the petitioner two certified checks, in the amounts of $12,000 and $25,000, drawn on the respondent Manufacturers Hanover Trust Company. Shortly thereafter, the petitioner lost, misplaced, or was criminally relieved of the said certified checks and has to this date been unable to locate them.

The petitioner notified the respondent Newman, who, in turn, requested that the respondent Manufacturers Hanover Trust Co. stop payment. To this date, the checks have not been presented to Manufacturers Hanover Trust Co. for payment.

The petitioner also contacted an unnamed officer of the respondent Manufacturers Hanover Trust Co., who informed her that the bank would not honor any replacement checks issued by the respondent Newman unless an indemnity bond was posted in twice the amount of the original checks. The petitioner avers that this is an onerous and unjust burden; justifiably so, as it would require the posting of $74,000 as security.

.... When a bank certifies a check, it accepts that check and has the obligation to pay the amount for which it is drawn.... The bank in certifying a check obligates itself to an innocent holder in due course to pay the amount for which the check is drawn. Thus, the respondent Manufacturers Hanover Trust Co., through its act of certification, assumed liability on the instruments.

> The owner of an instrument which is lost, whether by destruction, theft or otherwise, may maintain an action in his own name and recover from any party liable thereon upon due proof of his ownership, the facts which prevent his production of the instrument and its terms. The court shall require security, in an amount fixed by the court not less than twice the amount allegedly unpaid on the instrument, indemnifying the defendant, his heirs, personal representatives, successors and assigns against loss, including costs and expenses, by reason of further claims on the instrument, but this provision does not apply where an action is prosecuted or defended by the state or by a public officer in its behalf. L.1962, c. 553; amended L.1963, c. 1003, § 9, eff. Sept. 27, 1964 (Uniform Commercial Code, § 3–804.)

While it is clear that the petitioner has the right to recover the amount of the checks upon sufficient proof that in fact the checks did at one time exist, were payable to her and cannot be produced, the issue to be decided is presented to this court as follows:

May the court order payment on a lost negotiable instrument without requiring the payee to post security as required in Uniform Commercial Code, § 3–804? In 487 Clinton Avenue v. Chase Manhattan, 63 Misc.2d 715, 313 N.Y.S.2d 445 (1970, Supreme Court, Kings County), the payee of a certified check was robbed of same at gun point and offered to pay the proceeds into an account controlled by the certifying bank. The court held that it had discretion to fix the security and that the security offered by the plaintiff was adequate.

The court notes that no appeal has been taken from the above decision, and thus no Appellate Court guidance is available. However, the Supreme Court in New York County in Guizani v. Manufacturers Hanover Trust, N.Y.L.J. October 12, 1971, p. 2, col. 5, held that under New York's version of this section (Uniform Commercial Code, § 3–804), the furnishing of the security is mandatory and not discretionary.

The section, as drawn by the drafters of the Uniform Commercial Code, and found in the Official Text and Official Commentaries, made the requirement for security discretionary with the court by the use of the word "*may.*" The Official Commentaries to the Uniform Commercial Code state as follows:

> "There may be cases in which so much time has elapsed, or there is so little possible doubt as to the destruction of the instrument and its ownership that there is no good reason to require the security."

The court, in 487 Clinton Avenue v. Chase Manhattan, supra, predicated its decision on the above reasoning. However, the New York version of section 3–804 of the Uniform Commercial Code pointedly changed the word "may" to "shall," and the Legislature in 1964 further amended this section to fix the amount of security to be not less than twice the amount allegedly unpaid on the instrument.... Thus, our Legislature appears to have considered the matter and amended the statute to make the furnishing of security not only mandatory but has also set the minimal amount at not less than twice the amount allegedly unpaid on the instrument.

....

The New York Commission Commentaries on section 3–804 of the Uniform Commercial Code leave little doubt that the express purpose of the Legislature was to make the furnishing of security mandatory rather than discretionary and thus conform to section 333 of the old Civil Practice Act.

....

If the court is to have the authority to determine the amount of security to be furnished, it would seem on the basis of the legislative history of this section that the change must come from the Legislature.

The court notes additionally that this section, as enacted by our Legislature, while being most positive in regard to the requirement of security and the amount thereof, fails to set any limit whatsoever as to the amount of time the security shall remain posted. The problem of the longevity of a certified check no doubt rendered the Legislature unable to fix a time limit. There being no legislative scheme to either limit the life of a certified check or the duration of time for which a bond must be posted, an unfortunate gap exists into which the petitioner's prayer must fall. It is the opinion of this court that further revision of this section of the Uniform Commercial Code is mandated, or in the alternative, legislation dealing with the valid life of certified checks must be enacted. Simple justice cries out for remedial legislation at the next session of the Legislature. The petitioner is being deprived of her life savings; the bank receives no benefit from the funds which are necessarily frozen. Under the present posture of the law, the funds will remain in that condition until the end of time or it escheats to the state, whichever comes first.

In light of the above, the court is constrained to reject the petitioner's application for recovery without posting of security as required by section 3–804 of the Uniform Commercial Code.

PROBLEMS

How does 3–312 resolve the following problems? Comment 4 to 3–312.

Claimant lives in New York and has her life savings, amounting to almost $100,000, in First Bank. She decided to retire and move to Miami Beach to be near her sister. In anticipation of the move she obtained a cashier's check, dated January 2, from First Bank for $90,000 payable to her order. Her deposit account was immediately debited for $90,000.

1. On January 5, Thief stole Claimant's purse that contained the cashier's check. The check was not indorsed by Claimant. She immediately called First Bank and asked that payment be stopped. An employee explained to her that if she would come in and sign a form asserting a claim to the check she could get her money back 90 days after the date of the check, but if she wanted her money immediately, she would have to provide a bond to protect the bank. 3–309. Having no resources to obtain a bond, Claimant went to First Bank on January 6 and signed a form asserting her rights under 3–312(b). Included in the form was a declaration of loss complying with 3–312(a)(3). Thief forged Claimant's signature as an indorsement of the cashier's check and deposited the check in his account in Second Bank on January 8. The check was promptly presented to First Bank for payment. First Bank paid the check. Thief withdrew the proceeds of the check from his account in Second Bank and absconded. Ninety days after the date of the check, Claimant demanded payment of $90,000 from First Bank. What are Claimant's rights against First Bank if it refuses to pay? If First Bank pays, what are its rights against Second Bank?

2. Change the facts in Problem 1. When First Bank issued the check to Claimant, she indorsed the check by writing her name on the back. She then mailed the check to her sister in Miami Beach who had agreed to deposit it in her account until Claimant could arrive and open her own account. The check was stolen from the mail by Thief who deposited it in his account in Second Bank. By January 10, Claimant realized that something had happened to the check. On that date, she went to First Bank and requested that payment be stopped. She was given the same information that was given in Problem 1 and on January 10 executed the necessary form to claim her rights under 3–312(b). On January 11, Second Bank presented the check to First Bank for payment. First Bank paid the check. Ninety days after the date of the check, Claimant sought $90,000 from First Bank and it refused to pay. What are Claimant's rights against First Bank?

3. Change the facts in Problem 2 in one respect. The check was deposited by Thief in Second Bank on May 10. Second Bank promptly presented the check to First Bank for payment. At the time the check was presented for payment, First Bank had already paid $90,000 to Claimant because 90 days had elapsed since the date of the check. First Bank dishonored the check. What are Second Bank's rights against First Bank and Claimant?

F. ACCOMMODATION PARTIES

1. LIABILITY OF ACCOMMODATION PARTY AND RIGHTS AGAINST ACCOMMODATED PARTY

a. ACCOMMODATED PARTY IS INDIVIDUAL

The issues raised in this basic Problem are discussed in the text following the Problem.

PROBLEM

Bank would lend Son the $25,000 that he needed to start his own business only if his Mother would "co-sign" the note. Mother reluctantly did so by signing her name on the face of the note in the lower right hand corner beneath that of Son. Bank advanced the money to Son. Mother was paid nothing by Son for her cooperation and she received none of the proceeds of the loan. When Son went into default in his payments on the note, Bank asked Mother to pay the note. Mother, who had broken with Son by this time, was reluctant to do so. When Bank threatened to sue her, she demanded that Bank sue Son first, and only if he could not pay the judgment should Bank be allowed to sue her. (1) Is Mother correct on this issue? In what capacity did Mother sign within the meaning of 3–419(b)? (2) If Mother pays the note, what are her rights against Son? (3) If Son pays the note, what are his rights against Mother?

A creditor taking the promissory note of a debtor who is not a good credit risk may require that a third party act as guarantor of the debtor's obligation to pay the note. Sometimes this guaranty is expressly stated. In many cases, however, a person who intends to act as guarantor does not expressly state that intention and signs the note as co-maker or indorser. For example, Son wants to buy equipment from Dealer for use in Son's business venture. Dealer is willing to sell to Son on credit only if Mother signs the note as co-maker along with Son. Two people who sign a note as co-makers are jointly and severally liable to pay the note. 3–412 and 3–116(a). Thus, if the note is not paid at the due date, Dealer, as holder, can enforce payment for the full amount against Son, or Mother, or both. If two people are jointly and severally liable to pay an obligation and one of the obligors pays the entire amount, the normal rule, in the absence of a contrary agreement between the two obligors, is that the burden is shared equally by the two obligors. This principle of equal sharing is expressed as a right of the obligor who pays the obligation to receive "contribution" from the other obligor. 3–116(b). The contribution rule is based on the assumption that the joint obligation was incurred for the joint benefit of the two obligors and that each should contribute equally in the payment of the obligation. But this assumption is not true if Mother did not have any property interest either in Son's business venture or in the equipment for which the note was given. There is a suretyship relationship between Son and Mother. Generically, Mother is referred to as the "surety" and Son is referred to as the "principal" or "principal debtor." In Article 3, the terminology is different. Mother is the "accommodation party," Son is the "accommodated party," and the note is signed by Mother "for accommodation." 3–419(a).

Mother, as accommodation party, has certain rights against Son. If Son doesn't pay the note when due and Mother has to pay, it is only fair that she be entitled to recover from Son the full amount that she paid. He got the full benefit of the transaction that gave rise to the note and, therefore, should have to bear the full burden. Otherwise, Son would be unjustly enriched at the expense of Mother. Instead of having the normal right of contribution from a co-obligor, Mother has a right of "reimbursement" for the amount she paid and has subrogation rights as well. By subrogation, she succeeds to the rights that Dealer had against Son on the note. 3–419(e). When she pays the note, she can require its surrender by Dealer (3–501(b)(2)) and becomes the person entitled to enforce the note. 3–301. Thus, if a note is secured by a security interest in collateral, the accommodation party who pays the note succeeds to the rights of the creditor with respect to the security interest (9–618(a)) and is entitled to a formal transfer of the note and security interest. Reimann v. Hybertsen, 550 P.2d 436 (Or. 1976).

If Son pays the note when due, Son has no right of contribution against Mother because she did not benefit from the transaction. 3–419(f) and 3–116(b).

Any type of instrument can be signed for accommodation, and an accommodation party can sign as maker, drawer, acceptor, or indorser. In the typical case, the instrument is a note and the accommodation party signs either as maker or indorser. We have examined the function of indorsement in the negotiation of an instrument and that is its primary function, but an indorsement can also be made for the purpose of incurring liability on the instrument. 3–204(a). In most cases, the negotiation and liability purposes coincide, but in some cases only one is present. For example, if an instrument is payable to an identified person, negotiation requires indorsement by the holder. 3–201(b). But the holder can negotiate the instrument without incurring liability as an indorser by indorsing without recourse. 3–415(b). The purpose of the indorsement is negotiation, not liability. An indorsement for accommodation is the converse; because it is not made by the holder of the instrument, it has no negotiation function and is referred to in 3–205(d) as an "anomalous indorsement." Its only purpose is to impose liability on the indorser.

PROBLEM

Bob and Ted borrowed money from Bank to set up their own business. Bank required that their wives, Carol (Bob) and Alice (Ted), and Bob's parents, Bill and Mildred, cosign the note. All signed the note in the lower right-hand corner. When Bob and Ted defaulted on the note, Bank demanded and received payment from Bill and Mildred. Neither Bill, Mildred, Carol nor Alice played any part in the business, and the property of the business was in the name of Bob and Ted. The facts in this Problem are based on Fithian v. Jamar, 410 A.2d 569 (Md. 1979).

(a) In a state that does not recognize community property, what are the rights of Bill and Mildred against Bob? Ted? Carol? Alice? See 3–116 and 3–419.

(b) Would your answer change in a community property state?

b. ACCOMMODATED PARTY IS BUSINESS ORGANIZATION

PROBLEM

X owned 50% of the capital stock of Corporation and was its President. Y and Z each owned 25%. Corporation needed money for working capital and borrowed it from Bank which insisted, as a condition to the loan, that X sign the note because of the precarious financial condition of Corporation. The note was signed as follows:

Corporation

By X, President

X, individually

The loan, which is unsecured, was made by crediting the entire principal amount to Corporation's account with Bank and was used entirely for corporate purposes. Corporation has defaulted on the loan. After Corporation's default on the loan to Bank, X paid Bank the entire unpaid balance amounting to $10,000. Is X an accommodation party? Is X entitled to reimbursement from Corporation for the $10,000 paid to Bank, or are X's rights limited to a claim for contribution? Would X's rights be any different if X owned 100% of the stock of Corporation rather than 50%? What do you learn about these questions from the following case?

Plein v. Lackey

Supreme Court of Washington, Third District, en banc, 2003.
67 P.3d 1061.

■ MADSEN, J.

Lee Cameron signed a promissory note both in his corporate capacity and individually, secured by a deed of trust, to purchase property from Sunset Investments for his corporation, Alpen Group, Inc. Later, Cameron paid off the Sunset note. He then sought to enforce the instrument and foreclose the deed of trust when Alpen defaulted. He claims he signed the note as an accommodation party and was therefore entitled to foreclose. We agree.... We reverse the Court of Appeals and reinstate the trial court's grant of summary judgment in favor of Cameron.

FACTS

In 1997, Paul Plein, Bruce White, and Lee Cameron formed Alpen Group Inc. to buy and sell real estate (the group formerly operated as a partnership). In April 1997, Alpen purchased a lot from Sunset Investments, issuing a promissory note for $75,000 to Sunset with the promise to pay stated: "For value received, ALPEN GROUP, INC., A WASHINGTON CORPORATION, promise(s) to pay to SUNSET INVESTMENTS...." The note was secured by a deed of trust naming Sunset as the beneficiary and Alpen as the grantor. It was signed by Cameron as "Secretary/Treasurer" and by White as "Vice–President". Cameron, his wife, Plein (who was president), and his wife each signed "individually."

Alpen also borrowed $136,500 from Columbia State Bank, executing a promissory note also secured by a deed of trust. Columbia loaned the money in part on Sunset's agreement to subordinate its interest in the property to Columbia's. Alpen commenced constructing a log home on the lot. However, more funds were needed, and Cameron advanced $30,000. The money was still insufficient to complete the project and trade creditors were owed an additional $45,000. Cameron declined to loan any more money to Alpen. The parties state that Plein, as president of Alpen, issued deeds of trust against the log home to secure the debt to the trade creditors.

At some point thereafter, Plein was ousted and Cameron became president. Alpen issued a promissory note for the $30,000 that Cameron had advanced to Alpen, secured by another deed of trust on the property. Then, one of the trade creditors sued Alpen in Thurston County Superior Court. The record does not contain any information about that suit beyond the parties' brief descriptions, but it evidently involved a number of claims and cross-claims resulting in payment to the creditor who sued and a judgment entered against Alpen in favor of Plein for $45,000, which Plein recorded. In addition, Cameron received all the stock in Alpen.

At this point, the creditors, in order of their secured interests in the log home property, were (1) Columbia, (2) Sunset, (3) the unpaid trade creditors, (4) Cameron, and (5) Plein. Any equity remaining in the property would be that of Alpen.

According to plaintiffs, "around the time the Thurston County suit was being litigated," the note to Columbia Bank came due and Columbia refused to extend the loan. Clerk's Papers (CP) at 105. In October 1998, Cameron paid the amount due to Columbia with his personal funds and Columbia endorsed the note to Cameron. In addition, Columbia assigned the beneficial interest in its deed of trust to Cameron. Then, in December 1998, the pivotal transaction in this case occurred. Cameron paid the amount due Sunset, Sunset endorsed the promissory note for this loan to Cameron, and Sunset assigned its beneficial interest in its deed of trust to Cameron.

By these two transactions, Cameron, as beneficiary of the two deeds of trust originally issued to Columbia Bank and Sunset, claimed secured interests in the property superior to all other secured interests. He also continued to have a secured interest junior to the trade creditors based on his loan of $30,000 to Alpen.

In October 1999, Cameron, as assignee of the Sunset note, hired attorney Chester Lackey to begin nonjudicial foreclosure proceedings as a result of Alpen's default on the Sunset note. All of the secured creditors received notice of the foreclosure informing them that the trustee's sale of the property would be held on March 31, 2000.

On February 7, 2000, Plein and the trade creditors (hereafter Plein) brought this suit against Cameron and Lackey (hereafter Cameron), seeking a permanent injunction barring the trustee's sale and a declaration that the deed of trust was void because the underlying debt had been paid, i.e., there was no default on the underlying debt. Plein did not seek a preliminary injunction or any other order restraining the sale. On March 28, three days before the scheduled sale, Plein filed a motion for summary judgment, claiming that undisputed facts showed that Cameron paid off the Sunset note on behalf of Alpen, thus extinguishing the debt. Plein further claimed that he was entitled to an order declaring that his and the trade creditors security interests were superior to Cameron's and that the foreclosure proceedings were void.

Plein did not obtain a preliminary injunction or restraining order restraining the sale, and on March 31, the trustee's sale occurred. Cameron, the only bidder, bought the property for $245,312.35 (approximately the total of the Columbia, Sunset, and Cameron notes).

On May 1, 2000, Cameron filed a cross-motion for summary judgment. He argued there was no evidence supporting Plein's motion for summary judgment because Mr. Plein's declaration, the only material submitted by Plein, was not made on personal knowledge. Cameron also argued he was entitled to summary judgment because the evidence indisputably established that Cameron purchased the Sunset and Columbia notes and obtained valid assignments of the promissory notes and deeds of trust for his personal benefit, rather than paying on behalf of Alpen. Cameron also argued that Plein failed to timely and properly object to the sale, pointing out Plein did not seek a preliminary injunction or a restraining order in time to restrain the trustee's sale.

The trial court granted Cameron's motion and dismissed Plein's complaint. Plein appealed and the Court of Appeals reversed. That court reasoned that where a person is individually liable on a note and pays it, the individual cannot also foreclose because the debt has been extinguished. The court held that there are disputed facts regarding Cameron's personal liability on the Sunset note that preclude summary judgment. In addition, the Court of Appeals reasoned that if Cameron was personally liable on the note, then Plein's failure to obtain an order restraining the foreclosure sale would make no difference because the debt would have been extinguished, Cameron would have nothing on which to foreclose, and the trustee's sale would be null and void.

Cameron petitioned for review by this court; his petition was granted. For the first time, he specifically relies on RCW 62A.3–419, a provision in the Uniform Commercial Code, to argue that he signed the Sunset note as an accommodation party, and that as such he had the right, once he paid the note, to enforce the instrument against Alpen and to foreclose the deed of trust....

ANALYSIS

Application of RCW 62A.3–419 resolves the first issue in this case, whether Cameron signed the Sunset note as an accommodation party....

Section 3–419(1) provides that

> [i]f an instrument is issued for value given for the benefit of a party to the instrument ("accommodated party") and another party to the instrument ("accommodation party") signs the instrument for the purpose of incurring liability on the instrument without being a direct beneficiary of the value given for the instrument, the instrument is signed by the accommodation party "for accommodation."

The comments to the statute explain that "[a]n accommodation party is a person who signs an instrument to benefit the accommodated party either by signing at the time value is obtained by the accommodated party or later, and who is not a direct beneficiary of the value obtained." RCWA 62A.3–419, cmt. 1, at 161. The issue whether a party is an accommodation party is a question of fact, comment 3 to section 3–419, and the party asserting accommodation party status bears the burden of proof.

Comment 1 to section .3–419 gives an example of accommodation party status that parallels the facts of this case:

> For example, if X cosigns a note of Corporation that is given for a loan to Corporation, X is an accommodation party if no part of the loan was paid to X or for X's direct benefit. This is true even though X may receive indirect benefit from the loan because X is employed by Corporation or is a stockholder of Corporation, or even if X is the sole stockholder so long as Corporation and X are recognized as separate entities.[2]

Here, the promissory note states that for value received, *Alpen* promised to repay the borrowed amount. The direct beneficiary of the loan was the corporation. As a stockholder of Alpen, any benefit obtained by Cameron was derivative and indirect. *See* Neil B. Cohen, *Suretyship Principles in the New Article 3: Clarifications and Substantive Changes,* 42 ALA. L. REV. 595, 600 (1991). Thus, Cameron received no proceeds from and no direct benefit from the loan.

In addition to the direct/indirect benefit inquiry, another factor that serves to establish accommodation party status is that the lender would not have made the loan in the absence of the party's signature on the note giving rise to liability. *Hendel v. Medley,* 66 Wash.App. 896, 899, 833 P.2d 448 (1992) (decided under former UCC provisions regarding accommodation parties); 11 AM.JUR.2D *Bills and Notes* § 85 (2002) (two primary factors that indicate accommodation party status are that the party received no direct benefit from the proceeds of the instrument and that the loan would not have been made unless the party signed the instrument). Here, Plein's complaint itself asserts that Sunset would not have loaned the money to Alpen, which had no assets, unless the corporate officers signed individually, thus incurring personal liability. Plein repeats this factual statement in his appellate brief. ("[b]ecause Alpen had virtually no other assets, as is customary in the business, Sunset demanded and obtained the personal guaranties of Alpen's owners"). Plein has repeatedly insisted that Cameron was a personal guarantor of the loan.

Because there are no disputed material questions of fact as to Cameron's status, we conclude as a matter of law that Cameron signed the Sunset note as an accommodation party.[3] Cameron obtained no direct benefit from the loan,

---

[2] There is no suggestion in this record or the briefing that Cameron and Alpen Group, Inc., were not separate entities.

[3] An accommodation party may be a maker, a drawer, an acceptor, or an indorser. Section .3–419(b). He or she is liable on the note in the capacity in which he or she signed, usually as a maker or indorser. Cmt. 4, § .3–419. However, the nature of the liability on the note does not dictate whether Cameron was an accommodation party. Instead, the absence of direct benefit, and the fact that Sunset would not have made the loan without individual liability on the part of the stockholders dictate that he signed as an accommodation party.

and Plein has conceded that the loan would not have been made unless the individual stockholders were subject to personal liability on the note.

. . . .

The Court of Appeals is reversed and the trial court's grant of summary judgment in favor of Cameron is reinstated.

---

2. SURETYSHIP DEFENSES

A surety, in addition to having rights against the principal debtor, also has certain rights which can be asserted against the creditor seeking enforcement of the surety's obligation to pay the debt. These rights are usually referred to as "suretyship defenses." Suretyship defenses relate to changes in the obligation of the principal debtor without the consent of the surety. For example, a surety guarantees performance of the principal debtor as buyer under a contract of sale of coal to be supplied on credit by a seller. The seller and the principal debtor agree to amend the contract so that it refers to fuel oil rather than coal. The surety didn't agree to the amendment. If the principal debtor fails to pay for fuel oil purchased under the amended contract and the seller demands payment, the surety has a complete defense. The surety's obligation related to a contract of the principal debtor to buy coal, not fuel oil. The seller and the principal debtor cannot impose a new contract on the surety.

However, in some cases, it cannot be said that the creditor and the principal debtor have attempted to impose an entirely new contract on the surety. There might be only some modification of the contract. In those cases, the existence of a defense may be justified only if the modification causes loss to the surety. A few examples illustrate the problem. The principal debtor borrows money from a lender. The debt is payable with interest and is secured by a security interest in personal property of the principal debtor. After the suretyship relationship arises, the lender agrees with the principal debtor to an amendment of the debt obligation as follows: (1) the amendment changes the interest rate; or (2) it extends the due date of the debt; or (3) it releases some of the collateral that secures the debt; or (4) it releases the principal debtor from any personal obligation to pay the debt. In each of these cases, if the surety does not agree to the change it may be unfair to allow the lender to enforce the surety's obligation to pay if, at the time the change was made, the lender had knowledge of the suretyship relationship. The suretyship defenses are intended to protect the surety by providing that, in some cases, a change in the terms of the debt may result in a total or partial discharge of the surety. See Restatement (Third) of Suretyship and Guaranty §§ 39–44 (1996).

Restatement § 4(1) provides that to the extent negotiable instruments law governs, it takes precedence over otherwise applicable rules in the Restatement. The suretyship defenses with respect to negotiable instruments are stated in 3–605. In 2002, this section was substantially rewritten to bring it into harmony with the principles of the Restatement. Readers of 3–605 will profit from having a copy of the Restatement at hand; frequent references are made to it in the Comments. However, 3–605 applies to some transactions beyond those covered in the Restatement, including indorsers of notes and checks, as well as co-makers, who are not accommodation parties.

We have eschewed an analysis of the complexities of 3–605 because suretyship defenses are almost always waived in instruments prepared by creditors. The most important provision in 3–605 is subsection (f), which authorizes waivers. Comment 9 says:

> The importance of the suretyship defenses provided in Section 3–605 is greatly diminished by the fact that the right to discharge can be waived as provided in subsection (f). The waiver can be effectuated by a provision in the instrument or in a separate agreement. It is standard practice to include such a waiver of suretyship defenses in notes prepared by financial institutions or other commercial creditors. Thus, Section 3–605 will result in the discharge of an accommodation party on a note only in the occasional case in which the note does not include such a waiver clause and the person entitled to enforce the note nevertheless takes actions that would give rise to a discharge under this section without obtaining the consent of the secondary obligor.

Even general language "indicating that the parties waive defenses based on suretyship or impairment of collateral" will suffice. 3–605(f). However, some note forms do not contain such waivers. This omission may be explained by 3–605(e), which provides that certain suretyship defenses cannot be asserted unless the creditor has knowledge of the accommodation. If this knowledge is present, the creditor may ask the accommodation party to sign a separate guaranty contract that contains the waivers.

Section 3–605 applies to only a narrow category of transactions, those in which the payment obligation is a negotiable instrument and the secondary obligor is a party to the instrument, such as an indorser or co-maker. The separate guaranty contracts that are more common in most commercial lending are not covered. The implied suretyship in the familiar real property transaction in which a grantee assumes existing financing is not covered because the assuming grantee is not a party to the instrument. See Comment 2.

The Restatement is generally regarded as a major advance in modernizing and clarifying the law of suretyship. A case can be made for the 2002 revisions of 3–605 on the ground that the Restatement rules constitute the prevailing law of the great majority of suretyship transactions. Since 3–605 applies to only narrow segment of suretyship transactions, conformity with the Restatement, when appropriate, is a desirable simplification.

G. Signatures by Representatives

A person is not liable on an instrument unless the instrument is signed personally by that person or by a representative who is authorized to sign for that person. 3–401(a). Whether a representative is authorized to sign for a represented person is determined by general principles of the law of agency. 3–402(a). Consider this case: Employer, an individual, has a checking account in Bank that is used to pay obligations incurred in Employer's business. Employer follows the practice of personally signing all checks, except that Employer authorizes Employee to sign Employer's name to checks during extended absences of Employer. Bank has paid all checks drawn on Employer's account whether Employer's name was written in Employer's handwriting or that of Employee. Employer never objected to the payment by Bank of any check on which Employer's name was written by Employee. On one occasion Employer was about to leave town and instructed Employee to pay all invoices arriving during Employer's absence except invoices of John Doe. In violation of these instructions Employee writes a check on Employer's account to John Doe in payment of a bill that Doe submitted. Employee's act of signing Employer's name to that particular check is not authorized by Employer in the sense that Employer never assented to it, but Employer nevertheless may be bound by the signature. The question of whether the signature is binding on Employer is determined by the law of agency. In our example, the probable result under agency law is that Employer is bound because Employee, although lacking actual authority to sign the Doe check, had apparent authority to do so because Employee had general authority to sign checks. In that event, under 3–401(a) and 3–402(a), the signature by Employee is effective as the authorized signature of Employer.

Signatures by agents on behalf of principals occur most often with respect to the obligations of organizations such as corporations whose signatures are made by its officers or employees. Two problems arise: Whether the corporation is bound by the signature of the officer or employee, and whether the officer or employee also becomes a party to the instrument by signing it on behalf of the principal. If it is clear that an agent is signing on behalf of a named principal, only the principal is bound. But sometimes it is not clear whether the agent's signature is on behalf of the principal or whether it is made to impose liability on the officer as an accommodation party.

1. LIABILITY OF AGENT ON NOTES

The problem of ambiguous signatures on notes by representatives is governed by 3–402(b). How does this provision resolve the cases in the following Problems?

PROBLEMS

Your client, Carolyn Park, has been appointed Treasurer of New Corp., Inc., a new enterprise. She is authorized to sign promissory notes on behalf of the company.

1. Before taking up her duties, she consults you about personal liabilities that she might incur in her new position. Among these is her concern about signing her name on notes given to evidence substantial bank loans and other credit extensions made to the company. Her fear is that if later on her new employer should fail and have to file in bankruptcy, holders of these notes might come after her as personally liable on the notes. How should she sign the company's notes to gain full protection from personal liability under 3–402(b)?

2. Are the following signatures "unambiguous" within the meaning of 3–402(b)?

(a) New Corp., Inc., by Carolyn Park

(b) New Corp., Inc., Carolyn Park, Treasurer

(c) Carolyn Park, Treasurer

(d) New Corp., Inc., Carolyn Park

3. Carolyn signed a note authorized by New Corp., Inc. merely by writing her name, "Carolyn Park."

(a) Is New Corp., Inc. liable on this note? See 3–401(a).

(b) This signature is clearly ambiguous. What would she have to prove under 3–402(b)(2) to avoid personal liability on the note against a non-holder in due course?

4. In order to evidence a loan obligation incurred by New Corp., Inc. to Lender, Carolyn signed on the front of the note: "New Corp., Inc., by Carolyn Park, Treasurer." On the back of the instrument, she signed "Carolyn Park." When New Corp., Inc. filed in bankruptcy, Lender sued Carolyn as indorser of the note. The usual reason one signs on the back of the note is to guarantee payment. Are there any facts that could be admitted into evidence to save Carolyn from personal liability against a non-holder in due course? Comment 2 to 3–402.

2. Liability of Agent on Checks

Section 3–402(c) states a different rule for checks than we saw in the prior section for notes. The thrust of this provision is to avoid windfall recoveries against agents signing checks who fail to disclose their agency. For example, Company authorizes Employee to sign its checks and Employee does so by writing her name on the line in the lower right hand corner of the check without disclosure of her agency. Company's name is imprinted on the check in the upper left hand corner of the check where the name of the account holder appears. When a check signed by Employee is returned marked NSF, Payee proceeds against Company, only to find that it is insolvent. Payee then proceeds against the hapless Employee as the drawer of the check because of her failure to reveal her agency status. Recovery against Employee in such a case would be an underserved windfall for Payee In an age of personalized printed checks, Payee was relying on the liability of Company, the account holder, and not that of the uninformed or careless signer. An occasional case had held the agent liable on these facts, e.g., Griffin v. Ellinger, 538 S.W.2d 97 (Tex. 1976), noted in Comment 3 as overruled by 3-402(c), which was added to protect the agent from personal liability in such cases.

PROBLEM

Section 3-402(c) relieves the drawer from liability on the check only if the check is payable from an account of the represented person "who is identified on the check." The provision does not state what is required for the represented person to be "identified." Suppose the legal name of the represented person is XYZ Corp. XYZ Corp.'s agent, with authority, draws a check with the name "XYZ" in the upper left hand corner, instead of "XYZ Corp." XYZ Corp.'s address appear on the check. Is the agent liable on the check? See Packaging Materials & Supply Co., Inc. v. Prater, 882 So. 2d 861 (Ala. Civ. App. 2003). Would the result be different if XYZ Corp.'s trade name "ABC" appeared on the check? See Peterson v. Holtrachem, Inc., 521 S.E.2d 648 (Ga. Ct. App. 1999).

H. Accord and Satisfaction

Before Revised Article 3, the UCC had no section on accord and satisfaction. One of the reasons for adding 3–311 was a deep division of authority over the meaning of 1–207 which provided that: "[a] party who, with explicit reservation of rights, performs or promises performance or assents to performance in a manner demanded or offered by the other party does not thereby prejudice the rights reserved. Such words as 'without prejudice', 'under protest' or the like are sufficient." The issue was whether, under this section, the recipient of a check marked "tendered in full satisfaction" could negate the effect of these words by merely writing "reserving all rights" or "under protest" on the check. The drafters of 3–311 took the position that the recipient of a full-satisfaction check could avoid an accord and satisfaction only by not cashing the check; words reserving rights were ineffective. This result was reached by adding a new subsection to 1–207: "(2) Subsection (1) does not apply to an accord and satisfaction." A new Comment 3 to 1–207 was added.

Effectuating an accord and satisfaction of a disputed claim by a "full satisfaction" legend on a check is a cheap and fast way in which to settle a claim. Section 3–311(a) and (b) provide that, as a general rule, if the legend on the check is conspicuous and the claim is subject to a bona fide dispute, the claimant cannot receive payment of the check without agreeing to the accord and satisfaction. If the claimant wishes to avoid settlement for the amount of the check, it may not cash the check or deposit it for collection. However, accord and satisfaction is a double-edged sword. As Comment 1 to 3–311 points out, accord and satisfaction by use of notations on checks is useful to consumers in disputes about the quality of goods or services purchased, but it is also commonly employed by insurance companies to settle claims of insured parties.

Section 3–311(c)(1) addresses a problem encountered by organizations like large retailers and other high volume recipients of checks who find it burdensome and wasteful to conduct a visual search of tens of thousands of checks to see if a handful contain a proposed accord and satisfaction legend. This provision allows such an organization to notify its customers to send any communications concerning disputed debts, including checks containing full satisfaction legends, to a specified address at which these checks and other communications can be examined and decisions made with respect to whether to accept them as settlement of claims. This allows retailers to rapidly process other checks without sight examination to detect accord and satisfaction language. Section 3–311(c)(2) is an alternative to 3–311(c)(1), which is designed to ameliorate the consequences of an inadvertent accord and satisfaction. It is explained in Comment 6 to 3–311.

The drafting of 3–311 was contentious; the final product is a series of compromises that can be detected by going through the section in the manner of an archeological dig. *Stage 1*. Subsections (a) and (b) codify the common law rule of accord and satisfaction. Ironically this was supported both by consumers, who saw it as the little person's way of settling disputes without having to litigate, as well as by insurance companies and other businesses that wanted to induce their customers to settle claims by sending them checks that they would be tempted to cash on the bird-in-the-hand principle.

Stage 2. Department stores, utilities and others who receive a huge volume of checks objected that the unadorned common law rule meant that they had to sift through thousands of checks each day to reach the few that contained the full-satisfaction legend. This was unduly expensive and, in consequence, the drafters were urged to get rid of the archaic rule that contract disputes can be settled by legends on checks. The drafters addressed these concerns in subsection (c)(1) which allows these organizations to require that customers send checks intended to pay disputed claims to a special office where the staff is trained to look for and deal with full-satisfaction checks. Subsection (c)(2) was a concession to companies that did not wish to use the somewhat cumbersome subsection (c)(1). Inadvertent accord and satisfaction could be avoided by allowing the claimant that had mistakenly deposited a full-satisfaction check to tender the money back to the drawer of the check within 90 days after payment. Organizations could opt for either (c)(1) or (c)(2), but not both. The second sentence in (c)(2) does not allow an organization that has set up a lockbox account under (c) (1) to escape an accord and satisfaction by returning money under (c)(2) if a full-satisfaction check had been sent to the lockbox account and deposited by the claimant.

Stage 3. Subsection (c) looked too pro-business to consumer representatives and they posed this case: Suppose Big Store sends out the notice under subsection (c)(1) that all checks for disputed claims must be sent to a certain post office box. Although Big Store complied fully with the requirements for notice under subsection (c)(1), Customer delivered her full-satisfaction check to the credit manager for the branch of Big Stores where she had always shopped. She had talked with him by telephone and he was aware of the dispute on the balance of her account. Big Store cashed her check and did not avail itself of the escape valve in subsection (c)(2). "Do you mean to tell me," the consumer representatives asked, "that there should be no accord and satisfaction in this case merely because Customer hadn't read all the periodic statements she received from Big Store (Do you read yours?), even though the person in charge of her account received the check bearing a conspicuous full-satisfaction legend and cashed the check?" This was a persuasive argument and subsection (d) was added to address this concern. Reaching consensus on the wording of subsection (d) was very difficult. IFC Credit Corp. v. Bulk Petroleum Corp. 403 F.3d 869 (7th Cir.2005), is the first decision we have seen that invokes subsection (d).

CHAPTER 3

Payment Systems: Checks and Cards

A. Check Collection

Noncash payments are made by transferring funds from a transferor's deposit account to a transferee through banking channels. Payments may be made by paper checks, debit cards, electronic orders, or, increasingly, by a combination of these methods. In this chapter, we will examine check transfers and debit and credit card transactions. In the following chapter, we will deal with funds transfers originated by electronic orders: big-dollar funds transfers under UCC Article 4A and transfers made through the Automated Clearing House (ACH) system.

By the end of the 20th century, the United States was the the only developed nation still using paper checks as its principal means of making noncash payments. The UCC Article 4 check collection process is slow and expensive. Tons of checks are lugged around by trucks, helicopters and airplanes all over the nation. Some checks are stolen; others are lost. In the digital age, why can't the immense cost of transporting and processing paper checks be greatly reduced by communicating the information on checks electronically or, better still, by getting rid of checks in favor of electronic payments?

The first decade of the 21st century has been the tipping point: the paper-based system changed materially. Each year fewer paper checks were collected through the Article 4 check collection channel. By 2006, the number of payments made by debit or credit cards surpassed the number of checks paid. Geoffrey R. Gerges, Recent Payment Trends in the United States, Fed. Res. Bull., Oct. 2008, at A101. The rapidly growing practice of converting paper checks into electronic payments communicated through the Automated Clearing House (ACH) under the National Automated Clearing House Association (NACHA) network has greatly reduced the number of checks collected under Article 4. Widespread acceptance of online banking also relieves consumers from having to write small checks to pay their bills. A leading article on the transformation is Stephanie Heller, An Endangered Species: The Increasing Irrelevance of the Article 4 of the UCC in an Electronics-Based Payments System, 40 Loyola L. Rev. 513 (2006). At the time of the article, Ms. Heller was Counsel and Vice President of the Federal Reserve Bank of New York.

These developments raise the question of what to teach about payments law in 2011 when we suspect that payments processes will continue to change, perhaps significantly, during the five-year lifetime of a casebook edition. Our judgment is that we should first examine the traditional check-oriented payment system set out in UCC Articles 3 and 4 as a template. The use of the banking system for transferring credits from an obligor's account to an obligee is the basis for all payment systems and it is best learned through the study of checks collected under Article 4. We will supplement this by discussing the new payments channels opened by NACHA and the debit and credit card networks.

1. Time Check Is Paid by Payor Bank

Article 4 governs the rights and obligations of commercial banks and their customers with respect to the collection of checks by the banking system. However, the Federal Reserve Board has always played a very important role in check collection. This role has been expanded by Regulation CC, 12 U.S.C. § 4001 et seq., which we discuss later in this chapter.

The check collection process consists of the movement of a check from the time the payee deposits it in its depository bank (4-105(2)), to its presentation to the payor bank (4–105(3)). If the payor bank wishes to dishonor the check, it must return the check; here the check moves from the payor bank back to the depository bank, and ultimately to the payee who deposited the check. To avoid liability for the check, the payor bank must return the dishonored check to the depository bank within a prescribed time. Article 4 sets a midnight deadline by which the payor bank must return the dishonored item to avoid liability. 4–104(a)(10). Section 4–301's midnight deadline applies when the payor bank has settled for an item and wishes to revoke settlement. In addition, 4–302(a)(1) requires the payor bank to return the item or make settlement by midnight of the banking day or receipt of the item unless the bank is a depository bank. Failure to comply with the midnight deadline makes a settlement final. The amount paid can't be recovered. When settlement hasn't occurred timely, tardy settlement makes the payor bank liable ("accountable") for the face amount of the item.

The process described in the preceding paragraph will be examined in detail in the following section, but some clarification may be helpful in understanding the statutes set out below that are not easy reading. The vast majority of checks presented to payor banks are paid. In these cases, the payor bank merely keeps the check when it arrives and adjusts the account of the bank's customer, the drawer of the check. The check will either be stored until the end of the billing cycle and returned to the drawer with its other checks or its digital image retained by the payor bank, depending on the bank-customer agreement. If the payor bank finds that the drawer's account is overdrawn, a stop payment order has been entered, or for other reasons the payor bank does not wish to pay the check, it must return the check to the depositary bank, which notifies its customer, the payee, of the dishonor. And it must do so by its midnight deadline—midnight of the day after receipt of the check. If it misses this deadline, it is accountable for, that is, liable for the face amount of the check. This is absolute liability. Even though the payee of the check has suffered no damages other than one or two day's interest on the amount of the check, it is liable for the face amount of the check; sometimes this amount may be in the millions of dollars. As we see later, bankers have always contended that this is an unfair rule that should be changed; so far, they have not been successful.

a. THE MIDNIGHT DEADLINE

Solve the following Problems on the basis of the text following the Problems and statutory provisions set out.

Section 4-104(a)

(9) "Item" means an instrument or a promise or order to pay money handled by a bank for collection or payment....

(10) "Midnight deadline" with respect to a bank is midnight on the next banking day following the banking day on which it receives the relevant item or notice...

Section 4-301. Deferred Posting; Recovery of Payment by Return of Items; Time of Dishonor; Return of Items by Payor Bank.

(a) If a payor bank settles for a demand item...before midnight of the banking day of receipt, the payor bank may revoke the settlement and recover the settlement if, before it has made final payment and before its midnight deadline, it

(1) returns the item;

(2) returns an image of the item, if the party to which the return is made has entered into an agreement to accept an image as a re-

turn of the item and the image returned is in accordance with that agreement; or

(3) sends a record providing notice of dishonor or nonpayment if the item is unavailable for return.

Section 4-302. Payor Bank's Responsibility for Late Return of Item.

(a) If an item is presented to and received by a payor bank, the bank is accountable for the amount of:

(1) a demand item,...whether properly payable or not, if the bank, in any case in which it is not also the depositary bank, retains the item beyond midnight of the banking day of receipt without settling for it or, whether or not it is also the depositary bank, does not pay or return the item or send notice of dishonor until after its midnight deadline....

....

4-301(d) An item is returned:

....

(2) in all other cases, when it is sent or delivered to the bank's customer or transferor or pursuant to instructions.

PROBLEMS

1. Drawer wrote a check for $10,000 (Check) on its account in Bank A payable to the order of Payee who deposited it in its account in Bank B, the "depositary bank" 4–105(2). Bank B gave Payee a provisional credit for the amount of Check and sent it to Bank A for payment. Check was presented to Bank A on Monday at 8:30 a.m. in a bundle of checks itemized in a cash letter, which listed each check and the total dollar amount for the bundle. Bank A provisionally settled for the checks by sending Bank B a Fedwire for the total amount of the cash letter on Monday afternoon. The checks in the bundle went through Bank A's reader-sorter computer on Monday afternoon.

(a) The reader-sorter selected out Check because Drawer's account balance was insufficient to pay it. On Tuesday morning, Bank A reviewed Drawer's account to ascertain whether Drawer had added funds sufficient to pay Check by that time. Finding none, Bank decided to dishonor Check and sent it to its check-return office on Tuesday afternoon, but owing to a mix-up, Check was not returned until the 3:00 a.m. courier on Wednesday. Check reached Bank B on Wednesday afternoon, and on Thursday, Bank B erased the provisional credit in Payee's account and delivered Check to Payee on Friday. Did Bank A revoke its settlement with Bank B under the time limits of 4–301(a)? Is Bank A accountable to Payee for the amount of the check under 4–302(a) even if Payee has suffered no damage?

(b) Check was selected out for visual inspection because of its relatively large amount. After Check was inspected, Bank A decided to pay it, and Drawer's account was debited for the amount of Check at 1:00 p.m. on Tuesday. Check was then routed to a filing clerk whose responsibility it was to place it with Drawer's other cancelled checks to be mailed to Drawer at the end of the monthly billing cycle. At 5:00 p.m. on Tuesday, Bank A learned that a mistake had been made and that Drawer's account was insufficient to cover the amount of Check, but the file clerk had left and the employees could not locate Check until 9:00 p.m., an hour after the 8:00 p.m. motor courier had left. They placed it in the mail at 10:00 p.m. addressed to the presenting bank, Bank B, where it arrived on Friday. Did Bank A revoke its settlement under 4–301(a) and (d)(2) or was Check finally paid at 1:00 p.m. on Tuesday under 4–215(a) when Bank A completed its processing? "Send" is defined in 1–201(b)(36).

2. Drawer drew a check (Check) on its account in Bank payable to the order of Payee. Upon receipt of Check, Payee deposited it in its account, which was also in Bank, on Monday. Hence, Bank is both the payor and depositary bank. Bank gave Payee a provisional settlement in its account on Tuesday for the amount of Check. On Wednesday morning, Bank discovered that Drawer's account was insufficient to pay Check. On Wednesday afternoon, Bank erased the credit from Payee's account and returned Check to Payee. Did Bank properly revoke the credit in Payee's account under 4–301(a) and (b)? Is Bank liable to Payee for the amount of the check under 4–302(a)(1)?

The *Blake* case that follows discusses the issue of when, under Article 4, the bank on which a check is drawn is deemed to have paid the check. This issue is presented in its most simple form if the holder of a check takes it to the drawee bank and asks for payment in cash over the counter. The check is paid when the bank gives cash equal to the amount of the check to the holder. 4–215(a)(1). However, most checks are not paid in cash but are deposited in the holder's bank for collection. That bank is the "depositary bank." 4-105(2).

To understand how Article 4 applies to checks deposited in a bank, it is necessary to understand the concept of settlement in Article 4. 4–104(a)(11) and 4–213. Typically, in the check-collection process, each bank that takes a check pays for it at, or shortly after, the time that the check is taken. Article 4 uses the terms "settlement" and "settle" to refer to this act of paying for the check. In the common case in which the depositary bank is not also the payor bank, the depositary bank is a "collecting bank" that acts as agent of the holder to obtain payment of the check. 4–105(5). The depositary bank will either present the check directly to the payor bank or it will negotiate the check to an "intermediary bank," which acts as a collecting bank to obtain payment of the check. 4–105(4) and (5). The intermediary bank is likely to be a Federal Reserve Bank and there may be more than one intermediary bank. Each collecting bank will give provisional settlement to the bank from which the check is received. The last collecting bank will present the check for payment to the payor bank, which will give provisional settlement to the presenting bank, usually on the date of receipt.

At the time a payor bank settles with the collecting bank for the check, it usually does not know whether it should pay the check. For example, if the balance in the drawer's account in payor bank is not sufficient to cover the amount of the check, it has has no obligation to the payee of the check to pay the check 3–408. Under Article 4, the payor bank is given a time-limited right to revoke or recover the settlement payment that it made to the collecting bank when that bank's account was credited. 4–301(a). The prescribed technique for accomplishing this result is to return the check to the holder and to debit ("charge-back") the holder's account in the amount of the check. The payor bank "pays the check" if and when it has not exercised its right to recover a provisional payment that it has made and the right of recovery no longer exists. 4–215(a)(3) and 4–301(a). This practice of settle-first-take-back-later is in effect because it is operationally efficient. Since payor banks have reason to refuse payment with respect to only a tiny percentage of the vast number of checks that are processed each day for payment, it is sensible to pay for all checks as they are received ("settlement") and to deal later with the small number of checks that turn out to be bad by revoking the settlement and returning the checks. Only 0.51% of total checks paid were returned in 2006. Fed. Res. Bull., Oct. 2008, at 75.

In transactions between banks, settlement is often made by a credit to the Federal Reserve account of the bank receiving the settlement. The payor bank may refuse payment of the check by returning it to the presenting bank and recovering the amount of the check from that bank. 4–301(a). In turn, the presenting bank and each collecting bank may return the check to the bank from which it received the check and recover the provisional payment. 4–214(a). As we will see, Regulation CC requires payor and collecting banks to expedite the return of checks and authorizes them to return checks directly to the depositary bank or to any bank that has agreed to handle the checks for expeditious return to the depositary bank. Any bank returning the check may obtain the amount of the check from the bank to which the check is transferred. When the depositary bank receives the returned check, it may recover the provisional payment given to the holder from whom it took the check for collection. 4–214(a).

Blake, which follows, relates the history of check collection and applies Article 4 check collection as it was before the 1990 Revision and the Federal Reserve reforms that followed. A cash management officer reading this case today would be appalled. The case also deals with one of the more common excuses for failing to meet the midnight deadline, delays recognized by 4–109 (formerly 4–108).

Blake v. Woodford Bank & Trust Co.

Court of Appeals of Kentucky, 1977.
555 S.W.2d 589.

■ PARK, JUDGE.

This case involves the liability of...Woodford Bank and Trust Company on two checks drawn on the Woodford Bank and Trust Company and payable to the order of...Wayne Blake. Following a trial without a jury, the Woodford Circuit Court found that the bank was excused from meeting its "midnight deadline" with respect to the two checks. Blake appeals from the judgment of the circuit court dismissing his complaint. The bank cross-appeals from that portion of the circuit court's opinion relating to the extent of the bank's liability on the two checks if it should be determined that the bank was not excused from meeting its midnight deadline.

BASIC FACTS

The basic facts are not in dispute. On December 6, 1973, Blake deposited a check in the amount of $16,449.84 to his account at the Morristown Bank, of Morristown, Ohio. This check was payable to Blake's order and was drawn on the K & K Farm Account at the Woodford Bank and Trust Company. The check was dated December 3, 1973.

On December 19, 1973, Blake deposited a second check in the amount of $11,200.00 to his account in the Morristown Bank. The second check was also drawn on the K & K Farm Account at the Woodford Bank and Trust Company and made payable to Blake's order. The second check was dated December 17, 1973.

When Blake deposited the second check on December 19, he was informed by the Morristown Bank that the first check had been dishonored and returned because of insufficient funds. Blake instructed the Morristown Bank to re-present the first check along with the second check. Blake was a cattle trader, and the two checks represented the purchase price for cattle sold by Blake to James Knight who maintained the K & K Farm Account. Blake testified that he had been doing business with Knight for several years. On other occasions, checks had been returned for insufficient funds but had been paid when re-presented.

The two checks were forwarded for collection through the Cincinnati Branch of the Federal Reserve Bank of Cleveland. From the Federal Reserve Bank, the two checks were delivered to the Woodford Bank and Trust

Company by means of the Purolator Courier Corp. The checks arrived at the Woodford Bank and Trust Company on Monday, December 24, 1973, shortly before the opening of the bank for business. The next day, Christmas, was not a banking day. The two checks were returned by the Woodford Bank and Trust Company to the Cincinnati Branch of the Federal Reserve Bank by means of Purolator on Thursday, December 27, 1973.

The two checks were received by the bank on Monday, December 24. The next banking day was Wednesday, December 26. Thus, the bank's "midnight deadline" was midnight on Wednesday, December 26. § 4–104(1)(h) [Revised § 4–104(a)(10)]. As the bank retained the two checks beyond its midnight deadline, Blake asserts that the bank is "accountable" for the amount of the two checks under § 4–302(1)(a) [Revised § 4–302(a)(1)].

HISTORY OF PAYOR BANK'S LIABILITY FOR RETAINING CHECK

Under the Uniform Negotiable Instruments Law a payor bank was not liable to the holder of a check drawn on the bank until the bank had accepted or certified the check.... Because of the payor bank's basic nonliability on a check, it was essential that some time limit be placed upon the right of the payor bank to dishonor a check when presented for payment. If a payor bank could hold a check indefinitely without incurring liability, the entire process of collection and payment of checks would be intolerably slow. To avoid this problem, a majority of courts construing § 136 and § 137 of the Uniform Negotiable Instruments Law held that a payor bank was deemed to have accepted a check if it held the check for 24 hours after the check was presented for payment.... Thus, in a majority of jurisdictions, the payor bank had only 24 hours to determine whether to pay a check or return it. However, in Kentucky and a few other jurisdictions, the courts held that § 136 and § 137 of the Uniform Negotiable Instruments Law applied only to checks which were presented for acceptance.... Consequently, the payor bank would be liable on the check only if it held the check "for an unreasonable length of time" and could thus be deemed to have converted the check.

In order to bring uniformity to the check collection process, the Bank Collection Code was proposed by the American Bankers' Association. The Bank Collection Code was adopted by Kentucky in 1930. Under § 3 of the Bank Collection Code, a payor bank could give provisional credit when a check was received, and the credit could be revoked at any time before the end of that business day. The payor bank became liable on the check if it retained the item beyond the end of the business day received....

Banks had only a few hours to determine whether a check should be returned because of insufficient funds. Banks were required to "dribble post checks" by sorting and sending the checks to the appropriate bookkeepers as the checks were received. This led to an uneven workload during the course of a business day. At times, the bookkeeping personnel might have nothing to do while at other times they would be required to process a very large number of checks in a very short time.... Because of the increasingly large number of checks processed each day and the shortage of qualified bank personnel during World War II, it became impossible for banks to determine whether a check was "good" in only 24 hours. The banks were forced to resort to the procedure of "paying" for a check on the day it was presented without posting it to the customer's account until the following day. See First National Bank of Elwood v. Universal C.I.T. Credit Corporation, 132 Ind.App. 353, 170 N.E.2d 238, at 244 (1960). To meet this situation, the American Banking Association proposed a Model Deferred Posting Statute....

Under the Model Deferred Posting Statute, a payor bank could give provisional credit for a check on the business day it was received, and the credit could be revoked at any time before midnight of the bank's next business day following receipt. A provisional credit was revoked "by returning the item, or if the item is held for protest or at the time is lost or is not in the possession of the bank, by giving written notice of dishonor, nonpayment, or revocation; provided that such item or notice is dispatched in the mails or by other expeditious means not later than midnight of the bank's next business day after the item was received."...If the payor bank failed to take advantage of the provisions of the deferred posting statute by revoking the provisional credit and returning the check within the time and in the manner provided by the act, the payor bank was deemed to have paid the check and was liable thereon to the holder....

The Model Deferred Posting Statute was the basis for the provisions of the Uniform Commercial Code. Under § 4–301(1) [Revised § 4–301(a)] of the Uniform Commercial Code (UCC), a payor bank may revoke a provisional "settlement" if it does so before its "midnight deadline" which is midnight of the next banking day following the banking day on which it received the check. Under the Model Deferred Posting Statute, the payor bank's liability for failing to meet its midnight deadline was to be inferred rather than being spelled out in the statute. Under UCC § 4–302 [Revised § 4–302], the payor bank's liability for missing its midnight deadline is explicit. If the payor bank misses its midnight deadline, the bank is "accountable" for the face amount of the check....

Like the Model Deferred Posting Statute, the Uniform Commercial Code seeks to decrease, rather than increase, the risk of liability to payor banks. By permitting deferred posting, the Uniform Commercial Code extends the time within which a payor bank must determine whether it will pay a check drawn on the bank. Unlike the Bank Collection Code or the Uniform Negotiable Instruments Law as construed by most courts, the Uniform Commercial Code does not require the payor bank to act on the day of receipt or within 24 hours of receipt of a check. The payor bank is granted until midnight of the next business day following the business day on which it received the check.

EXCUSE FOR FAILING TO MEET MIDNIGHT DEADLINE

UCC § 4–108(2) [Revised § 4–109(b)] provides:

> "Delay by a * * * payor bank beyond time limits prescribed or permitted by this Act * * * is excused if caused by interruption of communications facilities, suspension of payments by another bank, war, emergency conditions or other circumstances beyond the control of the bank provided it exercises such diligence as the circumstances require."

The circuit court found that the bank's failure to return the two checks by its midnight deadline was excused under the provisions of UCC § 4–108.

The circuit court dictated its findings of fact into the record:

> "From all of the evidence that was presented in this case, it would appear that there was no intentional action on the part of the bank to hold these checks beyond the normal course of business as an accommodation to its customer. In fact, the uncontroverted testimony of the bank officers was to the contrary. To say that the bank failed, through certain procedures, to return the checks by the midnight deadline does not, in the mind of this Court, imply or establish an intentional act on the part of the bank.
>
> ....
>
> "In this instance we have the Christmas Holiday, which caused in the bank, as in all businesses, certain emergency and overloaded situations. This is not unique to the banking industry; but is true of virtually every business in a christian society, in which the holiday of Christmas is observed as the major holiday of the year. Special considerations are always given to employees as well as customers of these banking institutions.
>
> ".... On the Christmas Holiday, two machines were broken down for periods of time during this critical day in question. There was an absence of a regular bookkeeper."

Under CR 52.01, these findings of fact cannot be set aside by this court unless they are clearly erroneous. The foregoing findings are supported by the record, and are not questioned by Blake on the appeal.

After making findings of fact, the circuit court dictated the following conclusions into the record:

> ".... The entire cumulative effect of what happened would constitute diligence on the part of the bank, as circumstances required.
>
> "It is the opinion of the Court and it is the Finding of the Court that the circumstances described by the banking officers, the standards of banking care, as described by expert witnesses, would bring the bank within 4–108(2), and the Court therefore, finds as a fact that there were circums-

> tances here beyond the control of the bank, and that it exercised such diligence as those circumstances required."

When the circuit court concluded "that there were circumstances here beyond the control of the bank, and that it exercised such diligence as those circumstances required," the circuit court was doing no more than repeating the words of the statute. This court must determine whether the circuit court's findings of fact support these conclusions.

. . . .

The basic facts found by the circuit court can be summarized as follows: a) the bank had no intention of holding the checks beyond the midnight deadline in order to accommodate its customer; b) there was an increased volume of checks to be handled by reason of the Christmas Holiday; c) two posting machines were broken down for a period of time on December 26; d) one regular bookkeeper was absent because of illness. Standing alone, the bank's intention not to favor its customer by retaining an item beyond the midnight deadline would not justify the application of § 4–108(2). The application of the exemption statute necessarily will turn upon the findings relating to heavy volume, machine breakdown, and absence of a bookkeeper.

The bank's president testified that 4,200 to 4,600 checks were processed on a normal day. Because the bank was closed for Christmas on Tuesday, the bank was required to process 6,995 checks on December 26. The bank had four posting machines. On the morning of December 26, two of the machines were temporarily inoperable. One of the machines required two and one half hours to repair. The second machine was repaired in one and one half hours. As the bank had four bookkeepers, the machine breakdown required the bookkeepers to take turns using the posting machines for a time in the morning. One of the four bookkeepers who regularly operated the posting machines was absent because of illness on December 26. This bookkeeper was replaced by the head bookkeeper who had experience on the posting machines, although he was not as proficient as a regular posting machine operator.

Because of the cumulative effect of the heavy volume, machine breakdown and absence of a regular bookkeeper, the bank claims it was unable to process the two checks in time to deliver them to the courier from Purolator for return to the Federal Reserve Bank on December 26. As the bank's president testified:

> "Because we couldn't get them ready for the Purolator carrier to pick them up by 4:00 and we tried to get all our work down there to him by 4:00, for him to pick up and these two checks were still being processed in our bookkeeping department and it was impossible for those to get into returns for that day."

. . . .

The increased volume of items to be processed the day after Christmas was clearly foreseeable. The breakdown of the posting machines was not an unusual occurrence, although it was unusual to have two machines broken down at the same time. In any event, it should have been foreseeable to the responsible officers of the bank that the bookkeepers would be delayed in completing posting of the checks on December 26. Nevertheless, the undisputed evidence establishes that no arrangements of any kind were made for return of "bad" items which might be discovered by the bookkeepers after the departure of the Purolator courier. The two checks in question were in fact determined by Mrs. Stratton to be "bad" on December 26. The checks were not returned because the regular employee responsible for handling "bad" checks had left for the day, and Mrs. Stratton had no instructions to cover the situation.

Even though the bank missed returning the two checks by the Purolator courier, it was still possible for the bank to have returned the checks by its midnight deadline. Under UCC § 4–301(4)(b) [Revised § 4–301(d)(2)] an item is returned when it is "sent" to the bank's transferor, in this case the Federal Reserve Bank. Under UCC § 1–201(38) an item is "sent" when it is deposited in the mail. 1 R. Anderson, Uniform Commercial Code § 1–201 pp. 118–119 (2d ed. 1970). Thus, the bank could have returned the two checks before the midnight deadline by the simple procedure of depositing the two checks in the mail, properly addressed to the Cincinnati branch of the Federal Reserve Bank.

This court concludes that circumstances beyond the control of the bank did not prevent it from returning the two checks in question before its midnight deadline on December 26. The circumstances causing delay in the bookkeeping department were foreseeable. On December 26, the bank actually discovered that the checks were "bad," but the responsible employees and officers had left the bank without leaving any instructions to the bookkeepers. The circuit court erred in holding that the bank was excused under § 4–108 from meeting its midnight deadline. The facts found by the circuit court do not support its conclusion that the circumstances in the case were beyond the control of the bank....

NOTES

1. In an omitted portion of the opinion, the court dealt with the question of whether the first check, which was re-presented on December 24, should be treated differently from the second check that was presented for the first time on that date. Woodford Bank argued that because the first check had been promptly returned the first time it was presented, it had no duty to return it in a timely manner a second time. The court rejected this contention.

Re-presentment of checks is common, and a substantial percentage are paid when presented the second time. The typical case is that of a customer who writes a check to be covered by a check contemporaneously deposited in the customer's account or which will be deposited in the very near future. If the customer's check is presented for payment before the deposited check is collected, the customer's check may be dishonored because of a temporary insufficiency of funds in the account. If the check is re-presented, it must be treated as a check presented for the first time because, if the midnight deadline does not apply to such checks, the depositary bank would have no basis for making a judgment whether the check was paid. The depositary bank receives notice that a check has been dishonored either by return of the check or by a separate notice of dishonor, but it is not told that a check has been paid. The bank normally determines that a check has been paid by the fact that it didn't receive the returned check or notice of dishonor within the normal time for receiving the check or notice.

2. Taken together, 4–301(a) and 4–302(a) provide that if a check arrives on Day 1, Payor Bank may avoid being held accountable for, meaning liable for, the amount of the check by returning it before its "midnight deadline" (midnight of Day 2, 4–104(a)(10)), only if it had settled for the check before midnight of Day 1. We discussed settlement briefly in the text preceding *Blake*. In Hanna v. First National Bank of Rochester, 661 N.E.2d 683 (N.Y. 1995), checks arrived at Payor Bank on November 12 and were returned on November 13, but Payor Bank was held accountable on the checks because it offered no proof that it had settled for the checks on November 12. Payor Bank objected to this result on the ground that it should not be liable for the full amount of the checks, $44,503, when Depositary Bank's loss was minimal. The court stated:

> Some commentators have questioned the wisdom of imposing liability under UCC 4–302(a) for a payor bank's failure to settle for the item on the day it is received when the bank has dishonored or returned the item within the midnight deadline because if the item has been dishonored before payment of it has become final, the only apparent harm that results is that the depositary bank has been deprived of one day's interest on the amount of the item. They maintain that holding the payor bank accountable for the face value of the item in the light of such minimum damages is an unduly harsh penalty (see 6 Hawkland, Leary & Alderman, UCC Series, § 4–302:02).... We do not similarly view the matter.

661 N.E.2d at 688.

The unusual aspect of *Hanna* is how the issue of failure to settle on Day 1 ever arose. *Hanna* is the first reported case we have seen in which there was no settlement on the date of delivery. A large percentage of checks are presented by Federal Reserve Banks, and, as to these checks, there is always settlement on the day of presentment. This is true because the Fed will not present a check to a payor bank unless that bank or its correspondent bank has an account in the Fed; this account will be promptly debited by the Fed. With respect to checks not presented by the Fed, settlement may be made by the payor bank's sending a Fedwire credit to the presenting bank's Fed account before the close of Fedwire (6:30 p.m. ET) on the day of delivery. If, as in *Hanna*, a check is presented through a clearing house, the banks that are members of the clearing house usually have agreements (4–213(a)) providing that as each member exchanges checks at the clearing with each other member, the amounts are netted out with debit balances to be paid that day by wire transfers to the account of the creditor bank in the Fed by an agreed time or by entries in accounts each of the members holds in the others. In short, in clearing house transactions, payor banks must settle for checks on the day the checks are delivered to it. The court has little to say about why this result didn't follow in *Hanna*, other than to observe, laconically, that the payor bank had presented no admissible evidence of settlement on November 12.

b. WHAT IS A PAYOR BANK?

Under 4–302(a), presentment to the payor bank starts the running of the midnight deadline period. But in the branch banking system so common today, what is the payor bank? In a branch banking system, checks drawn by customers having accounts in a branch will usually not be sent to the branch for payment initially but will be routed through a processing center where the checks are run through a reader/sorter machine and drawers' balances are adjusted in the bank's electronic data storage system. Checks meeting the bank's standards for sight review of signatures (usually large balance checks) may then be delivered to the branch where the drawer has an account and signature cards are kept. Which is the payor bank for the purpose of the midnight deadline: any branch in the system, the branch where the drawer maintains its account whose address is on the check, or the processing center? Section 4–107 states: "A branch or separate office of a bank is a separate bank for the purpose of computing the time within which and determining the place at or to which action may be taken or notices or orders shall be given under this Article and under Article 3." Comment 1 suggests that this is the best the drafters can do given the infinitely varying practices in the huge banking industry, and the courts will have to sort out the proper results "on the basis of the facts of each case." See the extensive discussion on this issue in 2 James J. White & Robert S. Summers, Uniform Commercial Code 20–4c. (4th Prac. ed. 1995).

c. CHECK KITING

Check kiting scams have placed pressure on the strict accountability rule of 4–302(a). Check kiting is a form of fraud. It is described in First National Bank v. Colonial Bank, 898 F. Supp. 1220 (N.D. Ill. 1995):

. . . The kiter opens accounts at two (or more) banks, writes checks on insufficient funds on one account, then covers the overdraft by depositing a check drawn on insufficient funds from the other account.

> To illustrate the operation, suppose that the defrauder opens two accounts with a deposit of $500 each at the First National Bank and a distant Second National Bank. (A really successful defrauder will have numerous accounts in fictitious names at banks in widely separated states.) The defrauder then issues for goods or cash checks totaling $3,000 against the First National Bank. But before they clear and overdraw the account, he covers the overdrafts with a check for $4,000 drawn on the Second National Bank. The Second National account will be overdrawn when the $4,000 check is presented; before that happens, however, the defrauder covers it with a check on the First National Bank. The process is repeated innumerable times until there is a constant float of worthless checks between the accounts and the defrauder has bilked the banks of a substantial sum of money.

John D. O'Malley, Common Check Frauds and the Uniform Commercial Code, 23 Rutgers L. Rev. 189, 194 n. 35 (1968–69). By timing the scheme correctly and repeating it over a period of time, the kiter can use the funds essentially as an interest-free loan.... Thus, when a kite is operating, the depositary bank allows the kiter to draw on uncollected funds based on a deposit of a check. The depositary bank presents that check to the payor bank, which must decide whether to pay or return the check before the midnight deadline. The check may appear to be covered by uncollected funds at the payor bank, and so the payor bank may decide to pay the check by allowing the midnight deadline to pass.

A kite crashes when one of the banks dishonors checks drawn on it and returns them to the other banks involved in the kite. Usually, such a dishonor occurs when one bank suspects a kite. However, an individual bank may have trouble detecting a check kiting scheme...[E]ach bank is usually able to monitor only its own account. Even if a bank suspects a kite, it might decide not to take any action for a number of reasons. First, it may be liable to its customer for wrongfully dishonoring checks. 4–202. Second, if it reports that a kite is operating and turns out to be wrong, it could find itself defending a defamation suit. Finally, if it errs in returning checks or reporting a kite, it may risk angering a large customer.

First National involved the fallout of a collapsed check kiting scheme. In substance, Bank Two presented to Bank One for payment on Day 1 checks drawn on Bank One (the "Bank One" checks) by Kiter A payable to Kiter B that had been deposited by Kiter B in Bank Two. Bank One examined Kiter A's account on Day 2 for the existence of a check kite and initially decided not to return the Bank One checks. Assume that Banks Two and One changed positions with respect to checks drawn by Kiter B on its account in Bank Two (the "Bank Two" checks) payable to Kiter A and deposited in Bank One. But, when Bank Two examined Kiter B's account on Day 2, it concluded that a kite was under way and returned the Bank Two checks before its midnight deadline. After its midnight deadline passed, further evidence of a check kiting scheme convinced Bank One that there was a check kite and it returned the Bank One checks late. The Kiters disappeared with the money. In litigation, Bank Two contended that Bank One was accountable for the amount of the Bank One checks because it missed its midnight deadline. Bank One asserted that Bank Two had a good faith duty to inform Bank One of the existence of the check kite; hence, the midnight deadline should not apply. Bank Two replied that banks deal with each other at arms length; in this case each bank made a business decision and Bank Two's turned out to be the correct one. In *First National,* Bank Two prevailed.

First National states the prevailing rule, but Oregon courts have taken the view that a depositary bank may be in bad faith if it presents checks knowing of a check kite while dishonoring checks drawn on it. Farmers & Merchants State Bank v. Western Bank, 841 F.2d 1433 (9th Cir.1987), applies Oregon law and reviews the state court authorities. 1 Barkley Clark & Barbara Clark, The Law of Bank Deposits, Check Collections and Credit Cards ¶ 9.03 (Rev. ed. 2009).

In the 1990 revision of Article 4, after much discussion, a new defense to the accountability rule was added by 4–302(b): "The liability of a payor bank to pay an item pursuant to subsection (a) is subject to defenses based on...proof that the person seeking enforcement of the liability presented or transferred the item for the purpose of defrauding the payor bank." Comment 3 says: "A payor bank that makes a late return of an item should not be liable to a defrauder operating a check kiting scheme." Why didn't the court in *First National* refer to 4–302(b) and the quoted Comment? The court was correct in not doing so; 4-302(b) was not intended to cover such a case. Bank Two was not "operating a check kiting scheme" when it presented checks to Bank One and had no intention of defrauding that bank.

The first authoritative holding on the application of 4-302(b) to check kiting is found in Bank of America NT & SA v. David W. Hubert, P.C., 101 P.3d 409 (Wash. 2004). In that case, Principal, an incorporated law firm, gave Agent complete control over a large deposit account of Principal in Bank A in which the proceeds from real estate closings were deposited. Agent, who was running a check kiting scheme, stole large sums from the account in Bank A and replenished the balance in the account by writing checks payable to

Principal on her empty account in Bank B, which she deposited in Principal's account in Bank A. When these checks were presented to Bank B for payment, they were returned for insufficient funds *after* Bank B's midnight deadline. Principal asserted that Bank B was accountable for the funds under 4-302 but the court held that 4-302(b) applied because Agent's fraudulent intent was imputed to the careless Principal.

d. EFFECT OF REGULATION CC ON THE MIDNIGHT DEADLINE

Regulation CC, 12 CFR pt. 229, § 229.30(c), is a major modification of the Article 4 midnight deadline. In this regulation the Fed attempts to speed the return of checks by *extending* the midnight deadline. How does this make returns swifter? The regulation is set out below.

> (c) Extension of deadline. The deadline for return or notice of nonpayment under the U.C.C.... is extended to the time of dispatch of such return or notice of nonpayment where a paying bank uses a means of delivery that would ordinarily result in receipt by the bank to which is sent
>
> (1) On or before the receiving bank's next banking day following the otherwise applicable deadline [the UCC midnight deadline], for all deadlines other than those described in paragraph (c)(2) of this section; this deadline is extended further if a paying bank uses a highly expeditious means of transportation, even if this means of transportation would ordinarily result in delivery after the receiving bank's next banking day; or
>
> (2) Prior to the cut-off hour for the next processing day (if sent to a returning bank), or on the next banking day (if sent to the depositary bank), for a deadline falling on a Saturday that is a banking day (as defined in the applicable U.C.C.) for the paying bank.

An example of how these provisions operate is found in the following case. In this case, Wooden wrote a check for $700,000 drawn on its account in Wells Fargo Bank payable to HMA, which deposited the check in its account in U.S. Bank on August 2. But on that date Wooden ordered Wells Fargo to stop payment on the check. U.S. Bank forwarded the check for presentment to Wells Fargo through the Boise Clearninghouse. The check was received by Wells Fargo on Friday, August 3. Since Saturday and Sunday were not banking days, Wells Fargo's midnight deadline under the UCC fell upon Monday, August 6. But as we see in the portion of the opinion set out below, instead of returning the check through the clearinghouse to U.S. Bank, Wells Fargo sent the check by courier to the Salt Lake Federal Reserve Bank either late Monday or very early Tuesday morning. HMA's claim was that Wells Fargo should have returned the check directly to U.S. Bank and that it missed its midnight deadline. In the portion of the opinion set out below, we see the court applying Regulation CC to these facts. The court took up a number of other issues that we have omitted.

U.S. Bank N.A. v. HMA, L.C.

Supreme Court of Utah, 2007.
169 P.3d 433.

■ NEHRING, JUSTICE:

. . ..

A bank that seeks to return a check because of insufficient funds, a stop-payment order, and the like must normally dispatch the check before the midnight deadline. *See* 4-301(1). The midnight deadline is defined by the U.C.C. as midnight on a bank's "next banking day following the banking day on which it receives the relevant item or notice or from which the time for taking action commences to run, whichever is later." *Id.* 4-104(1)(j).

Wells Fargo received the Woodson check as part of its Friday, August 3 banking day. This meant that the midnight deadline would occur at midnight on the bank's next banking day, Monday, August 6....

If the U.C.C. were the exclusive authority governing the return of checks, as it largely was before Congress enacted the Expedited Funds Availability Act (the Act) in 1987 the obligations of a paying bank, like Wells Fargo, would begin and end with meeting the midnight deadline. Banks could focus their attention on the sole mission of getting checks out the door. What happened to the checks after dispatch was of little concern. The U.C.C. check return scheme was unpopular with bank customers. Because banks were not accountable for delays in returning checks to depositary banks, customers who had deposited checks were frequently denied access to funds for lengthy periods of time. *See generally* 1 Barkley Clark & Barbara Clark, *The Law of Bank Deposits, Collections and Credit Cards* ¶ 7.02, at 7-2 (rev. ed. 2003). Customer unhappiness over these delays provided the primary impetus for congressional action. The Act empowered the Federal Board of Governors of the Federal Reserve System to promulgate regulations to implement the Act. The Federal Board exercised this grant of authority, mindful of its need to strike a balance between the interests of bank customers to enjoy speedier access to funds and the interests of banks in managing the risks they would assume by standing behind checks of dubious pedigree deposited by their customers. *See* 12 U.S.C. § 4008(b) (1987).

The product of the Federal Board's efforts was regulation CC and, in particular, its subpart C at 12 C.F.R. sections 229.30 to 229.43 (2001). Along with its predecessor, regulation J, regulation CC created a federal check management protocol that loosened to some degree the constraints of the U.C.C. midnight deadline, but added the obligations of expeditious return and prompt notice of dishonor to banks returning checks. The effect of regulation CC was to expand the check return mission of banks beyond their U.C.C. task of monitoring dispatch before the midnight deadline to include an interest in when dishonored checks were delivered to depositary banks. 12 C.F.R.

§§ 229.30-.31 (2001). Although it left the midnight deadline in place, regulation CC made its effect less Cinderella-like by authorizing an extension of the deadline to paying banks that met certain conditions.

Regulation CC at 12 C.F.R. section 229 extends the midnight deadline in two ways. First, a paying bank . . . may escape the midnight deadline by seeing to it that it dispatches the check in time to ordinarily reach the receiving bank, here the Federal Reserve Bank, on or before the bank's next banking day after the imposed midnight deadline, provided the bank uses any means of delivery that would ordinarily accomplish the safe arrival of the check at a returning or depositary bank on that day. 12 C.F.R. § 229.30(c) (2001). As an even more generous alternative, regulation CC extends the midnight deadline beyond the next banking day to a paying bank using a "highly expeditious" means of transporting the check to the receiving bank.[1] *Id.* One commentator has plausibly suggested that the Federal Board's decision to provide for an extension of the midnight deadline was prompted by the Board's desire to encourage banks to abandon the practice of using the mail to convey returned items in favor of couriers and other means of more expeditious transport. 1 Barkley Clark and Barbara Clark, *The Law of Bank Deposits, Collections and Credit Cards* ¶ 8.01[4], at 8-6 (rev. ed.2006). Irrespective of its possible objectives, the extension to the midnight deadline authorized by section 229.30(c) clearly replaces the midnight deadline's compliance, measured based on time of dispatch, with compliance measured by delivery. As our upcoming discussion will reveal, the delivery contemplated in section 229.30(c) is not necessarily limited, as HMA asserts, to the depositary bank, but includes delivery to Federal Reserve Banks in the manner Wells Fargo employed.

II.
WELLS FARGO'S DUTY OF EXPEDITIOUS RETURN WAS SATISFIED WHEN IT PLACED THE WOODSON CHECK IN THE HANDS OF THE FEDERAL RESERVE BANK IN SALT LAKE CITY

Wells Fargo placed the Woodson check in the hands of a courier who transported it from the Wells Fargo central operations building located near

---

[1] gulation CC at 12 C.F.R. section 229.30(c) (2001) states:

Extension of deadline. The deadline for return or notice of nonpayment under the U.C.C. or Regulation J (12 CFR part 210), or Sec. 229.36(f)(2) is extended to the time of dispatch of such return or notice of nonpayment where a paying bank uses a means of delivery that would ordinarily result in receipt by the bank to which it is sent-

(1) On or before the receiving bank's next banking day following the otherwise applicable deadline, for all deadlines other than those described in paragraph (c)(2) of this section; this deadline is extended further if a paying bank uses a highly expeditious means of transportation, even if this means of transportation would ordinarily result in delivery after the receiving bank's next banking day; or

(2) Prior to the cut-off hour for the next processing cycle (if sent to a returning bank), or on the next banking day (if sent to the depositary bank), for a deadline falling on a Saturday that is a banking day (as defined in the applicable U.C.C.) for the paying bank.

Salt Lake International Airport to the Federal Reserve Bank in Salt Lake City sometime either before or shortly after midnight on August 6. No one disputes that Wells Fargo's choice of transport, a courier, was a highly expeditious means of delivery that would ordinarily result in delivery of the Woodson check to the Federal Reserve Bank in Salt Lake City on August 7.

From the standpoint of HMA, the delivery of the Woodson check to the Salt Lake Reserve Bank was irrelevant because under HMA's interpretation of the applicable authority the only delivery destination that mattered was U.S. Bank. That delivery occurred on Wednesday, August 8, a date too late even if Wells Fargo were to enjoy the benefit of the section 229.30(c) exception. To succeed, HMA's argument depends on designating the Boise Clearinghouse rules as the authority governing the manner in which Wells Fargo could return checks. Those rules, HMA asserts, required Wells Fargo to return the Woodson check directly to U.S. Bank without interrupting the journey with stops at intermediary banks including the Federal Reserve Bank.

Any restriction imposed on the method of returning dishonored checks by the Boise Clearinghouse rules must contend with and account for 12 C.F.R. section 210.12(a)(2) (regulation J), which states:

> A paying bank that receives a check as defined in Sec. 229.2(k) of this chapter (Regulation CC), other than from a Reserve Bank, and that determines not to pay the check, may send the returned check to any Reserve Bank (unless its Administrative Reserve Bank directs it to send the returned check to a specific Reserve Bank) in accordance with subpart C of part 229 of this chapter (Regulation CC), the Uniform Commercial Code, and the Reserve Banks' operating circulars.

The Boise Clearinghouse rules surrender any claim as controlling authority, however, on the method of check return when this seemingly unambiguous grant of permission to return checks through the Federal Reserve System—checks like the Woodson check that were not presented for collection through the Federal Reserve System—is coupled with the assertion of the primacy of federal regulations over inconsistent provisions of the Uniform Commercial Code, any other state law, or regulation CC found in 12 C.F.R. section 210.3(f) of regulation J. The official commentary to regulation CC reinforces this point by explaining that section 229.30 supersedes provisions of the U.C.C. relating to the method of returning dishonored checks "in that instead of returning a check through a clearinghouse or to the presenting bank, a paying bank may send a returned check to the depositary bank or to a returning bank." 12 C.F.R. pt. 229, app. E, § 229.30(a), cmt. 10.a (2001).

Federal regulations not only authorize check return through the Federal Reserve System even where clearinghouse rules might be construed to prohibit it, but they also make clear that the successful transfer of a returned check to a Federal Reserve Bank satisfies the paying bank's duty of expeditious return.

The commentary to regulation CC notes that "[a]ll Federal Reserve Banks agree to handle returned checks expeditiously." *Id.* at cmt. 5.b.i (2001).

HMA resists this conclusion by going to considerable lengths to show that the Woodson check was not delivered within the time limits established by either the two-day/four-day test or the forward collection test, the two standards by which regulation CC measures expeditious return. HMA's labors in this cause were to no avail because whether the Woodson check met either test is irrelevant. Liability for untimely return attaches to a bank upon its failure to make expeditious return of a dishonored check. By agreeing to handle returned checks in an expeditious manner, Federal Reserve Banks impliedly acknowledge that their handling of the check will conform to the two-day/four-day and forward collection tests.

None of the authorities cited by HMA in support of its conclusion that Wells Fargo was obliged to deliver the Woodson check directly to U.S. Bank and not to use the Federal Reserve System alters our conclusion that Wells Fargo satisfied its duty of expeditious return when it delivered the check to the Federal Reserve Bank in Salt Lake City.

....

We accordingly hold that the district court properly granted U.S. Bank summary judgment on the issue of the timeliness of the Woodson check's return.

....

Affirmed.

NOTE

In Oak Brook Bank v. Northern Trust Co., 256 F.3d 638 (7th Cir.2001), a drawee of a check involved in a check kite did not decide to dishonor a $450,000 check presented on February 11 until shortly before 4 p.m. on the afternoon of February 13. Under Regulation CC, 12 CFR 229.30(c)(1), quoted at the beginning of this section, drawee could return the dishonored check during the "banking day" on the 13th. Drawee's courier raced across town to the Federal Reserve Bank of Chicago and arrived at 4:46 pm. Regulation CC defines "banking day" as "that part of any business day on which an office of a bank is open to the public for carrying on *substantially all of its banking functions.*" 12 C.F.R. § 229.2(f) (emphasis added).The question was whether the check arrived during the "banking day" on the 13th. Judge Posner concluded that since the principal function of a Federal Reserve bank is to process checks, which it does 24 hours a day, the drawee had until midnight of the 13th to return the check. The court leaves open the meaning of banking day for returning banks other than Federal Reserve Banks. Comment 2 to UCC 4–104 speaks to this issue: "Under [the definition of banking day in 4–

104(a)(3)] that part of a business day when a bank is open only for limited functions, e.g., to receive deposits and cash checks, but with loan, bookkeeping and other departments closed, is not part of a banking day."

2. Right of Collecting Bank to Revoke Settlement on Dishonored Check

We saw in the preceding section that a payor bank may inadvertently pay a check by failing to return the check within its midnight deadline. A collecting bank, including a depositary bank, is also subject to a midnight deadline in the case of return of a dishonored check to the bank. If a check forwarded to the payor bank is not paid, the depositary bank may revoke the provisional credit that it gave to its customer with respect to the check. 4–214(a). But the depositary bank is required either to return the check to its customer or to give notice of dishonor to the customer before the bank's midnight deadline. The case below discusses the Revised Article 4 provisions on notice of dishonor and the consequences of the failure of the depositary bank to act within its deadline.

Essex Construction Corp. v. Industrial Bank of Washington, Inc.

United States District Court, D. Maryland, 1995.
913 F.Supp. 416.

■ MOTZ, CHIEF JUDGE.

Plaintiff Essex Construction Corporation (Essex) claims violations of the...District of Columbia banking laws. Essex alleges that Defendant Industrial Bank of Washington, Inc. (Industrial)...failed to provide timely notice that the check had been dishonored. Plaintiff seeks the amount of the check as damages. Defendant moves to dismiss or for summary judgment, and plaintiff cross-moves for default or summary judgment.

The relevant facts are not in dispute. On March 31, 1995, plaintiff deposited into its account at Industrial a check in the amount of $120,710.70 from East Side Manor Cooperative Association (East Side). East Side's check was drawn against its account at Signet Bank (Signet). At the time of the deposit, Industrial provisionally credited Essex's account but provided written notice that all but $100 of the funds would not be available for withdrawal until April 6, 1995.

On April 6, Signet notified Industrial that East Side had stopped payment on the check. Industrial placed a permanent hold on the $120,710.70 deposit, effectively revoking the provisional credit to Essex's account. On April 7, Industrial mailed written notice (including the returned check itself) to Essex.

On April 7, Essex wrote two checks in the amount of $21,224 and $18,084.60 against the funds it thought were available in its account at Industrial. Essex received Industrial's written notice of dishonor on April 11....

...[A] depository bank's right to revoke or charge back an uncollectible deposit...must comply with applicable state law. The District of Columbia has adopted the Uniform Commercial Code's system for regulating check processing transactions. The U.C.C. observes a fundamental distinction between "payor" and "collecting" banks. A payor bank is the bank maintaining the account against which a check is drawn, in this case Signet. See § 4–105(3). A collecting bank is a bank handling a check for collection from the payor, in this case Industrial. See § 4–105(5).

Payor and collecting banks have distinct obligations. A payor bank must decide whether to reject a check by midnight on the day it receives a check for collection. Failure to respond by midnight constitutes "final payment," making the payor bank strictly liable for the amount of the check. See First Nat'l Bank in Harvey v. Colonial Bank, 898 F.Supp. 1220, 1226 (N.D.Ill.1995) (discussing U.C.C.'s "final payment" system and role of payor banks); see also § 4–302(a). A collecting bank, in contrast, retains the right to revoke or charge back funds that are provisionally credited to a customer until the collecting bank's settlement with the payor bank becomes final. See § 4–214(a). It is at the moment of "final payment" by the payor bank that the respective liabilities for a check become fixed: the payor bank is strictly liable to the collecting bank for the amount of the check, see § 4–302(a), and the collecting bank loses the ability to revoke a provisional settlement or charge back withdrawn funds. See §§ 4–215(d), 4–214(a).

Essex argues that on April 6 Industrial's provisional credit to its account became a final and irrevocable payment under § 4–215(a). This contention misunderstands the difference between payor and collecting banks. As discussed, a final payment occurs when a payor bank accepts or fails to promptly reject a check presented for collection by a collecting bank. Industrial was the collecting bank in this transaction. Essex's reliance on § 4–215(a) therefore is misplaced. See § 4–215(a) ("An item is finally paid by a *payor* bank when the bank has first done any of the following....") (emphasis added). Essex's right to the provisionally credited funds became irrevocable only upon "final payment" by Signet to Industrial, a condition that Essex does not allege occurred.

Essex also argues that Industrial's mailing of the returned check via first class mail on April 7 did not constitute timely notice of dishonor under D.C. law. § 4–214 provides in relevant part:

> § 4–214 Right of charge-back or refund; liability of collecting bank; return of item.

> (a) If a collecting bank has made a provisional settlement with its customer for an item and fails by reason of dishonor ... to receive settlement for the item which is or becomes final, the bank may revoke the settlement given by it, charge back the amount of any credit given for the item to its customer's account, or obtain refund from its customer ... if by its midnight deadline or within a longer reasonable time after it learns the facts it returns the item or sends notification of the facts....

There is no dispute that Industrial failed by reason of dishonor to receive a final payment from Signet, the payor bank. Section 4–214(a) therefore provides that Industrial could revoke the provisional credit "if by its midnight deadline or within a longer reasonable time after it learn[ed] the facts it return[ed] the item or sen[t] notification of the facts." A bank's "midnight deadline" is defined as "midnight on its next banking day following the banking day on which it receives the relevant item or notice." § 4–104(a)(10); see also § 3–503(c)(i) ("[W]ith respect to an instrument taken for collection by a collecting bank, notice of dishonor must be given by the bank before midnight of the next banking day following the banking day on which the bank receives notice of dishonor of the instrument."). The parties do not dispute that Industrial received notice of dishonor from Signet on April 6, that Industrial mailed the returned check to Essex before midnight on April 7 via first class mail, but that Essex did not receive it until April 11.

Essex argues that merely mailing the notice of dishonor before midnight on April 7 was insufficient. Industrial attempts to rely on § 3–508(4) for the proposition that "[w]ritten notice is given when sent although it is not received." However, the District of Columbia Council repealed § 3–508 effective March 27, 1995. See An Act to revise Articles 3 and 4 of the Uniform Commercial Code, 1994 D.C.Laws 10–249. Industrial's position finds alternative support, however, in § 4–214. Section 4–214(a) requires a bank to "*send* notification of the facts" or "return" the dishonored item. (emphasis added). Section 4–214(b) defines an item as "returned" "when it is *sent* or delivered to the bank's customer." In addition, § 3–503(b) provides that notice of dishonor may be given by "any commercially reasonable means, including an oral, written, or electronic communication." Industrial did not unduly delay notifying Essex, but instead took the reasonable step of promptly mailing the returned check. Although immediately telephoning Essex may have constituted better customer service, Industrial complied with D.C. notice requirements by mailing the returned check to Essex on April 7.

Moreover, even were I to find that Industrial's method of notice was not sufficient, Essex would not be entitled to the damages it seeks. In a case involving directly analogous provisions of the U.C.C. as enacted in Illinois, the Seventh Circuit has held that a depositor is entitled only to the damages actually resulting from a bank's failure to provide timely notice of dishonor. See Appliance Buyers Credit Corp. v. Prospect Nat'l Bank, 708 F.2d 290, 292–

95 (7th Cir.1983). Furthermore, although the Appliance Buyers court reached this well-reasoned conclusion by interpreting an Illinois statute that was silent as to damages,[4] here the D.C. provision contains additional language which expressly so limits a depositor's remedies: a bank that fails to provide timely notice retains its right to charge back dishonored deposits "but is liable for any loss *resulting from the delay*." § 4–214(a) (emphasis added).[5] Plaintiff therefore may have been able to assert a claim for the bank charges associated with the two checks written on April 7, or for other foreseeable damages.[6] Essex, however, has made no showing of damages actually suffered.

A separate order granting defendant's summary judgment motion and entering judgment on its behalf is being entered herewith.

NOTE

In Gordon v. Planters & Merchants Bancshares, Inc., 935 S.W.2d 544 (Ark.1996), a collecting bank charged back against a customer's account a check for which it had received final settlement in violation of 4–215(d). The customer sued for punitive damages and the trial court granted the bank a directed verdict. The Supreme Court of Arkansas (4 to 3) reversed and remanded for a new trial. In its view the customer had shown substantial evidence that the bank had acted in a willful or malicious manner, and the "other rule of law" language of 1–106(1) [1–305(a)] allows punitive damages even if not specifically provided for in the UCC. The court noted the "bad faith" language in 4–103(e). The dissenting judges were outraged; two judges didn't participate.

---

[4] In *Appliance Buyers*, the Seventh Circuit noted that because the charge-back provision at issue in that case did not expressly address damages—in contrast to other U.C.C. provisions that expressly do hold banks "accountable" for the amount of the check—the drafters could not have intended "that banks should be held strictly liable for the face value of dishonored checks." 708 F.2d at 293. Instead, the *Appliance Buyers* court turned to Illinois' general damages provision, which provided only for actual damages and which was identical to D.C.'s current provision. Compare § 4–103(e) with 708 F.2d at 293 (quoting IlL. Rev.Stat. ch. 26 § 4–103(5)).

[5] In fact, prior to revisions that became effective on March 27, 1995, the predecessor to § 4–214(a) was largely identical to the Illinois statute at issue in *Appliance Buyers*. In 1995, however, the D.C. Council revised its U.C.C. provisions to add, among other changes, the above-quoted language that expressly limits recovery to actual loss. See 1994 D.C.Laws 10–249.

[6] To recover the $120,710.70 from Industrial, therefore, Essex would have had to show that, absent the delay from April 7 to April 11, it would have been able to take action to collect from East Side. See Alioto v. United States, 593 F.Supp. 1402, 1416–17 (N.D. Ill. 1984) (discussing cases). The record indicates, however, that East Side stopped payment on the check because of its ongoing dispute with Essex, not that East Side lacked funds on April 11 (or any time thereafter) that it had on April 7. In addition, defendant points out that in a separate proceeding East Side has alleged that it directly informed Essex of the stop payment order on April 6, the same day Signet notified Industrial.

3. Check Encoding

The conservatism of the banking profession is snickered at by the following oft-told anecdote: When a retiring banker was asked what the single biggest change in banking had been during his long career, he replied, "air conditioning." In the 20th century, the biggest change in check collection to have gained wide-spread acceptance was an elementary technology invented in 1956 known as Magnetic Ink Character Recognition (MICR) encoding. In order to permit electronic processing of checks for presentment for payment, almost all checks in use today are preprinted with a row of numerals and symbols along the bottom of the check (the "MICR line") that can be read by machines that process the checks for payment. The preprinted MICR encoding identifies the payor bank, the Federal Reserve district in which the bank is located, the Federal Reserve Bank or branch that serves the payor bank, the number of the check, and the number of the account at the payor bank on which the check is drawn. When the check is deposited, either the depositary bank or the next collecting bank that has encoding equipment will add to the MICR line numerals that indicate the amount of the check. In some cases the encoding of the amount of the check will be done by the payee of the check before the check is deposited in the depositary bank. This can occur if the payee is a person receiving a very large volume of checks that are processed in processing centers operated by the payee. Examples of such payees are public utilities, insurance companies, and large retailers.

Most checks that have been encoded with the amount of the check will be processed by automated equipment by the payor bank and by collecting banks on the basis of the encoded information without any examination of the check by a human being. What happens if a check is payable in the amount of $123.45 but the person encoding the amount of the check erroneously encodes the amount as $12,345? The misencoding does not change the amount of the check. There has been no alteration of the check. But if the check is read by machines on the basis of the encoded amount, the bank that processes the check will treat it as a check in the amount of $12,345. If the payor bank pays the check, it has paid out the encoded amount to the presenting bank but will be entitled to debit the account of the drawer of the check only for the actual amount of the check. Alternatively, the payor bank might wrongfully dishonor the check because the balance in the drawer's account, although large enough to cover the actual amount of the check, is not enough to cover the encoded amount. Before the 1990 revision, Article 4 did not address the problem of misencoding because MICR encoding did not exist when Article 4 was drafted in the 1950s. Section 4–209 now addresses the consequences of misencoding.

PROBLEM

Drayton drew a check on Bank One for $10,000 payable to the order of Park Company. Park deposited the check in its account in Bank Two and was given a provisional credit for the amount of the check. Bank Two forwarded the check to Bank One for payment; it arrived on May 1.

(a) Bank Two misencoded the check for $1,000, and on May 1, Bank One sent Bank Two a wire transfer for $1,000 intended as provisional settlement. Bank One debited Drayton's account for that amount and retained the check for mailing to Drayton at the end of the billing cycle with her other cancelled checks. When Bank Two received only $1,000 for the check, it reduced the credit in Park's account to that amount. Park complained to Bank Two about its failure to give $10,000 final credit for the check. What are Bank Two's rights against Bank One under 4–302(a)? What are Bank One's rights against Bank Two under 4–209(a)? If Drayton's account exceeds $10,000, has Bank One suffered a loss under 4–209(c)? See Comment 2 to 4–209.

(b) The check was misencoded for $100,000. On May 1, Bank One provisionally settled for the check by sending Bank Two a wire transfer for $100,000.

(i) Drayton had more than $100,000 in her account and Bank One debited her account for $100,000. What are Drayton's rights against Bank One? 4–401(a). Bank One's rights against Bank Two? 4–209(a) and (c).

(ii) On May 2, Bank One discovered that Drayton had only $25,000 in her account and dishonored the check by returning it to Bank Two before midnight on that date. Does Drayton have rights against Bank One for wrongful dishonor under 4–402? If Bank One is liable for damages to Drayton, what is its recourse under 4–209(a) against Bank Two?

Courts have not warmed to 4-209. Although First Union National Bank v. Bank One, N.A., 2002 WL 501145 (E.D. Pa. 2002), concerned an under-encoding error of major proportions and was decided years after 4-209 became law, the court decided the case without a mention of the statute. In another case, Douglas Cos., Inc. v. Commercial National Bank of Texarkana, 419 F.3d 812 (8th Cir.2005), the district court was at least aware of § 4-209 but, in its concern about confusing the jury by requiring them "to sift through the intricacies of the UCC," chose to instruct on negligence. The Eighth Circuit approved this paternalistic approach on the ground that no harm was done.

NOTE: MISENCODING OR LATE RETURN?

Case #1. Drawer issues check for $10,000 to Payee on its account in Payor Bank (PB). Payee deposits the check in Depositary Bank (DB), which presents the check for payment to PB. Since Drawer has insufficient funds in its account, PB acts to dishonor the check by mailing it to DB within its midnight deadline at an incorrect address. Under 4-302, PB is liable for the full amount of the check because it has not properly returned the check under 4-301(d)(1) ("sent"). Under 1-201(b)(36)(A) ("send"), PB has not sent the check before the midnight deadline because the letter was not "properly addressed."

Case #2. Same facts as above, except that PB attached a magnetic tape to the check that made the check a "qualified return check," returnable by the Federal Reserve's automated processing system under Regulation CC. But PB misencoded the check by failing to encode DB's correct routing number on the tape, causing the check to go to another bank. Payee contends that PB is accountable for $10,000 because it did not properly return the check within the midnight deadline under 4-301(d). PB argues that this is a misencoding under 4-209, and, since no one suffered a loss (the check was worthless), PB has no liability.

In NBT Bank, N.A. v. First National Community Bank, 393 F.3d 404 (3d Cir.2004), on facts similar to Case #2, the court held that the provisions of Regulation CC applied to this case and damages under Subpart C of Regulation CC, which includes encoding standards, are limited to the amount of the loss incurred; hence, PB is not liable. 12 CFR § 229.30(a)(2)(iii) provides:

> A paying bank may convert a check to a qualified return check. A qualified returned check must be encoded in magnetic ink with the routing number of the depositary bank, the amount of the returned check, and a '2' in position 44 of the MICR line as a return identifier.

12 CFR § 229.38(a) provides:

> .... A bank that fails to exercise ordinary care or act in good faith under this subpart may be liable.... The measure of damages for failure to exercise ordinary care is the amount of the loss incurred, up to the amount of the check, reduced by the amount of the loss that party would have incurred even if the bank had exercised ordinary care.

Thus, even though the misencoding causing the check to be returned to an incorrect party might have been an ineffective return under the UCC 4-301(d) (the court didn't decide the issue), Regulation CC preempts the UCC's strict liability under 4-302 by its actual damages limitation set out above. Subpart C of Regulation CC, 12 C.F.R. §§ 229.30-.43, governs the collection, processing and return of checks, and the provisions of Subpart C "supersede any inconsistent provisions of the UCC as adopted in any state, or of any other state law, but only to the extent of the inconsistency."12 C.F.R. §229.41. Hence, with respect to "qualified return checks," Regulation CC preempts UCC 3-401 and 4-302 in providing that damages for a misencoding, even one affecting the midnight deadline, are limited to actual loss caused by the error. This is the same measure of damages for misencoding under 4-209. See 4-103(e).

4. ELECTRONIC PRESENTMENT

a. UNDER UCC

Illustration: Charles is an American Express cardholder and has a deposit account in the Bank of America. He used his Amex card to purchase goods for $875. When his Amex statement arrived, he was billed for $875, which he promptly paid by check number 2034 drawn on his BofA account. Later, when he returned from a hectic vacation trip, he was uncertain whether he had paid the $875 charge. His checkbook record showed that he had but when he looked through the cancelled checks that he had just received from BofA and found no cancelled check for the Amex bill, he was concerned. However, when he examined the BofA statement that accompanied the cancelled checks, he found under the column marked "Withdrawals, Transfers and Account Fees" a line stating "American Express DES: Checkpayment ID: 2034" followed by "INDN" and a very long number. Under the next column marked "Reference Number" he found a six digit number, and in the final column marked "Amount" the amount of the check, $875, appeared. From this, Charles concluded that he had paid the Amex bill, but he didn't understand how his account could have been debited for the payment if the BofA apparently had no check to return to him. The following material explains how Charles' check-originated payment was converted into electronic presentment pursuant to an agreement between BofA and Amex that allows Amex to collect all checks drawn on BofA that are payable to Amex by electronic presentment. Amex's depositary bank sends to BofA, in digitalized form, the information from the MICR line of the check or an image of the check. As we see below, this is a valid presentment within the provisions of the UCC. Conversion of paper checks to electronic presentment by agreement of the parties is increasingly common.

With respect to collection of checks by a depositary bank, the present system depends upon transportation of checks through the banking system from the depositary bank to the payor bank. The number of checks processed by the banking system each day is huge; the transportation of this volume of paper to the payor bank is very expensive and delays payment. It is not surprising that the banking system, which has been aggressively seeking methods of cutting costs, has considered alternatives to flying and trucking tons of checks across the nation each day. One method discussed is often referred to by bankers as "truncation," but this is a confusing term because it is used to describe two quite different transactions. One use of the term describes the practice of payor banks in retaining checks after payment rather than returning them to the drawers who wrote them. Some banks send customers an electronic image of their paid checks and destroy the originals after a period of time. We will discuss this matter later.

It is the second use of the term, sometimes described as "radical truncation," that we are concerned with at this point. In order to avoid confusing it with the other meaning of truncation, Revised Articles 3 and 4 refer to this process as "electronic presentment." 4–110. Under this process, most checks are retained by the depositary bank for destruction after a relatively short period of time. Presentment for payment of a check is to the payor bank by transmittal of an electronic image of the check rather than by delivery of the check. After the check is destroyed, an image of the check is stored electronically so that a copy of the check could be produced if needed at some later time.

Although under the traditional system the check itself was normally transported to the payor bank, most checks are not examined by anybody in the payor bank's process of payment. In these cases, the check serves only as the carrier of the electronic encoding on the MICR line, which is read by the automated machinery of the payor bank. Use of the paper check itself to convey the information contained on the MICR line is both inefficient and unnecessary. It is technologically feasible to provide this information to the payor bank by electronic transmission. Since a system of electronic presentment was believed to be a possible solution to the banking industry's difficulties with the present check payment system, much discussion during the drafting of Revised Articles 3 and 4 centered on how the revision should deal with electronic presentment. The agreement reached was that it was not the role of the UCC to mandate business practices in the banking industry. Electronic presentment, if found economically feasible, should come by interbank agreements or through the Federal Reserve pursuant to its broad regulatory authority. Thus, Articles 3 and 4 should be revised to remove any legal barriers to a regime of electronic presentment. The assumptions under which the Drafting Committee proceeded are set out in Comments 2 and 3 to 4–110. The changes made in Articles 3 and 4 to accommodate electronic presentment are explained in the following paragraphs.

With respect to collection of checks, presentment is simply a demand made to the drawee to pay the check. 3–501(a). The demand may be made by an electronic communication (3–501(b)(1)). But Revised Article 3 follows the pre-1990 law in preserving the right of the drawee to demand exhibition of the check and its surrender as a condition to payment (3–501(b)(2)). This right of the drawee to require exhibition and surrender of the check is subject, however, to rules stated in Article 4 and may be waived by the drawee by agreement. Section 4–110 permits electronic presentment by means of a "presentment notice," which is defined as "transmission of an image of an item or information describing the item." The presentment notice is in lieu of delivery of the check itself. Presentment under 4–110 requires an "agreement for electronic presentment" which provides for the presentment notice. The quoted term includes not only an agreement between the drawee and the presenting bank, but also a clearing-house rule or Federal Reserve regulation or operating circular providing for electronic presentment.

Electronic presentment raises a number of problems. Unless imaging is used, the payor bank will not be able to examine the signature of the drawer to detect a possible forgery, but this problem exists under current practice as well because most checks are not examined for forgery. Under the current practice, payor banks look at the drawer's signature only on some checks such as those in large dollar amounts. This practice could continue under a regime of electronic presentment by a requirement that large checks be excluded from electronic presentment. Alternatively, presentment might be made by transmitting an image of the check rather than information describing the check to allow examination of the drawer's signature. Current imaging technology allows depositary banks to send to payor banks miniature digitized images of checks, 15 or 20 to a page. The process, encouraged by 4–110(a), is described in 2 Barkley Clark & Barbara Clark, The Law of Bank Deposits, Check Collections and Credit Cards ¶ 16.02[1] (Rev. ed. 2009). Many banks, even small ones, appear to be either purchasing imaging technology or outsourcing the service. David Breitkof, Survey Finds Healthy Adoption of Imaging, Amer. Banker, Oct. 17, 2007, at 5. Imaging gives more information than that contained on the MICR line; the drawer's signature appears as well as the name of the payee.

The agreement for electronic presentment must provide for retention and destruction of the check in order to protect the drawer of the check against further negotiation of the check. Under present practice, some payor banks still return all cancelled checks to the drawer after the checks are paid. This will not be possible with respect to checks paid pursuant to electronic presentment. But the practice of returning checks to the drawer has become less prevalent in recent years. If the bank-customer agreement does not call for return of cancelled checks to the customer, the customer may be given a statement describing the checks paid, or better, is given an image of each check. Under electronic presentment, the payor bank would be able to obtain, at the request of a customer, a copy of any check paid for the customer's account for which the customer may have a particular need. The agreement for electronic presentment would provide for electronic storage of copies of checks presented electronically and would impose a duty on the storing bank to provide a copy of a check on request of the payor bank. 4–406(a) and (b).

The requirement of an interbank agreement for electronic presentment is the major barrier to adoption of this form of check collection. Requiring banks to enter into agreements with all the counterparties that they deal with in check collection seems almost impossible, but banks are dealing with it under the expansive definition of "agreement for electronic presentment" in 4-110(a) as including clearing house rules and Federal Reserve regulations or operating circulars. Geoffrey R. Gerdes, Recent Payment Trends in the United States, Fed. Res. Bull., October 2008, p. A91, predicted that "[i]n the long run, all depository institutions that process checks most likely will adopt electronic image processing methods." As we will see in the section on Check 21, the requirements of an interbank agreement has been avoided when substitute checks are used.

The Electronic Check Clearing House Association (ECCHO) is a non-profit national clearing house, formed by a number of member banks, to foster the electronic presentment of checks. It has a set of rules on electronic check presentment by imaging that are recognized by a number of organizations. The ECCHO rules are intended to qualify as agreements for electronic presentment under 4-110(a). An image of the check, front and back, would be sent electronically by the depositary bank, yielding more information and greater speed in check collection than Check 21, discussed below. The thrust of these rules would be to retain paper checks—some bank customers like them—but treat them as the source of information to be transmitted electronically.

b. UNDER FEDERAL LAW: "THE CHECK 21 ACT"

In the late 1980s, the prospects of federally mandated electronic presentment seemed bright. The Expedited Funds Availability Act, discussed in the next section, mandated that the Fed "shall consider...requiring by regulation, that...the Federal Reserve banks and depositary institutions provide for check truncation." 12 U.S.C. § 4008(b). The Fed has the power to mandate electronic presentment with no further authorization from Congress because 12 U.S.C. § 4008(c) gives the Fed the power to regulate any aspect of the payment system with respect to checks in order to carry out expedited funds availability. But after its 1988 post-EFTA study, the Fed declined to mandate electronic presentment. Although it conceded that electronic presentment was feasible givetn the technology at that time, the study concluded that the benefits of mandatory electronic presentment would be outweighed by the potential risks borne by the paying banks. It concluded that the matter should be left up to banks to choose to participate in voluntary interbank or multibank electronic presentment agreements with Reserve Banks or other presenting banks.

However, by 2000, the Fed had begun to investigate methods for improving the check-clearing process. Working with the industry, the Fed came up with a draft that Chairman Greenspan sent to the appropriate members and committees of the Senate and House at the end of 2001. In 2003, Congress enacted the Check Clearing for the 21st Century Act ("The Check 21 Act" or "Check 21"), with an effective date of October 2004. Pub. L. No. 108–100, 117 Stat. 1177 (2003). The Act allows the use of electronic presentment and return of checks without electronic truncation agreements between banks.

It does so by creating a new type of negotiable instrument: a "substitute check." A "substitute check" is a paper reproduction created from an electronic image of the original check and suitable for automated processing in the same manner as the original check. Section 3(16). A substitute check is the legal equivalent of the original check for all purposes if it accurately represents the information on the original check and contains the requisite legend ("This is a legal copy of your check. You can use it the same way you would use the original check."). Section 4(b). Check 21 requires a bank to handle a substitute check if warranties created by the legislation cover the check. Section 4(a). Banks are not required to accept presentation of checks in electronic form unless required to do so under an electronic truncation agreement. For a discussion of the events that led to enactment of Check 21 and a detailed critique of the law, see Carl Felsenfeld & Genci Bilali, The Check Clearing for the 21st Century Act—A Wrong Turn in the Road to Improvement of the U.S. Payments System, 85 Neb. L. Rev. 52 (2006).

Check 21 imposes a nondisclaimable warranty on a bank's use of a substitute check. §§ 5, 8. The bank warrants to downstream parties handling the check that the check is the legal equivalent of the original check and that they will not receive requests to pay the original or substitute check already paid. The warranty continues to apply even if the substitute check is converted into electronic form or reconverted back from an electronic form into another substitute check. § 5. Further, because the substitute check is the legal equivalent of the original check, any warranties that apply to the original check carry over to the substitute check. Check 21 also requires a bank transferring a substitute check to indemnify subsequent transferees for loss due to receipt of a substitute rather than original check. § 6. The legislation contains some consumer protection provisions that require expedited recrediting of consumer deposit accounts. In 2004, the Federal Reserve Board promulgated implementing regulations in 12 C.F.R. Subpart D, §§ 229.51-229.59, as part of Regulation CC, Availability of Funds and Collection of Checks.

A prototypic case follows: Payee deposits a check for $1,000 in Bank A in New York. The check is drawn on Payor Bank in Los Angeles. Bank A indorses and delivers the check to Bank B in New York for collection. Bank B is called the "truncating bank" because it truncates the check, that is, it takes the check out of the collection chain, creates an electronic image of the check, and sends the image to Bank C in Los Angeles. Bank C is called the "reconverting bank" because it reconverts the electronic information into a paper substitute check. Bank C presents the substitute check to Payor Bank, which pays the check. For this transaction to occur, Bank B and Bank C must have an agreement authorizing the actions taken. But there need be no agreement by Payor Bank that it will accept the paper substitute check as the equivalent of the original check. Check 21 requires Payor Bank to treat the paper check as the equivalent of the original check and deal with it accordingly. Hence, any payor bank in the United States must accept a substitute check, just as it would the original. Bank C, the reconverting bank, must warrant that the substitute check contains an accurate image of the front and back of the original check and a legend stating that it is the legal equivalent of the original check. Moreover, it must warrant that no depositary, drawee, drawer or indorser will be asked to pay a check that it has already paid. Any bank that presents, or otherwise transfers, a substituted check is responsible for indemnifying any person that suffers a loss owing to the receipt of the substituted check instead of the original check.

In this case, the paper check will not have to be flown across the country for presentment. When the substitute check is created by Bank C in Los Angeles, it can be presented to the payor bank on the day the check is created. Banks will have to invest in the electronic imaging equipment only if they agree to enter into such transactions as truncating or reconverting banks. Other banks need buy no new equipment because the paper substitute checks they receive may be processed in the same way as original checks. If the drawer requires the payor bank to deliver the cancelled checks to it at the end of each periodic account cycle, the paper substitute checks will serve as the cancelled checks. Of course, disclosure to customers of the nature of the substituted checks and of the customers' rights must be made.

Check 21's intended purpose is obscured by its provisions governing substitute checks. The legislation aims to facilitate electronic presentment without biasing the form check truncation might take. § 2(a)(3). As we saw in the preceding section, electronic presentment transfers electronic images of checks without the physical transfer of checks themselves. This does not require the creation and transfer of substitute checks. Check 21 facilitates electronic presentment merely by removing legal or contractual barriers that require transfer of original checks. It does this by giving substitute checks the same legal status as original checks. The legislation does not require banks to truncate checks electronically. § 2(b)(2). Nor does it require banks to create or transfer substitute checks. Check 21 simply requires banks to accept substitute checks when created and sent for collection or return, if a bank has made substitute check warranties as to it. § 4(a). In this way, the legislation is consistent with the demand for medium-neutrality required by other recent federal legislation (e.g., The Electronic Signatures in Global and National Commerce Act).

Electronic presentment can proceed without the creation or transfer of a substitute check. A substitute check is useful only when an individual or bank prefers (and pays) to create or receive a paper check. For instance, a substitute check can be created from an electronic image of an original check and presented to a payor bank without an interbank electronic presentment agreement. After payment, the payor bank can return the substitute check to the drawer with other cancelled checks. The same process can be used to return dishonored checks to the depository bank when the bank or the depositor insists on a paper check. Check 21 allows for the possibility that a demand for paper checks might remain as part of a market for electronic presentment. Its regulation of substitute checks is a way of accommodating this preference without interfering with the market for electronic presentment of checks. The unit cost of processing paper checks increases as the volume of paper checks processed declines. For banks and their customers who still want paper checks, substitute checks are cheaper to process than original checks. Electronic presentment has lower unit processing costs than both substitute and original (paper) checks, because it avoids use of paper checks entirely. Check 21 leaves to market participants the decision as to the optimal mix of electronic presentment and substitute checks.

As we saw in the previous section, banks engaged in electronic presentment must enter into an interbank agreement authorizing that manner of collection; moreover, electronic presentment requires banks to acquire expensive equipment and software. Check 21 addressed these impediments by creating a new paper negotiable instrument, the substitute check. Check 21 does not require banks to adopt electronic check processing, but it enables banks that wish to use electronic imaging technology to do so and creates substitute checks from the images for delivery to banks that do not accept electronic presentment. Hence, substitute checks are an intermediate step toward a full electronic processing system. By facilitating the settlement and return of checks electronically, the legislation reduces the time in which payees are denied access to deposited funds.

Check 21's impact on the market for electronic presentment of checks has been significant. The number of substitute checks grew rapidly but peaked at around 250 million items per month in 2008 and has declined since then. However, the number of checks sent for collection via electronic image during this period has increased much faster. See Digital Checks as Electronic Payment Orders, Fed. Res. Bank of Chicago, November 2009, at 8. The Government Accountability Office (GAO) Report on Check 21 Act, October 2008, at 14, found that some banks were moving directly to electronic processing in preference to making the investment to engage in substitute check processing because they thought that the check collection system would become predominantely electronic in only a few years. The GAO Report on p. 40 notes that the Federal Reserve Banks "expect that by year-end 2009, more than 90 percent of their check deposits and presentments will be electronic."

5. Funds Availability and Regulation CC

Suppose Father living in Sacramento, California, mails a check for $1,000, drawn on First Bank in Sacramento, to Daughter, attending school in College Town, New York, 80 miles from New York City. The check arrives on

Monday morning. Daughter takes it to Second Bank's College Town branch and deposits it in her account. On Monday night the check is driven by a courier to Second Bank's central check processing center in New York City and is run through a reader-sorter computer. On Tuesday morning, it is taken to the New York Fed where it goes through another reader-sorter and is sent by air courier on Tuesday night to the San Francisco Fed where it arrives early Wednesday morning. There it goes through a reader-sorter computer, and on Wednesday afternoon, is driven by courier to First Bank in Sacramento. By early Thursday morning, the check has been posted by automation to Father's account in First Bank, which was then debited. When Daughter deposited the check in Second Bank, she asked when she could withdraw her money; she was told it would be available for her in two weeks. She needed the money earlier and called Father to describe her plight. He was irritated to learn that although the banking system had withdrawn the amount of the check from his account on Thursday morning, Daughter would not be able to withdraw the funds until several days later.

Second Bank's action in placing a two-week "hold" period on Daughter's check was thought necessary to protect itself from the possibility that the check would not be paid by First Bank owing to insufficient funds in the account, entry of a stop-payment order or other reasons. Relatively long hold periods were thought to be necessary because of the slow and inefficient system banks use for returning checks that have been dishonored. Second Bank may not learn whether the check has been dishonored until the unpaid check is physically returned to it. The forward collection of the check in this case from College Town to Sacramento was fairly prompt because the MICR line enabled the collecting banks to utilize an automated system for sorting checks and directing them to the banks on which they are drawn. But there is no automated system for the return of checks. Each must be processed manually by clerks who must attempt to return the check to the proper bank by deciphering the sometimes unintelligible indorsements on the back of the check. Moreover, before institution of the reforms discussed below, the system of provisional credits made it desirable to send the check back through the same chain of banks as in the forward collection of the check. Thus, had First Bank dishonored the check that arrived there after that bank's 2:00 p.m. cutoff hour on Wednesday, it could have waited until its Friday night midnight deadline to send the check back to the San Francisco Fed. That bank would probably need a second banking day after the banking day of receipt for the manual processing of the check. The same is true for the New York Fed. Although the check would probably be returned by truck and air courier services, returning banks could slow the process down even more by mailing the returns back. One study found that although the forward collection process for checks averaged 1.6 days, the return averaged 5.2 days.

Barkley Clark & Barbara Clark, Regulation CC: Funds Availability and Check Collection ¶ 1.01[2] 1–4 (1988).

a. FUNDS AVAILABILITY

Banks met the growing chorus of customer complaints about what seemed to be excessive hold periods by justifying their actions as necessary to protect them from bad check losses. But in the 1980s several states passed laws limiting hold periods, and in 1987 Congress enacted the Expedited Funds Availability Act of 1987, 12 U.S.C. § 4001 et seq. The Board of Governors of the Federal Reserve System implemented this statute by promulgating Regulation CC in 1988, 12 C.F.R. Pt. 229. Subpart B of Regulation CC prescribes mandatory availability schedules. Next day availability is required for "low risk" deposits for which a hold period is not needed to protect the depositary bank from risk. Examples are cashier's checks, certified checks, teller's checks, electronic payments (wire transfers and ACH credits), "on us" items, Treasury and state and local government checks. § 229.10.

Until recently, Regulation CC had separate rules for local and nonlocal checks. Funds for local checks were required to be available not later than the second day after the banking day of deposit. § 229.12(b). For nonlocal checks, the Regulation set a maximum of five days after the banking day of deposit. § 229.12(c). However, effective February 10, 2010, the funds availability rules for nonlocal checks no longer apply. Changes in the clearing of checks, induced by the decline in the volume of checks, effectively eliminate the category of nonlocal checks. As of Februrary 10, 2010, a single regional Federal Reserve Bank (Cleveland) clears all checks in the United States. 75 Fed. Reg., January 5, 2010 (Docket No. R-1382). Thus, all checks are local because made payable by a bank located in the same check-clearing region as this Reserve Bank. Therefore, there are no longer nonlocal checks controlled by special availability rules for them. As a result, all check funds must be made available not later than the second business day following the banking day on which the funds are deposited. However, the depositor is allowed to withdraw up to $100 on the next banking day after deposit. § 229.10(c). Section 229.13 sets out exceptions to mandatory availability schedules with respect to new accounts, large deposits, redeposited checks, repeated overdrafts, and cases in which there is reasonable cause to doubt collectibility.

A 1994 American Bankers Association study showed that banks were generally making funds available to depositors earlier than Regulation CC required. For local checks drawn on consumer demand accounts, over 90% of the banks surveyed reported that they were making funds available on either the day of deposit or the next day. And over 50% of the banks were following the same practice for nonlocal checks on these accounts. Anecdotal evidence indicates that these percentages are probably much higher today. The reasons given for the banks' early availability policies are customer service and competition. The operational difficulties of dealing with the multiple availability schedules of Regulation CC may be another factor. Moreover, as indicated above, in cases in which a bank has reason to question the collectibility of a check it can protect itself by withholding payment. Clarks' Bank Deposits and Payments Monthly, Vol. 19, No. 2, Feb. 2010, at 5, states that now the FRB processes most checks electronically. This is owing to the development of check imaging, electronic check presentment, the conversion of paper checks to ACH debits, and the use of substitute checks under Check 21. The Clarks predict that it is only a matter of time before all checks are processed electronically.

b. CHECK COLLECTION AND RETURN

Today, the law of check collection and return is found in Regulation CC as well as in Article 4, to the extent that its provisions are not preempted by Regulation CC. Consideration in the revision of Article 4 was given to redrafting Article 4 in order to make it compatible with Regulation CC. This approach was rejected because of the likelihood that Regulation CC will continue to evolve, leaving inconsistencies between Article 4 and Regulation CC. Compatibility was again considered in the amending process that yielded the 2002 amendments to Articles 3 and 4, and was again rejected.

To allow the banking system to meet the funds availability standards set by Regulation CC without exposing depositary banks to excessive bad check losses, it was necessary to expedite the return system. Subpart C of Regulation CC sets out a sweeping revision of the law of check collection and return in order to speed the return of dishonored checks, thereby preempting portions of Article 4.

In the early stages of the revision of Article 4, before the EFAA had been enacted, the drafters had proposed several provisions designed to speed the return of dishonored checks. These provisions included: facilitating direct return of dishonored checks to depositary banks; reducing the number of returned checks by extending the payor bank's midnight deadline for checks under $100 (thus giving the drawer time to put enough money in the account to pay the check); requiring compliance with uniform indorsement standards governing the content and placement of bank indorsements; commencing the running of the midnight deadline for return from the time of delivery of checks to central bank processing centers; and imposing on payor banks the duty to give prompt notice of the nonpayment of items of $2,500 or more. Regulation CC incorporated all these provisions except the extension of the midnight deadline for small checks, which was not included in Regulation CC and dropped from later drafts of Article 4 because of the belief that it would slow the collection of checks; hence, all these provisions were deleted from the Article 4 draft.

But Regulation CC went far beyond these modest steps. In sections 229.30 and 229.31, it authorizes a payor or returning bank to return a check directly to the depositary bank or to any returning bank agreeing to handle the returned check for expeditious return to the depositary bank, regardless of whether the returning bank had handled the check for forward collection. The contemplation was that the banks most likely to agree to handle a returning check expeditiously were the regional Federal Reserve Banks. The consequences of allowing a check presented by one bank to be returned by the payor bank to a different bank undermined the usual methods of interbank settlements. Under these methods, the payor bank gives the presenting bank a provisional settlement, which it revokes when it returns the dishonored check to that bank. If the payor bank returns the check to a bank that was not the presenting bank, the payor bank cannot obtain settlement for the returned check by revoking the settlement with the presenting bank. Rather, it must recover settlement from the bank to which it returned the check. But in order to give banks incentive to make expeditious returns, even if the payor bank does return the dishonored check to the presenting bank, § 229.31(c) forbids a payor bank to obtain settlement for the check by charging back against a credit it had previously given the presenting bank. The payor bank cannot recover settlement from a bank to which it has returned a check until the check has reached the returning bank, as though in forward collection. In harmony with these two provisions, section 229.36(d) provides that all settlements between banks for the forward collection of checks are final when made.

The interbank settlement provisions of Article 4 are stated in terms of provisional settlements. 4–201(1). Bank credit given by a settling payor or collecting bank is provisional in the sense that it can be revoked upon return of the item. The Fed's decision in Regulation CC to make all settlements final meant that now the conceptual approach of Article 4 to inter-bank settlements differed from that of Regulation CC, though, at least with respect to the issues addressed by Article 4, there is little functional difference between the two laws. The fact that under Regulation CC any credit given for a check is final rather than provisional was not intended by the drafters of Regulation CC to limit the right of a payor or collecting bank to return a check and recover the amount of the check from the bank to which it was returned. After stating that settlement under Regulation CC is final rather than provisional, the commentary to § 229.36(d) of Regulation CC explains: "Settlement by a paying bank is not considered to be final payment for the purposes of U.C.C. [§ 4–215(a)], because a paying bank has the right to recover settlement from a returning or depositary bank to which it returns a check under this subpart." 12 C.F.R. Pt. 229, App. E. The check collection aspects of Regulation CC are discussed in detail in 1 Barkley Clark & Barbara Clark, Bank Deposits, Collections and Credit Cards, Chapter 8 (Rev. ed. 2009).

B. Credit and Debit Cards

1. Introduction

a. CREDIT CARDS

(1) HOW CREDIT CARDS FUNCTION

Credit cards fall into two broad categories: "restricted use" and "universal" cards. In the first category are credit cards issued by a merchant as a means of identifying customers who have charge accounts with the merchant. They are particularly convenient for merchants who have numerous retail outlets located over a large geographical area. These cards originally could be used to make purchases only from the merchant that issued the card, but in some cases use of the card to purchase from a limited number of other merchants is also permitted. "Restricted use" cards include, for instance, cards issued by oil companies for use at affiliated or independently owned service stations that sell products of the company that issued the card. The most important characteristic of this category of credit card is that the primary purpose of the issuer is to facilitate sales of goods or services of the issuer. Financial institutions have become involved in the merchant credit business by issuing "private-label" credit cards that appear to be issued by the merchant. The so-called co-branded card, bearing the names of both the merchant and the financer, have also become common.

"Universal" credit cards comprise cards issued by financial institutions that provide short-term credit, usually unsecured, to cardholders to allow them to make purchases from a multitude of merchants and other sellers of goods and services who are not related to the issuer of the card. These used to be called travel and entertainment cards; more often today they are referred to as bank cards because of the prominence of Visa and MasterCard in this category. This category of credit card has emerged as an important substitute for cash or personal checks in paying for goods or services. A merchant who accepts this type of credit card as the payment mechanism is party to a preexisting arrangement either directly with the issuer of the card or with an interbank system to which the issuer belongs, such as Visa USA or MasterCard International. Pursuant to this arrangement the merchant can obtain payment from the issuer for purchases made by use of the card. In a face-to-face purchase, the cardholder signs a credit card slip indicating the amount of the purchase and containing the card number and other information taken from the card.

The merchant is faced with several risks in honoring a credit card. First, the person using the card may not be a person authorized to use the card. Second, the card may have been revoked by the issuer. One common reason for revocation is a report to the issuer that the card has been lost or stolen. Third, the amount of credit given by the issuer to the cardholder may not be sufficient to cover the amount of the purchase. The merchant can normally avoid the last two risks. At the time a purchase is to be made, the merchant can determine, through telephonic or electronic access to a computer center having a record of the card, whether the card is valid and whether the charge is within the cardholder's line of credit. Through this process the merchant obtains approval of the charge before the purchase is made and has assurance of receiving payment in accordance with the arrangement to which the issuer and merchant are parties. As we see later, the merchant receives the amount of the charge less a discount to compensate the issuer for financing the purchase. The issuer receives this compensation by obtaining payment of the full amount of the charge from the cardholder. Thus, the credit risk of nonpayment by the cardholder is taken by the issuer. The issuer normally sends a monthly statement of charges to the cardholder. Under most plans, the cardholder has the option of paying the full amount by a specified date without an interest charge or of making payment in installments with an interest charge.

The growth of credit cards issued by financial institutions has been phenomenal. The Bank of America first issued its BankAmericard in the 1950s. A consortium of banks formed an association to issue a competing card, MasterCharge, in 1960. The BankAmericard was later taken over by an association of banks, Visa USA and renamed the Visa card. MasterCharge became MasterCard; its bank association is MasterCard International. Formerly these two companies were entirely owned and funded by their member banks, but now both are partially owned by public stockholders. In past years, many American banks issued both cards, but increasingly banks are required to choose between them. According to the Nilson Report, May 2008, Visa had 46% of the market, MasterCard 36%, American Express 12%, and Discover 6%. Most Amex cards are charge cards rather than credit cards; balances are payable a few days after receipt of the statement. More recently American Express also issues credit cards. According to the Federal Reserve's 2007 Survey of Consumer Finances, cited in Federal Reserve Bulletin of February 2009, 46.1% of Americans carry balances on their credit cards. They pay an average of 13.54% interest on these balances. See Consumer Action 2008 Credit Card Survey. American households that have credit cards maintain balances averaging $10,679.

Visa and MasterCard do not issue credit cards. They maintain networks of participating banks that handle the clearing and settlement of credit card debts. We will speak of this arrangement as the Visa or MasterCard network. The Visa and MasterCard entities are supported by periodic assessments on their member banks. For this, they provide computer networks through which messages between merchants and card issuers are exchanged, and card transactions are authorized. The Visa and Mastercard networks also pay for advertising and other marketing activities, as well as monitor the technology needed to keep their networks operating smoothly.

The process by which the participating banks are compensated is as follows: after a merchant authorized to honor Visa cards or MasterCards has sold goods or services to a cardholder, it will present to the "merchant bank" or "acquirer" a credit card slip signed by the cardholder at the time of purchase. The merchant bank will give the merchant a provisional credit in the amount of the purchase, less a discount, in its account with the merchant. The merchant bank functions as a processor; it sends by electronic transmission the amount of the credit card slip through the Visa or Mastercard network clearing system to the bank that issued the credit card to the cardholder (the "issuing bank"). The issuing bank, in turn, transfers funds for the amount of the slip, less an interchange fee, to the merchant bank through the settlement process of Visa or Mastercard and bills the cardholder for the full amount of its purchase. If the cardholder returns goods purchased, the issuing bank credits the cardholder's account and charges back this amount against the merchant bank.

The issuing bank is entitled to an "interchange fee" that is set by Visa and MasterCard, usually between 1 and 2% depending on the type of merchant and card being used; none of this fee is shared with Visa or MasterCard. According to Andrew Martin, Card Fees Pit Retailers Against Banks, N.Y. Times, July 16, 2009, at B1, annual revenue from interchange fees paid to issuing banks ranges between \$40 to \$50 billion. Merchants complain that interchange fees, which have to be passed on to consumers, are excessive and treated by issuing banks as nonnegotiable. Legislation is under consideration in Congress to address the merchants' concerns. The merchant bank must make its profit on the deal it makes with the merchant to handle the processing. Hard bargaining goes on. The merchant bank will take a smaller discount if dealing with a merchant that is a high volume grocery or pharmacy chain; a larger discount if it is a luxury store or expensive restaurant. Since being able to offer customers the convenience of a range of credit cards is essential to the merchant, the merchant bank is in a strong bargaining position against the merchant. But competition with other merchant banks, eager to take the merchant's processing business, is a moderating force. Thus, the merchant's profit on the sale is subject to two discounts: the interchange fee fixed by the network, going to the issuing bank and virtually nonnegotiable by merchants, and the merchant bank's discount. The two usually average at around 3%.

(2) THE PERILS OF SUCCESS

Credit cards have been so wildly successful in expanding the volume of consumer credit that they are often viewed, particularly in the bankruptcy context, as posing serious social problems for consumers. Visa claims that nearly 60% of consumers ages 18-25 use cards as their primary payment method. Elizabeth Holmes, Charge It!, Wall St. J., Aug. 20, 2007, at R8. Visa reports that there were more than 1.7 billion Visa-branded cards world-wide in 2009. Jay Miller and Kevin Kingsbury, Visa's Net Jumps 73% Even as Spending Falls, Wall St. J., July 30, 2009, at C3. In little more than 50 years, bank cards have completely replaced the traditional, highly inefficient, system in which merchants made their own decisions on the creditworthiness of their customers, relying on the often sketchy information the local credit bureau was able to gather on the prospective customer. For bank credit cards, the creditworthiness of the cardholder is determined by a professional credit grantor, the bank, at the time it issues the credit card, and it can impose spending limits consistent with the cardholder's credit record. The merchant is safe in relying on that decision of the bank and can devote its resources to selling rather than credit evaluation. The system is cheap and efficient.

In the early years bank credit cards were restricted to middle or upper income groups, but over time aggressive competition for market share led card issuers to lower their credit standards, sometimes with disastrous results for both card issuer and cardholder. In 2007, 5.2 billion offers for new cards were sent out and estimates are that in 2006 there were about 1.5 billion charge cards in circulation. James Surowiecki, House of Cards, The New Yorker, March 16, 2009, at Financial Page 5. According to Esperian, there were 5.4 credit cards per consumer in 2009. See Credit Cards.com. In recent years, credit card issuers have broadened their market by focusing on small business: a business simplifies its accounts payable by using a credit or charge card to pay all its suppliers and makes a single payment each month to the card issuer. Even the subprime market has become a target for credit card issuers. Direct mail solicitation with low temporary teaser rates (sometimes zero), followed by much higher regular reset rates, became standard, as did "pre-approved" card offers. By 2007 25.7% of households in the bottom quintile of income had credit cards. See 2007 Survey of Consumer Finances, Federal Reserve Bulletin, Feb. 2009. Only two percent of these households held credit cards in 1970. David S. Evans & Richard Schmalensee, Paying With Plastic 88-89 (2d ed. 2005).

Horror stories abound of bankrupts with 15 or 20 credit cards, all maxed out, seeking discharge of debt totals far exceeding annual income. Card issuers frequently opposed bankruptcy discharges in such cases by alleging fraud under BC 523(a)(2)(A). Cardholders fought back by asserting that card issuers could not have justifiably relied on the cardholder's representation of intent to repay because of inadequate inquiry into the cardholder's financial position.

For a good discussion of the issue, see In re Ellingsworth, 212 B.R. 326 (Bankr.W.D.Mo.1997). The abuse by some cardholders in excessive use of their cards was matched by the unwarranted lowering of credit standards by some card issuers in their relentless pursuit of market share. By 2009, in a period of high unemployment, credit card charge-offs had risen to the extent that card issuers were scrambling to drop cardholders that they believed were most likely to default and to limit the amount other customers could charge. Sorowiecki, supra.

Under the 2005 Bankruptcy Abuse Prevention and Consumer Protection Act (BAPCPA) amendments, credit card issuers substantially improved their position in bankruptcy under BC 523(a)(2)(C), which presumes nondischargeable all consumer debts to a single creditor aggregating more than $500 (formerly $1,225) incurred on or within 90 (formerly 60) days of filing if for "luxury goods or services." The quoted term "does not include goods or services reasonably necessary for the support or maintenance of the debtor or dependent of the debtor or a dependent of the debtor." BC 523(a)(C)(ii)(II). There is no positive definition of "luxury," and the extent to which goods and services not reasonably necessary for support or maintenance should be deemed luxury goods or services is not clear. Cash advances aggregating more than $750 (formerly ($1,225) obtained on or within 70 (formerly 60) days before filing are presumed nondischargeable, but only if made in an open end credit transaction, which is the kind of transaction used for cash advances on credit cards. So long as the loan transaction is an extension of consumer credit, that is, the loan was obtained for a personal, family or household purpose, there are no limits on the use of the loan proceeds. Thus, the original, sensible belief that credit card issuers deserve some protection against the excesses of a "credit card spree" that allowed debtors to acquire expensive luxuries on the eve of bankruptcy, now, as amended, applies to a huge swath of consumer sales transactions made by use of credit cards within three months before filing and cash advances made pursuant to credit cards within 70 days before filing.

In response to the 2007-2009 recession. Congress reacted to creditor abuses of credit cardholders by enacting the Credit Card Accountability, Responsibility and Disclosure (CARD) Act, Public Law 111-24, effective February 2010, which we will discuss in the chapter on the Bank-Customer Relationship.

b. DEBIT CARDS

Debit and credit cards transfer funds in different ways. In a credit card transaction the cardholder orders the issuing bank to pay an amount to a third person, for which the cardholder is billed. In a debit card transaction the cardholder authorizes a withdrawal from her bank account either for her benefit or to pay a third person. Thus, a major distinction between the two transactions is that a debit card does not function unless the cardholder has funds in her bank account. Credit cards function without respect to the existence of a bank account on the part of the cardholder; the cardholder may have multiple credit cards and no bank accounts.

Credit cards are regulated by §§ 1601-1666j of the Consumer Protection Act, 15 U.S.C. §§ 1601-1666j. Several kinds of consumer debit transfers are covered by the Electronic Fund Transfer Act, 15 U.S.C. § 1693 et seq. Regulation E, which implements the EFTA, defines "electronic fund transfer" as including "[t]ransfers resulting from debit card transactions, whether or not initiated through an electronic terminal." 12 CFR § 205.3(b)(5).

Debit cards have two common uses: to deposit or withdraw money from the cardholder's account and to transfer funds to another person as payment. The most popular use of debit cards is with respect to the ubiquitous automated teller machine (ATM) system, as a means of depositing and withdrawing funds. The customer can use the access card and a personal identification number (PIN) to make deposits and withdrawals from her account in a bank or other financial institution. The cost of human teller-handled deposits and withdrawals far exceeds the cost of deposits and withdrawals made by ATM.

One example of the way in which debit cards are used to transfer funds as payment is the point-of-sale (POS) retail transaction. Here, the buyer pays for goods or services by using a plastic coded card, called an access or debit card, inserted into an electronic terminal on the merchant's premises that is linked to the banks of both the merchant and the cardholder, usually through an interbank network. The debit card contains a machine-readable identification of the buyer's bank account. When the card is inserted into the terminal, the amount of the transaction and the buyer's personal identification number (PIN) are also entered. The result is that the buyer's account is immediatly debited and the merchant's account is credited in that amount at the same time.

As the language quoted above from Regulation E indicates, debit cards may also be used in transactions with merchants who do not maintain electronic terminals. The card authorizes the merchant to draw on the buyer's account in the issuing bank for the amount of the sales price. The cardholder signs for the transaction, as in a credit card transaction, rather than using a PIN in an electronic terminal. The transaction does not settle immediately. Rather an authorization query is sent from the merchant to the card issuer through the Visa or MasterCard network for verification to determine whether there is an available balance in the cardholder's account. If so, the issuing bank immediately debits the cardholder's account, instead of billing the cardholder as is done for credit cards. PIN-based clearing systems are cheaper. Estimates are that retailers pay from 11-38 cents for each PIN transaction but from 43-57 cents for each signature transaction. Chicago Fed Letter, Dec. 2005. Thus, the bank takes a larger interchange fee from the merchant's sale price in signature cases. Retailing trends show that major retailers like J.C. Penney and Sears are "steering" cutomers to PIN transactions. Robin Sidel, Cash Back: As Card Fees Fees Climb, Merchants Push PINs, Wall St. J., Jan. 16 2007, at A1.

The market for debit cards is growing faster than that for credit cards. According Geoffrey Gerdes, supra, the annual rate growth of debit cards is 17.5%; of credit cards, 4.6%, but the volume of the credit card market is still much larger than that for debit cards because the size of the transactions financed is greater. Consumers say that use of debit cards gives them a better sense of how they spend their money; in recession times, use of debit cards grows; more consumers want to pay as they go. Robin Sidel, Debit-Card Use Overtakes Credit, Wall St. J., April 30, 2009, at C1.

2. LIABILITY FOR UNAUTHORIZED USE OF CARDS

a. CREDIT CARDS

Hurried retail cashiers have little time to examine credit cards to be sure that the person presenting them is the true cardholder or that the card is genuine rather than counterfeit. Billions of dollars of payments for gasoline are made each year by running credit cards through strip-reading devices on the pumps with no human examination of the credit card or its bearer. A thief or counterfeiter has a good chance of not being caught. Credit card fraud is estimated to cause heavy losses with much of that owing to lost or stolen credit cards. How should the loss be allocated in unauthorized credit card cases: on the careless merchant, on the card owner who is slow in reporting the loss or theft, or on the credit card industry that has monitoring capacities that can stop multiple uses of lost, stolen or counterfeit cards?

In 1970, Congress decisively resolved this issue in the following statute. The provisions on credit cards are found in the Truth-in-Lending Act (TILA), which is Subchapter I of the Consumer Credit Protection Act (CCPA), 15 U.S.C. §§ 1601–1666j, which is a grab-bag of consumer protection provisions. In § 1602(k), "credit card" is defined as "any card, plate, coupon book or other credit device existing for the purpose of obtaining money, property, labor, or services on credit." An "accepted credit card" means one "which the cardholder has requested and received or has signed or has used, or authorized another to use for the purpose of obtaining money, property, labor, or services on credit." § 1602(l). "The term 'cardholder' means any person to whom a credit card is issued or any person who has agreed with the card issuer to pay obligations arising from the issuance of a credit card to another person." § 1602(m). "The term 'unauthorized use,' as used in § 1643, means a use of a credit card by a person other than the cardholder who does not have actual, implied, or apparent authority for such use and from which the cardholder receives no benefit." § 1602(*o*).

Section 1643. Liability of Holder of Credit Card

(a)(1) A cardholder shall be liable for the unauthorized use of a credit card only if

(A) the card is an accepted credit card;

(B) the liability is not in excess of $50;

(C) the card issuer gives adequate notice to the cardholder of the potential liability;

(D) the card issuer has provided the cardholder with a description of a means by which the card issuer may be notified of loss or theft of the card, which description may be provided on the face or reverse side of the statement required by section 1637(b) or on a separate notice accompanying such statement;

(E) the unauthorized use occurs before the card issuer has been notified that an unauthorized use of the credit card has occurred or may occur as the result of loss, theft, or otherwise; and

(F) the card issuer has provided a method whereby the user of such card can be identified as the person authorized to use it.

PROBLEMS

1. Oscar paid for his meal at a restaurant by use of his credit card. The waiter surreptitiously copied the information on Oscar's card by a device that he concealed in his belt and sold this information to an enterprise that fraudulently produced plastic cards that were replicas of Oscar's card. These cards were used to make purchases at retail establishments. When these purchases appeared on Oscar's monthly statement, he protested to the credit card issuer that he had not made the purchases. How does § 1643(a) apply to this Problem? How can fraud loss be reduced in cases such as this?

2. Oscar is absent minded, and his condition worsened in the months before his bar examination. He had obtained a credit card from Bank A but had forgotten to sign the back of the card. He used it only a couple of times by inserting it in the slot on gasoline pumps to buy gas; the mechanism on the pump did not search for the presence of a signature. He left the card unsigned on the top of a table in his bedroom in the house where he roomed. He wasn't aware that it had disappeared even though he was billed monthly for purchases that he had not made. The cause of his inattention was that he was so preoccupied in the weeks immediately before his exam that he had stopped opening his mail. After his exam, he discovered that the card had been stolen and that Bank A was demanding payment of $5,000 for a purchase made on

the card three months after the card disappeared and noted on Bank A's statements that Oscar had received. Not until then did Oscar notify Bank A of the unauthorized use of his card. How would this case be resolved under the statute set out above? See § 1643(d). Would the result be different if the $5,000 charge reflected 10 separate $500 purchases made by the thief?

What policy was Congress implementing in adopting the drastic limitation in § 1643(a) on the liability of cardholders? What incentive does a cardholder have to report the loss or theft of a credit card? Does the fact that the $50 limit on liability has not been changed since 1970 give you some insight on what Congress had in mind? For a discussion of a variety of explanations of the CCPA's allocation of risk between cardholder and card issuer, see Clayton P. Gillette, Rules, Standards, and Precautions in Payment Systems, 82 Va. L. Rev. 181 (1996).

b. DEBIT CARDS

Debit cards are governed by the Electronic Fund Transfer Act (EFTA). 15 U.S.C. § 1693(a)–(r). Definitions appear in § 1693a and consumer liability is covered by § 1693g, which affords debit cardholders much less protection than the TILA gives credit cardholders. If the debit cardholder notifies the card issuer of loss or theft of the card within two days of learning of the loss, liability for unauthorized use is limited to $50, otherwise liability may go as high as $500. However, there is no limit for liability for an unauthorized charge if the cardholder fails to report the unauthorized charge appearing on a periodic statement within 60 days of transmittal of the statement. Section 1693g(d) allows state law to reduce the cardholder's liability even below that set by § 1693a, and the law of several state has done so. See, e.g., Cal. Civ. Code § 1748.31(b); Mass. Gen. L. ch. 167B § 18. Why is the EFTA's limitation of the debit card liability different from, and less generous than, the TILA's limitation of the credit cardholder's liability?

Questions have arisen about which statute applies in cases in which the same card may be used as both a debit and credit card. Regulation E addresses the issue in 12 CFR § 205.12, which provides that if an electronic fund transfer is involved the EFTA provisions apply; TILA applies if the card is used as a credit card without an electronic fund transfer. 2 Barkley Clark & Barbara Clark, The Law of Bank Deposits, Collections and Credit Cards, ¶¶ 15.03[2][c], 16.06[2] (Rev. ed. 2009). The problem has been alleviated by the pledge on the part of both Visa and MasterCard in 1997 that they would voluntarily apply a "zero liability" policy to the unauthorized use of both kinds of cards. But this policy has only limited application to debit cards used for small business or commercial purposes.

PROBLEM

How would the case posed in Problem 2 above be resolved if Oscar's debit card had been stolen? Concerned that owing to his stressful preparation for the bar exam he would forget his PIN, Oscar had copied it on a post-it stuck to the card where it remained at the time of the theft.

A cardholder whose debit card is lost, stolen or counterfeited is in a somewhat less advantageous position than a credit cardholder in comparable circumstances because the money has already been removed from the cardholder's account, with bounced checks or overdraft fees as a possible consequence, and what can be a prolonged period before the card issuing bank restores the money taken. Despite bank promises of "zero liability" for customers victimized by ATM fraud, banks may take a tough stance on refunds in cases in which there is no hard evidence of fraud. During the delay, cardholders may be deprived of necessary funds. On the other hand, in the case of a lost, stolen or counterfeited credit card, the cardholder can merely refuse to pay for fraudulent transactions charged on her account until the issue is resolved.

3. When Is Use Authorized?

As we have seen, TILA's imposition of a $50 limit on liability shifts most of the risk of losses owing to unauthorized uses of credit cards from cardholders to card issuers. A use is unauthorized for the purpose of § 1643 if the card user lacks actual, implied or apparent authority to make a purchase with the card. § 1602(*o*). The card issuer bears the burden of proof as to unauthorized use. § 1643(b). The TILA allows state law to be more protective of cardholders, reducing their liability in such cases below $50. § 1643(c). Because the cardholder remains fully liable for charges from authorized use, litigation focuses on whether card use is authorized.

Most unauthorized use cases raise issues of apparent authority rather than of actual or implied authority. The card issuer contends that the card user had apparent authority to make purchases on the cardholder's account owing to the user's status as a member of the cardholder's family or, as in the following case, as an employee of the cardholder. In the case below, the court allows for "apparent authority created through the cardholder's negligence." Does the court allow for liability based on authorized use under the TILA or instead on the cardholder's grossly negligent behavior? In other words, does the court carefully distinguish between negligence by a cardholder which creates apparent authority for someone else's use of the credit card and negligent acts that enable someone else to use the credit card whether or not apparent authority existed?

Minskoff v. American Express Travel Related Services Co., Inc.

United States Court of Appeals, Second Circuit, 1996.
98 F.3d 703.

■ MAHONEY, CIRCUIT JUDGE.

Plaintiffs-appellants Edward J. Minskoff and Edward J. Minskoff Equities, Inc. ("Equities") appeal from a final judgment entered September 15, 1995 in the United States District Court for the Southern District of New York, Robert P. Patterson, Jr., Judge, that granted the motion of defendant-appellee American Express Travel Related Services Company, Inc. ("American Express") for summary judgment dismissing plaintiffs-appellants' complaint. The complaint asserted claims under 15 U.S.C. § 1643, a provision of the Truth in Lending Act, 15 U.S.C. § 1601 et seq. (the "TILA"), and New York General Business Law § 512 for recovery of $276,334.06 paid to American Express through checks forged by an Equities employee to cover charges incurred by that employee on American Express credit cards that were fraudulently obtained and used by the employee. * * * The complaint also sought a declaratory judgment that plaintiffs-appellants were not liable for the balance of the unpaid charges outstanding on those credit cards, but the district court granted American Express summary judgment in the amount of $51,657.71 on its counterclaim for that balance.

We vacate the judgment of the district court and remand for further proceedings.

BACKGROUND

Minskoff is the president and chief executive officer of Equities, a real estate holding and management firm. In 1988, Equities opened an American Express corporate card account (the "Corporate Account") for which one charge card was issued in Minskoff's name. Minskoff also maintained a personal American Express account, which was established in 1963.

In October 1991, Equities hired Susan Schrader Blumenfeld to serve as its assistant to the president/office manager. Blumenfeld was responsible for both the personal and business affairs of Minskoff, and her duties included screening Minskoff's mail, reviewing vendor invoices and credit card statements (including statements for the Corporate Account), and forwarding such invoices and statements to Equities' bookkeepers for payment. Prior to Blumenfeld's employment with Equities, Minskoff personally reviewed all Corporate Account statements; after hiring Blumenfeld, he no longer reviewed any of these statements.

In March 1992, defendant-appellee American Express received an application for an additional credit card to issue from the Corporate Account in Blumenfeld's name. The application had been pre-addressed by American Express and mailed to Minskoff at his business address. It had been completed and submitted by Blumenfeld without the knowledge or acquiescence of

Equities or Minskoff. American Express issued the supplemental card and mailed it to Equities' business address. From April 1992 to March 1993, Blumenfeld charged a total of $28,213.88 on that card.

During this period, American Express sent twelve monthly billing statements for the Corporate Account to Equities' business address. Each statement listed both Blumenfeld and Minskoff as cardholders on the Corporate Account, and separately itemized Corporate Account charges for Minskoff and Blumenfeld. These twelve statements show a total of $28,213.88 in charges attributed to Blumenfeld and $23,099.37 in charges attributed to Minskoff, for a total of $51,313.25. Between April 1992 and March 1993, American Express received twelve checks, drawn on accounts maintained by Minskoff or Equities at Manufacturers Hanover Trust ("MHT"), in payment of these charges, with each check made payable to American Express and bearing Equities' Corporate Account number. Minskoff did not review any statements or cancelled checks received during 1992 and 1993 from either his personal account with MHT or the Equities account with MHT.

In July 1992, American Express sent Minskoff an unsolicited invitation to apply for a platinum card. Blumenfeld accepted the invitation on behalf of Minskoff, again without the knowledge or acquiescence of either Minskoff or Equities.[3] Blumenfeld also submitted a request for a supplemental card to issue from this new account (the "Platinum Account") in her name. When platinum cards arrived in both Minskoff's and Blumenfeld's names, Blumenfeld gave Minskoff his card, claiming that it was an unsolicited upgrade of his American Express card privileges. Minskoff proceeded to use his platinum card for occasional purchases, and Blumenfeld charged approximately $300,000 to the Platinum Account between July 1992 and November 1993.

Between August 1992 and November 1993, American Express mailed sixteen Platinum Account monthly billing statements to Equities' business address. Each statement named Blumenfeld and Minskoff as cardholders and itemized charges for each separately. These statements attributed a total of $250,394.44 in charges to Blumenfeld and $10,497.31 to Minskoff, for a total of $260,891.75. These bills were paid in full with checks drawn on the MHT accounts, made payable to American Express, and bearing the Platinum Account number.

In November 1993, Equities' controller, Steven Marks, informed Minskoff that MHT had called to inquire about a check made payable to American Express for approximately $41,000 that had been written on Equities' MHT

[3] It is not clear from the record whether the invitation to receive a platinum American Express card was directed to Minskoff in his individual capacity or in his official position as president of Equities. The solicitation was preprinted with Minskoff's home address, and the record does not reveal how it ended up in Blumenfeld's hands at the Equities office.

account. Minskoff stopped payment on the check, initiated an internal investigation of Equities' accounts that revealed the full extent of Blumenfeld's fraudulent activities, and gave notice to American Express of Blumenfeld's unauthorized charges to the Platinum and Corporate Accounts. Blumenfeld subsequently stated in an affidavit that she had forged approximately sixty checks drawn on Equities' MHT account and Minskoff's personal MHT account, including at least twenty payments to American Express for charges to the Platinum and Corporate Accounts. Although some of these checks were used to pay legitimate obligations of plaintiffs-appellants, an accounting analysis attributed losses totalling $412,684.06 to Blumenfeld's theft. In January 1994, Blumenfeld agreed to repay $250,000 to Minskoff and Equities in return for their promise not to institute legal action against her.

Plaintiffs-appellants initiated this action in the United States District Court for the Southern District of New York on February 15, 1994. As previously noted, they sought (1) to recover $276,334.06 that had been paid to American Express in satisfaction of unauthorized charges by Blumenfeld, and (2) a declaration that they were not liable for the outstanding balances on the Platinum Account. The district court, however, dismissed their complaint and awarded American Express $51,657.71 on its counterclaim for that balance. The district court reasoned that the $50 limit on a cardholder's liability for the unauthorized use of the cardholder's credit card specified in 15 U.S.C. § 1643(a)(1)(B), see supra note 1, did not apply to plaintiffs-appellants because their negligence in failing to examine credit card statements that would have revealed Blumenfeld's fraudulent charges "resulted in an appearance of authority [to use the cards] in Blumenfeld."

This appeal followed.

DISCUSSION

....

Plaintiffs-appellants contend that because Blumenfeld obtained the platinum and corporate credit cards through forgery and fraud, her use of the cards is *per se* unauthorized under section 1643, see supra note 1, and plaintiffs-appellants' liability is therefore limited to $50 by section 1643(a)(1)(B). Section 1643 applies, however, only in the case of an "unauthorized use" of a credit card. See § 1643(a)(1), (d). The term "unauthorized use" is defined as "a use of a credit card by a person other than the cardholder who does not have actual, implied, or apparent authority for such use and from which the cardholder receives no benefit." 15 U.S.C. § 1602(o). In determining whether a use is unauthorized, "Congress apparently contemplated, and courts have accepted, primary reliance on background principles of agency law in determining the liability of cardholders for charges incurred by third-party card bearers." Towers World Airways v. PHH Aviation Systems, 933 F.2d 174, 176–77 (2d Cir.), cert. denied, 502 U.S. 823, 112 S.Ct. 87, 116 L.Ed.2d 59 (1991).

Under general principles of agency, the authority of an agent "is the power of the agent to do an act or to conduct a transaction on account of the principal which, with respect to the principal, he is privileged to do because of the principal's manifestations to him." Restatement (Second) of Agency (the "Restatement") § 7 cmt. a (1958). Such authority may be express or implied, but in either case it exists only where the agent may reasonably infer from the words or conduct of the principal that the principal has consented to the agent's performance of a particular act. See id. cmt. b.

Apparent authority is "entirely distinct from authority, either express or implied," id. § 8 cmt. a, and arises from the "written or spoken words or any other conduct of the principal which, reasonably interpreted, causes [a] third person to believe that the principal consents to have [an] act done on his behalf by the person purporting to act for him," id. § 27; see also Fennell v. TLB Kent Co., 865 F.2d 498, 502 (2d Cir.1989). Apparent authority, then, is normally created through the words and conduct of the principal as they are interpreted by a third party, and cannot be established by the actions or representations of the agent. See *Fennell*, 865 F.2d at 502 (collecting cases).

The existence of apparent authority is normally a question of fact, and therefore inappropriate for resolution on a motion for summary judgment.... However, a principal may be estopped from denying apparent authority if (1) the principal's intentional or negligent acts, including acts of omission, created an appearance of authority in the agent, (2) on which a third party reasonably and in good faith relied, and (3) such reliance resulted in a detrimental change in position on the part of the third party. See Restatement § 8–....

Viewing the facts in the light most favorable to plaintiffs-appellants, it is clear that Blumenfeld acted without actual or implied authority when she forged the platinum card acceptance form and supplemental card applications. Accordingly, plaintiff-appellants cannot be held accountable for Blumenfeld's initial possession of corporate and platinum cards. As we stated in *Towers*:

> Though a cardholder's [voluntary] relinquishment of possession may create in another the appearance of authority to use the card, [15 U.S.C. §§ 1602(o) and 1643] clearly preclude[ ] a finding of apparent authority where the transfer of the card was without the cardholder's consent, as in cases involving theft, loss, or fraud. However elastic the principle of apparent authority may be in theory, the language of the 1970 Amendments [to the TILA] demonstrates Congress's intent that the category of cases involving charges incurred as a result of *involuntary* card transfers are to be regarded as unauthorized under sections 1602(o) and 1643.

Towers, 933 F.2d at 177.

This result is consistent with the underlying policy of the TILA to protect credit card holders against losses due to theft or fraudulent use of credit cards on the theory that the card issuer is in the better position to prevent such losses.... We accordingly disagree with the decision of the district court insofar as it imposed upon plaintiffs-appellants the entire burden of the unauthorized charges made by Blumenfeld to the Corporate and Platinum Accounts.

However, while we accept the proposition that the *acquisition* of a credit card through fraud or theft cannot be said to occur under the apparent authority of the cardholder, our statement in *Towers* should not be interpreted to preclude a finding of apparent authority for the subsequent *use* of a credit card so obtained. Under the rule urged by plaintiffs-appellants, a cardholder could disregard both credit card and bank statements indefinitely, or even fail to act upon a discovery that an employee had fraudulently obtained and was fraudulently using a credit card, and still limit his liability for an employee's fraudulent purchases to $50. Cf. Transamerica Ins. Co. v. Standard Oil Co., 325 N.W.2d 210, 215 (N.D.1982) ("[A]n unscrupulous cardholder could allow another to charge hundreds of dollars in goods and services and then attempt to limit his liability to 50 dollars."). Nothing in the TILA suggests that Congress intended to sanction intentional or negligent conduct by the cardholder that furthers the fraud or theft of an unauthorized card user. We therefore agree with the district court to the extent that it decided that the negligent acts or omissions of a cardholder may create apparent authority to use the card in a person who obtained the card through theft or fraud. Apparent authority created through the cardholder's negligence does not, however, retroactively authorize charges incurred prior to the negligent acts that created the apparent authority of the user.

Applying these principles to the case at hand, we address the district court's conclusion that plaintiffs-appellants' failure to examine credit card and bank statements amounts to negligence which created an appearance of authority in Blumenfeld to use the card. Under New York law, consumers are obligated to "exercise reasonable care and promptness to examine [bank] statement[s] ... to discover [any] unauthorized signature or any alteration." § 4–406(1) * * *. This provision is derived from a common law obligation to examine bank statements and report forgeries or alterations, and it is based upon a determination that "the depositor [is] in the better position to discover an alteration of the check or forgery of his or her own signature." Woods v. MONY Legacy Life Ins. Co., 84 N.Y.2d 280, 284, 617 N.Y.S.2d 452, 453, 641 N.E.2d 1070, 1071 (1994) (extending application of § 4–406 to brokerage accounts).

This policy is no less applicable to credit card holders than it is to bank depositors. Once a cardholder has established a credit card account, and provided that the card issuer is in compliance with the billing statement disclosure requirements of 15 U.S.C. § 1637,[4] the cardholder is in a superior

[4] Section 1637(b) requires "[t]he creditor of any account under an open end consumer credit plan [to] transmit to the obligor, for each billing cycle at the end of which there is an outstanding

position to determine whether the charges reflected on his regular billing statements are legitimate. A cardholder's failure to examine credit card statements that would reveal fraudulent use of the card constitutes a negligent omission that creates apparent authority for charges that would otherwise be considered unauthorized under the TILA....

It is undisputed that between April 1992 and November 1993, American Express mailed to Equities' business address at least twenty-eight monthly billing statements documenting charges made to the Platinum and Corporate Accounts. Each of those statements clearly lists Blumenfeld as a cardholder, and each specifically itemizes those charges attributable to her credit card. During that same period, MHT mailed to Equities' business address numerous bank statements showing that checks made payable to American Express had been drawn on Equities' business account and Minskoff's personal account to pay these American Express charges. Minskoff concedes that he failed to examine any of these statements until November 1993, and no other employee or agent of Equities (other than Blumenfeld) became aware of the disputed monthly payments to American Express prior to the inquiry by Bankers Trust in November 1993. These omissions on the part of plaintiffs-appellants created apparent authority for Blumenfeld's continuing use of the cards, especially because it enabled Blumenfeld to pay all of the American Express statements with forged checks, thereby fortifying American Express' continuing impression that nothing was amiss with the Corporate and Platinum Accounts.

Plaintiffs-appellants argue that summary judgment is inappropriate because they exercised reasonable care in the hiring and supervision of Blumenfeld and in the implementation and administration of internal accounting procedures designed to detect and prevent fraud. In this case, however, while American Express concedes that Equities employed bookkeepers who were responsible, *inter alia*, for reviewing credit card statements and arranging for their payment, as well as reviewing bank statements and cancelled checks, the inadequate manner in which these procedures were performed from April 1992 to November 1993 enabled Blumenfeld to acquire unauthorized American Express credit cards, run up more than $300,000 in invalid American Express charges, and pay for them with approximately twenty forged checks drawn on Equities' MHT account and Minskoff's personal MHT account, without detection.

A cursory review of any of the American Express statements would have disclosed charges by Blumenfeld made with an unauthorized credit card. A

---

balance in that account or with respect to which a finance charge is imposed, a statement setting forth," *inter alia*, the outstanding balance in the account at the beginning and end of the statement period, the amount and date of each extension of credit during the period, the amount of any finance charge added to the account, and the date by which payment must be made to avoid finance charges.

review of any MHT statement would have disclosed one or more payments to American Express (or, if the cancelled checks had previously been removed by Blumenfeld, charges that could not be matched to cancelled checks) generally in amounts far exceeding Minskoff's habitual American Express charges. We are not dealing in this case with an occasional transgression buried in a welter of financial detail. In our view, once a cardholder receives a statement that reasonably puts him on notice that one or more fraudulent charges have been made, he cannot thereafter claim lack of knowledge. The district court was justified in determining that no reasonable jury could conclude that this standard had been satisfied as to plaintiffs-appellants on the record presented in this case, warranting summary judgment in favor of American Express to the extent that we have previously indicated.

In our view, the appropriate resolution in this case is provided by adapting the ruling in *Transamerica* to provide that

> [American Express] is liable for [Blumenfeld's] fraudulent purchases [as to each credit card] from the time the credit card was issued until [plaintiffs-appellants] received the first statement from [American Express] containing [Blumenfeld's] fraudulent charges plus a reasonable time to examine that statement. After that time, [plaintiffs-appellants are] liable for the remaining fraudulent charges.

325 N.W.2d at 216. We accordingly vacate the judgment of the district court and remand for further proceedings to make this determination. We leave it to the district court in the first instance to ascertain whether, as the record is developed on remand, any issues require submission to a jury.

NOTES

1. Most of the TILA's provisions govern only the consumer credit transactions, not business transactions. § 1603(1). An exception is the TILA's limitation on liability for unauthorized use, which applies to credit cards used for business purposes as well. § 1645. For business cardholders, the $50 limit on liability of § 1643(a) is a default rule. A business cardholder can assume greater liability for unauthorized card use by its employees if it does not impose liability on them for such use. See, e.g., American Express Travel Related Services Co. v. Web, Inc., 405 S.E.2d 652 (Ga. 1991).

2. In defining "unauthorized use" to mean the lack of actual, implied or apparent authority, the TILA (and implementing federal regulations; see 12 C.F.R. § 226.12(b)(1) (1997)) employs concepts borrowed from the law of agency. See Mary Elizabeth Matthews, Credit Cards—Authorized and Unauthorized Use, 13 Ann. Rev. Banking L. 233 (1994). Agency law can work to restrict the efficient allocation of loss from unauthorized card use, as determined by a court. In such cases, courts sometimes stretch agency principles or infer facts that make agency law consistent with efficient loss allocation. Apparent authority, for example, requires that the principal's acts create in third parties a reasonable belief that a designated person is acting on its behalf. See Restatement (Second) of Agency § 8 (1958). A finding of authorized credit card use by an agent, therefore, requires conduct by the cardholder that creates such beliefs in merchants. The question of whether the card issuer or the cardholder is in a superior position to control the designated person's conduct is not directly at issue. The *Minskoff* court took the cardholder's failure to examine its credit card statements as omissions which induced a belief that the charges were authorized. Stieger v. Chevy Chase Savings Bank, F.S.B., 666 A.2d 479 (D.C.1995), goes further, concluding that an employee had apparent authority to make charges when she signed her name only after the employer had authorized her to make other charges. The employers in both cases were in a superior position to control the use of their credit cards by employees. The TILA's incorporation of agency notions seems to demand more: conduct by the cardholder that leads a merchant to believe that the employee is authorized to act on the employer's behalf. D.B.I. Architects, P.C. v. Amex, 388 F.3d 886 (D.C. Cir.2004), follows *Minskoff* in holding a corporate credit cardholder liable for employee fraud under apparent authority.

PROBLEM

When Wife married Husband, she opened a credit card account with Bank and requested that Bank issue a credit card to her and a duplicate card to Husband in his name. When the marriage broke up, Wife notified Bank that she would no longer pay for Husband's charges on the credit card. The credit card agreement that Wife signed provided that an account could be closed by returning all cards. Bank immediately revoked both cards and gave numerous notifications to both parties of revocation and requests that the cards be returned. Both Wife and Husband continued to make charges on the cards. Wife contended that with respect to Husband's charges made after her notification to Bank, her liability should be limited to $50; the card should be treated as a lost or stolen card since she had no power to make her ungrateful spouse return it. Bank sued her for the balance of her account. What result? Which party was in the better position to prevent Husband's improper use of the card, Wife or Bank? These facts are based on Walker Bank & Trust Co. v. Jones, 672 P.2d 73 (Utah 1983).

4. ASSERTION OF CARDHOLDER DEFENSES

In the chapter on Negotiability and Holders in Due Course, with respect to a promissory note issued by a consumer to obtain goods or services, we saw that various doctrines of case law or provisions of statutory or administrative law have been used to allow the consumer to assert against a financial institution that holds the note claims and defenses that the consumer has against the seller of the goods or services. If a consumer uses a bank credit card to buy goods and the goods are either never delivered or are defective, should the cardholder be allowed to refuse to pay the issuer of the credit card to the extent that the cardholder would have been excused from paying the seller of the goods if the sale had been a credit sale by the seller? This question was hotly debated at the state level in the late 1960s. Financial institutions that were issuers of credit cards argued that they had only the most tenuous relationship with retailers honoring their cards, and should not be subjected to claims and defenses arising out of sales made pursuant to their cards. The card issuer, it was contended, should be no more involved in the sale transaction financed by a credit card than should a drawee bank in a sale paid for by a check drawn on the bank. Moreover, would not subjecting card issuers to sales defenses ultimately restrict the acceptability of credit cards by retailers? The concern of the retailer was that the card issuer would insist on a right to charge back against the retailer debts as to which the cardholder raised claims or defenses. Would a retailer in Maine feel secure in honoring a credit card presented by a cardholder who lives in California knowing that if the cardholder claims the goods are defective the retailer may end up with an unsecured claim against the debtor three thousand miles away?

In 1974, Congress enacted the Fair Credit Billing Act, stating rights and obligations of the cardholder and the issuer of the credit card with respect to the correction of a billing error that the cardholder believes has been made in the billing statement received from the issuer. These provisions now appear in the Consumer Credit Protection Act, "Correction of Billing Errors" in 15 U.S.C. § 1666. "Billing error" is defined in § 1666(b) and includes reflection on the statement of an extension of credit not made by the cardholder and reflection on the statement of goods or services not accepted by the cardholder or not delivered to the cardholder in accordance with the agreement made at the time of the sales transaction. The 1974 legislation covered a number of other aspects of the issuer-cardholder relationship in §§ 1666a–1666i. Section 1666i addressed the issue of the extent to which the cardholder can assert, as a defense to the obligation to pay the issuer, claims and defenses of the cardholder arising from the transaction in which the credit card was used. It is set out below:

Section 1666i. Assertion by Cardholder Against Card Issuer of Claims and Defenses Arising Out of Credit Card Transactions

(a) Subject to the limitation contained in subsection (b), a card issuer who has issued a credit card to a cardholder pursuant to an open end consumer credit plan shall be subject to all claims (other than tort claims)

> and defenses arising out of any transaction in which the credit card is used as a method of payment or extension of credit if (1) the obligor has made a good faith attempt to obtain satisfactory resolution of a disagreement or problem relative to the transaction from the person honoring the credit card; (2) the amount of the initial transaction exceeds $50; and (3) the place where the initial transaction occurred was in the same State as the mailing address previously provided by the cardholder or was within 100 miles from such address, except that the limitations set forth in clauses (2) and(3) with respect to an obligor's right to assert claims and defenses against a card issuer shall not be applicable to any transaction in which the person honoring the credit card (A) is the same person as the card issuer, (B) is controlled by the card issuer, (C) is under direct or indirect common control with the card issuer, (D) is a franchised dealer in the card issuer's products or services, or (E) has obtained the order for such transaction through a mail solicitation made by or participated in by the card issuer in which the cardholder is solicited to enter into such transaction by using the credit card issued by the card issuer....

PROBLEM

California tourist, Marcy Birkenstock, goes to Maine, loves the maple syrup, buys $1,500 of the precious stuff, pays with her Visa card, issued by a bank in South Dakota, has the syrup shipped to her LA home, but hates the stuff delivered to her. She is sure that she has been defrauded. First, she calls Seller who maintains that the syrup shipped was exactly what she sampled at his store in Maine and assures her that he won't take the syrup back if she returns it. In a surly mood, Marcy calls your law office to find out what she can do. If the Seller won't take the syrup back, she doesn't want to have to pay the bank issuing the Visa card when she is billed. (1) What do you tell her? (2) What is the purpose of the same-state or 100–mile limitation in the statute? (3) Where did the sale take place in this case? (4) What if Marcy had ordered the syrup by telephone after she had returned home? Or bought it on the Internet?

Section 1666i regulates only the rights between the cardholder and card issuer. The credit card systems, e.g., Visa USA and MasterCard International, have agreements governing the relationships between merchants, merchant banks, and issuing banks. These agreements allow limited recourse by an issuing bank against a merchant in defective merchandise cases. The issuing bank sends a chargeback to the merchant bank, requiring it to refund the payment made to it by the issuing bank. The merchant bank then charges back against the merchant's account. If there are too many complaints against a merchant, the merchant may be required to adopt fair policies for adjustment and return of defective merchandise in order to be allowed to continue to accept credit cards. See 2 Barkley Clark & Barbara Clark, The Law of Bank Deposits, Collections and Credit Cards ¶ 15.07[2] (Rev. ed. 2009).

Citibank (South Dakota) v. Mincks

Missouri Court of Appeals, 2004.
135 S.W.3d 545.

■ JEFFREY W. BATES, JUDGE.

Citibank (South Dakota), N.A. ("Citibank") sued defendant Mary Mincks ("Mary") for breach of contract after Mary refused to make any further payments on her Citibank credit card account.[1] Mary defended on the ground that: (1) the only unpaid charges on the account related to merchandise which was never delivered by the merchant; and (2) since her Citibank credit card was used to order the merchandise, she was entitled to assert the defense of non-delivery against Citibank in its action to recover the balance due on her credit card account. After a bench trial, judgment was entered in Mary's favor. On appeal, Citibank argues that the trial court's judgment should be reversed because it was not supported by substantial evidence, and it was based on an erroneous application of the provisions of the Truth-in-Lending-Act, 15 U.S.C. 1601, *et seq.* We affirm....

II. Factual and Procedural History

The facts in this case are relatively simple and virtually undisputed. The summary set forth below is a synthesis prepared from the pleadings, trial testimony and exhibits.

On September 18, 1999, Mary applied to have a credit card issued to her by Citibank. She filled out a document called a "Citibank Platinum Select Acceptance Form," which appears to be a typical application for personal credit. Nothing on the application indicates that credit was being sought by either a business or by an individual who intended to use the credit card for business purposes. The application listed Mary as the cardholder and showed her home address as the billing location. The form asked for the normal personal information (e.g., mother's maiden name, social security number, income) found in such personal applications. Mary applied for credit for herself, and she requested that her husband, Chuck, also be authorized to use

---

[1] We will refer to Mary Mincks and her husband, Chuck Mincks, collectively as "the Mincks." We will refer to them individually by their first names. We do so for purposes of clarity and intend no disrespect.

her credit card account. The application contained the familiar exhortation, typically found in consumer credit applications, offering an introductory period of very low interest. Such offers tend to encourage consumers to transfer balances from other credit cards to the new account in order to obtain the benefit of a lower rate of interest.

Mary's application was accepted, and Citibank issued a credit card to her with an $8,000 line of credit. On October 26, 1999, Mary transferred the existing balances from two other credit cards, totaling $7,213.50, to her Citibank account.[4] There is no indication in the record that these balance transfers were comprised of purchases for anything other than personal, family or household purposes.

Between November 1999 and January 2000, Mary purchased a few additional items with her credit card and made several payments on her account. Once again, nothing in the record demonstrates that these purchases were made for anything other than personal, family or household purposes. On January 27, 2000, Mary made a large payment on her account that reduced the outstanding balance to approximately $20.00.

In February 2000, Chuck received a solicitation to order merchandise from Purchase Plus Buyers Group ("PPBG"). PPBG sold products like mailing cards, telephone cards and other similar items which could be used to promote a home business. After reviewing the solicitation, Chuck decided to order some high-definition, high-color postcards that he could use to contact potential customers for a home business that he had started about three months earlier. On February 24, 2000, Chuck placed an order with PPBG for 4,000 postcards. The order form was sent by fax from Lamar, Missouri, to PPBG's office in Westerville, Ohio. Chuck used Mary's Citibank credit card to pay the $7,600 purchase price for the postcards. The charge for this purchase first appeared on Mary's Citibank statement in March 2000.

Four weeks after placing the order, Chuck contacted PPBG by telephone to find out why he had not yet received the postcards. He was told that the merchandise was on backorder and would not be available for another month. Having no reason to doubt that explanation at the time, he waited another month. When he still had not received the postcards, he contacted PPBG again by telephone. The persons with whom he spoke were very positive and continued to assure him that he would receive the postcards in time. Thereafter, he called PPBG "innumerable times" by telephone, and PPBG personnel kept reiterating that he would ultimately receive the postcards he ordered. In mid-May 2000, Chuck first learned from PPBG that the type of

[4] Mary transferred the $2,432.62 balance from her AT and T card and the $4,780.88 balance from her Discover card. On Mary's October 1999 Citibank statement, the line item entry for the two transactions noted that each was a balance transfer and stated "purchase charged to lower rate."

postcards he ordered had been discontinued in December 1999, even though the product continued to be offered for sale until April 2000. On May 18, 2000, he faxed a letter to PPBG requesting that he be given some other type of product that he could use since the postcards he wanted were no longer available. He received no response. He faxed the same letter to PPBG's executive committee on July 13, 2000, and again received no response.

Around August 1, 2000, Chuck decided he was never going to receive the postcards he ordered from PPBG. On August 4, 2000, he faxed a written demand for a full refund to PPBG because the company had failed to deliver either the postcards or a satisfactory alternative product. He sent this fax because he still believed he could get a refund for the undelivered merchandise. This belief changed on September 1, 2000, when he received a fax from PPBG stating the company had ceased operations and permanently closed its doors that day. Chuck knew then he would not be able to get a refund from PPBG.

On September 28, 2000, the Mincks sent a letter to Citibank. In sum, the letter provided Citibank with the following information: (1) Chuck's $7,600 postcard order from PPBG had never been delivered; (2) the charge for this order first appeared on Mary's March 2000 statement; (3) the facts showing that Chuck had made a good faith effort to resolve the issue with PPBG were recounted with considerable specificity and detail; (4) PPBG committed a breach of contract and fraud by failing to deliver the ordered merchandise and by continuing to sell a discontinued product; and (5) the Mincks were invoking their rights under Regulation Z of the federal Truth-in-Lending-Act to have their account credited in the amount of $7,600 and to have this sum charged back to PPBG.

On October 9, 2000, Citibank responded in a letter sent to Mary. Citibank took the position that it was not able to assist the Mincks because it had not received their letter "within 60 days of the disputed charge." Citibank advised the Mincks to pursue the matter with the merchant or through some alternative means available to them.

After receiving the October 9, 2000, letter from Citibank, the Mincks continued to use Mary's credit card. They made a few additional purchases with the card, and they continued to make payments on the account. That changed in February 2002, when the Mincks stopped making any payments on the Citibank account. The outstanding account balance at this time was comprised solely of the remaining amount due for the undelivered postcards ordered from PPBG, plus accrued interest and late charges.[6] Citibank

---

[6] At trial, Mary's monthly Citibank statements from October 1999 through October 2002 were admitted in evidence. The statements show that from September 2000 through August 2001, the Mincks used Mary's Citibank card to make $337 in new purchases. The Mincks continued to make payments on Mary's account from September 2000 through January 2002. The total

continued to add interest charges, over credit limit fees, and late fees to Mary's credit card account until July 2002. As of that date, the outstanding account balance was $9,048.49.

On October 7, 2002, Citibank sued Mary for breach of contract and sought to recover the $9,048.49 then due, accrued interest at the rate of 24.99% per annum and a 15% attorney fee. Insofar as pertinent to the issues here, the petition alleged that: (1) Citibank had issued a credit card to Mary; (2) by acceptance and use of the credit card, Mary had agreed to make the monthly payments described in the Citibank Card Agreement attached to the petition; (3) Citibank had advanced credit to Mary, through the use of the credit card, to certain persons or firms shown on her account statements; (4) Citibank had made demand on Mary to pay the amount due on her account, but she refused to do so for more than 25 days; and (5) Citibank had "paid valuable consideration to each of said issuers of the credit to Defendant [Mary], and that as consideration therefore [sic] each of said issuers of credit has assigned to Plaintiff [Citibank] the rights to receive payment evidenced in each of the transactions making up the balance due...." Thus, it is apparent from Citibank's petition that it was suing as the assignee of the individual merchants from whom Mary or Chuck had made purchases using Mary's Citibank credit card. It is also undisputed that the entire account balance which Citibank sought to recover from Mary resulted from the direct and collateral charges associated with the single $7,600 transaction in which PPBG was the merchant. In Mary's answer, she specifically asserted non-delivery of the merchandise ordered from PPBG as a defense against Citibank's claim.[7]

At trial, the sole dispute was whether Mary was entitled to assert PPBG's non-delivery as a defense against Citibank, which sought to recover the purchase price of the postcards as PPBG's assignee. Citibank argued that the non-delivery defense should not be permitted on two grounds. First, the PPBG postcard order, which was the only transaction at issue, was not within the scope of Regulation Z since this specific purchase was for a business or commercial purpose. Second, even if Regulation Z did apply, non-delivery of merchandise constitutes a "billing error" within the meaning of the regulation. According to Citibank, Mary lost the ability to assert non-delivery as a defense in this lawsuit because she did not give Citibank notice of this "billing error" within 60 days after the charge first appeared on her credit card statement. In

---

amount of these payments was $2,194. The outstanding account balance shown in the January 2002 statement was $7,734.47.

[7] Paragraph 3 of Mary's answer stated, in pertinent part, as follows: "[T]he goods and services purchased by Defendant were never delivered to Defendant and Defendant received nothing in consideration of the charges. Defendant notified Plaintiff of the non-delivery of the items purchased as soon as it was apparent to Defendant she had been defrauded. Under Federal Law, Defendant has no liability to Plaintiff. Federal Reserve Board Regulation Z; 12 Code of Federal Regulations 226.12(c)."

response, Mary argued that Regulation Z imposed no time limit that precluded her from asserting non-delivery as a defense in Citibank's lawsuit against her, and she denied that this was a "billing error" within the meaning of the regulation. At the conclusion of the case, the trial court made the following ruling from the bench:

> I think that Reg Z does apply, and I don't think this is a billing error. And I think that the provision of Reg Z that allows the cardholder to assert any differences-any defenses that they could assert against the provider of the product is against the-the credit card company. Court's going to find the issues in favor of the Defendant and enter a judgment for the Defendant against the Plaintiff.

Judgment was entered in accordance with the trial court's pronouncement, and Citibank appealed.

III. Discussion and Decision

Citibank's appeal presents two points for us to decide. Each point relied on is a rescript of the arguments Citibank made below.

Point I

In Citibank's first point, it contends the trial court erred in permitting Mary to assert PPBG's non-delivery as a defense in Citibank's breach of contract action. Specifically, Citibank argues that the trial court's judgment is not supported by substantial evidence and is based on a misapplication of the law because "Regulation Z" should not have been applied in this lawsuit, in that the PPBG transaction was primarily for a business or commercial purpose. Citibank's argument is grounded upon on two implicit premises: (1) the Truth-in-Lending-Act and its implementing regulations do not apply to this lawsuit if the single PPBG transaction at issue was for a business purpose; and (2) Mary's ability to assert non-delivery as a defense against Citibank in this contract action is derived solely from the Truth-in-Lending-Act and Regulation Z. Citibank's first point fails because neither implicit premise is correct.

The Truth-in-Lending-Act and Regulation Z
Do Apply to Mary's Open End Consumer Credit Plan

....

The Truth-in-Lending-Act governs a number of different types of consumer credit, including one type described as an "open end consumer credit plan." *See* 15 U.S.C. § 1637. This phrase is derived from a combination of two other statutory definitions found in 15 U.S.C. § 1602:

> (h) The adjective "consumer", used with reference to a credit transaction, characterizes the transaction as one in which the party to whom credit is offered or extended is a natural person, and the money, property, or servic-

es which are the subject of the transaction are primarily for personal, family, or household purposes.

(i) The term, "open end credit plan" means a plan under which the creditor reasonably contemplates repeated transactions, which prescribes the terms of such transactions, and which provides for a finance charge which may be computed from time to time on the outstanding unpaid balance. A credit plan which is an open end credit plan within the meaning of the preceding sentence is an open end credit plan even if credit information is verified from time to time.

.... We have previously summarized the evidence presented at trial concerning how Mary's account was established and used prior to the single PPBG purchase at issue here. We find this evidence sufficient to support the conclusion that Mary's account was an open end consumer credit plan within the meaning of the Truth-in-Lending-Act. Furthermore, Citibank's counsel forthrightly conceded during oral argument that Mary's account was this type of plan.

Since Mary's open end consumer credit plan involved the use of a credit card, the Truth-in-Lending-Act specifically preserves her right to assert defenses against Citibank arising out of the PPBG transaction. Section 1666i states, in pertinent part:

(a) Claims and defenses assertible

Subject to the limitation contained in subsection (b) of this section, a card issuer who has issued a credit card to a cardholder pursuant to an open end consumer credit plan shall be subject to all claims (other than tort claims) and defenses arising out of any transaction in which the credit card is used as a method of payment or extension of credit if (1) the obligor has made a good faith attempt to obtain satisfactory resolution of a disagreement or problem relative to the transaction from the person honoring the credit card; (2) the amount of the initial transaction exceeds $50; and (3) the place where the initial transaction occurred was in the same State as the mailing address previously provided by the cardholder or was within 100 miles from such address....

(b) Amount of claims and defenses assertible

The amount of claims and defenses asserted by the cardholder may not exceed the amount of credit outstanding with respect to such transaction at the time the cardholder first notifies the card issuer or the person honoring the credit card of such claim or defense....

15 U.S.C. § 1666i. This same rule is repeated in 12 C.F.R. § 226.12(c). Hereinafter, we generically refer to the consumer protections contained in this statute and regulation as the "claims and defenses rule."

At the trial, Mary presented substantial evidence proving that she met each statutory element necessary to successfully assert the defense of non-delivery against Citibank under the Truth-in-Lending-Act claims and defenses rule:

1. The defense arose out of the PPBG transaction, and Mary's credit card was used as the method of payment for that purchase.

2. The Mincks made a good faith attempt to resolve the issue with PPBG.

3. The amount of this transaction greatly exceeded the $50 minimum.

4. The PPBG transaction occurred in Missouri, which is the same state as the mailing address shown on Mary's billing statements from Citibank.[8]

5. The non-delivery defense was used solely to extinguish the remaining indebtedness on Mary's Citibank account resulting from the single PPBG transaction at issue.

Therefore, we hold that the trial court committed no error in concluding Mary was entitled to assert the non-delivery defense against Citibank. The Truth-in-Lending-Act claims and defenses rule authorized Mary to assert non-delivery as a defense because her Citibank credit card account was an open end consumer credit plan, and her credit card was used to make the PPBG purchase at issue.

In so holding, we have given due consideration to Citibank's assertion that the Truth-in-Lending-Act claims and defenses rule does not apply because the single PPBG purchase was for a business or commercial purpose. Citibank's argument is based on the 15 U.S.C. § 1603(1), which defines what transactions are exempted from the scope of the Truth-in-Lending-Act. This statute states, in pertinent part:

> This subchapter does not apply to the following: (1) Credit transactions involving extensions of credit primarily for business, commercial, or agricultural purposes, or to government or governmental agencies or instrumentalities, or to organizations.

We find this argument unpersuasive for two reasons.

First, Citibank's argument is inconsistent with the plain language of 15 U.S.C. § 1666i. When an open end consumer credit plan is involved, this statute explicitly authorizes a cardholder (*i.e.*, Mary) to assert a defense against

---

[8] Courts deem a contract to have been made where the parties to the contract perform the last act necessary to complete the contract. *Gash v. Black and Veatch,* 976 S.W.2d 31, 32 (Mo.App.1998). Here, Chuck accepted PPBG's offer to sell the postcards by (a) filling out the written order form, (b) including Mary's Citibank credit card information on the form for use as the method of payment, (c) signing the form and (d) faxing the order from Lamar, Missouri, to PPBG's offices in Ohio. Since acceptance of PPBG's offer occurred in Missouri, the contract is deemed to have been made in this state. *See Johnson Heater Corp. v. Deppe,* 86 S.W.3d 114, 119 (Mo.App.2002); *Whiteman v. Del-Jen Const., Inc.,* 37 S.W.3d 823, 831 (Mo.App.2001); *Garrity v. A.I. Processors,* 850 S.W.2d 413, 416 (Mo.App.1993).

the card issuer (*i.e.,* Citibank) "arising out of *any transaction* in which the credit card is used as a method of payment or extension of credit...." 15 U.S.C. § 1666i(a) (emphasis added.) Since we are required to liberally construe this language in Mary's favor, we interpret the phrase, "any transaction," to mean exactly what it says. So long as a credit card was used to make a purchase on an open end consumer credit plan, the claims and defenses rule in 15 U.S.C. § 1666i applies to "any transaction" meeting the other requirements set forth in the statute. Any less expansive interpretation of this phrase would constitute a strict, rather than a liberal, construction of this remedial statute. We decline Citibank's invitation that we do so.

Second, Citibank's argument ignores the fact that the relevant "transaction" here was the initial extension of credit to Mary when her Citibank account was opened, rather than the specific transaction involving the postcard purchase from PPBG. We find the initial transaction controlling because it resulted in the creation of an open end consumer credit plan for Mary. It was this occurrence which inexorably led us to conclude that Mary was authorized by statute and regulation to assert non-delivery as a defense against Citibank in its lawsuit.

We believe this result is entirely consistent with the discussion of the Truth-in-Lending-Act by the United States Supreme Court in *American Express Company v. Koerner,* 452 U.S. 233, 101 S.Ct. 2281, 68 L.Ed.2d 803 (1981), upon which Citibank relies. In *Koerner,* the Supreme Court acknowledged that there can be an extension of consumer credit when an open end consumer credit account is created or renewed, as well as when individual credit card transactions occur. *Id.* at 240-42, 101 S.Ct. 2281. For the purpose of determining when the provisions of the Truth-in-Lending-Act apply, the Supreme Court described three possible alternative tests:

> The language of does not distinguish between the two types of transactions included in the definition of "credit" or indicate which of them must satisfy the definition of "consumer" in order for the section to be applicable. There are several possibilities. The relevant extension of credit may be only the creation or renewal of the account. Under this view, adopted by the District Court, [*Koerner v. American Express Co.,* 444 F.Supp. at 340 (E.D.La.1977)], if an account is opened by a natural person, its overall purpose must be considered. If the account is opened primarily for consumer purposes, applies, even if the cardholder uses the card for an occasional nonconsumer purchase. On the other hand, the language might be interpreted to call for a transaction-by-transaction approach. With such an approach, would apply if the transaction that is the subject of the dispute is a consumer credit transaction, regardless of the overall purpose of the account. A third alternative would be to combine the two approaches by holding applicable to all disputes that arise under an account that is characterized as a consumer credit account as well as to any dispute concern-

ing an individual transaction that is an extension of consumer credit, even if the overall purpose of the account is primarily a business one.

Id. at. 242, 101 S.Ct. 2281. The Supreme Court, however, was not required to decide which approach should be used because it determined there had not been an extension of consumer credit under any of the alternative tests.

In the case at bar, we do reach the issue which was deferred in *Koerner* and conclude that the first of the three alternatives, which we denominate the "overall purpose" test, is the one that should be used when an open end consumer credit plan is involved. Under this test, the overall purpose of an account opened by a natural person must be considered. If the account was opened primarily for consumer purposes, the statutory and regulatory framework of the Truth-in-Lending-Act applies, even if the cardholder occasionally uses the card for a nonconsumer purchase.

We find support for this conclusion in the Official Staff Interpretations of Regulation Z. *See* Supplement I to part 226, 12 C.F.R. p. 357 (1-1-04 edition). The Official Staff Commentary dealing with 12 C.F.R. § 226.3 (exempt transactions) notes that a creditor must determine in each case whether the extension of credit "is primarily for an exempt purpose." Pt. 226, Supp. I p. 369. "Examples of business-purpose credit include:.... A business account used occasionally for consumer purposes. Examples of consumer-purpose credit include:.... A personal account used occasionally for business purposes." *Id.* Therefore, we disagree with Citibank's contention that the use of Mary's Citibank credit card account to purchase nonconsumer goods on one occasion prevents her from taking advantage of the Truth-in-Lending-Act's claims and defenses rule in this case.

Mary's Use of Non-delivery as a Defense Against Citibank Also Is Authorized by State Law

Even if we accepted Citibank's argument in Point I that the Truth-in-Lending-Act does not apply, our decision would not change. Like Ulysses' unfortunate sailors in *The Odyssey,* Citibank would successfully navigate past the Charybdis of federal law only to be devoured by the Scylla of state law. Expressed in less metaphorical terms, the trial court's decision to enter judgment for Mary is still correct, based exclusively on Missouri common law and statutory principles. We must affirm the judgment under any reasonable theory supported by the evidence, even if the reasons advanced by the trial court are wrong or insufficient....

Citibank brought a breach of contract action against Mary for failing to pay her credit card account. The only unpaid charge on Mary's account was the PPBG purchase. As the petition expressly acknowledged, Citibank was suing Mary as PPBG's assignee.

"Missouri law is well-settled that an assignee acquires no greater rights than the assignor had at the time of the assignment." *Carlund Corp. v. Crown*

Center Redevelopment, 849 S.W.2d 647, 650 (Mo.App.1993).... As a result, Citibank stands in PPBG's shoes and can occupy no better position than PPBG would if it sued Mary directly.... These common law principles compel the conclusion that any defense valid against PPBG is valid against its assignee, Citibank.... The same is true under Missouri statutory law.... Therefore, without regard to the provisions of the federal Truth-in-Lending-Act, Missouri law gave Mary a common law and statutory right to assert any defense against Citibank that she could have asserted against its assignor, PPBG.

Assuming PPBG had sued Mary for breach of contract and sought to recover the cost of the postcards, would she have had a valid defense against that claim? We answer this question affirmatively because PPBG never delivered the merchandise for which Mary was charged.... This defense is just as effective against Citibank as it would have been against PPBG.

Regardless of whether the trial court's decision is reviewed by using the federal Truth-in-Lending-Act or state law standards, the judgment is correct. The trial court committed no error by ruling in Mary's favor and denying Citibank any recovery on its action for breach of contract. Citibank's first point is denied.

Point II

In Citibank's second point, it contends the judgment is not supported by substantial evidence and is based on a misapplication of the law because, even if Regulation Z does apply, PPBG's non-delivery of the postcards constituted a "billing error" within the meaning of the regulation. Assuming that to be true, Citibank then argues Mary could not avoid responsibility for the PPBG purchase unless she gave Citibank notice of the error within 60 days after the charge first appeared on her credit card statement. According to Citibank, failure to invoke the billing error provisions of the Truth-in-Lending-Act prohibits a consumer from thereafter relying on the claims and defenses rule if he or she is sued on the debt by the creditor.

The relevant statutory and regulatory provisions of the Truth-in-Lending-Act dealing with billing errors are found in 15 U.S.C. § 1666 and 12 C.F.R. § 226.13. Hereinafter, we generically refer to the consumer protections contained in this statute and regulation as the "billing error rule." The billing error rule gives a consumer the right, upon proper written notice, to request correction of billing errors. The notice must be received within 60 days after the creditor has sent the consumer a statement reflecting a billing error. *See* 15 U.S.C. § 1666(a); 12 C.F.R. § 226.13(b). If the consumer properly invokes the billing error rule by giving timely written notice, the creditor is required to investigate the claim. 15 U.S.C. § 1666(a); 12 C.F.R. § 226.13(b) and (c). While the investigation is pending, the consumer may withhold payment of the disputed sum, and the creditor is prohibited from both collection and adverse credit reporting activity. 15 U.S.C. § 1666(c); 12 C.F.R. § 226.13(d). As defined in 15 U.S.C. § 1666(b)(3) a billing error includes "[a] reflection on a statement of goods or services ... not delivered to the obligor or his designee in accordance with the agreement made at the time of a transaction." Essentially the same definition of a billing error is found in 12 C.F.R. § 226.13(a)(3).

The trial court concluded that PPBG's failure to deliver the postcards did not constitute a "billing error" within the meaning of 15 U.S.C. § 1666 and 12 C.F.R. § 226.13. We interpret this decision to be a rejection of Citibank's position that the 60 day time limit for giving written notice began running in March 2000 when the PPBG charge first appeared on Mary's statement because the Mincks did not know, during any portion of this 60 day period, that they would never receive the postcards, an acceptable substitute product, or a refund from PPBG. In order to dispose of Citibank's second point on appeal, however, it is unnecessary for us to decide whether this ruling was in error. Assuming PPBG's non-delivery of the postcards did constitute a "billing error" within the meaning of the Truth-in-Lending-Act, Mary still was entitled to invoke the claims and defenses rule in 15 U.S.C. § 1666i and 12 C.F.R. § 226.12(c). This statute and regulation are stand-alone provisions that operate independently of 15 U.S.C. § 1666 and 12 C.F.R. § 226.13, which give a consumer separate and distinct rights and remedies when seeking to correct a billing error. We find support for our conclusion through a textual analysis of 15 U.S.C. § 1666 and an examination of the Official Staff Interpretations of Regulation Z.

The only obligation imposed upon a consumer by 15 U.S.C. § 1666 is the transmittal of an adequate written notice to the creditor within 60 days after receiving a statement containing a billing error.[14] Once the billing error process is properly initiated, the consumer may withhold payment of the disputed sum and obtain an abatement of collection and adverse reporting activity while the creditor investigates the issue. Nothing in the statute affirmatively imposes any penalty on the consumer for failing to take advantage of the benefits of this statute. The only penalty which can even be inferred is the loss of the abatement rights contained therein. We accept as accurate the way in which the Texas Court of Appeals summed up the purpose of 15 U.S.C. § 1666:

> The purpose of the protections afforded a consumer under section 1666 is not, after all, to change the substantive law with regard to his liability for the underlying debt, but to protect him from the intimidating process of bargaining over a disputed debt with a creditor in a superior bargaining position. Without such protections, the creditor may use that bargaining power to encourage payment of even an illegitimate debt by threatening to

[14] The notice must identify the consumer by name and account number, indicate that a billing error has occurred and what the amount of the error is, and explain why the consumer believes the charge is a billing error. 15 U.S.C. § 1666(a)(1-3).

force the consumer to expend substantial time and money to protect his rights.

Dillard Department Stores, Inc. v. Owens, 951 S.W.2d 915, 918 (Tex.App.1997).

In contrast, the statute does affirmatively impose a penalty upon *a creditor* that ignores the provisions of this statute. This conclusion follows from 15 U.S.C. § 1666(e), which states:

(e) Effect of noncompliance with requirements by creditor

Any creditor who fails to comply with the requirements of this section or section 1666a of this title forfeits any right to collect from the obligor the amount indicated by the obligor under paragraph (2) of subsection (a) of this section, and any finance charges thereon, except that the amount required to be forfeited under this subsection may not exceed $50.

Thus, § 1666 only affects the amount of the debt in the event of a creditor's noncompliance with the statute. When this occurs, however, the creditor may still sue on the debt if there is a remaining balance due after subtracting the $50 forfeiture sum. If we were to accept Citibank's argument, it would mean that a consumer who failed to utilize this billing error statute-through ignorance, inadvertence, or purposeful action-would completely forfeit his right to contest the debt owed in a collection lawsuit. The creditor, on the other hand, could knowingly and willfully ignore its responsibilities under this statute and only be penalized a maximum of $50. In our view, this interpretation of the statute leads to an absurd result and turns topsy-turvy our duty to liberally construe the Truth-in-Lending-Act in a consumer's favor. Again, we decline to do so.

Our construction of how the billing error rule operates also is supported by the Official Staff Interpretations of Regulation Z. As the United States Supreme Court stated in *Ford Motor Credit Company v. Milhollin,* 444 U.S. 555, 100 S.Ct. 790, 63 L.Ed.2d 22 (1980):

At the very least, ... caution requires attentiveness to the views of the administrative entity appointed to apply and enforce a statute. And deference is especially appropriate in the process of interpreting the Truth in Lending Act and Regulation Z. Unless demonstrably irrational, Federal Reserve Board staff opinions construing the Act or Regulation should be dispositive....

Id. at 565, 100 S.Ct. 790. We wholeheartedly agree. In this very specialized area of law governing commerce in credit, we believe the Federal Reserve Board's interpretation of the Truth-in-Lending-Act and its implementing regulations are entitled to substantial deference as we analyze the issues presented in Citibank's appeal.

The regulation dealing with a consumer's right to correct billing errors is 12 C.F.R. § 226.13. The regulation dealing with a consumer's right to assert claims and defenses is 12 C.F.R. § 226.12. The Official Staff Commentary for 12 C.F.R. § 226.12 states, in pertinent part:

> *12(c) Right of cardholder to assert claims or defenses against card issuer.*
>
> *1. Relationship to § 226.13.* The § 226.12(c) credit card "holder in due course" provision deals with the consumer's right to assert against the card issuer a claim or defense concerning property or services purchased with a credit card, if the merchant has been unwilling to resolve the dispute. Even though certain merchandise disputes, such as non-delivery of goods, may also constitute "billing errors" under § 226.13, that section operates independently of § 226.12(c). The cardholder whose asserted billing error involves undelivered goods may institute the error resolution procedures of § 266.13; but whether or not the cardholder has done so, the cardholder may assert claims or defenses under § 226.12(c). Conversely, the consumer may pay a disputed balance and thus have no further right to assert claims and defenses, but still may assert a billing error if notice of that billing error is given in the proper time and manner. An assertion that a particular transaction resulted from unauthorized use of the card could also be both a "defense" and a billing error.

See Pt. 226, Supp. I p. 419. Thus, the Federal Reserve Board recognizes that the claims and defenses rule operates independently of the billing error rule. As the Board's analysis of the proper relationship between these two different rules and their respective remedies is not demonstrably irrational, we accept it as dispositive here.

For all of the foregoing reasons, we reject Citibank's argument that a consumer's failure to give a creditor timely notice of a billing error precludes the consumer from later invoking the claim and defense provisions of 15 U.S.C. § 1666i and 12 C.F.R. § 226.12(c) if the creditor sues on the debt. Citibank's second point is denied.

IV. Conclusion

Mary was entitled to assert non-delivery as a valid defense against Citibank in its action for breach of contract. The use of this non-delivery defense was authorized both by the Truth-in-Lending-Act and by state law. Furthermore, the use of this defense was not precluded by the billing error rule found in the Truth-in-Lending-Act. Therefore, the trial court ruled correctly when it denied Citibank any recovery and entered judgment in Mary's favor.

The judgment is affirmed.

NOTES

1. 15 U.S.C. § 1666i's geographic limitation on the cardholder's use of defenses to payment against the card issuer does not specify where the "initial transaction occurred." The court in Izraelewitz v. Manufacturers Hanover Trust Co., 465 N.Y.S.2d 486 (N.Y. Civ. Ct. 1983), states that the determination, instead, is left to state law. In Plutchok v. European American Bank, 540 N.Y.S.2d 135 (N.Y.Dist.Ct. 1989), the court determined that under New York state law a contract concluded by telephone occurs where the acceptance occurs.

2. Although an informal policy argument might prefer eliminating § 1666i's geographic limit, the case for doing so is far from decisive. A card issuer has an advantage over the cardholder at monitoring and gaining information about merchants who have accounts with it, wherever the merchant is located. Repeat business between the merchant and card issuer also reduces the merchant's incentive and ability to engage in sharp practice when it affects the issuer. These considerations favor always allowing the cardholder to use whatever defense it has against the merchant to resist paying the card issuer. Cf. Singer v. Chase Manhattan Bank, 890 P.2d 1305 (Nev.1995). Against this, sharp practice by cardholders in transactions in distant locations also must be considered. There is also the possibility that local merchants might be well positioned to share information about the patterns of behavior of remote cardholders purchasing in their locality. If cardholders tend to "misbehave" differently in transactions entered into far from home, where reputational constraints are slight and such transactions are sporadic enough to make monitoring by card issuers costly, for instance, eliminating the geographic limit increases the cost to remote merchants of accepting payment by credit card. Thus, the likely source of misbehavior (merchant or cardholder) as well as its costs do not unambiguously favor doing away with a limit.

5. INTERNET FRAUD

Most Internet sales are paid for by credit cards, and security problems are mounting. Losses may result from counterfeit credit cards in which the information on the card (credit card number and name of cardholder) is stolen and a new plastic card is manufactured from that information that can be used in face-to-face transactions, or, more commonly, use of fraudulently obtained information in telephone, Internet sales or other remote transactions in which no plastic card is required. How are losses in Internet sales allocated? The following Problem raises the issue in a common fact situation.

PROBLEM

Brentwood Books (BB) sells rare books all over the world on its Website. It accepts Visa, MasterCard and Amex in payment, but for sales over $250,

BB checks with the relevant network to verify that a card bearing the name and number submitted by the buyer has, in fact, been issued to the buyer. BB received a $1,000 order on the Internet purportedly from Lin Jong in Hong Kong, China, a well known book dealer, which directed that the sale be charged to Lin Jong's Visa card, with the credit card number and expiration date stated. BB verified with Visa International that a card bearing the stated number and expiration date had been issued to Lin Jong. When BB shipped the goods, it sent a memorandum to Union Bank, its California merchant bank (MB), that a sale had been made to be charged to Lin Jong's Visa card; MB credited BB's account for the amount of the sale and sent a charge message through the Visa International network to Hong Kong Bank, Lin Jong's issuing bank (IB), which debited Lin Jong's account for the amount of the sale. When Lin Jong saw the $1,000 charge on his statement, he protested to IB that he had not purchased the goods and demanded a chargeback. IB complied and sent a chargeback to MB, which erased the credit for that amount in BB's account. It became apparent that someone had stolen the information from Lin Jong's credit card and had ordered the goods sent to a Hong Kong address different from that of Lin Jong's business. Who should bear the loss in this case? How can the parties avoid losses of this kind on Internet sales?

Brentwood Books' difficulty is that it can't prove that Lin Jong received the goods because it doesn't have his signature. A typical online sale is considered a "card-not-present" transaction as opposed to a "card-present" sale at a brick-and-mortar store, where shoppers sign receipts. Thomas E. Weber, What Do You Risk Using a Credit Card to Shop on the Net, Wall. St. J., Dec. 10, 2001, at B1, states the understanding to be: "When a consumer challenges a card-not-present charge, the merchant is liable for the loss." Julia Angwin, Credit–Card Scams Bedevil E–Stores, Wall St. J., Sept. 19, 2000, at B1, reports that more Internet transactions are charged back (1.25%) than catalog transactions by telephone (0.33%) or storefront retail transactions (0.14%). She notes that one survey of 156 of the largest retailers showed that 2.64% of their Internet transactions are charged back. She interviewed online retailers whose chargeback losses have driven them to require that all deliveries be made only to the address of the cardholder and, for larger orders, to telephone the cardholder to confirm the order. The assumption is that a large portion of Internet chargeback losses are caused by use of stolen credit card numbers. Software has been developed to spot potential fraud cases, and Visa and MasterCard have developed new systems, "Verified by Visa" and "MasterCard SureCode," under which the cardholder receives a password resembling a PIN that only the cardholder can use in online sales. These systems will be phased in over the next few years. The intent is to have the use of the password treated as the equivalent to the cardholder's signature. Paul Beckett & Jathon

Sapsford, As Credit–Card Theft Grows, A Tussle Over Paying to Stop It, Wall St. J., May 1, 2003, at A1.

Identity theft has brought credit card fraud to a new level of criminal professionalism. Individuals are duped by fraudsters into divulging confidential information: account numbers, home addresses, Social Security numbers, date of birth, even driver's license numbers. This information is collected on Web sites that sell or share stolen credit card information. In a recent year the MasterCard International security office detected 35,045 MasterCard numbers for sale or trade on the Internet; these numbers can be used in telephone or Internet transactions. In 2005, there were 8.3 million cases of identity theft in all its forms. 2006 Identity Theft Report, Federal Trade Commission. As Internet sales grow, identity fraud becomes more costly; it's hard for merchants to recognize crooks with stolen identities. As merchants and banks become more wary, fraudsters become more sophisticated. As a harassed merchant put it: "[I]t's a cat-and-mouse game. As we get better, they get better." Mitchell Pacelle, At Online Stores, Sniffing Out Crooks Is a Matter of Survival, Wall St. J., Aug. 4, 2005, at A1. In 2004, an alliance of international law-enforcement agencies coordinated a global crackdown on illegal trade in stolen credit card numbers on the Internet: "Operation Firewall." The results are shown by the title of the following article. Riva Richmond, Trade in Stolen Credit-Card Data on the Internet Shows Resiliency, Wall St. J., June 1, 2005, at B5C.

CHAPTER 4

PAYMENT SYSTEMS: ELECTRONIC TRANSFERS

A. ELECTRONIC FUNDS TRANSFERS UNDER ARTICLE 4A

1. THE BASIC TRANSACTIONS COVERED BY ARTICLE 4A

Article 4A was promulgated by ALI and National Conference in 1989. By 1996 it had been enacted in all 50 states. Representatives of the Federal Reserve Board and of the New York Federal Reserve Bank were very active in the four-year drafting process of Article 4A, and, after Article 4A was completed, Regulation J, which governs Fedwire (described below), was revised by the Federal Reserve Board to bring it into conformity with Article 4A. 12 C.F.R. § 210.25 et seq. The Fed's stated policy in doing so was to provide a "level playing field" in which the rights and obligations of the parties in all funds transfers would be governed by essentially the same set of rules. Ernest T. Patrikis, Thomas C. Baxter, Jr. & Raj K. Bhala, Wire Transfers 140 (1993) (hereafter Patrikis et al., Wire Transfers).

Section 4A-108 provides that Article 4A does not apply to consumer electronic funds transfers governed by the Electronic Fund Transfer Act (EFTA), 15 U.S.C. § 1693 et seq., discussed later in this chapter. Typical transactions covered by the EFTA are: point-of-sale transactions in which retail customers pay for purchases by use of an access or debit card inserted in a terminal at a retail store that allows the bank account of the customer to be debited; automated teller machine transactions; direct deposit of paychecks in consumer accounts and preauthorized withdrawals from consumer accounts to pay consumer obligations like insurance premiums. 15 U.S.C. § 1693a(6). "Small dollar" wire transfers by Western Union and its competitors are not covered by Article 4A because payment orders are defined in 4A–103 as orders to banks and Western Union and its competitors are not banks.

The typical funds transfer transaction covered by Article 4A is a large payment of money from one business or financial organization to another made through the banking system by electronic means. The average size of a wire transfer is measured in the millions of dollars. A common wire transfer might be: Los Angeles Seller is selling $100 million in property to a New York Buyer. The closing is in Buyer's counsel's office in New York. When negotiations are concluded and the deal is made, Buyer calls its office and requests that an instruction be given to its bank, New York Bank (NYB), to transfer $100 million to Seller's account in Seller's bank, Los Angeles Bank (LAB). Within a few hours, Seller receives a call from its office stating that it has been notified by LAB that the funds are now in Seller's account in LAB and available for withdrawal by Seller. The deal is done.

What went on behind the scenes to move $100 million from New York to Los Angeles in a few hours? Some of the alternative methods follow. These are described in detail in Patrikis et al., Wire Transfers, Chapter 2.

(a) *Two bank transfer*. Buyer, the "originator" (4A–104(c)), instructs NYB, the "originator's bank" (4A–104(d)), to send $100 million to LAB, the "beneficiary's bank" (4A–103(a)(3)), to the account of the Seller, the "beneficiary" (4A–103(a)(2)). The instruction is a "payment order" (4A–103(a)(1)) and it may be transmitted "orally [e.g., by telephone], electronically, or in writing." NYB "accepts" (4A–209(a)) the payment order when it "execute[s]" (4A–301(a)) that order by sending a payment order to LAB intended to carry out the payment order it received from Buyer. LAB accepts the payment order of NYB by crediting the Seller's account and notifying Seller of this fact. 4A–209(b)(1). When LAB accepted the payment order, the "funds transfer" (4A–104(a)) was completed. Since Seller has received payment, Buyer's obligation to pay Seller for the property is discharged. 4A–406.

This transaction involved two payment orders: the first, from Buyer to NYB and the second, from NYB to LAB. With respect to the first, Buyer is the "sender" (4A–103(a)(5)), and NYB is the "receiving bank" (4A–103(a)(4)). With respect to the second, NYB is the sender and LAB is the receiving bank. In crediting Seller's account, LAB was not sending a payment order.

It is important to understand that Article 4A prescribes the liability of the parties to a funds transfer; it does not mandate a mode of settlement. That is, when NYB accepted Buyer's payment order, Buyer, as sender, became liable to pay the amount of that payment order to NYB, the receiving bank. 4A–402(c). When LAB, the beneficiary's bank, accepted NYB's payment order, NYB became liable to pay the amount of the order to LAB. 4A–402(b). When LAB credited Seller's account and gave notice to Seller, LAB paid Seller and Seller can withdraw the funds.

How these debts are settled, that is, how the money changes hands, is not covered by Article 4A, which merely provides for a series of bank credits, usually ending in a credit in the beneficiary's account in the beneficiary bank. NYB became a creditor of Buyer when it accepted Buyer's payment order by sending its own order to LAB. Buyer will pay its debt to NYB either by having enough money in its account in NYB that NYB can debit to cover the payment or by depositing enough money into the account, usually by the end of the banking day, to cover the payment made on Buyer's behalf. If no satisfactory agreement has been reached in advance between Buyer and NYB to fund the payment order, NYB would probably not accept the order.

LAB became a creditor of NYB when it accepted NYB's payment order by crediting Seller's account. Unless NYB and LAB have some agreement on how NYB will pay this debt, LAB probably would not accept the payment order. Usually in two-bank cases, settlement will be accomplished either through "cross accounts" or a "common account." In a cross-account situation, each bank will have an account in the other. When NYB accepts Buyer's payment order, it will debit Buyer's account and credit LAB's account. When LAB accepts NYB's payment order, it will debit NYB's account and credit Seller's account. Common-account settlement is possible when both NYB and LAB have accounts in a common correspondent bank. The correspondent bank will debit NYB's account and credit that of LAB.

(b) *CHIPS*. If both NYB and LAB are participants in the Clearing House Interbank Payments System (CHIPS) of the New York Clearing House Association, they can utilize the CHIPS facilities for both transmission of the payment order and settlement of the ensuing obligations. Members of The New York Clearing House Association are Bank of America, New York Mellon, Citibank, J.P. Morgan Chase, Wells Fargo and other banking giants. CHIPS is one of the two major wire transfer systems in the nation; it handles a large volume of international transfers in dollars and a number of its participants are foreign banks. Under CHIPS, NYB will send its payment order to LAB through the central CHIPS clearing system. At the end of the day, CHIPS computers will net out the difference between the total value of payments orders NYB has sent to LAB on that day, and vice versa, and the net balance debtor will pay through Fedwire the amount of the debit balance to the CHIPS Settlement Account at the New York Federal Reserve Bank (FRBNY); the net balance creditor will receive the amount of the credit balance from this account through Fedwire sent by the FRBNY at the end of the day. Patrikis et al., Wire Transfers, Chapter 17.

(c) *Fedwire*. This system is owned and operated by the 12 Federal Reserve banks and is the other major domestic wire transfer system. It can be used only by banks in privity with Reserve banks. These banks must have accounts in the Fed. However, other banks can use Fedwire through correspondent banks that are in privity with the Fed. If both LAB and NYB have access to

Fedwire, the transaction would go like this: Buyer instructs NYB to send the funds to LAB for credit to Seller's account. NYB instructs the New York Fed to send the funds to LAB, for Seller. The NY Fed will instruct the San Francisco Fed to send funds to LAB for Seller's account. The SF Fed will instruct LAB to credit Seller's account. LAB will notify Seller that the money is available for withdrawal. In this case four payment orders have been sent: from Buyer to NYB, from NYB to NY Fed, from NY Fed to SF Fed, and from SF Fed to LAB.

Fedwire is not only a communication system that receives and sends payment orders, but, like CHIPS, it is also a settlement system. However, there is a difference: under Fedwire, as soon as the NY Fed sends the instruction to the SF Fed, it debits NYB's Federal Reserve account and credits the Federal Reserve account of the SF Fed. As soon as the SF Fed sends the instruction to LAB, it debits the NY Fed's Federal Reserve account and credits the Federal Reserve account of LAB. As they say in the business, with Fedwire "the message is the money." By the time LAB receives the payment order, all prior payment orders are settled. No end-of-day settlement, as in CHIPS, is necessary. Each sender's payment order is settled for at the time of acceptance by the receiving bank by debiting the Federal Reserve account of the sender and crediting the Federal Reserve account of the receiving bank.

(d) *SWIFT*. The Society For Worldwide Interbank Financial Telecommunications (SWIFT), a Belgium-based consortium, is owned and operated by some of the world's largest financial institutions: Bank of America, JPMorgan Chase and Citigroup and large European banks such as Deutsche Bank in Germany. The SWIFT network was founded in 1973 to replace telex and is used primarily for non-dollar transfers between financial institutions in more than 200 countries. It has almost 7,900 participating institutions and only 16% of its traffic is American. Like CHIPS, SWIFT does not transfer funds between banks; it transmits payment orders and settlement takes place through the Fed and its international counterparts. Josh Meyer & Greg Miller, U.S. Secretly Tracks Global Bank Data, LA Times, June 23, 2006, at A1.

At the time Article 4A was being written, the United Nations Commission on International Trade Law (UNCITRAL) was drafting the Model Law on International Credit Transfers that is intended to be a model for any nation that wishes to have legislation on the subject. Advisers who had been active in the Article 4A project served as members of the U.S. delegation to the Working Group that constituted the drafting committee for the Model Law. Article 4A and the Model Law bear many similarities but there are differences as well. As yet no nation has adopted the Model Law and it is exceedingly unlikely the U.S. will do so. The Model Law is discussed extensively in Patrikis et al., Wire Transfers, Chapters 19–23.

2. PAYMENT ORDERS

A funds transfer involves a series of payment orders, defined in 4A-103(a)(1) as meaning "an instruction of a sender to a receiving bank, transmitted orally, electronically, or in writing to pay, or to cause another bank to pay, a fixed or determinable amount of money to a beneficiary...." Why did the customer's instructions to its bank in the following case not constitute a payment order?

Trustmark Insurance Co. v. Bank One, Arizona, NA

Court of Appeals of Arizona, 2002.
48 P.3d 485.

■ GEMMILL, JUDGE.

If a banking customer sends a bank a letter of instructions requesting wire transfers of funds upon future occurrences of a specified balance condition in the customer's account, does the letter of instructions constitute a "payment order" under Article 4A of Arizona's Uniform Commercial Code ("UCC")? We address this question, and others, in this decision.

Bank One, Arizona, NA ("Bank One") appeals from a jury verdict for Trustmark Insurance Company ("Trustmark") on Trustmark's claim under Article 4A of the UCC.... We reverse the judgment on the UCC claim....

FACTUAL AND PROCEDURAL BACKGROUND

This case involves a commercial dispute between Bank One and Trustmark over a wire transfer arrangement. In February 1995, Trustmark set up a deposit account ("Account One") at Bank One governed by Bank One's deposit account rules. At the same time, Trustmark executed a wire transfer agreement with Bank One.

In May 1995, Trustmark sent Bank One a letter (the "Letter of Instructions") regarding a second deposit account ("Account Two"). Account Two was subject to the same deposit account rules and wire transfer agreement as Account One. In the Letter of Instructions, Trustmark instructed Bank One to (1) retain a daily balance of $10,000 in Account Two and (2) transfer funds in Account Two automatically to a Trustmark account at the Harris Bank ("Harris Account") whenever Account Two reached a balance of $110,000 or more. In September 1995, Trustmark's Arizona agent began depositing funds into Account Two. Bank One began transferring funds to the Harris Account whenever the Account Two balance rose above $110,000....

In September 1996, the Account Two balance rose above $110,000 for the first time since the July 19, 1996 deadline. Bank One did not transfer funds from Account Two into the Harris Account. Bank One sent regular account statements to Trustmark showing the balances in Account Two, but received no further instructions from Trustmark. The Account Two balance continued to grow until December 1997, when Bank One brought the balance to the specific attention of Trustmark's Arizona agent, who contacted Trustmark's management. Bank One transferred $19,220,099.80 to the Harris Account, leaving $10,000 in Account Two. In early 1998, Trustmark instructed Bank One to transfer Account Two's remaining funds to the Harris Account and thereafter closed Account Two.

Trustmark then filed this action against Bank One, alleging a claim under Article 4A of the UCC , as well as claims for unjust enrichment and negligence. Trustmark alleged that Bank One failed to complete wire transfers from Trustmark's non-interest bearing account at Bank One (Account Two) to Trustmark's investment account at Harris Bank (Harris Account), contrary to the Letter of Instructions. Trustmark asserted a loss of more than $500,000 in interest on its funds as a result of Bank One's inaction, and that Bank One reaped a corresponding windfall profit through interest Bank One earned on Trustmark's money. Trustmark did not assert a breach of contract claim. According to Bank One, the contractual documents eliminated recovery or significantly limited the amount recoverable for breach of contract. However, Article 4A—if applicable—restricts the right of a bank to limit its liability regarding funds transfers. *See* A.R.S. § 47-4A305(F) (1997).[2]

Bank One filed motions to dismiss and for summary judgment on the UCC claim, arguing that the wire transfers at issue were not subject to Article 4A because the Letter of Instructions was not a "payment order" under Article 4A. The trial court denied Bank One's motions, and the case proceeded to a jury trial. At the close of evidence, the court granted Bank One's motion for judgment as a matter of law on the unjust enrichment claim, but continued to reject Bank One's argument that Article 4A of the UCC was not applicable. The court submitted Trustmark's UCC claim and its negligence claim to the jury.

The jury returned a verdict for Trustmark on the UCC claim and found damages of $573,197.02.... The trial court entered judgment for Trustmark with damages of $573,197.02, as well as pre-judgment interest, attorneys' fees, and taxable costs.

---

[2] Section 47-4A305 specifies the liability of a bank under UCC Article 4A for late or improper execution of, or failure to execute, a payment order. *See* A.R.S. § 47-4A305(A), (B), and (D). Trustmark sought recovery under A.R.S. § § 47-4A305 and 47-4A506 (1997). Bank One argued these provisions were not applicable.

ISSUES ON APPEAL AND CROSS APPEAL

Bank One argues on appeal that Trustmark's judgment should be reversed as a matter of law because Article 4A of the UCC is not applicable. According to Bank One, the Letter of Instructions was not a "payment order" under Article 4A, and the trial court should not have sent this UCC claim to the jury....

BANK ONE'S APPEAL

Bank One challenges the trial court's submission of the UCC claim to the jury on the basis that the Letter of Instructions is not a "payment order" under Article 4A; therefore the UCC is not applicable, and this claim should have been dismissed as a matter of law....

As a Matter of Law, the UCC Does Not Apply Because the Letter of Instructions Was Not a "Payment Order" Under Article 4A

....

Article 4A applies only to "funds transfers" as defined in the statute. A.R.S. § 47-4A102 (1997). A "funds transfer" is "the series of transactions, beginning with the originator's *payment order*, made for the purpose of making payment to the beneficiary of the order." A.R.S. § 47- 4A104(1) (1997) (emphasis added). Accordingly, to fall within the scope of Article 4A, a transaction must begin with a "payment order."

A "payment order" is defined by the UCC, in pertinent part, as:

> [A]n instruction of a sender to a receiving bank, transmitted orally, electronically, or in writing, to pay, or to cause another bank to pay, a *fixed or determinable amount of money* to a beneficiary if:
>
> (a) *The instruction does not state a condition to payment* to the beneficiary *other than time of payment.* ...

A.R.S. § 47-4A103(A)(1) (1997) (emphasis added). A recent law review article explains:

> By definition, an Article 4A payment order must be unconditional. Therefore, an important scope issue in determining whether Article 4A applies is whether the payment order in question is or is not conditional.

Alvin C. Harrell, *UCC Article 4A,* 25 Okla. City U.L.Rev. 293 (2000) (footnote omitted).

Bank One argues that the Letter of Instructions was not a payment order, because the Letter was not for a "fixed or determinable amount of money" and imposed two conditions other than time of payment: that the account balance always remain $10,000 ("balance condition") and that transfers not occur until subsequent deposits have raised the balance to $110,000 or more ("deposit condition").[4] Trustmark argues that the conditions at issue were merely conditions regarding the time of payment—that the balance and deposit conditions essentially determined when transfers were to be made. Trustmark asserts that time of payment need not be set by a specific date, but may be set by events such as the bank's receipt of an incoming wire or deposit. However, the amounts to be transferred did not relate to incoming wires for the same amounts or even wires received on the same day of each month. Rather, Trustmark's agent made deposits sporadically and in varying amounts. Therefore, the conditions in the Letter of Instructions required Bank One to continuously monitor Trustmark's account balance to determine whether sufficient deposits had been made to enable the bank to make a transfer that satisfied both the deposit and balance conditions.

Neither party has cited, nor has our own research revealed, any reported decision addressing the precise issue presented: whether a letter of instructions from an account holder to its bank, requesting automatic wire transfers of funds in excess of a minimum balance whenever the total balance equals or exceeds a specified amount, constitutes a "payment order" governed by UCC Article 4A. We conclude that the Letter of Instructions was not a "payment order," because the Letter subjected Bank One to a condition to payment other than the time of payment.

Article 4A applies to discrete, mechanical transfers of funds. Comment 3 to UCC § 4A-104 (A.R.S. § 47-4A104) provides:

> The function of banks in a funds transfer under Article 4A is comparable to their role in the collection and payment of checks in that it is essentially mechanical in nature. The low price and high speed that characterize funds transfers reflect this fact. Conditions to payment ... other than time of payment impose responsibilities on [the] bank that go beyond those in Article 4A funds transfers.

See also Centre-Point Merchant Bank v. Am. Express Bank, 913 F.Supp. 202, 208 (S.D.N.Y.1996) (payment orders under Article 4A are not intended to require banks to "engag[e] in inquiries as to whether conditions have been satisfied.").

Bank One's obligation to make an ongoing inquiry as to Account Two's balance status removes the Letter of Instructions from the Article 4A definition of a "payment order." A.R.S. § 47-4A103(A)(1)(a); Comment 3 to UCC § 4A-104 (A.R.S. § 47-4A104), (quoted in , *supra*). Conditions other than time of payment "are anathema to [A]rticle 4A, which facilitates the low price, high speed, and mechanical nature of funds transfers." *Grabowski,* 997

---

[4] Because we base our resolution on the definition of "payment order," we do not reach Bank One's argument that the Letter of Instructions was not for a "fixed or determinable amount of money."

F.Supp. at 121 (citing Mass. Gen. L. ch. 106, § 4A-104, cmt. 3). In their treatise on the UCC, James J. White & Robert S. Summers further explain:

> A payment order must not "state a condition to payment of the beneficiary other than time of payment." Few transactions will include such conditions. The exception for "time of payment" means that a payment order need not order immediate payment, though most do. For example, a payment order may specify that a certain amount of money must be paid on a certain date to a particular beneficiary.

3 James J. White & Robert S. Summers, *Uniform Commercial Code* § 22-2 (4th ed.1995) (citation omitted). White & Summers then quoted the same language from Comment 3 that we quote in to explain that "the drafters did not wish to involve banks in [inquiries] into whether other conditions have occurred." *Id.*

Based on the language defining "payment order," the purpose of Article 4A, and the drafters' intent that payment orders be virtually unconditional, we conclude that requiring the bank to continually examine the account balance is a condition to payment other than time of payment under A.R.S. § 47-4A103(A)(1)(a). We perceive a qualitative difference between a condition requiring daily monitoring of the account balance and an instruction to wire funds on a specific day....

We conclude, as a matter of law, that Trustmark does not have a claim under UCC Article 4A, because the Letter of Instructions is not an Article 4A "payment order." Therefore, we reverse the judgment against Bank One on Trustmark's UCC claim....

CONCLUSION

We reverse the judgment in favor of Trustmark on the UCC claim....

3. ACCEPTANCE OF PAYMENT ORDER

By Receiving Bank. "Acceptance," defined in 4A–209, is a core concept of Article 4A. The rights and obligations of the participants to a funds transfer under Article 4A arise as a result of acceptance. A payment order instructs a receiving bank to accept the payment order, but the receiving bank may either accept or reject. If a receiving bank accepts a sender's payment order, the sender becomes liable to the receiving bank for the amount of the payment order (4A–402(c)), and the receiving bank is obliged to issue a payment order complying with the sender's payment order (4A–302(a)(1)). A receiving bank, other than the beneficiary's bank, accepts the sender's payment order by executing the order (4A–209(a)), that is, by issuing a payment order intended to carry out the payment order received by the bank (4A–301(a)). An originator is a sender and an originator's bank is a receiving bank. When the originator's bank executes the payment order by sending it to a receiving bank, the originator's bank becomes a sender.

By Beneficiary's Bank. The last receiving bank in the chain is the beneficiary's bank, the one identified in the payment order as the bank in which the account of the beneficiary is to be credited. 4A–103(a)(3). Section 4A–209(b) spells out when a beneficiary's bank accepts a payment order. In the most common case, this occurs when the beneficiary's bank credits the beneficiary's account and notifies the beneficiary that it may withdraw the credit. 4A–405(a). At this point the beneficiary's bank becomes liable for the amount of the payment order to the beneficiary. 4A–404(a). The beneficiary has bank credit in its account in the amount of the funds transfer—"money in the bank"—that it can withdraw. The purpose of the funds transfer has been achieved: the beneficiary is paid and the underlying obligation that the originator owed the beneficiary is discharged. 4A–406(a)-(b). Bank credit has been transferred from the originator's bank to the beneficiary's bank. Settlement between the banks may occur later.

PROBLEM

Beneficiary's Bank (BB) received a payment order for $10,000 and credited Beneficiary's (B) account for that amount. A few hours later BB notified B that the credit had been received but said nothing about its availability. However, the evidence was uncontradicted that B had been given immediate access to the funds in its account at the time the account was credited. The issue before the court was whether payment was made at the time of the credit or at the time of the notice. Section 4A–405(a) states that payment is made "when ... (i) the beneficiary is notified of the right to withdraw the credit,...or (iii) funds with respect to the order are otherwise made available to the beneficiary by the bank." The court in First Security Bank of New Mexico v. Pan American Bank, 215 F.3d 1147 (10th Cir.2000), held that payment occurred as soon as B had immediate access to the funds under 4A–405(a)(iii) even though BB had not given B notice of its right to withdraw the funds. The only discussion in Article 4A of this provision appears in Comment 5 to 4A–209 and is not clearly on point. Do you agree with the court's decision? What position does *Aleo*, following, take on this issue?

4. RECEIVER FINALITY

a. CANCELLATION

In an earlier chapter we discussed why obligees might not choose to take payment in uncertified checks or even in cashier's checks. At that point we suggested that they might demand to be paid by wire transfer in order to provide maximum safety. In the following case we see why this is so.

Aleo International, Ltd. v. Citibank

Supreme Court, New York County, 1994.
160 Misc.2d 950, 612 N.Y.S.2d 540.

■ HERMAN CAHN, JUSTICE.

Defendant Citibank, N.A. ("Citibank") moves for an order, pursuant to CPLR 3212, granting it summary judgment dismissing the complaint.

Plaintiff Aleo International, Ltd. ("Aleo") is a domestic corporation. On October 13, 1992, one of Aleo's vice-presidents, Vera Eyzerovich ("Ms. Eyzerovich"), entered her local Citibank branch and instructed Citibank to make an electronic transfer of $284,563 US dollars to the Dresdner Bank in Berlin, Germany, to the account of an individual named Behzad Hermatjou ("Hermatjou"). The documentary evidence submitted shows that at 5:27 p.m. on October 13, 1992, Citibank sent the payment order to the Dresdner Bank by electronic message. Dresdner Bank later sent Citibank an electronic message: "Regarding your payment for USD 284.563,00 DD 13.10.92 [indecipherable] f/o Behzad Hermatjou, Pls be advised that we have credited A.M. beneficiary DD 14.10.92 val 16.10.92 with the net amount of USD 284.136,16." This information was confirmed by the Dresdner Bank by fax to Citibank on July 29, 1993: "Please be advised that on 14.10.92 at 09:59 o'clock Berlin time Dresdner Bank credited the account of Behzad Hermatjou with USD 284.136,16 (USD 284.563,00 less our charges)." It is undisputed that Berlin time is six hours ahead of New York time, and that 9:59 a.m. Berlin time would be 3:59 a.m. New York time. At approximately 9 a.m. on October 14, 1992, Ms. Eyzerovich instructed Citibank to stop the transfer. When Citibank did not, this action ensued.

Article 4A of the Uniform Commercial Code ("UCC") governs electronic "funds transfers." The Official Comment to UCC § 4A–102 states that the provisions of Article 4A

> are intended to be the exclusive means of determining the rights, duties and liabilities of the affected parties in any situation covered by particular

> provisions of the Article. Consequently, resort to principles of law or equity outside of Article 4A is not appropriate to create rights, duties and liabilities inconsistent with those stated in this Article.

Article 4A does not include any provision for a cause of action in negligence. Thus, unless Citibank's failure to cancel Ms. Eyzerovich's transfer order was not in conformity with Article 4A, plaintiff Aleo has failed to state a cause of action, and this action must be dismissed.

UCC 4A–211(2), which governs the cancellation and amendment of payment orders, provides that

> A communication by the sender cancelling or amending a payment order is effective to cancel or amend the order if notice of the communication is received at a time and in a manner affording the receiving bank a reasonable opportunity to act on the communication before the bank accepts the payment order.

"Acceptance of Payment Order" is defined by UCC 4A–209 (2), which provides that:

> a beneficiary's bank accepts a payment order at the earliest of the following times: (a) when the bank (i) pays the beneficiary ... or (ii) notifies the beneficiary of receipt of the order or that the account of the beneficiary has been credited with respect to the order....

The documentary evidence shows that Hermatjou's account was credited on October 14, 1992 at 9:59 a.m. Berlin time. Thus, as of 3:59 a.m. New York time, the Dresdner Bank "paid the beneficiary" and thereby accepted the payment order. Because this payment and acceptance occurred prior to Ms. Eyzerovich's stop transfer order at 9 a.m. on that day, according to UCC 4A–211(2), Ms. Eyzerovich's attempt to cancel the payment order was ineffective, and Citibank may not be held liable for failing to honor it.

"Summary judgment is designed to expedite all civil cases by eliminating from the Trial Calendar claims which can properly be resolved as a matter of law.... [W]hen there is no genuine issue to be resolved at trial, the case should be summarily decided." Andre v. Pomeroy, 35 N.Y.2d 361, 364, 362 N.Y.S.2d 131, 320 N.E.2d 853.

Accordingly, defendant's motion is granted and this action is dismissed.

NOTES

1. The attractions of the wholesale wire transfer system, as regulated by Article 4A, are that it is cheap, fast and final. After LAB accepted the payment order in the hypothetical case at the beginning of the chapter by crediting Seller's account and notifying Seller of its right to withdraw, Buyer could not stop payment by canceling the payment order unless LAB agreed to do so, and then only in the four cases set out in 4A–211(c)(2). These are that the payment order was: (i) unauthorized; (ii) a duplicate; (iii) made to the wrong beneficiary; or (iv) in an excessive amount. "Buyer's remorse" is not listed. Since LAB will have little incentive to antagonize its customer, Seller, by agreeing to the cancellation of the payment order and may not be sure whether any of the four events has actually occurred, it is unlikely that many beneficiary banks will agree to cancel.

2. A concern often expressed by banks during the process of drafting Article 4A was that a beneficiary bank might need protection against the insolvency of prior banks in the chain. If the payment order is sent through Fedwire, the beneficiary's bank is fully protected because "the message is the money," and the beneficiary's bank is paid as soon as it receives the Fedwire payment order. 4A–209(b)(2) and 4A–403(a)(1). But in most other cases, the beneficiary's bank will not receive settlement on the payment order until after it has received the order. If it turns the money over to the beneficiary as soon as it receives the credit, it faces the risk that a prior bank in the chain may suspend payments before it settles with the beneficiary bank. Some banks wanted to solve this problem by being allowed to make provisional payments to their customers that would allow the beneficiary's bank to grab back the money paid out to the beneficiary if a prior bank failed before settlement. Strong arguments were made against this view by both users of the wire transfer system and the Fed; they contended that once the beneficiary's bank had made the money available to the beneficiary, it should be able to keep it. Receiver finality should be the goal of Article 4A. The users won this argument. Section 4A–405(c) invalidates provisional payments to beneficiaries, except in case of ACH transfers (4A–405(d), Comment 3) or, with respect to CHIPS transfers, in case of a meltdown of the entire American banking system (4A–405(e)), an event that Comment 4 cheerfully assures us "should never occur."

3. If a beneficiary bank cannot protect itself against up-stream insolvencies by making provisional payments to its customers, what can it do to guard against this risk? Patrikis et al., Wire Transfers, Chapter 10. First, it can reject the payment order if it doubts the solvency of the sending bank. 4A–210. Second, it can notify the beneficiary that it will not be allowed to withdraw the funds until the bank receives settlement from the sender of the order. 4A–209(b)(1). Third, it can withhold the funds until an hour after the opening of business on the day after receipt, by which time, if it has not already received settlement, it must reject to avoid acceptance. 4A–209(b)(3). But the competitive pressure on beneficiary's banks to afford their customers prompt payment upon receipt of payment orders is great. This is particularly true with respect to CHIPS banks that are in direct competition with the Fedwire system that offers beneficiaries of Fedwire payments immediate access to the incoming funds. By adoption of new rules after the completion of Article 4A, CHIPS has created a loss-sharing system that requires CHIPS banks to contribute funds to allow the system to settle for payment orders sent over the system during a given day in the event that one or more banks are unable to meet their settlement obligations. Patrikis et al., Wire Transfers, Chapter 18. The level playing field between CHIPS and Fedwire has been achieved with respect to the early release of funds to beneficiaries.

b. AMENDMENT

Under 4A-211(b), a sender can cancel or amend a payment order only if notice is received affording the receiving bank a reasonable opportunity to act before the bank accepts the payment order. Section 4A-211(d) provides that an unaccepted payment order is cancelled by operation of law at the close of the fifth funds-transfer business day of the receiving bank after the execution date or payment date of the order. Thus, amendment is not possible after expiration of the five day period.

PROBLEM

Day 1. Originator (O) instructed Originator's Bank (OB) to send $1.5 million to Beneficiary's Bank (BB) for the account of Bradford (B). OB accepted the payment order by sending the funds to BB.

Day 2. BB discovered that it could not accept OB's payment order because it had no account in the name of Bradford. BB took no further action.

Day 3. O discovered its error and instructed OB to send a payment order of $1.5 million to the correct beneficiary, Blue Star. OB sent the payment order and BB accepted it by crediting Blue Star's account and notifying the beneficiary.

Day 4. A review of O's wire transfer transactions showed irregularities with respect to the first payment order, and the decision was made to amend the Day 1 payment order by instructing OB to send a communication to BB to amend the payment order by inserting the name Blue Star as that of the beneficiary. BB complied and credited Blue Star's account with an additional $1.5 million.

Day 5. Blue Star withdrew the additional $1.5 million. The whereabouts of Blue Star are unknown.

O sued BB for the excess $1.5 million on the ground that the Day 4 amendment to the Day 1 payment order was ineffective; since no valid beneficiary was named on that payment order, it was cancelled by operation of law and could not be amended. BB replied that 4A-211(d) cancels an unaccepted payment order by operation of law only after expiration of five days after the execution or payment date of the order. Initially ineffective payment orders can be amended within that five-day period to allow acceptance. Hence, BB acted properly with respect to both payment orders. Which party should prevail? See Phil & Kathy's, Inc. v. Safra Nat'l Bank of N.Y., 595 F. Supp. 2d 330 (S.D.N.Y. 2009).

5. THE "MONEY–BACK GUARANTEE"

The general rule is that an originator owes the originator's bank the amount of the payment order when the bank accepts the payment order. 4A–402(c) (second sentence). But what if payment never reaches the beneficiary intended by the originator? That is, the "funds transfer" (4A–104(a)) is not completed. For example, the payment is made to the wrong beneficiary or not made at all. As between the originator and its bank, which should bear the risk of loss? The originator still owes the beneficiary, and, if it is liable to its bank as well, it may have to pay twice. We see that under the "money-back guarantee" rule of 4A–402(c) (last sentence), the policy decision is made that the originator is not liable to its bank, and, if it has already paid, it may recover the payment. 4A–402(d). But what if the originator designated that the transfer be made by the originator's bank through a specified intermediary bank, and it is that bank that is at fault or doesn't send the payment because it has suspended payments? The originator's bank is required by 4A–302 to follow the originator's instructions with respect to intermediary banks. See 4A–402(e).

The first authoritative holding on these matters is Grain Traders, Inc. v. Citibank, N.A., 160 F.3d 97 (2d Cir.1998). The facts are complicated. Grain Traders (GT), the Originator, issued a payment order to BCN, the Originator's Bank, to send $310,000 to Kraemer, the Beneficiary. GT instructed BCN to issue a payment order to Citibank, an intermediate bank, that held accounts for both BCN and BCIL. The payment order directed Citibank to: (1) debit BCN's account in Citibank for the amount of the transfer, (2) issue a payment order to BCIL, instructing it to transfer $310,000 to Extrader, the beneficiary's bank, to be credited to Kraemer's account in Extrader, and (3) credit BCIL's account in Citibank. Citibank accepted BCN's payment order by issuing a payment order to BCIL regarding the transfer to Extrader. Citibank then debited BCN's account and credited that of BCIL. BCIL did not accept Citibank's payment order by sending one to Extrader. Apparently this was related to BCIL's financial condition. GT's payment order was sent on December 22 and on December 31, BCIL "began closing its offices." Extrader also became insolvent late in December or early the next year. Since Kraemer was not paid, GT requested BCN to ask Citibank to return the money. BCN made the request, but Citibank did not return the money. BCIL owed Citibank money on dealings having nothing to do with the wire transfer; and, when it learned of BCIL's insolvency, froze its account. Hence, Citibank was able to tell BCN that it couldn't return the money because BCIL had insufficient funds in its account in Citibank. Citibank seemed to have a windfall, and GT brought suit against it to get its money back. GT still owed Kraemer, and BCN had been paid by GT, so GT was out $310,000. The court treated the case as an application of the "money-back guarantee" rule and held, by summary judgment, that GT sued the wrong party. Since the funds transfer was not completed, 4A-402(c) provides that GT's obligation to pay BCN was excused, and 4A-402(d) provides that, if BCN had already received payment, it was obliged to return the money to GT. As Comment 2 to 4A-402 points out, BCN then "has the burden of obtaining refund from the intermediary bank that it paid," Citibank. This would leave Citibank with the burden of establishing its rights against BCIL's receiver.

The court applauded the "money-back guarantee" rule as offering an orderly process for unraveling failed funds transfers, one that promotes certainty and finality. A receiving bank is liable only to its sender, with which it is presumably familiar, rather than to remote entities. All this is true, but there is more to it than that. The "money-back guarantee" rule affords the users, here GT and Kraemer, a measure of protection against bank insolvencies and, as we see in the next section, errors. GT gets its money back from its own bank and walks away, leaving to the banking system the cost of sorting out the ultimate responsibility for the loss. This has the effect of making the banking system internalize the costs of establishing the responsibility for these losses.

6. Garnishment

Creditors may garnish deposit accounts of debtors only so long as the funds remain in the deposit account. When Originator's Bank sends the funds to an Intermediary Bank, Originator's creditors lose their power to seize the funds. See Comment to 4A-503. This issue has assumed importance in cases in which foreign banks send funds through New York banks as intermediaries. In a disastrous opinion, Winter Storm Shipping Ltd. v. TPI, 310 F.3d 263 (2d Cir.2002), the court, relying on federal law, allowed a foreign originator's creditors to attach funds in the intermediary bank, the Bank of New York. Chaos ensued; hundreds of creditors of foreign companies lined up with attachment writs to grab funds being transferred by wire through New York intermediaries. The story is told in Clarks' Bank Deposits and Payments Monthly, Vol. 18, No. 10, Oct. 2009. *Winter Storm* was mercifully overruled seven years later by The Shipping Corp. of India LTD. v. Jaldhi Overseas Pet LTD., 585 F.3d 58 (2d Cir.2009), which found error in *Winter Storm* on the ground that that no federal law controlled and relied on 4A-503 of the New York Commercial Code and its Comment. The court remarked that the effects of that case on the federal courts and international banks in New York were too significant to avoid overturning a recent precedent.

NOTE: ARTICLE 4A AND COMMON LAW PRINCIPLES

The issue of the degree to which Article 4A displaces common law principles has probably been the most widely litigated issue in funds transfer cases. Section 1–103(b) allows courts to invoke principles of law and equity to "supplement" the provisions of the Code, unless "displaced by the particular provisions of this [Act]." Anyone who has participated as a drafter of UCC provisions becomes familiar with the persistent gripe of advisors that something more specific than 1–103(b) should be drafted to deter courts from ignoring the Code provisions that the courts don't like in favor of judicial remedies such as restitution, negligence, money had and received, and the like, that empower courts to reach results more in keeping with their notions of justice. This is particularly true in cases involving consumers. But there are no consumers affected by Article 4A; funds transfers amount to more than a trillion dollars a day. Hence, the final draft was a series of compromises made among powerful, well represented interests (money center banks, Board of Governors of Federal Reserve System, the New York Federal Reserve Bank, and giant corporate users), and these behemoths wanted some assurance that the bargained-for advantages that Article 4A gave them would not be taken away by courts using common law principles to change the intended meaning of the statute.

The result was the inclusion of Comment to 4A–102, quoted in part in *Grain Traders*:

> Funds transfers involve competing interests—those of the banks that provide funds transfer services and the commercial and financial organizations that use the services, as well as the public interest. These competing interests were represented in the drafting process and they were thoroughly considered. The rules that emerged represent a careful and delicate balancing of those interests and are intended to be the exclusive means of determining the rights, duties and liabilities of the affected parties in any situation covered by particular provisions of the Article. Consequently, resort to principles of law or equity outside of Article 4A is not appropriate to create rights, duties and liabilities inconsistent with those stated in this Article.

The plea by the drafters made in this Comment is that Article 4A is the result of long years of hard bargaining, and that the final draft is a good faith attempt to balance the various competing interests. It will come as no surprise to learn that the success of this Comment in taking the pen out of the judge's hand in order to assure Article 4A's displacement of the common law has been spotty. Some commentators see it as manifesting a touch of hubris on the part of the drafters. Some courts believe that common law principles can be applied in wire transfer cases so long as they are not "inconsistent" with specific Article 4A provisions. In a broad holding, Zengen, Inc. v. Comerica Bank, 158 P.3d 800 (Cal. 2007), the California Supreme Court relied on the quoted Comment in deciding that where the circumstances giving rise to the common law claims are specifically covered by the provisions of [Article 4A] these claims must be displaced. *Zengen* is followed by the Second Circuit in ReAmerica, S.A. v. Wells Fargo Bank International, 577 F.3d 102 (2d Cir.2009). The case law is fully analyzed in 2 Barkley Clark & Barbara Clark, Law of Bank Deposits, Collections and Credit Cards ¶17.01[1], ¶17.02[3] (Rev. ed. 2009). The authors conclude a long discussion by observing rather generously, in our view: "In all of these cases, the courts appeared to hold that (1) Article 4A does not preempt common-law causes of action in all cases, but that (2) preemption will be determined in each case by the extent to which the rules of Article 4A occupy the field covered by the particular common-law cause of action." The drafters did not expect more.

7. ERRONEOUS EXECUTION OF PAYMENT ORDERS

a. SENDING BANK'S ERRORS

A fertile field of litigation with respect to wire transfers is the case in which the receiving bank executes the sender's payment order by sending an erroneous payment order. In such cases, the general principle adhered to by Article 4A is that the sender is liable for its own errors. The subject is discussed in Richard F. Dole, Jr., Receiving Bank Liability for Errors in Wholesale Wire Transfers, 69 Tul. L. Rev. 877 (1995).

For illustration, assume these facts. Originator (O) instructs its bank, Originator's Bank (OB), to send $100,000 to the account of Beneficiary (B) in Beneficiary's Bank (BB). OB executed O's payment order by instructing its correspondent bank, Intermediary Bank (IB) (4A–104(b)), to pay BB as indicated in the cases below. With respect to the payment order, O, OB and IB are senders and OB, IB and BB are receiving banks, and BB is also the beneficiary's bank. Thus, the funds transfer looks like this:

O———OB———IB———BB———B

Work through these elementary problems:

Case #1. OB executed the payment order by instructing IB to pay BB $100,000 for the account of B. IB mistakenly instructed BB to pay $100,000 for the account of X.

a. Did IB execute the payment order of OB? 4A–301(a).

b. Is OB entitled to payment from O? 4A–402(c).

c. Is IB entitled to payment from OB? 4A–402(c).

d. Is BB entitled to payment from IB? 4A–402(b).

e. Is IB entitled to recover from X? 4A–303(c).

Case #2. OB mistakenly instructed IB to pay BB $200,000 for B's account. IB executed OB's payment order by sending the same payment order to BB. BB deposited the funds in B's account and B withdrew the money. What are OB's rights against O and B under 4A–303(a)?

b. DISCHARGE-FOR-VALUE RULE

Obligor instructed Bank A to pay $100,000 to Bank B for the account of X. Bank A mistakenly instructed Bank B to pay $100,000 for the account of Y. If Obligor owed a debt to Y in an amount in excess of $100,000, Y may claim that it is entitled to retain the funds under the discharge-for-value rule of the Restatement (First) of Restitution § 14 (1937), under which a creditor is under no duty to make restitution even though the third party sent the money by mistake, so long as the creditor had no notice that the payment order was erroneously made. Some courts decline to follow the rule and hold that the money can be retained only if the recipient changed its position in reliance on the mistaken payment. The court in Banque Worms v. BankAmerica Intn'l, 570 N.E.2d 189 (N.Y. 1991), adopted the discharge-for-value rule in a funds transfer transaction that went awry. Although the facts in that case occurred before enactment of Article 4A, the court viewed the rule as consistent with the policies of Article 4A. The court relied on Comment 2 to 4A–303 as showing that the drafters of Article 4A thought the discharge-for-value rule was appropriate in an analogous situation involving an erroneous payment order.

Finality of payment and the low cost of funds transfers are policy considerations that the *Banque Worms* court believed support the discharge-for-value rule. Cf. Credit Lyonnais N.Y. Branch v. Koval, 745 So.2d 837 (Miss.1999) (finality); Gen. Elec. Capital Corp. v. Cen. Bank, 49 F.3d 280 (7th Cir.1995) (finality and efficiency). Clearly, finality favors the rule. A beneficiary-creditor receiving funds can retain them as long as it received the funds without knowing or having notice that the payment was a mistake. Because detrimental reliance by the beneficiary is unnecessary, there are fewer occasions in which the transfer of funds will be disturbed than under a "mistake of fact" rule. In fact, finality favors allowing the recipient of a mistaken payment to keep it even if the recipient knew of the mistake.

In re Calumet Farm, Inc., 398 F.3d 555 (6th Cir.2005), is the first court of appeals analysis of the intricacies of precisely when discharge takes place in an overpayment case. In this case, the overpayment funds were received by the beneficiary's bank before the beneficiary learned of the overpayment, but the beneficiary did not *apply* them by crediting the originator's debt until after it learned of the error. In overruling the district court, the Sixth Circuit held that the discharge-for-value rule did not apply because the crucial time was not when the beneficiary received the funds but when it applied them to the originator's obligation. The court's rule probably limits the application of the discharge-for-value doctrine somewhat.

Whether the discharge-for-value rule optimally lowers the cost of funds transfers compared to the "mistake of fact" rule is a closer question. A receiving bank issuing a payment order faces a risk that its sender will be unwilling or unable to reimburse it for the amount of the order. Both rules allocate this credit risk as between the receiving bank and the beneficiary, but they do so differently. The discharge-for-value rule increases the credit risk to the receiving bank as compared to the "mistake of fact" rule because there are fewer circumstances in which it can recover the funds from the beneficiary. Given this risk, the receiving bank can take precautions to avoid making mistaken payments or simply increase the price of executing a payment order. The "mistake of fact" rule shifts the receiving bank's credit risk to the beneficiary when the beneficiary does not detrimentally rely on the mistaken payment. This increases the cost to the beneficiary of dealing with the sender, and the increased cost presumably will be reflected in the price the beneficiary demands from it. The discharge-for-value rule optimally lowers the cost of funds transfers only if the marginal costs to the receiving bank associated with the rule are less than the marginal costs to the beneficiary associated with the "mistake of fact" rule. In estimating these costs, it is significant that the beneficiary in *Banque Worms* was a creditor who had entered into a revolving loan arrangement with the sender-debtor. Such arrangements almost always require the creditor to monitor its debtor. If so, the marginal costs to the beneficiary-creditor of detecting a mistaken payment might be slight.

8. Failure of Receiving Bank to Execute Payment Order

Since payments of obligations in very large transactions are made through the funds transfer system, the potential for large consequential damages to flow from a receiving bank's failure to execute a payment order is great. One of the major policy decisions to be resolved in the drafting of Article 4A was whether receiving banks should be liable for consequential damages for failure to execute payment orders. Banking advisors saw this decision as crucial for their industry; they contended that they could not continue to offer cheap and fast service all over the world if they bore the risk of unlimited liability for consequential damages; imposition of such liability would force them to recast their industry in a form very different from the robust and flourishing enterprise it was at the time Article 4A was drafted. They relied for support of their position on the decision in Evra Corp. v. Swiss Bank Corp., 673 F.2d 951 (7th Cir.1982).

In *Evra,* Hyman–Michaels chartered a ship, the Pandora, from the ship's Owner under an agreement to make semi-monthly payments for hire in advance. If a payment was late, Owner could cancel the charter. Payments were to be made by deposit in the Banque de Paris in Geneva for the account of Owner. With the intention of making a periodic payment, Hyman–Michaels (Originator) issued a payment order to Continental (Chicago) to pay $27,000 to Banque de Paris in Geneva for the account of Owner. Continental (Chicago) executed the order by issuing a payment order to Continental (London) and debited the account of Hyman–Michaels in the amount of the order. Continental (London) executed the payment order of Continental (Chicago) by issuing a payment order to Swiss Bank in Geneva. Swiss Bank was instructed to issue a payment order to Banque de Paris to complete the funds transfer, but, for unknown reasons, failed to do so. Market conditions changed after the ship was chartered, and the hire payments required by the ship charter were below market rates. Because the beneficiary did not receive timely payment, Originator lost a valuable ship charter. The lower court awarded the Originator $2.1 million for lost profits even though the amount of the payment order was only $27,000. The appellate court reversed, in part on the basis of the common law rule of Hadley v. Baxendale that consequential damages may not be awarded unless the defendant is put on notice of the special circumstances giving rise to them. Swiss Bank did not have enough information to infer that if it lost a $27,000 payment order it would face liability in excess of $2 million.

PROBLEMS

1. How would the following case be decided under Article 4A? Under Article 4A, Hyman–Michaels is the originator of the funds transfer, Continental (Chicago) is the originator's bank, and Continental (London) and Swiss Bank are both "intermediary banks" (4A–104(b)). Each of the three banks is also a receiving bank with respect to the payment order it received. The duty of a receiving bank with respect to a payment order that it receives is stated in 4A–212. The duty of a receiving bank in executing a payment order is stated in 4A–302. The extent of liability of a receiving bank for late or improper execution or for failure to execute a payment order is stated in 4A–305. The right of the originator or other sender of a payment order to refund of amounts paid by them if the funds transfer is not completed is stated in 4A–402(c) and (d).

2. What is the policy basis of 4A–305's hard-hearted denial of consequential damages? Who is in the best position to evaluate the risk that a funds transfer will not be made on time and to manage that risk? The drafters' justification for 4A-305 is set out in detail in Comment 2 to 4A–305.

NOTE

Evra announces a default rule to the effect that a receiving bank is not liable for consequential damages resulting from its erroneous exclusion of a payment order unless it has notice of the type or extent of damage at the time it executes the order. Thus, to avoid liability for consequential damages, receiving banks with such notice must contract around the rule. Section 4A–305(d) rejects that part of *Evra*'s default rule allowing recovery when the bank has the requisite notice. Under 4A–305(d), consequential damages are recoverable from the receiving bank only "to the extent provided in an express written agreement." Comment 2 to 4A–305 judges that, to effect low-cost and speedy funds transfers, most receiving banks are in a comparatively poor position against their senders to reduce the risk of issuing erroneous payment orders. This may remain true even when the receiving bank has notice of special circumstances bearing on the type or extent of loss resulting from its erroneous execution of a payment order. See Comment 2 (paragraph 3) to 4A–305. If so, parties to most funds transfers, therefore, prefer to contract around *Evra*'s default rule. Section 4A–305(d) saves them the cost of having to do so because under it consequential damages aren't recoverable from the receiving bank without an express written agreement allowing recovery. Section 4A–305(d)'s default rule denying recovery of consequential damages, therefore. may optimally reduce contracting costs associated with funds transfers. Presumably 4A-305(d) requires opting out to be by "express written agreement" to reduce proof and other litigation costs incurred in establishing an agreement to opt out.

9. Fraudulent Payment Orders

A funds transfer is a very efficient method of payment. Large amounts can be transferred in a short time at low cost. But this great efficiency also provides a highly efficient method for the theft of money. The thief might steal funds in a bank account by fraudulently inducing either the bank or the owner of the account to make a wire transfer of the funds to an account controlled by the thief in some other bank. For example, the thief might electronically transmit to the bank a payment order purporting to be that of the owner of the account. If the bank is unaware that its customer did not send the order, the fraud can succeed. If the bank executes the fraudulent payment order, it has transferred funds on behalf of the customer without authority of the customer to do so. Who takes the loss? Has the thief stolen funds of the customer or funds of the bank? Under Article 4A, a receiving bank that executes a payment order is not acting as the agent of the sender. §4A–212. But if the bank executes an order that it believes to be the order of its customer but which in fact was issued by a person not authorized to act for its customer, should the law of agency determine whether the customer is bound by the unauthorized payment order issued in its name? If agency law applies, the customer is not bound by the unauthorized order, the bank has no authority to debit the customer's account, and the bank takes the loss.

But the law of agency is not very useful in determining whether the risk of loss with respect to an unauthorized payment order transmitted electronically should fall upon the receiving bank's customer, the purported sender of the fraudulent payment order, or the receiving bank that accepted it. The agency doctrines of actual, implied, and apparent authority grew out of cases in which the person purporting to be the agent and the third party acting in reliance on the acts of the purported agent have some personal contact with each other. These doctrines do not work well in cases in which a commercial transaction normally is carried out in the name of a principal by a person who is anonymous and who has no direct contact with the third person. In the case of electronic transmission of a payment order, the receiving bank is acting on the basis of a message that appears on a computer screen. There is no way of determining the identity or authority of the person who caused the message to be sent. The receiving bank is not relying on the authority of any particular person to act for its customer. Instead, the receiving bank relies on a security procedure pursuant to which the authenticity of the message can be "tested" by various devices such as identification codes or other security information in the control of the customer designed to provide certainty that the message is that of the customer identified in the payment order as its sender.

In the funds transfer business, the concept of "authorized" is different from the concept found in agency law. A payment order is treated as the order of the person in whose name it is issued if it is properly tested pursuant to a security procedure and the order passes the test. Risk of loss rules regarding unauthorized payment orders with respect to which verification pursuant to a security procedure is in effect are stated in 4A–202 and 4A–203. The general rule is that a payment order is effective as the order of the customer, whether or not authorized, if the security procedure is commercially reasonable and the receiving bank proves that it accepted the order in good faith after verifying the order in compliance with the security procedure. There are certain exceptions and qualifications to this rule that are explained in the Comments to 4A–203. The general rule is based on the assumption that losses due to unauthorized payment orders can best be avoided by the use of commercially reasonable security procedures, and that the use of such procedures should be encouraged. If a commercially reasonable security procedure is not in effect or if the bank fails to comply with a commercially reasonable procedure, ordinary rules of agency apply with the effect that, if the payment order was not authorized by the customer, the receiving bank acts at its peril in accepting the order.

The Article 4A rules are designed to protect both the customer and the receiving bank. A receiving bank needs to be able to rely on objective criteria to determine whether it can safely act on a payment order. Employees of that bank can be trained to "test" a payment order according to the various steps specified in the security procedure. The bank is responsible for the acts of these employees. The interests of the customer are protected by providing an incentive to a receiving bank to make available to the customer a security procedure that is commercially reasonable. Prudent banking practice may require that security procedures be utilized with respect to virtually all payment orders except for those in which personal contact between the customer and the bank eliminates the possibility of an unauthorized order. The burden of making available commercially reasonable security procedures is imposed on receiving banks because, generally. they determine what security procedures can be used and are in the best position to evaluate the efficacy of procedures offered to customers to combat fraud. The burden on the customer is to supervise its employees to assure compliance with the security procedure, to safeguard confidential security information, and to restrict access to transmitting facilities so that the security procedure cannot be breached.

Sections 4A–202 and 4A–203 were among the most contentious provisions in the drafting of Article 4A. Customers strongly believed that they should not be liable for unauthorized funds transfers; the banks control the security procedures and if a fraudulent payment order penetrates the security controls the bank should bear the loss. Bank representatives were just as firm in their belief that they could not transfer trillions of dollars a day all over the world at great speed in a highly automated process if they had to be concerned about whether the customer had actually authorized the payment order; if the payment order "tests," that is, meets their security procedures, they should be able to send the order without fear of liability. Sections 4A–202 and 4A–203 represent a compromise solution which satisfied neither side. Each time the authorization issue was discussed, customer representatives brought up the possibility that a brilliant hacker might crack even the most sophisticated security procedure and pull off the world's biggest bank robbery at the expense of the customer. Bankers said that it was tried every day and just couldn't be done.

PROBLEMS

1. Bank One received a payment order to send $1 million to Account #567891234 in Bank Two for Boniface, a customer of Bank Two. The originator's name on the payment order was SoCorp, a customer of Bank One.

The payment order complied with all security procedures agreed to by SoCorp and was accepted by Bank One and, subsequently, by Bank Two. Boniface disappeared after withdrawing the money from its account in Bank Two. When SoCorp learned of the transaction, it denied that it had authorized the payment order and demanded its money back from Bank One, which had deducted the amount of the transfer from SoCorp's account. An investigation showed that SoCorp did not authorize the payment order. As between SoCorp and Bank One, who should bear the loss of the funds that resulted from the fraud under 4A–202 and 4A–203? What additional information do you need before you can decide this case?

2. Under the heading "Cyber Caper," the Wall Street Journal reported that a 28–year–old Russian biochemistry grad student, "Vova," who worked for a trading company in St. Petersburg, broke into Citicorp's computers on Wall Street and, over a period of months, transferred about $12 million from customer's accounts to banks in Finland, Israel, the Netherlands, San Francisco and Switzerland, where his confederates attempted to withdraw the funds. They succeeded in getting $400,000 out before the accounts were traced and frozen. Since, according to the Journal article, Citicorp moves about $500 billion a day in funds transfers, Vova seemed almost restrained in his thievery. Customers of Citicorp in Buenos Aires and Jakarta were shocked to learn that unauthorized transfers had been made from their accounts. In order to get into Citicorp's computers, Vova had to penetrate a security system so sophisticated that industry experts said what he did was "almost impossible." William M. Carley & Timothy L. O'Brien, Cyber Caper: How Citicorp System Was Raided and Funds Moved Around World, Wall St. J., Sept. 12, 1995, at A1. Assume that Vova was a brilliant hacker who penetrated the security system without the assistance of anyone associated with Citicorp or its customers whose accounts were debited. As between the customers whose accounts were charged and Citicorp, where would 4A–202 and 4A–203 throw the loss in the Cyber Caper case?

By way of a postscript, when Vova was eventually extradited to this country, he pled guilty to charges of conspiracy to commit bank, wire and computer fraud. He admitted that he had used passwords acquired from "another Russian." Citibank doesn't know how the accomplice obtained the passwords, but there is no evidence that its employees were involved. Citibank has beefed up its security system since that time. Dean Starkman, Russian Hacker Enters Fraud Plea in Citicorp Case, Wall St. J., Jan. 26, 1998, at B9A.

10. Incorrectly Identified Beneficiary

When 4A–207 was conceived, the drafters had in mind the type of fraud transaction involved in the following Problem in which the name identifies one person and the account number identifies a different person. The hypothetical case set out in Comment 2 to 4A–207 is similar to this Problem.

PROBLEM

In the 1990s, billions of dollars flowed into stock and bond mutual funds; new funds sprung up daily. These developments caught the attention of Thief who reasoned that these novice funds were unlikely to be as fraud-sensitive as his old prey, commercial banks. Thief developed a new MO for mutual funds and he employed it with success in the following case: He impersonated Investor, who owned shares in a mutual fund (Fund) worth more than $1 million, by sending forged documents to Fund requesting redemption of $1 million of his shares and the wire transfer of these funds to Investor's account number 987654 in Dallas Bank. Thief preceded the redemption by agreeing to pay Coin Dealer $1 million for gold coins (impossible to trace) by wiring the funds to Coin Dealer's account in Dallas Bank. Fund was taken in by the impersonation and sent a payment order to Boston Bank requesting it to transfer $1 million to Investor as beneficiary to be credited to account number 987654 in Dallas Bank. Boston Bank carried out the instructions. When Dallas Bank received the payment order, designating the Investor as the beneficiary and the account number as 987654, it credited the designated account number that, of course, was the account of Coin Dealer, not Investor, who had no account in this bank. When Dallas Bank notified Coin Dealer of the credit, Coin Dealer released the gold coins to Thief who absconded. After Fund learned of the theft, it recredited Investor's account and sued Dallas Bank for return of the money, relying on 4A–207(b)(1), (c) and (d). Dallas Bank relied on a pre-Article 4A case, Bradford Trust Co. of Boston v. Texas American Bank-Houston, 790 F.2d 407 (5th Cir.1986), that held, on similar facts, that Fund should take the loss because it was the party in the best position to avoid the loss, it dealt directly with the impostor, and it sent the funds to the wrong account. What result under 4A–207? See Comments 2 and 3 to 4A–207.

Murphy's Law being what it is, one of the first cases to arise under 4A–207 was *Corfan* in which the account number identified *no one*.

Corfan Banco Asuncion Paraguay v. Ocean Bank

District Court of Appeal of Florida, 1998.
715 So.2d 967.

■ SORONDO, JUDGE.

Corfan Banco Asuncion Paraguay, a foreign banking corporation (Corfan Bank), appeals the lower court's entry of a Final Summary Judgment in favor of Ocean Bank, a Florida bank.

On March 22, 1995, Corfan Bank originated a wire transfer of $72,972.00 via its intermediary Swiss Bank to the account of its customer, Jorge Alberto Dos Santos Silva (Silva), in Ocean Bank. The transfer order bore Silva's name as the recipient and indicated that his account number was 010070210400 (in fact, this was a nonexistent account). Upon receipt of the wire transfer, Ocean Bank noticed a discrepancy in this number and before depositing the money, confirmed with Silva that his correct account number was 010076216406. Ocean Bank did not, however, inform Corfan Bank or Swiss Bank of the error. Once the correct number was confirmed by Silva, Ocean Bank accepted the wire transfer and credited Silva's account.

The next day, Corfan Bank became aware of the account number discrepancy and, without first checking with either Silva or Ocean Bank, sent a second wire transfer of $72,972.00 to Silva's correct account number at Ocean Bank. The second transfer order did not indicate that it was a correction, replacement or amendment of the March 22nd transfer. Because the information of the transfer was correct, it was automatically processed at Ocean Bank and was credited to Silva's account. Several days later, Corfan Bank inquired of Ocean Bank regarding the two transfers, maintaining that only one transfer was intended. By that time, Silva had withdrawn the proceeds of both wire transfers. When Ocean Bank refused to repay $72,972.00 to Corfan Bank, this litigation ensued. Corfan Bank proceeded on two claims, one based on the section 670.207, Florida Statutes (1995), which codifies as Florida law section 4A–207 of the Uniform Commercial Code (UCC), and one based on common law negligence. Ocean Bank answered denying liability under the statute and also contending that the negligence claim was precluded by the preemptive statutory scheme.

The trial court, emphasizing that Florida's adoption of the UCC sections concerning wire transfers did not abrogate the basic tenets of commercial law, found that Ocean Bank had not contravened § 4A–207 by crediting the erroneous March 22nd wire transfer to Silva's account. Finding that Corfan Bank was the party best situated to have avoided this loss, the court held that Corfan Bank must bear that loss and, therefore, the court granted Ocean Bank's motion for summary judgment as to count one (the UCC count). Additionally, the court dismissed count two (the negligence count).

We begin with a review of the exact language of § 4A–207(a):

> (a) Subject to subsection (b), if, in a payment order received by the beneficiary's bank, the name, bank account number, *or* other identification of the beneficiary refers to a nonexistent or unidentifiable person or account, no person has rights as a beneficiary of the order and acceptance of the order cannot occur.

Corfan Bank argues that this language is clear and unambiguous, where a name or bank account number, or other identification refers either to a nonexistent or unidentified person *or* a nonexistent account, the order *cannot* be accepted. Ocean Bank responds that such a "highly technical" reading of the statute is "contrary to commercial and practical considerations and common sense." It suggests that we look to the legislative intent and conclude that the "or" in the statute should be given conjunctive rather than disjunctive effect. We respectfully decline Ocean Bank's invitation to look behind the plain language of the statute and conclude that given its clarity it must be read as written.

In Capers v. State, 678 So.2d 330 (Fla. 1996), the Florida Supreme Court stated:

> [T]he plain meaning of statutory language is the first consideration of statutory construction. St. Petersburg Bank & Trust Co. v. Hamm, 414 So.2d 1071, 1073 (Fla. 1982). Only when a statute is of doubtful meaning should matters extrinsic to the statute be considered in construing the language employed by the legislature. Florida State Racing Comm'n v. McLaughlin, 102 So.2d 574, 576 (Fla. 1958).

Id. at 332.... These cases preclude the analysis urged by Ocean Bank. Although Ocean Bank's position has been noted in the legal literature,[4]

---

[4] One respected treatise on the Uniform Commercial Code analyzes the code provision, 4A–207(a), which is identical to the statute in question, as follows:

> The requirements of subsection 4A–207(a) are stated in the disjunctive. Thus, apparently, if the payment order name and bank account number provide an identifiable or known person but "other identification of the beneficiary" refers to a nonexistent or unidentifiable person or account, subsection 4A–207(a) is literally applicable. The express deference in subsection 4A–207(a) to subsection 4A–207(b) does not appear to resolve this conundrum. Subsection 4A–207(b) provides rules only for payment orders in which the beneficiary is identified "by both name and an identifying or bank account number" in the instance in which the name and the number identify different persons.
>
> *It does not appear that this anomaly in subsection 4A–207(a) was intended; nonetheless, the subsection 4A–207(a) suggests only one preventive mechanism for avoiding this conundrum: the sender should include no "other identification of the beneficiary" which might "refer ... to a nonexistent or unidentifiable person or account."* Then subsection 4A–207(a) would be harmonized with subsection 4A–207(b) as long as the name and account number refer to the same identifiable person or account. If they refer to different identifiable persons or accounts then subsection 4A–207(b) controls. If either the name or account number refers to a nonexistent or unidentifiable person then subsection 4A–207(a) is again applicable.

"unambiguous language is not subject to judicial construction, however wise it may seem to alter the plain language." *Jett*, 626 So.2d at 693. * * *

....

The Supreme Court of Florida has fashioned only one exception to this general rule: "[t]his Court will not go behind the plain and ordinary meaning of the words used in the statute unless an unreasonable or ridiculous conclusion would result from failure to do so." Holly v. Auld, 450 So.2d 217, 219 (Fla. 1984). The plain and ordinary meaning of the words of the statute under review do not lead to either an unreasonable or ridiculous result. As discussed more thoroughly below, one of the critical considerations in the drafting of Article 4A was that parties to funds transfers should be able to "predict risk with certainty, to insure risk with certainty, to adjust operational and security procedures, and to price funds transfer services appropriately." See 19A Fla. Stat. Ann. 15 (U.C.C. cmt. 1995). All of these goals are reasonable and assured by the plain statutory language.

In the present case, although the payment order correctly identified the beneficiary, it referred to a nonexistent account number. Under the clear and unambiguous terms of the statute, acceptance of the order could not have occurred. As the Florida Supreme Court stated in *Jett*:

> We trust that if the legislature did not intend the result mandated by the statute's plain language, the legislature itself will amend the statute at the next opportunity.

Jett, 626 So.2d at 693.

As indicated above, the trial court dismissed count two of the complaint which sounded in negligence. The court concluded that the statutory scheme preempts the common law remedy of negligence....

In addressing this issue we restrict our analysis to the pleadings and facts of this case. In pertinent part, count two reads as follows:

Ocean Bank owed Corfan Bank a duty of care to follow the accepted banking practice of the community, and to return the funds from the first transfer to Corfan Bank upon receipt due to the reference in the first transfer to a non-existent account number.

The duty claimed to have been breached by Ocean Bank in its negligence count is exactly the same duty established and now governed by the statute. Under such circumstances we agree with the trial judge that the statutory scheme preempts the negligence claim in this case and affirm the dismissal of

---

William D. Hawkland & Richard Moreno, Uniform Commercial Code Series, § 4A-207:01 (1993)(emphasis added).

count two.[5] We do not reach the issue of whether the adoption of Article 4A of the UCC preempts negligence claims in all cases.

We reverse the Final Summary Judgment entered by the trial court in favor of Ocean Bank as to count one of the complaint and affirm the dismissal of count two. We remand this case for further proceedings consistent with this opinion.

■ LEVY, J., CONCURS.

■ NESBITT, JUDGE, DISSENTING: [OPINION OMITTED.]

NOTE

In a case like *Corfan* in which the account number identifies no one, 4A–207 doesn't work as intended. Corfan Bank is responsible for the error and should bear the loss, but under the plain meaning of the statute, the court placed the loss on Ocean Bank. Section 4A–207(b) contains a drafting error and should be amended. One solution would be to amend subsection (b) by deleting the words in brackets and adding the underlined words as follows:

(b) If a payment order received by the beneficiary's bank identifies the beneficiary both by name and by an identifying or bank account number and the name and number [identify different persons] <u>do not refer to the same person</u>, the following rules apply:

(1) Except as otherwise provided in subsection (c), if the beneficiary's bank does not know that the name and number [refer to different persons] <u>do not refer to the same person</u>, it may rely on the number as the proper identification of the beneficiary of the order. The beneficiary's bank need not determine whether the name and number refer to the same person.

(2) If the beneficiary's bank pays the person identified by name or knows that the name and number [identify different persons] <u>do not refer to the same person</u>, no person has rights as beneficiary except the person paid by the beneficiary's bank if that person was en-

[5] We note that allowing a negligence claim in this case would "create rights, duties and liabilities inconsistent" with those set forth in § 4A-207. In a negligence cause of action, Ocean Bank would be entitled to defend on a theory of comparative negligence because Corfan Bank provided the erroneous account number which created the problem at issue and then initiated the second transfer without communicating with Ocean Bank. Section 670.207 does not contemplate such a defense. (Oddly enough, allowing Corfan Bank's negligence claim in this case might actually inure to Ocean Bank's benefit). As explained in the comment, one of the primary purposes of the section is to enable the parties to wire funds transfers to predict risk with certainty and to insure against risk. The uniformity and certainty sought by the statute for these transactions could not possibly exist if parties could opt to sue by way of pre-Code remedies where the statute has specifically defined the duties, rights and liabilities of the parties.

> titled to receive payment from the originator of the funds transfer. If no person has rights as beneficiary, acceptance of the order cannot occur.

Since subsection (a) is subject to (b), if subsection (b) were amended as indicated, that subsection would apply to a case like *Corfan* because the name on the payment order referred to Silva and the account number did not refer to anyone. Thus, the name and number did not refer to the same person. Subsection (b)(2) would control.

11. Bank-Customer Agreement

The issue taken up by *Regatos* has been hotly debated by funds transfer participants. Although Article 4 is drafted almost entirely as a default statute, courts have placed limits on what statutory rights of customers can be limited by agreement, and there are many cases on the issue. Article 4A has taken a more restrictive approach; certain provisions designated in the statute may not be varied by agreement. 4A-501. The question before the court in *Regatos* is whether there are other provisions of the statute (4A-505 in this case) that are so basic to the operation of the statute that courts should not allow agreements to vary them. Provisions reducing the one-year period in 4A-505 to a much shorter time are presumably present in most funds transfer agreements; hence, the clamor about the *Regatos* case as it has proceeded through the courts.

Regatos v. North Fork Bank

Court of Appeals of New York, 2005.
838 N.E. 2d 629.

■ ROSENBLATT, J.

The United States Court of Appeals for the Second Circuit, by certified questions, asks us whether a commercial bank customer can recover funds that the bank improperly transferred out of his account, even though he did not notify the bank of the unauthorized transfer until well after the time limit stated in his account agreement. This issue requires us to decide whether the one-year period of repose in our Uniform Commercial Code § 4-A-505 may be modified by agreement. We also resolve whether UCC 4-A-204 (1) requires the bank actually to send the customer notice of an unauthorized transfer in order to trigger the running of a "reasonable time" within the meaning of that section, or whether a private agreement to hold a customer's mail can allow constructive notice to start that period. These are questions of first impression in this Court, and apparently in every other court of last resort in states that have adopted the relevant statutes.

In accord with the United States District Court for the Southern District of New York, we hold for the customer on both questions. The one-year period of repose in UCC 4-A-505, governing the customer's time in which to notify the bank of the unauthorized transfer, may not be modified by contract. Furthermore, both the one-year statute of repose and the "reasonable time" referred to in section 4-A-204 (1), which determines the customer's ability to recover interest on the misallocated money, begin to run when the customer receives actual notice of the improper transfer.

I.

Tomáz Mendes Regatos held a commercial account with Commercial Bank of New York, the predecessor to North Fork Bank. His agreement with the bank required him to notify the bank of any irregularity regarding his account within 15 days after the bank statement and items were first mailed or made available to him.[1] The agreement did not provide for notice to him of electronic funds transfers, except to the extent those transfers appeared on his monthly statements. The bank adopted a practice of holding Regatos's bank statements rather than mailing them to him, and expected him to request the statements when he wanted to see them.

On March 23, 2001, the bank received a funds transfer order from someone it believed to be Regatos, but failed to follow agreed security procedures[2] to confirm the order. Without authorization, the bank then transferred $450,000 out of his account. On April 6, 2001, the bank received another transfer order, again failed to follow its security procedures and without authorization transferred an additional $150,000 out of his account. Together, these transfers represented most of the value of the account.

Regatos did not learn of the unauthorized transfers until he checked his accumulated account statements on August 9, 2001. The transfers were reflected on statements issued on March 23, 2001 and April 25, 2001, but the

---

[1] The relevant part of the account agreement stated that

"[t]he depositor will exercise reasonable care and promptness in examining such statement and items to discover any irregularity including, but not limited to, any unauthorized signature or alteration and will notify the Bank promptly in writing of any such discovery, and in no event more than fifteen (15) calendar days subsequent to the time that such statement and items were first mailed or available to the depositor. In those situations in which the depositor has authorized the Bank to hold his correspondence, this section shall apply as if the depositor received such statement on the date shown on the statement."

[2] The security procedures here involved nothing more than checking Regatos's signature against the signature on the faxed transfer order and calling him to confirm (*cf.* UCC 4-A-201 ["Comparison of a signature on a payment order or communication with an authorized specimen signature of the customer is not by itself a security procedure"]). Apparently, the bank did not require any password, even for large sums. Here, the bank compared the signature on the fax to its signature on file, but did not realize that the fax signature had been forged. The jury found that the bank did not telephone Regatos to confirm that the order was legitimate.

bank held these statements until he asked for them, following its standard practice in relation to him. He informed the bank of the unauthorized transfers on the day he learned of them, August 9, 2001.

When the bank refused to reimburse Regatos for the lost funds, he sued in the United States District Court for the Southern District of New York. In a comprehensive, well-reasoned opinion, District Judge Shira Scheindlin denied the bank's motion for summary judgment and held that the one-year statute of repose may not be shortened by agreement. The court ruled that, in any event, the 15-day notice period set by the account agreement was unreasonable and invalid. The Federal District Court further held that the UCC 4-A-505 period to notify the bank began to run when Regatos received actual notice of the error on August 9, 2001 (*Regatos v. North Fork Bank,* 257 F.Supp.2d 632 [S.D.N.Y.2003]).

A federal jury found in favor of Regatos. Following UCC 4-A-204, the court awarded him both the principal ($600,000) and the interest from the date the bank improperly transferred the funds.

The bank appealed, and the United States Court of Appeals for the Second Circuit determined that the legal issues necessary to dispose of the case were novel, important questions of New York law. The Second Circuit certified to this Court, and we accepted, the following questions:

> " Can the one-year statute of repose established by New York U.C.C. [ ] 4-A-505 be varied by agreement? If so, are there any minimum limits on the variation thereof (such as 'reasonable time') that estop [the bank] from denying Regatos recovery in this case? ...
>
> " In the absence of agreement, does New York U.C.C. Article 4-A require actual notice, rather than merely constructive notice? If so, can this requirement be altered by agreement of the parties and was such achieved here?" (*Regatos v. North Fork Bank,* 396 F.3d 493, 498-499 [Wesley, J.].)

We answer the first part of the first question "no," rendering the second part academic. We answer the first part of the second question "yes" and the second part of the second question "no."

II.

UCC 4-A-204 establishes a bank's basic obligation to make good on unauthorized and ineffective transfers and, with one exception, forbids any variation of that obligation by agreement. UCC 4-A-204 reads as follows:

> "(1) If a receiving bank accepts a payment order issued in the name of its customer as sender which is (a) not authorized and not effective as the order of the customer under Section 4-A-202, ... the bank shall refund any payment of the payment order received from the customer to the extent the bank is not entitled to enforce payment and shall pay interest on the refundable amount calculated from the date the bank received payment to

the date of the refund. However, the customer is not entitled to interest from the bank on the amount to be refunded if the customer fails to exercise ordinary care to determine that the order was not authorized by the customer and to notify the bank of the relevant facts within a reasonable time not exceeding ninety days after the date the customer received notification from the bank that the order was accepted or that the customer's account was debited with respect to the order. The bank is not entitled to any recovery from the customer on account of a failure by the customer to give notification as stated in this section.

"(2) Reasonable time under subsection (1) may be fixed by agreement as stated in subsection (1) of Section 1-204, but the obligation of a receiving bank to refund payment as stated in subsection (1) may not otherwise be varied by agreement."

Furthermore, UCC 4-A-505 provides that

"[i]f a receiving bank has received payment from its customer with respect to a payment order issued in the name of the customer as sender and accepted by the bank, and the customer received notification reasonably identifying the order, the customer is precluded from asserting that the bank is not entitled to retain the payment unless the customer notifies the bank of the customer's objection to the payment within one year after the notification was received by the customer." (UCC 4-A-505.)

Regatos argues that the one-year statutory period is an integral part of the bank's "obligation ... to refund payment" under UCC 4-A-204 (1) and so, pursuant to UCC 4-A-204 (2), "may not ... be varied by agreement." The bank and its supporting amici point out that the notice provision is in section 4-A-505, not section 4-A-204 (1), and rely on UCC 4-A-501 (1), which declares that "[e]xcept as otherwise provided ... the rights and obligations of a party to a funds transfer may be varied by agreement of the affected party."[5] The bank maintains that the customer's duty to notify the bank of the error before recovering misallocated funds is an "obligation" separate from that created by section 4-A-204 (1) and therefore modifiable.

We agree with Regatos's reading of the statutes. In context, the policy behind article 4-A encourages banks to adopt appropriate security procedures. Only when a commercially reasonable security procedure is in place (or has been offered to the customer) may the bank disclaim its liability for unauthorized transfers (UCC 4-A-202). Permitting banks to vary the notice period by

[5] In support of this position, the amici urge that article 4-A is not a consumer protection statute, especially considering that it applies solely to presumably sophisticated commercial parties. While this is true to some extent, the provision in section 4-A-204 refusing to allow parties to modify the bank's basic obligation to refund unauthorized transfer funds contradicts the amici's argument because the provision clearly protects consumers, even commercial consumers, from bearing the burden of this type of bank error.

agreement would reduce the effectiveness of the statute's one-year period of repose as an incentive for banks to create and follow security procedures.

While the issue is close, we cannot accept the bank's argument that the customer's responsibility to notify the bank of its error is modifiable. UCC 4-A-204 (1) states that "[t]he bank is not entitled to any recovery from the customer on account of a failure by the customer to give notification as stated in this section."[6] Accordingly, a bank has an obligation to refund the principal regardless of notice, provided such notice is given within one year in accordance with UCC 4-A-505 (*see* 3 James J. White & Robert S. Summers, Uniform Commercial Code § 22-4). Moreover, as the District Court pointed out, section 4-A-505 (the one-year notice period) appears in the "Miscellaneous Provisions" part of the article, not the parts touching upon substantive rights and obligations (*Regatos,* 257 F.Supp.2d 632, 644 n. 19). The period of repose in section 4-A-505 is essentially a jurisdictional attribute of the "rights and obligations" contained in UCC 4-A-204 (1). To vary the period of repose would, in effect, impair the customer's section 4-A-204 (1) right to a refund, a modification that section 4-A-204 (2) forbids.

Article 4-A was intended, in significant part, to promote finality of banking operations and to give the bank relief from unknown liabilities of potentially indefinite duration (*see Banque Worms v. BankAmerica Intl.,* 77 N.Y.2d 362, 371, 568 N.Y.S.2d 541, 570 N.E.2d 189). This legislative purpose does not suggest that those interests alter (or should alter) the statute's fine-tuned balance between the customer and the bank as to who should bear the burden of unauthorized transfers.

Therefore, we hold that the one-year repose period in section 4-A-505 cannot be modified by agreement. By notifying the bank on August 9, 2001, the day he received actual notice, and four or five months after the statements were available, Regatos acted either way within the year-long period of repose. This clearly satisfied the statutory requirement and he is entitled to recover at least his $600,000 principal.

III.

The Second Circuit next asks whether actual notice is required under article 4-A (or whether mere constructive notice will do) and, consequently, whether Regatos is also entitled to recover interest on the misdirected funds....

---

[6] "A customer that acts promptly is entitled to interest from the time the customer's account was debited or the customer otherwise made payment.... But the bank is not entitled to any recovery from the customer based on negligence for failure to inform the bank. Loss of interest is in the nature of a penalty on the customer designed to provide an incentive for the customer to police its account. There is no intention to impose a duty on the customer that might result in shifting loss from the unauthorized order to the customer" (UCC 4-A-204, Comment 2, reprinted in McKinney's Cons Laws of NY, Book 62 1/2 , UCC 4-A-204, at 622).

Even where customers enter "hold mail" agreements with their banks, the actual notice rule still applies. Just as the one-year notice limitation is an inherent aspect of the customer's right to recover unauthorized payments, the actual notice requirement provides the bedrock for the exercise of that right. Permitting banks to enforce "agreements" to accept constructive notice would defeat article 4-A's guarantee of recovery for unauthorized payments.

In response to the second certified question, we answer that article 4-A requires actual notice, and that this requirement cannot be varied by a "hold mail" agreement, neither to begin the statute of repose, nor to begin "reasonable time" under the account agreement. Regatos notified the bank of his loss within an indisputably reasonable time after receiving actual notice, and is therefore entitled to recover the interest on his lost principal (UCC 4-A-204).

Accordingly, the first part of certified question 1 should be answered in the negative and the second part not answered as unnecessary, and the first part of certified question 2 should be answered in the affirmative and the second part in the negative.

Chief Judge KAYE and Judges G.B. SMITH, CIPARICK, GRAFFEO, READ and R.S. SMITH concur.

Following certification of questions by the United States Court of Appeals for the Second Circuit and acceptance of the questions by this Court pursuant to section 500.27 of the Rules of the Court of Appeals (22 NYCRR 500.27), and after hearing argument by counsel for the parties and consideration of the briefs and the record submitted, certified questions answered as follows: the first part of question 1 answered in the negative, and the second part of question 1 not answered as academic; and the first part of question 2 answered in the affirmative, and the second part of question 2 answered in the negative.

NOTE

As the *Regatos* court recognizes, the question whether 4A-505's one-year rule is mandatory is "close." A strong argument can be made that it is only a default rule. Article 4A carefully identifies the mandatory rules within its scope. Section 4A-501 state that Article 4A's rules may be varied by agreement, "[e]xcept as otherwise provided in this Article." Mandatory rules are expressly provided in 4A-202(f), 4A-204(b), 4A-402(f), and 4A-404(c). Article 4A does not designate 4A-505's one-year rule as mandatory. Given that the interests of both financial instututitions and nonfinancial users of funds transfers were well represented in Article 4A's drafting (Comment 2 to 4A-102), the failure to deem 4A-505's rule mandatory suggests that it is a default rule.

More general considerations reinforce this conclusion. Mandatory rules typically are justifiable on either of two grounds: paternalism or market failure. Paternalism has no role in Article 4A's rules because parties to funds transfers covered by the Article are nonconsumers. Consumer funds transfers, instead, are covered by the EFTA and excluded from Article 4A's scope. 4A-108. Market failure can occur only when the contract governing a funds transfer produces negative externalities (costs created for nonparties to the funds transfer that are not internalized by either the sender of the payment order or the receiving bank). There is no reason to believe that a contractual provision reducing 4A-505's one-year period produces externalities. Instead, 4A-505, in effect, functions as a sort of statutory limitation on the sender's recoverable damages. Under the section, the sender cannot recover a payment made to the receiving bank if it fails to give notice of objection within a year after it received notice identifying the payment order. As such, the provision allocates the costs and benefits of the limitation between the sender and the receiving bank. Because neither paternalistic concerns nor externalities plausibly are implicated by such allocations, 4A-505's one-year rule is best treated as a default rule.

B. OTHER ELECTRONIC FUNDS TRANSFERS

1. ELECTRONIC FUND TRANSFERS ACT

Consumer electronic funds transfers are governed by the Electronic Fund Transfers Act of 1978, 15 U.S.C. § 1693 et seq., of 1978. Regulation E, 12 C.F.R. Part 205, issued by the Federal Reserve Board, prescribes regulations to carry out the purposes of the Act. Section 1693a(6) states that the "term 'electronic fund transfer' means any transfer of funds, other than a transaction originated by check, draft, or similar paper instrument, which is initiated through an electronic terminal, telephonic instrument, or computer or magnetic tape so as to order, instruct, or authorize a financial institution to debit or credit an account. Such term includes, but is not limited to, point-of-sale transfers, automated teller machine transactions, direct deposits or withdrawals of funds, and transfers initiated by telephone." "Account" is defined as meaning an account in a financial institution established for consumer purposes § 1693a(2). "Financial institution" includes banks, credit unions, and savings and loan associations. In short, the EFTA applies to any electronic fund transfer that authorizes a bank to debit or credit a consumer's account. Section 4A-108 provides that Article 4A does not apply to a funds transfer any part of which is governed by the EFTA. The Comment to 4A-108 states that the intent of that section is to make Article 4A and the EFTA mutually exclusive. Thus, the EFTA preempts any application of Article 4A to consumer transactions.

The EFTA requires full disclosure of the terms and conditions of electronic funds transfers involving the consumer's account (§ 1693c), written documentation to the consumer for each transfer, and periodic statements for each account of the consumer accessed by electronic funds transfers (§ 1693d). Periodic statements must be sent for each monthly cycle in which an electronic fund transfer has been made. (§ 205.9(b)).The periodic statement must show the name of the person paid. § 205.9(b)(1)(v). As we will see in the next chapter, the absence of the names of payees on bank statements is a major gripe of drawers of checks. Written authorization is required for any preauthorized transfers with a copy provided to the consumer when made § 1693e. Among the most important consumer protection provisions are those in §§ 1693f and 205.11 for error resolution. The consumer has 60 days after receiving its periodic statement or other documentation to give the financial institution oral or written notice of error. A financial institution may require the consumer to give written confirmation of an error within 10 business days after oral notice of error § 205.11(b)(2). Within 10 business days of receiving notice of error, the financial institution must determine if an error occurred and report the results of its investigation to the consumer within three days after completion of the investigation.

The financial institution must correct any error discovered within one business day after discovery of the error. If the financial institution is unable to complete its investigation within 10 days, it may take up to 45 days from receipt of the notice of error to investigate further but only if it provisionally recredits the consumer's account in the amount of the alleged error. The 45-day period may be extended to 90 days in certain cases. § 205.11(c). Acts constituting error include unauthorized transfers and billing errors by the financial institution. § 205.11(a). For violation of the error resolution provisions, the financial institution may be subject to treble damages under §§ 1693f(e) and 1693m. Consumer liability for unauthorized funds transfers is detailed in § 1693g and was discussed in detail earlier in this chapter in our comparison of credit cards (covered by the Truth in Lending Act) and debit cards (covered by the ETFA) with respect to unauthorized use. We noted there that the lesser protection accorded holders of debit cards under § 1693g, has been largely offset, at least for the time being, by the voluntary pledges of Visa, MasterCard and other networks to observe "zero liability" on the part of cardholders. Section 1693m prescribes civil liability for financial institutions that fail to comply with the Act.

2. AUTOMATED CLEARING HOUSE (ACH)

a. DIRECT DEPOSITS AND PAYMENTS

The Automated Clearing House (ACH) is an electronic network for direct deposits, direct payments and check conversions. It operates separately from the networks used for credit and debt card transactions. ACH was established by the National Automated Clearing House Association (NACHA), a non-profit organization, and is governed by the NACHA Operating Rules. Several thousand banks are members and a number of ACH regional clearing house associations serve as operators. Recurring direct deposits (credits) and direct payments (debits) have been made through the ACH system for several decades, but check conversions began only in 2000. Although NACHA is a private organization, Federal Reserve Banks serve as clearing house operators in most cases; the Electronic Payment Network, a private processor, serves as operator in the remaining cases. An ACH transaction is a low cost, value-dated electronic funds transfer between originating and receiving banks. NACHA reports that there were more than 18.2 billion ACH payments in 2008, an increase of 1.2 billion over 2007. By 2010 the ACH system rivaled the UCC Article 4 check collection process and the Visa and MasterCard credit-debit card networks for moving funds in consumer transactions.

A typical ACH recurring credit transaction is one in which an employer (Originator) pays its employees (Receivers) by direct deposits to their bank accounts. Suppose its employees have accounts in ten banks in the area. In such a case, the employer will prepare an electronic file with information concerning the bank accounts of each employee in which a deposit is to be made. This information will go to the employer's bank (Originating Depositary Financial Institution—ODFI) "in batches" that it then forwards to an ACH facility (ACH Operator). (The "batches" terminology is a holdover from the early years of ACH when magnetic tapes were used by the employer to send information to the bank—the information about all the employees was "batched" on a single tape.) The ACH performs its clearing house function by repackaging this information for each bank in which the employees have accounts, which it forwards to these banks (Receiving Depositary Financial Institution—RDFI). ACH allows the party initiating the transfer to time the dates when the payments will be credited to the employees' accounts by their banks (RDFI) and when the debits will be made to the originator's account in its bank (ODFI). After the ACH has determined the net balances between the employer's bank and the employees' banks, these banks will settle through the Federal Reserve System. Numerous government payments, such as social security and other benefits and pensions, are made in this manner. The ACH Operator charges a small per-transaction fee to both the ODFI and the RDFI.

Equally common is the recurring debit transaction. An example is one in which the debtor (Receiver) authorizes its creditor (Originator) to draw each month on its bank account to make its monthly mortgage payments. The mortgage lender Originator will prepare an electronic file giving information on all mortgagors whose payments are due on a given date and send this file to its bank (ODFI). The bank will forward this information in batches to an ACH Operator that will send the relevant information to each bank (RDFI) in which mortgagors have accounts. These banks will debit the mortgagors' accounts on the prescribed date. The mortgagee's bank (ODFI) will credit the mortgagee's account on that date and settlement between the banks will be made through the Federal Reserve System. Insurance premiums and other recurring payments are frequently made in this manner.

b. CHECK CONVERSION

In 2000, the sedate business of recurring ACH credit and debit transfers radically expanded. In that year, NACHA authorized one-time ACH debits to consumer bank accounts, and a series of developments generally referred to as "check conversions" remade the check payments world. The first is referred to as the one-time point-of-purchase (POP) transfer. The cashier who receives a check in payment for goods or services runs the check through a MICR reader and returns the check, marked void, to the purchaser. The MICR line contains the payor bank's routing number, the customer's account number, and the number of the check. From this point on, the check is treated merely as authorization for an ACH debit to the purchaser's account in the payor bank; funds are transferred on the ACH electronic network from the purchaser's account to that of the merchant. Thus, in a POP transaction, the check functions only as a source of information for the creation of the POP transfer.

Another check conversion product is the accounts receivable conversion transaction (ARC). Here, the purchaser buys on credit; when the invoice is received, it contains a clause authorizing the creditor to use the information on the purchaser's check to make an ACH debit transfer. When the creditor receives the purchaser's check, it uses the information from the check's MICR line to make the ACH transfer. Pursuant to NACHA rules, the check is stored for two years by the creditor. Comparable check conversion products are telephone sales (TEL) and Internet sales (WEB). In these cases, the purchaser authorizes the ACH transfer and provides the MICR line information on the telephone in TEL or on the Internet in WEB. See the Heller article, supra, for a discussion of these transactions.

In 2006, NACHA authorized Back Office Conversion (BOC) in a reaction to some of POP's perceived shortcomings. The BOC regime allows cashiers to accept paper checks from customers and have those checks processed later for

ACH transfers in the "back office." In POP, each cashier must have a scanner; in BOC, one scanner per store may be enough. Retail cashiers are often inexperienced owing to the high turnover. Placing the burden on them to deal with a POP scanner in a busy checkout line, while attempting to explain why a customer's check is being returned marked void, may lead to mistakes as well as unhappy customers. BOC not only solves these problems but also allows the larger merchants to outsource ACH check processing. In the competition between POP and BOC, smaller retail outlets tend to prefer POP while the larger ones elect BOC. Both POP and BOC check conversions have experienced huge growth. For instance, even with BOC competition, in 2006, there were 269.4 million POP transactions, but in 2007, there were 462.8 million transactions, up an astonishing 71.8% from the previous year. See Nadia Oehlson, Merchants Tackle Two Fronts with ACH Check Conversion, 2 Cards & Payments, No. 8 (Aug. 2008).

It is no wonder that check conversions have grown so rapidly: ACH has invented a better mousetrap. A merchant accepting a check might have to wait days before its account was credited under the Article 4 check collection process described in the preceding chapter. Under check conversion, in which the check merely serves as the information source for an ACH electronic transfer, the merchant's account may be credited the same day. By 2010, most noncash consumer retail payments had an electronic component: (i) credit and debit cards account for a large percentage of retail payments and these are processed through the Visa and MasterCard electronic network; (ii) direct electronic presentment and Check 21 payments account for a growing number of payments; and (iii) to the extent that retail purchasers still pay by checks, ACH check conversions are rapidly converting checks into ACH electronic payments.

c. WHAT LAW GOVERNS ACH TRANSFERS?

The NACHA Operating Rules govern every aspect of ACH payments. The substance of these detailed rules is beyond the scope of this course, but issues arise as to the extent that other payments laws that we deal with bear on ACH payments. The relationship of Article 4A to NACHA rules is explicitly set out in 4A-501(b), which provides that a "funds-transfer system rule" (NACHA) is effective even if it conflicts with Article 4A. See Comment 2.

As noted in the preceding section, the EFTA, which applies to "electronic funds transfers," defines the term as meaning "any transfer of funds, *other than a transaction originated by a check, draft, or similar paper instrument*, which is initiated through an electronic terminal."(emphasis added).15 U.S.C. § 1693a(6). The issue arose whether this provision excludes check conversions from the EFTA because they are originated by checks. The problem was removed when the definition of electronic funds transfers (EFTs) in 12 C.F.R. § 205.3(b)(2) was revised to include: "Electronic fund transfer[s] (i) This part applies where a check, draft, or similar paper instrument is used as a source of information to initiate a one-time electronic fund transfer from a consumer's account. The consumer must authorize the transfer." Clearly, both POP and ARC transactions are electronic funds transfers covered by Regulation E. Hence, the consumer safeguards discussed in the preceding section apply: authorization, limiting error resolution liability for fraudulent or unauthorized conduct; and disclosures. Extensive treatment of these subjects is found in 2 Barkley Clark & Barbara Clark, supra, ¶16.06 [12] et seq. (Rev. ed. 2009); and 3 James J. White & Robert S. Summers, Commercial Law § 22-3 (5th. ed. 2002). How courts will deal with NACHA products such as check conversions will be the stuff of future litigation. The extent to which courts will be influenced by the solutions worked out in UCC Article 3 and 4 remains to be seen.

d. DIGITAL CHECKS

As we have seen, the "back end" of the check processing system (in which checks clear and settle) has been greatly modernized by image technology. Most paper checks written by individual consumers and businesses are now converted to images early in the clearing process, resulting in substantial efficiency gains. Why not get rid of paper checks altogether? A study by the Federal Reserve Bank of Chicago, Digital Checks as Electronic Payment Orders, Nov. 17, 2009, proposes that consumers wishing to make a payment be able to do so by use of a hand-held smart mobile phone. They would access their address book for the name of the payee, select the amount and date and write their signature on the screen, just as buyers write signatures on screens at checkout counters. The software check program would then create a visual image of both the front and back of the check and automatically take a screen shot of the image. The screen-shot image would be identical to an image of a paper check. The program would then automatically transmit an encrypted version of the imaged check to the payee and the payee would would deposit it electronically into its own bank account. Such an electronification procedure could completely eliminate the remaining paper part of the check process by pushing the point of imaging all the way back to the check writer.

Check 21 replaced one form of paper with another, the substitute check, but it jumpstarted imaging, which has greatly overtaken substitute checks. As noted earlier, the Fed has been able to reduce its check processing centers from 45 to 1 at great cost savings. The 2010 study's contention is that by electronifying the front-end (from the drafting of the check until its delivery at the depositary bank) costs of transportation, printing and processing checks could be reduced dramatically. According to the study, in 2009, checks continued to be the second largest non-cash payment method in terms of the volume of payments (debit cards, 33 billion; transactions originated by checks, 24 billion; credit cards, 23 billion). P.12 n.26. So there are many potential digital check customers. Currently, the legal standing of digital checks must be based on private agreements; there is no statutory or regulatory foundation for them. Developments in payment devices in the past have been unpredictable; banks might find reason to object to digital checks while mobile phone manufacturers may cheer. A near certainty is that Congressional or state legislative action will not be forthcoming for a long period of gestation, and the Federal Reserve Board, a self-supporting agency, is not known for alacrity in giving up lucrative fields like check processing.

3. INTERNET PAYMENTS

a. PAYMENTS THROUGH ONLINE PAYMENT SERVICES

The Internet has become a powerful global medium for the sale of goods, the providing of services, particularly financial services, and information of all kinds. The volume of goods sold on the Internet is huge and growing. Online stock transactions are vast. A growing percent of mortgage loans originate online. The examples of the commercial use of the Internet are endless. Not only the largest merchants have Web sites but tiny boutiques do so as well. The electronic catalog function of the Internet is inexpensive and unbounded in territory.

The use of the Internet for remote shopping is well established. For a remote payments system to develop on a large scale, there must be a means of moving credit through the banking system. Leaving aside the wholesale funds transfer systems of Fedwire and CHIPS, the two means commonly used for this task are the credit card clearing and settlement systems (e.g., the Visa and MasterCard networks) and the automated clearing house (ACH) system that connects nearly all banks. By far, the most popular method of paying for consumer obligations incurred in Internet shopping is by credit cards.

Person-to-Person (P2P)

But what of cases in which the seller is not authorized to accept credit cards? Programs have been developed that allow person-to-person payments to be made online. The need arose out of the great success of online auction selling by eBay. Many of the noncommercial auction sellers on eBay, some of whom may have just cleaned out their attics, cannot be expected to be authorized credit card merchants. This is also true for some small merchants who sell by auction over the Internet. Online payment services companies have been created to meet the needs of these sellers. PayPal, founded in 1998, is the leader in online payments. The procedure is for online senders (buyers) and recipients (sellers) to set up accounts with an online payment service provider, e.g., PayPal. A sender's account may be funded from the sender's bank account through an ACH bank transfer, a credit or debit card, or check or money order. The sender can activate a transfer of funds from this account through the service company provider to another account holder of the company merely by sending an e-mail. After an online auction in which the sender makes a purchase, the payment, less a discount for the online payment service (usually about 2% of the amount of the transaction), is added to the recipient's account. If the recipient doesn't have an account with the online payments service at the time of the sale, the service may notify it that the sender's money has arrived and will be added to the seller's account when one is opened. Recipients may withdraw the money from their accounts by debit cards issued by the service provider, by credits to a credit card account, or by ACH transfers made to their bank accounts. PayPal is now owned by eBay; Google has entered the field. According to a 2009 PayPal fact sheet, its revenues for the first quarter of 2009 were $ 643 million, and it moved $16 billion during that period.

Even merchants who are authorized to accept credit cards sometimes prefer to use an online payment service because the costs of online payments made through the ACH batching system are lower than the charges made by the credit card networks for the clearing and settlement of credit card payments. For a discussion of the laws governing online payments, see Anita Ramasastry, Confusion and Convergence in Consumer Payments: Is Coherence in Error Resolution Appropriate?, 83 Chi.-Kent L. Rev. 813 (2008). In the future, interbank agreements may reduce the need for an intermediary such as an online payment service entity. For a detailed treatment of Internet person-to-person payments, see Melanie L. Fein, Law of Electronic Banking § 6.05[B] (2003 Supp.), and Clarks' Bank Deposits and Payments Monthly, Vol. 9, No. 9, at. 4, Mar. 2000.

b. ONLINE BANKING AND BILL PAYING

Banks are pressing their customers to do their banking and bill paying online. They have strong incentives to do so; most charge their customers fees for online payment services; online payment users tend to stay with their banks longer and hold higher balances; and a banking transaction completed over the Internet costs the bank only a penny, compared with 27 cents for an ATM and $1.07 for a teller. Some banks give premiums to customers who convert to online bill paying. Optimistic estimates are that as many as 70 million households use online banking, Nearly 70 Million Households Now Use Online Banking, Bus. J. Milwaukee, July 15, 2009, including four of five households with Internet access. All the customer need do is to go to her bank's Web site, create a user name and password and indicate which account is to be accessed. At this point, the customer can do just about anything online that can be done on a telephone: pay bills, transfer money between accounts, apply for credit cards, mortgages or other loans. Major banks are adding personal finance tools to allow customers to manage their money online. Customers avoid the monthly chore of writing checks to pay their bills; no more searching for stamps and licking envelopes; busy customers save time and banks make money.

Customers can use online bill paying to make payments to anyone having a bank account, and the payments can be scheduled a year in advance. Thus, at the beginning of the year, a customer can schedule all recurring payments to be made during the year; can keep her money in interest bearing savings accounts until the time of payment when the money can be transferred into a checking account; and can get a confirmation on the screen for every transaction. A problem is that a transfer can be made electronically only to a payee whose bank and account number are known either to the customer or the payor bank. To meet this problem, banks have signed up large numbers of businesses that are prepared to accept electronic payments to their accounts. Thus, in the usual case of a payment to a business, all the customer has to be sure about is the name and address of the payee, for the bank will know its account number. In cases in which the databank does not contain the payee's account number and the payee has not provided that number to the customer, payment may be made by the customer's bank's sending that person a paper check drawn on the customer's account. This must also be done when the payee is not equipped to receive electronic payments. Some large organizations outsource their bill paying function to companies that maintain large directories (the "yellow pages").

An alternative method of online bill paying is to accept the invitation of a growing number of companies that encourage debtors to pay their bills directly at the biller's Web site by authorizing the biller to charge the debtor's bank account or credit card. After giving the biller the information about the debtor's bank account or credit card to be charged the first time a payment is made, subsequently, all the debtor has to do is to click the "pay" button on the biller's Web site and the money is withdrawn from the bank account or charged to the credit card. Clearing can be done through the ACH system if a credit card is not used. The downside of direct billing is that the debtor must visit each Web site in order to pay. Customers can also arrange for automatic deductions to pay periodic bills.

There is wide-spread belief that online bill paying will not replace checks until the industry has incorporated electronic bill presentment or delivery as a feature of online bill paying. At present, the customer usually receives bills by mail, but systems have been developed in which bills are received online. These systems turn paper bills into electronic bills if the customer arranges for her bills to be sent to a processing facility. This enables customers, having been alerted by a message "You have bills," to log onto a Web site and view any bills that had been presented; payment can be made by a click. Electronic bill presentment is regarded as likely to lead to much broader acceptance of computer banking.

4. STORED VALUE OR PREPAID CARDS

The plastic cards that we call credit or debit cards are merely bearers of information encoded in machine readable form on a magnetic strip on the back of a card. A stored value (or "prepaid" or "value-added") card uses a computer chip or magnetic strip to hold information that allows the cardholder to make purchases. More recent stored value cards ("smart" cards) use computer chips that reliably retain information and allow encryption to avoid duplication or unauthorized use of the card. Long used in Europe and Asia, "smart" cards are less used in the United States. In Hong Kong, they are used in subways, movie theaters, parking meters, and even McDonald's, as well as for security purposes at schools and residential complexes. Stacy Forster, Smart Cards Escape the U.S. Mind, Wall St. J., July 16, 2002, at D2. Because they can store large quantities of information, their potential use is unlimited. "Smart" cards can serve as a health insurance card, containing the patient's medical records, or as electronic "dog tags" for soldiers. China used these cards to allow their security authorities to store personal information about its citizens on ID cards with embedded microchips. Andrew Batson, China Orders Up a Billion Smart Cards, Wall St. J., Aug. 12, 2003, at A10.

When used as a means of payment, the cards store a "value" of funds available for the cardholder's use. The balance of funds recorded on the card is debited at the merchant's terminal when the cardholder makes a purchase. Stored value cards, therefore, serve as substitutes for cash, although the information stored on the cards is not itself cash. Use of the card does not transfer funds to the merchant, it only transfers information telling it of its right to be paid by the card sponsor. Stored value cards are extensively treated in Donald I. Baker & Roland E. Brandel, The Law of Electronic Fund Transfer Systems, Chapter 9 (1988, Cum. Supp. 1995), and in 2 Barkley Clark & Barbara Clark, The Law of Bank Deposits, Collections and Credit Cards ¶ 16.07 (Rev. ed. 2009).

Our interest in stored value cards is in their function as cash substitutes. Stored value card systems are of two basic sorts: "online" and "off line" systems. The stored value card systems differ as to whether transactions are made with or without communication with a central data facility operated by the system provider. "Online" systems process use of the card by communication from the facility giving authorization for a transaction. A record of the balance of funds available to the cardholder is maintained only at a central data facility. Off line systems involve card use without contact with a central data facility. These systems differ, in turn, according to where the primary record of the balance of funds on the card is maintained. If the primary record is maintained at a central data facility, the system is considered an off line "accountable" system. If the primary record is maintained on the card itself, the system is an off line "unaccountable" system. Almost all stored value card systems currently in use are off line unaccountable systems.

A simple example of card use in an off line unaccountable system is one in which the card is "loaded" with a sum of money, say $500, that the cardholder can use to purchase goods or services from participating merchants, telephone companies, transit systems and the like. The cardholder obtains the card by buying it from a bank teller, retailer, or by using a bank dispenser by inserting money or an ATM or credit card. It is disposable; when used up, it is worthless and may be thrown away. If the cardholder makes a purchase from a merchant, no identification is sought; the card has its own verification and passwords. The merchant deducts the sale price by running the card through a terminal. The balance record contained in the card in turn is reduced by the amount of the sale price and is ascertainable by ATM or POS terminals. (In an off line accountable system, the primary balance record is reduced at the central data storage facility as well.) The merchant aggregates balances stored in its transaction records, usually on a daily basis, and transmits them electronically in a batched transmission to the system provider. Upon verifying the validity of the transmission, the provider transfers funds to the merchant equal to the aggregate amount of the transmissions minus a discount fee reflecting the system provider's expenses. At least with respect to the cardholder and participating merchant, the card is a complete substitute for cash.

More sophisticated cards may be "reloadable" by accessing the cardholder's bank account through an ATM machine or the Internet. They may be online through the use of ATM or POS terminals and, like debit cards, the cardholder's bank account is debited upon use. However, until reloaded, these cards can transfer value only to the extent of the amount stored on the card. College students are familiar with these cards because a growing number of universities have combined them with the student's identification card, allowing the student to make on-campus purchases. Credit card companies have developed technologies that allow consumers to download dollar amounts from their bank accounts onto the cards.

The question facing banks and merchants is whether the potential for stored value cards justifies the costs of converting from the present magnetic strip technology to one that will accommodate these cards. If sufficiently high volume can be obtained, banks may profit handsomely from stored value cards by the "float," that is, having cardholder's money until the card is used up, by charging fees from participating merchants, and by keeping the few cents left on the card when the cardholder discards it. (In principle, competitive pressure could force card providers to pay interest on unused funds deposited with the provider, thus reducing profit from the "float.") As is true with the introduction of any new operational technology, the chicken-and-egg dilemma arises: banks and merchants would prefer not to convert to stored value cards until there are enough customers to promise ultimate profitability; customers would like not to go to the trouble of obtaining stored value cards until enough providers of goods and services are prepared to accept them.

Stored value cards have had a slow start in this country. Banks made a major promotional effort to popularize them in connection with the 1996 Olympic Games in Atlanta. They signed up merchants with some 1500 retail outlets, mostly fast food outlets and gas stations, and the Atlanta transit system. There results were encouraging but hardly a gold medal performance. Nikhil Deogun, The Smart Money is on "Smart Cards," but Electronic Cash Seems Dumb to Some, Wall St. J., Aug. 5, 1996, at B1. In 1997, VisaUSA, MasterCard International, Citibank and Chase Manhattan distributed 80,000 stored value cards to New Yorkers on Manhattan's Upper West Side; 700 merchants signed up to accept them. In 1998 they ended the program, citing little support from consumers and merchant complaints of slow processing. Brian Tracey, The Color of Money, Wall St. J., Nov. 16, 1998, at R28. Smart cards have been more successful in continental Europe, where governments along with some banks have ensured demand by installing pay telephones, bus-ticket machines and parking meters that accept (sometimes exclusively) smart cards. In America and Britain, where such decisions are more decentralized, guaranteeing demand for smart cards is harder. Keep the Change, Economist, Nov. 21, 1998, at 73.

In the article cited above, Stacy Forster concludes that so far, stored value cards have been a failure in the U.S. in part because retailers have been reluctant to install the higher-end processing equipment necessary to read them. He refers to the Upper West Side flop and the view of Americans that the cards have to do more than serve as cash-substitutes before they will embrace them. Kathy Chu, Prepaid Cash Cards Win Fans but Struggle to Make Impact, Wall St. J., Sept.10, 2003, at B4, chronicles the lack of success of prepaid, reloadable cash cards aimed at teenagers and college students. Things may change. Prepaid cards may become popular with college students (or their parents) after the Credit Card Accountability, Responsibility and Disclosure Act, Pub.L. No. 111-24 (2009), has made it more difficult for them to be approved for credit cards. Will Hernandez, New Law May Increase Use of Prepaid Cards Among Students, Am. Banker, Sept. 1, 2009, at 7.

"Payroll cards" have become popular. Employers arrange with a bank to issue employees a magnetic stripe-back card that accesses an account. Each payday, the employer credits the account for the amount of the employee's compensation. The employee may access the account at an ATM or make purchases from merchants in the same manner that they would with debit cards. This allows employees who do not have bank accounts to avoid having to cash paychecks at check cashing agencies that charge hefty fees. Giant Wal-Mart is moving toward making all payroll payments either by payroll debit cards or direct deposits to the employee's bank account. Miguel Bustillo, Wal-Mart to Pay Via Check Cards, Wall St. J., Sept. 3, 2009, at B6. Effective July 1, 2007, Fed regulations brought payroll card transactions within Regulation E. 71 FR 1437 (January 10, 2006). The regulation is discussed in 2 Barkley Clark & Barbara Clark, The Law of Bank Deposits, Collections and Credit Cards, ¶ 16.07 [5] (Rev. ed. 2009).

5. UNIFORMITY AND DIVERSITY IN PAYMENT SYSTEMS

Payment by check, credit or debit card, wholesale wire transfer or letter of credit occurs through different payment systems. Current law adopts separate rules depending on the payment system. Thus, the allocation of loss from unauthorized payment, erroneous payment, and the reversibility of instructions to pay varies according to whether payment is made by check, credit or debit card, wholesale wire transfer or letter of credit. (1) *Unauthorized payment*: If unauthorized payment is by check, funds transfer or letter of credit, the drawer, originator and applicant generally are not liable for the payment. 4-401(a). 5-108(i), 4A-202(a)-(b). Unauthorized payment by credit card leaves the cardholder with a maximum liability of $50 and the debit card holder with a maximum liability of $500. 15 U.S.C. §§1643(a) and 1693g(a). Different notions of authorization applicable to these payment devices result in different allocations of loss for unauthorized payments, as do different limitations on the recovery. (2) *Payment error*: Rules governing errors in payment are more uniform across payment systems. As between the owner of an account erroneously charged and the payment provider, the latter generally bears the risk of errors in the transfer of payment. Cf. 4-209, 4A-303, 5-111(i), 15 U.S.C. §§ 1666(a)-(b), and 15 U.S.C. 1693f(a).

(3) *Reversibility of payment instruction*: Reversibility allows the owner of the account to shift the risk of its dissatisfaction with the underlying transaction to the system provider or merchant. Denial of reversibility leaves the risk with the account owner. Reversibility rules differ significantly between payment systems and sometimes even within a system. Payment by cash, for example, does not allow reversibility: the payor must pursue the merchant to retrieve the cash paid. The drawer of a check may stop payment on its account if it gives the drawee timely notice. However, the dissatisfied buyer cannot countermand payment of a cashier's or teller's check. 4-402 and 3-411. Senders of wire transfers can cancel or amend their payment orders if their instruction to do so leaves the receiving bank a reasonable opportunity to act. 4A-211(b). By contrast, applicants of letters of credit can prevent their issuers from paying against complying presentations only in narrowly defined circumstances. 5-109(a). A credit card user can countermand its instruction to the credit card issuer to pay a seller, depending on the natures of the

underlying dispute, the location of the transaction, and the extent to which the user has notified the card issuer of the dispute. 15 U.S.C. § 1666i(a). By contrast, a consumer debit card user has no similar right. 15 U.S.C. § 1693f. Her right to have her account recredited is greater than the right of a cash buyer to retrieve her cash (none) but more limited than the right of a credit card user to have her account recredited.

Some scholars believe that the main rules in payments law should be the same. In their view, payment systems differ merely in the technology they use to transfer value. Applicable legal rules, therefore, should not vary according to the payment system a user happens to select. See, e.g., Ronald J. Mann, Making Sense of Payments Policy in the Information Age, 93 Geo. L.J. 633 (2005); Fred H. Miller, A Report on the New Payments Code, 39 Bus. Law. 1215 (1984). This view led to the drafting of the proposed (but not adopted) 1983 Uniform New Payments Code and remains influential. A case against uniform payment systems rules nonetheless can be made. The following is based on Clayton P. Gillette & Steven D. Walt, Uniformity and Diversity in Payments Systems 83 Chi-Kent L. Rev. 499 (2008).

Diverse legal rules among payment systems offer users a choice. Users can select the payment device to suit the underlying transaction of which it is a part. Payment systems themselves entail multiple risks, each of which is likely to be priced into the transaction. Accordingly, as with any contract term, parties choose a payment device to optimally minimize these risks. The device that optimally minimizes their risks, in turn, depends on their preferences and abilities to control or shift them. From this perspective, payment systems can be thought of as "products," each consisting of rules allocating the risk of unauthorized payment, payment error and reversibility of payment instructions, among others. Parties select from a menu of different products the product suitable for their transaction. Uniformity among payment system "products" creates standardization, and standardization has benefits. It saves users the cost of having to learn about the different legal rules associated with each payment system. Confusion, therefore, is also avoided. But standardization has a significant cost: it makes selection of a payment device tailored to particular transactions costly. A shopper in the market for a car would not be happy being offered a choice among "uniform" cars. This is part of what makes Henry Ford's statement about his Model T customers' choice of color amusing: "Any customer can have a car painted any color he wants so long as it's black." Just as the customer might want a color other than black, a payment system user might prefer to select among a menu of payment devices with different risk allocations.

Payment systems law consists primarily of default rules: Parties for the most part can alter applicable rules to suit their preferences. The range of preferences and transactions makes it unlikely that a uniform set of default rules suits the majority of transactors. Deviating from a uniform set of defaults arguably is more expensive than selecting the desired defaults from within a menu of different payment systems defaults. This is not to say that existing payment rules provide the optimal degree of diversity. However, the optimal degree of diversity is likely to be above zero. For instance, a buyer might be particularly concerned about fraud or error in the underlying transaction. Payment by check allows a period of time in which to issue a stop payment order (short with electronic check collection); payment by credit card allows a charge-back within a billing cycle. By contrast, payment by debit card, cash or letter of credit do not generally allow reversibility in similar circumstances. In addition, different transaction structures might warrant different allocations of relevant payment risks. A long-distance sale of goods may call for different payment rules than the rules applicable in a face-to-face transaction. Finally, different transactors might be concerned differently with credit risk. Checks put the risk of the drawer's insolvency on the payee, at least initially. Debit and credit cards, as well as letters of credit, avoid that risk. For these reasons, a menu of different payment devices with separate rules allows transactors to choose the rules that suit their preferences.

The case for diversity comes with two caveats. Neither undermines the case. First, there might be objectives other than efficient risk bearing that payment systems law properly should take into account. For instance, an efficient risk allocation might systematically burden vulnerable social groups that deserve protection. These concerns could justify a uniform mandatory rule applicable across payment systems used by these groups. However, this possibility leaves unaffected diverse payments systems rules that apply to all other transactors. Second, consumer protection might also justify special rules. There is an ongoing debate about the tendency of consumers to make systematic cognitive errors and the ability of payment systems operators to take advantage of them. Orin Bar-Gill, Seduction by Plastic, 98 Nw. U .L. Rev. 1373 (2004); Jon D. Hanson & Douglas A. Kysar, Taking Behavioralism Seriously: The Problem of Market Manipulation, 74 N.Y.U.L. Rev. 630 (1999). The capacity of legal rules to identify these disabilities and to track them over time is questionable. As important, special consumer protection rules can work to benefit some consumers at the expense of others. For example, the TILA rule limiting a consumer credit cardholder's $50 maximum liability for unauthorized use of his credit card subsidizes the negligent cardholder at the expense of the non-negligent cardholder. Even if workable and defensible, uniform payment system rules protecting consumers remain consistent with diverse rules for nonconsumer transactors.

CHAPTER 5

FRAUD, FORGERY, AND ALTERATION

A. FORGERY

1. ALLOCATION OF LOSS BETWEEN CUSTOMER AND PAYOR BANK

a. INTRODUCTION

Suppose Customer has a checking account in Payor Bank. Thief steals Customer's checkbook, writes a check payable to Payee, and signs Customer's name to the check as drawer. Because Thief was not authorized to sign Customer's name, the signature is ineffective as the signature of Customer unless some provision of Article 3 or Article 4 makes it effective. 3–403(a). Since Customer did not sign the check and did not authorize Thief to sign the check, Customer is not liable on the check. 3–401(a). The check, however, is not a nullity. Although it is not Customer's check, Article 3 treats it as Thief's check even though Thief signed it by using Customer's name. 3–403(a) and 3–401(b). Checks such as the check in this example, i.e., a check bearing a forged drawer's signature, are known as "forged checks." Such checks are sometimes transferred for value and paid by the drawee bank. Rights of a holder with respect to such checks can be acquired by persons who take them.

A more common type of forgery can be illustrated by the following example. Customer writes a check to the order of Payee, signs it as drawer, and mails it to Payee. Thief steals the check from Payee, indorses the check by signing Payee's name on the back of the check, and obtains payment of the check from Payor Bank. The check in this example is not a forged check because Customer's signature was not forged. Rather, the infirmity of the check is that it bears a "forged indorsement." Under 3–403(a) and 3–401, the signature by Thief is ineffective as the indorsement of Payee. Since Payee did not indorse the check, Thief cannot negotiate the check and no one can obtain rights as a holder unless some provision of Article 3 otherwise provides. 3–201(b) and 3–109(b).

What are the rights of Customer and Payor Bank toward each other if Payor Bank pays the forged check in the first example or the check bearing the forged indorsement in the second example? Under 4–401(a), a payor bank "may charge against the account of a customer an item that is properly payable from that account" and, to be properly payable, the check must be "authorized by the customer." Thus, in the case of the forged check, the Payor Bank may not debit Customer's account and is not entitled to reimbursement from Customer. The risk of loss falls on Payor Bank even though it may have had no way of discovering the forgery.

The result is the same in the case of the check bearing the forged indorsement. By the terms of the check, Payor Bank was ordered by Customer to pay the check to the order of Payee. Since Payee did not receive payment and did not order payment to anybody else, Payor Bank did not comply with the terms of the check. Since Payor Bank did not pay a holder or other person entitled to receive payment, it has no right to reimbursement from Customer.

The general rule protecting Customer from loss from forgery is changed in some cases by other provisions of Article 3 or Article 4. Two of the most important provisions that may allow Payor Bank to shift the forgery loss to Customer are 3–406(a), discussed in *Thompson Maple Products,* and 4–406, discussed in *Espresso Roma*.

b. NEGLIGENCE OF CUSTOMER CONTRIBUTING TO FORGERY

With respect to payment by a payor bank of a forged check or a check bearing a forged indorsement, if the bank can prove a failure by the customer to exercise ordinary care that substantially contributed to the making of the forged signature, the customer is precluded from asserting the forgery. 3–406(a). "Ordinary care" is defined in 3–103(a)(9). The leading case on the meaning of the words "substantially contributes to...the making of a forged signature" in 3–406(a) is *Thompson Maple Products,* the case that follows. Comment 2 to 3–406 discusses the meaning of the quoted words. In the absence of proof of negligence by the bank contributing to the loss, the effect of the preclusion is to give to the bank a right to reimbursement from the customer for the amount paid on the check. Under former 3–406, discussed in *Thompson Maple Products,* the preclusion against the customer did not occur if the bank was negligent in paying the check. This result is changed by Revised 3–406. Negligence by the bank does not prevent the preclusion from arising but, under subsection (b), the loss from the forgery can be apportioned between the negligent customer and the negligent bank.

Thompson Maple Products, Inc. v. Citizens National Bank

Superior Court of Pennsylvania, 1967.
234 A.2d 32.

■ HOFFMAN, JUDGE.

....

The plaintiff [Thompson Maple Products] is a small, closely-held corporation, principally engaged in the manufacture of bowling pin "blanks" from maple logs. Some knowledge of its operations from 1959 to 1962 is essential to an understanding of this litigation.

The plaintiff purchased logs from timber owners in the vicinity of its mill. Since these timber owners rarely had facilities for hauling logs, such transportation was furnished by a few local truckers, including Emery Albers.

At the mill site, newly delivered logs were "scaled" by mill personnel, to determine their quantity and grade. The employee on duty noted this information, together with the name of the owner of the logs, as furnished by the hauler, on duplicate "scaling slips."

In theory, the copy of the scaling slip was to be given to the hauler, and the original was to be retained by the mill employee until transmitted by him directly to the company's bookkeeper. This ideal procedure, however, was rarely followed. Instead, in a great many instances, the mill employee simply gave both slips to the hauler for delivery to the company office. Office personnel then prepared checks in payment for the logs, naming as payee the owner indicated on the scaling slips. Blank sets of slips were readily accessible on the company premises.

Sometime prior to February, 1959, Emery Albers conceived the scheme which led to the forgeries at issue here. Albers was an independent log hauler who for many years had transported logs to the company mill. For a brief period in 1952, he had been employed by the plaintiff, and he was a trusted friend of the Thompson family. After procuring blank sets of scaling slips, Albers filled them in to show substantial, wholly fictitious deliveries of logs, together with the names of local timber owners as suppliers. He then delivered the slips to the company bookkeeper, who prepared checks payable to the purported owners. Finally, he volunteered to deliver the checks to the owners. The bookkeeper customarily entrusted the checks to him for that purpose.

Albers then forged the payee's signature and either cashed the checks or deposited them to his account at the defendant bank, where he was well known....

In 1963, when the forgeries were uncovered, Albers confessed and was imprisoned. The plaintiff then instituted this suit against the drawee bank, asserting that the bank had breached its contract of deposit by paying the checks over forged endorsements....

The trial court determined that the plaintiff's own negligent activities had materially contributed to the unauthorized endorsements, and it therefore dismissed the substantial part of plaintiff's claim. We affirm the action of the trial court.

Both parties agree that, as between the payor bank and its customer, ordinarily the bank must bear the loss occasioned by the forgery of a payee's endorsement.

....

The trial court concluded, however, that the plaintiff-drawer, by virtue of its conduct, could not avail itself of that rule, citing § 3–406 of the Code: "Any person who by his negligence substantially contributes to.... the making of an unauthorized signature is precluded from asserting the.... lack of authority against.... a drawee or other payor who pays the instrument in good faith and in accordance with the reasonable commercial standards of the drawee's or payor's business."

Before this Court, the plaintiff Company argues strenuously that this language is a mere restatement of pre-Code law in Pennsylvania. Under those earlier cases, it is argued, the term "precluded" is equivalent to "estopped," and negligence which will work an estoppel is only such as "directly and proximately affects the conduct of the bank in passing the forgery * * *." See, e.g., Coffin v. Fidelity–Philadelphia Trust Company, 374 Pa. 378, 393, 97 A.2d 857, 39 A.L.R.2d 625 (1953); Land Title Bank and Trust Company v. Cheltenham National Bank, 362 Pa. 30, 66 A.2d 768 (1949). The plaintiff further asserts that those decisions hold that "negligence in the conduct of the drawer's business," such as appears on this record, cannot serve to work an estoppel.

Even if that was the law in this Commonwealth prior to the passage of the Commercial Code, it is not the law today. The language of the new Act is determinative in all cases arising after its passage. This controversy must be decided, therefore, by construction of the statute and application of the negligence doctrine as it appears in § 3–406 of the Code....

Had the legislature intended simply to continue the strict estoppel doctrine of the pre-Code cases, it could have employed the term "precluded," without qualification, as in § 23 of the old Negotiable Instruments Law, 56 P.S. § 28 (repealed). However, it chose to modify that doctrine in § 3–406, by specifying that negligence which "*substantially contributes to...the making of an unauthorized signature*...." will preclude the drawer from asserting a forgery. [emphasis supplied]. The Code has thus abandoned the language of the older cases (negligence which "directly and proximately affects the conduct of the bank in passing the forgery") and shortened the chain of causation which the defendant bank must establish. "[N]o attempt is made," according to the Official Comment to § 3–406, "to specify what is negligence, and the question is one for the court or jury on the facts of the particular case."

In the instant case, the trial court could readily have concluded that plaintiff's business affairs were conducted in so negligent a fashion as to have "substantially contributed" to the Albers forgeries, within the meaning of § 3–406.

Thus, the record shows that pads of plaintiff's blank logging slips were left in areas near the mill which were readily accessible to any of the haulers. Moreover, on at least two occasions, Albers was given whole pads of these blank logging slips to use as he chose. Mrs. Vinora Curtis, an employee of the plaintiff, testified:

"Q. Did you ever give any of these logging slips to Mr. Albers or any pads of these slips to Mr. Albers?

"A. Yes.

....

"Q. What was the reason for giving [a pad of the slips] to him, Mrs. Curtis?

"A. Well, he came up and said he needed it for [scaling] the logs, so I gave it to him."

Mrs. Amy Thompson, who also served as a bookkeeper for the plaintiff, testified:

"Q. As a matter of fact, you gave Mr. Albers the pack of your logging slips, did you not?

"A. Yes, I did once.

"Q. Do you remember what you gave them to him for?

"A. I don't right offhand, but it seems to me he said he was going out to look for some logs or timber or something and he needed them to mark some figures on * * *.

"Q. Well, if he was going to use them for scratch pads, why didn't you give him a scratch pad that you had in the office?

"A. That's what I should have done."

In addition, the plaintiff's printed scaling slips were not consecutively numbered. Unauthorized use of the slips, therefore, could easily go undetected. Thus, Mr. Nelson Thompson testified:

"Q. Mr. Thompson, were your slips you gave these haulers numbered?

"A. No, they were not.

"Q. They are now, aren't they?

"A. Yes.

"Q. Had you used numbered logging slips, this would have prevented anybody getting logging slips out of the ordinary channel of business and using it to defraud you?

"A. Yes."

Moreover, in 1960, when the company became concerned about the possible unauthorized use of its scaling slips, it required its own personnel to initial the slips when a new shipment of logs was scaled. However, this protective measure was largely ignored in practice. Mrs. Amy Thompson testified:

"Q. And later on in the course of your business, if you remember Mr. Thompson said he wanted the logging slips initialed by one of the so-called authorized people?

"A. Yes.

"Q. [D]idn't you really not pay too much attention to them at all?

"A. Well, I know we didn't send them back to be sure they were initialed. We might have noticed it but we didn't send them back to the mill.

"Q. In other words, if they came to you uninitialed, you might have noticed it but didn't do anything about it.

"A. Didn't do anything about it."

The principal default of the plaintiff, however, was its failure to use reasonable diligence in insuring honesty from its log haulers including Emery Albers. For many years, the haulers were permitted to deliver both the original and the duplicate of the scaling slip to the company office, and the company tolerated this practice. These slips supplied the bookkeeper with the payees' names for the checks she was to draw in payment for log deliveries. Only by having the company at all times retain possession of the original slip could the plaintiff have assured that no disbursements were made except for logs received, and that the proper amounts were paid to the proper persons. The practice tolerated by the plaintiff effectively removed the only immediate safeguard in the entire procedure against dishonesty on the part of the haulers.

Finally, of course, the company regularly entrusted the completed checks to the haulers for delivery to the named payees, without any explicit authorization from the latter to do so.

While none of these practices, in isolation, might be sufficient to charge the plaintiff with negligence within the meaning of § 3–406, the company's course of conduct, viewed in its entirety, is surely sufficient to support the trial judge's determination that it substantially contributed to the making of the unauthorized signatures.[6] In his words, that conduct was "no different than had the plaintiff simply given Albers a series of checks signed in blank for his unlimited, unrestricted use."

....

Judgment affirmed.

■ WATKINS, J., DISSENTS.

---

[6] In this connection, the trial court also noted that the plaintiff at all times prior to the commencement of this litigation failed to keep an accurate inventory account. It could not therefore verify, at any given point in time, that it actually possessed the logs which it had paid for.

NOTES

1. In Bank/First Citizens Bank v. Citizens & Associates, 82 S.W.3d 259 (Tenn. 2002), Drawer (D) was induced to invest in Payee by fraudulent representations made by Agent of Payee that she had the authority to grant franchise rights to investors. D entrusted checks payable to Payee to Agent for delivery to Payee. But Agent forged Payee's indorsement and deposited the checks in her account in Depositary Bank (DB), which obtained payment from Drawee Bank. In order to avoid liability on the presentment warranty it breached for collecting a check that contained forged indorsements, DB sued D on ground that D's act of negligence in failing to inquire of Payee about Agent's authority substantially contributed to the forgery. The court held that D was indeed negligent in giving Agent the checks without inquiring of Payee about Agent's authority but that this negligence did not substantially contribute to Agent's forgery of Payee's name in indorsing the checks for deposit in DB. Thus, the court reasoned, DB could not use the negligent drawer claim to relieve itself of liability. There was no causal connection between D's negligence and Agent's forgery. D's negligence did not increase the possibility that Agent would forge the indorsement. The court favorably cited a line of cases holding that only negligence that "proximately relates or contributes to the forgery, and not merely issuance of the checks, would relieve a collecting bank of liability for improper payment of a fraudulently endorsed check." Id. at 266. Is this case contrary to *Thompson* on the "substantially contributes" issue? See Case #2 in Comment 3 to 3-406.

2. Do the comparative fault provisions of 3-406(b) create a new affirmative cause of action for negligence? The answer has practical consequences. Suppose the drawee pays a forged check under circumstances in which both the drawee and drawers' negligence contributed to the resulting loss. The drawee in turn debits the drawer's account in the amount of the check. By its terms, 3-406(a) precludes the drawee from recovering its apportioned loss from the drawer. Unless 3-406(a) gives the drawee a cause of action to recover the apportioned loss from the drawer, it bears the entire loss from the forgery. Commentators contend that 3-406(b) is not limited to the drawer-drawee relationship and that it creates a new cause of action that would allow the drawer to sue a depositary bank for that part of the the loss that the bank should bear for its negligence. 2 James J.White & Robert S. Summers, Uniform Commercial Code § 19-3 (5th ed. 2002). Not so, said the Supreme Court of Virginia in Halifax Corp. v. Wachovia, 604 S.E.2d 403 (Va. 2004). When the drafters of Revised Article 3 wished to give the person bearing the loss an affirmative cause of action, they said so in 3-404(d) and 3-405(b). There is no such language in 3-406(b). Nor is there any indication in the extensive Comments that the drafters intended to create an affirmative cause of action in forged signature cases for recovery by the drawer against a depositary bank. Section 3-406(b) appears to give only an affirmative defense based on the loss attributable to the other person's negligence. Thus, in the example above, in a suit by the drawee to recover from the drawer the amount of the check it paid, the drawee can raise the drawee's negligence to allocate to the drawee a portion of the loss. The defense reduces the drawer's liability to the drawee by the proportion of the loss allocated to the drawee.

PROBLEMS

1. In *Thompson Maple Products,* Albers either cashed or deposited the checks with his forged indorsement in the same bank on which they were drawn by the Thompson company. Banks call this an "on us" check, meaning the drawee bank is also the depositary bank. Note that 3–406(b) embraces a form of comparative negligence. If this case had been decided under Revised Article 3, could a case be made that Bank's conduct in *Thompson Maple Products* was not in exercise of ordinary care in paying the checks that were presented to it by Albers over a period of years that were payable to timber producers? Is there any legitimate reason why the payees would transfer the checks to Albers? Wouldn't the payees normally deposit these checks to their accounts?

2. Assume that the facts in *Thompson* were these: the checks made to the timber companies were made to corporate payees; the indorsements of these companies would ordinarily be printed and "look official." Albers forged the indorsements of these companies by handwritten indorsements that were crudely done. Albers then wrote his own name under each of these indorsements. He deposited these checks in his account in Depositary Bank and withdrew the proceeds of the checks once they cleared. The checks were presented to the drawee, Citizens National Bank, which paid the checks. In subsequent litigation, the drawer, Thompson Maple Products, contended that the drawee bank was precluded from relying upon the drawer's negligence as a defense under 3–406 because of the drawee's failure to verify the indorsements. The drawee bank defended on the ground that a drawee has no duty to examine indorsements on checks that it has received from a depositary bank. Under the facts in this Problem, Albers had no deposit account in drawee bank and the drawee had no reason to be familiar with his signature. Is drawee bank correct in this case? See Guardian Life Ins. Co. of Am. v. Weisman, 223 F.3d 229 (3d Cir.2000).

c. FAILURE OF CUSTOMER TO REPORT FORGERY

In cases involving forged checks, the malefactor often forges a series of checks on the same account over a period of time. Forgery with respect to a single check is much more likely to involve a forged indorsement rather than a forgery of the drawer's signature. Typically, repeated forged check cases involve a dishonest employee of the person whose signature is forged. Usually the employee has access to the employer's checkbook and often has duties related to bookkeeping. In the case of repeated forgeries, the later forgeries could have been easily prevented if the person whose signature was forged had detected the earlier forgeries. Such detection is relatively easy because in most cases the payor bank, after paying a check, returns the cancelled check to the customer on whose account the check was drawn. The customer should be able to determine whether a check written on its account is a forgery. On the other hand, it may be very difficult for the payor bank to detect forgery. Since it is easy for the customer to detect a forgery, 4–406 imposes a duty on the customer to report forged checks to the bank. Failure of the customer to comply with this duty can, in some cases, result in a shifting of the loss from the bank to the customer. Although 3–406 applies to checks bearing a forged indorsement as well as forged checks, 4–406 does not apply to forged indorsements. Both sections also apply to altered checks which are discussed later in this chapter.

Given the rule that a payor bank bears the loss on a check it pays over a forged drawer's signature, banks had traditionally engaged in the labor intensive activity of sight review of all checks drawn on the bank. Bank employees compared the signature on each check with that on the signature specimen card on file. For a large bank, a typical setting was a big room, crammed with desks, with soft music, free softdrinks and aspirin, and other amenities designed to keep these unfortunate workers from losing their minds. As the volume of checks grew and automation became the norm, banks abandoned sight review except for checks that met certain risk criteria, the principal one being the amount of the check.

Now that forgers utilize desktop printers, sight review has become obsolete for the large volume of corporate and government checks on which signatures are printed. Even on personal checks in which a signature is written in ink, a sight reviewer, who can normally spend only a few seconds on each check, is no match for a skillful forger. Thus, banks came to the conclusion that sight review was not cost effective. Some banks purported to find no greater forgery losses without sight review than with it, and others contended that whatever losses they might suffer on the payment of forged checks of relatively small amounts did not justify the heavy labor costs involved. As we shall see, payor banks have better ways of fighting forgeries than sight review.

The legal problems raised by the abandonment of sight review occupied the courts for years. Julianna J. Zekan, Comparative Negligence Under the Code: Protecting Negligent Banks Against Negligent Customers, 26 U. Mich. J.L. Reform 125, 166–178 (1992). Under 4–406, the customer is obliged to examine its cancelled checks for forgeries and to notify the payor bank if any are found. If it fails to do so in a timely manner, the customer is precluded from raising the forgery *unless the bank fails to exercise ordinary care.* Before the 1990 revision of Articles 3 and 4 became effective, the case law was sharply divided on the issue of whether a bank that did not conduct sight review of the checks in question was exercising ordinary care. In Medford Irrigation District v. Western Bank, 676 P.2d 329 (Or.Ct.App.1984), the bank's automated system was programmed to pay all checks of $5,000 or less unless there was a hold or stop order on the check; checks for amounts in excess of that sum were selected out by the check sorting machine and individually reviewed. The court held that the bank was precluded from raising the customer's negligence on the ground that in order to exercise ordinary care a bank's system must be reasonably related to the detection of forged signatures. Since, in this case, the bank had no procedure for detecting forgeries in checks under $5,000 the bank was negligent *as a matter of law*.

The *Medford* view has been rejected in a number of cases. The Illinois Supreme Court held in Wilder Binding Co. v. Oak Park Trust & Savings Bank, 552 N.E.2d 783 (Ill. 1990), that whether a bank exercised ordinary care in paying a check is a question of fact. In Rhode Island Hospital Trust Nat'l Bank v. Zapata Corp., 848 F.2d 291 (1st Cir.1988) (Breyer, J.), the court approved the cost-benefit analysis rejected in *Medford*. Judge Breyer opined that there was no evidence that any increased forgery loss from the bank's automated system was unreasonable in light of the costs that the new practices would save. He relied on Learned Hand's view that duty should be defined by calculating the probability of injury times the gravity of harm to determine the burden of precaution that is warranted. United States v. Carroll Towing Co., 159 F.2d 169 (2d Cir.1947).

In the revision of Articles 3 and 4, the Drafting Committee was mindful of the need to make sure that Revised Article 4 would accommodate a system of electronic presentment, discussed in the preceding chapter, if such a system were developed. This tipped the scale in favor of adopting the line of authority rejecting *Medford*. This was implemented in the definition of "ordinary care" in 3–103(a)(9), discussed in Comment 5 to 3–103 and Comment 4 to 4–406. The following case discusses 3–103(a)(9) and is instructive in showing how banks attempt to prove ordinary care under that provision.

Espresso Roma Corp. v. Bank Of America, N.A.

Court of Appeal, First District, California, 2002.
124 Cal.Rptr.2d 549.

■ STEIN, ACTING P.J.

Espresso Roma Corporation, Pacific Espresso Corporation, and David S. Boyd dba Hillside Residence Hall (appellants) appeal from a judgment dismissing their complaint alleging several causes of action against Bank of America, N.A. (Bank), based upon its payment of forged checks drawn on appellants' accounts by one of their former employees. The court entered judgment in favor of the Bank after it granted the Bank's motion for summary judgment on the ground that appellants were precluded by California Uniform Commercial Code section 4406, subdivisions (d) and (e) from asserting any claims against the Bank for unauthorized payment of checks drawn on their accounts. We shall affirm the judgment.

David S. Boyd is the president of Espresso Roma and Pacific Espresso Corporations and also runs Hillside Residence Hall. All three businesses had checking accounts with the Bank.

From late 1996 through April 1999, appellants employed Joseph Montanez, who eventually assumed certain bookkeeping responsibilities, learned how to generate company checks on the computer, and had access to blank checks. Starting in October 1997, Montanez downloaded company computer programs, stole blank checks, and printed company checks on his home computer which he used to pay his personal bills, and for personal purchases. He concealed his actions by removing the forged checks from the bank statements when he sorted the mail.

Boyd did not discover the forgeries, or report them to the Bank until May 1999. After Montanez left the company, a check was returned by a stereo company, bearing a signature that Boyd did not recognize. Boyd then reviewed the records and discovered that, from October 1997 through April 1999, Montanez had forged company checks in an amount totaling more than $330,000.

The Bank's motion for summary judgment was based upon section 4406, which limits a payor bank's liability to its customer for making payment upon checks with alterations or unauthorized signatures.

Pursuant to subdivision (f) of section 4406, the Bank asserted that appellants were absolutely precluded from asserting forgeries processed more than one year before the forgery was reported. By its terms subdivision (f) applies, "[*w*]ithout regard to care or lack of care of either the customer or the bank," (italics added) and precludes "a customer who does not within one year after the statement or items are made available to the customer...discover and report the customer's unauthorized signature" from asserting it against the Bank. The Bank also relied upon the conditional preclusion established by subdivisions (d) and (e) of section 4406. Subdivision (c) of section 4406 imposes a duty upon the customer promptly to review monthly statements or checks made available to the customer by the bank, to exercise reasonable care in discovering any unauthorized signature or alteration, and promptly to notify the bank of the discovery of such items. Pursuant to subdivision (d), if the customer fails to comply with these duties, when the same person has forged checks on the account, the customer is precluded from making a claim against the bank for the unauthorized payment unless the customer notified the bank no more than 30 days after the first forged item was included in the monthly statement or canceled checks, and should have been discovered. (§ 4406, subd. (d)(2).) This preclusion is conditional because the customer may avoid its application by establishing that the bank "failed to exercise ordinary care in paying the item and that the failure contributed to [the] loss." (§ 4406, subd. (e)....

In its order granting summary judgment, the court held that appellants were precluded by "sections 4406(d) and 4406(e) from asserting claims against the [B]ank for unauthorized payments of checks drawn on [appellants'] checking accounts." The court specifically ruled that appellants failed to create a triable issue of fact as to whether "the [B]ank's system of processing checks for [appellants' accounts] violated the [B]ank's ... procedures" or varied unreasonably from general banking usage in the area. The court also ruled that the declaration of appellant's expert failed to create a triable issue of fact "as to whether the [B]ank failed to exercise ordinary care," and that the Bank had no duty to sight review the checks.[2]

Appellants argue that the burden never shifted to them to create a triable issue of fact because the Bank failed to meet its "burden of production to make a prima facie showing of the nonexistence of any triable issue of fact," that (1) despite the availability of monthly statements and canceled checks, appellants failed to discover and notify the Bank of the forgery within 30 days, and (2) it exercised ordinary care in paying the item.... Appellants further contend that, even if the burden did shift to them, the declaration of their own expert created a triable issue of fact on the issue whether the bank exercised ordinary care, precluding summary judgment in the Bank's favor.

1. APPELLANTS' FAILURE TO DISCOVER AND REPORT THE FORGERIES

Pursuant to section 4406, subdivision (d), the customer is precluded from making a claim against the bank for unauthorized payment unless the customer notified the bank no more than 30 days after the *first* forged item was included in the monthly statement or canceled checks and should have been discovered. (§ 4406, subd. (d)(2); see also Official Comments on U. Com. Code, West's Ann. Cal. U. Com.Code, (2002 ed.) com. 2, § 4406, p. 190.)[3]

---

[2] The Bank contends that, even if triable issues of fact existed on the issue of exercise of ordinary care, the absolute preclusion set forth in section 4406, subdivision (f) applied, and was shortened by contract to a period of six months, thereby barring nearly half of appellants' claim without regard to exercise of ordinary care. We need not reach this contention because we shall uphold the summary judgment upon the ground that no triable issue of fact existed with respect to the application of the conditional preclusion set forth in section 4406, subdivisions (d) and (e).

[3] The California Uniform Commercial Code comment 2 explains: "Subsection (d)(2) applies to cases in which the customer fails to report an unauthorized signature or alteration with respect to an item ... and the bank subsequently pays other items of the customer with respect to which there is an alteration or unauthorized signature of the customer and the same wrongdoer is involved. If the payment of the subsequent items occurred after the customer has had a

According to the complaint, the forged checks were presented for payment between October 1997 and May 1999, but appellants did not discover or report them until on or about May 15, 1999. To establish its prima facie case that the conditional issue preclusion created by section 4406, subdivision (d) applied, the Bank presented the deposition testimony of Boyd, that it made monthly account statements and canceled checks available to appellants shortly after the closing period of each statement. Boyd testified that he received statements on a monthly basis, and they included canceled checks. When Boyd began to suspect unauthorized checks were being written and reviewed the statements and checks in May 1999, he was able to identify, and reported, the forgery. This evidence supports the inference that the first monthly statement that would have reflected the forgery by Montanez would have been in November 1997.... Yet, despite having the means to discover the forgeries, more than a year and a half elapsed before appellants discovered and reported any of them, far beyond the 30 days specified in section 4406, subdivision (d)....

2. EVIDENCE THAT THE BANK EXERCISED ORDINARY CARE

Having established a prima facie case that the Bank made monthly statements and checks available, and that appellants failed to notify the Bank within 30 days, the issue preclusion pursuant to section 4406, subdivision (d) applies unless the customer can establish that the bank, "failed to exercise ordinary care in paying the item and that the failure contributed to [the] loss." (§ 4406, subd. (e).) "Ordinary care" is defined by section 3103, subdivision (a)(7) as follows: "'Ordinary care' in the case of a person engaged in business means observance of reasonable commercial standards, prevailing in the area in which the person is located, with respect to the business in which the person is engaged. In the case of a bank that takes an instrument for processing for collection or payment by automated means, reasonable commercial standards do not require the bank to examine the instrument if the failure to examine does not violate the bank's prescribed procedures and the bank's procedures do not vary unreasonably from general banking usage not disapproved by this [D]ivision or Division 4 (commencing with Section 4104.)"

As explained in *Story Road Flea Market, Inc. v. Wells Fargo Bank* (1996), 42 Cal.App.4th 1733, 1742, 50 Cal.Rptr.2d 524, a case in which the court upheld a motion for summary judgment in the Bank's favor based upon section 4406, subdivisions (d) and (e), ordinary care as used in section 4406 is a "'professional negligence' standard of care which looks at the procedures utilized in the banking industry rather than what a 'reasonable person' might have done under the circumstances." (*Id.* at p. 1741, 50 Cal.Rptr.2d 524.)

---

reasonable time, (not exceeding 30 days) to report *with respect to the first item,* and before the bank received notice of the unauthorized signature or alteration *of the first item,* the customer is precluded from asserting the alteration or unauthorized signature with respect to the subsequent items." (Official Comments on U. Com. Code, 23B West's Ann. Cal. U. Com.Code, *supra,* Com. 2, foll. § 4406 (2002 ed.) p. 190, italics added.)

"'[R]easonable commercial standards do not require the bank to *examine the instrument* if the failure to examine does not violate the bank's prescribed procedures and the bank's procedures do not vary unreasonably from general banking usage.'" (*Id.* at p. 1742, 50 Cal.Rptr.2d 524, italics added.)

The Bank, in support of its motion for summary judgment, presented a prima facie showing that it exercised ordinary care, through the declaration of its expert, Jack Thomas. In addition to stating his qualifications as an expert in the field, Thomas declared that he was "familiar with the check processing strategies and procedures employed by banks similarly sized to Bank of America, including those within the San Francisco Bay area, which are 'bulk file bookkeeping' banks." He further explained that "Bank of America is a 'bulk file bookkeeping' check processor," meaning that it processes checks automatically and does not visually examine individual checks or verify signatures. Thomas declared that Bank of America processes in excess of one million checks per day in California, and although it uses fraud filters, they are not designed to "catch a crooked employee who forges his employer's checks, which only the employer would know are forged." Thomas declared that the Bank's "practices and procedures are consistent with those of all other large 'bulk file bookkeeping' banks in California." Thomas also "verified with the responsible [B]ank officer that [the Bank] followed its procedures with respect to the checks at issue in this litigation when it processed the checks." He concluded that the Bank "exercised ordinary care in processing [appellants'] checks ... in observance of reasonable commercial standards prevailing in the area in which Bank of America is located, and where [appellants] maintained their accounts."

Appellants argue that this declaration was insufficient to define the reasonable commercial standard "in the area," (§ 3103, subd. (a)(7)) and failed to demonstrate that the Bank's automated check processing did not vary unreasonably from general banking usage, because the expert stated that the Bank's practices conformed to commercial standards for "bulk file bookkeeping" in all of California and considered only the practices of similarly sized banks. Appellant, however, takes the reference to the entire State of California in isolation and out of context, because the expert specifically stated that he was also familiar with the practices of similarly sized banks in the "San Francisco Bay area." Thus, read as a whole, the expert's declaration expressed the opinion that the Bank's practices conformed not only with those of similarly sized banks in the Bay Area, but also with similarly sized banks in the State of California. Nor are we persuaded by appellant's contention that it was necessary to offer expert opinion that the Bank's practices were consistent with those of *all* banks in the area, not just those of similarly sized banks. To the contrary, section 3103, subdivision (a)(7) defines ordinary care as "observance of reasonable commercial standards, prevailing in the area in which the person is located, with respect to the business in which the person is engaged," meaning the standard of reasonableness is set by comparable businesses. (See Com. com. 4, West's Ann.Cal. U. Com.Code, § 4406, p. 191 [ordinary care is established if the bank's "procedure is reasonable and is commonly followed by other comparable banks in the area" and was followed by the bank in processing the checks in issue.] Size is a relevant factor in identifying comparable businesses because, in the banking context, a reasonable commercial standard for processing checks at a small bank with a relatively small volume of checks, and personal familiarity with its customers, would be quite different than what is reasonable for a large bank that processes upwards of a million checks per day. Thomas's declaration therefore established that the reasonable industry standard prevailing in the area for similarly sized banks was to bulk process checks through an automated system that employs fraud filters, but does not include sight review of individual checks for signature verification. The Bank's procedures conformed to this standard, which also was consistent with general bank usage as reflected by the practices of other bulk file bookkeeping banks in California, and it followed those procedures in this case. We conclude that Thomas's declaration was sufficient to establish a prima facie case that the Bank exercised ordinary care, thereby shifting the burden to appellant to create a triable issue of fact. (*Story Road Flea Market, Inc. v. Wells Fargo Bank, supra,* 42 Cal.App.4th 1733, 1738, 1743, 50 Cal.Rptr.2d 524 [expert declaration that bank processed checks, none of which were selected for sight review, in accordance with its own procedures, and consistent with reasonable commercial standards in the area, and general banking practices, shifted burden to plaintiff to create a triable issue of fact].)

Although appellants submitted the declaration of its own expert, John Moulton, in opposition, the trial court correctly concluded that it failed to create a triable issue of fact on the question whether the Bank "failed to exercise ordinary care in paying the item *and* that the failure contributed to [the] loss." (§ 4406, subd. (e), italics added.) Moulton declared that he called upon "large and small banks in Alameda County to inquire of their actual practices." These banks make decisions for payment of items at the branch where the account is kept and have the "means to check signatures for forgeries" present, whether it be by signature card or digital imaging. He also declared that these banks would manually examine checks which resulted in an overdraft, were unsigned, or exceeded a certain amount. He further declared that there were four instances of daily overdrafts occurring on days in which forged checks were processed, and one unsigned check that was processed and paid, all without selecting the checks for manual review.

The fundamental defect in Moulton's declaration is that, instead of defining the applicable reasonable commercial standard of care by looking at comparably sized banks using bulk file bookkeeping, he bases his opinion that the standard of care requires certain checks be selected for sight review, or other special handling, upon the practices of large and small banks. Without a showing that *comparable* banks in the area select individual checks for sight review, the fact that the Bank's system did not select individual checks for sight review, or signature verification, is insufficient to create a material issue of fact because section 3103, subdivision (a)(7) specifies that "reasonable commercial standards *do not require the bank to examine the instrument if the failure to examine does not violate the bank's prescribed procedures and the bank's procedures do not vary unreasonably from general banking usage.*" (Italics added.) Therefore, Moulton's declaration does not create a triable issue of fact with respect to the Bank's showing that its system of bulk processing of checks, which does not include sight review for signature verification, is commercially reasonable, and consistent with the practice of other comparably large banks in the area and in California.

Moreover, assuming arguendo that reasonable commercial standards did require that the Bank have established criteria for selecting some checks for sight review, Moulton's declaration still fails to create a triable issue of fact because it provides no basis to infer that the failure to have such a system *contributed to the loss.* (§ 4406, subd. (e) [the customer must show the Bank "failed to exercise ordinary care in paying the item *and* that the failure contributed to [the] loss" (italics added)].) Moulton does not specify what the criteria should be, in an automated check processing system that selects some checks for sight review, other than reviewing a check that causes an overdraft, or is in excess of some unspecified amount. Although Moulton declares that daily overdrafts occurred on four of the days forged items were processed, Moulton does not declare that it was forged checks which caused the overdrafts. Similarly, although Moulton identifies a check that was paid without a signature, he does not state whether this check is one of the items that appellants contend were paid without authorization, or how such a check would be identified and selected for sight review under the criteria he declares are commercially reasonable. Nor does he declare that any forged check was in an amount that, pursuant to the criteria he suggests, would have resulted in its selection for sight review. Therefore, even if such a system of selection for sight review had been used by the Bank, the declaration provides no basis for inferring that any of the unauthorized checks would have been selected for sight review, resulting in earlier discovery of the forgeries. Therefore, the declaration does not create a triable issue that the failure to have such a system contributed to the loss. (See *Story Road Flea Market, Inc. v. Wells Fargo Bank, supra,* 42 Cal.App.4th 1733, 1744, 50 Cal.Rptr.2d 524 [expert declaration that unauthorized checks were out of sequence failed to create an issue of fact, because under stated criteria for selecting checks for sight review, unauthorized checks would still not have been selected for sight review])....

We conclude that the court properly granted the Bank's motion for summary judgment on the ground that section 4406, subdivisions (d) and (e) precluded appellants from asserting claims against the Bank for unauthorized payments of checks drawn on their checking accounts, and that appellants failed to create a triable issue of fact as to whether they failed to exercise ordinary care in paying the items and that the failure contributed to their loss.

The judgment is affirmed.

NOTES

1. Should a bank be allowed to raise the 4–406(f) one-year bar if it was in bad faith when it paid the check? The subsection and the Comments are silent on the issue. Take this case: Drawer Company (D) employed Margaret Marvic in its accounts payable department. She fraudulently signed the name of D's treasurer, Travis, to a number of checks over a three-year period. These checks were all made payable to Margaret and drawn on D's account in Bank. Margaret's husband, Lazlo Marvic, an officer of Bank made certain that no questions were raised about the validity of the checks upon payment. When D finally began to raise questions about Margaret's honesty, she and Lazlo disappeared. When D demanded recredit of its account in Bank for the amount of the forged checks, Bank raised the one-year bar of 4–406(f). D countered by contending that Bank could not raise this barrier because it paid the checks in bad faith.

The authorities are divided on the bad faith issue. The thrust of 4–406 is to place on the drawer the burdens of discovering a forged signature when the bank has returned the periodic bank statement and notifying the bank of the forgery. Under 4–406(f), without respect to the lack of due care of the bank, if the drawer has not reported the forgery within a year, the drawer is precluded from raising the forgery. But, under the hypothetical facts given, the drawer has been hindered in performance of its duties to discover forgeries and give the requisite notice of the bad faith intervention of an officer of the bank. This is different from mere lack of care. Falk v. Northern Trust Co., 763 N.E.2d 380 (Ill. App. Ct. 2001), held that the one-year limitation does not apply if the bank is in bad faith. But, Halifax Corp. v. First Union National Bank, 546 S.E.2d 696 (Va. 2001), noting that 4–406(f) says nothing about good faith while 4–406(d) and (e) do mention it, drew the negative implication and held the contrary. In neither case was there a clear case of bad faith. See 1–201(b)(20) "good faith." Unless the statute is amended, more judicial analysis will be required before we can be confident of the trend of the law in this area.

2. If the customer and payor bank enter into the increasingly common agreement that allows the bank to retain the cancelled checks and to send the customer a periodic statement of account, does the customer have enough information to detect forged checks drawn on its account? 4–406(a)-(b). Comment 1 to 4–406. Some banks send digital copies of the customer's checks and destroy the originals after a period of time. Does this practice allow customers enough information to detect forgery?

3. There has been disagreement in the courts on the question of what constitutes reasonable promptness by the customer in discovering an unauthorized signature and in notifying the bank when the wrongdoer is the person designated by the customer to check the monthly statement. Under 1–202(f), the customer would seem to be bound by the information supplied by the bank when that information reaches the customer's employee who is authorized to receive it and act on it. Under the law of agency, if that employee fails to notify the bank of the forgery, the customer should be bound by the employee's conduct regardless of whether the employee's failure to notify is due to negligence or is the deliberate act of the employee to cover up the employee's wrongdoing. The issue should not be whether the customer was negligent in the procedure chosen for reviewing the bank statements if the employee receiving and acting on the statements was the designated agent of the customer for that purpose. See Warren A. Seavey, Notice Through An Agent, 65 U. Pa.L. Rev. 1, 7–8 (1916).

PROBLEMS

The agreement between Bank and its corporate customer, Company, is that Bank is authorized to pay checks drawn on Company's account only if they are signed by the chief financial officer, Hardy, and her deputy, Olsen. Signature specimens of these two parties were on file with Bank.

1. Olsen signed his name to the check in dispute but Hardy did not. Bank paid the check. When Company demanded that Bank re-credit its account with the amount of the check, Bank contended that this should not be treated as an unauthorized signature on the part of Company because the signature on the check was not forged. Is Bank correct? See 3–403(b).

2. Olsen fraudulently wrote three checks on Company's account payable to the order of Olsen. Olsen signed his name to each check and forged the name of Hardy.

a. The first check, in the amount of $1,000, was paid by Bank on January 2 by automated equipment without any human examination of the check. The cancelled check was returned to Company on January 4.

b. The second check, in the amount of $2,000, was paid by Bank on February 20 by automated equipment without any human examination of the check. The cancelled check was returned to Company on March 3.

c. The third check, in the amount of $5,000, was paid by Bank on February 28. Before the check was paid, an employee of Bank examined the check but failed to detect the forgery of Hardy's signature. The cancelled check was returned to Company on March 3.

Under the established procedures of Bank, checks presented for payment in amounts less than $2,500 were not examined by anybody before payment. All checks paid by Bank were returned to Company each month along with the monthly statement of account.

The fraud by Olsen was discovered by Company in June. Olsen, who is insolvent, used the proceeds of the three checks to pay gambling debts. Company notified Bank of the forged checks on June 7, immediately after discovery of the fraud. Company demanded that Bank restore to Company account the $8,000 debited to the account as a result of payment of the checks.

With respect to each of the checks, state your opinion whether, under 4–406, Company is entitled to recover from Bank.

NOTE: FRAUD PREVENTION MEASURES

Banks have attempted to reduce fraud losses by adopting fraud prevention measures. These are described in 1 Barkley Clark & Barbara Clark, The Law of Bank Deposits, Collections and Credit Cards ¶ 10.01 (Rev. ed. 2009). Traditional methods involving sight review or random examination are not very effective against professionals who have desktop computers, color printers and copiers available that can scan and alter documents to produce accurate reproductions, as well as color printers and copiers, unless precautions are taken by the customer or bank.

A common protection against alteration and counterfeiting (producing checks like those of the drawer) is the use of paper stock with securities features for checks. Examination of checks will normally warn a potential forger that the check has safety features. Some of these are visible, like the legend "original document" which has a ghostly presence on the back of some checks and is difficult to copy. Others are warnings, such as the admonition that some awful things will happen to the check if photocopied. Still others are not revealed at all, leaving the would-be malefactor to worry about what he might be up against if he transgresses. Of course, security devices in the paper stock are not effective in the common insider case in which the forger has access to the genuine checks of the customer. 1 Clark & Clark, supra, ¶ 10.01[8][2].

Some banks offer a service identified as "positive pay." In its most common form the bank's business customers notify the bank daily of the checks drawn by them. The information provided to the bank typically includes the MICR line, dollar amounts and, under some plans, payee identification. When checks drawn by that customer are presented for payment, the bank compares these checks with the list given by the customer. If the checks don't match, they are returned to the presenting bank. See ABA Subcommittee on Payments, Deterring Check Fraud: The Model Positive Pay Services Agreement and

Commentary, 54 Bus. Law. 637 (1999). Banks have begun to offer imaging positive pay services under which the bank posts online for the customer's benefit the entire image of suspect checks, not just their MICR line. When the returned checks reach the depositary bank, it will erase the provisional credit given its depositor. If the depositary bank has already allowed the depositor to withdraw the funds, it has the burden of pursuing this person to get the money back. Since banks under Regulation CC are making funds available for most checks either on the day of deposit or the next day, as we indicated in an earlier chapter, it is likely that the money has been withdrawn in cases in which the forger is the depositor.

After Regulation CC, one of the favorite handiworks of skilled forgers has been cashier's checks, the proceeds of which must be available for withdrawal by the depositor the day after deposit. Some banks take thumb prints of persons cashing checks that can then be compared with FBI files to identify a forger.

Software companies have developed programs that allow banks to scan accounts for possible forgeries without the assistance of customers. The program allows a bank to review the past activity of customers' accounts in order to construct an archive for each account that shows a profile of the customer's usage. Checks presented for payment on these accounts will be reviewed for aberrations from this profile that may point to suspect checks. Fraud detection factors may include whether the check is larger in amount than checks drawn on this account in the past, whether the check number duplicates other checks already paid, whether the check number is out of sequence with other checks the customer is currently drawing, whether the check lacks any check number, and whether the volume of activity in the customer's account exceeds past levels. 1 Barkley Clark and Barbara Clark, supra, ¶ 10.01[6]

d. VALIDITY OF CONTRACTUAL "CUTDOWN" CLAUSES

Section 4–406 states two time limitations bearing on the customer's duty to discover and report unauthorized signatures or alterations. One appears in 4–406(d)(2) and bears on the repeat forgery issue. It provides that if there is a repeat forgery, the customer is precluded from asserting the forgery against the bank if payment was made before the bank received notice of the forgery "after the customer had been afforded a reasonable period of time, not exceeding 30 days, in which to examine the item or statement of account and notify the bank." The other is the overriding one-year notice preclusion in 4–406(f) that we discussed in Note 1 in the previous section. This is a strong statement of the policy of giving banks an outer time limit beyond which they no longer need to be concerned about forged checks even if the bank's negligence had led to the forgery. But 4–103(a) allows the parties to vary the effect of the terms of Article 4 by agreement, a subject that we will discuss in greater detail in the next chapter. Does this mean that the deposit agreement between the bank and its customer can cutdown this one-year period to six months, or 60 days, or 20 days? If so, the risk of forgery loss on the part of banks may be substantially reduced.

National Title Insurance Corp. Agency v. First Union National Bank

Supreme Court of Virginia, 2002.
559 S.E.2d 668.

■ OPINION BY JUSTICE CYNTHIA D. KISNER.

Pursuant to the provisions of Code § 8.4–406(f), a bank's customer is precluded from asserting against the bank an unauthorized signature or alteration on an item if the customer fails to report such fact to the bank within one year after a statement of account showing payment of the item is made available to the customer. The dispositive issue in this appeal is whether a bank and its customer may, by contractual agreement, shorten the one-year period provided in Code § 8.4–406(f). Because we conclude that Code § 8.4–103(a) permits the parties to vary that time period, we will affirm the judgment of the circuit court holding that an agreement reducing the period to 60 days is binding on the parties.

National Title Insurance Corporation Agency (National Title) opened an escrow checking account with First Union National Bank (First Union) in April 1996. At that time, the parties entered into a "DEPOSIT AGREEMENT AND DISCLOSURES For Non–Personal Accounts" (Deposit Agreement) that defined and governed the relationship between them. The provisions of Paragraph 12 of that Deposit Agreement, which are at issue in this appeal, absolve First Union of any liability for paying an item containing an unauthorized signature, an unauthorized indorsement, or a material alteration if National Title does not report such fact to First Union within 60 days of the mailing of the account statement describing the questioned item. In pertinent part, Paragraph 12 states:

> You should carefully examine the statement and canceled checks when you receive them. If you feel there is an error on the statement, or that some unauthorized person has withdrawn funds from the account, notify us immediately. The statement is considered correct unless you notify us promptly after any error is discovered. Moreover, because you are in the best position to discover an unauthorized signature, an unauthorized [i]ndorsement or a material alteration, you agree that we will not be liable for paying such items if ... (b) you have not reported an unauthorized signature, an unauthorized [i]ndorsement or material alterations to us within 60 days of the mailing date of the earliest statement describing these items....

Subsequently, First Union paid two checks ostensibly drawn on National Title's account, both of which were counterfeit checks and were not executed by an authorized signatory to the account. The first check, paid in November 1998, was described in an account statement mailed on December 5, 1998, and the second check, paid in December 1998, was described in National Title's account statement mailed on January 5, 1999. National Title did not report either of the unauthorized signatures to First Union within 60 days of the mailing of the respective account statements describing the two checks.

After First Union refused to credit National Title's account in the amounts paid on the two checks bearing unauthorized signatures, National Title filed a motion for judgment seeking to recover its losses from First Union. In its answer, First Union asserted, among other things, that National Title was precluded from making this claim because it had failed to report the unauthorized signatures within the 60–day time period specified in Paragraph 12 of the Deposit Agreement between the parties.

Ruling on the parties' cross-motions for summary judgment, the trial court concluded that First Union and National Title could contractually reduce the one-year period for reporting unauthorized signatures set forth in Code § 8.4–406(f) and that the 60–day period agreed upon by the parties in this case is not "manifestly unreasonable" under the provisions of Code § 8.4–103. The court therefore denied National Title's motion for summary judgment and granted First Union's motion, entering judgment in favor of First Union. National Title now appeals from that final judgment.

Title 8.4 of Virginia's Uniform Commercial Code (UCC) establishes the rights and duties between banks and their customers with regard to deposits and collections. A bank may charge against the account of its customer only those items that are properly payable from that account. *See* Code § 8.4–401(a). Items bearing unauthorized signatures, such as the checks in this case, are not properly payable. *Id.*

However, a customer has certain duties with regard to discovering and reporting an unauthorized signature or alteration on an item. If a bank sends or makes available to its customer a statement of account showing payment of items for the account, "the customer must exercise reasonable promptness in examining the statement or the items to determine whether any payment was not authorized because of an alteration of an item or because a purported signature by or on behalf of the customer was not authorized." Code § 8.4–406(c). A customer must promptly report to the bank any unauthorized payment that the customer "should reasonably have discovered" based on the statement or items provided. *Id.*

If a customer fails to comply with these duties, the customer is precluded from asserting against the bank the unauthorized signature or alteration on the item. Code § 8.4–406(d)(1). However, if a customer establishes that the bank "failed to exercise ordinary care in paying the item and that the failure substantially contributed to loss, the loss is allocated between the customer precluded and the bank asserting the preclusion according to the extent" that the failure of each party contributed to the loss. Code § 8.4–406(e).[2] Finally, if a customer does not discover and report an unauthorized signature or alteration on an item within one year after the statement or items are made available to the customer, the customer is thereafter precluded from asserting against the bank the unauthorized signature or alteration. Code § 8.4–406(f). This preclusion applies irrespective of whether the bank paid the item containing the unauthorized signature or alteration in good faith. *Halifax Corp. v. First Union Nat'l Bank,* 262 Va. 91, 101, 546 S.E.2d 696, 703 (2001).

On appeal, National Title first argues that Code § 8.4–406(f) is a statute of repose, i.e., a rule of substantive law, and that the one-year period set forth in that section is, therefore, not subject to contractual modification by the parties. Next, National Title posits that Paragraph 12 of the Deposit Agreement imports the time bar established in Code § 8.4–406(f) into subsection (c), thereby rendering the preclusion in subsection (f) meaningless. National Title further asserts that Paragraph 12 impermissibly changes the comparative negligence provisions established in Code § 8.4–406(e) and reinstates the concept of contributory negligence into Code § 8.4–406(c). Finally, National Title contends that the 60–day time limit for reporting an unauthorized signature or alteration on an item is "manifestly unreasonable," but that, if Paragraph 12 is enforceable, the 60–day limit should be construed as the parties' definition of "reasonable promptness" in determining comparative negligence, rather than as an absolute bar to National Title's claim against First Union. We do not agree with National Title.

The issue in this appeal is whether a bank may, through a contractual agreement with its customer, shorten the one-year period provided in Code § 8.4–406(f) to a period of 60 days. In *Halifax Corp.,* 262 Va. at 101, 546 S.E.2d at 703, we characterized that one-year period as a statutorily prescribed notice that operates as "a condition precedent to the customer's right to file an action against the bank to recover losses caused by the unauthorized signature or alteration."…. This condition precedent does not limit a customer's claim against a bank but requires that the customer first perform the duty to discover and report any unauthorized signature or alteration on an item before bringing suit against the bank. However, that characterization of subsection (f) as a condition precedent is not, as National Title suggests, determinative of the question whether a customer and a bank can, by agreement, shorten the one-year period. The provisions of Code § 8.4–103(a) provide the analytical framework for resolving that question.

---

[2] If a bank does not pay an item in good faith, the preclusion under Code § 8.4–406(d) as to the customer does not apply. Code § 4.6–406(e).

Code § 8.4–103(a) states that

> [t]he effect of the provisions of this title may be varied by agreement but the parties to the agreement cannot disclaim a bank's responsibility for its lack of good faith or failure to exercise ordinary care or limit the measure of damages for the lack or failure. However, the parties may determine by agreement the standards by which the bank's responsibility is to be measured if those standards are not manifestly unreasonable.

According to Official Comment 2 regarding § 4–103 of the UCC, "[s]ubsection (a) confers blanket power to vary all provisions of the Article by agreements of the ordinary kind." Thus, this statute allows a bank and its customer to vary by agreement the effect of the provisions of Title 8.4 as long as the agreement does not: "disclaim a bank's responsibility for its lack of good faith," "[disclaim a bank's responsibility for its] failure to exercise ordinary care," or "limit the measure of damages for the lack or failure." Code § 8.4–103(a).

The clause in Paragraph 12 of the Deposit Agreement reducing the one-year period in Code § 8.4–406(f) to a period of 60 days does not run afoul of these limitations on the authority to vary the effect of the provisions of Title 8.4. The Deposit Agreement does not absolve First Union of its duty to exercise ordinary care or good faith, nor does it limit the measure of damages. Instead, Paragraph 12 merely varies the effect of Code § 8.4–406(f) in that the period of time in which National Title must report an unauthorized signature or alteration on an item, without having its claim for losses precluded by the bar in subsection (f), is shortened from one year to 60 days.... This reduction in the length of the statutory notice period is consistent with the concept embodied in Code § 8.4–406(f) that a bank can be held potentially liable for paying an item containing an unauthorized signature or alteration only for a limited period of time. Thus, we conclude that a bank and its customer may contractually shorten the one-year period contained in Code § 8.4–406(f) and that First Union and National Title did so in Paragraph 12 of the Deposit Agreement.

Notwithstanding this reduced time period, if National Title complies with its duty to exercise reasonable promptness in examining its account statement and reporting any unauthorized signature or altered item, First Union remains liable for paying an item bearing an unauthorized signature or alteration. Likewise, the comparative negligence provisions contained in Code § 8.4–406(e) remain in effect during the 60–day period after First Union makes available to National Title a statement showing payment of items from National Title's account. Thus, the provisions of Paragraph 12 at issue do not alter the scheme of liability between banks and their customers as set forth in Code § 8.4–406....

Finally, National Title contends that the 60–day period for reporting unauthorized signatures or alterations is "manifestly unreasonable" under Code § 8.4–103(a). As used in subsection (a), this term is the test for determining the validity of an agreement that sets the standards by which a bank's responsibility for its lack of good faith or failure to exercise ordinary care is to be measured. While it is not necessary for us to decide in this case whether the test of manifest unreasonableness also applies to a determination regarding the validity of a reduction in the time period contained in Code § 8.4–406(f), we will utilize that standard in this appeal since it is the one advanced by National Title. In doing so, we conclude that the 60–day time limitation set forth in Paragraph 12 of the Deposit Agreement is not "manifestly unreasonable." Other jurisdictions have likewise upheld the validity of reductions in the one-year period provided in Code § 8.4–406(f) to periods similar to or shorter than 60 days....[4]

A condition precedent such as the one set forth in Code § 8.4–406(f) recognizes that a customer is in a better position than a bank to know whether a signature is authorized or an item has been altered.... A reduction in the one-year period allowed in subsection (f) to a period of 60 days encourages diligence by a customer and is "'in accord with public policy by limiting disputes in a society where millions of bank transactions occur every day.'" *Basse Truck Line, Inc. v. First State Bank,* 949 S.W.2d 17, 22 (Tex.App.1997) (quoting *Parent Teacher Ass'n,* 524 N.Y.S.2d at 340).

For these reasons, we will affirm the judgment of the circuit court.

NOTE

The validity of cut-down clauses has been much litigated. Barkley Clark & Barbara Clark, supra, ¶ 10.05[1][c][i] (Rev. ed. 2009). If a 60–day limitation is permissible, what about a 20–day limit? See Stowell v. Cloquet Co–Op Credit Union, 557 N.W.2d 567 (Minn. 1997). What if the customer is mentally incompetent? See Peters v. Riggs Nat'l Bank, 942 A.2d 1163 (D.C. App. 2008).

2. Right of Payor Bank to Recover Mistaken Payment of Check

a. FORGED CHECKS

The law of mistake and restitution recognizes the general principle that a person who confers a benefit upon another person because of a mistake is

[4] We do not decide today whether a period shorter than 60 days would be "manifestly unreasonable."

entitled to restitution from the person receiving the benefit. For example, a shopkeeper receives a $10 bill from a customer in payment of goods purchased by the customer for a price of $8. The shopkeeper, who has an obligation to give the customer $2 change, gives the customer $12 because of a mistaken belief that the customer had paid with a $20 bill. The shopkeeper is entitled to get back the $10 paid by mistake. Restatement (First) of Restitution § 19 (1937).

Mistake can also occur when money is paid for a negotiable instrument either by a person who buys the instrument or by a person, such as a payor bank, who pays the instrument. The law of mistake and restitution applies to negotiable instrument cases, but special rules apply in some cases. The mistake cases fall into various categories and most of the cases involve payment or acceptance of a check or other draft by the drawee. The principal categories involve forged checks, checks bearing a forged indorsement, altered checks, checks on which the drawer has stopped payment, and checks drawn on an account with insufficient funds to cover the check.

The seminal case in this area is Price v. Neal, (1762) 3 Burr. 1354, 97 Eng. Rep. 871 (K.B.), which involved two forged bills of exchange drawn on Price and indorsed to Neal, a bona fide purchaser for value. Price paid Neal on the first bill and then accepted the second bill which was subsequently purchased by Neal. After Price paid the second bill he learned that the signature of the drawer of the bills had been forged. Price sued Neal to get his money back. Lord Mansfield, in deciding in favor of the defendant, stated:

> It is an action upon the case, for money had and received to the plaintiff's use. In which action, the plaintiff can not recover the money, unless it be against conscience in the defendant, to retain it: and great liberality is always allowed, in this sort of action.
>
> But it can never be thought unconscientious in the defendant, to retain this money, when he has once received it upon a bill of exchange indorsed to him for a fair and valuable consideration, which he had bona fide paid, without the least priority or suspicion of any forgery.
>
> Here was no fraud: no wrong. It was incumbent upon the plaintiff, to be satisfied "that the bill drawn upon him was the drawer's hand," before he accepted or paid it: but it was not incumbent upon the defendant, to inquire into it. Here was notice given by the defendant to the plaintiff of a bill drawn upon him: and he sends his servant to pay it and take it up. The other bill he actually accepts; after which acceptance, the defendant innocently and bona fide discounts it. The plaintiff lies by, for a considerable time after he has paid these bills; and then found out "that they were forged:" and the forger comes to be hanged. He made no objection to them, at the time of paying them. Whatever neglect there was, was on his side. The defendant had actual encouragement from the plaintiff himself, for

negotiating the second bill, from the plaintiff's having without any scruple or hesitation paid the first: and he paid the whole value, bona fide. It is a misfortune which has happened without the defendant's fault or neglect. If there was no neglect in the plaintiff, yet there is no reason to throw off the loss from one innocent man upon another innocent man: but, in this case, if there was any fault or negligence in any one, it certainly was in the plaintiff, and not in the defendant.

Payment or acceptance by the drawee of a forged check or other draft is addressed in 3–418(a), (c) and 3–417(a)(3). Under these provisions, the rule of Price v. Neal is preserved. Section 4–208(a)(3) is identical in effect to 3–417(a)(3) and applies specifically to warranties made in the bank-collection process to a payor bank with respect to an Article 4 "draft" (4–104(a)(7)), which includes a check.

PROBLEM

Taylor, an employee of Juliet, needed money to meet overdue bills. He broke into a storeroom and stole a pad of company checks. Taylor forged Juliet's name to a check for $307 drawn on Payor Bank which he made payable to him. He used the check to pay for groceries at Best Foods whose policy was to accept third-party checks only if they appeared to be paychecks, which this check clearly did. The name printed at the top of the check was Juliet's d/b/a, "Juliet Company," and Taylor typed the company name on the signature line, followed by a written signature of Juliet. The forgery was skillfully done and even a handwriting expert would have had difficulty in detecting it. Best Foods deposited the check in its account in Depositary Bank which presented the check to Payor Bank for payment. Payor Bank paid the check in ordinary course and Best Foods withdrew the amount from its account in Depositary Bank. Taylor shortly filed in bankruptcy.

(a) When Payor Bank learned of the forgery, it demanded that Depositary Bank reimburse it for the amount of the check. Is it entitled to recover on the basis of the Code provisions set out in the paragraph preceding the Problem?

(b) When Payor Bank learned of the forgery, it demanded that Best Foods, the party that dealt with the forger, reimburse it for the amount of the check. Is it entitled to recover? See the Code provisions set out above and, in addition, 3–416(a)(2) and its Article 4 counterpart, 4–207(a).

(c) Did Depositary Bank breach the warranty stated in 3–417(a)(1)?

During the redraft of Articles 3 and 4, active consideration was given to rejecting the rule of Price v. Neal, but the doctrine has been retained. Does that doctrine allocate the loss resulting from forged checks in a fair manner in this Problem? For an article strongly supporting Price v. Neal, see James Steven Rogers, The Basic Principle of Loss Allocation for Unauthorized Checks, 39 Wake Forest L. Rev. 453 (2004). Professor Rogers believes that the fundamental principle of the check system and all other payment systems is that the burden of unpreventable losses should rest with the providers of the payment system rather than with the users of that system. Price v. Neal is entirely consistent with the basic principle of loss allocation for the check system.

b. FORGED INDORSEMENT

PROBLEM

Drawer drew a check to the order of Payee. The check was stolen from Payee by Thief who signed Payee's name to the check as a blank indorsement. Thief then delivered the check to Jennifer, who purchased for value, in good faith and without notice that the indorsement was forged. Jennifer indorsed and deposited the check with Depositary Bank which presented the check and received payment from Payor Bank. Depositary Bank credited Jennifer's account and the credit was withdrawn. Payee then notified Drawer of the theft. Drawer notified Payor Bank but was told that the check had already been paid. Is Payor Bank entitled to recover the amount of the check from either Depositary Bank or Jennifer? 3–417(a)(1), 4–208(a)(1), and Comments 3 and 4 to 3–417. If Depositary Bank has to pay, is Depositary Bank entitled to recover from Jennifer? 3–416(a)(1)- (2) and 4–207(a)(1)-(2).

How can you reconcile this case with Price v. Neal? That case announced a finality policy for forged checks: it is better to end the transaction on an instrument when it is paid rather than reopen and upset a series of transactions at a later date when forgery is discovered. But the result reached in the Problem above with respect to forged indorsements is inconsistent with a finality policy. Is it justified because a transferee from a forger may achieve some protection against a forged indorsement by requiring identification while a drawee cannot? For a judicial discussion of these issues, see Perini Corp. v. First National Bank of Habersham County, 553 F.2d 398 (5th Cir.1977).

c. ALTERATION

(1) COMPLETE INSTRUMENTS

"Alteration," defined in 3–407(a), refers to a change that purports to modify the obligation of a party to an instrument if the change is unauthorized. Thus, if the payee raises the amount of a check without the consent of the drawer, the check has been altered. But if the payee's act is authorized by the drawer before any other person becomes obligated on the check, the check has not been altered; the change is treated as a change made by the drawer.

The definition of alteration is very broad. It includes fraudulent changes as well as changes made in good faith. For example, the holder of a note changes the due date of the note because the holder believes in good faith that the original due date was erroneous. Even if the holder was mistaken, the alteration is not fraudulent. Under the second sentence of 3–407(b), the non-fraudulent alteration is ineffective to modify the obligation of the maker and the note is enforceable according to its original terms. Non-fraudulent alteration is described in the first paragraph of Comment 1 to 3–407.

The concept of alteration can apply to incomplete instruments, described in 3–115, as well as complete instruments, but the effect of alteration is not the same in each case. A discussion of alteration of incomplete instruments follows later section.

Fraudulent alteration is the principal focus of 3–407 and can be illustrated by the following hypothetical case:

> An authorized employee of Drawer, a large corporation, signed and delivered a typewritten check for $10 payable to the order of Payee. Without Drawer's consent, Payee raised the amount of the check to $10,000 by adding a comma and three zeroes after the figure "10" and the word "thousand" after the word "ten." Payee deposited the check in Payee's account with Depositary Bank and the bank obtained $10,000 from Drawee in payment of the check. Drawee then debited Drawer's account in the same amount. Payee withdrew the $10,000 that had been credited to Payee's account in Depositary Bank with respect to the check. When Drawer learned that Drawee had debited $10,000 to Drawer's account with respect to the check, Drawer notified Drawee of the alteration.

Who takes the loss in the hypothetical case? The liability of the drawer with respect to a check is based on the terms of the order to pay made by the person against whom the drawer's liability is asserted. Liability on an altered check can be compared to liability on a forged check. In the absence of fault, the person whose signature as drawer is forged has no liability on the check because the order to pay on which liability is asserted was not made by that person. In the case of the check in the hypothetical case, Drawer can reasonably be held liable with respect to the order to pay $10 because that order was made by Drawer, but, in the absence of fault by Drawer, it is not reasonable to hold Drawer liable with respect to the raised amount because Drawer did not order payment of that amount.

How is this analysis reflected in 3–407? In the hypothetical case, to what extent is Drawee entitled to debit Drawer's account with respect to the check? 3–407(c). If Drawee had dishonored the check, to what extent would Depositary Bank have had a right to recover from Drawer? 3–414(b) and 3–

407(c). What is the significance of the first sentence of 3–407(b), which states that "a party whose obligation is affected by the alteration" is discharged? See Comment 1 (second paragraph) to 3–407. If Depositary Bank is liable to Drawee, what recourse does Depositary Bank have against Payee? 3–416(a)(3) and (b).

Suppose, in the hypothetical case, that the employee who wrote the check on behalf of Drawer left blank spaces in the amount lines on the check, allowing Payee to raise the amount of the check without leaving any easily detectable evidence that the check had been altered. How does 3–406 apply to this case? See HSBC Bank USA v. F&M Bank N.V., 246 F.3d 335 (4th Cir.2001).

(2) ALTERATION OR FORGERY?

A person presenting a check to a drawee bank warrants that the check has not been altered (3-417(a)(2)), but only that it has no knowledge that the signature of the drawer is forged (3-417(a)(3)). Developments in check processing have made it more difficult to determine whether the check was altered or forged; alteration has gone far beyond whiting out. Paper checks are usually destroyed after a period; the digitalized copies may be hard to read. Cases arise in which the name of the payee on the check presented for payment is not the same as that on the original check. Courts are puzzled by how to decide whether the new name on the check was the result of an alteration of the old check or whether the wrongdoer created a counterfeit check containing the new name. Business checks are almost entirely printed, including the drawer's signature, and modern technology can produce counterfeit versions of these checks with ease. In such a case, Wachovia Bank, N.A. v. Foster Bancshares, Inc., 457 F.3d 619 (7th Cir.2006), Judge Posner comes very close to deciding the case by flipping a coin. He holds that in cases of doubt whether there has been forgery or alteration, the "tie should go to the drawee bank," that is, an alteration should be assumed. The following case is useful because of its dissenting opinion that shows the kinds of evidence used by counsel in arguing these cases. The reference to positive pay in the dissent relates to the fact that most positive pay plans at the time the facts of this case took place did not contain the name of the payee.

Chevy Chase Bank, F.S.B. v. Wachovia Bank, N.A.

United States Court of Appeals, Fourth Circuit, 2006.
208 F. Appx. 232.

■ SHEDD, CIRCUIT JUDGE:

Wachovia Bank, N.A. ("Wachovia") brings this appeal, asserting that the district court erred when it denied its motion for summary judgment and granted summary judgment in favor of Chevy Chase, F.S.B. ("Chevy Chase"). Finding no error, we affirm.

I

This case involves a dispute over a check in the amount of $341,187.45 issued on July 19, 2002. The check, drawn on the account of Young & Rubicam ("Y & R") at Wachovia, was deposited into an account maintained at Chevy Chase. Subsequently, Chevy Chase presented the check to Wachovia, which paid the check and debited Y & R's account for the amount of the check. When issued, the check was made payable to Hearst Magazines Division. Upon deposit at Chevy Chase, however, the name of the payee was Kon Pesicka/CJ International.

Y & R and Wachovia operate under a "positive pay" agreement, whereby Y & R drafts a check on its account and identifies key features of the check to Wachovia. Specifically, Y & R informs Wachovia of the date, check number, and dollar amount on each check. When the check is later presented to Wachovia for payment, Wachovia verifies each of these identifiers and pays the check unless one of them differs from the information supplied by Y & R.

The check presented to Wachovia matched the information provided by Y & R. Wachovia accordingly paid the check without verifying the name of the payee. Y & R subsequently discovered that there were problems with the check, notified Wachovia, and requested that Wachovia produce the original check. However, Wachovia was unable to locate and produce the original check because, pursuant to its policy, Wachovia had destroyed the original check after storing a digital copy. Wachovia, citing "business" reasons, then credited Y & R's account for the value of the check.

Thereafter, Wachovia sought repayment of the check from Chevy Chase based on an assertion of breach of presentment warranty. Upon receiving this request, Chevy Chase launched an investigation to determine whether the check had been forged or altered. Chevy Chase, however, was unable to determine with certainty what type of fraud was committed. More specifically, Chevy Chase could not determine whether the check it received was the check which Y & R had issued but with the name of the payee altered or whether it was a different check which was a forgery or a counterfeit.

Chevy Chase then filed this action, seeking a declaratory judgment regarding its obligations to Wachovia. Wachovia, in turn, sought to hold Chevy Chase liable for breach of presentment warranty under the Virginia Commercial Code. After discovery, both parties moved for summary judgment. The district court, holding that Wachovia had failed to produce sufficient evidence showing that the check had been altered, granted summary judgment in favor of Chevy Chase. Further, the district court alternatively held that Wachovia was precluded from recovery because, under its positive pay agreement, it was not obligated to credit Y & R's account upon discovery of check fraud. Thus, any loss was voluntarily borne by Wachovia, meaning that Wachovia suffered no damages. This appeal followed....

III

Both parties agree that the check received by Chevy Chase and the check issued by Y & R had different payees. This being the case, the check received by Chevy Chase-and paid by Wachovia-could have been the original check issued by Y & R (and subsequently altered by an unknown party) or the check could have been a counterfeit check (or a check with a forged drawer signature). The primary factual dispute centers on this distinction. Wachovia contends that the check was altered, while Chevy Chase maintains that the check was forged. The outcome of this factual dispute determines who must bear the loss incurred when the check was paid.

The Virginia Commercial Code provides that a party presenting a check for payment makes a warranty of presentment to the party paying the check. Va.Code Ann. § 8.4-207.2. One of the guarantees included in the warranty of presentment is that the check presented has not been "altered." *Id.* § 8.4-207.2(a)(2). An alteration is defined as:

> (I) an unauthorized change in an instrument that purports to modify in any respect the obligation of a party, or (ii) an unauthorized addition of words or numbers or other change to an incomplete instrument relating to the obligation of a party.

Id. § 8.3A-407(a). However, the presentment warranty does not include a guarantee that the drawer's signature on the check is authorized. Instead, it provides only that a presenting party *has no knowledge* that a check bears an unauthorized (or forged) drawer's signature. *Id.* §§ 8.4-207.2(a)(3), 8.1A-201(41). Similarly, a party seeking payment warrants that he has no knowledge that a check is counterfeit....

Wachovia has alleged that Chevy Chase breached its presentment warranty by presenting an altered check for payment. Specifically, Wachovia asserts that the check it received from Chevy Chase was the original check which Y & R issued to Hearst Magazine Services. Because this check contained an amount, check number, and date identical to the one Y & R issued, Wachovia concludes that the change in the name of the payee can only be an alteration. Accordingly, Wachovia maintains that it is entitled to recover the amount it paid Chevy Chase upon presentment of the check. *See* Va.Code Ann. § 8.4-207.2(b).

Wachovia may not recover on its claim for breach of warranty unless it proves that the check it received from Chevy Chase was altered. The district court found that Wachovia failed to carry its burden on this issue. We agree.

In support of its position that the check was altered, Wachovia presented nothing more than an assertion that the check it paid differed from the check which Y & R issued. This fact, of course, is obvious. Beyond this, Wachovia must show that the check it received from Chevy Chase was the original check issued by Y & R but with an altered payee. Wachovia has failed to do this.

Wachovia has presented no witnesses who can testify regarding Wachovia's receipt of the check, meaning that no one can offer evidence regarding the condition of the check when it was presented for payment. More importantly, Wachovia cannot present the original check, having destroyed it after making a digital copy. If Wachovia had produced the actual check itself, an examination of the check may have shed light on whether the check was altered. For example, the check may have contained smudges, erasures, chemical bleach marks, broken fibers, or other signs of alteration. Without the original, even Wachovia's own forensic expert testified that he could not say, with a reasonable degree of scientific certainty, that the check had been altered rather than forged or copied (and therefore counterfeit).

In these circumstances, Wachovia has failed to offer any evidence from which a reasonable factfinder could conclude that the check was altered as opposed to counterfeited. Accordingly, Wachovia cannot carry its burden of proving that Chevy Chase breached its warranty of presentment, and its claim against Chevy Chase fails. Having reached this conclusion, we need not address Chevy Chase's alternative argument that Wachovia's claim must fail for lack of damages.

IV

Based on the foregoing, we affirm the judgment of the district court.

AFFIRMED.

NIEMEYER, Circuit Judge, dissenting:

The facts of this case demonstrate, more likely than not, that the check issued by Young & Rubicam, drawn on Wachovia Bank, and presented to Chevy Chase Bank was an altered check, not a forged or counterfeit check. Under the Uniform Commercial Code, therefore, risk of loss by payment on the instrument must be borne by Chevy Chase Bank, and Wachovia Bank is entitled to relief against Chevy Chase Bank for breach of its presentment warranty. *See* Va.Code Ann. § 8.4-207.2. I believe the majority misapplies the summary judgment standard, which requires only that Wachovia create a "genuine issue as to any material fact." Fed.R.Civ.P. 56(c).

The image of the check presented to Chevy Chase Bank contained numerous indications that it was the image of the actual check issued by Young & Rubicam but with the payee altered: (1) the number on the image agreed with the number on the check issued by Young & Rubicam; (2) the date on the image agreed with the date on the check issued by Young & Rubicam; (3) the amount of the check on the image agreed with the amount of the check issued by Young & Rubicam; (4) the machine-embossed signature of Young & Rubicam agreed with its signature on the actual checks issued contemporaneously; (5) the image had the same front-to-back alignment as other checks in the same batch as the check issued by Young & Rubicam; and (6) the image perfectly overlapped with the typographical features of other checks in the batch issued by Young & Rubicam. Additional circumstantial evidence also supports the claim that the image in question was that of the actual check issued by Young & Rubicam: (7) The actual check issued by Young & Rubicam was never returned, except in its altered form, as shown in the image. If the check presented to Chevy Chase Bank was a counterfeit check, then the original check issued by Young & Rubicam would likely have been returned in the ordinary course of banking procedures. (8) The font used in the payee's name on the image check was different from the font otherwise used on the check and was consistent with alteration by typewriter. This indicates that the payee's name was added by alteration. One counterfeiting a Young & Rubicam check would logically have used the same font type throughout, as Young & Rubicam did when it issued the check. Finally, (9) fraud by alteration of the payee was known to be the common form of fraud used to circumvent the "positive-pay" type of arrangement in place between Young & Rubicam and Wachovia Bank. Such fraud is much harder to detect during the routine, high-volume banking process than a check issued with a forged signature on counterfeit check stock.

Because I conclude that the facts presented by Wachovia make it more likely than not that the image was an image of the original check issued Young & Rubicam but altered, I would conclude, *a fortiori,* that Wachovia's evidence was sufficient to create a question of fact, requiring us to deny Chevy Chase Bank's motion for summary judgment.

The majority opinion seems to absolve Chevy Chase Bank of any need to rebut Wachovia's evidence, permitting it rely simply on the bare assertion that the check might have been counterfeit, rather than altered. In addition, the majority enters into needless conflict with our sister circuit in the law of negotiated instruments under the Uniform Commercial Code. *See Wachovia Bank, N.A. v. Foster Bancshares, Inc.,* 457 F.3d 619 (7th Cir.2006). This is unfortunate in an area of law where the need for national uniformity is greatest.

(3) INCOMPLETE INSTRUMENTS

Section 3–115(a). Incomplete Instrument.

(a) "Incomplete instrument" means a signed writing, whether or not issued by the signer, the contents of which show at the time of signing that it is incomplete but that the signer intended it to be completed by the addition of words or numbers.

Assume that A is indebted to B but is not sure of the precise amount of the debt. In payment of the debt, A sends to B a check payable to B, leaving the amount of the check blank. A instructs B to complete the check by filling in the amount of the debt. If the amount of the debt is $10 and B fills in the check for that amount, there is no difficulty in enforcing the check against A. The intent of A has been carried out by B's completion of the check. The result is the same as if A had personally completed the check. When the check was received by B, the check was an "incomplete instrument," defined in 3–115(a). Because the amount of the check was not stated, the check was not a negotiable instrument under 3–104 and the last sentence of 3–115(b) applies. If B completes the check by writing in $10 as its amount, the check becomes an instrument under 3–104 and the last sentence of 3–115(b) states that the check can be enforced as completed. There is no alteration.

But if B fills in $10,000 rather than $10, the act of B is not authorized by A. Under 3–115(c), there is an alteration of the incomplete instrument and 3–407 applies. The case is analogous to the hypothetical case in the material in the previous section in which a check payable in the amount of $10 was altered by changing the amount to $10,000. In each case the drawer intended a check in the amount of $10 and in each case the payee raised the intended amount to $10,000.

Suppose B deposited the altered check in B's account in Depositary Bank and the bank obtained $10,000 from Drawee Bank in payment of the check. Drawee Bank then debited A's account in the same amount. B withdrew the $10,000 that had been credited to B's account in Depositary Bank with respect to the check. When A learned that Drawee Bank had debited $10,000 to A's account with respect to the check, A notified Drawee Bank of the alteration. Who takes the loss in this case? To what extent is Drawee Bank entitled to debit A's account with respect to the check? 3–407(c). If Drawee Bank had dishonored the check, to what extent would Depositary Bank have had a right to recover from A? 3–414(b) & 3–407(c).

Compare the results in this case with the results in the hypothetical case in Section 1 above. Why are the results different? Is there any relationship between 3–406 and 3–407(c) as they apply to fraudulent completion of incomplete instruments?

d. REMOTELY CREATED CHECKS

Telemarketing has proved effective in selling goods and services. In the usual transaction the payment mechanism is a credit card; the buyer gives the credit card number to the telemarketer caller and is charged for the sale on its next statement. What if the buyer wants the article being offered but has no credit card or her credit cards are "maxed out"? No problem. If the buyer has a bank account, the telemarketer asks the buyer to read off the information on the MICR line (the payor bank's routing and transit number and the buyer's account number) of a check. If the buyer is willing to provide this information, the telemarketer prints a check drawn on buyer's account in the payor bank payable to itself, stamps on the signature line "customer authorized draft," or words to that effect, and deposits the check for collection in telemarketer's depositary bank. Unless the buyer stops payment, the check will be paid by the payor bank on the basis of the MICR information with no review of the signature.

If the buyer did not authorize the check, the rule of Price v. Neal places the loss of the unauthorized signature on the payor bank rather than the depositary bank. Interbank of New York v. Fleet Bank, 781 N.Y.S.2d 393 (N.Y. App. Div. 2004). This is a bad result because the depositary bank is in a better position to monitor the behavior of its customer, the telemarketer, than the payor bank. The 2002 revisions of Article 3 impose the risk of an unauthorized signature on the depositary bank, following the lead of several states that had done so by amendments earlier. "Remotely-created consumer item" is defined in 3–103(a)(16) as meaning a check that "does not bear a handwritten signature purporting to be the signature of the drawer." Under 3–416(a)(6), the telemarketer warrants to the depositary bank that the check is authorized by the person on whom the check is drawn, and 3–417(a)(4) provides that the telemarketer and depositary bank warrant the same to the payor bank. These amendments are described in Comment 8 to 3–416 as implementing "a limited rejection of Price v. Neal." A minority of states have adopted the relevant revisions of Article 3, and none has adopted all of them.

In 2006, the Fed partly preempted these provisions. 12 CFR § 229.2(fff) defines a remotely created check as one "that does not bear a signature applied, or purported to be applied, by the person on whose account the check is drawn." 12 CFR § 229.34(d) provides that "[a] bank that transfers or presents a remotely created check and receives a settlement or other consideration warrants to the transferee bank, any subsequent collecting bank, and the paying bank that the person on whose account the remotely created check is drawn authorized the issuance of the check in the amount stated on the check and to the payee stated on the check." Unlike 3-416(a)(6) and 3-417(a)(4), the federally created warranty is not limited to remotely created consumer checks. It applies to remotely created checks drawn on the account of any person, including a business. However, in one respect the federal transfer and presenting warranties are narrower than the UCC warranties; they apply only to banks transferring and presenting remotely created checks, not to nonbanks. Thus, the warranties do not apply to telemarketers creating the telechecks. Because most states have not adopted the relevant revisions to Article 3, Article 3 warranties frequently will also not apply to the telemarketer.

Neither the UCC amendments nor the Fed changes directly address the concern that the use of "remotely-created" checks by telemarketers is subject to abuse. Congress intervened to provide a degree of consumer protection by enacting the Telemarketing and Consumer Fraud and Abuse Prevention Act in 1994, which requires the Federal Trade Commission to issue rules "prohibiting deceptive telemarketing acts or practices." 15 U.S.C. § 6102(a)(1). Pursuant to this, the FTC rule provides that it is a deceptive telemarketing practice to submit for payment a draft drawn on a person's deposit account without that person's "express verifiable authorization." Authorization is deemed verifiable if the customer's authorization is obtained either in writing or on tape or if written confirmation of the transaction is sent to the customer prior to submission for payment of the customer's draft. 16 CFR § 310.3(a)(3). The burden of policing the activities of telemarketers or other users of remotely recreated checks ultimately falls on the bank closest to those persons, the bank of first deposit. The remotely created check issue is extensively discussed in 1 Barkley Clark & Barbara Clark, supra, ¶ 10.02[2] (Rev. ed. 2009).

The FTC's Telemarketing Sales Rule, establishing the "Do–Not–Call" registry, 16 CFR § 310.4(b)(1)(iii), Mar. 31, 2003, should reduce the volume of telemarketing sales, and, presumably, the abuses associated with telemarketing. Congress ratified the FTC Rule in H.R. 3161, 108th Cong., 1st Sess. (2003).

e. OVERDRAFTS

If a payor bank pays a check that is forged or which bears a forged indorsement, it is clear that the bank paid the check by mistake. No bank would knowingly pay such a check because the check is not properly payable and the payor bank is not entitled to charge the account of the drawer. The payment of a check drawn on an account in which there are insufficient funds to cover the check is different. Under 4–401(a), such a check is properly payable and the drawer's account can be charged. Thus, it may not be clear at the time of payment whether the payor bank paid by mistake or intended to grant credit to the drawer. Intentional payment of checks that create overdrafts is very common. There is some authority denying a payor bank any right of restitution in overdraft cases, but most courts follow Restatement (First) of Restitution § 29 (1937), which recognizes a limited right of restitution in such cases. In Article 3, overdraft cases are governed by 3–418(b), which gives to the payor bank a right to recover "to the extent permitted by the law governing mistake and restitution." But 3–418(b) is subject to 3–418(c). No right of restitution may be asserted against a person who took the check in good faith and for value or who in good faith changed position in reliance on payment of the check.

3. Conversion Actions Regarding Checks Bearing Forged Indorsement

a. ACTION BY PAYEE

(1) INTRODUCTION

Section 3–420(a) restates the common law rule: "An instrument is...converted if it is taken by transfer, other than a negotiation, from a person not entitled to enforce the instrument or a bank makes or obtains payment with respect to the instrument for a person not entitled to enforce the instrument or receive payment." Thus, a person, including a depositary bank, taking after a forged indorsement is a converter, as is a drawee bank that pays such an instrument. A payee or other holder from whom the instrument has been taken has a choice of suing either the depositary bank (3–420(c)) or the drawee bank for the conversion even though neither knew that the indorsement was forged. Solve the following Problem on the basis of the text set out below the Problem and the statutes cited.

PROBLEM

Electronic Supply Co. (ESC) sells products by mail order and over the Internet as well as at its retail store, which also serves as its headquarters. Most of its sales are paid for by credit cards or cash but some are by checks drawn on banks throughout the nation. Thief, a former employee, broke into the retail store after the close of business and stole cash and unindorsed checks payable to ESC from buyers. He had prepared a stamp, bearing ESC's name, which he used to indorse the stolen checks. Beneath the stamped indorsement, Thief signed the name he used as an account holder at Depositary Bank (DB) and made an ATM deposit of the stolen checks in DB before dawn. The various payor banks on which the checks were drawn paid the checks when presented by DB through banking channels. DB allowed Thief to withdraw the proceeds of the checks before the forgeries were discovered. What are ESC's remedies with respect to (i) the drawers of the checks, (ii) the several payor banks on which the checks were drawn, and (iii) DB? Which remedy would you advise ESC to use? Why?

In a common type of forged indorsement case, the check is stolen by an employee of the payee. The check is an ordinary check mailed to the payee by the drawer in payment of an obligation owed to the payee. The check is received by the payee when the mail delivery is made and the payee becomes a holder of the check at that time. Suppose the check is stolen by an employee of the payee who works as a clerk in the payee's mailroom. The employee forges the payee's name as an indorsement of the check and obtains payment from the drawee bank. How does the theft of the check and its collection affect the payee's rights with respect to the check and the obligation of the drawer to the payee that the check was intended to pay? Under 3–310(b), the obligation for which the check was received becomes "suspended" at the time the payee receives the check. In the hands of the payee, the check represents a right to receive money, which is a property right of the payee. This property right is provisionally substituted for the right of the payee to enforce the obligation for which the check was received. If the payee receives payment of the check, the obligation for which the check was received is discharged to the extent of the payment. 3–310(b)(1). If the payee presents the check for payment and the check is dishonored, the payee has a cause of action against the drawer of the check either on the check (3–414(b)) or on the obligation for which the check was received (3–310(b)(3)).

What rights does the payee have if the check is stolen from the payee and the thief obtains payment from the drawee? Under 3–310(b)(1), "[p]ayment...of the check" results in discharge of the obligation for which a check was taken, but under 3–602(a), the check is not paid unless payment is made to a person entitled to enforce the check. Payment to the thief or a transferee of the thief does not result in payment of the check, and the obligation of the drawer on the check is not discharged. The payee of the check remains the owner of the check and the person entitled to enforce it. 3–301 and 3–309 (lost instruments). The drawee's payment to a person not entitled to enforce the check does not affect the payee's rights in the check. The payee, however, does not have a right to enforce the obligation for which the check was received. That obligation remains suspended under 3–310(b) because neither dishonor nor payment of the check has occurred. Under the last sentence of 3–310(b)(4), the payee of a stolen check who is not in possession of the check, has rights against the drawer only on the check. 3–309, 3–414, and Comment 4 to 3–310. Thus, the payee has the burden of asserting rights with respect to the stolen check, and there are several possible courses of action available to the payee against third parties as well as the drawer.

Although the payee from whom a check has been stolen has no right to obtain a substitute check from the drawer, sometimes the drawer will issue such a check. In the case in which payment with respect to the stolen check has not yet been made by the drawee, the drawee can be informed of the theft and payment to the thief may be avoided. If payment by the drawee has already been made, the drawer can insist that the drawee recredit the drawer's account because payment to the thief did not entitle the drawee to debit the drawer's account. 4–401. If the drawer refuses to issue a replacement check, the payee has a remedy against the drawer on the stolen check, but that remedy may not be convenient. 3–309. Often a forged indorsement case involves thefts of many checks from one payee by the same thief. Actions against the various drawers of the stolen checks may not be feasible. An action against the person who took the checks from the thief is usually a better remedy.

In the hands of the payee, a check is property and, if that property is stolen, the rules of conversion applying to personal property also apply to the check. Thus, the payee of the stolen check has an action in conversion against the thief for the amount of the check. But the law of conversion also allows an action to be brought against "innocent converters," i.e. persons who exercise dominion over stolen property without knowledge that it was stolen. Thus, if a thief sells stolen goods to a good faith purchaser for value, the owner has an action against the BFP as well. A stolen check bearing the forged indorsement of the payee can be turned into money by selling it to a depositary bank or other purchaser for cash, by depositing it to the thief's bank account for bank credit that can subsequently be withdrawn, or by presenting the check for payment to the drawee bank. Each of these takers of the check is a potential defendant. The common law was clear that a conversion action could be brought by the payee against the person who bought the check. The common law cases were divided on the issue of whether the drawee bank was liable in conversion if it paid a stolen check bearing a forged indorsement, but most courts held that a conversion action was available and that view was adopted by Article 3. Article 3 states the rules regarding conversion in 3–420.

(2) DELIVERY OF CHECK TO PAYEE

Pre-revision authorities were divided on whether the payee of a check could sue a depositary bank for conversion when the check had been stolen before it was delivered to the payee. Section 3–420(a)(ii) states that a payee cannot bring conversion unless it has received delivery. Comment 1 explains that a payee has no interest in the check until it receives delivery. If a check has not been delivered to the payee, its rights against the drawer have not been affected by the theft; the drawer is still liable to the payee on the underlying obligation.

Article 3 does not define "delivery." It states only that delivery may either be made directly to the payee or to an agent or co-payee. 3–420(a)(ii). Comment 1 to 3–420 states that a payee receives delivery when the check comes into the payee's possession. Words like "delivery," "agency," and "possession" are familiar but inexact terms, and Article 9 leaves their meaning to the body of common law that has grown around them. Clearly, delivery of a settlement check to the plaintiff's dishonest attorney is delivery to the plaintiff's agent. Leeds v. Chase Manhattan Bank, N.A., 752 A.2d 332 (N.J. Super.Ct. App. Div. 2000). Comment 1 opines on a recurring issue when it observes that a payee has possession when a check is put into its mailbox. The court in Hancock Bank v. Ensenat, 819 So.2d 3 (Miss. Ct. App. 2001), relied on this Comment to hold that possession occurs when the check arrives at the payee's home mailing address.

(3) LIABILITY OF DEPOSITARY BANK AS AGENT FOR COLLECTION

When a check is transferred to a depositary bank by its customer, the bank sometimes purchases the check from the customer by giving cash for it or by giving the customer a credit to the customer's account immediately available for withdrawal as of right. More commonly, the depositary bank doesn't buy the check. Rather, it takes the check as agent of the customer to obtain payment of the check from the payor bank and pays the proceeds of the check to the customer after the check is paid. This distinction can have some importance in Article 3 because the status of the depositary bank as a holder in due course may depend upon whether it had given value for the check at the time the check was presented for payment. But, in Article 4, the depositary bank is normally treated as an agent for collection whether or not the bank gave value to the customer for the check. 4–201(a).

Under former Article 3, the statute appeared to provide that a depositary bank, as well as subsequent collecting banks, was not liable for conversion if it acted merely as an agent for collection. This was a reversal of the common law rule, and some courts, by using creative statutory construction, refused to follow the literal wording of the statute. In justifying their deliberate misreading of the statute, courts pointed out that to do otherwise produced the ridiculous result that forced the payee to sue the payor bank in conversion and the payor bank to proceed against the depositary bank for breach of its presentment warranty; two lawsuits instead of one. The issue is well discussed in Denn v. First State Bank, 316 N.W.2d 532 (Minn.1982), in which the court reluctantly read the statute literally but acknowledged that to do so produced a bad result.

Section 3–420(a) and (c) return to the pre-UCC rule that allowed the payee to sue the depositary bank directly in conversion. Not only is judicial economy served because the bank of first deposit is ultimately liable in forged indorsement cases owing to its presentment warranty to the payor bank under 3–417(a)(1) and 4–208(a)(1), but, also, it is usually the most convenient defendant for the payee to sue in the common case of multiple forgeries in which an employee has forged the indorsement of the employer on checks drawn on many different payor banks, some in different states. Comment 3 to 3-420.

(4) UNAUTHORIZED INDORSEMENT

If a check is made payable to two persons, ambiguity sometimes arises whether both must indorse for the instrument to be negotiated or whether either may do so. Section 3–110(d) provides that if an instrument is payable to two or more persons alternatively, either may indorse, but if it is payable to them "not alternatively," all signatures are required. Section 3–403(b) states that the signature of an organization is unauthorized if one of the required signatures is lacking. How can we be sure when an instrument is payable to them alternatively so that one signature may constitute a negotiation?

PROBLEM

In each of the following cases, the check was indorsed only by Michael Bijlani & Assoc. and was deposited in Bank. Under 3–110(d), in which case or cases should Bank have demanded Bay Village Inc.'s signature before taking the check?

Case #1. The check was payable to "Bay Village Inc. Michael Bijlani & Assoc." See Bijlani v. Nationsbank of Florida, 1995 WL 264180 (Fla. Cir. Ct. 1995).

Case #2. How would Case #1 be decided if there were a slash (/) or virgule between "Inc." and "Michael"? See Purina Mills, Inc. v. Sec. Bank & Trust, 547 N.W.2d 336 (Mich. Ct. App.1996); Danco, Inc. v. Commerce Bank/Shore, N.A., 675 A.2d 663 (N.J.Sup.Ct. App. Div. 1996).

Case #3. How would Case #1 be decided if there were a hyphen between "Inc." and "Michael"? See J.R. Simplot, Inc. v. Knight, 988 P.2d 955 (Wash. 1999).

(5) FORGERY BY ENTRUSTED EMPLOYEE OF PAYEE

As we stated earlier, perhaps the most common cases of forged indorsements are the "inside jobs." An employee entrusted with the responsibility of dealing with checks payable to the employer forges the indorsement of the employer and covers up the forgery in the reconcilement process. Section 3–406(a) provides that if the payor bank can prove that the employer's failure to supervise the employee's activities and to monitor the financial records that the employee kept substantially contributed to the forgery, it can throw the forgery loss back on the employer. In the drafting of Revised Article 3, the contention was made that it was unfair to impose on the bank the burden of proving the employer's negligence. If the employer chose to entrust responsibility to an employee and the employee betrayed the trust, isn't it fair to put the risk of loss with respect to the employee's misconduct on the employer rather than the bank? The original Code recognized in Comment 4 to former 3–405 that in such cases the loss should fall on the employer as the risk of its business enterprise because it is normally in a better position to prevent forgeries by reasonable care in selecting or supervising employees "or if he is not, is at least in a better position to cover the loss by fidelity insurance." Section 3–405 implements this policy.

The following scenario is a summary of some of the facts, somewhat modified, of Cooper v. Union Bank, 507 P.2d 609 (Cal. 1973). This fact situation is one of the templates the drafters had in mind in writing 3–405 and its analysis offers an informative journey through the statute. See Comment 3, Case #3.

> Stell, a lawyer, was retained by Ruff to represent her in connection with her insolvency and litigation brought against her by several creditors. She informed Stell that her financial difficulties were primarily due to gambling losses she had sustained. A short time later, Stell hired Ruff as a secretary and bookkeeper. Ruff's duties included posting the amounts of checks received by Stell to the proper accounts in Stell's accounting records and reconciling the monthly bank statement of deposits and withdrawals with respect to Stell's checking account with Stell's accounting records. Over a period of a year and a half, Ruff stole 29 checks payable to Stell that were received in the mail, and forged Stell's indorsement to these checks. Most of these checks were cashed over the counter at Depositary Bank at which both Stell and Ruff had checking accounts. A few of the checks were deposited to Ruff's account in Depositary Bank. Stell was well known to the tellers at the bank as a customer of the bank and Ruff was well known as Stell's secretary. It was the policy of Depositary Bank to allow checks payable to known customers to be cashed over the counter by the customer or the customer's secretary. The forgeries by Ruff were so well done that only a handwriting expert could have detected them.
>
> Stell exercised almost no supervision over Ruff, never reviewed the books that she kept, and never checked the bank reconciliation of deposits to Stell's checking account. Stell brought an action in conversion against Depositary Bank with respect to the 29 checks that were transferred by Ruff to that bank.

Under the second sentence of 3–420(a), Depositary Bank is liable to Stell as a converter of the 29 checks that Ruff transferred to it if: (1) Depositary Bank did not become the holder of the checks as a result of the transfer, i.e., the transfer was not a negotiation, and (2) Ruff was not a person entitled to enforce the checks when she transferred them to Depositary Bank, i.e., she was not a holder at the time of the transfer. Both of these elements depend upon whether the forgery by Ruff of Stell's signature was effective as Stell's indorsement in spite of the fact that it was a forgery. Section 3–405 addresses this issue.

Section 3–405 applies to this case if a "fraudulent indorsement" (3–405(a)(2)) was made by Ruff, and Ruff was entrusted by Stell, her employer, with "responsibility" (3–405(a)(3)) with respect to the checks that she transferred to Depositary Bank. Under the first sentence of 3–405(b), is the indorsement by Ruff effective as the indorsement of Stell? The first and last paragraphs of Comment 1 to 3–405 address this issue. The Ruff–Stell scenario should be compared with Case #1, Case #3, and Case #4 of Comment 3 to 3–405. If Stell is not entitled to recover from Depositary Bank as a converter of the 29 checks because of the first sentence of 3–405(b), is Stell entitled to any recovery against Depositary Bank based on the last sentence of 3–405(b)? Under that sentence, is there any difference in result with respect to the checks cashed over the counter and the checks deposited to Ruff's account?

b. ACTION BY DRAWER

Forged indorsement cases usually involve a theft of the check from the payee, but sometimes the theft of the check occurs before the check is received by the payee. In *Stone & Webster,* which follows, an employee of the drawer of several checks stole the checks from the drawer before the checks could be mailed to the payee. The stolen checks were intended to pay debts of the drawer to the payee. In such a case, the payee has no legal claim with respect to the checks because the payee never received them. The theft of the check and payment by the drawee to the thief do not change payee's rights with respect to the debt for which the check was written. The payee never became the owner of the check and the drawer's debt to the payee remains unpaid; 3–310(b) does not apply. The drawer of the stolen check has a continuing obligation to pay the debt for which the check was issued and, thus, is obliged to issue a replacement check to the payee.

The drawer normally will not suffer any loss with respect to a check bearing a forged indorsement if the drawer is free of negligence contributing to the theft and forgery. 3–406. The payor bank may not charge the drawer's account because a check bearing a forged indorsement is not properly payable according to Comment 1 to 4–401(a). Thus, the drawer is entitled to have the account in the payor bank credited for the amount of the payment. This remedy of the drawer is clear and convenient, since in most cases, the drawer's account will be in a local bank. Nevertheless, there have been a number of cases in which the drawer, instead of suing the payor bank, sued the depositary bank. Such a suit might be brought in the uncommon case in which the depositary bank is a local bank and the payor bank is out of state, or the drawer may simply be reluctant to sue the payor bank with which the drawer has a favorable business relationship. The issue in these cases is whether the drawer of a check stolen from it has a property right in the check that can be asserted in a conversion action. The authority on the issue was divided under original Article 3. The view expressed in the seminal case of *Stone & Webster* was adopted by 3–420(a)(i).

Stone & Webster Engineering Corp. v. First National Bank & Trust Co.

Supreme Judicial Court of Massachusetts, 1962.
345 Mass. 1, 184 N.E.2d 358.

■ WILKINS, CHIEF JUSTICE.

In this action of contract or tort in four counts for the same cause of action a demurrer to the declaration was sustained, and the plaintiff, described in the writ as having a usual place of business in Boston, appealed. G.L. (Ter.Ed.) c. 231, § 96. The questions argued concern the rights of the drawer against a collecting bank which "cashed" checks for an individual who had forged the payee's indorsement on the checks, which were never delivered to the payee.

In the first count, which is in contract, the plaintiff alleges that between January 1, 1960, and May 15, 1960, it was indebted at various times to Westinghouse Electric Corporation (Westinghouse) for goods and services furnished to it by Westinghouse; that in order to pay the indebtedness the plaintiff drew three checks within that period on its checking account in The First National Bank of Boston (First National) payable to Westinghouse in the total amount of $64,755.44; that before delivery of the checks to Westinghouse an employee of the plaintiff in possession of the checks forged the indorsement of Westinghouse and presented the checks to the defendant; that the defendant "cashed" the checks and delivered the proceeds to the plaintiff's employee who devoted the proceeds to his own use; that the defendant forwarded the checks to First National and received from First National the full amounts thereof; and that First National charged the account of the plaintiff with the full amounts of the checks and has refused to recredit the plaintiff's checking account; wherefore the defendant owes the plaintiff $64,755.44 with interest.

Count 2, also in contract, is on an account annexed for money owed, namely $64,755.44, the proceeds of checks of the plaintiff "cashed" by the defendant on forged indorsements between January 1, 1960, and May 15, 1960.

Counts 3 and 4 in tort are respectively for conversion of the checks and for negligence in "cashing" the checks with forged indorsements.

By order, copies of the three checks were filed in court. The checks are respectively dated at Rowe in this Commonwealth on January 5, March 8, and May 9, 1960. Their respective amounts are $36,982.86, $10,416.58 and $17,355. They are payable to the order of "Westinghouse Electric Corporation, 10 High Street, Boston." The first two checks are indorsed in typewriting, "For Deposit Only: Westinghouse Electric Corporation By: Mr. O. D. Costine, Treasury Representative" followed by an ink signature "O. D. Costine." The Third check is indorsed in typewriting, "Westinghouse Electric Corporation By: [Sgd.] O. D. Costine Treasury Representative." All three checks also bear the indorsement by rubber stamp, "Pay to the order of any bank, banker or trust co. prior indorsements guaranteed...[date][1] The First National Bank & Trust Co. Greenfield, Mass."

The demurrer, in so far as it has been argued, is to each count for failure to state a cause of action.

....

1. Count 1, the plaintiff contends, is for money had and received. We shall so regard it. "An action for money had and received lies to recover money which should not in justice be retained by the defendant, and which in equity and good conscience should be paid to the plaintiff." Cobb v. Library Bureau, 268 Mass. 311, 316, 167 N.E. 765, 767; Adams v. First Nat. Bank, 321 Mass. 693, 694, 75 N.E.2d 502; Trafton v. Custeau, 338 Mass. 305, 308, 155 N.E.2d 159.

The defendant has no money in its hands which belongs to the plaintiff. The latter had no right in the proceeds of its own check payable to Westinghouse. Not being a holder or an agent for a holder, it could not have presented the check to the drawee for payment. * * * See Uniform Commercial Code § 3–419, comment 2: "A negotiable instrument is the property of the holder." See also Restatement 2d: Torts, Tent. draft no. 3, 1958, § 241A. The plaintiff contends that "First National paid or credited the proceeds of the checks to the defendant and charged the account of the plaintiff, and consequently, the plaintiff was deprived of a credit, and the defendant received funds or a credit which 'in equity and good conscience' belonged to the plaintiff."

In our opinion this argument is a non sequitur. The plaintiff as a depositor in First National was merely in a contractual relationship of creditor and debtor.... The amounts the defendant received from First National to cover the checks "cashed" were the bank's funds and not the plaintiff's. The Uniform Commercial Code does not purport to change the relationship.... Section 3–409(1) provides: "A check or other draft does not of itself operate as an assignment of any funds in the hands of the drawee available for its payment, and the drawee is not liable on the instrument until he accepts it.".... Whether the plaintiff was rightfully deprived of a credit is a matter between it and the drawee, First National.

If we treat the first count as seeking to base a cause of action for money had and received upon a waiver of the tort of conversion—a matter which it is not clear is argued—the result will be the same. In this aspect the question presented is whether a drawer has a right of action for conversion against a collecting bank which handles its checks in the bank collection process. Unless there be such a right, there is no tort which can be waived.

---

[1] The respective dates are January 13, March 9, and May 11, 1960. Each check bears the stamped indorsement of the Federal Reserve Bank of Boston and on its face the paid stamp of The First National Bank of Boston.

The plaintiff relies upon the Uniform Commercial Code § 3–419, which provides, "(1) An instrument is converted when...(c) it is paid on a forged indorsement." This, however, could not apply to the defendant, which is not a "payor bank," defined in the Code, § 4–105(b), as "a bank by which an item is payable as drawn or accepted."....

A conversion provision of the Uniform Commercial Code which might have some bearing on this case is § 3–419(3). This section implicitly recognizes that, subject to defences, including the one stated in it, a collecting bank, defined in the Code, § 4–105(d), may be liable in conversion. In the case at bar the forged indorsements were "wholly inoperative" as the signatures of the payee, Code §§ 3–404(1), 1–201(43), and equally so both as to the restrictive indorsements for deposits, see § 3–205(c), and as to the indorsement in blank, see § 3–204(2). When the forger transferred the checks to the collecting bank, no negotiation under § 3–202(1) occurred, because there was lacking the necessary indorsement of the payee. For the same reason, the collecting bank could not become a "holder" as defined in § 1–201(20), and so could not become a holder in due course under § 3–302(1). Accordingly, we assume that the collecting bank may be liable in conversion to a proper party, subject to defences, including that in § 3–419(3). See A. Blum, Jr.'s, Sons v. Whipple, 194 Mass. 253, 255, 80 N.E. 501, 13 L.R.A.,N.S., 211. But there is no explicit provision in the Code purporting to determine to whom the collecting bank may be liable, and consequently, the drawer's right to enforce such a liability must be found elsewhere. Therefore, we conclude that the case must be decided on our own law, which, on the issue we are discussing, has been left untouched by the Uniform Commercial Code in any specific section....

The authorities are hopelessly divided. We think that the preferable view is that there is no right of action....

We state what appears to us to be the proper analysis. Had the checks been delivered to the payee Westinghouse, the defendant might have been liable for conversion to the payee. The checks, if delivered, in the hands of the payee would have been valuable property which could have been transferred for value or presented for payment; and, had a check been dishonored, the payee would have had a right of recourse against the drawer on the instrument under § 3–413(2). Here the plaintiff drawer of the checks, which were never delivered to the payee..., had no valuable rights in them. Since, as we have seen, it did not have the right of a payee or subsequent holder to present them to the drawee for payment, the value of its rights was limited to the physical paper on which they were written, and was not measured by their payable amounts....

The enactment of the Uniform Commercial Code opens the road for the adoption of what seems the preferable view. An action by the drawer against the collecting bank might have some theoretical appeal as avoiding circuity of action.... It would have been in the interest of speedy and complete justice had the case been tried with the action by the drawer against the drawee and with an action by the drawee against the collecting bank.... So one might ask: If the drawee is liable to the drawer and the collecting bank is liable to the drawee, why not let the drawer sue the collecting bank direct? We believe that the answer lies in the applicable defences set up in the Code.

The drawer can insist that the drawee recredit his account with the amount of any unauthorized payment. Such was our common law.... This is, in effect, retained by the Code §§ 4–401(1), 4–406(4). But the drawee has defences based upon the drawer's substantial negligence, if "contributing," or upon his duty to discover and report unauthorized signatures and alterations. §§ 3–406, 4–406. As to unauthorized indorsements, see § 4–406(4). Then, if the drawee has a valid defence which it waives or fails upon request to assert, the drawee may not assert against the collecting bank or other prior party presenting or transferring the check a claim which is based on the forged indorsement. § 4–406(5). If the drawee recredits the drawer's account and is not precluded by § 4–406(5), it may claim against the presenting bank on the relevant warranties in §§ 3–417 and 4–207, and each transferee has rights against his transferor under those sections.

If the drawer's rights are limited to requiring the drawee to recredit his account, the drawee will have the defences noted above and perhaps others; and the collecting bank or banks will have the defences in § 4–207(4) and § 4–406(5), and perhaps others. If the drawer is allowed in the present case to sue the collecting bank, the assertion of the defences, for all practical purposes, would be difficult. The possibilities of such a result would tend to compel resort to litigation in every case involving a forgery of commercial paper. It is a result to be avoided.

The court sustained demurrers to all plaintiff's counts.

PROBLEM

Employee stole an unindorsed check from her employer, Payee, forged Payee's indorsement and deposited it in Depositary Bank (DB) for collection. Payor Bank (PB) paid the check upon presentment and debited Drawer's account for the amount of the check. When the forgery was discovered, PB erased the debit to Drawer's account and relied on DB's breach of presentment warranty in demanding the return of the amount that it paid DB in settlement for the check. DB defended on the ground that Drawer's lack of due care substantially contributed to the forgery and that PB should debit Drawer's account under 3–405 or 3–406 rather than proceeding against DB for breach of its warranty. If Drawer's conduct contributed to the forgery, should PB be allowed to shift the loss from the drawer to DB? See 3–417(c), Comment 6 to 3–417, and 4–208(c). DB's liability to PB is only to reimburse it for any loss resulting from the breach of warranty. 3–417(b), 4–208(b). If Drawer may not raise the forgery against PB because of 3–405 or 3–406, has PB been damaged by DB's breach of presentment warranty?

4. IMPOSTORS AND FICTITIOUS PAYEES

We have seen that in forged indorsement cases, as a general rule, the loss falls on the bank of first deposit, the bank that dealt with the forger. But exceptions to this rule have been made in certain situations in which it seems unfair to allocate the loss in this manner. One of these exceptions is the impostor cases, covered by 3–404(a). Another is the fictitious payee cases governed by 3–404(b). Still another is the payroll-padding cases to which 3–405 and other provisions apply. The drafting stratagem used to identify these cases in Article 3 is largely based on the intent of the issuer of the instrument with respect to the person to whom the instrument is payable. Hence, before looking at the exceptions, we examine the intent issue.

a. INTENT OF ISSUER

In some cases in which a forged indorsement is alleged, it may not be clear whether there is a forged indorsement because it is not clear to whom the instrument is payable. In identifying the person to whom the instrument is payable, the starting point is 3–110.

Suppose Jane Doe writes a check to the order of Richard Roe. Under 3–110(a), the intent of Doe determines to whom the check is payable. There may be many people in the world named Richard Roe, but only the Richard Roe intended by Doe is the payee of the check. If the check gets into the hands of a different Richard Roe, an indorsement by that Richard Roe is ineffective as an indorsement of the payee of the check.

Change the facts. Suppose Doe made a mistake in writing the check. Intending to issue a check to a person that she thinks is Richard Roe, she writes that name as the payee of the check. In fact, the name of the person to whom she intended to issue the check is Peter Poe and Poe has never used the name Richard Roe. If Doe delivers the check to Poe, Poe becomes the holder of the check even though the check states that it is payable to Richard Roe. An indorsement by Poe is effective because Poe is the payee of the check. Poe may indorse by signing either the name on the check or Poe's name. 3–110(a) and 3–204(d).

The rules stated in 3–110(a) apply to the issuer of a negotiable instrument in determining to whom the instrument is initially payable and the same rules apply in determining to whom an instrument is subsequently made payable by a holder making a special indorsement. 3–205(a). Thus, if Jane Doe is the payee of the check rather than the drawer and she indorses the check with the indorsement "Pay to Richard Roe," the person to whom the check becomes payable is determined by Doe's intent according to the rules in 3–110.

Section 3–110 is also important with respect to forged checks. Suppose Thief steals Jane Doe's checkbook and forges her name to a check on her bank account. The check is made payable to Richard Roe. Although Thief's act of signing Doe's name to the check is ineffective as the signature of Doe, the signature is effective as Thief's signature. 3–403(a). Under 3–110(a), it is the intention of Thief, the drawer of the check, that determines to whom the check is payable.

An organization such as a corporation must act through human agents in the drawing of checks, and the organization normally identifies officers who are authorized to sign checks in behalf of the organization. Often, the organization requires that its checks be signed by more than one authorized officer. Under 3–110(a), the intent of the authorized officer or officers signing in behalf of the organization determines to whom the check is payable. But in many cases, checks of organizations do not bear any manually-made signature on behalf of the organization. Rather, the check is produced by a check-writing machine and the signature of the drawer is a printed or facsimile signature. The terms of the check, including the name of the payee, are determined by information entered into the computer that controls the check-writing machine. The person providing the information usually is an authorized employee acting in good faith on behalf of the organization, but sometimes the person providing the information is acting fraudulently and might be either an employee authorized to operate the machine or a wholly unauthorized person. In all of these cases, the intention of the person supplying the information determines to whom the check is payable. 3–110(b).

People engaged in fraud usually try to mask the fraud. For example, an employee authorized to operate a corporation's check-writing machine wishes to steal money by obtaining payment of checks produced by the machine. Instead of causing the machine to produce checks payable to the employee, the employee causes the machine to produce checks payable to a different payee. The payee named on the check may be an imaginary person, a so-called "fictitious payee," or the check may name as payee a real person who is not intended to have any interest in the check. In either case, the intent of the dishonest employee is to produce a check for the employee's benefit that the employee can turn into cash after indorsing it by signing the name of the payee indicated on the check. In either case, to whom is the check payable? Is the indorsement by the employee an effective indorsement or a forgery? These cases are governed by 3–404(b), which validates the indorsement and allows the check to be negotiated by the employee.

b. IMPOSTORS

Although 3–110(a) states that the intent of the person writing the check determines to whom the check is payable, in some cases, it is not possible to clearly identify the payee that way. These cases involve issuance of checks to impostors. For example, if Rogers by impersonating Jacobs induces Drawer to issue to her an instrument payable to Jacobs, Drawer might well have dual intent: to make the check payable to the person to whom he issued the instrument (Rogers) and to the person he thought Rogers was (Jacobs). In this case, the statute resolves the case by providing that if Rogers induced Drawer to issue the instrument to him by impersonating Jacobs, Roger's indorsement of Jacobs' name on the instrument is effective. 3–404(a). Since business organizations must operate through the acts of their agents, cases involving malefactors who impersonate agents are common. Unlike its predecessor, 3–404(a) applies to such impersonations.

PROBLEMS

1. Pauley fraudulently induced Martini to write a check on Bank One for $5,000 payable to Herman by convincing Martini that Pauley was Herman, a person of high repute. Pauley took the check from Martini, indorsed Herman's name on the back of the check and deposited the check in Pauley's account in Bank Two. The check was presented by Bank Two to Bank One, Martini's bank, which paid the check. Pauley withdrew all the funds in his account in Bank Two and absconded. Martini claims that Bank One cannot debit his account for the amount of the check because Herman's indorsement was forged. Is Martini correct? See 3–404(a).

2. Pauley induced Martini to write a check on Bank One for $5,000 to the Red Cross of Cook County by leading Martini to believe that Pauley was chair of the local Red Cross chapter. Pauley wrote two indorsements on the check: first, "Cook County Red Cross", and second, "Pauley". Pauley deposited the check in his account in Bank Two, which presented it to Bank One, Martini's bank, which paid the check. Pauley withdrew the funds representing the check from his account and absconded. Martini claims that Bank One cannot debit his account for the amount of the check because Pauley forged the indorsement by writing "Cook County Red Cross" on the back of the check. Is Martini correct? See Comment 1 to 3–404.

The following case compares the former and the present impostor provisions with respect to agency impersonations. How does it help you solve the preceding problems?

Title Insurance Co. of Minnesota v. Comerica Bank–California

Court of Appeal, Sixth District, 1994.
27 Cal.App.4th 800, 32 Cal.Rptr.2d 735.

■ MIHARA, ASSOCIATE JUSTICE.

At issue in this appeal is the applicability and scope of the "impostor rule," which makes an indorsed check effective if the drawer was induced to issue the check by an impersonator of the payee. (Com.Code, § 3404, subd. (a); former Com.Code, § 3405, subd. (1)(a).) Plaintiff Title Insurance Company of Minnesota contends the trial court erroneously applied this rule in sustaining the demurrer of the drawee bank, respondent Comerica Bank–California ("Bank"), to plaintiff's complaint for negligence. We agree that the impostor rule is not applicable under the circumstances presented, and accordingly reverse the judgment of dismissal.

ALLEGATIONS OF THE COMPLAINT

....

Plaintiff is the assignee of the interests of First National Mortgage Company ("FNMC"), who made two equity loans to Helen Nastor ("Helen"), secured by deeds of trust. Plaintiff issued a policy of land title insurance for each of these loans.

On September 22, 1988, FNMC issued a check payable to Helen in the amount of $58,659.29, the proceeds of the first loan. FNMC gave the check to Helen's son, Rudy Nastor ("Rudy"), for delivery to Helen. That day, someone impersonating Helen indorsed the check and presented it to Bank, where FNMC held an account. Bank paid the impersonator the full amount of the check.

On December 29, 1988, FNMC made a second loan to Helen in the amount of $108,300. Part of the proceeds of this loan were used to pay off the first loan. The remainder was issued to Rudy in the form of a check made payable to him.

When FNMC failed to receive payment on the $108,300 loan, it initiated nonjudicial foreclosure proceedings against Helen's property. On October 17, 1989, Helen's attorney informed FNMC that its deed of trust on the property was invalid because it had been executed by Rudy using a forged power of attorney. Helen thereafter testified by deposition that she had not executed the power of attorney, nor had she indorsed or presented the check to Bank for payment.

FNMC made a claim for payment under the second title insurance policy, and plaintiff paid FNMC $108,300. Plaintiff, acting as subrogee and assignee with respect to FNMC's claim, then sued Bank for negligence, seeking recovery of the $108,000. According to the first amended complaint, Bank had a duty "to establish and practice such procedures and business practices as are or may be reasonably necessary and effective to avoid a breach of any of the duties of care owed by BANK ... to the depositors and customers of BANK ... including therein a duty to immediately inform customers such as FNMC when impostors and/or forgers attempt to cash a check drawn on such customers' accounts with BANK." Bank breached this duty, plaintiff alleged, by failing to ensure "that only properly endorsed and presented checks of its depositors [were] paid." Had Bank "caught" the impostor trying to cash the check payable to Helen, it would have informed FNMC of the attempt, and FNMC would have discovered the forged power of attorney before it made the second loan.

APPLICABILITY OF THE IMPOSTOR RULE

Bank's demurrer is based entirely on the asserted applicability of the impostor rule, which, according to Bank, interposes an "absolute defense" against plaintiff's allegations of negligence. Bank relies on the current provisions of section 3404, subdivision (a) (hereafter, "section 3404(a)"), which makes an indorsement by any person effective if an impostor had induced the issuance of the instrument to either the impostor or "a person acting in concert with the impostor."[1] In this case, argues Bank, Rudy was acting in concert with the impostor (the impersonator of Helen), who presented the check to Bank for payment.

Plaintiff responds that section 3404(a) is not applicable, because it was not enacted until 1992, after the events alleged in the complaint. Instead, plaintiff maintains, this case is controlled by former section 3405, subdivision (1)(a) (hereafter, "former section 3405(1)(a)"). The expression of the rule in the latter statute is substantially the same as that of the current provisions, but excluded from its reach are false representations of agency. Because Rudy obtained the check from FNMC by falsely representing that he was authorized to act as Helen's agent, plaintiff argues the transaction at issue is outside the scope of the impostor rule.

We agree with plaintiff that former section 3405(1)(a) governs the disposition of this case, since the events at issue took place in 1988, while that statute was still in effect. Former section 3405(1)(a) provided: "An indorsement by any person in the name of a named payee is effective if (a) An impostor by use of the mails or otherwise has induced the maker or drawer to issue the instrument to him or his confederate in the name of the payee...."

---

[1] Section 3404(a) states: "If an impostor, by use of the mails or otherwise, induces the issuer of an instrument to issue the instrument to the impostor, or to a person acting in concert with the impostor, by impersonating the payee of the instrument or a person authorized to act for the payee, an indorsement of the instrument by any person in the name of the payee is effective as the indorsement of the payee in favor of a person who, in good faith, pays the instrument or takes it for value or for collection."

This section does not protect Bank from liability under the circumstances presented. As one California court explained prior to the enactment of former section 3405, the impostor rule is applicable only when the issuance of the check has been accomplished through *impersonation* of the payee: "[W]here a check is delivered to an impostor as payee and the drawer believes that the impostor is the person upon whose endorsement it will be paid, the endorsement by such impostor in the name which he is using to impersonate another is not a forgery.... The soundness of the rule obtains in the fact that the money has actually been paid to the person for whom it was really intended. Because another person might bear the very name assumed by the impostor and might have some contractual relationships with the impostor does not subject to a loss the drawee bank when it has paid the check to the person intended as the payee." (Schweitzer v. Bank of America (1941) 42 Cal. App.2d 536, 540, 109 P.2d 441.)....

The reasoning of the *Schweitzer* court directs our analysis in the present case. If FNMC (the drawer) had been induced *by an impostor* of Helen to issue the check either to Rudy or to the impostor, then the indorsement would be considered effective as to FNMC under the impostor rule. The rationale for this result is that Bank has paid the person whom FNMC intended to receive the money. When viewed under principles of negligence or estoppel, the outcome of this scenario would be the same: the risk of loss would be shifted to the drawer of the instrument (FNMC), who was in a better position to detect the fraud. (See Fireman's Fund Ins. Co. v. Security Pacific Nat. Bank (1978) 85 Cal. App.3d 797, 830, 149 Cal. Rptr. 883 [burden of loss on party who deals with the forger]; Intelogic v. Merchants Nat. Bank (Ind.App. 2 Dist.1993) 626 N.E.2d 839, 842 [under UCC, loss resulting from forged indorsement should fall upon party best able to prevent it]; East Gadsden Bank v. First City Nat. Bank of Gadsden (1973) 50 Ala.App. 576, 281 So.2d 431, 433 [intended payee theory distinguished from negligence or estoppel theory].)

This case presents different facts, however. Here, FNMC made the check payable to the true Helen, not to an impostor representing herself as Helen. FNMC intended that Helen herself—not a person it believed to be Helen—indorse the check and receive the proceeds. There is no question that FNMC intended to deal solely with Helen. The rationale underlying the protection of the impostor rule thus does not apply here....

A person's false representation that he or she is an agent of the payee is not sufficient. Uniform Commercial Code Comment 2 to former section 3405 notes: "'Impostor' refers to impersonation, and does not extend to a false representation that the party is the authorized agent of the payee. The maker or drawer who takes the precaution of making the instrument payable to the principal is entitled to have his indorsement." (See Uniform Com.Code com., 23B to § 3405.) Here, Rudy obtained issuance of the check to Helen not by impersonating her, but by falsely representing that he was authorized to act on her behalf. Although clearly fraudulent, this conduct does not constitute impersonation and thus cannot be considered an inducement to issue the instrument within the meaning of former section 3405(1)(a)....

Bank's emphasis on the asserted fact that Rudy was acting in concert with Helen's impostor is of no consequence. To invoke the protection of former section 3405(1)(a) Bank would have to point to facts showing that *by impersonation* the impostor induced FNMC to issue the check either to her or to Rudy, her confederate. The complaint alleges no such facts, however. The only impersonation that took place was in the presentation of the check to Bank....

The result is no different even under section 3404(a), the current version of the rule. The only significant change in this section is its recognition that the impostor may pretend to be either the payee or the payee's agent. As the Uniform Commercial Code Comment to the revised law notes, "Under former Section 3–405(1)(a), if Impostor impersonated Smith and induced the drawer to draw a check to the order of Smith, Impostor could negotiate the check. If Impostor impersonated Smith, the president of Smith Corporation, and the check was payable to the order of Smith Corporation, the section did not apply.... Section 3–404(a) gives Impostor the power to negotiate the check in both cases." (See Uniform Com.Code com., 23B to § 3404.) This comment makes it clear that impersonation is still required to invoke the impostor rule, whether the perpetrator of the deception pretends to be the principal or the agent. Misrepresentation of the perpetrator's agency status does not suffice....

We must conclude, therefore, that the impostor rule is inapplicable under these circumstances. By correctly identifying himself as Rudy but falsely representing himself to be Helen's agent Rudy did not engage in the impersonation required by the impostor rule, as expressed both in former section 3405, which was applicable at the time of the transactions at issue, and in its contemporary form, section 3404(a). The impersonation by Helen's impostor cannot be said to have induced FNMC to issue the check, since it took place only afterward, when the impostor presented the check to Bank.

Bank does not challenge the legal sufficiency of the complaint in any respect other than the asserted bar of the impostor rule. Accordingly, we hold that the trial court incorrectly sustained Bank's demurrer based on the application of the impostor rule....

NOTE

Contrast these two cases: Case #1. Rudy induced Drawer to issue a check to Helen Corporation by falsely representing that he was the treasurer of that organization. Case #2. Rudy induced Drawer to issue a check to Helen Corporation by representing that he was Barnes, who actually was the treasurer of Helen Corporation. How would 3–404(a) apply to these cases? Which of these cases most resembles *Title Insurance Company*?

c. FICTITIOUS PAYEES

The two basic fictitious payee cases are set out in Comment 2 to 3–404. In Case #1, Treasurer, authorized to draw checks on behalf of Corporation, fraudulently draws a corporate check to Supplier Co., a non-existent company. 3–404(b)(ii). In Case #2, the facts are the same except that Supplier Co. is an actual company that does business with Corporation, but Treasurer does not intend Supplier Co. to have any interest in the check. 3–404(b)(i). In both cases, the Treasurer indorses the checks in the name of Supplier Co and deposits them in Depositary Bank in an account controlled by Treasurer. Some cases had distinguished between Case #1 in which the payee is truly fictitious and Case #2 in which the payee is an actual person with which Corporation does business. Section 3–404(b) sweeps away this distinction and treats the indorsements as effective as the indorsement of the payee in both cases in favor of Corporation's Payor Bank and the Depositary Bank, if, in good faith, the Payor Bank paid the check or the Depositary Bank cashed the check over the counter or took it for collection.

The effect of the fictitious payee rule under 3–404(b) is to shift the loss to the Drawer instead of the Depositary Bank. Since the indorsement is effective as the indorsement of the payee, Payor Bank can charge Drawer's account because the check is properly payable under 4–401. The statement in Comment 1 to 4–401 that a check containing a forged indorsement is not properly payable does not apply because there is no forged indorsement. If Payor Bank does not charge Drawer's account and elects to proceed against Depositary Bank on breach of its presentment warranty under 4–208(a)(1), it cannot succeed because, at the time of presentment, Depositary Bank was a holder under 3–404(b)(1). Section 4–208(c) specifically empowers Depositary Bank to defend a breach of warranty suit by Payor Bank by proving that the indorsement is effective under 3–404(b).

Pre-revision 3–405(1) provided that "[a]n indorsement by any person in the name of a named payee is effective" if the drawer did not intend the payee to have an interest in the instrument. Some courts frustrated the manifest policy of this section by holding that even a slight variation between the indorsement and the name of the "named payee" precluded the section from applying, thereby making the indorsement a forgery, with the loss falling on the innocent depositary bank. Section 3–404(c)(i) addresses this problem by providing that an indorsement is made in the name of the person to whom the instrument is payable if it is made in a name substantially similar to the name of that person. Perhaps of greater importance is the provision in 3–404(c)(ii) stating that no indorsement at all is needed if the check is deposited in an account in a name substantially similar to the name of the person to whom the instrument is made payable.

The most important novelty in 3–404 is subsection (d) which allows "the person bearing the loss" in a fictitious payee case—usually the drawer—to recover from a person who fails to exercise due care in paying or taking an instrument for collection—usually the depositary bank—if that failure substantially contributes to the loss resulting from the payment of the instrument. See Comment 3 to 3–404. An example of the kind of case this provision is intended to deal with is set out in Comment 4 to 3–405: Malefactor works the fictitious payee scam and possesses a check for a large amount payable to the Ford Motor Company, a supplier of Malefactor's employer; Malefactor opens an account in Ford's name in Depositary Bank, asserting that he is the manager of a new Ford branch; he indorses the check in Ford's name, deposits the check and withdraws the proceeds by a wire transfer to a foreign country. Depositary Bank failed to require Malefactor to produce a corporate resolution or other evidence of authorization to act for the corporation when the account was opened. The premise of 3–404(d) is that, in some cases, the person taking the check might have detected the fraud and prevented the loss through exercise of ordinary care. If that person did not exercise ordinary care, it is reasonable to impose loss on that person to the extent its failure contributed to the loss. Comment 3. We see an application of this provision in *Gina Chin* in the next section.

An unusual application of 3-404(d) is found in State Security Check Cashing, Inc. v. American General Financial Services, 972 A.2d 882 (Ct. App. Md. 2009). There a financial services company (Drawer) issued a check for $18,000 to Impostor who cashed the check at a check cashing facility (Holder). Holder sued Drawer to recover for the check's proceeds paid to Impostor. The court applied 3-404(a) to hold the impostor rule applied and the indorsement of Impostor was effective as the indorsement of Payee, a credit-worthy person. Holder, who took for value and in good faith, was a holder in due course. Section 3-404(d), a comparative fault provision, was raised by Drawer to shift the loss to Holder. As we have seen, 3-404(d) provides that if a person who takes a check for value fails to exercise ordinary care and that failure substantially contributes to the loss, "the person bearing the loss may recover from the person failing to exercise ordinary care to the extent that the failure to exercise ordinary care contributed to the loss." Here the court reversed the usual application of 3-404(d) and held that Holder was the person bearing the entire loss and Drawer, who was in the best position to avoid the fraud, was the person failing to exercise ordinary care. Drawer could shift none of the loss to Holder.

5. THE DOUBLE FORGERY

We have seen that in cases of a forged drawer's signature, the loss is generally borne by the payor bank and, in cases of a forged indorsement, the loss usually falls on the depositary bank, subject to the important exceptions discussed in this chapter. But what of the case—the all-time favorite negotiable instruments examination question—in which both the drawer's signature and the payee's indorsement are forged, the so-called double forgery? In the following case, Lehman, an employee of Chin, forged the signature of one of Chin's officers on checks payable to Chin's suppliers; Lehman then forged the indorsement of the payee of these checks and deposited them in his account in First Union. Before revision of Article 3, the courts had reached consensus that such cases should be treated as forged check cases, not as forged indorsement cases. The loss should fall on the drawee bank and not the depositary bank because the indorsement is not forged. In short, there is no double forgery; there is only one, the signature of the drawer. How would this case be decided under 3–404(b)? See Case #5 in Comment 2 to 3–404. How does 3–404(d) change this result? Comment 3 to 3–404. 1 Barkley Clark & Barbara Clark, supra, ¶ 12.07[3][b] (Rev. ed. 2009); James J. White & Robert S. Summers, Uniform Commercial Code §§ 18–5, 19–4e (5th ed. 2002).

Gina Chin & Associates, Inc. v. First Union Bank

Supreme Court of Virginia, 1998.
500 S.E.2d 516.

■ LACY, JUSTICE.

Gina Chin & Associates, Inc. (Chin) filed a motion for judgment against First Union Bank alleging that First Union was negligent when it accepted checks drawn on Chin's accounts bearing both forged signatures of the drawer and forged indorsements of the payees. The trial court sustained First Union's demurrer and entered summary judgment. We awarded Chin an appeal, and we will reverse the judgment of the trial court because we conclude that Chin's motion for judgment pled a cause of action pursuant to §§ 3–404 and –405 of the Uniform Commercial Code.

In reviewing a case decided on a demurrer, we accept as true the facts alleged in the motion for judgment and all reasonable inferences to be drawn therefrom.... Chin, a food wholesaler, maintained checking accounts at Signet Bank and Citizens Bank of Washington, D.C. (the drawee banks). During 1994 and 1995, an employee of Chin, Amie Cheryl Lehman, forged the signature of one of Chin's officers on a number of checks that were payable to

Chin's suppliers. Lehman then forged the payees' indorsements and, with the assistance of a First Union teller, deposited the checks in an account which she held at First Union. The drawee banks then paid the checks and debited a total amount of $270,488.72 from Chin's accounts.

First Union asserts that, under the UCC, it is amenable to suit only by the drawee banks based on a breach of warranty of title theory. § 4–207. Chin's sole cause of action, according to First Union, is against the drawee banks for improperly charging Chin's accounts for the amount of the forged checks. See §§ 4–401–406. Under First Union's interpretation of §§ 3–404 and –405, Chin does not have a cause of action against it pursuant to those sections because they only apply to instances involving a forged indorsement of the payee and not to the circumstances where both the payee's indorsement and the signature of the drawer were forged.

While First Union correctly states that the UCC provides a drawer with a cause of action against a drawee bank that charges a drawer's account based on checks containing a forged signature of the drawer, its conclusion that §§ 3–404 and –405 cannot be utilized by a drawer against the depositary bank in a double forgery situation is erroneous.

Sections 3–404 and –405 were part of the 1992 revisions to the UCC. Revised § 3–404(b) provides that where the payee on a check is fictitious or not the person intended to have an interest in the check by the person determining to whom the check is payable, a forged payee's indorsement on the check is nevertheless effective for one who takes the check in good faith.[2] Similarly, where an employee vested with the responsibility for processing, signing, or indorsing the employer's check makes a fraudulent indorsement of such check, revised § 3–405 continues the prior provision's rule that the indorsement is effective if taken or paid in good faith. However, both revised sections provide that if the person taking the check fails to exercise ordinary care, "the person bearing the loss may recover from the person failing to exercise ordinary care to the extent the failure to exercise ordinary care contributed to the loss." §§ 3–404(d)–405(b).

The revisions to §§ 3–404 and –405 changed the previous law by allowing "the person bearing the loss" to seek recovery for a loss caused by the negligence of any person paying the instrument or taking it for value based on comparative negligence principles. The concept of comparative negligence introduced in the revised sections reflects a determination that all participants in the process have a duty to exercise ordinary care in the drawing and handling of instruments and that the failure to exercise that duty will result in liability to the person sustaining the loss. Nothing in the statutory language indicates that, where the signature of the drawer is forged, the drawer cannot

---

[2] The person whose intent determines to whom an instrument is payable includes a person who forges the drawer's signature. See § 3–110(a).

qualify as a "person bearing the loss" or that the drawer is otherwise precluded from seeking recovery from a depositary bank under these sections. In the absence of any specific exclusion, we conclude that the sections are applicable in double forgery situations.

This conclusion is consistent with Comment 2 of the Official Comments to § 3–404, which states that subsection (b) "also applies to forged check cases." Another commentary also concludes that § 3–404 applies to double forgery situations. Remarking that under the previous law, double forgery cases were treated solely as forged drawer's signature cases, allowing the depositary bank to avoid liability, the commentary concludes that the result under the revised section "differs sharply."

> In fictitious payee double forgeries under the Revision, some of the ultimate loss will end up on the shoulders of the company that hired the dishonest bookkeeper and failed to supervise the miscreant. The rest will be shouldered by the depositary bank for [its] negligence....

Barkley Clark & Barbara Clark, The Law of Bank Deposits, Collections and Credit Cards ¶ 12.07[3][b] (Rev. ed. 1995).

Accordingly, we hold that Chin was not precluded from asserting a cause of action against First Union pursuant to §§ 3–404 or –405. In light of this conclusion, we next examine Chin's motion for judgment to determine whether it is sufficient to state a cause of action under these sections.

Chin seeks recovery for a loss sustained as a result of the negligent actions of First Union. Chin alleged that its employee, Lehman, forged both its signature and the indorsement of the payees on a number of checks and, with the cooperation of an employee of First Union, deposited the checks into Lehman's account at First Union. The motion for judgment specifically alleged that the acceptance of the forged checks by First Union for payment "was negligent and was in contravention of established banking customs and standards" and "was due to the negligent failure of First Union Bank to supervise its employee." The pleading further asserts that this negligence caused Chin to suffer a loss of over $270,000.

These allegations are sufficient to state a cause of action against First Union pursuant to §§ 3–404 and –405. Accordingly, the trial court erred in sustaining First Union's demurrer. The judgment of the trial court is reversed and the case is remanded for further proceedings.

NOTE

Since Chin's signature on the checks was forged, under 4–401(a), the drawee banks were not entitled to charge Chin's account, unless 3–406 or 4–406 applies, and these are not atissue in this case. If the drawee banks cannot charge Chin's account, how does Chin qualify as a "person bearing the loss" under 3–404(d)? In the last paragraph of Comment 3 to 3–404, the statement is made that in Case #5, which is a double forgery case in which the indorsement is effective under 3–404(b), the drawee bank has a cause of action under subsection (d).

6. PAYROLL PADDING

We have seen examples of employee fraud that involve forgery of the employer's signature either as an indorsement of checks payable to the employer or as drawer of a check drawn on the employer's bank account. Another common type of employee fraud does not involve forgery of the employer's signature. This type of fraud is sometimes referred to as "payroll padding," and it can be illustrated by the following cases.

Case #1. Corporation pays its employees by check. Treasurer is authorized to sign checks on behalf of Corporation, but a signature by one other officer of Corporation is also necessary. Treasurer signed checks to pay employees on the April payroll. Intending to defraud Corporation, Treasurer included in the checks for that month three checks payable either to fictitious people or real people who sometimes work for Corporation but who did not work in April and therefore were not entitled to any pay. At the request of Treasurer, Vice President also signed the checks. Vice President did not know who was entitled to payment and did not raise any question about the checks. The checks were returned to Treasurer after they were signed. Treasurer took the three fraudulent checks and indorsed each of them by signing the name of the payee. She then deposited each of the checks in a bank in which she had an account. The checks were paid and Treasurer withdrew the proceeds of the checks. Assume Treasurer is judgment proof. If the indorsements by Treasurer are effective as indorsements of the payees of the three checks, Corporation takes the loss. If the indorsements are treated as forged indorsements, the depositary banks that collected the checks will take the loss. 3–417(a)(1) and 4–208(a)(1). In this case, the intent of Treasurer determines the person to whom each of the three checks is payable. 3–110(a) (last sentence). Under 3–404(b), Treasurer became the holder of each check and her indorsement in the name of the stated payee was effective as the indorsement of the payee of the check. Thus, Corporation takes the loss.

Case #2. Same as Case #1 except that Corporation's checks are produced by a check-writing or facsimile signature machine. Treasurer had access to the computer that operates the machine. She made entries in the computer that caused the machine to issue the three fraudulent checks. She obtained possession of the checks and then proceeded as in Case #1. Under 3–110(b), the intent of Treasurer determines the person to whom each of the three checks is payable. The analysis of Case #2 is identical to that of Case #1.

Case #3. Treasurer signs checks on behalf of Corporation to pay employees, but Clerk prepares the April payroll that tells Treasurer to whom to issue the checks and in what amount. This time the culprit is Clerk. Intending to defraud Corporation, Clerk includes in the payroll the names of three people who work part time for Corporation, but who performed no work during April. Clerk prepared checks of Corporation in accordance with the payroll and gave them to Treasurer for signature. Treasurer signed the checks and returned them to Clerk. Clerk took the three fraudulent checks, indorsed each in the name of the payee named in the check, and dealt with the checks as Treasurer did in Case #1. This case is more complex. Assume Treasurer knew each of the three employees named in the three fraudulent checks, but she did not know that they did not work in April. Treasurer intended each check to be payable to the payee named in the check and, under 3–110(a), Treasurer's intent controls; hence 3–404(b) doesn't apply. Thus, Clerk's indorsements are forged indorsements and the normal result is that the loss is taken by the depositary bank that collected the check. In Case #1 and Case #2, Corporation took the loss because it was held responsible for the conduct of Treasurer, its faithless employee. In Case #3, the faithless employee is Clerk. Is there any good reason why Corporation should not also be responsible for the conduct of Clerk? In each case, the faithless employee had duties with respect to the issuance of checks. The three cases are essentially similar. In Case #3, Treasurer performed the same function as Vice President did in Case #1 and the check writing machine did in Case #2. By preparing the payroll, Clerk, as a practical matter, determined to whom Corporation's checks were to be made payable. However, the result in Case #3 is not determined solely by 3–110(a) because 3–405 also applies. We previously examined cases covered by 3–405(a)(2)(i). This time the relevant provision is 3–405(a)(2)(ii).

7. Allocation of Loss By Contract

How far can banks go in protecting themselves from fraud or forgery losses by contracts with their customers? Section 4–103(a) gives broad authority to vary the effect of the statute by agreement, but there are limits beyond which banks cannot go in disclaiming their liability. We will discuss these limits in more detail in the next chapter. At this point, we include a case on a bank's attempt to disclaim liability for paying counterfeit checks containing unauthorized facsimile signatures. We place the case here rather than in the next chapter so that you can assess the reasonableness of the bank's broad disclaimer provisions in the context of the material you have just studied on fraud and forgery.

Jefferson Parish School Board v. First Commerce Corp.

Court of Appeal of Louisiana, Fourth Circuit, 1996.
669 So.2d 1298.

■ JONES, JUDGE.

Jefferson Parish School Board appeals a judgment of the trial court granting defendant First National Bank of Commerce's ("First NBC") Motion for Summary Judgment.

Appellant Jefferson Parish School Board maintained a checking account titled "general account," number 7003–42931, with appellee, First NBC. Appellant desired to utilize a facsimile signature machine, and accordingly, adopted a facsimile signature resolution with First NBC.

In November of 1992, various instruments purporting to be checks made by appellant and drawn on the subject account were presented for payment and paid by First NBC. Upon receiving the monthly bank statement, appellant observed the instruments to be counterfeit. The checks were returned to First NBC each with an individual "Affidavit of Forgery, Alteration, Loss or Threat of Instrument." First NBC maintained that, pursuant to the resolution adopted by appellant, they were entitled to honor the instruments and appellant should bear the loss.

Appellant filed suit in the Civil District Court for the Parish of Orleans in October of 1993 seeking recovery of the amount paid on the checks. First NBC filed a motion for summary judgment alleging that the resolution adopted by appellant precludes such an action. The district court agreed and granted First NBC's Motion for Summary Judgment.

In their only assignment of error, appellant argues that the trial court erred in dismissing their case based on the adoption of the facsimile signature resolution. This assignment of error has no merit. The resolution contains the following provision:

> RESOLVED: That the First National Bank of Commerce, New Orleans, hereinafter referred to as "Bank", as a designated depository of this corporation, be and it is hereby requested, authorized and directed to honor, for the account and to the debit of the corporation, all checks, drafts, or other orders for the payment of money (inclusive of any such as may be payable to any of the officers of this Corporation or other persons hereinafter specified or whose names appear thereon as signor or signors thereof) drawn in the name of this Corporation on the account(s) of this Corporation with the Bank when bearing *or purporting to bear* the facsi-

> mile signatures as of any of the following: [facsimile signatures] and the Bank is and shall be entitled to honor and to charge this Corporation for all such checks, drafts, or other orders, *regardless of by whom or by what means the actual or purported facsimile signature or signatures thereon may have been affixed thereto, if such facsimile signature or signatures resemble the facsimile specimens* from time to time duly certified to or filed with the Bank by the Secretary or other officer of the Corporation. (emphasis added).

The resolution further provides:

> *That the said bank may rely on these resolutions until the receipt by the Bank of a certified copy of a resolution by the Board of Directors of this Corporation revoking the same, this Corporation expressly assuming all risks involved in any unauthorized use of such facsimile signature and agreeing that this Corporation shall be responsible for and chargeable with the amount of all checks, drafts, or other orders bearing such facsimile signature or signatures resembling the same, whether or not placed thereon by the authority of this Corporation.* (emphasis added).

The language of the facsimile agreement, a contract between the parties, is clear and unambiguous. The bank is authorized to honor *all checks* "purporting to bear" the facsimile signatures, "regardless of by what means" the actual or purported signature is affixed as long as the "signatures resemble the facsimile specimens." This is the only requirement imposed on the bank by the contract between the parties—to insure that any signatures "resemble" those provided by the Board on the signature card. This comports with the provision of § 4–103(1) in effect at the time of the agreement. The provision provides:

> The effect of the provisions of this chapter may be varied by agreement except that no agreement can disclaim a bank's responsibility for its own lack of good faith or failure to exercise ordinary care or can limit the measure of damages for such lack of failure; *but the parties may agree to determine the standards by which such responsibility is to be measured if those standards are not manifestly unreasonable.* (emphasis added).

Agreements confected pursuant to this statute are not unusual. See Springhill Bank and Trust Co. v. Citizens Bank and Trust Co., 505 So.2d 867 (La.App. 2d Cir.1987), and Perini Corp. v. First National Bank of Habersham County, 553 F.2d 398 (5th Cir.1977). In *Perini*, the court held that there was no cause of action for recovery of funds paid on forged checks where a resolution was adopted authorizing the drawee's payment of checks bearing signatures resembling the machine-endorsed facsimile signature.

The appellant erroneously argues that First NBC cannot prove any negligence on the part of the appellant's employees regarding the safeguarding of their checks on that account and of the facsimile signature plates of the employees used on that account. This argument incorrectly suggests that the appellant should not bear the burden of the loss if the facsimile plates were not used in the forgery. This position is clearly contrary to the resolution adopted by the appellants. As previously stated, the resolution provides that the bank is authorized to honor checks "regardless of by whom or by what means" the actual or purported signature is affixed as long as the "signatures resemble the facsimile specimens."

Additionally, appellants contend that the checks at issue contained errors that a diligent perusal of the documents would have revealed to experienced bank employees. Appellants base this argument on the fact that the checks in question were printed on different paper. This argument also lacks merit. First NBC is obligated to pay on any paper on which the signature of the drawer matches the signature on file. It is very common for customers to order their checks from different sources.

When reviewing trial court judgments on motions for summary judgment, appellate courts must use the same criteria applied by the trial courts. Thus, a summary judgment should be affirmed when "the pleadings, depositions, answers to interrogatories, and admissions on file, together with affidavits, if any, show that there is no genuine issue of material fact, and that the mover is entitled to judgment as a matter of law."...The only material fact in this case is the nature of the signatures and there is no dispute that the signatures are nearly identical to the facsimile signatures submitted by the appellants.

Therefore, for the reasons stated above, the judgment of the trial court is affirmed.

PROBLEM

A fundamental principle of banking law, established in Price v. Neal, is that the drawee bank bears the loss in forged check cases. *Jefferson Parish* allowed Bank to contract out of this basic liability by obtaining a resolution from the Board exculpating Bank from liability for paying forged facsimile checks bearing a drawer's signature that resembles the Board's signature specimens. Would a resolution be valid that extends the bank's protection from facsimile machine forgery losses to all cases in which the drawer's signature, whether written by *hand* or by machine, resembles that of the drawer's signature specimens?

NOTE

The School Board was not negligent in this case and its facsimile machine was not used by the counterfeiter; none of its employees had any connection with the counterfeiter. The Board saw itself as an innocent bystander. In this light, why isn't the disclaimer clause "manifestly unreasonable" as applied to this case? Compare Cumis Ins. Soc'y, Inc. v. Girard Bank, 522 F.Supp. 414 (E.D.Pa.1981), in which the court reached a different result in a forged facsimile signature case. See 1 Barkley Clark & Barbara Clark, supra, ¶ 10.02[1] (Rev. ed. 2009). For a critique of *Jefferson Parish*, see James Steven Rogers, The Basic Principle of Loss Allocation for Unauthorized Checks, 39 Wake Forest L.Rev. 453, 484-509 (2004). Professor Rogers believes this case poses the issue of whether the basic loss allocation scheme of the check system should be variable by agreement. If so, are there any fundamental principles of loss allocation in Article 4?

The limits of parties under 4–103(a) to vary their statutory rights and obligations has also been tested with respect to stop payment orders, discussed further in the next chapter. Section 4–403(a) obligates a bank to stop payment on a check when ordered to do so by its customer or authorized drawer if it has a reasonable opportunity to act. Banks' deposit contracts with customers frequently specify the conditions under which stop payment orders will be honored, and the litigated issue has been whether the specified conditions are "manifestly unreasonable" under 4–103(a). The results have been mixed. Compare Poullier v. Nacua Motors, Inc., 439 N.Y.S.2d 85 (N.Y.Sup.Ct. 1981) (bank's stipulation of information needed for stop payment orders to be executed upheld), with FJS Elec's, Inc. v. Fid. Bank, 431 A.2d 326 (Pa.Super.Ct. 1981) (refusing to give effect to stipulation when inaccuracy in stop payment order insignificant). Some refusals to enforce contractually imposed restrictions are based on the extrastatutory requirement that the bank clearly disclose them to the customer; see, e.g., Staff Ser.Assoc., Inc. v. Midlantic Nat'l Bank, 504 A.2d 148 (N.J.Super.Ct. 1985). Is there a problem of nondisclosure in *Jefferson Parish*, where the Parish School Board's resolution authorized honor of instruments containing signatures "purporting to bear" the facsimile signature? Cf. SOS Oil Corp. v. Norstar Bank of Long Island, 563 N.E.2d 258 (N.Y. 1990). Or, is the *Jefferson Parish* court simply refusing to regulate the substantive allocation of forgery risk between the customer and the bank?

B. Restrictive Indorsements

Indorsement of an instrument may serve several purposes, but most commonly an indorsement is made in order to negotiate the instrument. 3–204(a). The form of the indorsement can affect rights with respect to the instrument if it is stolen and collected or transferred to a third party. If a check indorsed in blank by the holder is stolen, the thief may negotiate the check to a transferee who may obtain rights as a holder in due course. If the stolen check was payable to an identified person and the payee made a special indorsement or did not indorse the check at all, the thief cannot negotiate the check and nobody taking through the thief can become a person entitled to enforce the check. Thus, the rights of a person taking a stolen check may depend upon whether an indorsement by the holder was made and whether the indorsement was special or in blank. The rights of the taker, however, can also depend upon whether the holder made a "restrictive indorsement" governed by 3–206.

The purpose of a restrictive indorsement is to restrict payment of the instrument. That restriction can be expressed as part of a special indorsement or an indorsement in blank. For example, an indorsement of a check consisting solely of the signature of the holder under the words "for deposit only" is a blank indorsement because it does not identify a person to whom it makes the check payable, and is a restrictive indorsement because it indicates that the check is to be deposited to an account. This restrictive indorsement is governed by 3–206(c). Comment 3 to 3–206. An indorsement "Pay to John Doe in trust for Jane Doe" is a special indorsement because it identifies John Doe as the person to whom the check is payable, and is a restrictive indorsement because it indicates that the proceeds of the check are to be paid for the benefit of Jane Doe. This restrictive indorsement is governed by 3–206(d). Comment 4 to 3–206.

Some attempts to restrict payment of an instrument by an indorser are nullified by 3–206. An indorsement "Pay to John Doe only" is ineffective to prohibit payment to any other holder. In spite of the indorsement, John Doe may indorse the instrument to another person and that person may become entitled to enforce the instrument. 3–206(a). An indorsement that attempts to prohibit payment unless a stated condition is satisfied is also ineffective to restrict payment. 3–206(b). Invalid restrictions are discussed in Comment 2 to 3–206.

PROBLEM

Banking by mail is a common practice. This problem considers the degree of protection the payee of a check gains by using a restrictive indorsement under 3–206. Peter, the payee of a check for $10,000 drawn on Payor Bank, indorsed and mailed the check to Bank One where he had an account. Before the check arrived at Bank One, Thief stole the check and wrote Thief's name under Peter's indorsement. Thief then deposited the check to Thief's account in Bank Two. Bank Two presented the check to Payor Bank and Payor Bank paid the check. Thief then withdrew the $10,000 that had been credited to Thief's account in Bank Two with respect to the check.

What are Peter's rights against Bank Two and Payor Bank if Peter's indorsement were as follows?

Case #1

For deposit only

Peter

Case #2

Pay to Bank One for Account No. 1234321

Peter

Case #3

Peter

For deposit only

When we are sending checks to our bank for deposit by mail, many of us use the kinds of restrictive indorsements set out in either Case #1 or Case #3. You may be surprised to learn that the court in Spencer v. Sterling Bank, 74 Cal.Rptr.2d 576 (Cal.Ct.App.1998), tells us that what we've been doing accomplishes nothing. The court held that under the plain meaning of 3–206(c)(2), a check indorsed "X, for deposit only" can be deposited in anyone's account in any bank; the depositary bank need not deposit the proceeds in the account of the person indorsing the check, usually the payee of the check, because the blank indorsement does not specify where or for whose benefit such a check is to be deposited. A few cases agree with *Spencer*, but the majority does not. The following case states the majority view. Which view do you believe is a correct interpretation of the statute?

State of Qatar v. First American Bank

United States District Court, E.D. Virginia, 1995.
885 F.Supp. 849.

■ ELLIS, DISTRICT JUDGE.

At issue in this sequel to State of Qatar v. First American Bank of Virginia ("Qatar I")[1] is the meaning and legal significance of the phrase "for deposit only" following an indorsement on the back of a check. More specifically, the question presented is whether a depositary bank complies with the restrictive indorsement "for deposit only" when it deposits a check bearing that restriction into *any* person's account, or whether that restriction requires a depositary bank to deposit the check's proceeds only into the account of the

[1] 880 F.Supp. 463 (E.D.Va.1995).

named payee. For the reasons that follow, the Court holds that the unqualified language "for deposit only" following an indorsement on the back of a check requires a depositary bank to place the check's proceeds into the payee's[2] account, and the bank violates that restrictive indorsement when it credits the check to any other account.

The facts underlying this case are more fully set forth in *Qatar I* and are only briefly reiterated here. Plaintiffs are the State of Qatar and certain of its agencies (collectively, "Qatar"). From approximately 1986 to 1992, one of Qatar's employees, Bassam Salous, defrauded his employer by having checks drawn on Qatar's account in purported payment of false or duplicate invoices that he had created. Although all of the unauthorized checks were made payable to individuals and entities other than Salous, he nonetheless successfully deposited the checks into his own personal accounts with Defendant First American Bank of Virginia ("First American") and Central Fidelity Banks, Inc. (collectively, "the depositary banks").

After Qatar discovered this fraudulent scheme in 1992, it brought suit against the depositary banks for conversion....

Only one category of checks remains in dispute. These checks all bear the forged indorsement of the payee named on the face of the check, followed by a stamped "for deposit only" restriction. In *Qatar I*, the Court denied the depositary banks' motion for summary judgment with respect to these checks on the ground that the depositary banks could be held liable for applying the proceeds of the checks in violation of the restrictive indorsements. *Qatar I*, 880 F.Supp. at 469, 470–71. Specifically, the Court stated:

> [W]hile the forged signature presented no barrier to payment given the effect of [U.C.C.] § 3–405, the accompanying restriction ("FOR DEPOSIT ONLY") provided a clear instruction to the depositary banks to deposit the funds only into the account of the last indorser—here, the named payee.

The Court did not hold the depositary banks liable as a matter of law with respect to these checks, but decided to await the banks' presentation of defenses, if any, at trial. At trial, the depositary banks raised no defenses, but instead challenged for the first time the Court's assumption in *Qatar I* that the phrase "for deposit only", without further specification, directs a depositary bank to deposit the funds only into the account of the named payee. An indorsement in this form, they argued, is far less restrictive, as it merely directs that the check's proceeds be *deposited* in an account, not that they be deposited into a particular account. Thus, the depositary banks urged, they fully complied with the restrictive indorsements on these checks when they deposited the proceeds into Salous' account. Although this issue properly

---

[2] Throughout this Memorandum Opinion, "payee" is intended to refer to the last purported indorser.

should have been raised at the summary judgment stage, the Court permitted the parties to research the matter and submit post-trial legal memoranda regarding this final, narrow issue. Qatar and First American did so, and the matter is now ripe for disposition.

It is now established that First American may be liable to Qatar for handling a check's proceeds in violation of a restrictive indorsement. *Qatar I*, 880 F.Supp. at 469, 470–71.[8] Under § 3–205(c) of the pre–1993 Uniform Commercial Code ("U.C.C." or "Code"),[9] restrictive indorsements are defined to "include the words 'for collection,' 'for deposit,' 'pay any bank,' or like terms signifying a purpose of deposit or collection." Thus, the U.C.C. makes clear that the phrase "for deposit only" is, in fact, a restrictive indorsement. But the Code does not define "for deposit only" or specify what bank conduct would be inconsistent with that restriction.[10] Nor does Virginia decisional law provide any guidance on this issue. As a result, reference to decisional law from other jurisdictions is appropriate.

Not surprisingly, most courts confronted with this issue have held that the restriction "for deposit only", without additional specification or directive, instructs depositary banks to deposit the funds only into the payee's account. In addition, commentators on commercial law uniformly agree that the function of such a restriction is to ensure that the checks' proceeds be deposited into the payee's account.[11]

---

[8] It is important to note for the reader unfamiliar with *Qatar I* that First American is liable in conversion to Qatar, the drawer, for violating restrictive indorsements only because the forged indorsements are "effective" pursuant to former § 3–405(1)(c). Were this not a § 3–405(1)(c) case, the forged indorsements would be ineffective to negotiate the instrument, and any money paid to the depositary banks on the forged checks would be deemed to come from the drawee bank's own funds, not from Qatar's account. See *Qatar I*, 880 F.Supp. at 467–68.

[9] Article three of the U.C.C. governs the law of negotiable instruments and was substantially amended effective January 1, 1993. Because all of the relevant events surrounding this case occurred prior to 1993, the former U.C.C. provisions apply here. All U.C.C. citations are to Va.Code, Title 8.3, amended by Va.Code, Title 8.3A (Supp.1994).

[10] The amended Code provision on restrictive indorsements provides more guidance on the meaning of "for deposit only." § 3–206. Specifically, in describing particular types of restrictive indorsements, § 3–206(c)(ii) refers to indorsements "using the words 'for deposit,' 'for collection,' *or other words indicating a purpose of having the instrument collected by a bank for the indorser or for a particular account*" (emphasis added).

[11] See, e.g., 1 William H. Lawrence, Commercial Paper and Payment Systems § 3.6[b][3], at 3–37 (1990) ("A payee who endorses a check 'for deposit only' provides notice to the depository [sic] bank that the check is to be credited to the payee's account.... The only way that a depository [sic] bank can apply value consistently with the endorsement is to credit the payee's account"); 4 William D. Hawkland and Lary Lawrence, U.C.C. Series § 3–206:05 (Art. 3), at 366 (1994) (rejecting proposition that "for deposit only" "would permit the proceeds to be credited to any account"); 2 Frederick M. Hart and William F. Willier, Bender's Uniform Commercial Code Service, Commercial Paper under the Uniform Commercial Code § 3A.02 (1994) ("When an instrument is indorsed 'For Deposit,' the indorsee, almost always a bank, is obligated to put any money received for the instrument in the indorser's account"); Julian B. McDonnell, Bank Liability for Fraudulent Checks: the Clash of the Utilitarian and Paternalist

This construction of "for deposit only" is commercially sensible and is adopted here. The clear purpose of the restriction is to avoid the hazards of indorsing a check in blank. Pursuant to former § 3–204(2), a check indorsed in blank "becomes payable to bearer." It is, essentially, cash. Thus, a payee who indorses her check in blank runs the risk of having the check stolen and freely negotiated before the check reaches its intended destination. To protect against this vulnerability, the payee can add the restriction "for deposit only" to the indorsement, and the depositary bank is required to handle the check in a manner consistent with that restriction. § 3–206(3). And in so adding the restriction, the payee's intent plainly is to direct that the funds be deposited into her own account, not simply that the funds be deposited into some account.[14] See 1 William H. Lawrence, Commercial Paper and Payment Systems § 3.6[b][3] (1990). Any other construction of the phrase "for deposit only" is illogical and without commercial justification or utility. Indeed, it is virtually impossible to imagine a scenario in which a payee cared that her check be deposited, but was indifferent with respect to the particular account to which the funds would be credited.

First American opposes this result, contending that the unqualified restriction "for deposit only" merely requires a depositary bank to deposit the check into an account, irrespective of which one....

While it is true that the literal command of the bare words "for deposit only" is simply that the check be deposited, such rigid reliance on linguistics in disregard of practical considerations and plain common sense is both unwarranted and imprudent. This is especially so given that the individuals writing and relying upon these restrictive indorsements are not apt to be well versed in the subtleties of negotiable instruments law. As evidenced by numerous authorities, see supra note 12, and common experience, the unqualified phrase "for deposit only" is almost universally taken to mean "for deposit only *into the payee's account.*" To disregard this common understanding in support of an illogical construction is to elevate form over substance. First American's argument to the contrary is a little like saying that a store sign reading "shirts and shoes required" does not restrict a trouserless man from entering the store.

Creeds under the Uniform Commercial Code, 73 Geo.L.J. 1399, 1415 (1985) ("indorsers must deposit checks restrictively indorsed 'for deposit only' into the account of the indorser, rather than cash the check or deposit it into another's account"); James S. Rogers, Negotiability as a System of Title Recognition, 48 Ohio St.L.J. 197, 223 n. 94 (1987) ("the mechanism of restrictive indorsement 'for deposit only' enables a payee to [indorse a check in blank] without facing any of the risks that would otherwise flow from converting the instrument into bearer form"). See also 1 James J. White & Robert S. Summers, Uniform Commercial Code § 13–10 (3d ed. 1994 Supp.).

[14] Of course, the payee can direct that the funds be delivered into someone else's account by including the particular account name or number in the restriction (e.g., "for deposit only into account of X" or "for deposit only into account #123456").

Finally, it is worth noting that the new revisions to the negotiable instruments provisions of the U.C.C., see supra note 10, support the result reached here. Although these revisions are inapplicable to this case, the commentary following § 3–206 states that the new subdivision dealing with "for deposit only" and like restrictions "continues previous law." § 3–206 comment 3. Shortly thereafter, the commentary provides an example in which a check bears the words "for deposit only" above the indorsement. In those circumstances, the commentary states, the depositary bank acts inconsistently with the restrictive indorsement where it deposits the check into an account other than that of the payee. Id. Although the restriction in that example precedes the signature, whereas the restrictions on the checks at issue here follow the signature, this distinction is immaterial. The clear meaning of the restriction in both circumstances is that the funds should be placed into the payee's account.[17]

Therefore, First American violated the restrictive indorsements in depositing into Bassam Salous' account checks made payable to others and restrictively indorsed "for deposit only." Pursuant to the holding in *Qatar I*, then, First American is liable to Qatar for conversion in the amount of the total face values of these checks.

PROBLEM

Peter, the payee of a check for $10,000 drawn on Payor Bank, gave the check to Faith, the legal guardian of Ward, her elderly father who had become legally incompetent. Peter told Faith that the check was a contribution to defray Ward's nursing home expenses. Before giving the check to Faith, Peter indorsed the check as follows:

Pay to Faith as Guardian for Ward

Peter

Faith indorsed the check by signing her name under Peter's indorsement and deposited the check to her personal account in Depositary Bank. Faith also had a fiduciary account as guardian for Ward in the same bank. Pursuant to her instructions, Depositary Bank credited Faith's personal account $10,000 and obtained payment of the check from Payor Bank. Faith subsequently

---

[17] The facts of this case are unusual in that it was the forger, Bassam Salous, who added the restriction "for deposit only." While *his* intent clearly was not to direct that the funds be placed into the account of the named payee, the general purpose and meaning of the phrase "for deposit only" is unaltered. Cf. Society Nat'l Bank v. Security Fed. Sav. and Loan, 71 Ohio St.3d 321, 643 N.E.2d 1090 (1994). Although it is difficult to speculate regarding why Salous so indorsed the checks, Salous' idiosyncratic subjective intent is immaterial to First American's obligation to abide by the terms of the restrictive indorsement, an obligation which, if fulfilled, would have put an earlier stop to the ongoing fraud.

withdrew the $10,000 that had been credited to her personal account by writing checks on the account for her personal expenses.

Suit on behalf of Ward has been brought against Faith for breach of trust and against Depositary Bank and Payor Bank. Faith is insolvent and has no funds. What is the liability of Depositary Bank and Payor Bank? 3–206.

CHAPTER 6

THE BANK–CUSTOMER RELATIONSHIP

A. INTRODUCTION

A customer with a deposit account in a bank has a contractual relationship with the bank that is governed by Part 4 of Article 4. If the bank pays a check written on the customer's account, 4–401(a) allows the bank to charge the customer's account only if the check is "properly payable," that is, if the customer has authorized the payment and it violates no agreement between the customer and the bank. Thus, a bank cannot charge a customer's account if the customer's signature is forged, but may charge the account even though the charge creates an overdraft. Of course, the bank does not have to pay an overdraft unless it has agreed to do so. 4–402(a). Agreements by banks to pay overdrafts up to specified limits are common. If a bank fails to pay a check that is properly payable and covered by funds in the customer's account, the bank has wrongfully dishonored the check under 4–402(a) and may be liable for damages under 4–402(b). A customer has the right for any reason or no reason to order a bank to stop payment of checks on the customer's account or to close the account and, if the bank fails to do so, it may be liable for the loss caused by its failure. 4–403. However, a bank is not liable for dishonoring a "stale" check, one presented more than six months after its date. 4–404.

The provisions of Article 4 are only one source of rules concerning the bank-customer relationship. Federal statutes and Federal Reserve regulations are another source. The Truth-in-Savings Act, discussed later, became effective in 1992; it requires disclosure of the terms of consumer deposit accounts. The Expedited Funds Availability Act and Regulation CC expressly override the UCC. Regulation J does so as well. Still another source is provided by 4–103(a) under which the "effect of the provisions" of Article 4 may be varied by bank-customer agreements; it is customary for banks to have some form of deposit agreement with their customers. Section 4–103(a) restates and even enlarges upon the "freedom of contract" principle embodied in 1–302. Comment 1 to 4–103 says: "This section, therefore, permits within wide limits variation of the effect of provisions of the Article by agreement." Since deposit agreements have aspects of contracts of adhesion, a continuing matter of dispute between banks and their customers concerns the extent of the "wide limits" referred to in the Comment. We discuss this issue later in this chapter.

B. Stop–Payment Orders

Section 4–403(a) affords a customer an unrestricted right to stop payment on checks drawn on the customer's account or to close the account. Comment 1 to 4–403 is a ringing affirmation of this cherished right of bank customers, and Comment 7 adds that a payment in violation of a stop order is an improper payment even if made by inadvertence or mistake. The broad right given drawers by 4–403(a) to stop payment of checks is unique in payment systems and it can be very valuable to drawers. Even if the check was given in payment of an obligation of the drawer on a valid contract, a stop payment order by the drawer deprives the payee of the coveted status of being a paid obligee, forcing the payee to proceed against the obligor by legal process for payment of the obligation. When a contract is breaking down, this is a tactical advantage for the drawer; facing the expense of enforcing its rights at law, the payee-obligee may give up and let the drawer out of the contract. But it must be noted that developments discussed in earlier chapters in which the check payments process has been greatly speeded up (Check 21, truncation, and electronic check conversion) have significantly limited the importance of stop orders.

Answer these elementary introductory questions about 4–403.

Question #1. Saxton is the remitter of a cashier's check issued by Bank. She learns that the payee of the check, who now has possession of the check, has possibly defrauded her. She orders Bank to stop payment of the check. Must Bank do so?

Question #2. Payee learns that his paycheck has been stolen from his wallet. He immediately notifies Bank on which the check was drawn to stop payment of the check. Must Bank do so?

Question #3. Baker and Able are partners but they don't trust each other. Their agreement with Bank is that both must sign any partnership check. Both signed a check for $10,000 payable to Payton. After the check had been delivered to Payton, Baker had second thoughts and ordered Bank to stop payment on the check. Must Bank do so?

Question #4. Husband and Wife have a joint account in Bank. Wife disapproved of some checks that Husband had been writing on the account and, without Husband's consent, ordered Bank to close the account even though this would result in the dishonor of several checks Husband had already written. Must Bank do so?

1. Proving Loss under 4–403(c)

Subsection 4–403(a) grants a drawer an unlimited right to stop payment on checks and Comment 1 to 4–403 states that this right is a basic service that bank customers are entitled to receive whatever the inconvenience to the bank, but, in a seeming contradiction, subsection (c) imposes the burden of establishing any loss resulting from a bank's violation of a stop order on the customer. What justification is there for this provision? If the bank is the wrongdoer, shouldn't it bear the burden of proving absence of loss?

Although the meaning of 4–403(c) seems clear, courts have disagreed widely on its import. We use the facts of Hughes v. Marine Midland Bank, N.A., 484 N.Y.S.2d 1000 (N.Y. City Ct. 1985), as the basis for discussing the divergence of views:

Customer wrote a check payable to a real estate agent for advance rental on a vacation cottage in Florida. When Customer arrived at the cottage she found that it was not as advertised and stopped payment on the check in ample time for her Bank, located in New York, to act on the stop order. When Customer received her cancelled checks at the end of the month, she found, to her surprise, that Bank had mistakenly paid the check. She immediately demanded that Bank recredit her account for the amount of the check. Bank declined to recredit the account on the ground that Customer had not established her loss by merely showing that Bank had violated the stop order and had refused to recredit her account. The real estate agent was located in Florida, and Bank had no way of knowing about the transaction between Customer and the agent. For all Bank knew, Customer may have owed the money to the agent, thus Bank's payment might have paid a legitimate debt of Customer. Since only Customer knew these facts, Bank argued that she should have the burden of convincing Bank before it returned the money to her.

Minority view. Customer sued Bank for the amount of the check. Her proof of loss was her showing that Bank had paid the check over her valid stop order and had refused to recredit her account. A summary judgment for Customer was entered. The court held that Bank should have recredited Customer's account immediately and sought its remedy under 4–407. Under that provision, if Bank can show that its payment was made either to a holder in due course (4–407(1)) or to a holder of the check who was entitled to payment from Customer (4–407(2)), Bank is subrogated to the right of the holder to recover the amount of the check from Customer in order to prevent unjust enrichment. If Bank finds that it has paid a holder who was not entitled to payment from Customer (e.g., this would be true if the agent had defrauded

Customer), Bank is subrogated to Customer's right to get the money back from the holder (4–407(3)) in order to prevent unjust enrichment.

Majority view. Most courts believe that holdings like *Hughes* do not give adequate weight to the requirement of 4–403(c) that the customer must establish the loss. A statement of this view is found in the following quotation from Siegel v. New England Merchants National Bank, 437 N.E.2d 218, 222–223 (Mass. 1982):

> The rule of § 4–403(3), that a depositor must prove his loss, may at first seem at odds with our earlier conclusion that § 4–401(1) provides the depositor with a claim against the bank in the amount of the check, leaving the bank with recourse through subrogation under § 4–407.... We believe, however, that § 4–403(3) was intended to operate within the process of credit and subrogation established by §§ 4–401(1) and 4–407. See § 4–403, comment 8. When a bank pays an item improperly, the depositor loses his ability to exercise any right he had to withhold payment of the check. His "loss," in other words, is equivalent to his rights and defenses against the parties to whose rights the bank is subrogated—the other party to the initial transaction and other holders of the instrument. Section 4–403(3) simply protects the bank against the need to prove events familiar to the depositor, and far removed from the bank, before it can realize its subrogation rights. The depositor, who participated in the initial transaction, knows whether the payee was entitled to eventual payment and whether any defenses arose. Therefore, § 4–403(3) requires that he, rather than the bank, prove these matters....
>
> This view of the three relevant sections of the code suggests a fair allocation of the burden of proof. The bank, which has departed from authorized bookkeeping, must acknowledge a credit to the depositor's account. It must then assert its subrogation rights, and in doing so must identify the status of the parties in whose place it claims. If the bank's subrogation claims are based on the check, this would entail proof that the third party subrogor was a holder, or perhaps a holder in due course. This responsibility falls reasonably upon the bank, because it has received the check from the most recent holder and is in at least as good a position as the depositor to trace its history.
>
> The depositor must then prove any facts that might demonstrate a loss. He must establish defenses good against a holder or holder in due course, as the case may be. See UCC §§ 3–305, 3–306. If the initial transaction is at issue, he must prove either that he did not incur a liability to the other party, or that he has a defense to liability. Thus, the bank, if it asserts rights based on the transaction, need not make out a claim on the part of its subrogor against the depositor. Responsibility in this area rests entirely with the depositor, who participated in the transaction and is aware of its details. Further, the depositor must establish any consequential loss.

A few courts have adopted a variant of the majority rule, assigning shifting burdens of production. See, e.g., Mitchell v. Republic Bank & Trust Co., 239 S.E.2d 867 (N.C.Ct.App.1978); Thomas v. Marine Midland Tinkers Nat'l Bank, 381 N.Y.S.2d 797 (N.Y.City Civ.Ct. 1976). These courts allocate the burden of proof as to loss to the customer. However, burdens of production of evidence of loss are allocated between the customer and the bank. The customer must present evidence that the bank paid a check against an effective stop-payment order. Thereafter, the bank must present evidence that the customer did not suffer a loss when it paid against the order. The variant of the majority rule apparently does not read 4–403(c)'s requirement that customer bears "[t]he burden of establishing the fact and amount of loss" as including both burdens of production and proof.

Section 4–403(c) has long been a bone of contention between customers and banks. In violating a customer's stop-payment order, even if the payment is made to a holder on a valid debt of the customer, the bank has deprived the customer of the tactical advantage of forcing the holder to proceed against the customer for payment. Had the stop order in *Hughes* been honored by the bank, the agent might well have been unwilling to undertake the expense of suing the customer for the amount of the check, and might have given up on the transaction. But there is no basis in 4–403 or 4–407 for compensating a customer for this kind of loss.

A major difference between the majority and minority views is that under the majority view the bank usually keeps the money while the parties litigate; under the minority view the bank must recredit the customer's account upon learning that it has paid over a valid stop-payment order and then must proceed under 4–407 to get its money back from either the holder or the customer. The banks seek to shore up the policy of the majority view by claiming that many stop-payment orders are the result of "buyer's remorse" rather than valid defenses on the part of the customer; moreover, they strongly object to getting tied up in messy contract disputes between obligors and obligees. Customers find unfairness in a system that allows a bank that has wrongfully paid out over a stop-payment order to sit back and force the customer to proceed against it to get its money back.

A number of attempts were made to redraft 4–403(c) during the revision of Article 4, but no solution found consensus. The only substantive change made was the addition of the last sentence in 4–403(c), which clarified an issue on which there was some dispute in the case law. If a customer's checks presented subsequent to the violation of the stop order are dishonored because the check that should not have been paid depleted the customer's account balance, the customer can proceed against the bank under 4–402 to recover damages for wrongful dishonor. Since it costs money to attract customers and banks are reluctant to lose them, anecdotal evidence indicates that banks have worked out informal procedures to satisfy meritorious customer demands for a recredit after the bank violates a stop order. Under one plan, discussed by the Drafting Committee as a possible model for the redraft of Article 4, if the bank believes the customer's representations that it had paid out money the customer did not owe, it required the customer (1) to sign an affidavit stating facts indicating that the payment was made on a debt for which the customer was not liable, and (2) to enter into an agreement that it would cooperate in any litigation the bank might have to bring against the person who received the mistaken payment. Once this was done, the bank would recredit the customer's account and initiate proceedings against the person who received payment.

2. Operational Issues

If the customer gives an oral order to stop-payment, 4–403(b) provides that the order lapses after 14 calendar days unless confirmed in writing within that period. Usually the check will be presented and dishonored within the 14–day period after the oral order was given, but if the check is not presented during that period and the customer fails to confirm the order in writing, the bank may have a customer relations problem. Although 4–403(b) allows the bank to treat an unconfirmed oral stop-payment order as having no effect after the 14–day period, if the bank later pays the check, the customer may contend that it had not understood that it had to confirm in writing within a short period of time. Playing back the tape recording of the conversation regarding the stop-payment order to the customer is not likely to placate the customer; the directions to the customer may have been couched in banker's talk that customers (and sympathetic juries) find difficult to understand. On the other hand, if the bank suspects that the customer wants the stop-payment order to continue even though not confirmed and dishonors the subsequently presented check, the bank risks being held for wrongful dishonor. Banks customarily try to prevent misunderstandings in these cases by sending a written confirmation form to the customer as quickly as possible after the oral order is received with an exhortation to the customer to return the form immediately. The matter is discussed in 1 Barkley Clark & Barbara Clark, The Law of Bank Deposits, Collections and Credit Cards ¶ 3.06[1][b] (Rev. ed. 2009).

PROBLEMS

1. Customers ordered Bank to stop-payment on check number 292 drawn on their account number 315–726 for $1000. The stop order was communicated to Bank in plenty of time to act on it. However, since the correct number of the check in question was 280 and not 292, Bank's computer, which was directed to identify only checks on a customer's account which bore the correct check number, did not identify the check, and it was paid. Bank

denied liability for violating the stop order because under 4–403(a) banks must stop-payment on a check only if the check is described by the customer "with reasonable certainty." Bank conceded that its computer could have been directed to stop-payment by (1) check number alone, (2) by check number and amount of check, or (3) by amount of check alone. Did Customers identify the check with reasonable certainty? See Comment 5 to 4–403.

2. Would the decision in Problem 1 be affected by a clause in the bank's stop order form stating: "In order to stop-payment on a check, you must inform the bank of the exact amount of the item, the number of the check, and your account number; otherwise, our computer may not catch the stop order. Unless this is done the bank will not be responsible for any loss resulting from its failure to stop-payment." 1 Barkley Clark & Barbara Clark, supra, ¶3.06[1][b] and [d] (Rev. ed. 2009). Is this clause valid under 4–103(a) as determining "the standards by which the bank's responsibility is to be measured" or is it invalid as an attempt to disclaim the bank's responsibility for its "failure to exercise ordinary care"? Comment 1 to 4–403.

3. Suppose Bank induces its customer to sign a stop-payment form containing the following clause: "In requesting you to stop payment of this or any other item, the undersigned agrees to hold you harmless for all expenses and costs incurred by you on account of refusing payment of said item, and further agrees not to hold you liable on account of payment contrary to this request if same occurs through inadvertence, accident or oversight, or, if by reason of such payment, other items drawn by the undersigned are returned insufficient." Is this clause, or any part of it, enforceable? 4–103(a) and 4–403. See Comment 7 to 4-403; Opinion of Attorney General of Connecticut, 1978 WL 23495 (1978).

4. Given that the customer has an absolute right to stop-payment by complying with 4–403, is the drawee bank entitled to impose a charge for processing a stop-payment order? See Opinion of Attorney General of Michigan, 1981 WL 137970 (1981); 1981 WL 138014 (1981). 1 Barkley Clark & Barbara Clark, supra, ¶ 3.06[1][b]. If a typical charge for a stop order is $30, could a bank legally impose a $250 charge?

NOTE: POSTDATED CHECKS

A luxury that manual processing of checks allowed customers was the postdated check. The customer could hold off an impatient creditor by writing a check for the debt and could control the time of payment by postdating the check. The customer could be confident that the check would not be paid before its date because a bank clerk would examine the check for date before payment by the bank. Under original Article 3 and pre–1990 Article 4, the check was not properly payable until the date of the check, and the bank could not charge the customer's account until that time. But when automated processing of checks became universal in the 1960s, there was no visual examination of the vast majority of checks. Checks were paid or dishonored on the basis of the balance in the account and the machine-readable information on the MICR line. Since there is no space on that line for the date of the check, the usual result is that the check is paid or dishonored without regard to its date. A bank prematurely paying a postdated check that depleted the customer's account balance could be liable for wrongfully dishonoring subsequent checks that would have been paid had the postdated check not been paid. A bank might seek protection against this liability by a clause in the bank-customer agreement allowing payment of any check at the time of presentment regardless of the date of the check. To the extent such a clause is enforceable, it deprives the customer of the ability to rely on postdating.

Section 4–401(c) offers a compromise that enables customers to postdate checks while protecting banks from potential liability for failure to examine each check for its date. Under this provision, the bank can pay all checks at the time of presentment unless it has received a notice of postdating from the customer. This allows the bank time to order its computer to identify the described check when it is presented so that its date may be examined before a decision to pay is made. Banks charge a fee for processing notices of postdating just as they charge for stop-payment orders.

C. Section 4–303 and the "Four Legals"

1. Claims Affecting the Customer's Account

In an earlier chapter we considered when a check is paid in order to determine how long a payor bank has to decide whether to dishonor. A related issue concerns the priority of parties who assert rights that affect the customer's bank account as against a check that is presented for payment from that account. Whether a payor bank will pay a check depends on whether the balance in the customer's account is large enough to cover the check. A number of events may occur after a check has been presented for payment that give rise to claims that affect the size of the customer's balance. The priority between these claims, often referred to as the "four legals," and the right of the holder of the check to be paid is governed by 4–303(a). The events enumerated in 4–303(a) are (1) knowledge or notice by the bank of the customer's death, incompetence or bankruptcy; (2) a customer's order received by the bank to stop payment; (3) legal process (e.g., garnishment) served on the bank by a creditor of the customer; and (4) setoff against the customer's account exercised by the payor bank. The "four legals" are discussed in 1

Barkley Clark & Barbara Clark, supra, ¶ 6.03 (Rev. ed. 2009); 2 James J. White & Robert S. Summers, Uniform Commercial Code § 21–7 (5th. ed. 2002).

We have seen in the previous section that a customer has an absolute right to stop payment on a check under 4–403(a), and the payor bank must honor a stop order received at a time that gives the bank "a reasonable opportunity" to act on it. Just as a bank's authority to pay a check of a customer may be revoked by the express direction of the customer, as in the case of a stop-payment order, it may also be revoked by operation of law as in the case of the death, adjudication of incompetence or bankruptcy of the customer. The risk to the bank in making unauthorized payment in these cases is similar to that involved in the case of stop-payment orders. Section 4–405(a) deals specifically with the bank's authority in the case of death or incapacity and 4–405(b) gives to the bank additional authority in the case of death. On the latter point see Comments 2 and 3 to 4–405.

The authority of the bank to act in the case of the bankruptcy of the customer is not dealt with by the UCC because the question is governed by federal rather than state law. Under Bankruptcy Code § 541(a), the property of the bankrupt (including bank accounts) passes to the estate in bankruptcy when the bankruptcy case is commenced. Thus, after bankruptcy, payment by the bank of a check drawn on the account would be a payment of funds owned by the bankruptcy estate rather than by the bankrupt customer. Authority to dispose of property of the bankruptcy estate rests with the trustee in bankruptcy, and in the case of a Chapter 7 bankruptcy, this means that the bankrupt has no right to dispose of assets of the estate. But, under Bankruptcy Code § 542(c), a bank, until it has "actual notice [or] actual knowledge" of the bankruptcy of its customer, may continue to pay checks of the customer. The latter provision codifies the result of Bank of Marin v. England, 385 U.S. 99 (1966), which recognized the same right of the bank under the previous statute, the Bankruptcy Act of 1898.

Attaching and judgment creditors of the customer are given the right, under conditions set out in state statutes, to reach the customer's bank accounts by legal process. The asset reached is the debt the payor bank owes the customer for the amount of the account. The process used is generally described as garnishment, under which a writ is served on the payor bank notifying it to pay over to a judicial officer for the benefit of the creditor the amount in the account up to the unpaid balance of the claim.

If the payor bank itself is a creditor of the customer, the bank may collect its debt extrajudicially by exercise of its traditional right of setoff. The bank may offset debts the customer owes the bank (loans the bank has made to the customer) against the debt the bank owes the customer (the balance of the customer's bank account). No legal process is involved in the bank's exercise of its right of setoff; bookkeeping entries indicating that the money has been withdrawn from the account suffice to effectuate the setoff.

2. Priority Rules of Section 4–303

The problem that must be solved is at what point a check has reached the stage in the payor bank's payment process that the amount of that check can no longer be considered part of the customer's account balance and subject to the "legals." Section 4–303(a) addresses this issue. Under 4–303(a)(1), when a bank certifies a check, the amount of that check is no longer considered to be in the customer's account for purpose of the legals. The same is true when the check is presented over the counter for immediate payment and the presenter receives cash (4–303(a)(2)) or a cashier's or teller's check (4–303(a)(3)). See Comment 3 to 4–303. If the check has been effectively paid by expiration of the midnight deadline, any subsequent claim under one of the legals comes too late to be prior to the check. 4–303(a)(4).

A special rule is set out in 4–303(a)(5) for checks that will apply to the great bulk of checks that are presented to payor banks through banking channels. This provides that if a check is presented to a payor bank on Day 1, the amount of that check is no longer considered to be included in the customer's account for purposes of the legals after the close of the banking day on Day 2. However, the bank can shorten that period by setting a cutoff hour on Day 2 no earlier than one hour after the opening of business. This means that if a garnishment order is served on the payor bank after that cutoff hour, the balance of the account subject to the garnishment does not include the amount of the check in question, and the bank is protected if it pays the check. By the same token, the balance of the account subject to the payor's bank's right of setoff is similarly reduced after this point. Nor can a customer stop payment on the check after the cutoff hour. However, if a bankruptcy proceeding has been commenced involving the customer, Bankruptcy Code § 362(a)(7) prevents the bank from exercising its setoff right even if the bank does not know that the proceeding has been commenced. In this case, the bank must obtain the permission of the bankruptcy court to do so.

W & D Acquisition, LLC v. First Union Nat'l Bank

Supreme Court of Connecticut, 2003.
817 A.2d 91.

■ BORDEN, J.

The dispositive issue in this appeal is whether, as a matter of law, a banking institution has until the "midnight deadline" described in General Statutes § 42a–4–104(a)(10) to comply with garnishment process under General Statutes § 42a–4–303(a). The plaintiff, W & D Acquisition, LLC, claims that the duration of the "reasonable time" period in which to comply with garnishment process pursuant to § 42a–4–303(a) is not defined by the midnight deadline, but is to be measured by a "reasonable time," considering the facts of the case. We agree with the plaintiff and, accordingly, we reverse the judgment of the trial court to the contrary.

The plaintiff brought this writ of scire facias alleging that the defendant, First Union National Bank, had failed to secure garnished funds held in the accounts of one of its customers, R.K.E. Associates (R.K.E.), which was a defendant in the underlying action. The defendant moved for summary judgment, arguing that it was not obligated to secure the garnished funds until its midnight deadline,[5] at which time only a nominal sum remained in the accounts subject to garnishment. The trial court ruled that, as a matter of law, a banking institution has until that time to secure garnished funds. Accordingly, the court granted the defendant's motion for summary judgment, except as to the nominal sum that remained in the accounts at the midnight deadline, as to which the court rendered judgment for the plaintiff. This appeal followed.

The parties presented the following undisputed facts on the motion for summary judgment. The plaintiff is a construction materials supplier that brought an action against R.K.E., a building contractor, for breach of a provisional credit contract. In that action, the plaintiff alleged that it had supplied R.K.E. with $45,436.40 worth of construction materials on credit and that R.K.E. had failed to pay any of that balance. After demonstrating to the trial court that there was probable cause to believe that a judgment would enter in its favor, the plaintiff obtained an ex parte prejudgment garnishment order for up to $70,000 of the goods or estate of R.K.E. to secure the potential judgment. The defendant was one of four named garnishees, all of which were banking institutions where R.K.E. allegedly had deposited funds. At approximately noon on October 27, 1997, the plaintiff served a copy of the writ of garnishment and a copy of the complaint on the defendant at one of the defendant's branch locations in Danbury. At that time, R.K.E. held two accounts with the defendant, which are known here as account 1 and account 2. The balance in account 1 was $34,163.79, and it fluctuated with debits and credits throughout the ensuing hours. The balance in account 2 was $30.54, and it remained at that level throughout the entire relevant time period.

The defendant did not secure the money in either account when the garnishment papers were served. At 3:26 p.m. on that same day, an agent of R.K.E. entered the same Danbury branch location of the defendant and, by means of a counter withdrawal,[7] withdrew $32,318.26 in cash from account 1.

---

[5] In this case, the midnight deadline would be midnight of the banking day following service of the garnishment process.

[7] The term "counter withdrawal" refers to the common practice of withdrawing funds from a bank account in person by filling out, signing and presenting a withdrawal slip to a bank teller The withdrawal slip used in the transaction at issue in this case was a nonnegotiable encoded

leaving a balance of approximately $1845. Additional credits and debits reduced the balance of account 1 to $200.39 at the close of business on October 27, and $30.43 at the close of business on October 28. At midnight on October 28, 1997, the midnight deadline following the garnishment, the balance of account 1 remained at $30.43.

The plaintiff then brought this writ of scire facias to recover funds that it alleged the defendant should have secured in response to the garnishment. The defendant moved for summary judgment on the basis that it was not obligated to secure the garnished funds until the midnight deadline. The trial court granted the motion, and rendered judgment for the plaintiff in the amount of $60.97, the sum that remained in R.K.E.'s accounts at the midnight deadline.

On appeal, the plaintiff claims that the trial court improperly determined that, as a matter of law, a banking institution has until the midnight deadline described in § 42a–4–104(a)(10) to comply with garnishment process pursuant to § 42a–4–303(a). Specifically, the plaintiff claims that General Statutes §§ 42a–4–303(a) and 52–329[9] require a bank to comply with garnishment process within a "reasonable time" period, the precise duration of which will vary from case to case, depending upon the factual circumstances. We agree with the plaintiff....

The statutory provision primarily at issue in this appeal is § 42a-4–303(a). We first turn to its language. The language of § 42a–4–303(a) strongly suggests that the relevant time period is a reasonable time depending upon all of the relevant facts and circumstances, rather than a fixed period terminating on the bank's midnight deadline.

Section 42a–4–303(a) provides that "[a]ny ... legal process served upon ... a payor bank comes too late to terminate, suspend, or modify the bank's right or duty to pay an item or to charge its customer's account for the item if the ... legal process is received or served and *a reasonable time for the bank to act* thereon expires ... after the earliest of the following: (1) [t]he bank accepts ...

---

document, with fields for the account number, name of the account holder, authorized signature, date and dollar amount.

[9] General Statutes § 52–329 provides in relevant part that "*from the time of leaving [a] copy* [of the necessary garnishment process on a garnishee] all the effects of the defendant in the hands of any such garnishee, and any debt due from any such garnishee to the defendant ... shall be secured in the hands of such garnishee to pay such judgment as the plaintiff may recover...." (Emphasis added.) Nonetheless, the parties agree, as do we, that this provision cannot feasibly or fairly be applied literally, because a bank necessarily requires some period of time from the moment the process is left with it to take the practical steps necessary to secure the funds in its depositor's account.

Thus, both sides agree that this provision means that a bank has a reasonable time in which to act. They differ, however, regarding how to measure that reasonable time. The plaintiff contends that the reasonable time must be determined on a case-by-case basis, depending on all of the facts and circumstances. The defendant contends that, as a matter of law, its midnight deadline is the appropriate measurement of what is a reasonable time.

the item; (2) the bank pays the item in cash...." (Emphasis added.) In other words, under § 42a–4–303(a), a banking institution is obligated to secure funds within a "reasonable time" after receiving garnishment process, a form of "legal process," to prevent distribution of those funds in response to an "item." The "item[s]" at issue in this case include a withdrawal slip[10] tendered in exchange for $32,318.26 in cash as well as several checks drawn against account 1 in the hours that followed.[11]

Section 42a–4–303(a) expressly provides that a banking institution must act within a "reasonable time"; it does not expressly provide that a banking institution must act before its midnight deadline. We do not decide the meaning of "reasonable time," as used in § 42a–4–303(a), in a vacuum. General Statutes § 42a–1–[12] 204 further defines "reasonable time" as used in § 42a–4–303(a). Section 42a–1–204 (1) specifically provides that the standards that it contains apply to conduct governed by "this title...." "[T]his title" is title 42a of the General Statutes, the Uniform Commercial Code. The requirement in § 42a–4–303(a) that a bank act within a "reasonable time," is a provision of the Uniform Commercial Code. Thus, the standards set forth in § 42a–1–204, which define the phrase "reasonable time," apply to § 42a–4–303(a). Section 42a–1–204 (2) specifically provides: "What is a reasonable time for taking any action depends on the nature, purpose and circumstances of such action." Thus, textually, § 42a-4–303(a) strongly indicates, by its open-textured language and by virtue of § 42a–1–204 (2), that its meaning is what is normally meant by the statutory use of the phrase "reasonable time," namely, a fact-specific inquiry depending on all of the circumstances of the case.

The conclusion that the phrase "reasonable time" as used in § 42a–4–303(a) requires a fact-specific inquiry and is not synonymous with the midnight deadline is also consistent with the official commentary of the Uniform Commercial Code dealing with the very same "reasonable time" provision.

---

[10] See footnote 7 of this opinion.

[11] * * * [T]he withdrawal slip that R.K.E. handed to the defendant's teller was an "item" within the meaning of § 42a–4–303 (a). General Statutes § 42a–4–104 (a)(9) defines an " 'item' " as, inter alia, "an ... order to pay money handled by a bank for collection or payment...." An " '[o]rder' " is defined in General Statutes § 42a–3–103 (a)(6) as "a written instruction to pay money signed by the person giving the instruction...." The withdrawal slip at issue in this appeal was a written instruction to pay out $32,318.26 in cash, handled by a bank, namely, the defendant, for payment, and signed by the agent of R.K.E., who gave the bank the instruction to pay. See footnote 7 of this opinion.

[12] General Statutes § 42a–1–204 provides: "(1) Whenever this title requires any action to be taken within a reasonable time, any time which is not manifestly unreasonable may be fixed by agreement.

"(2) What is a reasonable time for taking any action depends on the nature, purpose and circumstances of such action.

"(3) An action is taken 'seasonably' when it is taken at or within the time agreed or if no time is agreed at or within a reasonable time."

Section 42a–4–303 is our state's version of § 4–303 of the Uniform Commercial Code. The official commentary to § 4–303 is a part of the circumstances surrounding the enactment of § 42a–4–303(a), and, as such, is relevant to the legislature's intent.... Official comment 6 to § 4–303 of the Uniform Commercial Code provides in relevant part: "In the case of ... legal process the effective time for determining whether [it was] received too late to affect the payment of an item and a charge to the customer's account by reason of such payment, is receipt plus a reasonable time for the bank to act on [the service of process].... Usually, a relatively short time is required to communicate to the accounting department advice of one of these events but certainly some time is necessary...." Thus, the official commentary unequivocally states that the time period is variable and depends upon the factual circumstances. It makes no mention of the bright-line rule created by the midnight deadline.

This conclusion is consistent with what we perceive to be the purpose of § 42a–4–303(a), namely, to balance the interests of the garnishor in securing its potential debtor's funds against the need for the bank to have the necessary time in which to take the steps necessary to effectuate that security. Although, as the defendant suggests, a midnight deadline would give a bank more certainty and, in all likelihood, more time to take those steps, we see nothing in either the language or the purpose of the statute to justify that bright-line rule....

The judgment is reversed and the case is remanded for further proceedings according to law.

PROBLEM

Payee deposited a check for $25,000 in Depositary Bank (DB) for collection. The check was drawn by Drawer on her account in Payor Bank (PB) and was presented through banking channels to PB at 10 a.m. on Day 1. At the time the check was presented, Drawer had $30,000 in collected funds in her account. At noon on Day 2, PB examined the check and noted that paying the check would leave only $5,000 in Drawer's account. This was of concern to PB because Drawer owed PB $20,000 on an overdue loan. At 2 p.m. on Day 2, PB made the bookkeeping entries that were required to setoff its $20,000 claim against Drawer's account. Since this act reduced Drawer's account to $10,000, PB returned the check, marked "not sufficient funds," to the presenting bank at 6 p.m. on Day 2. The close of PB's banking day was 5 p.m., and it had not opted for an earlier cutoff hour. Payee challenged PB's right to setoff against the check 26 hours after it had been presented to PB. Is Payee correct? See 4–303(a)(5) and Comment 4.

D. Wrongful Dishonor

Most business lawyers at some time receive a call from an irate client whose check has been bounced by a bank. Sometimes the bank has not been sufficiently contrite about its error, and your client wants to "teach that bank a lesson." What can you do for this client? As we will see, the answer in most cases is very little, other than to extract an apology from the chastened bank. Nonetheless, the lawyer would do well to ask the client some detailed questions about the facts surrounding the wrongful dishonor because, under certain circumstances, 4–402(b) not only offers the wronged customer direct damages but is one of the few provisions in the UCC that offers consequential damages.

Section 4–402(b) is only the latest step in a long series of judicial and legislative efforts to strike a balance between the erring bank and the wronged customer. In nineteenth century rural America where everyone knew everyone else's business, wrongful dishonor of checks was treated as slander against the character of a business person ("trader"). 1 Barkley Clark & Barbara Clark, supra, ¶ 3.05[9][c][i] (Rev. ed. 2009). Being a "no account" was a serious accusation. The so-called "trader rule" was stated in 2 Morse, Banks and Banking § 458, at 1007–1008 (6th ed. 1928):

> [T]he better authority seems to be, that, even if...actual loss or injury is not shown, yet more than nominal damages shall be given. It can hardly be possible that a customer's check can be wrongfully refused payment without some impeachment of his credit, which must in fact be an actual injury, though he cannot from the nature of the case furnish independent distinct proof thereof. It is as in cases of libel and slander, which description of suit, indeed, it closely resembles, inasmuch as it is a practical slur upon the plaintiff's credit and repute in the business world. Special damage may be shown, if the plaintiff be able; but, if he be not able, the jury may nevertheless give such [temperate] damages as they conceive to be a reasonable compensation for that indefinite mischief which such an act must be assumed to have inflicted, according to the ordinary course of human events.

This was a plaintiff's lawyer's dream: if a bank wrongfully dishonored the check of a business customer, the customer got to the jury without showing any actual damage, and juries weren't any more fond of banks then than now. The banks fought back in the legislatures. At the behest of the American Bankers Association, a number of states enacted a version of the following: "No bank shall be liable to a depositor because of the nonpayment through mistake or error, and without malice, of a check which should have been paid unless the depositor shall allege and prove actual damage by reason of such nonpayment and in such event the liability shall not exceed the amount of damage so proved." Cal. Civ. Code § 3320 (repealed).

The original version of what is now 4–402(b) read: "A payor bank is liable to its customer for damages proximately caused by the wrongful dishonor of an item. When the dishonor occurs through mistake liability is limited to actual damages proved. If so proximately caused and proved damages may include damages for an arrest or prosecution of the customer or other consequential damages. Whether any consequential damages are proximately caused by the wrongful dishonor is a question of fact to be determined in each case." Comment 1 to Revised 4–402 contains a critique of this language and discusses the changes made in the revision.

Loucks v. Albuquerque National Bank

Supreme Court of New Mexico, 1966.
76 N.M. 735, 418 P.2d 191.

■ LA FEL E. OMAN, JUDGE, COURT OF APPEALS.

The plaintiffs-appellants, Richard A. Loucks and Del Martinez, hereinafter referred to as plaintiffs, Mr. Loucks and Mr. Martinez, respectively, were partners engaged in a business at Albuquerque, New Mexico, under the partnership name of L & M Paint and Body Shop.

By their complaint they sought both compensatory and punitive damages on behalf of the partnership, on behalf of Mr. Loucks, and on behalf of Mr. Martinez against the defendants-appellees, Albuquerque National Bank and W. J. Kopp, hereinafter referred to as defendants, the bank, and Mr. Kopp, respectively.

Prior to March 15, 1962 Mr. Martinez had operated a business at Albuquerque, New Mexico, under the name of Del's Paint and Body Shop. He did his banking with defendant bank and he dealt with Mr. Kopp, a vice-president of the bank.

On February 8, 1962 Mr. Martinez borrowed $500 from the bank, which he deposited with the bank in the account of Del's Paint and Body Shop. He executed an installment note payable to the bank evidencing this indebtedness.

On March 15, 1962 the plaintiffs formed a partnership in the name of L & M Paint and Body Shop. On that date they opened a checking account with the bank in the name of L & M Paint and Body Shop and deposited $620 therein. The signatures of both Mr. Loucks and Mr. Martinez were required to draw money from this account. The balance in the account of Del's Paint and Body Shop as of this time was $2.67. This was drawn from this account by a cashier's check and deposited in the account of L & M Paint & Body Shop on April 18, 1962.

Two payments of $50.00 each were made on Mr. Martinez' note of February 8, 1962, or on notes given as a renewal thereof. These payments were made by checks drawn by plaintiffs on the account of L & M Paint and Body Shop. The checks were payable to the order of the bank and were dated June 29, 1962 and August 28, 1962. A subsequent installment note was executed by Mr. Martinez on October 17, 1962 in the principal amount of $462 payable to the order of the bank. This was given as a replacement or renewal of the prior notes which started with the note of February 8, 1962.

Mr. Martinez became delinquent in his payments on this note of October 17, 1962 and the bank sued him in a Justice of the Peace court to recover the delinquency.

As of March 14, 1963 Mr. Martinez was still indebted to the bank on this note in the amount of $402, and on that date, Mr. Kopp, on behalf of the bank, wrote L & M Paint and Body Shop advising that its account had been charged with $402 representing the balance due "on Del Martinez installment note," and the indebtedness was referred to in the letter as the "indebtedness of Mr. Del Martinez."

The charge of $402 against the account of L & M Paint and Body Shop was actually made on March 15, 1963, which was a Friday.

Although Mr. Martinez at one time testified he telephoned Mr. Kopp on either Friday or the following Monday about this charge, when he was questioned more closely he admitted he discussed the matter with Mr. Kopp by telephone on Friday. Mr. Loucks testified that as he recalled, it was on Monday. Both plaintiffs went to the bank on Monday, March 18, and talked with Mr. Kopp. They both told Mr. Kopp that the indebtedness represented by the note was the personal indebtedness of Mr. Martinez and was not a partnership obligation. Mr. Loucks explained that they had some outstanding checks against the partnership account. Mr. Kopp refused to return the money to the partnership account. There was evidence of some unpleasantness in the conversation. The partnership account, in which there was then a balance of only $3.66, was thereupon closed by the plaintiffs.

The bank refused to honor nine, and possibly ten, checks drawn on the account and dated between the dates of March 8 and 16, inclusive.

The checks dated prior to March 15 total $89.14, and those dated March 15 and 16 total $121.68. These figures do not include the tenth check to which some reference was made, but which was not offered into evidence and the amount of which does not appear in the record.

The case came on for trial before the court and a jury. The court submitted the case to the jury upon the question of whether or not the defendants wrongfully made the charge in the amount of $402 against the account of L &

M Paint and Body Shop. The allegations of the complaint concerning punitive damages and compensatory damages, other than the amount of $402 allegedly wrongfully charged by the defendants against the partnership account, were dismissed by the court before the case was submitted to the jury. The jury returned a verdict for the plaintiffs in the amount of $402.

The plaintiffs have appealed and assert error on the part of the trial court in taking from the jury the questions of (1) punitive damages, (2) damages to business reputation and credit, (3) damages for personal injuries allegedly sustained by Mr. Loucks, and (4) in disallowing certain costs claimed by plaintiffs.

....

The plaintiffs, as partners, sought recovery on behalf of the partnership of $402 allegedly wrongfully charged against the partnership account. This question was submitted to the jury, was decided in favor of the partnership, and against the defendants, and no appeal has been taken from the judgment entered on the verdict. They also sought recovery on behalf of the partnership of $5,000 for alleged damages to its credit, good reputation, and business standing in the community, $1,800 for its alleged loss of income, and $14,404 as punitive damages.

Each partner also sought recovery of $5,000 for alleged damages to his personal credit, good reputation and business standing. Mr. Martinez sought punitive damages individually in the amount of $10,000, and Mr. Loucks sought punitive damages individually in the amount of $60,000. Mr. Loucks also sought $25,000 by way of damages he allegedly sustained by reason of an ulcer which resulted from the wrongful acts of the defendants.

The parties have argued the case in their respective briefs and in their oral arguments upon the theory that the questions here involved, except for Point IV, which deals with the disallowance by the trial court of some claimed costs, are questions of the damages which can properly be claimed as a result of a wrongful dishonor by a bank of checks drawn by a customer or depositor on the bank, and of the sufficiency of the evidence offered by plaintiffs to support their claims for damages.

Both sides quote UCC § 4–402...[.]

It would appear that the first question to be resolved is that of the person, or persons, to whom a bank must respond in damages for a wrongful dishonor. Here, the account was a partnership account, and if there was in fact a wrongful dishonor of any checks, such were partnership checks.

We have adopted the Uniform Commercial Code in New Mexico. In UCC § 4–402 it is clearly stated that a bank "is liable to its customer." In UCC § 4–104(1)(e), entitled "Definitions and index of definitions" it is stated that:

"(1) In this article unless the context otherwise requires

> "(e) 'Customer' means any person having an account with a bank or for whom a bank has agreed to collect items and includes a bank carrying an account with another bank; * * * "

This requires us to determine who is a "person" within the contemplation of this definition. Under part II, article I of the Uniform Commercial Code, entitled "General Definitions and Principles of Interpretation," we find the term "person" defined in § 1–201(30) as follows: "'Person' includes an individual or an organization * * *."

Subsection (28) of the same section expressly includes a "partnership" as one of the legal or commercial entities embraced by the term "organization."

It would seem that logically the "customer" in this case to whom the bank was required to respond in damages for any wrongful dishonor was the partnership. The Uniform Commercial Code expressly regards a partnership as a legal entity. This is consistent with the ordinary mercantile conception of a partnership....

The Uniform Partnership Act, which has been adopted in New Mexico and appears as chapter 66, article I, N.M.S.A.1953, recognizes that a partnership has a separate legal entity for at least some purposes....

Suits may be brought in New Mexico by or against the partnership as such. * * * A partnership is a distinct legal entity to the extent that it may sue or be sued in the partnership name. National Surety Co. v. George E. Breece Lumber Co., 60 F.2d 847 (10th Cir. 1932).

....

The relationship, in connection with which the wrongful conduct of the bank arose, was the relationship between the bank and the partnership. The partnership was the customer, and any damages arising from the dishonor belonged to the partnership and not to the partners individually.

The damages claimed by Mr. Loucks as a result of the ulcer, which allegedly resulted from the wrongful acts of the defendants, are not consequential damages proximately caused by the wrongful dishonor as contemplated by § 4–402. In support of his right to recover for such claimed damages he relies upon the cases of Jones v. Citizens Bank of Clovis, 58 N.M. 48, 265 P.2d 366 and Weaver v. Bank of America Nat. Trust & Sav. Ass'n., 59 Cal.2d 428, 30 Cal. Rptr. 4, 380 P.2d 644. The California and New Mexico courts construed identical statutes in these cases. The New Mexico statute appeared as § 48–10–5, N.M.S.A.1953. This statute was repealed when the Uniform Commercial Code was adopted in 1961.

Assuming we were to hold that the decisions in those cases have not been affected by the repeal of the particular statutory provisions involved and the adoption of the Uniform Commercial Code, we are still compelled by our reasoning to reach the same result, because the plaintiffs in those cases were the depositor in the California case and the administratrix of the estate of the deceased depositor in the New Mexico case. In the present case, Mr. Loucks was not a depositor, as provided in the prior statute, nor a customer, as provided in our present statute. No duty was owed to him personally by reason of the debtor-creditor relationship between the bank and the partnership.

It is fundamental that compensatory damages are not recoverable unless they proximately result from some violation of a legally-recognized right of the person seeking the damages, whether such be a right in contract or tort....

Insofar as the damage questions are concerned, we must still consider the claims for damages to the partnership. As above stated, the claim on behalf of the partnership for the recovery of the $402 was concluded by judgment for plaintiffs in this amount. This leaves (1) the claim of $5,000 for alleged damage to credit, reputation and business standing, (2) the claim of $1,800 for alleged loss of income, and (3) the claim of $14,404 as punitive damages.

The question with which we are first confronted is that of whether or not the customer, whose checks are wrongfully dishonored, may recover damages merely because of the wrongful dishonor. We understand the provisions of UCC § 4–402 to limit the damages to those proximately caused by the wrongful dishonor, and such includes any consequential damages so proximately caused. If the dishonor occurs through mistake, the damages are limited to actual damages proved.

It is pointed out in the comments to this section of the Uniform Commercial Code that:

> "....
>
> "This section rejects decisions which have held that where the dishonored item has been drawn by a merchant, trader or fiduciary he is defamed in his business, trade or profession by a reflection on his credit and hence that substantial damages may be awarded on the basis of defamation 'per se' without proof that damage has occurred. * * * " Uniform Commercial Code, § 4–402, Comment 3.

If we can say as a matter of law that the dishonor here occurred through mistake, then the damages would be limited to the "actual damages proved." Even if we are able to agree, as contended by defendants in their answer brief, that the defendants acted under a mistake of fact in "...that Mr. Kopp acting on behalf of the bank thought that the money was invested in the partnership and could be traced directly from Mr. Martinez to the L & M Paint and Body Shop," still defendants cannot rely on such mistake after both Mr. Martinez and Mr. Loucks informed them on March 15 and 18 that this was a personal obligation of Mr. Martinez and that the partnership had outstanding checks. At least it then became a question for the jury to decide whether or not defendants had wrongfully dishonored the checks through mistake.

The problem then resolves itself into whether or not the evidence offered and received, together with any evidence properly offered and improperly excluded, was sufficient to establish a question as to whether the partnership credit and reputation were proximately damaged by the wrongful dishonors. There was evidence that ten checks were dishonored, that one parts dealer thereafter refused to accept a partnership check and Mr. Loucks was required to go to the bank, cash the check, and then take the cash to the parts dealer in order to get the parts; that some persons who had previously accepted the partnership checks now refused to accept them; that other places of business denied the partnership credit after the dishonors; and that a salesman, who had sold the partnership a map and for which he was paid by one of the dishonored checks, came to the partnership's place of business, and ripped the map off the wall because he had been given "a bad check for it."

This evidence was sufficient to raise a question of fact to be determined by the jury as to whether or not the partnership's credit had been damaged as a proximate result of the dishonors. This question should have been submitted to the jury.

Damages recoverable for injuries to credit as a result of a wrongful dishonor are more than mere nominal damages and are referred to as " ...compensatory, general, substantial, moderate, or temperate, damages as would be fair and reasonable compensation for the injury which he [the depositor] must have sustained, but not harsh or inordinate damages...." 5A Michie, Banks and Banking, § 243 at 576.

What are reasonable and temperate damages varies according to the circumstances of each case and the general extent to which it may be presumed the credit of the depositor would be injured.... The amount of such damages is to be determined by the sound discretion and dispassionate judgment of the jury....

The next item of damages claimed on behalf of the partnership, which was taken from the jury, was the claim for loss of income in the amount of $1,800 allegedly sustained by the partnership as a result of the illness and disability of Mr. Loucks by reason of his ulcer. We are of the opinion that the trial court properly dismissed this claim for the announced reason that no substantial evidence was offered to support the claim, and for the further reason that the partnership had no legally-enforceable right to recover for personal injuries inflicted upon a partner.

Even if we were to assume that a tortuous act had been committed by defendants which proximately resulted in the ulcer and the consequent personal injuries and disabilities of Mr. Loucks, the right to recover for such would be in him. An action for damages resulting from a tort can only be sustained by the person directly injured thereby, and not by one claiming to have suffered collateral or resulting injuries.

As was stated by Mr. Justice Holmes in Robins Dry Dock & Repair Co. v. Flint, 275 U.S. 303, 48 S.Ct. 134, 72 L.Ed. 290:

> "…no authority need be cited to show that, as a general rule, at least, a tort to the person or property of one man does not make the tort-feasor liable to another merely because the injured person was under a contract with that other, unknown to the doer of the wrong…. The law does not spread its protection so far."

The last question of damages concerns the claim for punitive damages. The trial court dismissed this claim for the reason that he was convinced there was no evidence of willful or wanton conduct on the part of defendants. Punitive or exemplary damages may be awarded only when the conduct of the wrongdoer may be said to be maliciously intentional, fraudulent, oppressive, or committed recklessly or with a wanton disregard of the plaintiffs' rights….

Malice as a basis for punitive damages means the intentional doing of a wrongful act without just cause or excuse. This means that the defendant not only intended to do the act which is ascertained to be wrongful, but that he knew it was wrong when he did it….

Although, as expressed above, we are of the opinion that there was a jury question as to whether defendants acted under a mistake of fact in dishonoring the checks, we do not feel that the unpleasant or intemperate remark or two claimed to have been made by Mr. Kopp, and his conduct, described by Mr. Martinez as having "run us out of the bank more or less," are sufficient upon which an award of punitive damages could properly have been made. Thus, the trial court was correct in taking this claim from the jury….

It follows from what has been said that this cause must be reversed and remanded for a new trial solely upon the questions of whether or not the partnership credit was damaged as a proximate result of the dishonors, and, if so, the amount of such damages.

NOTES

1. *"Liable to its customer."* Since *Loucks*, interesting developments have taken place on the issue of who can recover for damages incurred from a wrongful dishonor of the check of a corporate customer. Obviously a corporation cannot suffer emotional distress or acquire ulcers resulting from the bank's mistake, much less the personal embarrassment and social ostracism stemming from being jailed for writing a check that was wrongfully dishonored. But in a closely held corporation, these damages may well be sustained by the individuals who own and operate the business. In an era in which plaintiffs are successfully seeking more adequate awards for their injuries, it comes as no surprise that courts are finding ways of reading the term "customer" more flexibly or finding alternative bases for liability. In

Kendall Yacht Corp. v. United California Bank, 123 Cal.Rptr. 848 (Cal.Ct.App.1975), Corporation was the depositor and Laurence and Linda Kendall were officers and prospective shareholders who personally guaranteed Corporation's debts to Bank. Corporation never issued stock, and "it was, in effect, nothing but a transparent shell, having no viability as a separate and distinct legal entity." Id. at 853. The court held that the Kendalls were "customers" within the meaning of 4–402. "Thus it was entirely foreseeable that the dishonoring of the Corporation's check would reflect directly on the personal credit and reputation of the Kendalls and that they would suffer the adverse personal consequences which resulted when the Bank reneged on its commitments." Id.. at 853. The court allowed recovery by the Kendalls of damages for emotional distress under 4–402.

Parrett v. Platte Valley State Bank & Trust Co., 459 N.W.2d 371 (Neb. 1990), goes beyond *Kendall Yacht.* Parrett was the principal shareholder and president of the corporate customer. He personally participated in the business relationship between the corporate customer and the bank and entered into a personal guaranty for the corporation's obligations to the bank. When the bank wrongfully dishonored the corporate customer's check, Parrett was charged with felony theft and went to trial on the charge. At trial the charge was dismissed. Parrett sued for wrongful dishonor under 4–402. The lower court sustained the bank's demurrer on the ground that Parrett was not the customer. The Supreme Court of Nebraska, relying on *Kendall Yacht*, reversed and said:

> As reflected by Parrett's petition, the parties' business relationship, which included Parrett's personal guaranty for P & P Machinery's obligations to the bank, was such that it was foreseeable that dishonoring the corporation's check would reflect directly on Parrett. This is borne out by the fact that a criminal charge based on the dishonored check was brought against Parrett, but was dismissed during Parrett's trial. Since the consequences of the wrongful dishonor fell upon Parrett, it would elevate form over substance to say that he was not the bank's "customer" within the meaning of § 4–402. This is not to say that in every case a corporate officer has a wrongful dishonor action against the depository bank on which the corporation's check has been drawn and later dishonored. However, in view of the facts of this case alleged in Parrett's petition, Parrett has a cause of action against the bank.

Id. at 378. Although the majority opinion in *Parrett* purported to rely on *Kendall Yacht,* the dissent pointed out that the key factor in that case was that the corporation was not a separate legal entity; the decision was based on veil-piercing. But in *Parrett,* the corporate customer was clearly a separate legal entity and had always been treated as such by the bank.

Another line of decisions has held fast to the view expressed in *Loucks* that only the corporate customer can proceed under 4–402. See, e.g., Farmers Bank v. Sinwellan Corp., 367 A.2d 180 (Del.1976) (president of corporate customer denied right to sue under 4–402 for damages resulting from a criminal action brought against him because of the dishonor). See Jana v. Wachovia, N.A., 2006 WL 3731190 (Pa. Com. Pl. 2006). An approach to allowing insiders to recover in cases in which corporate checks have been dishonored, even in jurisdictions taking the *Sinwellan* point of view, is to contend that 4–402 does not displace any cause of action that such an insider may have had against the bank at common law. See 1–103(b) and Comment 5 to 4–402.

2. *Damages*. Section 4–402(b) provides very broadly that a bank is liable for any damages proximately caused by a wrongful dishonor. Comment 1 to 4–402 describes a customer's right to sue as a "statutory cause of action." In most cases, no damages can be proved, but if economic loss can be shown consequential damages will be awarded. Skov v. Chase Manhattan Bank, 407 F.2d 1318 (3d Cir.1969). The principal damages issue has been whether aggrieved customers can recover for emotional distress. Certainly a wrongful dishonor can proximately cause emotional distress, and this type of damage is within the limitation in the second sentence of 4–402(b) that the damages must be "actual." Although courts show their concern about the potential for abuse present in allowing damages for emotional distress, a number of courts have awarded customers damages for emotional distress in wrongful dishonor cases. The precedents are collected and discussed in Buckley v. Trenton Saving Fund Society, 544 A.2d 857 (N.J. 1988). In that case the court held that the facts did not justify recovery for mental anguish and said:

> To some extent, slight emotional distress arising from the occasional dishonor of a check is one of the regrettable aggravations of living in today's society. See *Restatement,* [(Second) of Torts], § 436A comment b. Accordingly, we are reluctant to allow compensation for the intentional infliction of emotional distress when a bank wrongfully dishonors a check unless the bank's conduct is intentional, as well as reckless or outrageous, and the distress is severe or results in bodily injury. See *Hume,* 178 N.J.Super. 310, 428 A.2d 966; *Restatement,* [(Second) of Torts], § 46. When those conditions are met, a customer should be compensated for the emotional distress that is caused by the wrongful dishonor of a check.

Id. at 864. Other courts are similarly restrictive on allowing damages for emotional distress in wrongful dishonor cases. See, e.g., Maryott v. First Nat'l Bank of Eden, 624 N.W.2d 96 (S.D. 2001).

Comment 1 to 4–402 points out in its last sentence that whether punitive damages are appropriate depends, under 1–305(a), on non–UCC state law. The matter is discussed in *Buckley*.

3. *Consequential damages.* Two further questions arise in connection with 4–402(b). First, why is the bank liable for consequential damages under 4–402(b) while a receiving bank that improperly executes or fails to execute a wire transfer is not liable for consequential damages under 4A–305(c)–(d), unless it expressly agrees to assume liability? Both 4–402(b) and 4A–305(c) set default rules; the question is why the default rules are set differently. The precaution-taking abilities of banks and customers, and the array of possible loss from wrongful dishonor of a check and improper execution of a wire transfer, seem to be the same. The costs of contracting around a default rule also do not appear to differ as between 4–402(b) and 4A–305(c). What, then, justifies setting different default rules? There might be a political explanation. Banks might have conceded an expanded potential liability under 4A–402(c)'s "money-back guarantee" and 4A–202 and 4A–203's unauthorized payment order provisions in exchange for limitations on recoverable damages under 4A–402(c). A similar sort of trade-off possibly was infeasible in the case of Article 4.

Second, does 4–402(b) set the default rule correctly with respect to consequential damages? There is room for doubt. Where contracting parties have asymmetric information and the less well informed party is the superior risk bearer, an important purpose of default rules can be to induce the party with the better information to disclose it to the less well informed party. See Ian Ayres & Robert Gertner, Filling Gaps in Incomplete Contracts: An Economic Theory of Default Rules, 99 Yale L.J. 87 (1989). This seems warranted in the context of wrongful dishonor of checks because customers typically are better informed than banks about the impact of wrongful dishonor on them. In order for banks to take the appropriate precautions, they need this information. However, allowing customers to recover consequential damages, including for emotional distress, under some plausible assumptions gives them a disincentive to disclose information to banks. As a result, banks might take inefficient precautions against wrongful dishonor. To see this, assume that customers are of two sorts, "low injury" and "high injury," and that banks cannot identify in advance a customer as being of one sort or another. "Low injury" customers suffer few consequential damages from wrongful dishonor, and no loss from emotional distress; "high injury" customers suffer significant consequential damages, including emotional distress.

Banks will charge each customer a rate reflecting its expected liability to a mixed population of low and high injury customers. Thus, each customer pays this blended charge. Low injury customers pay a higher rate, and high injury customers a lower rate than if banks could identify each customer's risk profile. Here, high injury customers are subsidized by low risk customers. Banks, in turn, take inefficient levels of precaution because they overinvest in preventative measures for low injury customers and underinvest in them for high injury customers. An efficient default rule gives high and low injury customers incentives to reveal information about their respective types to banks.

Section 4–402(b) doesn't induce customers to do so. By allowing recovery of consequential damages, including damages for emotional distress, 4–402(b) gives all customers an enhanced level of protection. High injury customers therefore have no incentive to disclose information about their likely emotional distress resulting from banks' wrongful dishonor. They are protected by 4–402(b) and already benefit from the cross-subsidy provided by low injury customers. Low injury customers, who don't need 4–402(b)'s enhanced protection, also might not have an incentive to disclose their type to banks. For instance, if the population of customers contains a significant number of high injury customers and relatively few low injury customers, the subsidy provided to high injury customers might be slight. Disclosure, therefore, would produce a modest reduction in rates charged to low injury customers. If so, the costs of contracting around 4–402(b), to reduce the banks potential liability, might exceed the benefits of doing so for low risk customers. On the other hand, if the default rule excluded particular sorts of consequential damages, such as damages for emotional distress, high injury customers would be unprotected. Low injury customers would not need to incur contracting costs because the default rule already protects them. High injury customers would have to contract with banks, thus disclosing information about their type, but they receive a benefit in the form of enhanced protection (for an enhanced charge). Thus, 4–402(b) might be an inferior default rule.

This conclusion obviously is sensitive to the assumptions made. A realistic estimate of the population of customers would not divide it into two simplified sorts of customer: low and high injury. The more accurate assumption is that customers come in a continuum of risk profiles, from businesses suffering no emotional distress from wrongful dishonor, to the thick-skinned customer, to the socially sensitive or financially precarious customer. The extent of other sorts of consequential damage also realistically varies among customers, as does the size of contracting costs for customers of bargaining around a default rule. Section 4–402(b)'s default rule might be superior to other candidates, given the limited information available to lawmakers in designing or applying default rules. For the important effect of such details on the choice of default rule, see Barry E. Adler, The Questionable Ascent of Hadley v. Baxendale, 51 Stan. L. Rev. 1547 (1999); Alan Schwartz, The Default Rule Paradigm and the Limits of Contract Law, 3 S. Cal. Interdisc. L.J. 389 (1993); Lucian Ayre Bebchuk & Steven Shavell, Information and the Scope of Liability for Breach of Contract: The Rule of Hadley v. Baxendale, 7 J.L. Econ. & Org. 284 (1991).

E. THE BANK–CUSTOMER AGREEMENT

1. DISCLOSURE: THE TRUTH–IN–SAVINGS ACT

Among the demands that consumer groups have made on deposit-holding institutions, one of the most persistent has been the call for improved disclosure of the terms of deposit accounts so that customers may better understand the agreements they are entering into with banks. The drive for improved disclosure was at the core of the consumer movement in the second half of the last century. At the earliest stage of this movement, Senator Paul Douglas of Illinois, a former economics professor, noted that financial institutions quoted their finance charges to consumers in several different ways: annual percentage rate, monthly percentage rate, annual dollar amount, and so forth. These practices made it difficult for consumers to do effective credit shopping because they could not be sure which creditor was offering the lowest rates. He proposed what sounded like a modest solution: require all creditors to state their finance charges as an annual percentage rate or "simple annual interest," as he liked to put it. Creditors, seeing the head of the federal camel under the tent, tried to head off the legislation by asserting that the variety and complexity of consumer credit transactions were so great that such a law would be operationally impossible for creditors to comply with. After many years of heated discussions about the subject, Congress passed the Truth-in-Lending Act in 1968, which required disclosure of finance charges in terms of an annual percentage rate. 15 U.S.C. § 1601 et seq. Congress passed on to a reluctant Federal Reserve Board (FRB) the task of solving by regulations the innumerable operational problems encountered. Regulation Z, 12 C.F.R. Part 226, resulted. Now there is a considerable body of legislative, administrative and case law on the subject of the disclosure of consumer finance charges. The Truth-in-Lending Act served as a model for the deposit account disclosure legislation that came along more than two decades later.

Consumers had the same problems in attempting to compare the terms offered by banks and other depository institutions with respect to deposit accounts. These terms are usually contained either in the bank-customer agreement or in a separate brochure and are selectively publicized in advertisements designed to attract more depositors. Consumers complained that although most deposit institutions disclosed the interest rates they were paying on deposit accounts as an annual percentage rate based on the full amount of the principal in the account, others used methods that made it appear that the interest rate offered was higher than it actually was. As was the case with Truth in Lending, negotiations leading to Truth-in-Savings went on for years in Congress before the Act was finally passed in 1991 as part of the Federal Deposit Insurance Act, 12 U.S.C. § 4301 et seq. Again, Congress gave the FRB the task of making the law workable, and Regulation DD, 12 C.F.R. Part 230, was completed in 1992 for this purpose. The Act and the Regulation are extensively discussed in 2 Barkley Clark & Barbara Clark, supra, Chapter 19 (Rev. ed. 2009).

(1) *Initial disclosure.* In brief, the Truth-in-Savings Act (TISA) requires federal and state deposit-holding institutions, e.g., banks, savings and loan associations, and credit unions, to disclose in a uniform manner the terms of their consumer deposit accounts at the time of entering into the deposit relationship with the customer. This initial disclosure must include interest rate information, the amounts of any service charges or other fees that may be imposed in connection with the account, and other salient features of the deposit account like minimum balance requirements, time account features (e.g., the effect of early withdrawal), and transaction limitations (e.g., limitations on the number of withdrawals or deposits). Regulation DD § 230.4.

The key items disclosed are the interest rate and the "annual percentage yield" (APY), which is the yield the interest rate produces with compounding. Regulation DD § 230.2(c). It is this figure that should be most useful to consumers in interest rate shopping. The model clause suggested by the Appendix to Regulation DD is:

> The interest rate on your account is _______% with an annual percentage yield of _______%.

(2) *Periodic statement disclosures.* Additional disclosures must be made in the periodic, usually monthly, statements that depository institutions send to their customers. Regulation DD § 230.6. These disclosures must include the "annual percentage yield earned" during the statement period, the dollar amount of the interest earned during that period, the dollar amounts and kinds of fees imposed and the number of days in the statement period or the beginning and ending dates of the period.

(3) *Advertising.* The third level of disclosure regulation relates to advertising. As is true with any law attempting to regulate advertising, Regulation DD § 230.8 is very complex. In an attempt to force the depository institution to be fair in its advertising, Regulation DD calls for so much explanatory language that it will probably result in either less advertising or an information overload in the ads that are published. If the printed ad states a rate of return, it must state the rate as an APY, but if it does so, it must include a host of additional disclosures if they relate to the kind of deposit being advertised, e.g., explanations concerning variable rates, the period of time the APY is offered, any minimum balance required to obtain the APY advertised, any minimum opening balance, a statement that the fees charged could reduce the earnings, a number of features of time accounts, and on and

on. However, if the advertising is being done on radio, TV or billboards, the disclosure requirements are drastically reduced.

(4) *Changes in the terms of the deposit account.* Advance notice, usually 30 days, is required for changes "if the change may reduce the annual percentage yield or adversely affect the consumer." Regulation DD § 230.5(a)(1). Normally, the bank-customer agreement will give the bank the right to change unilaterally certain terms of the account so long as some prior notice is given. Among the most common changes made are those in the service charges and fee amounts. Despite the specific reference in the quotation above to changes in annual percentage yield, 2 Barkley Clark & Barbara Clark, supra, ¶ 19.02[2][t] and ¶ 19.07[1][e][iv], points out that in the original version of Regulation DD, the broad definition of "variable-rate account," Regulation DD § 230.2(v), as "an account in which the interest rate may change after the account is opened," means that most interest rate changes need not be disclosed in a change-in-terms notice unless the bank specifically commits to give advance notice of rate decreases. This result flows from Regulation DD § 230.5(a)(2)(i), which provides that no notice of change need be given for changes in interest rates in variable rate accounts. Since all deposit accounts in which the bank has the power to change rates were arbitrarily considered to be variable rate accounts under the broad definition of the term in former Regulation DD § 230.2(v), which bears no relation to the common meaning of the term, the most important information that a customer needs to know, that the bank is lowering its interest rate, need be disclosed to the customer only if the bank has specifically agreed to make the disclosure. This wacky result was subsequently changed by adding to the definition of "variable-rate account," quoted above, the following: "unless the institution contracts to give at least 30 calendar days advance written notice of rate decreases." Under this amendment, a bank cannot lower rates unless it gives a 30-day notice.

(5) *Overdraft disclosures.* Bank customers may be offered overdraft protection as a feature of their deposit accounts, usually with a dollar limit stated. Although banks usually provide that overdraft protection is discretionary, the common practice is to allow qualified customers automatic protection. A flat fee is charged when an overdraft occurs; the usual assumption is that this fee is not a finance charge under Truth-in-Lending. Abuses have been alleged with respect to advertisements promoting overdraft programs as a reliable source of additional credit even though the fees may make it expensive to draw on them and the bank may have discretion whether to allow the overdraft. In 2006, Regulation DD was amended to add provisions prohibiting the advertising of an account as "free" or "no cost" if an activity fee is imposed. § 230.8(a)(2). Until 2010, only institutions promoting overdraft availability in advertisements had to comply with provisions that prescribed that (i) periodic statements must disclose on each statement the total of fees imposed for overdrafts as well as the total of all fees paid for

dishonoring items for the statement period and the calendar year to date (§ 230.11(a)(1)), and that (ii) advertising disclosures for overdrafts must include the fees for the payment of each overdraft, the time period within which the customer must repay or cover any overdraft, and the circumstances under which the institution will not pay an overdraft (§ 230.11(b)(1)). The 2010 change is described below.

(6) *The 2010 amendments to Regulation DD.* In the years since TISA was enacted in 1991, overdraft and returned item fees became increasingly important sources of revenue for banks and growing burdens on uninformed consumers. Automatic overdraft service was added to the bank-customer agreement without the consent or, in some cases, the knowledge of the consumer. Fees for overdraft services and returned items grew over the years to about $35 at the time the FRB amended Regulations DD and E in 2010. There was no proportionality in the imposition of these fees: a $1 overdraft cost the consumer $35. Regulation E, discussed in detail in the last section of this chapter, mandated an opt-in regime for overdraft fees with respect to one-time debit cards and ATMs. The bank cannot impose overdraft fees with respect to these two transactions unless the consumer has consented to the bank's overdraft services.

The 2010 amendments to Regulation DD expand the current requirements for disclosing totals for overdraft and returned item fees on periodic statements. The requirement is expanded to all institutions and not solely to institutions that promote the payment of overdrafts. § 230.11(a). Thus, all consumers that use overdraft services will receive additional information about fees to help them better understand the costs associated with their accounts, regardless of whether the services is marketed to them. Proximity and format requirements that are intended to enhance the effectiveness of disclosures and make them more noticeable to consumers are added under § 230.11(a)(3). Regulation DD is revised to address balance disclosures provided to consumers through automated systems. § 230.11(c). The FRB is not adopting the proposed format, content and timing requirements regarding a consumer's right to opt out of overdraft coverage under Regulation DD. Instead, these requirements are covered in Regulation E, discussed in the last section of this chapter.

2. "Freedom of Contract" Under Section 4–103(1)

The UCC adopts the principle of freedom of contract in 1–302(a), which provides that: "Except as otherwise provided in subsection (b) or elsewhere in [the Uniform Commercial Code], the effect of provisions of [the Uniform Commercial Code] may be varied by agreement." How far can the parties go in contracting away the provisions of the Code? Section 1–302(b) states that:

"The obligations of good faith, diligence, reasonableness, and care prescribed by [the Uniform Commercial Code] may not be disclaimed by agreement. The parties, by agreement, may determine the standards by which the performance of those obligations is to be measured if those standards are not manifestly unreasonable." Comment 1 to 1–302 cautions that it is only the "effect" of the provisions of the UCC that may be varied by agreement, but "[t]he meaning of the statute itself must be found in its text, including its definitions, and in appropriate extrinsic aids; it cannot be varied by agreement."

Section 4–103(a) reiterates the freedom-of-contract principle for Article 4: "The effect of the provisions of this Article may be varied by agreement...." At bottom, almost all of Article 4's provisions are default rules only. Comment 1 to 4–103 seems to go even further to say that constant technological changes affecting banking warrant giving parties even greater latitude than with respect to 1–302 to make changes by agreement. This seems to suggest that the provisions of Article 4 are even more subject to variation than other parts of the UCC. The Comment asserts that it would be unwise to interpret Article 4 as freezing the law in this dynamic area by mandatory rules. It concludes: "This section, therefore, permits within wide limits variation of the effect of provisions of the Article by agreement." This Comment impliedly recognizes two short-comings of the UCC. First, amending the provisions of the Code is a cumbersome procedure that usually takes a minimum of ten years before the changes are adopted in all states; thus the Code is not good at keeping up with technological change. Second, there is no state administrative agency devoted to keeping the Code up to date by issuance of regulations in the Article 4 area. To an extent, the Federal Reserve Board (FRB) serves as such an administrative agency. Section 4–103(b) recognizes the FRB's power to make regulations varying the provisions of Article 4, and the FRB's has frequently acted to modernize the law of bank collections. But the FRB is not particularly interested in bank-customer relations; its focus is on inter-bank relations.

Article 4's drafters concluded that private ordering is preferable to statutory regulation as a means of keeping the Code responsive to the needs of modern banking collection operations. Is this a defensible conclusion? The question raises the familiar problem of the comparative benefits and costs of setting contract terms by regulation or contract. The problem is a basic one of institutional design. Certainly there must be some limits on the degree to which terms in a deposit agreement can vary Article 4's provisions. It is difficult, however, to specify exactly those limits. True, deposit agreements have all the earmarks of contracts of adhesion: contracts drafted by the bank and offered to the prospective customer on a take-it-or-leave-it basis. If a customer does not like particular terms in the agreement, its only choice is to go to another bank. The recent trend in bank consolidations means that fewer competing banks are available and therefore there is possibly less variation in the terms of deposit agreements being offered. But it can't be concluded that the terms in deposit agreements, even if adhesion contracts, are adverse to the interests of customers. Adhesion contracts can be transaction cost saving devices and therefore consistent with either monopoly power or convergence of contract terms produced by market competition.

The prominent terms of deposit agreements, such as conditions placed on stop-payment orders, authorized signatures, and waiver provisions, implicate issues of fairness and efficiency. They affect the incentives of customers and banks, and alter the costs of banking services for classes of customers. The central issue of statutory drafting is whether fairness and efficiency are better pursued by the terms being set by private ordering or substantive regulation. Given the fast pace of technological change in banking services and their price impact on all depositors, the political and judicial barriers to updating statutes, and the demanding informational requirements for effective substantive regulation in the area, Article 4's drafters presumably favored private ordering announced by 4–103(a). It is perhaps significant that the Federal Reserve Board to date has taken the same view with respect to many of the terms governing electronic payments systems.

The only limitations stated in 4–103(a) are that "[t]he parties to the agreement cannot disclaim a bank's responsibility for its lack of good faith or failure to exercise ordinary care or limit the measure of damages for the lack or failure. However, the parties may determine by agreement the standards by which the bank's responsibility is to be measured if those standards are not manifestly unreasonable." Hostility to 4–103(a)'s freedom-of-contract principle is well expressed by Grant Gilmore, who described agreements that alter Article 4's default rules as "carrying a good joke too far." Grant Gilmore, The Uniform Commercial Code: A Reply to Professor Beutel, 61 Yale L.J. 364, 375 (1952). How should a court apply 4–103(a) to the following Problems? The issues raised by these Problems are discussed in detail in 1 Barkley Clark & Barbara Clark, supra, ¶ 3.01[3] (Rev. ed. 2009), and James J. White & Robert S. Summers, Uniform Commercial Code § 21–2 (5th ed. 2002).

PROBLEMS

1. Husband (H) and Wife (W) have a joint checking account in Bank. Their deposit agreement with Bank provides, among other matters: (1) that either party may write checks on the account, may stop-payment of any check drawn on the account, or may close the account, and (2) that Bank may pay an overdraft drawn by either party, the account may be debited for the overdraft, and either party is liable for the amount of the overdraft without respect to whether that party signed the check or benefited from the overdraft. H wrote a check which Bank paid that overdrew the account. W did not know of the overdraft and she did not benefit in any way from the proceeds of the

overdraft. H is insolvent and Bank seeks to hold W liable for the amount of the overdraft. May it do so? 4–401(b).

2. Corporate depositor (D) opens a demand deposit account in Bank from which D intends to pay its bills. The deposit agreement that D entered into with Bank contains the following clause: "You [D] may authorize the use of a facsimile signature device by a corporate resolution communicated to Bank. If you have authorized the use of a facsimile signature device, Bank may honor any check that bears or appears to bear your facsimile signature even if it was made by an unauthorized person or with a counterfeit facsimile device." Use of a facsimile device was duly authorized. Burglar breaks into D's premises and uses the facsimile machine to write a check to himself that Bank pays on presentment. May Bank debit D's account? Is the quoted clause enforceable in the face of 3–403(a), which provides that an unauthorized signature is ineffective, and 4–401(a), which provides that a bank may charge a customer's account only for checks that are properly payable? Comment 1 to 4–401 states that "[a]n item containing a forged drawer's signature...is not properly payable." 1 Barkley Clark & Barbara Clark, supra, ¶ 3.01[3][c][iii], cites cases on both sides of the question, and, like James J. White & Robert S. Summers, supra, § 18–2 a., favors upholding the exculpatory clause. The quoted clause is based on one that appears in a model deposit account set out in 1 Barkley Clark & Barbara Clark, supra, ¶ 3.13[1].

3. Corporate depositor (D) opens a demand deposit account in Bank from which D intends to pay its bills. The deposit agreement that D entered into with Bank contains the following clause: "Unless you [D] shall notify Bank within fifteen calendar days of the delivery or mailing to you of any statement of account and cancelled checks of any objection to any check or item on the account, all objections for any cause or reason whatsoever, whether known or unknown, shall be absolutely barred and waived." A forged check was returned by Bank to D on June 1; D's reconciliation process did not turn up the forgery until July 15, at which time D gave Bank prompt notice of the forgery. Bank claimed that because D had failed to give the notice within the 15–day period prescribed in the agreement, D had no right to challenge its payment of the check. D noted that under 4–406(f), it had a year in which to object. Is Bank protected by the quoted clause? Nat'l Title Ins. Corp. Agency v. First Union Nat'l Bank, 559 S.E.2d 668 (Va. 2002), reprinted in the previous chapter, upheld a 60–day contract cutdown clause; Stowell v. Cloquet Co–Op Credit Union, 557 N.W.2d 567 (Minn. 1997), upheld a 20–day contract cutdown clause. 1 Barkley Clark & Barbara Clark, supra, ¶ 3.01[3][c][ii], cites some cases tending to uphold similar clauses. James J. White & Robert S. Summers, supra, § 21–2 (5th ed. 2002), questions whether a clause with a 15–day cutoff date should be upheld. Herzog, Engstrom & Koplovitz P.C. v. Union Nat'l Bank, 640 N.Y.S.2d 703 (N.Y.App.Div.1996), refused to enforce a 14–day cutoff period.

Caution: At the time this casebook went to press in the summer of 2010, Congress had just enacted complex landmark financial markets legislation that includes establishing the Consumer Financial Protection Bureau, within the Federal Reserve, with rulemaking and enforcement power over banks and other financial companies engaged in consumer financial transactions. This agency is authorized to deal with a number of the issues that are taken up in this chapter. We are reluctant to speculate on what position the Bureau will take on these matters. Hence, our discussion of consumer issues in this Edition must be viewed as a statement of the law as it was on the eve of this broad reform legislation.

3. Service Charges and Fees

a. DEPOSIT CHARGES AND FEES

Most banks impose charges on depositors for services performed by banks in processing stop-payment orders, overdrafts, checks returned for insufficient funds (NSF) and other services. In recent years, banks have increased these charges and customers have become more resolute in challengening them in the courts and legislatures. Banks have turned to federal regulatory agencies to preempt state action. First, we will discuss some of these fees and their treatment in the courts, then we will examine federal preemption.

(1) NSF FEES AND HIGH-TO-LOW POSTING

Bank receives five checks drawn on Customer's account that are presented on the same day: $1500 mortgage payment, $500 car payment, $100 credit card payment, $65 florist payment, and $60 gift shop payment. But Customer's account contained only $1525 on that date. Bank paid the $1500 check and returned the four others, charging the customer a $35 NSF (not sufficient funds) fee for each returned check. When Customer learned that Bank could have paid the four smaller checks and assessed only a single $35 NSF fee, he complained loudly. Bank explained that, pursuant to the bank-customer agreement, it followed the "high-to-low" posting basis, which meant that its policy was to pay the largest check first; moreover, the law clearly gives it the option of choosing this payment basis. Section 4–303(b) states: "…items may be accepted, paid, certified, or charged to the indicated account of its customer *in any order* (emphasis added)."

In the past banks have used different posting rules. According to Rick Brooks, How Banks Make the Most of Bounced Checks, Wall St. J., Feb. 25, 1999, at B1, among the nation's five largest banks, three pay the largest checks first and two pay the smallest checks first. Other banks pay checks on the basis of check number. Some high-low banks justify their policy by maintaining that their customers tell them they want the largest checks paid first; they would rather owe the florist than have their mortgage check bounce. Before Revised Article 4, banks usually had clauses in their deposit agreements with their customers saying about what 4–303(b) now says. At the time Revised Article 4 was being drafted, the codification of these agreements was not controversial. But, during the enactment process, consumer groups in California and Texas were sufficiently concerned about the potential for abuse in 4–303(b) to persuade their legislatures to append the following to the Official Comments:

> The only restraint on the discretion given to the payor bank under subsection (b) is that the bank act in good faith. For example, the bank could not properly follow an established practice of maximizing the number of returned checks for the sole purpose of increasing the amount of returned check fees charged to the customer.

Over time, enough customers have become sufficiently aggrieved by high-low posting that lawsuits have challenged the practice as merely a device for increasing banks' income from NSF and overdraft fees. With NSF fees running up as high as $35 per check, the stakes are high. When pre-trial discovery in some of these suits turned up damaging intra-bank communications proposing that the high-low formula be adopted in order to increase revenue, the fat was in the fire. In the early years the banks were winning these cases. See, e.g., Hill v. St. Paul Federal Bank for Savings, 768 N.E.2d 322 (Ill. App. 2002), which held that even if the intention of the bank in adopting the high-low posting order was to maximize profits, the motive was irrelevant because 4–303(b) authorizes high-low posting. After issue in 2001 by the Comptroller of the Currency of Interpretative Letter #916 that is favorable to high-low posting, litigation was assumed to disappear.

That did not happen. Consumer class actions challenging high-low posting continue to be brought. A large majority of banks now use high-low posting, and NSF and overdraft fees are the source of a significant portion of their income. Given the existence of 4-303(b), the federal preemption action of Letter #916, and well drafted deposit contract provisions, consumers have had difficulty winning. In Hassler v. Sovereign Bank, 644 F.Supp.2d 509 (D. N.J. 2009), the bank prevailed, largely on the basis of a well drafted, "unmistakenly plain" customer agreement that allowed the bank to use high-low posting.

Other cases have viewed high-low posting, coupled with overdraft provisions, as predatory practices and have sought ways of flouting the pro-bank factors enumerated above. In Gutierrez v. Wells Fargo Bank, N.A., 2008 WL 4279550 (N.D. Cal. 2008), the court relied on a California Comment to 4-303 quoted above to conclude that the bank was not acting in good faith. It added: "From the viewpoint of customers, the facts must seem particularly alarming. Wells Fargo's business strategy is to maximize overdraft penalty revenue at their expense by sequencing debts so as to use up the available balances as quickly as possible and thus artificially increase the number of overdrafts." In White v. Wachovia Bank, N.A., 563 F.Supp.2d 1358 (N.D. Ga. 2008), the court found the bank to be in breach of the implied covenant of good faith in its use of high-low posting; federal law did not preempt state law on this subject. Authoritative appellate cases dealing with these issues have not come down.

With respect to credit cards, a cardholder may maintain balances with a card issuer bearing different interest rates. Before the Credit Card Act, card issuers frequently applied payments by cardholders to the balance with the lowest interest rate, leaving unpaid the balances with the highest rate. Under 12 CFR § 226.53, pursuant to the 2009 Credit Card Act, this procedure is prohibited: "[w]hen a consumer makes a payment in excess of the required minimum periodic payment for a credit card account under an open-end...consumer credit plan, the card issuer must allocate the excess amount first to the balance with the highest annual percentage rate and any remaining portion to the other balances in descending order based on the applicable annual percentage rate."

(2) OVERDRAFT FEES

If the bank bounces a check for insufficient funds, it charges the customer a NSF fee; if it pays the check it imposes an overdraft fee, often the same amount as the NFS fee. Current banking practice is to automatically enroll customers in an overdraft program. This is referred to as an "opt-out" plan; if the customer does not want overdraft protection, she must indicate so when she opens her account. If the overdraft is greater than a small amount ($5 or $10), a fee will automatically be assessed. A recent FDIC study shows that overdraft fees range from $10 to $38 per item in automatic overdraft programs. These charges may be applied multiple times in a single day. Dan Fitzpatrick, Damian Paletto, & Jane J. Kim, Wall St. J., Sept. 23, 2009, at C1. Candice Choi, AP Finance Writer, Yahoo! Finance, Sept. 23, 2009, cites Celent, a consulting firm for the banking industry, for the claim that in 2007 banks earned an astonishing $28 billion from overdraft fees!

(3) POTENTIAL LEGISLATION

Case law may continue to go in different directions on the validity of high-low posting, opt-out, and high-fee overdraft penalties, but the intense scrutiny being given these practices in Congressional committees has led several of the major banks to capitulate even before legislation is enacted on these issues. As indicated in the two articles cited above, among the reforms accepted by these banks are: (1) Adopting opt-in overdraft programs. This could be very expensive for banks; customers will have to be sold on the need for overdraft protection, with its high penalties. Existing customers can opt out.

(2) Lowering the cap on how many times each day the bank may collect overdraft fees. Bank of America is going from 10 to 4; J.P. Morgan from 6 to 3. (3) Bank of America will not impose fees if the overdraft is $10 or less; J.P.Morgan, if the overdraft is $5 or less. The Credit Card Act of 2009 provides that over-limit fees are prohibited unless the cardholder has opted in by expressly electing to permit such fees. § 226.53. Some survey evidence suggests that the vast majority of regular users of overdraft protection will choose to keep the service. Sara Lepro, Overdrafts' Demise Could be Overblown In Flux: Card Business, Am. Banker, Vol. 175, May 17, 2010 p. 1 .

b. PREEMPTION

(1) CLASS ACTIONS

The emergence of class actions to vindicate consumer rights allowed consumers to challenge banks on the validity of the terms of that classic example of a contract of adhesion, the bank-customer deposit agreement. The rules of the game were well known: if the class was certified and the plaintiff could get by a demurrer, the case could go to the jury. The plaintiffs had won the case because at this point, the bank would usually settle. It would be difficult to find a juror who does not believe that bank service charges are excessive. An early example of the ensuing blizzard of class action litigation against banks is the following oft-cited case. It is this litigation that brought on federal preemption

Perdue v. Crocker Nat'l Bank

Supreme Court of California, 1985.
702 P.2d 503.

■ BROUSSARD, JUSTICE.

Plaintiff filed this class action to challenge the validity of charges imposed by defendant Crocker National Bank for the processing of checks drawn on accounts without sufficient funds. (The parties refer to such checks as NSF checks and to the handling charge as an NSF charge.) He appeals from a judgment of the trial court entered after that court sustained defendant's general demurrer without leave to amend.

On July 3, 1978, plaintiff filed suit on behalf of all persons with checking accounts at defendant bank and a subclass of customers who have paid NSF charges to the bank. The complaint first alleges a contract under which the bank furnishes checking service in return for a maintenance charge. It then asserts that "It is the practice of defendants to impose and collect a unilaterally set charge for processing checks presented against plaintiffs' accounts when such accounts do not contain sufficient funds to cover the amount of the check." "Defendants have at various times unilaterally increased the NSF charge to an amount the defendants deemed appropriate, without reference to any criteria, and defendants imposed and collected the said increased amount without any explanation or justification by defendants to plaintiffs." At the time of filing of the suit, the charge was $6 for each NSF check, whether the check was honored or returned unpaid, even though "the actual cost incurred by the defendants in processing an NSF check is approximately $0.30."

The bank requires each depositor to sign a signature card which it uses "to determine and verify the authenticity of endorsements on checks". In extremely small (6 point) type, the signature card states that the undersigned depositors "agree with Crocker National Bank and with each other that ... this account and all deposits therein shall be ... subject to all applicable laws, to the Bank's present and future rules, regulations, practices and charges, and to its right of setoff for the obligations of any of us." The card does not identify the amount of the charge for NSF checks, and the bank does not furnish the depositor with a copy of the applicable bank rules and regulations.

On the basis of these allegations, plaintiff asserts...causes of action: (1) for a judicial declaration that the bank's signature card is not a contract authorizing NSF charges; [and] (2) for a judicial declaration that such charges are oppressive and unconscionable....

I. PLAINTIFF'S FIRST CAUSE OF ACTION: WHETHER THE SIGNATURE CARD IS A CONTRACT AUTHORIZING NSF CHARGES.

....

We conclude that plaintiff here is not entitled to a judicial declaration that the bank's signature card is not a contract authorizing NSF charges. To the contrary, we hold as a matter of law that the card is a contract authorizing the bank to impose such charges, subject to the bank's duty of good faith and fair dealing in setting or varying such charges. Plaintiff may, upon remand of this case, amend his complaint to seek a judicial declaration determining whether the charges actually set by the bank are consonant with that duty....

II. PLAINTIFF'S SECOND CAUSE OF ACTION: WHETHER THE BANK'S NSF CHARGES ARE OPPRESSIVE, UNREASONABLE, OR UNCONSCIONABLE.

Plaintiff's second cause of action alleges that the signature card is drafted by defendant bank which enjoys a superior bargaining position by reason of its greater economic power, knowledge, experience and resources. Depositors have no alternative but to acquiesce in the relationship as offered by defendant or to accept a similar arrangement with another bank. The complaint alleges that the card is vague and uncertain, that it is unclear whether it is intended as an identification card or a contract, that it imposes no obligation upon the bank, and permits the bank to alter or terminate the relationship at any time,[8] then asserts that "The disparity between the actual cost to defendants and the amount charged by defendants for processing an NSF check unreasonably and oppressively imposes excessive and unfair liability upon plaintiffs." Plaintiff seeks a declaratory judgment to determine the rights and duties of the parties.

Plaintiff's allegations point to the conclusion that the signature card, if it is a contract, is one of adhesion. The term contract of adhesion "signifies a standardized contract, which, imposed and drafted by the party of superior bargaining strength, relegates to the subscribing party only the opportunity to adhere to the contract or reject it." (Neal v. State Farm Ins. Co. (1961) 188 Cal. App.2d 690, 694, 10 Cal. Rptr. 781.... The signature card, drafted by the bank and offered to the customer without negotiation, is a classic example of a contract of adhesion; the bank concedes as much....

In 1979, the Legislature enacted Civil Code section 1670.5, which codified the established doctrine that a court can refuse to enforce an unconscionable provision in a contract. Section 1670.5 reads as follows: "(a) If the court as a matter of law finds the contract or any clause of the contract to have been unconscionable at the time it was made the court may refuse to enforce the contract, or it may enforce the remainder of the contract without the unconscionable clause, or it may so limit the application of any unconscionable clause as to avoid any unconscionable result. [¶] (b) When it is claimed or appears to the court that the contract or any clause thereof may be unconscionable the parties shall be afforded a reasonable opportunity to present evidence as to its commercial setting, purpose, and effect to aid the court in making the determination."

In construing this section, we cannot go so far as plaintiff, who contends that even a conclusory allegation of unconscionability requires an evidentiary hearing. We do view the section, however, as legislative recognition that a claim of unconscionability often cannot be determined merely by examining the face of the contract, but will require inquiry into its setting, purpose, and effect. Plaintiff bases his claim of unconscionability on the alleged 2,000 percent differential between the NSF charge of $6 and the alleged cost to the bank of $0.30.[11] The parties have cited numerous cases on whether the price of an item can be so excessive as to be unconscionable. The cited cases are from other jurisdictions, often from trial courts or intermediate appellate courts,

---

[8] The depositor also has the right to terminate the relationship at any time, but lacks the right asserted by the bank to alter the relationship without terminating it.

[11] The bank's briefs claim the alleged $0.30 cost is too low and plaintiff's briefs admit that a higher figure, but still $1 or less, might be more accurate. We do not, however, find in plaintiff's briefs a sufficiently clear concession to enable us to depart from the general principle that, in reviewing a judgment after the sustaining of a general demurrer without leave to amend, we must assume the truth of all material factual allegations in the complaint. (Alcorn v. Anbro Engineering, Inc., supra, 2 Cal. 3d 493, 496, 86 Cal. Rptr. 88, 468 P.2d 216.)

and none is truly authoritative on the issue. Taken together, however, they provide a useful guide to analysis of the claim that a price is so excessive as to be unconscionable....

[W]e cannot endorse defendant's argument that the $6 charge is so obviously reasonable that no inquiry into its basis or justification is necessary. In 1978 $6 for processing NSF checks may not seem exorbitant,[13] but price alone is not a reliable guide. Small charges applied to a large volume of transactions may yield a sizeable sum. The complaint asserts that the cost of processing NSF checks is only $0.30 per check, which means that a $6 charge would produce a 2,000 percent profit; even at the higher cost estimate of $1 a check mentioned in plaintiff's petition for hearing, the profit is 600 percent.[14] Such profit percentages may not be automatically unconscionable, but they indicate the need for further inquiry.

Other aspects of the transaction confirm plaintiff's right to a factual hearing. Defendant presents the depositor with a document which serves at least in part as a handwriting exemplar, and whose contractual character is not obvious. The contractual language appears in print so small that many could not read it. State law may impose obligations on the bank (e.g., the duty to honor a check when the account has sufficient funds (Allen v. Bank of America, supra, 58 Cal. App.2d 124, 127, 136 P.2d 345)), but so far as the signature card drafted by the bank is concerned, the bank has all the rights and the depositor all the duties. The signature card provides that the depositor will be bound by the bank's rules, regulations, practices and charges, but the bank does not furnish the depositor with a copy of the relevant documents. The bank reserves the power to change its practices and fees at any time, subject only to the notice requirements of state law.

In short, the bank structured a totally one-sided transaction. The absence of equality of bargaining power, open negotiation, full disclosure, and a contract which fairly sets out the rights and duties of each party demonstrates that the transaction lacks those checks and balances which would inhibit the charging of unconscionable fees. In such a setting, plaintiff's charge that the bank's NSF fee is exorbitant, yielding a profit far in excess of cost, cannot be dismissed on demurrer. Under Civil Code section 1670.5, the parties should be

---

[13] Defendant cites Merrel v. Research and Data, Inc., supra, 589 P.2d 120, which held a $5 fee imposed by merchants for NSF checks was a "modest" amount (p. 123) and not unconscionable. NSF checks pose a substantial inconvenience to a seller, who has been deceived into an involuntary extension of credit to a customer whose credit standing may not be very good. A bank, however, is not deceived. It checks the balance of the account, and may reject any overdraft. A fee reasonable to compensate the merchant for the cost, inconvenience, and risk of an NSF check may be excessive if exacted by a bank.

[14] The complaint does not state the market price for the service of processing NSF checks, although one might infer it is similar to defendant's price since plaintiff alleges that if he did not contract with defendant, he would be "forced to accept a similar arrangement with other banks." The complaint does not set a figure for the "fair" or "true" value or worth of the service.

afforded a reasonable opportunity to present evidence as to the commercial setting, purpose, and effect of the signature card and the NSF charge in order to determine whether that charge is unconscionable.

....

NOTES

1. *Perdue* was trouble for California banks. See Attorney Warns Perdue Case Only First of Upcoming Challenges to Bank Fees, 46 Wash. Fin. Rep. (BNA) No. 15, at 594 (1986). Now every deposit account fee charged was open to challenge on whether it was unconscionable. Anecdotal evidence suggests that virtually every bank in California was subjected to class actions on their service fees. Most of the cases were settled, after presumably enriching counsel on both sides of the suits. The Comptroller of the Currency found this situation intolerable.

2. Since *Perdue*, class actions have burgeoned in consumer cases, and financial institutions have joined with other potential defendants in demanding legislative reform. In 2005, Congress enacted the Class Action Fairness Act of 2005, Pub.L.109-2 , 119 Stat 4, aimed at curtailing abuses in consumer class actions. Congressional findings were that class members often receive little or no benefit from class actions, as in cases in which counsel are awarded large fees while leaving class members with awards of little or no value. The principal reform offered is to grant federal jurisdiction in class action cases in which the matter in controversy exceeds $5 million and any member of a class of plaintiffs is a citizen of a state different from any defendant. The district court may decline jurisdiction in certain cases in which more than one-third but less than two-thirds of the plaintiffs and the primary defendants are citizens of the state where the action was originally filed. The district court must decline jurisdiction if greater than two-thirds of the members of the proposed plaintiff class are citizens of the state where the action was originally filed. The objective is to curtail forum-shopping for courts and jury pools that are known to be overly hospitable to class actions.

(2) FEDERAL PREEMPTION AS THE SOLUTION

In a reaction to *Perdue* and the numerous class actions against banks that it spawned, the Office of the Comptroller of the Currency (OCC) intervened decisively to preempt the area of deposit-related charges. The effect has been to make national banks virtually immune to attacks on the validity of the deposit service charges. National banks have long justified this preemption on the ground that since they are regulated by federal authorities, state investigators must be precluded from taking their own enforcement actions. They contended that allowing concurring federal and state regulation would be burdensome and confusing.

The following provision concerning deposit account service charges for national banks is found in 12 C.F.R. § 7.4002.

(a) *Authority to impose charges and fees.* A national bank may charge its customers non-interest charges and fees, including deposit account service charges.

(b) *Considerations.* (1) All charges and fees should be arrived at by each bank on a competitive basis and not on the basis of any agreement, arrangement, undertaking, understanding, or discussion with other banks or their officers. (2) The establishment of non-interest charges and fees, their amounts, and the method of calculating them are business decisions to be made by each bank, in its discretion, according to sound banking judgment and safe and sound banking principles. A national bank establishes non-interest charges and fees in accordance with safe and sound banking principles if the bank employs a decision-making process through which it considers the following factors, among others:

(i) The cost incurred by the bank in providing the service;

(ii) The deterrence of misuse by customers of banking services;

(iii) The enhancement of the competitive position of the bank in accordance with the bank's business plan and marketing strategy; and

(iv) The maintenance of the safety and soundness of the institution.

(c) *Interest.* Charges and fees that are "interest" within the meaning of 12 U.S.C. 85 are governed by § 7.4001 and not by this section.

(d) *State law.* The OCC applies preemption principles derived from the United States Constitution, as interpreted through judicial precedent, when determining whether State laws apply that purport to limit or prohibit charges and fees described in this section....

PROBLEM

The practice of banks in State A is to impose an additional charge for the use of their ATM machines by non-customers. Two cities in State A passed ordinances prohibiting this practice. National banks in these cities sought to have these ordinances permanently enjoined on the authority of § 7.4002. What result? See Bank of America v. City and County of San Francisco, 309 F.3d 551 (9th Cir.2002).

In 2004, the OCC issued its boldest and most controversial preemption of state law in 12 C.F.R. §§ 7.4007 (deposit taking) and 7.4008 (lending). The latter is set out in part below:

Authority of national banks. A national bank may make, sell, purchase, participate in, or otherwise deal in loans that are not secured by liens on, or interest in, real estate, subject to such terms, conditions, and limitations prescribed by the Comptroller of the Currency and other applicable Federal law....

....

(c) *Unfair and deceptive practices.* A national bank shall not engage in unfair or deceptive practices within the meaning of section 5 of the Federal Trade Commission Act, 15 U.S.C. 45(a)(1), and regulations promulgated thereunder in connection with loans made under this § 7.4008.

(d) *Applicability of state law.* (1) Except where made applicable by Federal law, state laws that obstruct, impair, or condition a national bank's ability to fully exercise its Federally authorized non-real estate lending powers are not applicable to national banks. (2) A national bank may make non-real estate loans without regard to state law limitations concerning:

....

(iv) The terms of credit, including the schedule for repayment of principal and interest, amortization of loans, balance, payments due, minimum payments, or term of maturity of the loan, including the circumstances under which a loan may be called due and payable upon the passage of time or a specified event external to the loan;

....

(e) *State laws that are not preempted.* State laws on the following subjects are not inconsistent with the deposit-taking powers of national banks and apply to national banks to the extent that they only incidentally affect the exercise of national banks' deposit-taking powers:

Contracts;

Torts;

Criminal law;

Rights to collect debts;

(5) Acquisition and transfer of property;

(6) Taxation;

(7) Zoning; and

(8) Any other law the effect of which the OCC determines to be incidental to the non-real estate lending operations of national banks or otherwise consistent with the powers set out in paragraph (a) of this section.

The difficulties facing courts in interpreting preemption regulations are illustrated by two cases from the same judicial district concerning the same bank and involving identical issues. In Abel v. KeyBank USA, N.A., 313 F.Supp.2d 720 (N.D. Ohio 2004), a student signed a note payable to a school to evidence his educational loan; the note was assigned to KeyBank; the school closed before the student completed his education. In Blanco v. KeyBank USA, N.A., 2005 WL 4135013 (N.D. Ohio 2005), the school was different but otherwise the facts were the same. In both cases the students relied on the Ohio Retail Installment Sales Act (RISA), which was interpreted to allow the students to raise their defenses under RISA against the bank. In both cases, the bank contended that § 7.4008 preempted RISA. In *Abel,* the court held that the regulation preempted RISA because the state law significantly interfered with a national bank's ability to negotiate promissory notes and lend money. The value of such notes in Ohio will likely be worth less than notes issued in states not having RISA and the bank's ability to collect on notes will be impaired. In *Blanco,* the court held that RISA had only an incidental effect on the operation of the bank; consumer protection law is traditionally regulated by the states. Section 7.4008 was in effect in both cases and referred to by both courts. Go figure.

Section 7.4007(c) is comparable to § 7.4008(e) in setting out state laws that are not preempted by the two regulations. Do UCC Articles 3 and 4 come within the state laws that are exempt from preemption?

(3) A CHINK IN THE FEDERAL PREEMPTION WALL

In Cuomo v. Clearing House Association, L.L.C., 129 U.S. 2710 (2009), the Court allowed the New York Attorney General to gain access to non-public information from several national banks over the opposition of the Office of the Comptroller of the Currency (OCC), which argued that OCC regulations promulgated under the National Bank Act prohibited this form of state law enforcement against national banks. The information concerned the lending practices of these banks sought in order to determine whether the banks had violated the state's fair lending laws. In a surprise decision, a volatile 5-4 majority (Justice Scalia and four liberals) held that the OCC preemption regulation was invalid to the extent that it prohibited the Attorney General from bringing actions against national banks to enforce these fair lending laws. The Court concluded, broadly stated, that the National Bank Act preempts the powers to supervise the administration of national banks but not the power of states to enforce at least certain of their laws.

The scope of the holding has been the focus of intense speculation on the extent to which it allows states to enforce their consumer protection laws against national banks. See Damian Paletta & Brent Kendall, States Get More Power to Challenge National Banks, Wall St. J., June 30, 2009, at A4. The long standing bar against enforcement by states of their consumer protection laws against national banks has been a major consumer complaint and a potential target of federal legislation.

c. MANDATORY ARBITRATION WITH WAIVER OF CLASS ACTION OR ARBITRATION

In *Perdue,* bankers saw what they considered to be the perfect storm: a class action with the potential for a jury trial that might result in a large judgment even though members of the plaintiff class suffered what were, at best, only nominal damages. We have seen in this chapter the measures the banking industry has taken to prevent cases like this from occurring in the future. The 2005 federal class action legislation made it possible for banks in large dollar class actions to move such actions out of friendly state jurisdictions into the federal courts. The OCC has been moving to preempt state law with respect to bank fees and, after the amendments of 2004, a whole lot more. But the most effective weapon the banks have deployed is mandatory arbitration with a waiver of class actions and arbitrations. Arbitration clauses with these waivers rapidly found their way into bank-customer agreements with respect to deposit accounts, loans and credit cards. The enforceability and meaning of these clauses are the primary issues in bank-customer disputes today.

(1) ARBITRATION

*The Basics.*The Federal Arbitration Act (FAA), 9 U.S.C. § 1 et seq., applies to both federal and state courts if the contract evidences a transaction involving interstate or foreign commerce and contains an arbitration clause. Southland Corp. v. Keating, 465 U.S. 1 (1984). Hence, the FAA may apply even to cases involving state law claims brought in state courts if the transaction falls within the capacious scope of interstate commerce. Almost all states have enacted arbitration acts that apply to the extent that the FAA is inapplicable, and about half the states have modeled their arbitration acts on the FAA. Section § 2 of the FAA, 9 U.S.C. §2, states:

> A written provision in any maritime transaction or a contract evidencing a transaction involving commerce to settle by arbitration a controversy thereafter arising out of such contract or transaction, or the refusal to perform the whole or any part thereof, or an agreement in writing to submit to arbitration an existing controversy arising out of such a contract, transaction, or refusal, shall be valid, irrevocable, and enforceable, save upon such grounds as exist at law or in equity for the revocation of any contract.

Thus, in order to deal with the traditional hostility of courts toward arbitration as a method of dispute resolution, Congress saw fit to federalize arbitration procedure and availability by enacting the FAA, which applies to cases in which there is an agreement in writing to arbitrate controversies arising out of contracts involving interstate commerce. Arbitration clauses commonly expressly state that they are governed by the FAA.. Under §§ 3 and 4, a court may stay a proceeding on any issue referable to arbitration until the arbitration has been had; a party aggrieved by the failure of another party to arbitrate may seek an order directing that arbitration proceed. Congress saw many benefits in arbitration. In H.R.Rep. No. 97-542, at 13 (1982), it said: "The advantages of arbitration are many: it is usually cheaper and faster than litigation; it can have simpler procedural and evidentiary rules; it normally minimizes hostility and is less disruptive of ongoing and future business dealings among the parties; it is often more flexible in regard to scheduling of times and places of hearings and discovery devices...."

The Supreme Court has strongly supported arbitration. In Green Tree Financial Corp. v. Randolph, 531 U.S. 79 (2000), the contract provided that all disputes arising from or relating to the contract would be resolved by binding arbitration. In enlarged type the contract said: "The parties voluntarily and knowingly waive any right they have to a jury trial either pursuant to arbitration under this clause or pursuant to a court action by assignee (as provided herein)." Id. at 83, fn 1. The Court upheld Green Tree's motion to compel arbitration and said "[W]e are mindful of the Federal Arbitration Act's purpose 'to reverse the longstanding judicial hostility to arbitration agreements...and to place arbitration agreements upon the same footing as other contracts.' In the light of that purpose, we have recognized that federal statutory claims can be appropriately resolved through arbitration, and we have enforced agreements to arbitrate that involved such claims.... We have likewise rejected generalized attacks on arbitration that rest on 'suspicion of arbitration as a method of weakening the protection afforded in the substantive law to would-be complainants'.... In determining whether statutory claims may be arbitrated, we first ask whether the parties agreed to submit their claims to arbitration, and then ask whether Congress has evinced an intention to preclude a waiver of judicial remedies for the statutory rights at issue." Id. at 89–90. Courts agree that disputes may be arbitrated "so long as the prospective litigant effectively may vindicate [his or her] statutory cause of action in the arbitral forum." Id. at 90.

Defenses to Arbitration. Section 2 of the Act, 9 U.S.C. § 2, provides that an agreement to arbitrate made pursuant to that section "shall be valid, irrevocable, and enforceable, save upon such grounds as exist at law or in equity for the revocation of any contract." Generally applicable contract defenses such as fraud, duress or undue influence may be raised to invalidate an arbitration clause under this language. The accepted view is that this language also includes unconscionability. See Doctor's Associates, Inc. v. Casarotto, 517 U.S. 681, 682 (1996); "Generally applicable contract defenses, such as fraud, duress or unconscionability, may be applied to invalidate arbitration agreements without contravening § 2." Proof of unconscionability focuses on the existence of both procedural and substantive unconscionability. Procedural unconscionability examines the manner in which the contract was negotiated and the circumstances of the parties: inequality of bargaining power, lack of disclosure, such as a clause hidden in boiler-plate contract, or coercion on the part of the stronger party. Substantive unconscionability centers on whether the terms of the agreement are so one-sided as to shock the conscience.

Courts have divided over the unconscionability of arbitration clauses and there is no overriding trend in the recent case law. Cases finding arbitration clauses not unconscionable generally follow the reasoning at work in Hutcherson v. Sears Roebuck & Company, 793 N.E.2d 886 (Ill. App.Ct. 2003). In that case, the court held that there was no procedural unconscionability because there was a clearly stated, conspicuous arbitration clause that gave the debtor the right to opt out if it did not agree to arbitration. Substantive unconscionability was absent because the court found no unfairness in the agreement and, moreover, federal policy strongly favors enforcement of arbitration provisions, even at the cost of the debtor's waiving her right to a class action.

Other courts have refused to enforce arbitration agreements on unconscionability grounds, citing the inequality of bargaining power and the take-it-or-leave-it basis on which arbitration clauses are offered as proof of procedural unconscionability. The wholly one-sided terms of arbitration agreements are relied on as showing substantive unconscionability. Ingle v. Circuit City Stores, Inc., 328 F.3d 1165 (9th Cir.2003), forcefully presents this view.

The Decline of Mandatory Arbitration. In 2009, some major banks, e.g., Bank of America, ceased to require arbitration in consumer disputes. This action followed announcements by the National Arbitration Forum (NAF) and the American Arbitration Association (AAA) that they would no longer participate in consumer debt collection disputes. NAF had been sued by the Attorney General of Minnesota on grounds that its practices constituted consumer fraud under state law in that NAF was so close to creditor groups that it was deceptive to hold itself out as a neutral party. NAF agreed to a consent decree that would bar its participation in consumer debt collection; AAA quickly followed. The story is told in Clark's Secured Transactions Monthly, Vol 25, No. 7, July 2009. Whether other creditors will follow BofA's retreat remains to be see.

(2) WAIVER OF CLASS ACTIONS

In recent years, bank-customer arbitration agreements typically include waivers of class actions. Since under a valid arbitration agreement no action can be sustained, these clauses also include a bar against class arbitrations. A currently used clause provides:

> If either party elects to resolve a Claim by arbitration, that Claim shall be arbitrated on an individual basis. There shall be no right or authority for

any Claims to be arbitrated on a class action basis or on bases involving Claims brought in a purported representative capacity on behalf of the general public, other Cardmembers or other persons similarly situated.

It is noteworthy that when BofA publicly relinquished mandatory arbitration, it continued to require waivers of class actions. Customers who object to these waiver clauses usually do so on two grounds: (i) the inability to bring claims in a class action makes it infeasible to raise these claims because lawyers will not represent customers on an individual basis for small claims; and (ii) such a waiver is unconscionable under applicable state law. According to Alan S. Kaplinsky & Mark J. Levin, Consensus or Conflict? Most (But Not All) Courts Enforce Express Class Action Waivers in Consumer Arbitration Agreements, 60 Bus. Law. 775 (2005), a majority of courts have enforced clauses waiving class actions and arbitrations. But a strong trend is developing toward holding that waivers of class actions and arbitrations may be unenforceable as unconscionable. The following case is an example.

Chalk v. T-Mobile USA, Inc.

United States Court of Appeals, Ninth Circuit, 2009.
560 F.3d 1087.

■ REINHARDT, CIRCUIT JUDGE:

In this case, we consider whether the district court properly dismissed a consumer class action pursuant to an arbitration agreement between T-Mobile and its customers. We hold that the agreement's class action waiver is substantively unconscionable and therefore unenforceable under Oregon law. We also note that under the agreement the waiver is not severable. We reverse the district court's order dismissing the case pending arbitration.

I. Procedural and Factual Background

Plaintiffs-Appellants Paul Stewart and Ellen Chalk bought a GC79 GPRS/Wireless LAN PC card ("card"), a device manufactured by Defendant-Appellee Sony Ericsson Mobile Communications (USA), Inc. ("Sony") that enables computers to connect wirelessly to the Internet, from Defendant-Appellee T-Mobile USA, Inc. ("T-Mobile"). Plaintiffs also signed a one-year service agreement with T-Mobile. The Service Agreement provided:

BY SIGNING THIS FORM OR ACTIVATING OR USING T-MOBILE SERVICE I ACKNOWLEDGE AND AGREE THAT:....

I UNDERSTAND THAT THE SERVICE AGREEMENT AFFECTS MY AND T-MOBILE'S LEGAL RIGHTS. AMONG OTHER THINGS, IT:

REQUIRES MANDATORY ARBITRATION OF DISPUTES;

REQUIRES MANDATORY WAIVER OF THE RIGHT TO JURY TRIAL AND WAIVER OF ANY ABILITY TO PARTICIPATE IN A CLASS ACTION;

The box containing the card and Welcome Guide was sealed with a label that stated:

> IMPORTANT
>
> Read the enclosed T-Mobile Terms & Conditions. By using T-Mobile service, you agree to be bound by the Terms & Conditions, including the mandatory arbitration and early termination fee provisions.
>
> The first paragraph of the Terms and Conditions instructs purchasers to read the terms carefully and advises those who do not agree to refrain from using the service or the unit. Section Three of the Terms and Conditions contains a mandatory arbitration clause, which provides that the parties will arbitrate all claims, and, in doing so, will follow the American Arbitration Association's published wireless industry arbitration rules. The clause states that each party agrees to pay its "own other fees, costs and expenses including those for counsel, experts, and witnesses."
>
> That section also contains a class action waiver and a severability clause:
>
> Neither you nor we may be representative of other potential claimants or a class of potential claimants in any dispute ... YOU AND WE ACKNOWLEDGE AND AGREE THAT THIS SEC. 3 WAIVES ANY RIGHT TO A JURY TRIAL OR PARTICIPATION AS A PLAINTIFF IN A CLASS ACTION. IF A COURT OR ARBITRATOR DETERMINES THAT YOUR WAIVER OF YOUR ABILITY TO PURSUE CLASS OR REPRESENTATIVE CLAIMS IS UNENFORCEABLE, THE ARBITRATION AGREEMENT WILL NOT APPLY AND OUR DISPUTE WILL BE RESOLVED BY A COURT OF APPROPRIATE JURISDICTION.... SHOULD ANY OTHER PROVISION OF THIS ARBITRATION AGREEMENT BE DEEMED UNENFORCEABLE, THAT PROVISION SHALL BE REMOVED, AND THE AGREEMENT SHALL OTHERWISE REMAIN BINDING.

For approximately three weeks after the purchase of the card, Plaintiffs were able to insert it into their IBM ThinkPad laptop computer ("ThinkPad") and connect to the internet without any difficulty. They then did not attempt to use the card again for a few months, at which time they were unable to insert the card into their ThinkPad. They contacted T-Mobile technical support several times and received refurbished cards on three separate occasions. They could not, however, insert any of the refurbished cards into the Think-Pad. After they were unable to insert the third card, staff from T-Mobile technical support informed Plaintiffs that they would have to pursue the issue at the T-Mobile store where they purchased the original card. At the store, a Sony representative attempted to insert the card and he failed to succeed in this task as well. He then promised to contact Plaintiffs about how to solve the problem. Plaintiffs never heard back from him, despite multiple email inquiries.

Ultimately, Plaintiffs filed a class action lawsuit in federal district court against T-Mobile and Sony. Plaintiffs alleged violations of various federal and state laws, including Oregon's Unlawful Trade Practices Act ("UTPA"), OR. REV. STAT. § 646.605, the federal Magnuson-Moss Warranty Act, 15 U.S.C. § 2301, and the federal Lanham Act, 15 U.S.C. § 1125(a). Plaintiffs also raised a number of common law theories of liability, including negligence, unjust enrichment, fraud by concealment, negligent misrepresentation, breach of implied warranties, breach of express warranty, breach of implied warranty of merchantability, and breach of implied warranty of fitness. The complaint alleged that defendants knew or should have known that the card "was not compatible and/or did not fit into the IBM ThinkPad laptop" computers, and that Defendants allowed customers to purchase cards and enter into long-term service contracts from which consumers would receive no benefit without a compatible card.

Three months after Plaintiffs filed their lawsuit, Defendants filed a motion to dismiss the case or stay proceedings and compel arbitration under the Federal Arbitration Act, 9 U.S.C. § 1 *et seq.* ("FAA"). Plaintiffs opposed the motion, contending that the arbitration clause was unconscionable and therefore unenforceable. The district court granted Defendants' motion and dismissed the case. The court agreed with Plaintiffs that the provision requiring each party to bear its own attorney fees was unconscionable because Oregon's UTPA provides for prevailing party attorney fees, and severed that provision from the agreement. The court rejected Plaintiffs' remaining arguments, however, including the argument that the prohibition against class actions was unconscionable, and concluded that Plaintiffs were required to arbitrate their claims under the agreement. Plaintiffs filed a timely notice of appeal.

II. Standard of Review and Applicable Law

The Federal Arbitration Act provides that arbitration agreements "shall be valid, irrevocable, and enforceable, save upon such grounds as exist at law or in equity for the revocation of any contract." 9 U.S.C. § 2. Plaintiffs allege that T-Mobile's arbitration agreement is unconscionable. As we have repeatedly recognized, unconscionability is a generally applicable contract defense that may render an agreement to arbitrate unenforceable.

Both parties recognize that unconscionability is governed by state law-in this case, by Oregon law.... Where the state supreme court has not yet decided an issue but "there is relevant precedent from the state's intermediate appellate court, the federal court must follow the state intermediate appellate court decision unless the federal court finds convincing evidence that the state's supreme court likely would not follow it." Ryman v. Sears, Roebuck and Co., 505 F.3d 993, 994 (9th Cir.2007) (emphasis omitted).

III. Analysis

B. Unconscionability

In assessing a claim of unconscionability, Oregon courts consider both procedural and substantive unconscionability. See Vasquez-Lopez *v.* Beneficial Oregon, Inc., 152 P.3d 940, at 948 (Or.App. 2007) Although both forms of unconscionability "are relevant, ... only substantive unconscionability is absolutely necessary." *Id.*

1. Procedural Unconscionability

Procedural unconscionability focuses on two factors in contract formation: oppression and surprise.

Oppression arises when there is inequality in bargaining power between the parties to a contract, resulting in no real opportunity to negotiate the terms of the contract and the absence of meaningful choice. Surprise involves the extent to which the supposedly agreed terms were hidden from the party seeking to avoid enforcement of the agreement.

In Motsinger v. Lithia Rose-FT, Inc., 156 P.3d 156 (2007), the Oregon Court of Appeals explained that a contract of adhesion—an agreement presented on a take-it-or-leave-it basis—reflects unequal bargaining power, but the adhesive nature of a contract standing alone is insufficient to render an agreement procedurally unconscionable. The court declined to find procedural unconscionability where an arbitration clause was not hidden or disguised and where the plaintiff was given time to read the documents before assenting to their terms. *Id.* at 161 ("A party is presumed to be familiar with the contents of any document that bears the person's signature.") (internal quotations and citation omitted).

Under the circumstances of the present case, the district court properly concluded that T-Mobile's arbitration agreement is not procedurally unconscionable. The take-it-or-leave-it nature of T-Mobile's agreement is insufficient to render it unenforceable. Stewart's signature appears on the Service Agreement below the arbitration clause and class action waiver-both of which are featured in boldface and uppercase text. Although Plaintiffs are correct that the Welcome Guide contained additional terms, the box containing the device and Welcome Guide was sealed with a label that brought the Terms and Conditions to the buyer's attention. To access the equipment, Plaintiffs were required to break the seal of the label. Under these circumstances, there is insufficient evidence of oppression or surprise to render the agreement procedurally unconscionable under Oregon law.

2. Substantive Unconscionability

The arbitration agreement, while not procedurally unconscionable, was adhesive and therefore reflected an underlying inequality in the parties' ability to bargain. *See, e.g., Best v. U.S. Nat'l Bank of Oregon,* 303 Or. 557, 739 P.2d 554, 556 (1987); *see also Vasquez-Lopez,* 152 P.3d at 948. Because Oregon law does not *require* that a contract exhibit procedural unconscionability in order to be invalid, *see Vasquez-Lopez,* 152 P.3d at 948 ("[O]nly substantive unconscionability is absolutely necessary."), we must still determine whether the terms of T-Mobile's arbitration agreement are unfairly onesided. To determine whether the district court properly dismissed Plaintiffs' claims pending arbitration, "we must consider whether the arbitration clause is rendered unconscionable when the disparity in bargaining power" reflected in the clause's adhesive nature "is combined with terms that are unreasonably favorable to the party with the greater power." *Motsinger,* 156 P.3d at 161 (internal quotations and citation omitted); *see also Carey v. Lincoln Loan Co.,* 203 Or.App. 399, 125 P.3d 814, 830 (2005) ("Although there is no evidence of trickery or deceit, as there often is in unconscionability cases, the gross inequality in knowledge and bargaining power is sufficient to require us to consider the substance of the challenged provisions.").[4] Thus, if the terms of the agreement are unreasonably favorable to T-Mobile, the agreement may be unenforceable despite its lack of procedural unconscionability.

Plaintiffs allege that numerous provisions of the arbitration agreement are substantively unconscionable, but we need address only one to resolve the present dispute. In an opinion issued after the district court's order in this case, the Oregon Court of Appeals held that a class action waiver in an arbitration provision may be substantively unconscionable. *Vasquez-Lopez,* 152 P.3d at 949-50. Applying *Vasquez-Lopez,* we conclude that the class action waiver in the present case is substantively unconscionable and unenforceable under Oregon law.

The *Vasquez-Lopez* court explained that a class action waiver in a consumer contract is unreasonably favorable to a company like T-Mobile for two distinct reasons. First, such a waiver is inherently one-sided when contained in a consumer contract. Even if the waiver on its face applies equally to both parties, it is entirely unilateral in effect. Wryly noting the well-known literary passage that "'the majestic equality of the laws ... forbid[s] rich

---

[4] California courts take a similar approach, and have explained that they evaluate unconscionability on a sliding scale. The more substantively unconscionable a provision, the less procedural unconscionability is required. *Armendariz v. Found. Health Psychcare Servs., Inc.,* 24 Cal.4th 83, 114, 99 Cal.Rptr.2d 745, 6 P.3d 669 (2000) (" 'Essentially a sliding scale is invoked which disregards the regularity of the procedural process of the contract formation, that creates the terms, in proportion to the greater harshness or unreasonableness of the substantive terms themselves.' ") (quoting 15 *Williston on Contracts* (3d ed. 1972) § 1763A, pp. 226-27).

and poor alike to sleep under the bridges, to beg in the streets, and to steal their bread,'" the Oregon Court of Appeals observed, "Although the arbitration rider with majestic equality forbids lenders as well as borrowers from bringing class actions, the likelihood of the lender seeking to do so against its own customers is as likely as the rich seeking to sleep under bridges." *Id.* (quoting Anatole France, *The Red Lily* 95 (Winifred Stephens trans., Frederic Chapman ed., 1894)).

Second, a consumer class action waiver frequently prevents individuals from vindicating their rights. A ban on class action denies plaintiffs a crucial opportunity "without which many meritorious claims would simply not be filed" because the cost of pursuing each claim individually outweighs the potential relief. *Id.* at 950. "'The policy at the very core of the class action mechanism is to overcome the problem that small recoveries do not provide the incentive for any individual to bring a solo action prosecuting his or her rights.'" *Id.* (quoting *Amchem Products Inc. v. Windsor,* 521 U.S. 591, 617 (1997)). As *Vasquez-Lopez* explained, by preventing consumers from pursuing small but meritorious claims a class action waiver "gives defendant[s] a virtual license to commit, with impunity, millions of dollars' worth of small-scale fraud." *Id.* at 951.

Like the Supreme Courts of California and Washington, *see Discover Bank v. Superior Court,* 36 Cal.4th 148, 30 Cal.Rptr.3d 76, 113 P.3d 1100, 1116 (2005); *Scott v. Cingular Wireless,* 160 Wash.2d 843, 161 P.3d 1000, 1006 (2007), the *Vasquez-Lopez* court declared that a class action waiver in a contract where individual damages are likely to be small is substantively unconscionable as a matter of state contract law. Because Defendants have presented no convincing evidence that Oregon's Supreme Court would disagree with *Vasquez-Lopez,* we must follow *Vasquez-Lopez* in determining whether T-Mobile's waiver is substantively unconscionable. *Ryman,* 505 F.3d at 994.

The class action waiver in T-Mobile's Service Agreement presents the same problems that led the *Vasquez-Lopez* court to find substantive unconscionability in that case. First, like the class action waiver in *Vasquez-Lopez,* T-Mobile's waiver is unilateral in effect: It can hardly be imagined that T-Mobile or its suppliers would ever want or need to bring a class action against T-Mobile's customers.

Second, the class action waiver here creates the same disincentive to litigate recognized in *Vasquez-Lopez.* The actual damages alleged by Plaintiffs do not exceed $693.63, which includes the monthly service fee over the one-year contract duration and the cost of the card. *Cf. Shroyer,* 498 F.3d at 984 (noting that individual damages of less than $1,000 qualify as small amounts for the purpose of determining whether class action waivers are enforceable under California law). Moreover, many of the customer claims covered by the class action waiver will be much smaller than Plaintiffs' claim, because they will involve something less than a total hardware failure resulting in a complete loss of service. We must evaluate unconscionability "under the circumstances existing at the time of the making of the contract," *W.L. May Co., Inc. v. Philco-Ford Corp.,* 273 Or. 701, 543 P.2d 283, 286 (1975), and it is impossible to know at the time of formation whether a customer's future claims against T-Mobile will involve a total failure or something far less costly. These latter potential claims are as relevant to our analysis of the waiver's unconscionability as Plaintiffs' actual claim. *Compare Vasquez-Lopez,* 152 P.3d at 951 ("[W]e are simply unconvinced that any significant number of plaintiffs with claims under, say $50, would be sufficiently motivated to spend the time and risk the expense necessary to take the claim to arbitration."); *with id.* at 944 (noting that the jury had awarded $26,639.73 in economic damages to the plaintiffs). Given the small size of the individual claims covered by the arbitration agreement, the class action waiver here, like the waiver in *Vasquez-Lopez,* is likely to prevent T-Mobile's customers from vindicating their rights because the time and expense of prosecuting such claims makes it impracticable "to embark on litigation in which the optimum result might be more than consumed by the cost." *Id.* at 950 (quoting *Deposit Guar. Nat. Bank v. Roper,* 445 U.S. 326, 338, 100 S.Ct. 1166, 63 L.Ed.2d 427 (1980)).[7]

Because T-Mobile's class action waiver is identical in effect to the class action waiver in *Vasquez-Lopez,* it is substantively unconscionable as a matter of Oregon law. We recognize that, under Oregon law, "every case [involving an allegedly unconscionable contract] is decided on its own facts," *id.* at 948, and, as in *Shroyer,* "[w]e do not hold that all class action waivers are necessarily unconscionable." 498 F.3d at 983. Instead, our decision simply applies the holding of *Vasquez-Lopez*—that a class action waiver in a consumer contract involving small claims is substantively unconscionable—to the virtually identical class action waiver in T-Mobile's arbitration agreement. Defendants attempt to distinguish *Vasquez-Lopez* from the present case by pointing to the procedural unconscionability of the contract in *Vasquez-Lopez* and to the hardships resulting from that contract's cost-sharing provisions. Although these issues were relevant to the *Vasquez-Lopez* court's determina-

---

[7] We note that the substantive unconscionability of T-Mobile's class action waiver is magnified by its requirement that each party bear its own costs. We agree with the district court's decision that this provision is unconscionable as well, as it discourages individuals from litigating by precluding an award of otherwise available attorney fees to a prevailing plaintiff under the Oregon UTPA. OR. REV. STAT. § 646.638(3). *Vasquez-Lopez* held that, even when an award of attorney fees *is* available, individuals may not "sufficiently be motivated to spend the time and risk the expense necessary to take [their] claim[s] to arbitration." 152 P.3d at 951. Where the possibility of an award of attorney fees is eliminated, the costs of individual action become even more onerous and the likelihood that the class action waiver provides T-Mobile with a "license to commit, with impunity, millions of dollars' worth of small-scale fraud," *id., is even greater.*

tion that the contract *as a whole* was unenforceable, neither bears any relevance to the court's holding that the class action waiver in that contract was substantively unconscionable. That analysis was based entirely on the unilateral nature of the waiver and the disincentive to litigate it created, both of which are present here.

Defendants also attempt to distinguish *Vasquez-Lopez* by noting that Plaintiffs claim damages of more than $696.63, while *Vasquez-Lopez* discussed "claims of under, say, $50.00." *Vasquez-Lopez,* 152 P.3d at 951. Like Defendants' other efforts to distinguish *Vasquez-Lopez,* this argument is meritless. *Vasquez-Lopez* mentioned claims of less than $50 only in response to the defendant's argument that the availability of attorney fees under that contract provided a sufficient incentive to litigate. The court in no way limited its prior elaboration of the reasons why a class action waiver in a consumer contract involving small claims is substantively unconscionable. By noting that claims of under $50 were likely to be covered by the contract at issue in *Vasquez-Lopez,* the Oregon Court of Appeals simply demonstrated that the question under Oregon law, as under California law, is whether the contract "occurred 'in a setting in which disputes between the contracting parties predictably involve small amounts of damages.'" *Shroyer,* 498 F.3d at 984 (quoting *Discover Bank,* 30 Cal.Rptr.3d 76, 113 P.3d at 1110). For reasons already discussed, the T-Mobile class action waiver, like the waiver in *Vasquez-Lopez,* is likely to cover "claims of less than, say, $50.00." 152 P.3d at 951; *see also Shroyer,* 498 F.3d at 984 (finding "individual damages in the hundreds of dollars" to be "an objectively small amount" and "a small enough sum to satisfy" the requirement that the arbitration agreement occur in a setting in which disputes will predictably involve small amounts of damages). Accordingly, *Vasquez-Lopez* cannot be distinguished on the basis of the size of the claims at issue in this case.

In view of the above, it is plain that, under *Vasquez-Lopez,* T-Mobile's class action waiver is substantively unconscionable under Oregon law....

IV. Conclusion

Under Oregon law, "only substantive unconscionability is absolutely necessary" to find that an agreement is unenforceable. *Vasquez-Lopez,* 152 P.3d at 948. Because Oregon courts have declared that class action waivers in consumer contracts where individual damages are likely to be small are substantively unconscionable and the waiver here was contained in a contract of adhesion, the class action waiver in T-Mobile's arbitration agreement is not enforceable. *Id.* at 950. Because the arbitration agreement prohibits severance of the waiver, the agreement as a whole is unenforceable. We therefore reverse the district court's decision to dismiss the case pending arbitration.

REVERSED and REMANDED.

NOTE

Other appellate court decisions holding waiver of class actions unenforceable are: Homa v. American Express Co., 558 F.3d 225 (3d Cir.2009); Discover Bank v. Superior Court, 113 P.3d 1100 (Cal. 2005); Feeney v. Dell Inc., 908 N.E.2d 753 (Mass. 2009). Muhammad v. County Bank of Rehoboth Beach, 912 A.2d 88 (N.J. 2006); Tillman v. Commercial Credit Loans, Inc., 655 S.E.2d 362 (N.C. 2008), and Scott v. Cingular Wireless, 161 P.3d 1000 (Wash. 2007). See Jean R. Sternlight & Elizabeth J. Jensen, Mandatory Arbitration: Using Arbitration to Eliminate Consumer Class Actions: Efficient Business Practice or Unconscionable Abuse? 67 Law & Contemp. Probs. 75 (2004).

Choice of Law. In California, the history of Discover Bank v. Superior Court, 113 P.3d 1100 (Cal. 2005), shows the way for creditors to avoid having their waiver clauses rejected even in those states holding such clauses unconscionable. In that case, the Califorinia Supreme Court, in a 4 to 3 decision, reversed the appellate court and held the clause forbidding class-wide arbitration to be unconscionable, but, since the agreement had a Delaware choice-of-law provision, remanded the case to the appellate court to decide the choice-of-law issue. That court rapidly decided that enforceability of the waiver clause must be governed by Delaware law, under which such waiver clauses are upheld. Discover Bank v. Superior Court, 36 Cal. Rptr. 3d 456 (Cal. Ct. App. 2005).

Homa v. American Express Co., 558 F.3d 225 (3d Cir.2009), took a contrary view. In that case, the American Express Company (AEC), a New York corporation, established a subsidiary, American Express Centurian Bank (AECB), in Utah for the purpose of issuing American Express charge cards. Why Utah? Perhaps it is not coincidental that by statute Utah expressly allows class arbitration waivers in consumer credit agreements, to the knowledge of the court, the only state to do so. When Homa filed a class action in the district court of New Jersey charging that AEC and AECB misrepresented the actual terms of a credit card rewards program in violation of the New Jersey Consumer Fraud Act, AEC and AECB contended that Homa should be required to arbitrate his claims on an individual basis because the contract's choice of law provision indicated that any disputes arising out of the agreement would be governed by Utah law. The court said that ordinarily New Jersey courts would uphold a contractual choice of law provision, but only if it does not violate New Jersey's public policy, and in *Muhammad*, cited above, the New Jersey Supreme Court established that waiver of class arbitrations violated the fundamental public policy of New Jersey.

F. THE CREDIT CARD ACT OF 2009

In the early years, the credit card industry was run by responsible card issuers who issued cards only to creditworthy consumers at moderate rates and charges. But by the turn of the century, card issuers, in a reckless drive for market share, had made credit cards available to lower socioeconomic levels than ever before. Anecdotes about cards being issued to pets and infants were common. Credit cards seemed to offer consumers access to a middle class life style, while card issuers were able to finance their risky credit grants by securitizing their receivables. However, the severe 2007-2009 recession caused what some economists have described as the "democratization of credit" to crash, with profound consequences for both low income families and imprudent card issuers. See S. Mitra Kalita, The "Democratization of Credit" Is Over—Now It's Payback Time, Wall St. J., Oct.10, 2009, at A1. Cardholders flocked to bankruptcy, while card issuers scrambled to close the accounts of marginal cardholders.

Congress intervened with the Credit Card Act of 2009, Public Law No. 111-24, 123 Stat. 1734 (2009), which is, for the most part, a series of amendments to the Truth In Lending Act (TILA), 15 U.S.C. §§ 1601 et seq. The Federal Reserve Board (FRB) toiled for the better part of two years in drafting an immensely detailed set of regulations and commentary, informed by extensive consultation with bankers and consumers, among others. The regulations became effective on February 22, 2010. 12 CFR § 226. For casebook purposes, we paint with a broad brush in dealing with the Act and the regulations; in some instances we cite the regulations and in others we cite the sections of statute being amended.

1. LIMITATIONS ON INTEREST AND CHARGES BEFORE THE CREDIT CARD ACT

The National Bank Act, 12 U.S.C. § 85, provides that a national bank may charge "interest at the rate allowed by the laws of the State…where they bank is located…." In Marquette Nat'l. Bank of Minneapolis v. First Omaha Service Corp., 439 U.S. 299 (1978), the Court held that this provision authorizes a national bank to charge out-of-state credit cardholders an interest rate allowed by the *bank's* home state, even when that rate is higher than what is permitted by the states in which the cardholders reside. This holding allows national banks to charter banks, empowered to issue their credit cards, in a state with no limit on interest rates and, thereby, to deprive their cardholders of rate ceilings protection offered by the states in which the cardholders live. By using this ploy, national banks—which issue about 90% of the credit cards—have been able to deprive the great bulk of cardholders of any interest rate protection. South Dakota, which has no interest limitation, is now the "home" of most of the national banks for credit card purposes.

In Smiley v. Citibank (South Dakota), N.A., 517 U.S. 735 (1996), the Court went even further in upholding the regulation of the Comptroller of the Currency that proclaimed that late charges, over-limit fees, NSF fees, and annual fees were "interest" within the National Bank Act. 12 CFR § 7.40001(a). Thus, for South Dakota-issued cards there were no ceilings on credit cards with respect to the charges and fees that have proved so profitable to credit card issuers. These two Supreme Court cases, in holding, in effect, that whatever-the-traffic-will-bear prevails with respect to interest rates and charges and fees, contributed to the exorbitant rates and charges that buried consumers during the 2007-2009 crash.

2. Limitations on Annual Percentage Rates (APR) and Charges and Fees Under the Credit Card Act

Annual Percentage Rates. The Credit Card Act does not impose ceilings on interest rates (APRs) for credit cards. Attempts to persuade Congress to enact a 18% ceiling failed. With respect to rates, the thrust of the Act is to place limitations on raising rates rather than the adoption of absolute ceilings.

(1) *Existing balances*. Under § 226.55(a), card issuers may not increase rates on *existing* balances unless one of the exceptions in § 226.55(b) applies. The exceptions apply when a temporary rate lasting at least six months expires; when the rate is increased due to the operation of variable rate index; when a minimum payment has not been received within 60 days after the due date; and when the consumer successfully completes or fails to comply with the terms of a workout arrangement. Among these exceptions, the most important is the variable rate exception under which the APR may automatically increase or decrease on existing balances depending on movement of an index rate adopted in the agreement. § 226.55(b)(2). The index chosen may not be under the card issuer's control and must be available to the general public. Comments to § 226.55(b)(2) bar the establishment of a floor below which the index rate cannot go as an example of control on the part of the card issuer. An example of an index rate available to the general public used by a large card issuer is: "The Prime Rate for each billing period is the Prime Rate published in the Wall Street Journal 2 days before the closing Date of the billing period." There was a mass shift on the part of major card issuers before the effective date of the Act toward adopting variable rate programs. Under the delinquent payment exception, a card issuer may increase an annual rate if it has not

received the required minimum periodic payment within 60 days after the due date for that payment. § 226.55(b)(4). But if, subsequently, the card issuer receives six consecutive required periodic payments on time after the rate increase, the card issuer must reduce the required payments to the level that applied before the increase.

(2) *New balances.* For new transactions, card issuers may not impose increased rates during the first year after an account is opened. §226.55(b)(3)(iii). After the first year, the card issuer is permitted to increase the APR that applies to new balances so long as the issuer provides the consumer with 45 days advance notice of the increase. 15 U.S.C. § 1637(i)(1). The 45-day notice of an APR increase must be accompanied by notice that the cardholder may cancel the account without default. 15 U.S.C. § 1637(i)(3). If the debtor cancels it may find itself with a considerable outstanding balance owed to the card issuer. The Act prevents the card issuer from accelerating and demanding immediate payment of this balance by providing two methods for repayment of the outstanding balance: (1) repayment over an amortized period of not less than five years, or (2) required minimum payments that include a percentage of the outstanding balance that is equal to not more than twice the percentage required before the effective date of the increase.

Fees and Charges. Congress did not set limits on late payment fees, over-limit fees, or other penalty fees or charges, but decreed that they must be "reasonable and proportional to the omission or violation to which the fee or charge relates". 15 U.S.C. § 16665d(a). The Fed was given the task of fixing limits on fees and penalties in keeping with the Congressonal intent. It did so in amendments to §226.52 of Regulation Z. Among the principles embraced by the Fed was that "the punishment must fit the crime." That is, a fee is prohibited that exceeds an amount associated with the violation: if a payment is $10 short, the penalty cannot exceed that amount. In a more general vein, the fee must represent a reasonable proportion of the costs incurred by the issuer as a result of that type of violation; that is, the fee must be justified in relation to the costs of the violation. Issuers can also justify the amount of a fee by showing that the amount was reasonably necessary to deter that kind of violation. The burden on issuers to calculate penalty amounts complying with these test is ameliorated by offering a "safe harbor" for issuers. The issuer complies with the rule if the amount of the fee does not exceed the greater of an amount fixed periodically by the Fed, adjusted to reflect changes in the Consumer Price Index, or 5% of an amount associated with the violation, provided that the amount does not exceed an upper limit, to be set by the Fed. This is the Fed's first experience with price fixing. See Clarks' Bank Deposits and Payments Monthly, March 2010, Vol. No. 3.

Over-Limit Fees. Credit card accounts are usually subject to creditor-imposed limits on the amounts that can be charged on the card, which are stated in the credit card agreement and on periodic statements. The credit card network allows merchants to whom the card is presented to ascertain by electronic means whether the transaction exceeds those limits. Before the Act, if the merchant accepted a card exceeding the limits, the card issuer could exact an over-limit fee from the cardholder if the credit card agreement expressly provided for it. Abuses by some card issuers of over-limit fees was a major factor in leading to the adoption of the Act, which now prohibits such fees unless the cardholder has "opted in" by expressly electing to permit such charges in the future after receiving notice by the card issuer. Before obtaining this consent, the issuer must disclose the dollar amount of any fees or charges that will be assessed for an over-limit transaction as well as notice of any increased rate that may apply if the consumer exceeds the account's credit limit. The issuer must also provide a notice of the consumer's right to revoke that consent that must appear on any periodic statement sent to the consumer. Certain practices are prohibited with respect to over-limit transactions. For instance, the issuer can not impose more than one over-limit fee per billing cycle and cannot impose more than one fee on the account for the same over-limit transaction in more than three succeeding billing cycles unless the consumer has obtained an additional extension of the credit limit or reduces the outstanding balance below the credit limit as of the end of the subsequent period.§ 226.56.

Double-Cycle Billing. Card issuers are prohibited from imposing finance charges on balances for days in previous billing cycles imposd as a result of the loss of a grace period. This is referred to as "double cycle billing." In addition, when a consumer pays some, but not all, of a balance prior to expiration of a grace period, the issuer is prohibited from imposing finance charges on the portion of the balance that has been repaid. 15 U.S.C. § 1637(j).

3. PAYMENTS

Payment Allocation. Cardholders may maintain balances with their card issuer bearing different interest rates. Before the Credit Card Act, card issuers frequently applied payments by the cardholder to the balance with the lowest interest rate. As a result, balances with higher interest rates remained unpaid and the card users assessed the higher interest rates on these balances. The Credit Card Act bans this payment allocation. Under § 226.53(a), if a consumer makes a payment in excess of the required minimum periodic payment, the card issuer must allocate the excess amount first to the balance with the highest annual percentage rate and any remaining portion to other balances in descending order based on the applicable APR.

Payment Periods. Payments must be scheduled for the same day each month. But if the day is on a weekend or holiday, the creditor cannot treat a payment received on the next business day as late.15 U.S.C. § 1637(o). A creditor may not treat a payment as late unless the issuer has adopted reasonable procedures designed to ensure that periodic statements specifying the payment due date are mailed or delivered to the consumer not later than 21 days before the payment due date disclosed on the statement. 15 U.S.C. § 1666b(a). If the credit card agreement authorizes fees for late payments, the periodic statement must disclose in a conspicuous location the date on which the payment is due, together with the amount of the fee that will be charged, if payment is late. 15 U.S.C. § 1637(b)(12)(A). If a late payment may result in an increase in the APR, the periodic statement must include a conspicuous notice of this fact. 15 U.S.C. §1637(b)(12)(B).

Minimum Payments. Card issuers have made it easy for cardholders to get in over their heads by making only minimum payments, leaving balances that grow rather than decrease. Throw in a late charge here and there and a minimum payment consumer runs the risk of going into bankruptcy, where she will find that, under BC § 523(a)(2)(C), some of her credit card transactions made within 70 days of filing bankruptcy may be presumed to be nondischargeable. The Credit Card Act addresses this problem by disclosures in § 226.7(b)(12) (Repayment Disclosures), which requires the periodic statement to contain general warnings of the perils of making only minimum payments. Moreover, the statement must have in tabular form: (1) the amount of time and the total cost (interest and principal) involved in paying the balance in full making only minimum payments, and (2) the monthly payment amount required to payoff the balance in 36 months and the total cost (interest and principal) of repaying the balance in 36 months. Although the willingness of credit cardholders to read their card agreements and statements is questionable, for this important information it's worth a try. Under § 226.51, discussed in the following paragraph, card issuers can exert some control by imposing credit limits on cardholders and by requiring that payments be large enough to repay the balance over a reasonable period.

Evaluation of Consumer's Ability to Pay. A prevalent abuse has been the issuance of credit cards to consumers who are not creditworthy. Section 226.51 addresses this issue by prohibiting the card issuer from opening new accounts or increasing the credit limit for existing credit cards unless the issuer considers the consumer's ability to make the required minimum payments under the terms of the account based on the cardholder's income or assets and current obligations. How are card issuers supposed to do this? Can they rely on the information the consumer gives them about her income and assets, or must they seek credit reports on all applicants? The Regulation provides that the card issuers must establish "reasonable policies and procedures" to consider a consumer's income or assets and current obligations. These procedures must include at least one of the following: the ratio of debt to income; the ratio of debt to assets; or the income the consumer would have after paying the debt obligations. Under § 226.51(a)(2), the card issuer must use a reasonable method for estimating the minimum periodic payments the consumer would be required to pay under the terms of the account. It would be reasonable for an issuer to estimate minimum payments based on a consumer's utilization of the full credit line using the minimum payment formula employed by the issuer with respect to transaction for which the consumer is being considered. This requirement presses the card issuer to require minimum payments large enough to repay the balance incurred within a reasonable time, considering the amount of the debt and the interest rate.

Internet Disclosures. As the reading tastes of the public turn increasingly from the printed page to the Internet for information of all sorts, the requirement that creditors post credit card agreements on the Internet make sense. Section 226.58 sets out detailed requirements. Card issuers with fewer than 10,000 open end credit card accounts are excepted from this requirement as *de minimis*.

4. Minors and Students

Underage Consumers. Card issuers are prohibited from issuing a credit card to a consumer under the age of 21 unless the consumer has submitted a written application that either (1) contains information showing the consumer has the capacity to make the required payments, or (2) has the signature of a cosigner at least 21 years old who has the means to repay the debts under the account and who assumes joint liability on the account.The cosignor may be a parent. Cosignors must approve in writing any increase in the credit limit on the credit card. § 226.51(b).

College Students. Credit and debit cards are ubiquitous on the college scene. Colleges are reluctant to have cards marketed on their campus—unless they get a cut of the proceeds. This is done through "affinity" cards, issued pursuant to agreements for profit sharing between a college or alumni group and the card issuer. For example, the Bank of America has about 4,400 affinity cards, usually pitched through college alumni associations, social groups and charities. Robin Sidel, Card Issuers Retreat, Wall St. J., Mar. 23, 2010, at C1. Section 226.57 limits a creditor's ability to offer a student at an institution of higher education any tangible item to induce the student to apply for a plan offered by the creditor. Specifically, the regulation prohibits such offers on or near the campus of the institution or at an event sponsored or related to the institution. Such institutions must publicly disclose agreements with credit card issuers regarding the marketing of credit cards. Moreover, card issuers must make annual reports to the Board regarding any business, marketing or promotional agreements between the issuer and an institution of higher education regarding the issuance of credit cards to students at that institution.

G. Debit Cards and ATMs

Ron Lieber & Andrew Martin, in their article, Overspending on Debit Cards is Painful, but Not for Banks, N.Y. Times, Sept. 9, 2009, at A1, tell of a man (Customer) who turned to a debit card to help him spend his money more carefully. But Customer was stunned when his bank charged him seven $34 overdraft fees to cover seven purchases when there was not enough money in his account, notifying him only afterward. He paid $4.14 for a coffee at Starbucks—and a $34 fee. He got the $6.50 student discount at a movie theater—but no discount on the $34 fee. He paid $6.76 at Lowe's for screws—and yet another $34 fee. All told, he owed $238 in extra charges for just a day's activity. He didn't know that his account was overdrawn.

As we have seen, Congress has imposed detailed regulations on credit cards with respect to late charges, overdraft charges and other issues. But it has failed to do so with respect to debit cards, checks, ATMs and ACH transfers, even though the same abuses may be present. In 2009, the FRB addressed these concerns by amending Regulation E, which implements the Electronic Fund Transfer Act (15 U.S.C. 1693 et seq.) (EFTA). The rule became effective in January 2010, with mandatory compliance in July 2010; it is found in 12 CFR part 205. Its coverage is narrow: it applies only to one-time debit card transactions and ATM services. It does not apply to payments made by checks or ACH transactions, including checks converted to ACH debit entries. Its scope is limited to overdraft service transactions, defined as a service under which a financial institution assesses a fee or charge on a consumer's account for paying a transaction when the consumer has insufficient or unavailable funds in the account. 12 CFR 205.17.

Before 2010, consumers were often enrolled in overdraft services automatically without their consent. The major reform in the new rule is to require institutions to obtain a consumer's affirmative consent before they can impose fees for paying an overdraft with respect to an ATM or one-time debit card transaction. § 205.17(b)(1). The opt-in policy is justified by the belief that any benefit from permitting ATM and debit card overdrafts to be paid without prior consumer consent is outweighed by the the harm to consumers stemming from overdraft fees, which may be significantly higher than the transactions causing the overdraft. Notice of the opt-in right must be provided and the consumer's affirmative consent must be obtained before fees or charges may be assessed on the consumer's account for paying such over-drafts. The opt-in requirement applies to both existing and new accounts. The operational difficulties for banks in imposing the opt-in requirement on existing accounts are substantial.

Why did the FRB restrict its opt-in rule on overdraft fees to one-time debit cards and ATM transactions, thereby omitting the great volume of check and ACH transactions? The FRB did extensive consumer testing and concluded that participants would prefer to have their checks paid even though overdraft fees were incurred because these transactions represented important bills. This must also be true in recurring debit card usage in which mortgages or utility bills are paid. In contrast, participants would prefer to have ATM withdrawals and one-time debit card transactions declined if they had insufficient funds, rather than incur an overdraft fee, because these transactions tend to be more discretionary in nature. Then, too, if a check is an overdraft, whether the bank pays it and charges an overdraft fee or returns it and charges an NSF fee, the customer usually pays the same fee. Consumer testing indicated that many consumers are unaware that banks will pay overdrafts on ATMs.

The rule is solely a disclosure regulation. If Customer in the Liebow & Martin article had filled out and returned the consent form at the time he opened his account, he would be liable for the $238 fees because he was on notice that the $34 fee could be assessed each time he used the overdrawn debit card. He is held to know the balance of his account and must lookout for himself. The rule does not limit amounts that a bank can charge for overdraft fees, nor are there limits on the number of fees that can be charged for any time period. If Customer had been allowed to open his account without returning the consent form, the bank could not assess overdraft fees. It can protect itself by either refusing to open the account or declining to extend overdraft services.

Some major banks have reacted to the rule by eliminating overdraft services on debit card purchases entirely, thereby forgoing the concomitant overdraft fees. Any cardholder using a debit card issued by one of these banks who attempts to make a purchase with insufficient funds in her account will be denied at the point of sale. The Bank of America plan will allow holders of its cards to get cash from an ATM. If there is an overdraft, the $35 fee would still be imposed, with the customer notified of the withdrawal at the ATM machine. Dan Fitzpatrick & Robin Sidel, Bank of America Eliminates Overdraft Fees on Debit Buys, Wall. St. J., Mar. 10, 2010, at C3. Overdraft fees have been an important source of revenue for banks. The article cited above refers to a report by a banking service predicting that the banking industry was on pace to collect $38.5 billion in overdraft fees, much of it from debit cards, in 2009. Presumably, other fees and charges will be adjusted upward to replace the lost income.

CHAPTER 7

LETTERS OF CREDIT

A. INTRODUCTION

Parties and Functions. Letters of credit are ubiquitous and important financial instruments. They have a wide variety of uses, such as paying for goods, guaranteeing commercial paper and municipal and corporate bonds, and backing up the performance of nonfinancial contracts. Simply put, a letter of credit is an undertaking in a writing or other record by one person to pay or deliver an item of value to a named person on that person's satisfaction of documentary conditions, if any, stipulated in the record. 5–102(a)(10). In its most basic form the instrument involves three parties: the issuer, the applicant (or "customer") and the beneficiary. The issuer is the party making the record undertaking, the applicant is the party requesting the issuer to make the record undertaking (almost always for a fee), and the beneficiary is the party who is to receive payment or deliver an item of value. The letter of credit provides that the issuer will pay the beneficiary a stipulated amount upon the beneficiary's satisfaction of stipulated documentary conditions by a specified date. It may even provide that the issuer will deliver an item of value to the beneficiary, such as stock certificates. The legal relationship between the beneficiary and applicant may vary, as can their identity. The beneficiary and applicant may be, respectively, a seller and buyer in a sales contract, a contractor and owner in a construction contract, a creditor and debtor, or a donee and donor. Although the relationship between parties and the transactions can change, the elementary form of the letter of credit is the same: an issuer's record undertaking, made at the request of an applicant, to give specified value to a beneficiary upon its satisfaction of documentary conditions, if any, stated in the record.

A letter of credit may involve additional parties. The issuer can engage a party, called the adviser, to notify the beneficiary of the existence and terms of the credit. 5–102(a)(1), 5–107(c). Another party, called the confirmer, may be engaged by the issuer to pay the beneficiary upon the beneficiary's presentation of documents required by the confirmation. 5–102(a)(4). A confirmed letter of credit is a separate instrument from the issuer's letter of credit. 5–107(a). Often the same party may undertake both to advise and confirm the issuer's letter of credit. Letters of credit issued in international transactions frequently involve advisers and confirmers. This is because applicants and beneficiaries often are strangers to each other. An adviser local to the beneficiary can vouch reliably for the genuineness and accuracy of the terms of a foreign letter of credit. A local confirmer provides a convenient and reliable source of payment as well as other advantages such as avoidance of foreign currency exchange controls. Where an advice and confirmed letter of credit is warranted, a prudent beneficiary will require them as part of the terms of transaction that calls for the issuance of a letter of credit.

Issuer's Obligation. Letter of credit contracts are traditionally called commercial or mercantile "specialties." They are contracts subject to special rules, not the ordinary rules that apply to other contracts. Some commentators and courts describe the letter of credit as a "unique" or "idiosyncratic" instrument. For instance, the issuer's obligation to the beneficiary is not the product of the beneficiary's acceptance of an offer by the issuer. The issuer's obligation also is enforceable without consideration, although typically consideration will support its obligation. See 5–105. Essential to letter of credit law is the rule that the issuer's payment obligation to the beneficiary is conditioned only on the documentary terms described in the credit. Only these terms govern the issuer's obligation to the beneficiary. Terms or facts bearing on the relationship or contracts between the beneficiary and the applicant or between the applicant and issuer, have no effect on the issuer's obligation to the beneficiary. In this sense, the issuer's obligation to the beneficiary is "primary": it is independent of facts or terms bearing on relationships between other parties. The issuer's undertaking to the beneficiary alone controls its payment obligation to the beneficiary. Thus, a letter of credit isn't a guarantee because the issuer's obligation isn't conditional on the default of the principal obligor; the issuer's liability isn't "secondary." In contrast, the guarantor's liability is secondary. See Restatement (Third) of Suretyship and Guaranty § 34 (1996). The letter of credit contract also doesn't give the issuer or applicant rights of a third party beneficiary: neither can use the rights of others to affect the issuer's payment obligation to the beneficiary. Legally, the insulation of the issuer's payment obligation from other transactions makes the letter of credit a distinctive financial instrument. See Comment 1 to 5–102.

Three Contracts. In a typical transaction involving a letter of credit, three separate contracts are involved: (1) the contract between the beneficiary and the applicant that calls for the establishment of the credit or gives rise to it; (2) the contract between the issuer and beneficiary requiring payment against presentation of the documents; and (3) the contract of reimbursement between the issuer and the applicant. It is standard to refer to contract (1) as the underlying contract, contract (2) as the letter of credit contract, and contract (3) as the reimbursement contract. The distinctiveness of the letter of a credit as a financial instrument derives from the independence of the letter of credit contract from the other two sorts of contract. Thus, issuer's obligations to the beneficiary under the letter of credit are "primary" and, therefore, unaffected by the underlying or reimbursement contracts.

Commercial Letters of Credit. There are two types of letters of credit: commercial and standby letters of credit. They are distinguished by their intended financial purposes and the sorts of documentary conditions specified credits. A commercial letter of credit serves as a mechanism for payment owed on the underlying contract. For instance, a contract for the sale of goods might require the buyer-applicant to establish a letter of credit naming the seller as the beneficiary. The terms of the credit require the issuer to pay a specified amount equal to the contract price to the beneficiary upon the beneficiary's presentation to it of documents described in the credit. The described documents can be of any sort. They typically include a draft drawn by the seller on the buyer, a commercial invoice, a bill of lading or other document of title, and certificates of origin or inspection certificates. Where the underlying contract involves a sale of assets other than goods, such as real estate or securities, different documentation will be required. The seller is paid the contract price by the issuer if the seller-beneficiary presents documents to it that comply with the terms of the credit. Because the issuer undertakes to pay the seller-beneficiary, the commercial credit adds the issuer's obligation to that of the buyer. Thus, the seller won't receive the contract price only if both the buyer and issuer are unable or unwilling to pay it. Because issuers frequently are banks with low risks of insolvency and a great concern for their reputations as reputable financial intermediaries, a commercial credit reduces the seller-beneficiary's risk of nonpayment significantly. The use of commercial credits in sales transactions is discussed in Clayton P. Gillette & Steven D. Walt, Sales Law: Domestic and International 465–516 (2d ed. 2009).

Standby Letters of Credit. A standby letter of credit has a different purpose and specifies different documentary conditions. Standby letters of credit function to guarantee performance of an underlying contract or transaction. They do not serve as a risk-reducing device for payment of the contract price. Typically, a standby credit provides that the issuer will pay the beneficiary if the beneficiary presents specified documentary evidence of default by the applicant or some other party in an underlying contract or transactions. Unlike the commercial letter, the issuer of a standby credit does not usually expect the beneficiary to draw on the credit. ("Direct pay" credits are variant standby credits in which the credit serves as a payment mechanism for discharging financial obligations, and the issuer expects to pay upon the beneficiary's presentation of a draft or documentary demand.) Required documents generally include a draft and noncommercial documents, typically a certificate of default of specified content. Thus, presentation of documentary evidence of default allows the beneficiary to obtain payment from the issuer. In this way the issuer's obligation backs up the applicant or another's obligation under the underlying contract or transactions. The standby credit thereby shifts the risk of the applicant's insolvency, nonpayment or nonperformance from the beneficiary to the issuer. Standby credits that back up financial obligations owed in an underlying transaction are called "financial" standby credits. "Performance" standby credits back up nonmonetary obligations owed in the underlying transaction. As a standby credit, the issuer's obligation to the beneficiary in each case depends only on the beneficiary's presentation of documentary evidence of default in an underlying transaction, not on nondocumentary facts bearing on default.

Standby credits serve a guarantee function in a variety of underlying transactions. Issuers of commercial paper can market the paper at a higher price by backing it up with letters of credit. The credits can be drawn upon by the holders of the paper if the paper isn't paid at maturity. Purchasers of limited partnerships on credit can guarantee their partnership interests by having issued a credit that undertakes to pay the beneficiary-sellers upon certification of the purchasers' default on its payment obligations. In securitization transactions, standby credits serve to enhance the credit rating of securities issued by the securitization vehicle: the credit guarantees the payment of interest and principal on securities the vehicle issued. Finally, a standby credit might serve as an alternative to withholding progress payments under a construction contract. Rather than withhold progress payments, the owner can have the contractor-applicant establish a standby credit in the owner's favor. The credit can allow the owner-beneficiary to draw stipulated amounts if the owner presents documentary evidence to the issuer of the contractor's default. The same sort of scheme can allow the buyer-beneficiary in a sale of goods contract to prepay for the goods and draw on credit upon documentary presentation of the seller-applicant's default under the sales contract. Its wide range of uses and the comparatively low fees charged by issuers of standby credits apparently make the standby credit an attractive financial instrument. As indirect evidence, standby credits now drawf commercial credits. In 2008, U.S. FDIC-insured depository banks issued slightly more than 600 billion dollars in standby credits. During the same period they issued about 25 billion dollars in commercial credits. See FDIC Statistics on Banking (2008). A form standby letter of credit and reimbursement agreement appear at the end of this chapter.

B. SOURCES OF LETTER OF CREDIT LAW

Most letter of credit law consists of domestic law and institutional rules, and much of it is uniform across jurisdictions. Letter of credit law has five sources: (1) In the United States Article 5 of the UCC and extra-Code common law; (2) Publication Number 600 of the Uniform Customs and Practice for Documentary Credits of the International Chamber of Commerce ("UCP 600" or "UCP"); (3) the Uniform Law for Demand Guarantees of the International Chamber of Commerce; (4) the International Standby Practices of the International Chamber of Commerce ("ISP 98"); and (5) the United Nations Convention on Independent Guarantees and Standby Letters of Credit ("U.N. Convention"). To date, six countries have ratified the U.N. Convention; the United States has not done so. Thus, domestic law such as Article 5 and the International Chamber of Commerce's institutional rules remain the most important rules governing credits. Treatises describing the sources of letter of credit law include John F. Dolan, The Law of Letters of Credit: Commercial and Standby Credits (4th ed. 2007) (herein Dolan, Letters of Credit); 3 James J. White & Robert S. Summers, Uniform Commercial Code, Chapter 26 (5th Prac. ed. 2002).; and Brooke Wunnicke et al., Standby and Commercial Letters of Credit (3d ed. 2003). A brief summary appears in Boris Kozolchyk, Commercial and Standby Letters of Credit, in 3 United States Law of Trade and Investment, Chapter 24 (Boris Kozolchyk and John F. Molloy eds., 2001). This chapter focuses almost exclusively on Article 5 and the UCP.

Article 5 of the UCC governs both commercial and standby letters of credit. Since the International Chamber of Commerce has no legislative authority, its institutional rules apply only if the credit incorporates them. Credits frequently incorporate UCP 600 in particular as a source for principles governing letter of credit transactions. To be applicable, both UCP 600 and ISP 98 require that the incorporation be express. UCP 600 art. 1; ISP 98 art. 1.01(b). Almost all international credits and many domestic commercial credits issued in New York, for instance, are made subject to the UCP. Over half of the standby credits currently issued by Citibank and J.P. Morgan Chase are reported to be governed by the ISP 98. A few courts have held that the UCP can apply to a credit by virtue of trade usage even when the credit does not refer to the UCP. Article 5 governs credits issued by banks or other persons but excludes credit undertakings issued by consumers. UCP 600 applies to both commercial and standby credits issued only by banks. The ISP 98 applies to standby credits issued by any person. See UCP 600 art. 2; ISP 98 art. 1.04. Both UCP 600 and ISP 98 allow parties to opt-in to the respective rules by incorporation in the credit when the credit would not otherwise be covered. UCP 600 art. 1; ISP 98 art. 1.01(b); cf. U.N. Convention art. 1(2).

Incorporation of institutional rules in most cases displaces conflicting default rules under Article 5. Section 5–116(c) is clear that if a credit is made subject to the UCP or other "rules of custom or practice," the UCP or other rules of custom or practice displace Article 5 only if there is a conflict and the conflict involves a default rule of Article 5. See Comment 3 to 5–116. If Article 5's conflicting rule is mandatory, its rule continues to apply. Article 5's rules, default or mandatory, also continue to apply when they have no counterpart under UCP 600, such as rules concerning fraud or standards of documentary compliance. In these cases, there is no conflict between rules. For the most part, Article 5's very few mandatory rules are consistent with the UCP 600's rules, the current version of the UCP. This is true because the 1995 revision of Article 5 sought to remove the inconsistencies between Article 5 and the UCP that existed in 1995. However, in UCP 600, accepted by the ICC in 2007, art. 14b made a major revision with respect to the period the issuing bank has to determine whether the presentation is complying that is flatly inconsistent with 5-108(b). We will discuss UCP 600 art. 14b later in this chapter.

Article 5, along with most other domestic letter of credit law, allows parties virtually unrestricted freedom of choice over the terms of the credit. Almost all of Article 5's rules are default rules: they apply unless the parties agree to vary them. As just noted, very few of Article 5's rules are mandatory. Section 5–103(c) lists the following mandatory rules: the exclusion of consumer-issuers and noncredit undertakings from Article 5, restrictions on the stipulated expiration date for a credit, regulation of the issuer's withholding of consent to the assignment of credit proceeds, obligations of good faith, and subrogation rights. See 5–102(a)(8), (10), 5–106(d), 5–114(d), 1–302(b), 5–117(d). All of Article 5's other rules are default rules. In fact, even Article 5's mandatory rules are in effect default rules too. This is because Article 5 allows parties to select law governing the letter of credit without restriction. Section 5–116(a) provides that the law of the jurisdiction chosen by the "affected parties" controls the liability of the issuer, nominated person or adviser, and the law selected "need not bear any relation to the transaction." Parties, therefore, can select applicable law that does not contain Article 5's mandatory rules. Thus, Article 5's mandatory rules apply only if affected parties fail to select the law of a jurisdiction that does not contain the same rules. See Comment 2 to 5–103 (second paragraph).

C. FORMAL REQUIREMENTS

1. DURATION

Under 5–106(a), a letter of credit is enforceable when issued. The credit, in turn, is issued when the issuer sends or transmits the credit to the beneficiary. Because a credit is "sent" when it is mailed or delivered for transmission by the usual means (1–201(36)(A)), the credit becomes enforceable upon dispatch. Article 5 does not explicitly provide when a confirmed credit becomes enforceable. However, Comment 1 to 5–107 instructs us to treat the terms "confirmation" and "letter of credit" interchangeably throughout Article 5. Thus, the same rules concerning issuance and dispatch apply to confirmed letters of credit. Under 5–106(a), UCP 600 art. 7b., and ISP 98 art. 1.06(a), a letter of credit is irrevocable unless it states otherwise. Irrevocability means that the issuer cannot cancel or amend the credit without the beneficiary's consent. 5–106(b). This default rule makes sense for the vast majority of beneficiaries, who might want to rely on the credit in advance of drawing on it. Section 5–106(c) provides that if there is no stated expiration date in a credit, it expires one year after issuance, and 5–106(d) provides that if the credit purports to be perpetual, it expires five years after issuance. The latter is a mandatory rule.

PROBLEM

The credit issued by Bank to Company in 2005 stated:

> This credit shall expire one year from date provided that it shall be deemed automatically renewed without amendment for additional one year periods from the present or any future expiration date hereof, unless at least 30 days prior to any such date(s), Company shall have sent Bank notice that Company elects not to require this credit renewed for any such additional period.

Company drew on the credit in 2010. Bank dishonored on the ground that the effect of the duration clause was to make the duration period "perpetual," even though that term was not used; hence, the duration was limited to five years under 5-106(d): "A letter of credit that states that it is perpetual expires five years after its stated date of issuance, or if none is stated, after the date on which it is issued." Credits renewable at the option of the issuer bank are common and are not considered perpetual. See Comment 4. Should this be true in cases like this in which the option to renew is that of the beneficiary? See Golden West Refining Co. v. Suntrust Bank, 538 F.3d 1233 (9th Cir.2008).

NOTE

The credit in *Golden West* contained an "evergreen clause": a provision automatically extending the credit past its expiration date, unless the issuer or beneficiary gives notice that is not to be extended. The evergreen clause in the credit gave Company alone the right to elect not to have the credit renewed. Unless Company elected not to require Bank to renew the credit, the credit would be renewed annually, in perpetuity. The issue in the case was whether the credit was in form (not function) a perpetual letter of credit. This is a simple case: the credit by its terms was not perpetual, as 5-106(d) requires, and thus did not expire five years after its stated date of issue pursuant to 5-106(d). The plain language of the statute requires that the credit state that it is perpetual to qualify as a perpetual credit. The court held for Company.

Should the court have drawn a negative inference from the last sentence of Comment 4? We don't think so, for three reasons. First, Comment 4's last sentence makes a limited exception to (d)'s formal requirement to the effect that credits stated to be perpetual are perpetual. The Comment deems a credit non-perpetual (even if stated to be perpetual) if it gives the issuer a right to revoke the credit. As the court notes, the Comment doesn't address the converse situation: when a credit, stated to be non-perpetual, is *perpetual*. Second, and more important, the language of (d) doesn't support the relevant sentence in the Comment. The relevant sentence of the Comment and the language of 5-106(d) instead are in conflict. Although courts frequently treat Comments as part of the UCC text, text controls Comments. Third, (d) recites a sensible rule. It adopts a formal test for "perpetuality;" Comment 4 states a functional test. From an operational perspective, (d)'s formal test has a lot going for it. The test allows parties to the credit to determine easily whether the credit is perpetual or not. By contrast, a functional test makes things harder for them. For instance, we can imagine qualifying language bearing on revocation of the credit complex enough to make it hard to determine whether the credit is perpetual or not. Formal requirements make letters of credit cheaper to adminster and therefore more attractive to potential users.

2. Form

To be a letter of credit, a financial instrument must take a certain form. Section 5–104 sets out the formal requirements a credit must satisfy. However, to be a letter of credit in the first place, the financial instrument must contain a particular sort of undertaking. Since the essential feature of a letter of credit is that the credit is independent of the underlying contract, the instrument must reflect this fact. Form must reflect function. Thus, an instrument is a letter of credit only if it conditions the issuer's obligation on satisfaction of documentary conditions. Section 5–102(a)(10) defines a letter of credit as a "definite undertaking...to honor a documentary presentation by payment...." This definition describes a mandatory rule ((5–103(c)), and an agreement to treat an instrument that is not a letter of credit under 5–102(a)(1) therefore is ineffective. In the following case, Notes and Problems, we inquire about the conditions in a written undertaking that undermine the writing's character as a letter of credit. The Problems following the case also investigate 5–104's formal requirements.

Wichita Eagle and Beacon Publishing Co., Inc. v. Pacific National Bank of San Francisco

United States Court of Appeal, Ninth Circuit, 1974.
493 F.2d 1285.

■ BEFORE CHAMBERS AND BROWNING, CIRCUIT JUDGES, AND KING, DISTRICT JUDGE.

■ PER CURIAM:

The facts are summarized in the district court's opinion, 343 F.Supp. 332 (N.D.Cal.1971)....

[Summary by Eds. Lessors leased a site on which Lessee (Circular Ramp Garages), under the terms of the lease, undertook to build a parking garage. In order to assure Lessors that Lessee would perform, Lessee obtained from Bank (Pacific National Bank) a writing addressed to Lessors in which Bank established its "Letter of Credit No. 17084" in favor of Lessors for payment of $250,000 "available by drafts drawn at sight on the Pacific National Bank providing that all of the following conditions are met at the time said draft is received by the undersigned." The conditions were (1) that Lessee has failed to perform the terms of the lease; (2) that Lessors have given Bank an affidavit stating that it has given notice to Lessee and its contractor specifying how Lessee has failed to perform its lease; and (3) that either Lessee or its contractor has failed to cure defaults under the lease during a period of thirty days after receiving Lessor's notice. Lessee failed to obtain the financing necessary to build the parking garage and defaulted on the lease. Lessors' assignee (Plaintiff) presented to Bank a draft for $250,000 drawn upon Letter of Credit No. 17084, together with the required documents. When Bank refused payment, Plaintiff brought suit against Bank. The district court concluded that "Although the question is not free from doubt, the Instrument denominated 'Letter of Credit No. 17084' should be treated as a letter of credit and be subject to the law respecting letters of credit to the extent applicable and appropriate." Id. at 339.]

We do not agree with the district court that the instrument sued upon is a letter of credit, though it is so labeled. Rather, the instrument is an ordinary guaranty contract, obliging the defendant bank to pay whatever the lessee Circular Ramp Garages, Inc., owed on the underlying lease, up to the face amount of the guaranty. Since the underlying lease clearly contemplated the payment of $250,000 in case of default, and since this provision appears to be a valid liquidated damages clause, the judgment below must be modified to award the plaintiff $250,000 plus interest.

We do not base our holding that the instrument is not a letter of credit on the fact that payment was triggered by default rather than performance or on the fact that the instrument was written in a lease context, for we recognize that the commercial use of letters of credit has expanded far beyond the international sales context in which it originally developed....

The instrument involved here strays too far from the basic purpose of letters of credit, namely, providing a means of assuring payment cheaply by eliminating the need for the issuer to police the underlying contract.... The instrument neither evidences an intent that payment be made merely on presentation on a draft nor specifies the documents required for termination or payment. To the contrary, it requires the actual existence in fact of most of the conditions specified: ...for payment, that the lessee have failed to perform the terms of the lease and have failed to correct that default, in addition to an affidavit of notice.

True, in the text of the instrument itself the instruments is referred to as a "letter of credit," and we should, as the district court notes, "giv[e] effect wherever possible to the intent of the contracting parties." 343 F.Supp. at 338. But the relevant intent is manifested by the terms of the agreement, not by its label.... And where, as here, the substantive provisions require the issuer to deal not simply in documents alone, but in facts relating to the performance of a separate contract (the lease, in this case), all distinction between a letter of credit and an ordinary guaranty contract would be obliterated by regarding the instrument as a letter of credit.

It would hamper rather than advance the extension of the letter of credit concept to new situations if an instrument such as this were held to be a letter of credit. The loose terms of this instrument invited the very evil that letters of credit are meant to avoid—protracted, expensive litigation. If the letter of credit concept is to have value in new situations, the instrument must be tightly drawn to strictly and clearly limit the responsibility of the issuer.

NOTES

1. The conceptual issue presented in *Wichita Eagle* concerns the character of the instrument issued by the Bank: is it a guarantee or a standby letter of credit? The issue is important as a matter of bank regulation. Banks in the United States generally are not permitted to issue guarantees. They are permitted, however, to issue letters of credit, subject to regulation. As noted above, in function guarantees and standby letters of credit are indistinguishable, both involving the enhancement of an obligor's promise by adding the promise of a creditworthy third party. In fact, European banking terminology sometimes refers to standby credit as "bank guarantees." Conceptually they are distinguishable by the nature of the issuer's obligation and the conditions under which its obligation attaches. As to the issuer's obligation, it is primary: the issuer cannot invoke defenses against the beneficiary available to the applicant to resist honoring the credit. A guarantor's obligation is secondary: it can invoke defenses available to the obligor to resist payment to the obligee. Because banks generally can only issue letters of credit, the conceptual distinction between credits and guarantees is crucial.

The Office of the Comptroller of the Currency regulates the issuance of letters of credit by focusing on documentary conditions. By the Comptroller's interpretive ruling, national banks may issue letters of credit, including standby letters of credit, only if the obligation to honor "depends upon the presentation of specified documents and not upon nondocumentary conditions or resolution of questions of fact or law at issue between the applicant and the beneficiary." 12 C.F.R. 7.1016(a) (1998). State chartered banks usually are subject to a similar sort of regulation.

An important question is the effect of a bank issuing a guarantee in violation of bank regulations. Issuing banks or applicants sometimes adopt the odd litigation posture of urging the illegal issuance of a guarantee as a defense to enforcement of the guarantee. This is the "ultra vires" defense to honor. See Republic Nat'l Bank v. Northwest Nat'l Bank, 578 S.W.2d 109 (Tex.1978); *Wichita Eagle*. Although a few courts have accepted the ultra vires defense, the majority of case law has rejected it. See, e.g., Federal Dep. Ins. Corp. v. Freudenfeld, 492 F.Supp. 763 (E.D. Wis.1980); First Am. Nat'l Bank v. Alcorn, Inc., 361 So.2d 481 (Miss.1978); Dolan, Letters of Credit ¶ 12.03[2]. In *Wichita Eagle*, for instance, the court enforced the instrument as a guarantee. The rejection of the ultra vires defense makes a good deal of sense. The issuer or applicant almost always is in a better position than the beneficiary to avoid violating applicable bank regulations or detecting their violation. Bank regulating agencies also are better positioned than beneficiaries to monitor issuers and applicants. Accordingly, not allowing the defense to enforcement increases the cost to issuers of violating the regulation against the issuance of guarantees. It serves as a partial substitute for closer monitoring of a bank's investment activities by bank regulating agencies.

2. *Wichita Eagle* was decided under the version of Article 5 in effect before its revision in 1995. How would this case be decided under the current version of Article 5? See 5–102(a)(10) ("letter of credit") and Comment 6 to 5–102. How could the document in *Wichita Eagle* be rewritten to remove all doubt about its status as a letter of credit? Does 5–108(g) allow the court in this case to find that the writing is a valid letter of credit by disregarding the two nondocumentary conditions? Comment 9 to 5–108. See Dolan, Letters of Credit ¶ 2.05; 3 White & Summers, Prac. ed. § 26–2. If the undertaking is a letter of credit, the disregard of nondocumentary conditions does not mean that the issuer can ignore them. As a matter of the reimbursement agreement between the applicant and the issuer, their honor might be required. Section 5–108(g)'s injunction only means that the issuer's obligations to the beneficiary under the letter of credit do not depend on the satisfaction of nondocumentary conditions. See Comment 9 to 5–108.

3. The cardinal principle of letter of credit law, the "independence principle," is codified in 5–103(d). Section 5–104 recognizes that the day of an exclusively paper-based system of letter of credit transactions has long since passed. Comment 3 notes: "Many banking transactions, including the issuance of many letters of credit, are now conducted mostly by electronic means.... By declining to specify any particular medium in which the letter of credit must be established or communicated, Section 5–104 leaves room for future developments." See the definitions of "document" (5–102(a)(6)) and "record" (5–102(a)(14)).

4. The documents to be presented to the issuer of the letter of credit to obtain payment are usually accompanied by a draft drawn by the beneficiary (5–102(a)(3)) on the issuing bank (5–102(a)(9)) payable "at sight" (that is on presentment) to the order of the beneficiary. A sight draft is merely a demand for payment that may be negotiable in form, thus conferring upon the beneficiary the power to transfer the draft to a third person who may take the rights of a holder in due course. Comment 11 to 5–102.

PROBLEMS

1. Paysaver Credit Union executed the following writing at the request of Wells and Titan Tool, which owed Transparent Products $33,000 on open account:

> Transparent Products Corporation
> Bensenville, IL 60101
>
> RE: Thomas Wells
>
> Gentlemen:
>
> We hereby establish our letter of credit at the request of Thomas Wells of 1315 South 3rd Avenue, Maywood up to the aggregate amount of fifty-thousand dollars ($50,000).

Titan wanted to buy more plastics from Transparent and obtained Paysaver's issuance of the writing directed to Transparent to bolster Titan's creditworthiness. Wells is an employee of Titan who was not indebted to Transparent. It was Wells' $50,000 certificate of deposit with Paysaver that apparently persuaded Paysaver to issue this writing. Transparent ultimately declined to extend more credit to Titan, and when the latter filed in bankruptcy, Transparent demanded payment under Paysaver's "letter of credit" to defray the remaining $33,000 debt. Is the quoted writing sufficiently "definite" to be a letter of credit under 5–102(a)(10)? See Comment 6 to Rev. 5–102. If it is not, is the instrument effective as a guaranty? A guarantor undertakes to pay the debt of another and can raise the principal debtor's defenses; the issuer of a letter of credit is primarily liable and cannot set up defenses of the applicant. The facts are based on Transparent Products Corp. v. Paysaver Credit Union, 864 F.2d 60 (7th Cir.1988). Comment 1 to 5–104 states: ".... a letter of credit will typically specify the amount available, the expiration date, the place where presentation should be made, and the documents that must be presented to entitle a person to honor."

2. (a) What would be the result in Problem 1 if the body of the writing had said: "We hereby establish our letter of credit at the request of Thomas Wells of 1315 South 3rd Avenue, Maywood up to the aggregate amount of fifty-thousand dollars ($50,000) on which Transparent Products Corporation may draw at any time within the next year by presentation of a draft payable at sight for any amount up to the credit limit"? See 5–102(a)(6) ("document"), (10) ("letter of credit") and (12) ("presentation").

(b) What would be the result in Problem 1 if the body of the writing had said: "This is a guarantee, not a letter of credit. At the request of Thomas Wells of 1315 South 3rd Avenue, Maywood, we hereby undertake to pay Transparent Products Corporation up to the aggregate amount of fifty-thousand dollars ($50,000) at any time within the next year upon the following three conditions: (1) Transparent presents a written demand for payment; (2) Transparent not make the presentation before 1 p.m. eastern standard time; and (3) Transparent recites to our representative that the writing represented is a written demand for payment"?

D. Issuer's Duty to Honor or Dishonor

1. The Strict Compliance Standard

A letter of credit is a highly efficient instrument in which banks or others issue suitably definite undertakings to honor complying documentary presentations and the beneficiaries present the prescribed documents and are paid. Indirect evidence of the credit's efficiency is the comparatively low fees issuers charge compared to fees charged for other comparable financial instruments. Central to the credit's cost advantage is the issuer's duty to honor complying documentary presentations. Under 5–108(a), the standard of documentary compliance is strict: "... [A]n issuer shall honor a presentation that, as determined by the standard practice referred to in subsection (e), appears on its face strictly to comply with the terms and conditions of the letter of credit." The domestic law of most legal systems apparently also adopts the strict compliance standard. See Boris Kozolchyk, Commercial Letters of Credit in the Americas 72, 259 (1966). Neither the UCP nor ISP 98 expressly adopts a standard of documentary compliance. UCP 600 art. 14a states merely that "the issuing bank must examine a presentation to determine, on the basis of the documents alone, whether or not the documents appear on their face to constitute a complying presentation." See ISP 98 art. 4.01. Accordingly, in credits governed by the UCP or ISP 98 that otherwise do not address the standard of compliance, domestic law standards continue to apply. The strict compliance standard, therefore, likely will control under applicable law in these cases.

The importance of a documentary discrepancy is irrelevant under the standard. As a Law Lord put it in Equitable Trust Co. of New York v. Dawson Partners Ltd., (1927) 27 L.L.Rep. 49, 52, a leading letter of credit case, "[t]here is no room for documents which are almost the same, or which will do just as well." Of course, facts about the underlying transaction also are irrelevant to the issuer's duty to the beneficiary. If the documents presented correspond to the terms of the credit, the issuer must pay. Otherwise, not. As we will discuss below, an issuer who honors a noncomplying documentary presentation risks not being reimbursed by the applicant.

The strict compliance standard resists an informative and precise statement. Strict compliance does not require literal, letter-for-letter correspondence between the contents of prescribed documents and the credit's terms. Comment 1 to 5–108 states that the standard does not mean "slavish conformity to the terms of the credit." On the other hand, both the strict compliance standard and Comment 1 reject a substantial compliance standard, which judges compliance by an undefined measure of the degree to which documents comply with the credit's terms. Thus, the standard seems to treat documents as complying if they less than literally, but more than substantially, comply with the credit's terms. Courts and commentators have had trouble identifying the permissible range of less-than-perfect compliance. Even courts that do not insist on absolute compliance sometimes disagree on what is strict but less than literal compliance. A rough working notion of compliance under 5–108(a) finds that documents strictly comply when the issuer, using standard practices of issuers, determines that they correspond on their face with the credit's terms. Put another way, the notion is that the documents comply if a reasonable issuer, examining only the documents and the credit and charged with knowledge of the practices of issuers, would decide that a documentary discrepancy is not substantial. For a brief history of applications of the standard, see Peter Ellinger, The Doctrine of Strict Compliance: Its Development and Current Construction, in Lex Mercatoria: Essays on International Commercial Law in Honour of Francis Reynolds 187–198 (Francis D. Rose ed. 2000). The strict compliance standard and related issues are extensively discussed in 2 Barkley Clark & Barbara Clark, The Law of Bank Deposits, Collections and Credit Cards 14.05 (Rev. ed. 2009); Dolan, Letters of Credit, Ch. 6; and 3 James J. White & Robert S. Summers, Uniform Commercial Code, Prac. ed. § 26–6.

In this section we examine perhaps the most litigated issue in the letter of credit law: the duty of the issuer to both the beneficiary and applicant to honor or dishonor a presentation. At issue in most of the litigation is the application of the strict compliance standard in the face of documentary discrepancies. Strict compliance tests documentary presentations by the standard practice of financial institutions that regularly issue credits. Using slightly different terms, 5–108(a) and (e), UCP 600 art. 14d and ISP 98 art. 4.01(b) refer to such practice. Did the court in the following case rely on evidence of the standard practice of financial institutions to determine the appropriate compliance standard?

Carter Petroleum Products, Inc. v. Brotherhood Bank & Trust Co.

Court of Appeals of Kansas, 2004.
97 P.3d 505.

■ GREEN, P.J.

This action involves a bank's wrongful refusal to honor a letter of credit. Carter Petroleum Products, Inc. (Carter) sued Brotherhood Bank & Trust Company (Bank) for its failure to honor a letter of credit. The Bank appeals from a judgment of the trial court granting summary judgment in favor of Carter on the letter of credit. On appeal, the Bank contends that the untimely presentment of the letter of credit and the noncompliance of the submitted documents with the letter of credit relieved the Bank of its duty to honor the letter of credit. We disagree and affirm.

Carter is in the petroleum business and sells fuel products to Highway 210, LLC (Highway 210), which operates a gas station. Highway 210 is also a customer of the Bank. On October 19, 2001, the Bank issued a letter of credit, No.2001-270, in the aggregate amount of $175,000, for the benefit of Carter on the account of Highway 210.

By its terms, the letter of credit authorized Carter to draw on the Bank on the account of Highway 210, to the aggregate amount of $175,000 available by Carter's draft at sight accompanied by the following document:

"STATEMENT SIGNED BY CARTER PETROLEUM PRODUCTS STATING THAT HIGHWAY 210, LLC HAS FAILED TO PAY OUTSTANDING INVOICES IN ACCORDANCE WITH TERMS OF PAYMENT."

The letter of credit further provided that "[e]ach draft must state that it is 'Drawn under Brotherhood Bank & Trust Company's Letter of Credit # 2001-270 dated July 26, 2001.' This credit must accompany the draft(s)." The date of "July 26, 2001" in the aforementioned quotation was a typographical error because the letter of credit at issue was dated October 19, 2001. This letter of credit was a renewal of one of a series of previous letters of credit which were referenced in the lower margin of the letter of credit. The October letter of credit replaced the letter of credit dated July 26, 2001, in the amount of $125,000.

Additionally, the letter of credit stated "that all draft(s) drawn under and in compliance with the terms of this credit will be duly honored on delivery of documents as specified if presented at this office in Shawnee, KS no later than June 26, 2002." The letter of credit was also subject to the Uniform Customs and Practice for Documentary Credits, International Chamber of Commerce Publication No. 500 (1993 Revision) (UCP).

Hal O'Donnell, Carter's credit manager, delivered a draft request to the Bank for payment on June 26, 2002. Carter's draft request contained the following statement:

> "Pursuant to the terms stated in the Letter of Credit # 2001-270 dated October 19, 2001 (copy attached), Carter Petroleum Products, Inc., hereby exercises its option to draw against said Brotherhood Bank and Trust Company's Letter of Credit in the amount of $175,000 due to non-payment of invoices in accordance with terms of payment (copies also attached)."

The account name listed on the draft request was Highway 210 Texaco Travel Plaza, LLC, not Highway 210, LLC, as listed on the letter of credit. In addition, the draft request contained a statement that Highway 210 had failed to pay outstanding invoices and contained a statement that Carter was exercising its rights under the letter of credit. Carter's draft request was accompanied by the letter of credit and copies of Carter's outstanding invoices to Highway 210.

O'Donnell arrived at the Bank at approximately 5 p.m. on June 26, 2002, to present the draft request. When O'Donnell arrived at the Bank, the lobby doors were locked, but after O'Donnell knocked on the door, an employee of the Bank admitted O'Donnell into the lobby. O'Donnell indicated he was there to see Ward Kerby, the assistant vice president of the Bank. Upon meeting Kerby, O'Donnell handed him the draft request accompanied by the letter of credit and unpaid Carter invoices of Highway 210. The draft request was then stamped received on June 26, 2002, and was signed by Kerby with a notation that it was received at 5:05 p.m.

When O'Donnell delivered Carter's draft request to the Bank, the drive-through window was still open for business. O'Donnell maintained that had the employee of the Bank not opened the lobby, he would have delivered the draft request along with the attachments to the drive-through window attendant.

June 26, 2002, was a Wednesday. There is no dispute that the lobby of the Bank closed at 5 p.m. on Wednesdays. Similarly, there is no dispute that the drive-through lane at the Bank was open until 7 p.m. on Wednesdays. Additionally, inside the Bank there were several signs which alerted customers that any transactions occurring after 2 p.m. would be posted on the next business day.

The Bank dishonored Carter's draft request on the letter of credit on June 28, 2002. The Bank's dishonor notice stated two reasons: (1) The draft request was presented to the Bank after regular banking hours of the Bank on the date the letter of credit expired, and (2) the request failed to contain the specific language required by the letter of credit: "Drawn under Brotherhood Bank & Trust Company's Letter of Credit # 2001-270 dated July 26, 2001."

Carter sued the Bank for its failure to honor the letter of credit. Both parties both moved for summary judgment. The trial court ruled in favor of Carter and granted its motion for summary judgment. The Bank requested time to conduct further discovery concerning Highway 210's current debt to Carter. Carter furnished the Bank's counsel with copies of documents including an acknowledgment by Highway 210 that its debt to Carter exceeded the $175,000 face amount of the letter of credit. Later, the trial court entered its judgment in favor of Carter in the amount of $175,000, plus interest, costs, and attorney fees....

On appeal, the Bank relies on two theories. First, the Bank contends that the attempted presentment of the draft request was untimely. The Bank makes two separate arguments. It argues that the presentment was untimely either because it occurred past 2 p.m. and, thus, should be considered on the next day's business or because the presentment occurred past 5 p.m., after the regular banking hours of the Bank. Second, the Bank argues that the draft request did not strictly comply with the terms of the letter of credit.

Letters of credit are governed by Article 5 of the Uniform Commercial Code (UCC), K.S.A. 84-5-101 *et seq.* The pertinent statute is K.S.A. 84-5- 108. It states, in relevant part:

> "(a) Except as otherwise provided in K.S.A. 84-5-109, an issuer shall honor a presentation that, as determined by the standard practice referred to in subsection (e), appears on its face strictly to comply with the terms and conditions of the letter of credit. Except as otherwise provided in K.S.A. 84-5-113 and unless otherwise agreed with the applicant, an issuer shall dishonor a presentation that does not appear so to comply.
>
> ....
>
> "(e) An issuer shall observe standard practice of financial institutions that regularly issue letters of credit. Determination of the issuer's observance of the standard practice is a matter of interpretation for the court. The court shall offer the parties a reasonable opportunity to present evidence of the standard practice."

Strict compliance and standard practice are explained in the Official UCC Comment 1 to K.S.A. 84-5-108. The comment states:

> "The standard of strict compliance governs the issuer's obligation to the beneficiary and to the applicant. By requiring that a 'presentation' appear strictly to comply, the section requires not only that the documents themselves appear on their face strictly to comply, but also that the other terms of the letter of credit such as those dealing with the time and place of presentation are strictly complied with....
>
> ....
>
> "The section adopts strict compliance, rather than the standard that commentators have called 'substantial compliance[.]' ... Strict compliance does not mean slavish conformity to the terms of the letter of credit. For example, standard practice (what issuers do) may recognize certain presentations as complying that an unschooled layman would regard as discrepant....
>
> "Identifying and determining compliance with standard practice are matters of interpretation for the court, not for the jury.... Granting the court authority to make these decisions will also encourage the salutary practice of courts' granting summary judgment in circumstances where there are no significant factual disputes."

The Kansas Comment to K.S.A. 84-5-108, as it pertains to strict compliance and standard practice, mirrors the sentiments presented in the official comment.

Turning first to the issue of timeliness, we notice that there is no dispute that the letter of credit was subject to the UCP. Both parties agree that Article 45 of the UCP provides that "[b]anks are under no obligation to accept presentation of documents outside their banking hours."

Letters of credit are governed by the rules applicable to the construction of ordinary contracts. *Sports, Inc. v. The Sportshop, Inc.*, 14 Kan.App.2d 141, 142, 783 P.2d 1318 (1989). The document must be construed from its four corners and all provisions must be considered together and not in isolation. When an ambiguity appears in a document, the language is construed against the party who prepared the instrument. *Amoco Production Co. v. Wilson, Inc.*, 266 Kan. 1084, 1088, 976 P.2d 941 (1999). In the instant case, the Bank prepared the letter of credit.

The letter of credit first stated that $175,000 was available by Carter's draft at "sight" accompanied by certain documents. It then stated that the letter of credit would be honored "if presented at this office in Shawnee, KS no later than June 26, 2002." The only office referred to in the letter of credit is the Bank's office at 7499 Quivira, Shawnee, Kansas.

O'Donnell arrived at the Bank just after 5 p.m., and the lobby was closed. The drive-through window at the Bank, located at 7499 Quivira, was still open. The letter of credit made no reference that the sight draft must be presented before the lobby closed on June 26, 2002. Similarly, it did not state that the draft needed to be presented before 2 p.m. or before 5 p.m. The letter of credit did not state that the draft needed to be presented to a loan officer, a vice president, or any particular person. The letter of credit simply stated that the money was available by draft at "sight" and would be honored "if presented at this office in Shawnee, KS no later than June 26, 2002."

Under the rules of construction, the presentment of the draft did comply with the requirements set forth for the time and place of presentment. The draft was presented at the Bank on June 26, 2002, at a time when the Bank was still open for business. Although the lobby was closed, by the terms of the letter of credit, anyone working at the Bank was authorized and could have accepted the draft, including the drive-through teller who was open for business.

Although the Bank may have intended to limit the presentment of a sight draft to either before 2 p.m. or 5 p.m. on June 26, 2002, the Bank did not specify in the letter of credit that presentment was to be conducted in this way. This was the source of the confusion; other than the date, no specific time of day was mentioned as to when it must be presented. For example, the letter of credit could have stated that it must be presented "no later than 5 p.m., June

26, 2002, at which date and time the letter of credit expires." The letter of credit failed to contain such language or any similar language to that effect. "Any ambiguity in a letter of credit must be resolved against the party drafting it." *East Girard Sav. Ass'n v. Citizens Nat. Bank & Trust Co. of Baytown,* 593 F.2d 598, 602 (5th Cir.1979). The Bank was the sole drafter of the letter of credit. Accordingly, if the Bank wanted more specificity as to when and where Carter had to make presentment, the Bank could have included such provisions in its letter of credit. The ambiguities or lack of explicitness in the letter of credit stemmed from the Bank's own pen. As a result, the Bank's argument fails.

Next, we must consider whether the draft request strictly complied with the terms of the letter of credit. When do documents comply with the terms of the letter of credit so that a bank is forced to pay the draft is a difficult legal question. The UCC furnishes no easy answer to this question.

The Bank was to make funds available to Carter under its sight draft when it was accompanied by a "statement signed by Carter Petroleum Products stating that Highway 210, LLC has failed to pay outstanding invoices in accordance with terms of payment."

Additionally, the letter of credit required that "[e]ach draft must state that it is 'Drawn under Brotherhood Bank & Trust Company's Letter of Credit # 2001- 270 dated July 26, 2001.' This credit must accompany the draft(s)."

On June 26, 2002, Carter presented to the Bank a sight draft in the amount of $175,000. The account name on the draft was Highway 210 Texaco Travel Plaza, LLC. The draft contained the following statement:

> "Pursuant to the terms stated in the Letter of Credit # 2001-270 dated October 19, 2001 (copy attached), Carter Petroleum Products, Inc., hereby exercises its option to draw against said Brotherhood Bank and Trust Company's Letter of Credit in the amount of $175,000 due to non-payment of invoices in accordance with terms of payment (copies also attached)."

The draft was accompanied by the letter of credit and Carter's outstanding invoices to Highway 210.

On appeal, the Bank contends that the demand was not in strict compliance because (1) the draft request stated the account name as "Highway 210 Texaco Travel Plaza, LLC," not "Highway 210, LLC," and (2) the draft request did not contain the exact language from the letter of credit.

In support of its contentions, the Bank cites *American Coleman v. Intrawest Bank of Southglenn,* 887 F.2d 1382 (10th Cir.1989). The defendant bank in *Coleman* was to make funds available to plaintiff under its sight drafts to be accompanied by the "'[o]riginal Letter of Credit and your signed written statement that Jim Gammon and Associates is in default on the Note and Security Agreement dated November 21, 1984, between American Coleman and Jim Gammon and Associates.'" 887 F.2d at 1383. Plaintiff tendered to the bank a sight draft with the following attached statement: "[T]he American Coleman Company informs you that Jim Gammon and Associates is in default on the Note and Security Agreement dated November 21, 1984, *and the Promissory Note dated November 16, 1984,* between American Coleman and Jim Gammon and Associates." (Emphasis added.) 887 F.2d at 1384.

The bank dishonored the draft. In finding in favor of the bank, the trial judge stated:

> "In the present case, it is clear that [plaintiff's] request for payment presented November 13, 1986 was not in technical or literal compliance with the terms of the letter of credit. [Plaintiff's] reference to two different notes could easily have caused the bank's documents examiner some confusion. Accordingly, because I conclude that the rule of strict compliance, as it is applied in Colorado, requires literal compliance with the terms and requirements set forth in the letter of credit, and there was no such literal compliance in this case." 887 F.2d at 1385.

In affirming the decision of the trial court, the Tenth Circuit Court of Appeals stated:

> "While it is apparent from the cases that minute discrepancies which could not possibly mislead a document examiner are usually disregarded, this does not constitute a retreat from the strict compliance standard applicable in this case inasmuch as the district court found that '[plaintiff's] reference to two different notes could easily have caused the bank's documents examiner some confusion.'" 887 F.2d at 1386.

The *Coleman* court then held that the trial court did not err in applying the strict compliance standard. 887 F.2d at 1386. In rejecting plaintiff's argument that reference to the second note was mere surplusage, the *Coleman* court declared:

> "The apparent existence of two promissory notes supports the district court's finding that Bank could have been misled by [plaintiff's] November 13, 1986, draft. [Plaintiff's] contention that Bank could not have been misled by the draft because Bank drafted the letter of credit is without support in this record." 887 F.2d at 1386-87.

Thus, the *Coleman* court's decision was largely based upon whether the defendant bank could have been misled by the discrepancy in the draft.

In *American Airlines, Inc. v. Federal Deposit Ins.,* 610 F.Supp. 199 (D.Kan.1985), a bank had issued a letter of credit No. G-301, to American Airlines, Inc. (American). Unfortunately, American delivered a sight draft to the bank referring to the letter of credit No. G0391. The cover letter, however, correctly referred to the letter of credit as G-301. The bank refused to pay on the letter of credit. The bank maintained that the typographical error on the sight draft indicated that American had failed to strictly comply with the terms of the letter of credit. As a result, American was not entitled to payment.

In ruling in favor of American, the *American Airlines* court stated:

"In the case at hand, we conclude that there was no possibility that the Bank could have been misled by the documents submitted to it by [plaintiff]. Even under the rule of strict compliance, a beneficiary may establish compliance with the terms of a letter of credit via documents submitted in conjunction with the disputed draft. [Citation omitted.] Here, the documents submitted along with [plaintiff's] draft clearly indicated the correct letter of credit reference number and the proper drawee (the Bank)." 610 F.Supp. at 202.

Because the bank could not have been misled, even with the typographical error, the *American Airlines* court determined that the documents did strictly comply with the terms of the letter of credit. As a result, American was entitled to payment. 610 F.Supp. at 202.

In the instant case, although the draft request submitted by Carter was not in complete conformity with the letter of credit issued by the Bank, it did contain all the necessary information requested by the letter of credit. Moreover, the Bank could not have been misled by the nonconformity.

Although the draft request listed the account name as "Highway 210 Texaco Travel Plaza, LLC," not "Highway 210, LLC" as requested in the letter of credit, the draw request was accompanied by the letter of credit which properly named the account. Obviously, there was no confusion caused by the different name referred to in the draft request because the Bank did not rely on this ground in rejecting the letter of credit. Moreover, the Bank failed to raise this particular argument before the trial court. Issues not raised before the trial court cannot be raised on appeal. *Board of Lincoln County Comm'rs v. Nielander,* 275 Kan. 257, 268, 62 P.3d 247 (2003).

The draft request also contained all of the other pertinent information requested in the letter of credit. The letter of credit accompanied the draft, the draft stated it was drawn under Brotherhood Bank and Trust Company's letter of credit, and the draft contained the correct letter of credit number: # 2001-270. Additionally, as required by the letter of credit, the draft stated that Carter was exercising its option to draw against the Bank due to nonpayment of invoices in accordance with the terms of payment.

The draft request differed from the requirements stated in the letter of credit in that the letter of credit mistakenly referred to the letter of credit dated July 26, 2001. In its draft request, Carter properly referred to the letter of credit dated October 19, 2001. Had Carter referred to the incorrect date as specified in the letter of credit, it would have been likely to cause confusion on the part of the Bank because the October 19, 2001, letter of credit was for a different amount and superceded [sic] the July 26, 2001, letter of credit. As a result, the Bank's argument fails....

Affirmed.

NOTES

1. With respect to the timeliness issue, is the court saying that presentation of the $175,000 letter of credit in *Carter Petroleum* would have been timely if made to the bank's drive-through teller at 6:59 on June 26, 2002? Might the court have found the presentation untimely had Carter Petroleum drafted the letter of credit? What does this case teach banks to do in drafting letters of credit with respect to time and place of presentation?

With respect to the compliance issue, is the court saying that, in the absence of proof of standard practice to the contrary, the test of compliance under 5-108(a) is whether the error in compliance (here "October 19, 2001" in the draft instead of "July 26, 2001") is "misleading"? How does a "misleading" test vary from a substantial compliance standard? See Comment 1 to 5-108. The court says that it takes this standard from *American Coleman,* in which the triggering event for the bank's obligation to pay was presentation to the bank of a sight draft accompanied by a written statement by the beneficiary that the "Note and Security Agreement dated November 21, 1984" were in default. Even though there was no such note, the beneficiary's statement contained the required representation. However, out of an abundance of caution and because of its unease about representing that the customers were in default on a nonexistent note, the beneficiary *added* the fatal words "and the Promissory Note dated November 16, 1984," which described the true note on which the customers were actually in default. The court held that under former Article 5, the documentary presentation was not in compliance owing to the additional language, which could have caused the bank's documents examiner some confusion and misled the bank. Wasn't the potential for confusion just as great in *Carter Petroleum*?

2. Section 5–108(a)'s strict compliance standard is a default rule. As with most aspects of the letter of credit, it can be varied by the reimbursement agreement between the applicant and the issuer when their interests and capabilities favor doing so. See 5–103(c); Comment 2 to 5–103; Comment 1 to 5–108. Reimbursement agreements sometimes are altered accordingly. For example, see ¶ 8 of the Letter of Credit Agreement form reprinted at the end of this chapter. Another example is ISP 98 art. 4.09(c), which requires exact compliance in the documentary presentation when the credit calls for "exact" or "identical" wording in documents. Even when the parties do not opt out of the default rule, 1–102(3) allows the reimbursement agreement to set standards of documentary compliance. Thus, whether a strict compliance standard is preferable to an alternative compliance standard depends on the preferences and capacities of typical parties to a letter of credit. Which rule is likely to minimize the costs of effecting payment under a credit for the typical applicant?

In his article, Letters of Credit, 44 Bus. Law. 1567, 1589 (1989), Albert J. Givray, an experienced bank counsel, contended that the strict compliance rule is essential to the efficient operation of the letter of credit department of banks. The document examiner must lay the draft against the letter of credit in the bank's files. If there is a discrepancy the examiner is ill-equipped to deal with it: she is not a lawyer and may know nothing of the circumstances surrounding the transaction. The examiner's task should merely be to ask: do the presented documents *on their face* meet all the letter of credit's requirements? Do you agree with this view of the examiner's function?

3. Section 5–108(e) states that "[a]n issuer shall observe standard practice of financial institutions that regularly issue letters of credit. Determination of the issuer's observance of the standard practice is a matter of interpretation for the court." Under both 5–108(a) and UCP 600 art. 14d, the degree of documentary compliance is determined by "standard practice." However, although close in meaning, the two provisions are not identical. They differ in the "practice" referred to: 5–108(e)'s "standard practice" is that of financial institutions that regularly issue credits; UCP 600 art. 14d refers to "international standard banking practice." Comment 8 to 5–108 discusses the intended meaning of "standard practice."

The ICC has attempted to describe some of the specific "best practices" for examining documents among international banks. See ICC Document No. 645, International Standard Banking Practice (ISBP) (2003). For example, ISBP para. 69 finds acceptable a description of the quantity of goods in the invoice that varies by +-5% from the quantity required by the credit. ISBP para. 32 requires that each document be presented in at least one original, unless the credit allows otherwise. ISBP para. 28 considers misspellings or typographical errors in a document nondiscrepant as long as they do not alter the meaning of the word or sentence in which they occur.

Section 5–108(e) allocates to the court the determination of the issuer's observance of standard practice. Comment 1 explains, "...it is hoped that there will be more consistency in the outcomes and speedier resolution of disputes if the responsibility for determining the nature and scope of standard practice is granted to the court, not to a jury." Does this unconstitutionally deprive the parties of a jury trial? See Margaret L. Moses, The Uniform Commercial Code Meets the Seventh Amendment: The Demise of Jury Trials Under Article 5?, 72 Ind. L.J. 681 (1997). Compare also §§ 1–205(2), 2–202, 2–302 and 4A–202(c), which use a similar approach. Section 5–108(e)'s treatment of the issue of standard practice as a question of law is controversial. Three states have adopted nonuniform amendments to the subsection eliminating the offending portion of subsection (e). See N.Y. U.C.C. § 5–108(e) (McKinney 2003); Pa. Stat. Ann. 13 § 51–8(e) (2003); Wyo. Stat. Ann. § 34.1–5–108(e) (2003).

4. Does the strict compliance standard enhance the reliability of letters of credit as payment mechanisms? Or does it encourage an issuing bank to find a minor defect in the documents in cases in which the bank doesn't want to pay, such as cases in which the applicant has gone into bankruptcy and reimbursement of the bank's claim against the applicant may be difficult? Observers have consistently found a high frequency of noncomplying documentary presentations, typically exceeding 50%. In an informal survey of selected banks issuing commercial credits, the issuers reported that 73% of the documentary presentations contained discrepancies. See Ronald J. Mann, The Role of Letters of Credit in Payment Transactions, 98 Mich. L. Rev. 2494 (2000). Concerned about the number of discrepant presentations, the ICC has tried to create uniformity in international banking practices for handling documentary discrepancies by publishing a set of "best practices." See Document No. 645, ISBP.

In assessing the wisdom of the strict compliance standard, recognize three points. First, in most commercial credits the beneficiary doesn't care if the documents presented contain discrepancies because the issuer will honor the presentation anyway. Where the market price of goods contracted for in the underlying transaction is stable or rising, the applicant-buyer will want the goods and, therefore, will have the issuer waive its right to insist on conforming documents. Alternatively, under these markets conditions, the issuer may waive the discrepancy at its own risk. Thus, most of the time, obtaining conforming documents isn't cost-justified for beneficiary-sellers. See John F. Dolan, Why High Discrepancy Rates Do Not Discourage L/C Use, 2003 Ann. Survey Letter Credit L. & Prac. 36. The few beneficiaries who are concerned about the prospect of a falling market can opt-out of strict compliance by insisting that the reimbursement agreement provide a more forgiving standard of compliance.

Second, there is a powerful market mechanism controlling strategic rejections of discrepant documents by issuers. Issuers operate in a market in which reputation matters. Because issuance fees are comparatively low, an issuer's profit from operating a credit department depends on generating a high volume of credits. The issuer, therefore, must both obtain repeat business and attract potential applicants and beneficiaries. The number of issuers is relatively small, and information about their handling of credits often can be obtained from other issuers. An issuer may seize on a discrepancy to avoid honor because it fears not being reimbursed or is undercollaterized or wants to avoid involvement in the applicant's bankruptcy or simply wants to placate its applicant. But doing so risks a loss of credit business since potential beneficiaries will insist that credits be issued by issuers that are reliable sources of payment. The presenting beneficiary also is unlikely to do business with the issuer again. Thus, prospect of a loss in reputation often suffices to prevent issuers from strategic rejections even under a strict compliance standard.

Third, less stringent standards of compliance require judicial intervention, and courts are poorly positioned to intervene effectively. For instance, the court in Voest–Alpine Trading USA Corp. v. Bank of China, 167 F.Supp.2d 940 (S.D.Tex. 2000), considers and rejects a standard that finds documentary discrepancies when the deviation in the document risks harming the applicant in the underlying transaction. Application of this standard encourages parties to litigate the issuer's decision to honor or dishonor a documentary presentation. Courts and issuers may be unfamiliar with the facts necessary to make this determination of harm at the time the issuer must decide to honor the presentation. They may know nothing about industry practices bearing on the underlying transaction. Standards less stringent than strict compliance, therefore, undermine the credit's efficient payment function. Professor White reaches the same conclusion and states, without remorse, that "the issuer may examine the documents microscopically and may assert small discrepancies to excuse its duty to pay." 3 James J. White & Robert S. Summers, Uniform Commercial Code, Prac. ed. § 26–5, at 164.

5. Under 5–108(a), an issuing bank must honor a conforming presentation. Must it dishonor a nonconforming presentation? Suppose in the case of questionable documentation like that in *American Coleman*, the bank called the applicant and asked its consent to the bank's payment of the credit. If the applicant gave its consent, (1) may the bank safely pay the credit? (2) May it safely decline to pay the credit? 5–108(a) and Comment 7 to 5–108. (3) Does the issuer have a duty to seek a waiver from the applicant in the case of a nonconforming presentation? Comment 2 to 5–108; see Bombay Indus., Inc. v. Bank of N.Y., 649 N.Y.S.2d 784 (N.Y. App. Div.1996).

6. Matter of Coral Petroleum, Inc., 878 F.2d 830 (5th Cir.1989), presented the issue of whether impossibility excuses strict compliance with a letter of credit. Seller sold Buyer 31,000 barrels of West Texas Intermediate crude oil for $880,400 and required Buyer to obtain a standby letter of credit in a form acceptable to Seller for the price. Bank issued the letter of credit under Buyer's instructions that the credit would be payable upon receipt of certain documents including (1) a statement by Seller that West Texas Intermediate oil had been delivered to Buyer and (2) a copy of the shipper's transfer order showing transfer to Buyer of 31,000 barrels of "WTNM SO or SR." Buyer's instructions were mistaken. West Texas Intermediate crude is a sweet oil (meaning not containing certain undesirable elements found in sour oil), but "WTNM SO or SR" refers to sour oil. Thus, the letter of credit required two documents that were contradictory: a shipper's order showing transfer of sour oil to Buyer and a statement that sweet oil had been delivered to Buyer. After Buyer filed in bankruptcy under Chapter 11, Seller demanded payment under the letter of credit. Bank refused to pay because Seller's demand was accompanied by a shipper's order showing transfer of sweet oil to Buyer. Seller had inspected the letter of credit before accepting it and did not ask that the erroneous description be corrected. Seller argued that the terms of the credit were impossible to perform. Seller could not deliver sweet oil to Buyer and procure a shipper's transfer order showing that sour oil had been delivered. Seller also argued that the letter of credit was ambiguous and the ambiguity should be construed against Bank. The court held that the letter of credit was not ambiguous. The fact that it was impossible for Seller to comply did not excuse compliance by Seller. Bank is not required to know the meaning of technical trade terms used in the letter of credit. If Seller finds the terms of a shipping agreement impossible to fulfill, it should attempt to renegotiate them beforehand or refuse to sign the letter of credit. BM Electronics Corp. v. LaSalle, 59 UC.C. Rep. Serv. 2d 280 (N.D. Ill. 2006). See also In re Sanders–Langsam Tobacco Co., Inc., 224 B.R. 1 (Bankr. E.D.N.Y.1998). Moreover, Seller was negligent in accepting a letter of credit with requirements that could not be met. Accord First State Bank v. Diamond Plastics Corp., 891 P.2d 1262 (Okla.1995).

In Albert J. Givray, Letters of Credit, 44 Bus. Law. 1567, 1587 (1989), it is suggested that issuers add a conspicuous legend stating "Please examine this letter of credit at once. If you feel unable to meet any of its requirements, either singly or together, please contact customer immediately to see if the letter of credit can be amended. Otherwise, you risk losing payment under this letter of credit for failure to comply strictly with its terms as written." Would the suggested legend be likely to help parties in Seller's position in *Coral Petroleum*?

2. NOTICE OF DISCREPANCIES: WAIVER AND PRECLUSION

An issuer can respond to a documentary presentation in either of two ways: by honoring or dishonoring it. Both Article 5 and the UCP describe the steps that an issuer must take when documents are presented under a letter of credit and the consequence of failing to take them. The two sets of rules prescribe the same steps. If the documents appear to comply with the credit's terms, both 5–108(a) and UCP 600 art. 8a. require the issuer to honor the presentation. If the documents are discrepant and the discrepancy allows the issuer to refuse honor, the issuer has a choice: it can waive its right to insist on a complying presentation and honor the discrepant presentation or it can dishonor the presentation. An issuer who waives the discrepancy does so at its own risk, unless the customer has agreed to the waiver.

When the beneficiary of a letter of credit seeks payment, it presents the letter of credit and other documents, which will include a draft demanding payment, usually on sight. When we speak of the issuer honoring a letter of credit, we mean that the issuer pays the draft within the statutory period. If the issuer does not pay the draft within the statutory period, it has dishonored. Wrongful dishonor of the draft may subject the issuer to damages. Issues that have troubled courts and law drafters are (i.) how long an issuer has to examine the documents presented before deciding whether to honor or dishonor and (ii) the extent to which the issuer must disclose the reasons why it dishonored. We raise these issues in the following problem based on Esso Petroleum Canada v. Security Pacific Bank, 710 F.Supp. 275 (D. Or. 1989).

PROBLEM

Esso would not sell aviation fuel to Valley Oil unless the buyer obtained a standby letter of credit for the price of the oil. After Bank issued the requisite letter of credit, Esso shipped the oil. The expiry date for the letter of credit was Monday, November 16. At 1 p.m. on Friday, November 13, Esso presented its draft drawn on Bank pursuant to the letter of credit, which was accompanied by what Esso believed were documents fulfilling the terms and conditions of the letter of credit. At that time, Esso demanded immediate payment, and well it might have done so for within two months Valley Oil filed in bankruptcy. Bank informed Esso at 5:15 on Friday that it would dishonor because of discrepancies in the presentation, but, despite Esso's strong demand for more information, refused to state the discrepancies at that time. It promised a written response stating the discrepancies by 9 a.m. Monday when the officer who had to sign the letter relating the discrepancies would be back in the office. After receiving Bank's written statement of discrepancies on Monday, Esso made another presentation in which it attempted to correct its prior presentation. Bank again dishonored because of uncorrected discrepancies. No payment was made by Bank. Esso sued Bank for the amount of the credit, plus interest and costs. The lower court granted Esso summary judgment on its claims that Bank had wrongfully dishonored its letter of credit and had failed to notify Esso of the discrepancies in a timely manner.

On appeal, what decision should the court reach:

a. If UCC Article 5 governed the letter of credit? See Comment 4 to 5-108.

Section 5-108(b) and (c) state:

(b) An issuer has a reasonable time after presentation, but not beyond the end of the seventh business day of the issuer after the day of its receipt of documents:

(1) to honor,

(2) if the letter of credit provides for honor to be completed more than seven business days after presentation, to accept a draft or incur a deferred obligation, or

(3) to give notice to the presenter of discrepancies in the presentation.

(c) Except as otherwise provided in subsection (d), an issuer is precluded from asserting as a basis for dishonor any discrepancy if timely notice is not given, or any discrepancy not stated in the notice if timely notice is given.

Comment 2 to 5-108 states that the 7-day period is not a safe harbor: the issuer must act within a reasonable time but that period may not exceed seven days. Thus the time within which the issuer must give notice is the lesser of a reasonable time or seven business days.

b. If UCP 600 governed the letter of credit?

Art. 14b. states: [An] issuing bank shall…have a maximum of five banking days following the day of presentation to determine if a presentation is complying. This period is not curtailed or otherwise affected by the occurrence on or after the date of presentation or any expiry date or last day for presentation.

Art. 16 states:

a. When…the issuing bank determines that a presentation does not comply, it may refuse to honour….

b. When an issuing bank determines that a presentation does not comply, it may in its sole judgment approach the applicant for a waiver of the discrepancies. This does not, however, extend the period mentioned in sub-article 14b.

c. When…the issuing bank decides to refuse to honour…, it must give a single notice to that effect to the presenter.

   The notice must state:

   i. that the bank is refusing to honour…; and

   ii. each discrepancy in respect of which the bank refuses to honour…; and

   iii. a) that the bank is holding the documents until it receives a waiver from the applicant and agrees to accept it, or receives further instructions from the presenter prior to agreeing to accept a waiver; or

   b) that the issuing bank is holding the documents until it receives a waiver from the applicant and agrees to accept it, or receives further instructions from the presenter prior to agreeing to accept a waiver; or

   c) that the bank is returning the documents; or

   d) that the bank is acting in accordance with instructions previously received from the presenter.

d. The notice required in sub-article 16c must be given by telecommunication or, if that is not possible, by other expeditious means no later than the close of the fifth banking day following the day of presentation.

NOTE

How would the following case be decided under 5–108? See Comments 2 and 4 to 5–108. In Rhode Island Hospital Trust Nat'l Bank v. Eastern General Contractors, Inc., 674 A.2d 1227 (R.I. 1996), a UCP case, the beneficiary made presentation on Thursday, September 26, 1985. On Friday, September 27, the bank did not open for business owing to Hurricane Gloria. Monday, September 30 was the expiry date. On Tuesday, October 1, the bank notified the beneficiary of certain discrepancies and stated that it would hold the documents for beneficiary's disposal. The court concluded that the trial court erred in directing a verdict for the bank. Expert testimony was to the effect that the bank did not act within a reasonable time; if the date of receipt of the presentation to the issuing bank is close to the expiry date of the credit, common banking procedure is to act expeditiously, presumably so that any discrepancy can be cured before expiration of the credit. Article 13b of UCP 500, the version of the UCP relied on by the *Rhode Island Hospital* court, gave the issuer a "reasonable time" in which to examine documents, not to exceed seven banking days following the day they are presented. Article 14b of UCP 600 gives the issuer "a maximum" of five banking days following that day in which to do so. It does not contain a reference to a "reasonable time" in which a documentary examination is to occur within the five day period. How would the *Rhode Island Hospital* be decided under article 14b of UCP 600?

Waiver is an intentional relinquishment of a known legal right and applies to Article 5 via 1–103(a), as a supplementing principle of extra-UCC common law. A waiver can be oral, unless the reimbursement agreement requires otherwise. Paragraph 11 of the Letter of Credit Agreement Form at the end of this chapter requires that waivers be in writing. UCP 600 art. 16b allows the issuer to approach the applicant for a waiver. The UCP is silent as to the issuer's waiver against the beneficiary. A few courts have divided over whether common law doctrines such as waiver apply to credits subject to the UCP. Compare Banco General Runinahui, S.A. v. Citibank Int'l, 97 F.3d 480 (11th Cir.1996), with Alaska Textile Co., Inc. v. Chase Manhatten Bank, N.A., 982 F.2d 813 (2d Cir.1992).

In deciding whether to waive a documentary discrepancy, prudent issuers usually approach their applicants to obtain their consent. This is because the applicant's consent modifies the reimbursement agreement to allow for the issuer's reimbursement if it honors the presentation. Sometimes issuers waive discrepancies at their own risk, without the consent of their applicants. In all cases, waiver is a right of the issuer that it can exercise within its discretion. The issuer has no obligation to waive a discrepancy, even if the applicant consents to the waiver. See Suntex Industrial Corp., Ltd. v. The CIT Group/BBC, Inc., 2001 U.S. Dist. LEXIS 17656 (D. Del. 2001). It need not even approach the applicant to elicit the applicant's consent. See Note 6 above. ISP 98 arts. 5.05 and 5.06(a) are to the same effect. Comment 7 to 5–108 construes waiver narrowly, so that waiver of one or more presentations does not waive subsequent discrepant presentations.

The issuer's second alternative is to dishonor a discrepant documentary presentation. Article 5 follows the UCP's approach both to the sufficiency of notice that must be given to the presenter and the effect of the failure to give timely notice and sufficient notice of dishonor. Section 5–108(b) requires that, in the case of dishonor, the issuer must communicate both the fact and grounds of dishonor to the presenter. See Comment 2 to 5–108 (second paragraph); cf. UCP 600 art. 16d. i, and ii. Thus, 5–108(b) contemplates two possibilities: either the issuer fails to make a timely decision to honor or dishonor, or the issuer's timely decision fails to give timely notice of the grounds for dishonor. In both cases, 5–108(c) precludes the issuer from relying as a ground for dishonor on discrepancies it has delayed communicating to the presenter within 5–108(b)'s prescribed time limit.

Section 5–108(b)'s preclusion rule is not a rule concerning waiver or estoppel. Courts tend to mix waiver and estoppel together, and sometimes treat both as preclusion. See, e.g., *American Coleman,* 887 F.2d at 1387 ("waiver-estoppel rule"); *Banco General Runinahui, S.A.*, 97 F.3d at 485 n.11 (preclusion as "strict estoppel"). The notions are distinct. Preclusion isn't waiver because it doesn't require the issuer to intentionally relinquish its right to a complying presentation. Section 5–108(b)'s preclusion rule applies when the issuer simply fails to give timely notice of the grounds for dishonor within the prescribed period. Preclusion also isn't estoppel because estoppel requires detrimental reliance and 5–108(b)'s rule does not require reliance. It, therefore, requires no showing that the presenter has been harmed by the issuer's failure to give timely notice of the fact or grounds of dishonor. Unlike waiver and estoppel, Article 5's preclusion rules avoid the proof costs associated with litigating over relinquishment of a right to a complying presentation (waiver) or detrimental reliance on a failure to give timely notice of a discrepancy (estoppel). The UCP's rules are similar.

PROBLEMS

1. Over the period of a year, Beneficiary presented three drafts for payment to Issuer. Each presentation contained the same discrepancy. The first two times Issuer paid the draft without objection after receiving permission of the Applicant to pay despite the nonconformity. The third time Applicant refused to consent to payment and Issuer dishonored the draft on the ground that the presentation was nonconforming. Has Issuer wrongfully dishonored? Comment 7 to 5–108. 3 James J. White and Robert S. Summers, Uniform Commercial Code, § 26–9(a) (4th Prac.ed. 1995).

2. Bank issued a letter of credit subject to UCP 600. The credit recited that it was also "subject to provisions of Article 5 of the UCC to the extent that they are consistent with UCP 600." Among the documents required was a commercial invoice covering "toys." Beneficiary presented to Bank documents, including a commercial invoice covering "construction equipment," on day 1. Bank delayed examining the documents until day 4. On that date, it properly notified Beneficiary of the documentary discrepany and stated that it was refusing to honor Beneficiary's presentation. Assume that issuing banks in these circumstances always examine documents the day after they are presented. May Bank nonetheless rely on the documentary discrepancy to dishonor Beneficiary's presentation? If not, why?

3. Bank issued a letter of credit subject to UCP 600 and with an expiration date of January 9. The credit obligated Bank to pay Beneficiary $100,000 (U.S.) upon Beneficiary's presentation of three documents: a commercial invoice, a bill of lading and a certificate of inspection. The terms of the credit required the documents to cover "100 pounds of widgets," and invoice and certificate of inspection to state that the widgets were "quality 100%." On January 1, Beneficiary presented all three documents to Bank. The commercial invoice described the goods as "105 pounds of widgets of 95% quality." The bill of lading described the goods as "105 pounds of widgit ... all received on board for shipment." The certificate of origin described them as "105 pounds of WGS," "WGS" being an abbreviation for widgets commonly used in the widget trade.

Bank notified Beneficiary on January 2 to the effect that it "finds discrepancies in the invoice presented by you going to the quantity and quality of widgets described." On January 5, it notified Beneficiary that it "rejects the bill of lading based on the failure of the description of the goods in the bill ('105 pounds of widgit') to conform to the terms of the credit." Bank gave notice to Beneficiary on January 6 that it "rejects the certificate of inspection because the description of goods ('WGS') fail to conform to the terms of the credit." Each notice was accompanied by Bank's statement that it was returning the documents to Beneficiary, and Bank did so. This did Beneficiary no good because Beneficiary was unable to make another presentation by January 9, the date on which the credit expired. Bank refused to pay Beneficiary $100,000.

(1) Did Beneficiary's documentary presentation comply with the terms of the credit? Consult ISBP paras. 25 and 65 reproduced below. (2) If not, is Bank entitled to dishonor Beneficiary's noncomplying documentary presentation? See UCP 600 arts. 16d.i, ii, f.

ICC, International Standard Banking Practices (ISBP) (2007)

25. Misspellings or typing errors that do not affect the meaning of a word or the sentence in which it occurs, do not make a document discrepant....

However, a description as "model 123" instead of "model 321" would not be regarded as a typing error and would constitute a discrepancy.

65. The quantity of the goods required in the credit may vary within a tolerance of +/–5%. This does not apply if the a credit stipulates that the quantity must not be exceeded or reduced, or if a credit stipulates the quantity in terms of a stated number of packing units or individual items."

3. ISSUER'S RIGHT TO REIMBURSEMENT AND OTHER REMEDIES

a. REIMBURSEMENT

Section 5–108(i) arms the issuer with a statutory right of reimbursement against the applicant. Credits usually also provide for reimbursement, as in the opening paragraph of the Letter of Credit Agreement at the end of this chapter.

The credit risk that an issuer takes with respect to payment of a letter of credit depends on whether the transaction involves a commercial or a standby letter of credit. Commercial letters of credit are payment mechanisms and are meant to be paid in every case, usually upon presentation of the seller-beneficiary's bill of lading covering the goods sold to the buyer-applicant. When the issuer has paid, it receives possession of the bill of lading which the applicant must obtain from the issuer in order to receive the goods from the carrier that issued the bill of lading. 5–108(i)(2). The issuer can secure its claim for reimbursement by holding the bill of lading until the applicant either pays or arranges for credit.

A standby letter of credit functions as a guaranty and is usually meant to be paid only in case of the applicant's failure to perform the underlying contract. When the issuer pays a standby letter of credit, it receives no bill of lading or similar document that can be used to induce the applicant to pay. Functionally, a letter of credit is a conditional loan made to the applicant by the issuer, and issuing banks treat it as such. Since it is a loan that will usually not have to be funded unless the applicant is in financial difficulty, as when the applicant is in bankruptcy, the statutory reimbursement right under 5–108(i) is invariably supplemented with an express reimbursement agreement between the issuer and applicant containing the usual terms of commercial loans with respect to security, interest rates, set-off, and the like. See ¶¶ 4, 5 and 9 of the Letter of Credit Agreement form reprinted at the end of this chapter.

As we have said before, if obligees are able to obtain standby letters of credit from their obligors, they are in a position far superior to that of secured parties under Article 9. Upon default by their obligor, they can go to the issuing bank and obtain prompt payment of the obligation. They do not need to engage in the expensive and time-consuming exercise of collecting the debt by repossessing and foreclosing on collateral, with all the attendant problems that we raised in the preceding chapters of this book, problems that are exacerbated by the obligor's bankruptcy. If no rational obligee would take a security interest in preference to a standby letter of credit, does this mean the death of security interests? Not at all; it merely changes the identity of the secured party from the obligee to the bank issuing the letter of credit. Unless the applicant is a customer who could borrow money on unsecured credit, banks will usually not issue standby letters of credit without receiving a security interest in the applicant's property. Efficiencies flowing from this tripartite arrangement have contributed to the great popularity of standby letters of credit. The creditworthiness of the obligor is determined by the bank, a professional credit grantor, rather than by the obligee who may be a seller of goods, a centerfielder, or others who are not in the business of credit granting. In this respect, the efficiency of the standby letter of credit resembles that present in the consumer bank credit card transaction. Retail stores, hotels, restaurants and others who sell goods and services can rely on a credit card issued by a bank that will guarantee payment on transactions made pursuant to the card; they don't need to maintain credit departments making costly credit evaluations of their customers. Banks will make the determination of the consumer's creditworthiness in deciding whether to issue the credit card.

b. STANDARD OF COMPLIANCE

Under 5–108(i), an issuer is entitled to reimbursement from the applicant only if it "has honored a presentation as permitted or required by this article." Under 5–108(a), an issuer must dishonor a presentation that does not strictly comply with the terms of the letter of credit. Comment 1 to 5–108 says that "[t]he standard of strict compliance governs the issuer's obligation to the beneficiary and to the applicant." The view adopted by Article 5 that an issuing bank that pays on a presentation that does not strictly comply with the terms of the letter of credit cannot receive reimbursement from the applicant was rejected by some cases under the old law which applied a "bifurcated" standard of compliance. This approach applied a strict compliance standard for the issuer's liability to the beneficiary for wrongful dishonor but a substantial compliance standard for the issuer's liability to the applicant for wrongful honor. The bifurcation view was thought to be justified by an appreciation of the difficulty an issuing bank experiences in a case in which the applicant is demanding that the bank dishonor while the beneficiary is threatening suit if the bank does not pay.

In rejecting the bifurcated approach, Article 5 takes the realistic position that institutions issuing letters of credit, usually commercial banks, are sophisticated parties that are eminently capable of looking out for themselves. Section 5–108(a) recognizes that an issuing bank can safely pay on a noncomplying presentation if the applicant will waive the discrepancy and consent to the payment. But what if the bank is uncertain about whether there is a discrepancy in the presentation and the applicant will not waive the potential discrepancy? Section 5–103(c) allows the parties to contract around 5–108(a)'s standard of compliance as it applies to the issuer's right to reimbursement. Prudent issuers will safeguard themselves against liability for wrongful payment by including exculpatory clauses in the reimbursement agreement designed to allow them to obtain reimbursement, even when they honor a credit in which a discrepant presentation has been made. See ¶ 8 of the Letter of Credit Agreement form reprinted at the end of this chapter. Provisions imposing a standard of only substantial compliance on issuing banks with respect to their duty to dishonor are clearly enforceable. Comment 2 to 5–103. However, under the last sentence of 5–103(c), terms "generally excusing liability or generally limiting remedies for failure to perform obligations" are unenforceable.

c. SUBROGATION, RESTITUTION AND BREACH OF WARRANTY

As we have seen, the prudent issuer of a standby letter of credit makes sure that if it has to pay the credit the applicant will be able to reimburse it. This is usually done by requiring that the applicant give security for its reimbursement obligation. However, if the security proves worthless and the applicant is insolvent, the issuer is unable to obtain reimbursement from the applicant. In these cases, the issuer will explore alternative remedies. If the applicant has given the beneficiary security, the issuer may seek to be subrogated to the beneficiary's rights to the security. If the issuer can claim to have paid because of fraud or mistake, it may demand restitution from the beneficiary, or the issuer may claim that the beneficiary has breached its presentation warranties to the issuer. In the materials below we will examine the availability of these remedies.

Whether an issuer, having paid the beneficiary of a letter of credit, is entitled to the equitable remedy of subrogation has been much litigated. For reasons discussed in *Ochoco Lumber Co.* below, a majority of courts have denied issuers the right to subrogation. Section 5–117(a) recognizes subrogation for issuers: "An issuer that honors a beneficiary's presentation is subrogated to the rights of the beneficiary to the same extent as if the issuer were a secondary obligor of the underlying obligation owed to the beneficiary and of the applicant to the same extent as if the issuer were the secondary obligor of the underlying obligation owed to the applicant." The subsection does not itself give an issuer a right of subrogation. It instead gives the issuer whatever rights a secondary obligor would have in the same circumstances ("as if the issuer were a secondary obligor..."). Thus, 5–117(a) removes a doctrinal barrier based on the issuer's "primary obligation" to granting issuers rights of subrogation. *Ochoco Lumber Co.*, below, adopts Judge Becker's dissenting opinion in Tudor Development Group, Inc. v. United States Fidelity & Guaranty Co., 968 F.2d 357 (3d Cir.1992). Professor White, the Reporter of Revised Article 5, states in 3 James J. White & Robert S. Summers, Uniform Commercial Code, Prac. ed. § 26–15, at 212–14 (4th Prac. ed. 1995), that Judge Becker's dissenting opinion in *Tudor* is the correct analysis of the problem, and Comment 1 to 5–117 indorses the Becker position. *Ochoco Lumber Co.* shares this understanding of 5–117(a).

Ochoco Lumber Co. v. Fibrex & Shipping Co., Inc.

Court of Appeals of Oregon, 2000.
994 P.2d 793.

■ KISTLER, J.

The trial court ruled that neither the applicant nor the issuer on a standby letter of credit can be subrogated to the beneficiary's claims. The court accordingly granted defendants' motion to dismiss plaintiff's equitable subrogation claims, denied plaintiff leave to replead, and entered judgment on those claims. We reverse and remand.

In 1993, defendant Fibrex & Shipping Co., Inc., entered into an agreement to purchase timber in Montana. To fund the purchase, Fibrex borrowed $3,900,000 from West One Idaho Bank.[1] West One imposed two conditions on the loan. First, it required that Fibrex's sole shareholder, Akira Saheki, and his wife, Saeko Saheki, personally guarantee the loan. Second, "[a]s security for repayment of [Fibrex's] note," West One required a standby letter of credit "in an amount no less than the amount of the principal balance of th[e] note."

Fibrex obtained the letter of credit by entering into an agreement with plaintiff Ochoco Lumber Company. Fibrex agreed to sell and Ochoco agreed to buy up to six and one-half million board feet of harvested ponderosa pine logs. As part of their agreement, Ochoco provided for an irrevocable standby letter of credit for $3,900,000, which First Interstate Bank issued for the benefit of West One. The letter of credit both served as security for Ochoco's performance under its agreement with Fibrex and also "was used by Fibrex to fulfill its obligations under [its loan from West One]."[2]

In 1994 and 1995, Fibrex failed to fulfill its obligations under its agreement with Ochoco. In May 1995, Ochoco and Fibrex renegotiated their agreement. In August 1995, Fibrex, Ochoco, and the persons who owned the timber

---

[1] West One Idaho Bank has since been acquired by U.S. Bank.

[2] Fibrex agreed to use the funds it received from Ochoco's log purchases to reduce the balance on its loan with West One and thus reduce Ochoco's exposure on the letter of credit.

entered into an amended timber purchase agreement. In September 1996, Fibrex's loan from West One came due. Fibrex failed to pay the loan, and West One drew over two million dollars on First Interstate's letter of credit. Ochoco reimbursed First Interstate Bank in full.[3] Ochoco then demanded repayment from Fibrex. After Fibrex refused to repay Ochoco, Ochoco notified West One that it was subrogated to West One's rights against both Fibrex and the Sahekis, the guarantors of Fibrex's loan.

When West One refused to acknowledge Ochoco's equitable subrogation rights, Ochoco brought an action alleging, among other things, four claims for relief that were based on equitable subrogation. Ochoco sought a declaration that it is subrogated to West One's rights, it sued Fibrex on the note that Fibrex had given West One, and it sued the Sahekis on their guarantee. Ochoco also sought injunctive relief against Fibrex and the Sahekis.[4] Defendants moved to dismiss Ochoco's claims for relief that were based on equitable subrogation. Relying on *Tudor Dev. Group, Inc. v. U.S. Fid. & Guar. Co.,* 968 F.2d 357 (3d Cir.1992), and *Shokai v. U.S. National Bank of Oregon,* 126 F.3d 1135 (9th Cir.1997), defendants argued that equitable subrogation is not available to the parties on a standby letter of credit. The trial court agreed. It dismissed Ochoco's subrogation claims without leave to replead and entered judgment on those claims pursuant to ORCP 67 B.

On appeal, defendants advance two arguments. They argue initially that equitable subrogation is available only to persons who are secondarily liable for a debt. They reason that the issuer's contractual obligation to pay on a standby letter of credit[5] [previous fn is in wrong place] means that the issuer is

---

[3] The complaint does not allege specifically that Ochoco reimbursed First Interstate. Ochoco acknowledged this oversight at the Rule 21 hearing and stated that it would replead to include that allegation. The trial court, however, dismissed Ochoco's subrogation claims without leave to replead, thereby preventing Ochoco from alleging that it had reimbursed First Interstate pursuant to its obligations under the letter of credit. Fibrex neither objected to Ochoco's request to replead at the Rule 21 hearing nor disputes Ochoco's contention on appeal that it reimbursed First Interstate in full. We accordingly assume that Ochoco has paid First Interstate the amount it paid West One.

[4] Ochoco alleged other claims for relief, but only its first, second, and third claims for relief and the first count of its thirteenth claim for relief are based on equitable subrogation and are at issue here.

[5] A letter of credit "is an engagement by an issuer, usually a bank, made at the request of the [applicant] for a fee, to honor a beneficiary's drafts or other demands for payment upon satisfaction of the conditions set forth in the letter of credit." *Tudor Dev. Group, Inc.,* 968 F.2d at 360; *accord* Peter R. Jarvis, *Standby Letters of Credit—Issuers' Subrogation and Assignment Rights,* 9 UCC LJ 356, 356–60 (1977). There are two major types of letters of credit transactions. A commercial letter of credit is typically used when the seller is unfamiliar or uncertain about the buyer's credit history. *Id.* The beneficiary of a commercial letter of credit (usually the seller) may draw upon the letter by showing that it has performed and is entitled to the funds. *Id.* A standby letter of credit, on the other hand, typically requires the production of documents showing that the applicant has defaulted on its obligation to the beneficiary, which triggers the beneficiary's right to draw on the letter. *Id.*

primarily, not secondarily, liable. They argue alternatively that, in any event, the particular facts of this transaction make subrogation inappropriate. Ochoco responds that a standby letter of credit is no different from a surety bond or a guarantee in that the issuer's obligation to pay on a standby letter of credit does not arise until there is a default. It follows, Ochoco reasons, that equitable subrogation should be equally available to the parties to a standby letter of credit; the transactions are in substance no different.

We begin with the statutes that govern letters of credit. When First Interstate issued the letter of credit in this case, the Oregon statutes did not address whether equitable subrogation was available on a standby letter of credit. Nothing should be inferred from that omission, however. ORS 75.1020(3) (1991) specifically recognized that "ORS 75.1010 to 75.1170 deal with some but not all the rules and concepts of letters of credit as such rules or concepts have developed * * * or may hereafter develop." It added: "The fact that ORS 75.1010 to 75.1170 state a rule does not by itself require, imply or negate application of the same or a converse rule to a situation not provided for...by ORS 75.1010 to 75.1170." ORS 75.1020(3) (1991). The statute thus explicitly left to judicial development those rules that were not codified in ORS chapter 75.

In 1997, the legislature authorized issuers of and applicants for letters of credit to seek equitable subrogation but made the new statute applicable to letters of credit issued on or after January 1, 1998.[6] Or. Laws 1997, ch. 150, §§ 20, 27 & 29. The Ninth Circuit has concluded that because Oregon's 1997 law applies prospectively, the Oregon legislature must have believed that prior law did not allow subrogation. *See Shokai,* 126 F.3d at 1136. Defendants find the Ninth Circuit's reasoning "instructive" and urge us to follow it. We decline to do so.

The 1997 Legislature amended many of the provisions in ORS chapter 75 governing letters of credit. *See* Or. Laws 1997, ch. 150, §§ 3–20. The fact that the legislature provided that all those amendments would apply prospectively hardly reflects a judgment on the existing state of the law with respect to each or any of them. *See* Or. Laws 1997, ch. 150, § 27. The inference the Ninth

---

[6] Oregon Laws 1997, chapter 150, section 20, provides:

"(1) An issuer that honors a beneficiary's presentation is subrogated to the rights of the beneficiary to the same extent as if the issuer were a secondary obligor of the underlying obligation owed to the beneficiary and of the applicant to the same extent as if the issuer were the secondary obligor of the underlying obligation owed to the applicant.

"(2) An applicant that reimburses an issuer is subrogated to the rights of the issuer against any beneficiary, presenter or nominated person to the same extent as if the applicant were the secondary obligor of the obligations owed to the issuer and has the rights of subrogation of the issuer to the rights of the beneficiary stated in subsection (1) of this section."

By its terms, this law applies only to letters of credit issued on or after January 1, 1998. Or. Laws 1997, ch. 150, §§ 27 and 29.

Circuit drew is, at best, a weak one and is at odds with the long-standing principle that one legislature's view on an earlier state of the law is entitled to little or no weight. *Cf. DeFazio v. WPPSS,* 296 Or. 550, 561, 679 P.2d 1316 (1984) ("[t]he views legislators have of existing law may shed light on a new enactment, but it is of no weight in interpreting a law enacted by their predecessors"). Even if, however, the inference that defendants urge were textually permissible, it is not required and the legislative history points in the opposite direction. The Oregon Bankers' Association, which sponsored the 1997 legislation, told the legislature that the courts had not agreed on the availability of equitable subrogation, giving rise to confusion in the law. Testimony, Senate Committee on Business, Law and Government, SB 246, January 22, 1997, Ex H (statement of Frank E. Brawner). Although the legislature sought to clarify the law for letters of credit issued after the effective date of the act, the text, context, and the legislative history of the 1997 act do not suggest that the legislature made any judgment about the parties' right to equitable subrogation for letters of credit issued before the act's effective date. We are accordingly left to resolve that issue under common-law principles.

The court has explained that subrogation is "'the substitution of another person in place of the creditor to whose rights he succeeds in relation to the debt, and gives to the substitute all of the rights, priorities, remedies, liens and securities of the party for whom he is substituted.' " *Maine Bonding v. Centennial Ins. Co.,* 298 Or. 514, 521, 693 P.2d 1296 (1985) (quoting *United States F. & G. Co. v. Bramwell,* 108 Or. 261, 277, 217 P. 332 (1923)). The purpose of subrogation is to prevent unjust enrichment. *See Barnes v. Eastern & Western Lbr. Co.,* 205 Or. 553, 596, 287 P.2d 929 (1955). Simply stated, subrogation is an equitable device used "'to compel ultimate discharge of a debt by [the person] who in equity and good conscience ought to pay it....' " *Maine Bonding,* 298 Or. at 521, 693 P.2d 1296 (quoting *United States F. & G. Co.,* 108 Or. at 277, 217 P. 332).

As a general rule, the courts have required that the party seeking subrogation must have paid a debt for which it was secondarily liable. *Wasco Co. v. New England E. Ins. Co.,* 88 Or. 465, 469–71, 172 P. 126 (1918); *accord Tudor Dev. Group, Inc.,* 968 F.2d at 361. The party must not have acted as a volunteer but must have paid to protect its own interests. *Id.* Finally, equitable subrogation "will not be enforced where it will work injustice to those having equal equities." *Id.* The Oregon courts have not specifically addressed how these requirements apply to standby letters of credit.[7] A handful of courts and commentators have done so, although their decisions

[7] In *Marshall-Wells Co. v. Tenney,* 118 Or. 373, 244 P. 84 (1926), the court used the terms letter of credit and guarantee interchangeably, but its reasoning reveals that it was considering the parties' rights under a guarantee, not a letter of credit. *See* Jarvis, 9 UCC LJ at 375.

have not been uniform. *See Tudor Dev. Group, Inc.*, 968 F.2d at 361–62 (collecting cases).

The majority and minority views are perhaps best illustrated by the two opinions in *Tudor Dev. Group, Inc.* The majority in *Tudor* focused on whether the issuer is primarily or secondarily liable for the debt. 968 F.2d at 362. It reasoned, as a majority of courts have, that the issuer is primarily liable because a letter of credit imposes an independent obligation on the issuer to pay. *Id.* The majority reasoned that the issuer is "satisfying its own absolute and primary obligation to make payment rather than satisfying an obligation of its customer." *Id.* The majority recognized that the issuer's obligation on a standby letter of credit is secondary in the sense that it does not arise until the applicant has defaulted, but it still declined to view an issuer as comparable to a guarantor.

The dissent in *Tudor* responded that the majority's reasoning proved too much. A surety also has a contractual obligation to pay, but that fact neither means that the surety is primarily liable nor prevents it from seeking equitable subrogation. In the dissent's view, the fact that there is a contractual obligation to pay provides no basis for saying that the issuer of a standby letter of credit is not secondarily liable. Rather, like a surety or guarantor, the issuer of a standby letter of credit only has an obligation to pay if and when there is a default. In this case, for example, the note between West One and Fibrex required Fibrex to obtain a letter of credit as "security for repayment of [Fibrex's] note."

The relevant question, in the dissent's view, was whether allowing equitable subrogation would defeat the independence principle that distinguishes letters of credit from guarantees and suretyships. Guarantors generally may assert defenses available to the party whose obligation is guaranteed. *Tudor Dev. Group, Inc.*, 968 F.2d at 366. Under the independence principle, however, the issuer of a standby letter of credit may not assert those defenses. Rather, it must pay if the documents presented by the beneficiary satisfy the conditions set out in the letter of credit. *Id.*

In the dissent's view, once the issuer has honored the letter of credit, the purpose of the independence principle—ensuring prompt payment on the letter of credit according to its terms—has been satisfied. *Id.* at 368. The dissent reasoned that denying equitable subrogation after the issuer had paid the letter of credit would not advance the purposes of the one principle that distinguishes letters of credit from guarantees. *Id.* Rather, in the dissent's view, denying subrogation after payment amounts to "[i]nsistence on...pointless formalism." *Id.* Although the dissent's view has only gained minority support among the courts, it has been generally supported by the commentators. *See* James J. White & Robert S. Summers, *Uniform Commercial Code* § 26–15 (4th ed. 1995); Peter R. Jarvis, *Standby Letters of Credit, Issuers' Subrogation and Assignment Rights,* 10 UCC L.J. 38 (1977); *cf.* Task

Force on the Study of U.C.C. Article 5, *An Examination of U.C.C. Article 5 (Letters of Credit)* 21 (Sept. 29, 1989), *reprinted in* 45 Bus.L. 1527 (1990).

Faced with these two positions, we conclude that the minority view is more persuasive. It recognizes that First Interstate was a *de facto* surety for Fibrex's obligations and is thus consistent with the long-standing principle in Oregon law that equity looks to the substance of the transaction rather than its form. *General Electric Co. v. Wahle,* 207 Or. 302, 317, 296 P.2d 635 (1956); *Decker v. Berean Baptist Church,* 51 Or.App. 191, 199, 624 P.2d 1094 (1981).[8] It is also consistent with the general practice on standby letters of credit—that the issuer's obligation to pay on the letter of credit only arises if there is a default. *See* Jarvis, 9 UCC LJ at 368–71 (comparing standby letters of credit and guarantees). More importantly, it is consistent with our legislature's recognition that having paid the beneficiary, the issuer (and the applicant if it has reimbursed the issuer) should be able to step into the beneficiary's shoes and assert its rights. Accordingly, we hold that equitable subrogation is available to both the issuer and the applicant on a standby letter of credit....

Reversed and remanded.

NOTE

The most common case in which the subrogation issue is litigated concerns the applicability of Bankruptcy Code 509(a), which states: "Except as provided in subsection (b) or (c) of this section, an entity that is *liable with the debtor* on, or that has secured, a claim of a creditor against the debtor, and that pays such claim, is subrogated to the rights of such creditor to the extent of such payment" (emphasis added). In In re Slamans, 69 F.3d 468 (10th Cir.1995), the court held that the independence principle under which an issuer is not "liable with the debtor" precluded subrogating an issuer to the beneficiary's right to setoff against funds of the applicant that the beneficiary had collected on behalf of the applicant. Accord In re Hamada, 291 F.3d 645 (9th Cir.2002). Although 5–117 was not yet law in the jurisdiction in question, the court was aware of it and said: "Although the revised Article Five provides an issuer with the remedy of subrogation, the UCC does not determine the availability of subrogation in a bankruptcy proceeding. Rather, 509 of the Bankruptcy Code governs an entity's eligibility for subrogation in a bankruptcy proceeding. Thus, the effect of the Rev. 5–117 on 509 subrogation is

---

[8] Defendants argue that the court's reasoning in *Newell v. Taylor,* 212 Or. 522, 532–33, 321 P.2d 294 (1958), supports a contrary position, but the court's reasoning in that case cannot be divorced from the statutory rights established by the workers' compensation laws. As the court explained, the Workers' Compensation Commission had a statutory obligation to pay the injured worker, regardless of whether the injury was due to a third party's negligence. *Id.* at 532, 321 P.2d 294. This case is far closer to the court's later. decision in *Jenks Hatchery v. Elliott,* 252 Or. 25, 30–31, 448 P.2d 370 (1968), where the court held, under common-law principles, that an accommodation maker that had paid on a note could sue on it.

presently undecided, and suitable for resolution by a future court." In re Slamans, at 476 n.7.

Courts remain uncertain about whether BC 509 provides the exclusive source of subrogation in bankruptcy or whether equitable subrogation instead continues to be available. The issue is one of bankruptcy law and is unaffected by nonbankruptcy law such as 5–117(a). In concluding that the issuer lacked subrogation rights in bankruptcy, the *Hamada* court analyzed the issuer's rights under both BC 509 and state law of equitable subrogation. In re AGF Direct Gas Sales & Servicing, Inc., 47 UCC Rep. Serv.2d 445 (D. N.H. 2002), offered the same analysis, adding in passing that it is not "apparent" that a ruling to the effect that BC 509 preempted state law of equitable subrogation would constitute legal error. Id. at 449. The court's analysis didn't rely on this observation.

NOTE: RESTITUTION AND BREACH OF WARRANTY

Issuers who have honored a draft drawn under a letter of credit but have been unable to obtain reimbursement from the applicant may attempt to get their money back from the beneficiary under doctrines of restitution or breach of warranty. The applicable common law of restitution may allow one who has paid out under mistake or who has honored a forged or fraudulent presentation to recover the payment. Former Article 5 was silent on the subject. Section 5–108(i)(4) provides that an issuer who has honored a presentation is "except as otherwise provided in Sections 5–110 and 5–117, precluded from restitution of money paid or other value given by mistake to the extent the mistake concerns discrepancies in the documents or tender which are apparent on the face of the presentation...." Section 5–110 states: "(a) If its presentation is honored, the beneficiary warrants: (1) to the issuer, any other person to whom presentation is made, and the applicant that there is no fraud or forgery of the kind described in § 5–109(a); and (2) to the applicant that the drawing does not violate any agreement between the applicant and beneficiary or any other agreement intended by them to be augmented by the letter of credit."

Under 5–110, after its presentation has been honored, the beneficiary makes two warranties. One warranty, created by 5–110(a)(1), is to the applicant, issuer and persons who received the presentation. The beneficiary warrants that there is no forgery or material fraud. As is made clear below, forgery involves a document presented whereas material fraud need not. Material fraud may involve fraud in the nondocumentary aspects of the underlying transaction. A party protected by 5–110(a)(1)'s warranty might prefer to recover under it even when the party can recover on some other basis, such as in tort. This is because forgery or documentary fraud typically presents fewer problems of proof than other bases of recovery.

A second warranty, created by 5–110(a)(2), runs only to the applicant. The beneficiary warrants that the drawing did not violate either an agreement between the applicant and beneficiary or any other agreement underlying the credit. Section 5–110(a)(2)'s warranty is more complicated than 5–110(a)(2)'s warranty, and leaves some uncertainty. It applies to any agreement that is part of the transaction underlying the letter of credit. Thus, even if the applicant isn't a party to the underlying agreement, the beneficiary breaches its 5–110(a)(2) warranty to the applicant if its draw "violates" the agreement. For instance, the warranty applies when an applicant has a credit issued at the request of a party to an underlying agreement other than the beneficiary. Usually, of course, the applicant has no need for 5–110(a)(2)'s warranty when it is a party to the agreement with the beneficiary. It can rely on warranties created by the underlying agreement. See Comment 2 to 5–110.

An uncertainty remains with respect to the "violations" referred to in 5–110(a)(2). Does a draw following any breach of the underlying agreement constitute a "violation" or must the breach rise to the level of seriousness on par with forgery or material fraud? Comment 2 (last sentence) to 5–110 suggests the former: the beneficiary warrants that it has performed all acts under the underlying agreement necessary for it to demand honor. If so, a beneficiary's draw upon presentation of documents indicating "due performance" of the underlying contract breaches the beneficiary's 5–114(a)(2) warranty to the applicant when the beneficiary has breached the underlying contract. Professor White agrees; 3 White & Summers, § 26-7 (Prac. ed. 2002). The position has a lot going for it. After the issuer has honored a presentation and paid, none of the concerns about disturbing the credit's payment function apply. Finality of payment by the issuer isn't jeopardized by the beneficiary's warranty against "violations" because the warranty runs only to the applicant against the beneficiary. In any case, finality of payment isn't a first principle of letter of credit law. Its principle, if any, is "pay first, litigate later." Both of 5–110's warranties arise only if honor has occurred. Thus, there seems to be no good reason to restrict 5–110(a)(2)'s warranty to breaches ("violations") of the underlying agreement on the order of forgery or material fraud. For an argument reaching the opposite conclusion, see Richard F. Dole, Jr., Warranties by Beneficiaries of Letters of Credit Under Revised Article 5 of the UCC: The Truth and Nothing But the Truth, 39 Houston L. Rev. 375, 394–97 (2002).

The UCP contains no warranties. Professor White, the Reporter for Revised Article 5, notes that of the "hotly debated issues" in Article 5's drafting, 5–110(a)'s warranty provision was the only one that "went against" the UCP. See James J. White, The Influence of International Practice on the Revision of Article 5 of the UCC, 16 Nw. J. Int'l L. & Bus. 189, 207 (1995). This does not mean that the UCP conflicts with 5–110(a)'s warranties. It merely means that the ICC's representatives preferred that warranty provisions not apply to a credit also subject to the UCP. They were disappointed. Given 5–110(a), its warranties apply to credits subject to the UCP, unless Article 5 is otherwise inapplicable or the credit excludes 5–110(a)'s application.

PROBLEMS

In the following Problems assume the following facts: Applicant, a movie producer with limited assets, engaged Beneficiary to appear in a new film, entitled "Legal Nights." In order to induce Beneficiary to agree to perform, Applicant caused Bank to issue a standby letter of credit to her payable on presentation to Bank of the letter of credit, a draft drawn on Bank payable 15 days after the date of presentation, and an affidavit that Beneficiary had satisfactorily completed the film and had not been paid by Applicant. Upon presentation by Beneficiary, Bank honored the draft but was unable to obtain reimbursement from Applicant. Bank proceeded against Beneficiary invoking the remedies of restitution and breach of warranty. What result in the following two cases under Article 5? The issues in these Problems are discussed in 3 James J. White & Robert S. Summers, Uniform Commercial Code, Prac. ed. § 26–7 (warranties), § 26–8(c) (restitution) (5th Prac. ed. (2002).

1. The documents presented by Beneficiary included a draft drawn on Bank "at sight," meaning at the time of presentation. Bank did not notice that the draft did not comply with the documents specified by the letter of credit and paid the draft according to its terms. Had the draft complied with the terms of the credit, Bank might not have paid it at all because during the 15–day period Applicant filed in bankruptcy and Bank's right of reimbursement became virtually worthless.

2. The documents presented by Beneficiary complied with the requirements of the credit, including the affidavit of completion. After honoring the draft, Bank learned that Beneficiary had not completed the film and had breached her contract with Applicant.

4. DAMAGES FOR WRONGFUL DISHONOR

As we have seen, it is fundamental that the letter of credit undertaking between an issuer and a beneficiary is independent of the underlying contract between the beneficiary and the applicant. 5–103(d). Does it follow that if the issuer wrongfully dishonors a draft presented under a letter of credit, the beneficiary can recover the full amount of the draw from the issuer, leaving the applicant to litigate with the beneficiary in a separate action over any amount the beneficiary has received in excess of its rights on the underlying contract? Yes. Under 5–111(a), the beneficiary or any other presenter can recover from the issuer the face amount of the draw under the credit if the issuer wrongfully dishonors the draw. The presenter also can recover incidental damages, but not consequential damages. Section 5–111(a) doesn't require the presenter to mitigate its damages in these circumstances. Because the issuer will have paid the presenter according to the credit's terms, as required by 5–111(a) (the dishonor was wrongful), the issuer's reimbursement agreement requires the applicant to reimburse it. The applicant, in turn, is left to recover from the beneficiary or other presenter in a separate action.

Section 5–111(b) governs the remedies of an applicant against the issuer. Under 5–111(b), the applicant can recover damages from the issuer who wrongfully dishonors a draft or other presentation under the credit. As under 5–111(a), incidental damages are recoverable but not consequential damages. Unlike 5–111(a)'s recovery, the applicant is required to mitigate its damages under 5–111(b). Article 5 does not provide a remedy in cases of improper honor by the issuer. Instead, recoverable damages are left to the courts. See Comment 2 to 5–111.

Section 5–111(e) requires courts to award reasonable attorney's fees and other litigation expenses to the prevailing party for any action in which a remedy is obtained under Article 5. The subsection overrules the "American rule" under which each party bears its own litigation costs. Section 5–111(e)'s mandatory award is not limited to remedies available under 5–111. The operative language of 5–111(e) is "under Article 5." Thus, a party prevailing on a breach of warranty claim against a beneficiary under 5–110, for instance, must be awarded reasonable attorney's fees and other litigation expenses. Would an injunction issued to prevent a materially fraudulent draw, discussed below, be a "remedy...obtained under Article 5"? Unsurprisingly, both 5–111(e) and the exclusion of consequential damages have proven controversial. Connecticut and Louisiana have adopted nonuniform amendments to 5–111 allowing recovery of consequential damages, and several states have enacted nonuniform versions of 5–111(e). New Jersey and Texas, for instance, simply allow the award of attorney's fees and litigation expenses. New York's enactment of Article 5, significantly, omits 5–111(e) entirely. See 2B U.L.A. § 5–111 (2003). How would you apply 5–111 to the following Problems?

PROBLEMS

1. Seller in New York agreed to sell goods to Buyer in Los Angeles by rail shipment with payment to be made pursuant to a commercial letter of credit. Buyer obtained issuance of a letter of credit by Issuer, Buyer's bank. The credit was payable to Seller on presentation to Issuer of a bill of lading, invoice, inspection and insurance certificates, sight draft drawn on Issuer, and the letter of credit. Issuer sent the letter of credit to Seller in New York (this is usually done through an "adviser" bank (5–102(a)(1)). Seller shipped the goods

and obtained an order bill of lading from the carrier. Seller then assembled the required documents and sent them through banking channels to Issuer for payment. Buyer decided that it had made a bad bargain and urged Issuer to dishonor the credit. Buyer threatened that if Issuer honored the letter of credit, Buyer would take its business elsewhere. Issuer reluctantly dishonored. When the goods arrived in Los Angeles, Seller ordered the carrier to store them in a warehouse. Several months later, Seller sold the goods for only a fraction of their invoice price. Seller sued Issuer for wrongful dishonor and sought the face amount of the draft drawn pursuant to the letter of credit in damages. Issuer contended that Seller should have mitigated damages, and that the goods should have been sold for a much higher price; moreover, at the very least, Seller must offset the amount actually recovered from the resale against its claim on the letter of credit.

(a) What result under 5–111(a)? See Comment 1 to 5–111. (b) What incentive does an Issuer have not to dishonor wrongfully? Comment 6 to 5–111. The explanation of the phrase "expenses of litigation" in that comment should be enough to chill the blood of any banker. (c) When might Seller have an incentive to seek recovery under law other than Article 5? See 5–111(e).

2. Applicant planned to develop a recreational community. County approval of Applicant's subdivision was conditional on Applicant's agreement to provide a standby letter of credit payable to the County as beneficiary to ensure that Applicant would complete roads and related improvements in accordance with subdivision design specifications. The required letter of credit was obtained from Issuer. Applicant never commenced construction of the roads or other improvements. Issuer wrongfully dishonored the letter of credit upon presentation. The County sued Issuer for the face amount of the credit plus interest from the date of the demand for payment. Issuer defended on the ground that the County would receive a windfall since it had not expended or committed itself to expend any funds to complete the improvements. The facts are based on Colorado National Bank v. Board of County Commissioners, 634 P.2d 32 (Colo.1981). What result under 5–111(a)? Dolan, Letters of Credit ¶ 9.02[5][b][ii] and 3 James J. White & Robert S. Summers, Uniform Commercial Code, § 26–13(b) (5th Prac ed. 2002), discuss the existing law.

3. Sport manufactured running shoes for various retail chains. It made the shoes to the specifications of retailers who sold the shoes under their own brand names. Sport was thinly capitalized and the business was highly competitive. Sport had contracts for large deliveries to Retailer A on March 1, Retailer B on June 1, and Retailer C on September 1. Sport required A to obtain a standby letter of credit for the invoice price of the goods on which Sport could draw if A failed to pay for the goods within 15 days of delivery. When the shoes arrived, A contended that they were defective and ordered Issuer not to honor the letter of credit. Sport made timely presentation to Issuer of the required documents and Issuer wrongfully dishonored. Sport immediately implored Issuer to pay, explaining that without the proceeds of this large sale it would be unable to fulfill its obligations to B and C and would lose the profits that it anticipated making on these contracts. When Issuer continued to refuse payment, Sport sued Issuer for wrongful dishonor and claimed damages measured by the face amount of the credit plus the amount of lost profits on its contracts with B and C. What result under 5–111(a)? Do you believe that this is a desirable result? See Comment 4 to 5–111.

E. FORGERY AND FRAUD

The influential pre-Code case, Sztejn v. J. Henry Schroder Banking Corp., 31 N.Y.S.2d 631 (N.Y. Sup. Ct. 1941), was a concession to the reality that the independence principle, however important, must have limits. The facts of *Sztejn* are summarized as follows: In brief, the contract of sale between the applicant and beneficiary was for the beneficiary to ship bristles to the applicant. Payment was to be made by a letter of credit calling for presentation of a draft along with a bill of lading describing the goods as bristles. The beneficiary's agent presented these documents to the issuer. However, the applicant discovered that the beneficiary had actually shipped what the court described as "rubbish" before the issuer honored the draft. It sought to enjoin the issuer from honoring the draft on the ground of fraud. On the pleadings, assuming the applicant was correct about the fraud, the court held for the applicant. Although the documents were in compliance on their face, they were not genuine and therefore the issuer did not have to honor.

This case seemed to undermine the independence principle in that it allowed the court to look outside the documents presented to determine whether the issuer must honor. Would this mean that honor could be enjoined if the applicant could make a showing that the goods shipped by the beneficiary were defective in a degree amounting to a breach of warranty of quality? Or if the applicant could show that it had been induced to enter into the underlying sale transaction by misrepresentations by the beneficiary about the goods? Former 5–114 attempted to codify and delimit *Sztejn*. It allowed the applicant to obtain an injunction against honor even though the documents appear on their face to be in compliance so long as a required document "is forged or fraudulent or there is fraud in the transaction." The breadth of the "fraud in the transaction" test seemed to place the independence principle in peril.

Intraworld Industries, Inc. v. Girard Trust Bank, 336 A.2d 316 (Penn. 1975), is the leading case in interpreting former 5-114 in a manner that preserved the independence principle by limiting "fraud in the transaction" to cases in which the beneficiary had no bona fide claim to payment or that its claim had absolutely no basis in fact. It required that the beneficiary's alleged wrongdoings had so vitiated the transaction that the legitimate ends of the independence principle would no longer be served. Comment 1 to 5-109 incorporates the *Intraworld* standards as the intended meaning of "material fraud."

There are two conceptual problems inherent in the test: describing behavior that constitutes fraud and identifying the transaction in which fraud occurs. In part to clarify the "fraud in the transaction" test, 5-109 to Revised Article 5 redrafts former 5-114. The following case discusses and applies the test in connection with a request for a preliminary injunction against honor. For an extensive discussion of fraud in the transaction, see Dolan, Letters of Credit ¶ 7.04.

Levin v. Meagher

Court of Appeals, First District, California, 2004.
2004 WL 1664864.

■ MARGULIES, J.

Plaintiffs Adam Levin and Credit.Com, Inc. obtained a preliminary injunction that prevents defendant Todd A. Meagher from drawing on a letter of credit. Defendant contends that the trial judge 'misunderstood and misapplied' the statutory fraud standard governing the issuance of an injunction against drawing on a letter of credit, that plaintiffs failed to demonstrate irreparable harm, and that the preliminary injunction is overbroad. We affirm.

BACKGROUND

Todd Meagher and Adam Levin are former business partners. Until early 2003, Meagher, Levin and Levin's wife owned 100 percent of the stock of Credit.Com, Inc. (Credit.Com). In 2002, however, Meagher and Levin had a falling out, which they resolved by agreeing that Levin would purchase Meagher's interest in Credit.Com. The various agreements associated with the buyout were signed in March 2003. Levin paid the purchase price partially in cash and partially by way of a $331,000 promissory note to Meagher, secured by a letter of credit. The promissory note provided that upon certain events of default, Meagher could declare the entirety of its unpaid principal immediately due and payable and draw down the letter of credit.

At the time of the buyout, Credit.Com was obligated on a line of credit extended by Wells Fargo Bank on which Meagher was a guarantor. Although Meagher had long since 'closed' the line of credit, meaning that it could no longer be drawn upon, an outstanding balance of over $70,000 remained. To assure Meagher of a safe release from his guarantee, section 7.2.1 of the buyout agreement required Credit.Com to 'either pay off and terminate its line of credit with Wells Fargo Bank, or . . . . arrange for the release of [Meagher] as a guarantor thereof, as soon as practicable, and in any event not later than' April 21, 2003. Failure to satisfy this obligation within the applicable time period was included as an event of default under the promissory note. Accordingly, a breach of section 7.2.1 would permit Meagher to declare the note due and draw on the line of credit.

On the morning of April 17, 2003, four days before the deadline for paying off the line of credit, Levin visited a San Francisco branch of Wells Fargo. Working with Megan Taub-Smith, the Premier Banking Manager at the branch, Levin drew against his personal line of credit sufficient funds to pay off the Credit.Com line of credit. Ms. Taub-Smith transferred these funds into the Credit.Com checking account and then applied them against the line of credit, paying it off in full.

The next day, Friday, April 18, Meagher encountered Levin at the offices of Credit.Com, which Meagher continued to share. Meagher asked whether the line of credit had been paid off, and Levin said that it had. Apparently not trusting Levin's assurance, later that day Meagher went to a Wells Fargo branch in the City of Alameda and asked whether the loan balance had been paid off. An employee there reported that the bank's computer continued to show an open balance. The employee recommended that Meagher talk to Mike Tonelli, who worked at the bank's Business Direct division in Phoenix. The employee then called Tonelli and handed the telephone to Meagher. Meagher confirmed with Tonelli that the bank's computer continued to display an outstanding balance on the line of credit.

The disparity resulted from internal bank accounting procedures. Wells Fargo may take several days to 'process' a loan payment and reflect the payment in its computer records, even though (as in this case) the bank is merely taking money from one of its own pockets and putting it in another. As a result, while Levin in fact paid off the loan on April 17, employees of the bank other than Taub-Smith would not have known of the payment because the bank did not immediately process that payment and 'post' it to the computer system. In fact, the payment was not posted to the bank's computers until April 28.

Early in the afternoon of April 18, Meagher's attorney, George Hisert, sent an e-mail to Levin's attorney, J. Anthony Vittal, noting that Meagher had received mixed information regarding payment of the line of credit and asking whether the line of credit had been paid off. Vittal responded, '[Y]ou may rest assured that the release of Mr. Meagher from his guaranty obligations . . . . will be effective before the contractual deadline.' Presented with this equivocal response, Hisert concluded in a responsive e-mail that afternoon that 'the Wells Fargo business line on which [Meagher] is the guarantor has not been paid,' although he acknowledged that Levin had stated the contrary.

To resolve the confusion, Hisert asked for written confirmation of the payment. Although Vittal responded promptly, his e-mail merely noted that he would 'endeavor to obtain' written proof of the payoff by April 21, leaving the then-current status of the line uncertain. Vittal did not commit to supplying such proof by the 21st, noting, '[I]f it takes a few days to generate the proof you request, I trust you will understand.'

Meagher could have confirmed that the line of credit had been paid if he had called Taub-Smith, but because Vittal did not confirm that the payment had been made or explain in what manner, it appears that neither Meagher nor his attorney knew that it was Taub-Smith who had received payment. Moreover, Meagher and his counsel believed they had reason to doubt Levin's word as a result of Vittal's equivocal messages and the apparently contrary information from Tonelli of Wells Fargo.

The day after the deadline for payment passed, April 22, Meagher called Tonelli again and was again told that there was an outstanding balance on the line of credit, which Tonelli confirmed in a letter. During this conversation with Tonelli, Meagher did not mention that Levin claimed to have paid off the line of credit already. Tonelli later asserted that if he had known about 'even the allegation of such a pay off,' he would have referred Meagher to another banking division to find out the true current status of the line.

Meagher's counsel then delivered a letter from Meagher to Levin declaring Levin to be in default and the full amount under the promissory note immediately due, demanding payment, and providing wire transfer instructions for the payment. Levin's counsel, Vittal, became aware of the letter of default that afternoon. At the same time, he also discovered that he had received a facsimile of a letter from Taub-Smith confirming in writing that the line of credit had been paid off and inviting any questions to be directed to her. Vittal responded to Meagher's default notice with his own letter disputing the default, describing when and how Levin paid off the line of credit, and enclosing the letter from Taub-Smith. The facsimile receipt shows that Vittal's letter was received by Meagher's counsel's office at approximately 8:20 p.m. on April 22.

In order to draw on the letter of credit, its terms required Meagher to present a draft to Wachovia Bank accompanied by a dated certificate from Meagher made under penalty of perjury that (1) he was the payee on the letter of credit, (2) Levin had defaulted in his obligations under the promissory note, and (3) neither Meagher nor his company, Credit 411, Inc., was in material breach of any of the covenants under paragraph 6.1 of the stock purchase agreement, relating to Meagher's and Levin's obligations after the closing. Meagher signed such a certification, stating that Levin had defaulted on his contractual obligations and that Meagher was entitled to the full amount due under the promissory note. Meagher's counsel, Hisert, had instructed a North

Carolina attorney to present this certification to the home office of Wachovia Bank, the issuer of the letter of credit, along with a demand that Meagher be paid over $330,000 on the letter of credit. The North Carolina attorney took the documents to the bank at approximately 10:00 a.m. Eastern Daylight Time on April 23, 2003. Although Hisert is vague about the time at which he authorized the delivery of these documents, it appears that after delivery of the notice of default he made no further inquiry of Vittal regarding written proof that Levin had paid off the line of credit or Levin's response to the notice of default, and he gave no warning to Levin or Vittal that the letter of credit was to be drawn on. It was not until '[l]ater on the morning of April 23' that Hisert learned that, the night before, Vittal had provided the written proof of payment that had been promised.

Despite receiving a copy of Taub-Smith's confirmation that the line of credit had been paid, neither Meagher nor his counsel called Taub-Smith for an explanation. Instead, they reported the discrepancy to Tonelli, who himself called Taub-Smith. Later on April 23, Tonelli told Meagher's counsel that Taub-Smith had confirmed that full payment had been made. Tonelli noted, however, that the payment had yet to be reflected in the bank's computer system and expressed his opinion that Meagher remained guarantor on the loan until the payment had posted. Based upon this information, on April 24, Meagher's counsel wrote a letter to Vittal claiming that Tonelli told them that 'the loan was still outstanding,' that 'Mr. Meagher had not been released as guarantor,' and that 'no payment had been posted.' The letter did not mention that Taub-Smith had confirmed to Tonelli that full payment had been made a week before, despite the fact that the payment had not 'posted.'

Although Tonelli confirmed Taub-Smith's report that the line of credit had been paid off by midday on April 23, Meagher continued, through his counsel, to assert that the bank's failure internally to post the payoff transaction by April 21 created a default. In addition to the April 24 letter noted above, Hisert took the same position in an e-mail of April 25, despite his hearing directly from Taub-Smith, who told him in a voicemail that the failure of the bank to post the transaction was due to 'an internal accounting error.' In light of Meagher's refusal to withdraw his request to draw on the letter of credit, on April 29, 2003, Levin filed a complaint and an ex parte application for a temporary restraining order (TRO) to prevent Meagher from drawing on the letter of credit. The TRO was granted the same day. Following further briefing and a hearing, the trial court entered a preliminary injunction enjoining Meagher 'from making any draw request or 'presentation' to Wachovia Bank or taking possession of or control over any draw on the Letter of Credit without prior leave from this Court.' Meagher appeals entry of the preliminary injunction.

DISCUSSION

....

B. Likelihood of Success on the Merits

The first half of the 'interrelated' standard for grant of a preliminary injunction is a likelihood of success on the merits. (Hunt v. Superior Court, supra, 21 Cal.4th at p. 999.) Of the various express requirements for an injunction under California Uniform Commercial Code section 5109, subdivision (b), Meagher challenges only the trial judge's conclusion that Levin is likely to succeed in demonstrating that Meagher committed a 'material fraud' on the issuer. * * *

Under the so-called 'independence principle,' the issuer's decision to honor a draft on a letter of credit must be based solely on compliance with the requirements of the presentation terms of the letter of credit itself, rather than on the parties' compliance (or lack thereof) with their obligations under the underlying contract. (Mitsui Manufacturers Bank v. Texas Commerce Bank-Fort Worth (1984) 159 Cal.App.3d 1051, 1955.) As summarized in Intraworld Industries, Inc. v. Girard Trust Bank (1975) 336 A.2d 316, 'unless otherwise agreed, the issuer deals only in documents. If the documents presented conform to the requirements of the credit, the issuer may and must honor demands for payment, regardless of whether the goods conform to the underlying contract between beneficiary and customer. Absent its agreement to the contrary, the issuer is, under the general rule, not required or even permitted to go behind the documents to determine if the beneficiary has performed in conformance with the underlying contract.' (Id. at p. 323.) Accordingly, the issuer of a letter of credit is required to honor a draft that 'appears on its face strictly to comply with the terms and conditions of the letter of credit.' (Cal.U.Com.Code, § 5108, subd. (a).)

There is one narrow exception to the independence principle. An issuer is not required to honor a draft if 'a required document is forged or materially fraudulent, or honor of the presentation would facilitate a material fraud by the beneficiary on the issuer or applicant.' (Cal.U.Com.Code, § 5109, subd. (a).) Where such fraud exists, a third party can obtain an injunction against the issuer's honor of the presentation, as Levin did here. (Cal.U.Com.Code, § 5109, subd. (b).)

This case demonstrates that the term 'fraud' in section 5109 is ambiguous. It can be argued that the term incorporates the elements of the common law tort of 'fraud,' one of which requires the maker of a false statement to possess an active intent to deceive. On the other hand, it can also be argued that any time an issuer releases funds under a letter of credit in reliance on false statements, there has been a 'material fraud . . . . on the issuer' because the funds were released under false pretenses. The latter is true regardless of whether the maker of the statements knew they were false and intended to deceive. Meagher argues that the standard governing his submission to Wachovia Bank should incorporate the subjective 'intent' element of common law fraud. In support of this legal argument, Meagher cites TMTI v. Empresa Nacional de Comercializacion (9th Cir.1987) 829 F.2d 949, 956 (TMTI), which held that a finding of 'active intentional fraud' or 'evil intent' was required before an injunction could issue under a similar provision of the California Uniform Commercial Code that preceded section 5109.

The fraud exception of California Uniform Commercial Code section 5109, enacted in its current form in 1996, has yet to be construed by a California appellate court, but the official code comment to section 5109, citing to several decisions from other jurisdictions, provides guidance regarding the proper legal standard for fraud. It is these cases that must guide our decision in interpreting section 5109, and TMTI, supra, is not cited in the official code comment. What unifies the various standards formulated in the cases cited in the official code comment is their requirement that fraud be determined by an objective examination of the circumstances, rather than by reference to the subjective beliefs of the beneficiary. The leading case in the area, recognized as such in the official code comment, is Intraworld Industries, Inc. v. Girard Trust Bank, supra, 336 A.2d 316, which construes the predecessor to section 5109. Intraworld Industries held that an injunction would not issue to prevent a draw on a letter of credit unless the beneficiary's presentation 'had absolutely no basis in fact' or there was 'no bona fide claim to payment under the [underlying contract].' (Id. at pp. 325, 327.) This standard requires the court to make an evaluation of the beneficiary's entitlement to payment under the letter of credit, rather than to inquire into the beneficiary's state of mind. No injunction will issue if the circumstances demonstrate that the beneficiary has a 'colorable' (or stronger) claim of entitlement to draw. (Itek Corp. v. First Nat. Bank of Boston (1st Cir.1984) 730 F.2d 19, 25.).... The most recent decision on this issue, 3Com Corp. v. Banco do Brasil, S.A. (2nd Cir.1999) 171 F.3d 739, similarly adopts an objective standard, precluding an injunction unless the beneficiary's claim to payment is 'clearly untenable.' (Id. at p. 747.)[3]

The issue before us is therefore whether there is substantial evidence in the record to support the conclusion that Levin is likely to demonstrate that Meagher has no colorable claim of default under the promissory note. (14859 Moorpark Homeowner's Assn. v. VRT Corp., supra, 63 Cal.App.4th at p. 1402.) That standard is satisfied on this record. Levin's obligation under the parties' agreement was to 'either pay off and terminate [the line of credit] or . .

---

[3] The adoption of an objective standard is consistent with the contractual nature of letters of credit. Under such contracts, a beneficiary has the right to draw on the letter of credit only if certain conditions are met. If there is 'no bona fide claim' that those conditions have been met-in other words, if it is clear that the beneficiary has no right to draw on the letter of credit-the beneficiary should not be permitted to draw on the line of credit merely because the beneficiary has formed a good faith but mistaken belief that conditions permitting a draw do exist.

. . arrange for the release of [Meagher] as a guarantor.' (Italics added.) Because the line of credit had already been terminated by Meagher months before, Levin could satisfy this obligation merely by paying off the line of credit by April 21, regardless of whether Meagher remained a guarantor. The evidence that Levin did so is undisputed. Accordingly, Levin was never in default under the promissory note.

Tonelli's repeated mistaken statements that a balance remained on the line of credit, based on the fact that the bank's accounting system did not accurately reflect the payment that had been made, are simply irrelevant. Under the express terms of the promissory note, Levin's obligation was to pay off the line of credit by April 21, not to cause the bank's accounting system to reflect that payment-a process over which Levin had no control. Tonelli's apparent insistence that Meagher remained liable on the note is similarly irrelevant to the issue of default, since Levin's obligation was stated in the alternative: either to pay off the line or secure a release of liability. When Levin paid off the note, he satisfied his contractual obligation, regardless of whether Meagher continued as a guarantor. Finally, the equivocal messages of Levin's attorney, Vittal, and his failure to obtain written confirmation of the payoff prior to April 22, while they contributed to Meagher's suspicion that a default had occurred, were similarly irrelevant. Levin's obligation was merely to pay off the line of credit, not to inform Meagher or provide written proof that payoff had occurred. Because there is no truth to Meagher's statement that Levin had defaulted in his obligations under the promissory note, Levin is virtually certain to demonstrate that Meagher's claim to payment under the letter of credit was not even 'colorable.' The trial court's conclusion on this issue was therefore fully supported by the evidence and the law.

C. The Balance of Interim Harms

The second element of the 'two interrelated factors' governing the issuance of a preliminary injunction is 'the relative interim harm to the parties from the issuance or nonissuance of the injunction.' (Hunt v. Superior Court, supra, 21 Cal.4th at p. 999.) 'in evaluation of the relative harm to the parties upon the granting or denial of a preliminary injunction requires consideration of: '(1) the inadequacy of any other remedy; (2) the degree of irreparable injury the denial of the injunction will cause; (3) the necessity to preserve the status quo; [and] (4) the degree of adverse effect on the public interest or interests of third parties the granting of the injunction will cause.' (Vo v. City of Garden Grove (2004) 115 Cal.App.4th 425, 435, quoting Cohen v. Board of Supervisors (1985) 40 Cal.3d 277, 286, footnote 5; 14859 Moorpark Homeowner's Assn. v. VRT Corp., supra, 63 Cal.App .4th at p. 1402.)

Of these various factors, Meagher challenges only Levin's showing of irreparable injury. 'Irreparable injury' is harm that cannot be fully compensated by money damages. (Tahoe Keys Property Owners' Assn. v. State Water Resources Control Bd. (1994) 23 Cal.App.4th 1459, 1471.) Although a showing of irreparable injury is 'ordinarily' a requirement for preliminary injunctive relief (Intel Corp. v. Hamidi (2003) 30 Cal.4th 1342, 1352), irreparable injury is only one element of the calculus required of the trial court in its balance of the hardships. Moreover, '[t]he more likely it is that plaintiffs will ultimately prevail, the less severe must be the harm that they allege will occur if the injunction does not issue. This is especially true when the requested injunction maintains, rather than alters, the status quo. [Citation.]' Thus, ' . . . . if the party seeking the injunction can make a sufficiently strong showing of likelihood of success on the merits, the trial court has discretion to issue the injunction notwithstanding that party's inability to show that the balance of harms tips in his favor. [Citation.]' (14859 Moorpark Homeowner's Assn. v. VRT Corp., supra, 63 Cal.App.4th at p. 1407.) It is important to remember that '[t]he ultimate goal of any test to be used in deciding whether a preliminary injunction should issue is to minimize the harm which an erroneous interim decision may cause. [Citation.]' (White v. Davis (2003) 30 Cal.4th 528, 554, quoting IT Corp. v. County of Imperial (1983) 35 Cal.3d 63, 73.)

Measured by the proper objective standard, Levin's likelihood of success is very great, lowering the degree of harm necessary to sustain the balance of hardships in his favor. In addition, the injunction as entered maintains the status quo, similarly lowering the standard for harm. Particularly in light of these two mitigating factors, Levin's demonstration of irreparable injury was adequate. It is true that some of the potential harm cited by Levin appears compensable in damages, such as the acceleration of his liability under the note and Meagher's possible violation of a noncompetition clause, but some is not. The potential loss of investment gains in the securities that would be liquidated to fund the payout and the harm to the business reputation and interests of Levin and his company as a result of a draw on the letter of credit, while plausible consequences of a wrongful draft, are sufficiently difficult to quantify that they would be difficult, if not legally impossible, to compensate in damages. Both of these types of damage have been held to constitute irreparable harm. (See, e.g., Heckmann v. Ahmanson (1985) 168 Cal.App.3d 119, 136; Hubbard Business Plaza v. Lincoln Liberty Life Ins. (D.Nev.1986) 649 F.Supp. 1310, 1317, affd. (9th Cir.1988) 844 F.2d 792 [damage to business reputation and interests from allegedly fraudulent draw of letter of credit constitutes irreparable injury supporting preliminary injunction]; but cf. Foxboro Co. v. Arabian American Oil Co. (1st Cir.1986) 805 F.2d 34, 37 [rejecting damage to business reputation as a basis for enjoining allegedly fraudulent draw on a letter of credit].) Although Meagher objected to evidence of certain of these possible harms as speculative, it is the degree and impact of these events that is speculative, not the fact that they pose a realistic risk. Weighed against these possible harms is the relative lack of harm to Meagher from grant of the preliminary injunction. In spite of the injunction, the letter of credit remains in place to secure Meagher's recovery under the promissory note. All he has lost through entry of the preliminary injunction is the acceleration of that debt, which remains payable according to its terms. Accordingly, the trial court did not abuse its discretion in finding that Levin provided sufficient evidence of irreparable injury, viewed in the context of the other factors relevant to the balance of harms.

....

NOTES

1. As *Levin* shows, applicants seeking to enjoin honor by issuers have more than the tough *Intraworld* standards to contend with. The applicant must show that it is more likely than not to succeed on the merits of the fraud or forgery issue (5–109(b)(4)), and it must also comply with the law of the jurisdiction on granting injunctions (5–109(b)(3)). This normally requires a showing of irreparable harm. An equitable suit for an injunction is not appropriate if there is an adequate remedy at law. Since the remedy would usually be an action by the applicant against the beneficiary for a money judgment, an injunction would usually be inappropriate if the beneficiary were solvent and subject to service of process. See Hendricks v. Bank of America, 408 F.3d 1127 (9th Cir.2004) (injunction granted where beneficiary is insolvent). *Levin* has a very sophisticated analysis of irreparable injury that balances the applicant's likelihood of success in proving fraud with the degree of harm that must be shown. The damage to the applicant's business reputation in having to liquidate securities in order to pay the draft may be difficult if not impossible to quantify.

2. Professor White concedes that the Drafting Committee was unable to agree on a definition of fraud. 3 James J. White & Robert S. Summers, Uniform Commercial Code, § 26–9, at 185 (5th Prac. ed. 2002). Section 5–109(a) adopts the standard of "material fraud." Comment 1 states: "Material fraud by the beneficiary occurs only when the beneficiary has no colorable right to expect honor and where there is no basis in fact to support such a right to honor." Does the addition of the adjective "material" make the inquiry as to fraud any more manageable? Without a working notion of fraud, 5–109(a)'s requirement that the fraud be material is unhelpful. The U.N. Convention on Independent Guarantees tries, without using the term, to make the fraud inquiry more manageable. It does not obligate an issuer to pay when it is "manifest and clear" that payment is not due on the basis asserted in the demand or documents presented. See U.N. Convention art. 19(1).

The *Sztejn* court distinguished between what it called "active fraud" and a "mere" breach of warranty without precisely characterizing the distinction. See *Sztejn*, 31 N.Y.S.2d at 634–635. To see the difficulty, consider a sales contract calling for Seller to deliver new widgets and a letter of credit requiring documents describing the goods delivered as "new widgets." Is there fraud in

Seller's performance of the sales contract in the following four circumstances? (1) Seller intentionally delivers an automobile, not new widgets. (2) Seller intentionally delivers new widgets with very minor scratches. (3) The same as (2) except the market price for widgets has increased so that scratched widgets sell for more than new widgets were previously sold. (4) Seller intentionally delivers seriously malfunctioning new widgets. Notice that Seller has breached an express warranty in all four circumstances. Circumstance (4) arguably is an easy case: deliberately delivering seriously defective goods is egregious behavior characteristic of fraud. The extent of breach differs in the other three circumstances, and a standard is needed to find fraud nonarbitrarily in one or more of them. Article 5 apparently decided not to provide one.

Section 5–109(a) also abandons the "fraud in the transaction" formulation that had led scholars and courts to differ on whether the transaction meant was only the credit transaction or whether it extended to the underlying transaction as well. A critique of the differing positions on this issue appears in 3 James J. White & Robert S. Summers, Uniform Commercial Code, § 26–10, at 179–80 (5th Prac. ed. 2002). With the addition of "or honor of the presentation would facilitate a material fraud by the beneficiary on the issuer or applicant," 5–109(a) expressly applies to fraud in the underlying transaction. Prevailing authority finds that Article 5's fraud exception continues to apply to credits governed by the UCP. See Mid–Am. Tire, Inc. v. PTZ Trading Ltd., 768 N.E.2d 619 (Ohio 2002).

3. Section 5–109(a)'s fraud provision is not limited to forgery or fraud by the beneficiary. By its terms, 5–109(a) applies when "a required document is forged or materially fraudulent." Thus, if 5–109(b)'s conditions for injunctive relief are satisfied, an applicant can enjoin an issuer from honoring a draw by the beneficiary even if the beneficiary has not perpetrated the forgery or fraud.

In some cases, applicants have attempted to forestall payment under a letter of credit by seeking to enjoin the beneficiary from making presentation to the issuer. An occasional opinion has applied a lesser standard for granting an injunction in such a case than in the usual case of an injunction against the issuer. Dolan, Letters of Credit ¶ 7.04[4][f]. Section 5–109(b) makes clear that the same standards must apply to limit injunctions in both cases by the addition of the language: "or grant similar relief against the issuer or other persons." Comment 5 to 5–109.

4. Article 5 distinguishes between two classes of presenters: presenters whose conforming documentary presentations the issuer must honor even if there is fraud in the transaction and presenters whose conforming presentations the issuer in good faith is permitted to honor or dishonor when there is fraud. See 5–109(a)(1), (b). The former class of presenters are protected against dishonor: fraud does not allow the issuer to dishonor their conforming presentations. Under 5–109(b)(4), the issuer also cannot be enjoined from honoring the draw. Protected presenters are all transferees of documents under the letter of credit. See 5–109(a)(1)(i)–(iv). (Recognizing developments in letter of credit practice, 5–109(a)(1)(iv) protects an assignee under a deferred obligation credit, a relatively recent type of credit first issued in Southeast Asia.) For instance, a negotiating bank, holder of a draft, or good faith purchaser of documents can be protected purchasers. To be protected, the presenter must take the documents or draft in good faith and without notice of the fraud. See 5–109(a)(1). All other presenters are not protected, and the issuer, therefore, in good faith can dishonor conforming presentations by them. Because a beneficiary under the credit does not purchase the draft or documents, it is a not transferee and, therefore, not a protected presenter.

Section 5–109(a)(2) deals with the rights of the issuer against unprotected presenters. It allows the issuer to honor ("may honor") presentations by them, even when the presentation involves forgery or material fraud, as long as the issuer does so in good faith. Is an issuer acting in good faith if it honors after the applicant has given it notice of the fraud or forgery? A common tactic used by applicants is to send a barrage of evidence to the issuer in advance of honor documenting the alleged fraud. The purpose is to present a risk to the issuer that a judge or jury ex post will find the issuer to have honored the draw in bad faith. Prudent practice sometimes leads issuers to resort to interpleader in these and other circumstances. See Dolan, Letters of Credit 7.04[4][g]. James J. White & Robert S. Summers, Uniform Commercial Code,. § 26–9 (5th Prac. ed. 2002), disapproves of the practice.

Note how 5–109 allocates the risk of the beneficiary's fraud. In the case of a protected presenter, the applicant bears this risk. This is because the issuer honoring the draw is entitled to be reimbursed by the applicant either by contract or by statute, or both. 5–108(i)(1). The applicant therefore must recover from the beneficiary. Because the issuer can dishonor an unprotected presenter's conforming presentation, the presenter bears the risk of the beneficiary's fraud when dishonor occurs. It must recover from the beneficiary (or its transferor, who ultimately must recover from the beneficiary). Thus, the unprotected presenter bears the risk of the beneficiary's fraud. Article 5's implicit judgment is that protected presenters are in an inferior position to the applicant or issuer to detect the beneficiary's fraud. Allocating fraud risk to either the applicant or unprotected presenters but never to protected presenters is thought to be the cost-minimizing solution. Is this judgment sound? In support, it is usually observed that the applicant has dealt with the beneficiary whereas a presenter may have purchased a draft or documents from a remote transferor and never have dealt directly with the applicant. See United Bank Ltd. v. Cambridge Sporting Goods Corp., 360 N.E.2d 943, 949 n. 6 (N.Y.1976). The applicant's costs in taking appropriate precautions, therefore, are thought generally to be lower than those facing the ultimate transferee's precaution costs. The observation has no force when the presenter purchases directly from the beneficiary. Consider also that often issuers or confirmers are local banks who know the beneficiary or can easily acquire information about it. Article 5's allocation of fraud risk is justifiable only if most documentary drafts are discounted in markets to strangers to the underlying contract. Neither the Comments to 5–109 nor its drafting history discuss this assumed empirical generalization.

5. "Good faith" is defined in 5–102(a)(7) as "honesty in fact." This is a subjective standard. Section 1–201(b)(20) contains the operative standard of good faith in the Articles of the UCC: "'Good faith,' except as otherwise provided in Article 5, means honesty in fact and the observance of reasonable commercial reasonable." The generally applicable definition includes both subjective and objective elements. Why is the "commercially reasonable standards" language not included in the Article 5 definition of good faith? See Comment 3 to 5–102. Professor White reports that in Article 5's drafting, representatives of a banking industry trade group argued that "Europeans and other non-Americans were frightened by the threat of a runaway good faith doctrine, particularly by American courts' applying good faith in unforeseen cases." James J. White, The Influence of International Practice on the Revision of Article 5 of the UCC, 16 Nw. J. Int'l L. & Bus. 189, 205 (1995).

Comment 3 finds 5–102(a)(7)'s subjective standard of good faith appropriate because it "creates greater certainty" in the issuer's obligations. The finding goes against the usual assessment of the effects of subjective standards. Standards such as "honesty in fact" make potentially relevant large bodies of evidence, encourage prelitigation coaching of witnesses, and potentially extend the course of judicial proceedings going to the issue of good faith. Objective standards of good faith, by contrast, typically involve more limited evidence, less prelitigation jockeying, and more truncated proceedings. The usual assessment is that subjective standards produce indeterminacy and high costs in the application of otherwise clear rules. See, e.g., Richard A. Epstein, Simple Rules for a Complex World (Harvard University Press 1995); Robert D. Cooter & Edward L. Rubin, A Theory of Loss Allocation for Consumer Payments, 66 Tex. L. Rev. 63 (1987). Comment 3's different assessment depends on a confidence that the requisite showing of "honesty in fact" is so easy (and a showing of "dishonesty in fact" so hard) as to discourage investment in litigation of the issue.

PROBLEM

At Buyer's request, Bank One issued a letter of credit in Beneficiary's favor. At Beneficiary's-Seller's insistence, Buyer also asked Bank One to have a bank known to Beneficiary, Bank Two, confirm the credit, and Bank One did so. Bank Two accordingly notified Beneficiary of its confirmation. Later, Buyer learns that Beneficiary has intentionally breached the underlying sales contract by shipping nothing but will present documents to Bank Two for payment under Bank Two's credit. The documents will evidence shipment in accordance with the sales contract, as required under the credit. (a) At Buyer's urging, can Bank One obtain an injunction to prevent Bank Two from honoring Beneficiary's presentation? See 5–107(a), 5–109(b). (b) Can Buyer obtain an injunction against Bank Two in these circumstances? See 5–109(b); 5–107(a); Comment 1 to 5–107 (third paragraph); International Trade Relationship & Export v. Citibank, N.A., 41 UCC Rep. Serv.2d 626 (S.D.N.Y. 2000).

F. TRANSFER, ASSIGNMENT AND SECURITY INTERESTS

1. TRANSFER AND ASSIGNMENT

There are two ways to transfer rights in a letter of credit: by "transferring" the credit and by assigning the proceeds of the credit. The two notions are different. Section 5–112(a) defines "transfer" to mean the transfer of the beneficiary's right to draw on the letter of credit. Transferring the credit changes the party who must present documents to the issuer for honor. See also UCP 600 art. 38b. Section 5–114 defines "proceeds of a letter of credit" to mean cash, checks or other items of value paid by the issuer upon honor of the letter of credit. Thus, assignment of the proceeds merely changes the party entitled to receive them. Assignment doesn't change the party who must present the documents for honor.

Letter of credit law treats transfer of the credit very differently from assignment of the credit's proceeds. Under 5–112(a), transfer conveys to a third party the beneficiary's right to draw on the credit by signing and presenting its own draft and other documents. See UCP 600 art. 38b. Further, in the words of Comment 2 to 5–112, "[i]t contemplates not merely payment to but also performance by the transferee." That is, the beneficiary's duties are delegated to the transferee, and it may submit documents showing that it rather than the beneficiary performed the underlying contract. The applicant loses control over the identity of the person who will perform. In short, it is analogous to a novation. Comment 2 to 5–112.

Transfer of the right to draw is a radical change in the original deal in which an applicant obtained an issuer's undertaking to pay a beneficiary, who is usually a party to whom the applicant is or will be indebted for performance. In the commercial letter of credit setting, the applicant is usually a buyer and the beneficiary a seller. Since after the transfer, the issuer's undertaking is to pay another person who may perform the beneficiary's contract, how are the applicant's rights protected in transfer cases? A letter of credit can be transferred only if the credit provides that it is transferable. 5–112(a); see also UCP 600 art. 38a. Section 5–112(a) sets the default rule against transfer to reflect the preferences of most applicants. If the applicant doesn't want to give the beneficiary the right to transfer, it must be sure that the credit it procures from the issuer does not permit transfer. In this case, the issuing bank must dishonor any presentation of invoices of third persons; the applicant bargained for performance by its beneficiary and only its invoices will do. But if the credit is transferable on its face, Comment 2 to 5–112 states: "The issuance of a transferable letter of credit with the concurrence of the applicant is ipso facto an agreement by the issuer and applicant to permit a beneficiary to transfer its drawing right and permit a nominated person to recognize and carry out that transfer without further notice to them." Issuing banks may counter this by a requirement in the letter of credit that the beneficiary obtain the bank's permission before transfer so that the bank can anticipate who will make the presentation. 5–112(b)(2).

Transferable credits often are used by intermediate sellers to finance sales to their buyers. In the simplest form of such transactions, the intermediate seller has its buyer have issued a transferable credit in the amount of the contract price naming the seller as the beneficiary. Typically, the credit requires the seller to present its invoice and draft. The seller, in turn. asks the issuer to transfer part of the credit to the supplier of the goods it is selling to its buyer. This is called a "partial transfer" of the credit because the issuer is being asked to allow the transferee to draw less than the full amount payable under the credit. The issuer notifies the supplier of the terms of the transfer, agreeing to pay the amount of the supplier's invoice and draft upon the supplier's presentation of conforming documents. If the documents comply with the notice of transfer, the issuer pays the supplier the face amount of the supplier's draft. It also pays over to the intermediate seller the difference between the amount it paid to the supplier and the amount of the credit—the seller's profit from the sale to its buyer. The issuer substitutes the intermediate seller's invoice, draft and other documents it has received from the seller for the supplier's documents. This is done in order to avoid disclosing to the buyer the supplier's identity and its lower invoice price. See UCP 600 art. 38i. The issuer then delivers the substituted documents to the buyer. Transferable credits usually involve more parties, such as advisers of the credit, who may themselves undertake to allow transfer.

The notion of assignment is straightforward; it simply means assignment by the beneficiary of the proceeds that it is entitled to receive upon honor of the credit by the issuer. Proceeds are always assignable. Assignment of proceeds does not include the beneficiary's drawing rights. 5–114(a). The right to draw on the credit remains in the beneficiary, and the assignee's rights are contingent upon whether the beneficiary's presentation for honor complies with the terms and conditions of the credit. See Comment 2 to 5–112 and 5–114(b). Further, the issuer and the beneficiary can amend the credit without the assignee's consent. The beneficiary may assign its rights to part or all of the proceeds, and it may do so after the credit is established but before presentation. Presumably, the beneficiary may also assign the proceeds even after presentation if the issuer wrongfully dishonors. In re XYZ Options, Inc., 154 F.3d 1276 (11th Cir.1998), so held, interpreting former Article 5. Comment 1 to 5–114 appears to support this sensible holding by its statement that assignments of proceeds are valid if made after the credit is established "but before the proceeds are realized." Section 5–114(a)'s default rule allowing assignment presumably reflects the preferences of most beneficiaries under credits.

Section 5–114(c) provides that an issuing bank can ignore an assignment of proceeds "until it consents to the assignment." Professor White, Reporter for the 1995 Revision to Article 5, describes this as a "significant concession" to issuing banks. 3 James J. White & Robert S. Summers, Uniform Commercial Code,. § 26–12, at 200 (4th Prac. ed. 1995). Comment 3 to 5–114 states that the requirement of the issuer's consent conforms to "recognized national and international letter of credit practices." Common practice is for the beneficiary to sign a form giving the issuer notice of the assignment and instructing the issuer to pay the assignee directly upon presentation. Noting that it is always advisable for assignees to obtain the consent of the issuer, the Comment says: "When notice of an assignment has been received, issuers normally have required signatures on a consent form. This practice is reflected in the revision. By unconditionally consenting to such an assignment, the issuer or nominated person becomes bound...to pay the assignee the assigned letter of credit proceeds that the issuer or nominated person would otherwise pay to the beneficiary or another assignee."

Thus, does banking practice become law. Some amelioration is found in 5–114(d), which provides that though an issuer is not obliged to consent, "consent may not be unreasonably withheld if the assignee possesses and exhibits the letter of credit and presentation of the letter of credit is a condition to honor." The assignee's exhibition to the issuer of a letter of credit presumably gives the issuer sufficient evidence of the assignment to make unreasonable its refusal to consent. Presumably, the issuer may consent in advance to assignments by a provision in the letter of credit. Dolan, Letters of Credit, Ch. 10 contains an extensive discussion of transfer and assignment of letters of credit. The subject is also treated in Barkley Clark, The Law of Secured Transactions Under the Uniform Commercial Code, Ch. 7 (rev. ed. 2009), and 3 James J. White & Robert S. Summers, Uniform Commercial Code, Prac. Ed. § 26–11 (5th Prac. ed. 2002).

2. SECURITY INTERESTS

The most common reason for a beneficiary to assign the proceeds of a letter of credit is to secure the beneficiary's obligation to a creditor. Security interests in the proceeds of a credit fall within Article 9. Section 5–114(f) provides that "[t]he mode of creating and perfecting a security interest in or granting an assignment of a beneficiary's rights to proceeds is governed by Article 9 or other law." Article 9 governs only the right to proceeds of the credit; it does not control rights in the letter of credit itself. Article 9 calls the right to proceeds of the credit "a letter-of-credit right." Comment 5(e) to 5–102. Under 9–102(a)(51), a letter-of-credit right is "a right to payment or performance under a letter of credit...The term does not include the right of a beneficiary to demand payment or performance under a letter of credit." Thus, the term does not include the right to draw on the credit. The transfer of rights to draw is controlled by Article 5. 5–114(e).

To obtain a property right in a letter-of-credit right, the creditor's security interest must attach to it. Attachment allows enforcement of the right against the debtor. It occurs when three conditions are satisfied. § 9–203(b). Two of the conditions are easily met in letter of credit contexts involving a loan or other value provided to the beneficiary: that the creditor give value to the debtor-beneficiary, and that the debtor-beneficiary have a right to the letter of credit proceeds. The third condition is disjunctive: the debtor must either authenticate a security agreement describing the letter-of-credit right or the secured creditor obtain "control" of the right pursuant to the debtor's security agreement or the secured creditor obtain a security interest in collateral for which the letter-of-credit right is a "supporting obligation." 9–203(b)(3).

Thus, under the third condition, a security interest can attach to the letter-of-credit right in either of two different ways. Attachment occurs if the right is described in a security agreement authenticated by the debtor or the creditor obtains control of the letter-of-credit right pursuant to the debtor's security agreement. Alternatively, the security interest attaches to the letter-of-credit right if it attaches to collateral for which the letter-of-credit right is a "supporting obligation." The next section discusses the letter-of-credit right as a "supporting obligation." Section 9–409(a) treats as ineffective restrictions on the creation of security interests in letter of credit proceeds. This allows a security interest to attach when the restriction otherwise would prevent attachment. Comment 2 to 9–409.

Perfection of a security interest allows enforcement of a security interest against third parties. It requires attachment plus the secured creditor to take steps, usually acts of public notice, prescribed by Article 9. 9–308(a), 9–310. Under 9–312(b)(2), a security interest in a letter-of-credit right as original collateral may be perfected only by "control." Thus, control is a particularly effective (but sometimes costly) means of attachment because a security interest that attaches by control also is perfected. Control, according to 9–107, occurs when the issuer "has consented to an assignment of proceeds of the letter of credit under Section 5–114(c)." Section 5–114(c), in turn, provides that an issuer need not recognize an assignment of credit proceeds until it consents to the assignment. Where the assignee possesses and exhibits the credit to the issuer, the issuer cannot withhold its consent unreasonably. Article 5 gives no further guidance on obtaining the issuer's consent, and Comment 2 to 9–107 states that the details of the consenting issuer's duty to pay the assignee are left to the parties' agreement.

Article 9's use of the concept of control is borrowed from Article 8. First used in Article 8 to govern the rights of purchasers and secured parties in investment property, Article 9 adapts and applies the concept to security interests in deposit accounts, electronic chattel paper, letter-of-credit rights, and investment property. It replaces the old system of requiring possession of the credit by the assignee in order to perfect a security interest in the credit proceeds. The requirement of possession was cumbersome, contrary to industry practice and, in the case of partial assignments of the credit, sometimes impossible to satisfy. See Barkley Clark, The Law of Secured Transactions Under the Uniform Commercial Code 7.14[1] (Rev. ed. 2010). Control doesn't require possession of the credit.

In the two cases below determine whether the secured parties have control over the described letter-of-credit proceeds.

> Case #1. Beneficiary assigned 1/3 of the credit proceeds to A1, its secured creditor, and delivered possession of the letter of credit to A1. Subsequently, Beneficiary assigned 1/3 of the letter-of-credit proceeds to each A2 and A3. Beneficiary notified the issuer of all three assignments.
>
> Case #2. Foreign Buyer had issued a letter of credit for $1,000,000 from Foreign Issuer payable to US Seller. Issuer sent the letter of credit to its US correspondent bank to serve as an advising and confirming bank, which delivered Issuer's letter of credit to Seller. Seller granted a security interest to SP Bank in the credit proceeds to secure a loan of $500,000, and a second security interest to US Distributor to secure an existing $250,000 obligation. Advising Bank's invariable practice when notified of assignments of letter-of-credit rights was to demand and retain possession of the credit and note on it the terms of the assignment. It followed the practice in this case. When Seller filed a bankruptcy petition, its trustee sought to avoid the security interests of SP Bank and Distributor in the proceeds of the letter of credit. Seller's trustee can avoid their security interests if the interests are unperfected.

Revised Article 9 leaves unaddressed the rights and priority of a secured creditor when it becomes the transferee of a letter of credit. A transferee acquires all of the beneficiary's rights under the letter of credit, and, therefore, transferring the credit is a good way to secure the beneficiary's obligations. Section 9–109(c)(4) makes Article 9 inapplicable to the rights of a transferee beneficiary given priority under 5–114(e). And Section 5–114(e), in turn, gives the transferee priority over the assignee's right to credit proceeds as well as over claims of competing secured creditors in the proceeds. See Comment 3 to 9–329. Thus, Article 9 leaves undisturbed 5–114(e)'s grant of paramount rights in the letter of credit proceeds to the transferee beneficiary, even when the transferee is a secured creditor. Article 9, therefore, does not govern at least two situations: (1) the rights of a beneficiary-debtor against the transferee beneficiary-secured creditor; and (2) the priority of the transferee beneficiary-secured creditor against competing secured creditors. In situation (1), a distinction between an outright transfer and the grant of a security interest has to be made. In situation (2), a conflict between Article 9's priority rules and 5–114(e)'s priority rule is possible. Section 9–329's "control priority" rule gives priority to the security party first obtaining control of the letter-of-credit right. Section 5–114(e), however, gives priority to the transferee beneficiary over competing claimants to the letter of credit proceeds. Suppose Secured Creditor 1 obtains control over credit proceeds of a transferable letter of credit. Later, Secured Creditor 2 becomes a transferee beneficiary under the same letter. It never obtains control over the credit proceeds. Section 9–329(1) awards priority to Secured Creditor 1. Section 5–114(e) awards it to Secured Creditor 2. Comment 4 to 9–329 recognizes the two unaddressed situations and simply counsels courts to give "appropriate consideration to the policies and provisions of Article 5 and letter-of-credit practice as well as Article 9."

3. Letters of Credit as Supporting Obligations

Article 9 has special rules that apply to letter-of-credit rights when the letter of credit is a "supporting obligation" under 9–102(a)(77). This term "means a letter-of-credit right or secondary obligation that supports the payment or performance of an account, chattel paper, a document, a general intangible, an instrument, or investment property." Collateral described in (a)(77) is the "supported obligation," and the letter-of-credit right is the "supporting obligation." When a letter-of-credit right "supports" the sort of collateral described in 9–102(a)(77), it serves to enhance the value of the supported collateral. Given the frequent use of standby credits as credit enhancement devices, our guess is that in the great majority of cases letter-of-credit rights will be supporting obligations. If a sports franchise assures a basketball player that if its promissory note for the athlete's salary is not paid, the athlete can rely on a standby letter of credit, the letter of credit is a supporting obligation. The same is true when a dealer assigns its accounts to a financer and backs the accounts by a letter of credit. The examples are endless.

Article 9's special rules for attachment, perfection and priority of a security interest in a letter-of-credit right treat the right as an incident of the collateral it supports. Comment 5f. to 9–102. Accordingly, the secured creditor's rights in the credit proceeds derive from its rights in the collateral supported by the credit proceeds. Thus, under 9–203(f), a security interest automatically attaches to the letter-of-credit right when it attaches to the supported collateral. So, for example, there is no need for an authenticated security agreement describing the supported obligation to describe or contain any reference to the letter-of-credit right supporting it. Under 9–308(d) perfection in the supported collateral is perfection in the letter-of-credit right. And under 9–322(c), with one significant exception, priority in the supported collateral is priority in the letter-of-credit right.

Article 9's control concept must be understood taking into account its special rules for supporting obligations. Two points are important. First, the role of control is significantly qualified for letter-of-credit rights when they are supporting obligations. If a letter-of-credit right is not a supporting obligation, 9–312(b)(2) provides that perfection may be achieved only by control. But the requirement doesn't apply to supporting obligations. In this case, perfection of the security interest in the supported collateral automatically perfects a security interest in the supported obligation. Some commercial and most standby transactions letter-of-credit rights are supporting obligations. Thus, in many cases, attachment and perfection in these rights is automatic. Control isn't necessary and will be a more expensive alternative.

Second, and by far more important, are Article 9's special priority rule for supporting obligations. Section 9–322(b)(2) describes Article 9's basic priority rule for supporting obligations. Under it the time for filing and perfection as to the supported obligation is also the time of filing and perfection as to the supported obligation. This priority rule treats priority in the supporting obligation as derivative: the priority of the supporting obligation is the priority of the supported collateral. However, 9–322(b)(2)'s basic rule is subject to an important exception contained in 9–322(c). Section 9–322(c)(1) provides in relevant part that the rule that a security interest in the supporting obligation takes the priority of a security interest in the supported collateral, subject to 9–329(1). Section 9–329(1), in turn, provides that if there are conflicting security interests in the same letter-of-credit right, the security interest of the secured party having control has priority over a security interest of a secured party that does not have control. Hence, for example, if a bank files first against accounts, it is perfected with respect to a supporting letter-of-credit right. However, it will not be prior as to that right if a financer who filed second against the same accounts but perfected its security interest in the supporting letter- of-credit- right by control. Thus, to be sure of their priority, secured parties claiming security interests in letter-of-credit rights that are supporting obligations must obtain control. Control remains the central tenet of the law of secured transactions in letter-of-credit rights.

G. LETTERS OF CREDIT IN BANKRUPTCY

If a standby letter of credit is to be useful as the functional equivalent of a guaranty, it must pass muster in bankruptcy. So far, it has. Discharge of the applicant in bankruptcy does not effect the liability of the issuer on a letter of credit. BC 524(e). The initial question is whether the automatic stay of BC 362(a) restrains the beneficiary from drawing on the issuer after the applicant's bankruptcy. If it does, the utility of letters of credit is greatly impaired because the beneficiary would be forced to go through the expensive and time-consuming procedure to lift the stay under BC 362(d). As we have shown, the usual letter of credit transaction involves three undertakings: the letter of credit between the issuer and the beneficiary; the underlying contract between the applicant and the beneficiary; and the reimbursement contract between the applicant and the issuer. There is no question that the automatic stay precludes any action by the beneficiary against the applicant on the underlying contract as well as any action by the issuer against the applicant on the reimbursement agreement.

That BC 362(a) does not stay the beneficiary's draw against the issuer was decided in In re Page, 18 B.R. 713 (D. D.C.1982), and has been widely accepted. Accord In re War Eagle Construction Co., Inc., 283 B.R. 193 (S.D.Va. 2002). The applicant in *Page* granted security interests in its assets to issuer to secure its obligation to reimburse the issuer if the issuer had to pay the letter of credit. Later, the applicant filed in bankruptcy and the beneficiary presented the letter of credit for honor. The bankruptcy court held that unless payment of the letter of credit were stayed, the issuer, after payment, would be able to realize on its security interest in debtor's property, thereby reducing the assets available to the other creditors. The district court reversed on the ground that before the applicant had filed in bankruptcy the issuer already had a perfected security interest in the applicant's assets to secure its contingent claim for reimbursement. In its payment of the letter of credit, the issuer merely liquidated its claim against the applicant for reimbursement, and applicant's other creditors are no worse off because the property of the applicant's bankruptcy estate has not been depleted. The letter of credit was not, of course, property of the applicant's estate. The court demonstrated its respect for the importance of the independence principle of letter of credit law:

"Moreover, enjoining the payment of the letter of credit, even temporarily, would frustrate the commercial purposes of letters of credit to the detriment of financial institutions as well as their customers.... If payment on a letter of credit could be routinely delayed by the filing of a Chapter 11 petition, the intended substitution of a bank for its less credit-worthy customer would be defeated." 18 B.R. at 717.

The more difficult problems concerning letters of credit in bankruptcy have arisen in the area of voidable preference law. Sometimes clients come to believe that obtaining a letter of credit fully insulates them from the risks attending the bankruptcy of their obligors. But under preference law, this view may not be true in certain situations.

In the common case, there is no preference because the letter of credit is given for contemporaneous consideration. Usually, a letter of credit is issued at the inception of a credit sale transaction. To assure payment, the seller requires the buyer to obtain a letter of credit obliging the issuing bank to pay the sale price if the buyer doesn't pay when it becomes due. To induce the bank to issue the letter of credit, the buyer grants the bank a security interest in the buyer's property to secure the buyer's obligation to reimburse the bank if the bank is required to pay the seller. The letter of credit transaction is a substitute for a secured transaction between the seller and buyer. After the letter of credit is issued, the seller delivers the goods to the buyer. If the buyer doesn't pay and files in bankruptcy, the seller obtains payment from the bank. The bank has a secured claim in bankruptcy. There is no preference to either the seller or the bank in this kind of case. Although the security interest granted to the bank is a transfer of property by the buyer for the benefit of the seller, it is not a preference to the seller because the transfer is not on account of an antecedent debt. Rather, it is a contemporaneous exchange for new value by the seller. The seller obligates itself to make a credit sale of goods to the buyer in exchange for issuance of the letter of credit. There is no preference to the bank because the security interest does not secure an antecedent debt owed to the bank. The transfer of property to the bank is a contemporaneous exchange for new value by the bank, the bank's issuance of the letter of credit.

The result may be different if the letter of credit is given to the creditor for antecedent consideration. Suppose that Debtor, an insolvent company, owed Creditor $500,000, and Creditor was pressing Debtor for payment. When it became convinced that Debtor was unable to pay at that time, Creditor accepted a letter of credit issued by Bank for $500,000 payable to Creditor a year later if Debtor had not paid Creditor its debt by that time. In order to induce Bank to issue the letter of credit, Debtor granted Bank a security interest in its property to secure its obligation to reimburse Bank for any payment Bank has to make on the letter of credit to Creditor. Debtor failed to pay its obligation to Creditor within the one-year deadline, and Bank paid Creditor the amount owing on the letter of credit. Debtor filed in bankruptcy and its assets were liquidated. Bank received full payment from Debtor's estate on its secured claim. Debtor's trustee brought an action against Creditor to recover the amount paid to Bank on the secured claim on the ground that Creditor had received a voidable preference.

If Debtor had granted Creditor a security interest in its property rather than a letter of credit, there clearly would have been an avoidable preference: there would be a transfer of an interest in Debtor's property for the benefit of a creditor for the account of an antecedent debt made while Debtor was insolvent. The use by Debtor of a letter of credit does not change this result. The court in Matter of Compton Corp., 831 F.2d 586 (5th Cir.1987), held that there was a preferential transfer to Creditor even though Debtor transferred no property to Creditor. There is no requirement that the transfer of Debtor's property be to Creditor. A transfer of Debtor's property "to or for the benefit of" Creditor is sufficient under § 547(b)(1). Since the transfer was made on account of the past-due debt to Creditor, § 547(b)(2) is satisfied as well. Thus, there was a voidable preference to Creditor. However, there was no preference to the Bank because the transfer of the security interest to the Bank was a contemporaneous exchange for new value by Bank, the Bank's undertaking on the letter of credit.

FORM. LETTER OF CREDIT APPLICATION AND AGREEMENT

When an applicant requests a standby letter of credit, banks require completion of the following form which states the agreement between the applicant and issuing bank and the terms under which the bank must honor upon presentation of the letter of credit.

CITY NATIONAL BANK

INTERNATIONAL OPERATIONS CENTER

606 South Olive Street, Suite 300 Date:_______

CABLE ADDRESS "CINABANK LSA" Los Angeles, California 90014
TELEX 825717

IRREVOCABLE STANDBY LETTER OF CREDIT APPLICATION AND LETTER OF CREDIT AGREEMENT

TO: CITY NATIONAL BANK
(CNB)

We (Applicant) request you to establish by

- ☐ Cable
- ☐ Overnight courier service
- ☐ Same day messenger service

an irrevocable standby Letter of Credit on

the following terms and conditions:

ADVISING BANK (name and address)	APPLICANT (name and address)
BENEFICIARY (name and address)	AMOUNT indicate currency—i.e., U.S. $—and specify amount in figures and words
EXCEPT SO FAR AS OTHERWISE EXPRESSLY STATED THIS CREDIT WILL BE SUBJECT TO INTERNATIONAL STANDBY PRACTICES 1998 (ISP98), INTERNATIONAL CHAMBER OF COMMERCE PUBLICATION AS IN FORCE AS OF THE DATE OF ISSUANCE OF THE LETTER OF CREDIT	EXPIRY DATE AT CNB'S ISSUING OFFICE

available by Draft(s) at sight on CNB and accompanied by the following:

APPLICANT'S AGREEMENT TO PAY CNB

Applicant agrees immediately upon CNB's demand or if no demand is made then on_____, to repay to CNB the total amount of each disbursement by CNB under this Letter of Credit, together with interest thereon at the rate of____ percent per year in excess of the Prime Rate. The "Prime Rate" shall mean the floating loan rate of CNB announced from time to time as its "Prime Rate". Any change in the interest rate resulting from a change in the Prime Rate shall be effective on the effective date of change in the Prime Rate. Interest shall be calculated on a basis of a 360-day year and actual days elapsed. We further authorize you to charge, without further notice, our account, (or an account of any of us) for all such amounts when and as such are due and payable.

THE OPENING OF THIS CREDIT IS SUBJECT TO THE TERMS AND CONDITIONS AS SET FORTH IN THE LETTER OF CREDIT AGREEMENT APPEARING ON THE REVERSE HEREOF TO WHICH WE AGREE. WE FURTHER AGREE THAT THE CREDIT AS ISSUED SHALL INCLUDE SUCH REVISIONS OF THE LANGUAGE SET FORTH ABOVE AS YOU DEEM NECESSARY.

(APPLICANT)

FOR BANK USE ONLY:
APPROVAL OF CREDIT:
Lending Officer

Sr. Loan Officer (when applicable)

Branch

ACCOUNT TO BE DEBITED:
( ) Branch G/L No. 11305000
( ) Customer Acct. No.

FIRM NAME

AUTHORIZED SIGNATURE

SOCIAL SECURITY/TAXPAYER I.D. NO.

LETTER OF CREDIT AGREEMENT

In consideration of your opening, at our request, a letter of Credit (herein called "the Credit"), the terms and conditions of which appear on the reverse side hereof we hereby agree as follows:

1. As to drafts under or purporting to be under the Credit, which are payable in lawful United States funds, we agree to pay you on demand at your issuing office in lawful United States funds, the amount of such draft(s) on the presentment to you thereof or, at your request in advance.
2. As to drafts under or purporting to be under the Credit, which are payable in foreign currency, we agree to pay you at your office on demand, the equivalent of each such draft in lawful United States funds at your then prevailing rate of exchange effective for sales of that other currency for cable transfer to the country of which it is the currency.
3. We also agree to pay to you any attorneys' fees incurred in the enforcement of this Letter of Credit Agreement, your service charge in accordance with your Schedule of Fees and Charges now existing or as hereafter adopted, and all other charges and expenses paid or incurred by you in connection therewith.

4. We agree to reimburse you for any losses and charges incurred by you or made against you in connection with this Agreement and related to the reevaluation or fluctuations in the exchange rate of any currency whether United States or any other.
5. We hereby convey and transfer to you a security interest in all goods, documents and instruments which shall come into your control or into your possession or that of any of your correspondents as the result of opening or in connection with any transactions under the Credit, which goods, documents and instruments are and shall be granted to you as security (a) for all payments made or to be made by you or your correspondents under the Credit; (b) for any interest, commission or other customary charges in relation to the Credit and (c) for any other obligations or liabilities (absolute or contingent) of us to you, which now exist or are hereafter created. Upon any default by us in any of the undertakings set forth in this Letter of Credit Agreement, you are authorized to sell, under the provisions of the Commercial Code of the State of California, any or all goods, documents and instruments; in the event of any deficiency, we will pay the same to you immediately or in the event of any surplus, you shall pay the same to us or to the persons entitled thereto. In the event such described property should suffer any decline in value we will upon demand, deliver to you additional collateral to your satisfaction.
6. We agree that your rights and duties under the Credit are, except as otherwise provided herein, governed by the International Standby Practices 1998 (ISP98), International Chamber of Commerce Publication as in force on the date of issuance of the Credit.
7. We agree that in the event of any amendments or modifications of the terms of the Credit, this Agreement shall be binding upon us with regard to the Credit so amended. You may (at your option) issue the requested Credit through a correspondent of your choice.
8. The users of the Letter of Credit shall be deemed our agents and we assume all risks of their acts of omissions. Neither you nor your correspondents shall be responsible for/or: the validity, sufficiency, or genuineness of documents, even if such documents should in fact prove to be in any or all respects invalid, insufficient, fraudulent or forged; the solvency or responsibility of any party issuing any documents; delay in arrival or failure to arrive of any documents; delay in giving or failure to give notice of arrival or any other notice; failure of any draft to bear adequate reference to the Credit; failure of documents to accompany any draft at negotiation, or failure of any person to note the amount of any draft on the reverse of the Credit, to surrender or take up the Credit or to send documents apart from drafts as required by the terms of the Credit, each of which provisions, if contained in the Credit itself, it is agreed may be waived by you; errors, or omissions, or interruptions or delays in transmission or delivery of any message by mail, cable, telegraph, wireless or otherwise; nor shall you be responsible for any error, neglect, or default of any of your correspondents; and none of the above shall affect, impair, or prevent the vesting of any of your rights or powers hereunder. In furtherance and extension and not in limitation of the specific provisions hereinbefore set forth, we agree that any action taken by you or any correspondent of you under or in connection with the Credit or relative drafts or documents, if taken in good faith, shall be binding on us and shall not put you or your correspondent under any resulting liability to us.
9. We agree at any time and from time to time, on demand, to deliver, convey, transfer, or assign to you, as security for any and all of our obligations and liabilities hereunder, and also for any and all other obligations and liabilities, absolute or contingent, due or to become due, which are or may at any time hereafter be owing to you, additional security of a value and character satisfactory to you, or to make such cash payment as you may require. We agree that all property belonging to us, or in which we may have an interest, conveyed, transferred, assigned, or paid to you, or coming into your possession or into the possession of anyone for you in any manner whatsoever, whether expressly as security, or for safekeeping or otherwise including any items received for collection or transmission and the proceeds thereof, whether or not such property is in whole or in part released to us on trust of bailee receipt, is security for each and all such obligations and liabilities. We agree that upon our failure at all times to keep a margin of security with you satisfactory to you, or upon the making by us of any assignments for the benefit of creditors, or upon the filing of any voluntary or involuntary petition in bankruptcy by or against us, or upon any application for the appointment of a receiver of any of our

property, or upon any act of bankruptcy or state of insolvency of us, or if you in good faith deem yourself insecure at any time, or upon the death of any of us, all of such obligations and liabilities shall become and be immediately due and payable without demand or notice notwithstanding any credit or time allowed to us, or any instrument evidencing any such obligation or otherwise; and each of us, and all of us, as to property in which we may have any interest, expressly authorize you in any such event or upon our failure to pay any of such obligations or liabilities when it or they shall become or be made due, to sell all such property, in accordance with the Commercial Code of the State of California and to apply the net proceeds of such sale or sales, together with any balance of deposits and any sum credited by or due from you to us, in general accounts or otherwise, to the payment of all of our obligations or liabilities to you however arising.

10. Your rights specified in this Agreement are in addition to any created by statute or rule of law. You are expressly given the right to execute and file and record endorsements, assignments, financing statements, and other instruments in the name of any of us with respect to documents, property and interests relative to the Credit or any property of any of us in which you have a security interest which may at any time come into your possession under the Credit or by virtue of this Agreement. We agree to pay all expenses, filing fees and other charges incurred by you relative to the perfection or enforcement of your rights and security interests hereunder.
11. You shall not be deemed to have waived any of your rights hereunder, unless you or your authorized agent shall have signed such waiver, in writing. No such waiver unless expressly stated therein shall be effective as to any transaction which occurs subsequent to the date of such waiver, nor as to any continuance of a breach after such waiver.
12. We understand that any credit issued pursuant to this Agreement is the direct obligation of you established in favor of our designated beneficiaries. Once established, such credit is irrevocable and is not subject to recall or stop payment, and any claim or demand by us to stop payment thereunder is void and of no effect.
13. The word "property" as used in this Agreement includes goods, merchandise, securities, funds, choses in action, and any and all other forms of property, whether real, personal or mixed and any right or interest therein.
14. This Agreement incorporates the provisions on the reverse hereof. Time is of the essence. Acceptance by you of partial or delinquent payments or your failure to exercise any right, power or remedy shall not waive any obligation of us or modify this Agreement. You, your successors and assigns have all rights, powers and remedies herein and as provided by law, and may exercise the same and effect any set-off and proceed against any security for the obligations of us at any time notwithstanding any cessation of our liability or running of any statute of limitations, which we hereby waive to the fullest extent permitted by law. Notice to you must be given at the office of City National Bank to which this Credit and Agreement is addressed.
15. We hereby agree to pay all reasonable fees and costs incurred by you and arising out of any act or action you may take to enforce any provision of this Agreement or to enforce collection of any sums, payments or obligations owing from us to you.
16. If this Agreement is signed by one individual the terms, "we", "our", "us", shall be read throughout as "I", "my", "me", as the case may be. If this Agreement is signed by two or more parties, it shall be the joint and several Agreement of such parties.

APPENDIX

PROMISSORY NOTES

On *, *, the undersigned, * ("Borrower"), promises to pay to the order of City National Bank, a national banking association ("CNB"), at its office in this city, in lawful money of the United States of America and in immediately available funds, the principal sum of * Dollars ($*), or so much thereof as may be advanced and be outstanding, with interest thereon to be computed on each advance from the date of its disbursement at a rate computed on the basis of a 360–day year, actual days elapsed, equal to the Prime Rate of CNB, as it exists from time to time, plus * percent (*%) per year. "Prime Rate" shall mean the rate most recently announced by CNB at its principal office in Beverly Hills, California, as its "Prime Rate." Any change in the Prime Rate shall become effective on the same business day on which the Prime Rate shall change, without prior notice to Borrower.

All or any portion of the principal of this Note may be borrowed, repaid and reborrowed from time to time prior to maturity, provided at the time of any borrowing no Event of Default (as herein defined) exists, and provided further that the total borrowings outstanding at any one time shall not exceed the principal amount stated above. Each borrowing and repayment hereunder shall be noted in the books and records of CNB. The excess of borrowings over repayments shall evidence the principal balance due hereon from time to time and at any time. Borrowings hereunder shall be conclusively presumed to have been made to or for the benefit of Borrower when made as noted in such books and records.

Interest accrued on this Note shall be payable on the * day of each *, commencing *, *.

The occurrence of any of the following with respect to any Borrower or any guarantor of this Note or any general partner of such Borrower or guarantor, shall constitute an "Event of Default" hereunder:

1. The failure to make any payment of principal or interest when due under this Note;
2. The filing of a petition by or against any of such parties under any provisions of the Bankruptcy Code;
3. The appointment of a receiver or an assignee for the benefit of creditors;

4. The commencement of dissolution or liquidation proceedings or the disqualification of any such parties which is a corporation, partnership, joint venture or any other type of entity;

5. The death or incapacity of any of such parties who is an individual;

6. The revocation of any guaranty of this Note, or any guaranty becomes unenforceable as to any future advances under this Note;

7. Any financial statement provided by any of such parties to CNB is false or misleading;

8. Any material default in the payment or performance of any obligation, or any default under any provisions of any contract or instrument pursuant to which any of such parties has incurred any obligation for borrowed money, any purchase obligation or any other liability of any kind to any person or entity, including CNB;

9. Any sale or transfer of all or a substantial or material part of the assets of any of such parties other than in the ordinary course of business; or

10. Any violation, breach or default under any letter agreement, guaranty, security agreement, deed of trust or any other contract or instrument executed in connection with this Note or securing this Note.

Upon the occurrence of any Event of Default, CNB, at its option, may declare all sums of principal and interest outstanding hereunder to be immediately due and payable without presentment, demand, protest or notice of dishonor all of which are expressly waived by each Borrower, and CNB shall have no obligation to make any further advances hereunder. Each Borrower agrees to pay all costs and expenses, including reasonable attorneys' fees, expended or incurred by CNB (or allocable to CNB's in-house counsel) in connection with the enforcement of this Note or the collection of any sums due hereunder and irrespective of whether suit is filed. Any principal or interest not paid when due hereunder shall thereafter bear additional interest from its due date at a rate of five percent (5.0%) per year higher than the interest rate as determined and computed above, and continuing thereafter until paid.

Should more than one person or entity execute this Note as a Borrower, the obligations of each Borrower shall be joint and several.

This Note and all matters relating thereto, shall be governed by the laws of the State of California.

REVOLVING NOTE (With Accounts Receivable Borrowing Base)

On *, *, a * ("Borrower"), promises to pay to the order of City National Bank, a national banking association ("CNB"), at its office in this city, in United States Dollars and in immediately available funds, the principal sum of * Dollars ($*) ("Revolving Credit Commitment"), or so much thereof as may be advanced and be outstanding, with interest thereon to be computed on each advance from the date of its disbursement at a rate computed on a basis of a

360–day year, actual days elapsed, equal to the "Prime Rate" of CNB, as it exists from time to time, plus * percent (*%) per year. "Prime Rate" shall mean the rate most recently announced by CNB at its principal office in Beverly Hills, California, as its "Prime Rate." Any change in the Prime Rate shall become effective on the same business day on which the Prime Rate shall change, without prior notice to Borrower.

As provided herein, the principal of this Note may be borrowed, repaid and reborrowed from time to time prior to maturity, provided at the time of any borrowing no Event of Default (as hereinafter defined) exists, and provided further that the total borrowings outstanding at any one time shall not exceed the lesser of (i) the Revolving Credit Commitment or (ii) * percent (*%) of the total Eligible Accounts Receivable owing to Borrower from time to time. Each borrowing and repayment hereunder shall be noted in the books and records of CNB. The excess of borrowings over repayments shall evidence the principal balance due hereon from time to time and at any time. Borrowings hereunder shall be presumed to have been made to or for the benefit of Borrower when made as noted in such books and records.

Interest accruing on this Note shall be payable on the * day of each month, commencing *, *.

Eligible Accounts Receivable shall mean those accounts receivable owed to Borrower:

A. Upon which Borrower's right to receive payment is absolute and not contingent upon the fulfillment of any condition whatsoever;

B. Against which is asserted no defense, counterclaim, discount or setoff, whether well-founded or otherwise;

C. That is a true and correct statement of a bona fide indebtedness incurred in the amount of the account receivable for goods sold or leased and delivered to, or for services rendered to and accepted by, the account debtor;

D. That is owned by Borrower free and clear of all liens, encumbrances, charges, interests and rights of others, except security interests granted to CNB;

E. That does not arise from a sale or lease to or for services rendered to any employee, stockholder, director, *[S]ubsidiary or affiliate of Borrower or any entity in which any employee, stockholder, director, *[S]ubsidiary or affiliate of Borrower has any interest;

F. That is not the obligation of an account debtor that is the federal government unless perfected under the Assignment of Claims Act;

G. That is not the obligation of an account debtor located in a foreign country;

H. That is due and payable not more than thirty (30) days from the date of the billing therefor unless otherwise agreed to in writing by CNB;

I. As to which not more than ninety (90) days have elapsed since the original invoice date;

J. As to which the account debtor has not:

(i) died, suspended business, made a general assignment for the benefit of creditors, become the subject of a petition under the *Bankruptcy Code* or consented to or applied for the appointment of a receiver, trustee, custodian or liquidator for itself or any of its property;

(ii) become more than sixty (60) days past due, under the original terms of sale, with respect to 20% or more of the amounts owed by such account debtor to Borrower;

(iii) had its check in payment of an account receivable returned unpaid; or

(iv) become or appear to have become unable, in the opinion of CNB, to pay the account receivable in accordance with its terms; and

K. That does not, when added to all other accounts receivable that are obligations of the account debtor to Borrower, at any time result in a total sum that exceeds twenty percent (20%) of the total balance then due on all accounts receivable.

The occurrence of any of the following with respect to any Borrower or guarantor of this Note or any general partner of such Borrower or guarantor, shall constitute an "Event of Default" hereunder:

1. Failure to make any payment of principal or interest when due under this Note;

2. Filing of a petition by or against any of such parties under any provision of the *Bankruptcy Code*;

3. Appointment of a receiver or an assignee for the benefit of creditors;

4. Commencement of dissolution or liquidation proceedings or the disqualification (under any applicable law or regulation) of any of such parties which is a corporation, partnership, joint venture or any other type of entity;

5. Death or incapacity of any of such parties which is an individual;

6. Revocation of any guaranty of this Note, or any guaranty of this Note becomes unenforceable as to any future advances under this Note;

7. Any financial statement provided by any of such parties to CNB is false or materially misleading;

8. Any material default in the payment or performance of any obligation, or any default under any provision of any contract or instrument pursuant to which any of such parties has incurred any obligation for borrowed

money, any purchase obligation or any other liability of any kind to any person or entity, including CNB;

9. Any sale or transfer of all or a substantial part of the assets of any of such parties other than in the ordinary course of business;

10. Any violation, breach or default under this Note, any letter agreement, guaranty, security agreement, deed of trust, subordination agreement or any other contract or instrument executed in connection with this Note or securing this Note;

11. Failure of Borrower, after twenty (20) days' written notice from CNB to Borrower, to reduce the principal balance hereunder to * percent (*%) of the total Eligible Accounts Receivable owing to Borrower;

12. Any obligee of *[S]*ubordinated *[D]*ebt shall fail to comply with the subordination provisions of the documents or instruments, including, without limitation, any subordination agreement, evidencing or relating to such *[S]*ubordinated *[D]*ebt;

13. Failure of Borrower to furnish CNB, within the times specified, the following statements:

13.1. Within *[forty-five (45)/sixty (60)]* days after the end of each quarterly accounting period of each fiscal year, a financial statement consisting of not less than a balance sheet, *[and income statement, reconciliation of net worth and statement of cash flows,]* with notes thereto, prepared in accordance with generally accepted accounting principles consistently applied, which financial statement may be internally prepared;

13.2. Within *[ninety (90)/one hundred twenty (120)]* days after the close of each fiscal year, a copy of the annual *[audit report/review report/compilation report]* for such year for Borrower and the Subsidiaries including therein a balance sheet, income statement, reconciliation of net worth and statement of cash flows, with notes thereto, the balance sheet, income statement and statement of cash flows to be *[audited/reviewed/ compiled]* by a certified public accountant acceptable to CNB, and *[certified by such accountants to have been]* prepared in accordance with generally accepted accounting principles consistently applied and accompanied by Borrower's certification as to whether any event has occurred which constitutes an Event of Default, and if so, stating the facts with respect thereto;

13.3. *[Monthly/quarterly]* reports of agings of Borrower's accounts payable and accounts receivable, together with a current list of names and addresses of all account debtors, as soon as available, but in no event later than thirty (30) days after the end of each *[month/fiscal quarter]*;

13.4. The Federal Income Tax Return for Borrower and each guarantor of this Note, *[and each general partner of Borrower or guarantor,]* within ten (10) days after its filing of each Return, respectively; and

13.5. Such additional information, reports and/or statements as CNB may, from time to time, reasonably request.

14. Failure of Borrower to furnish current financial statements of each guarantor of this Note *[and each general partner of Borrower or such guarantor]* on CNB's form or in such other form acceptable to CNB, certified by such guarantor *[or general partner]* to be true and correct, delivered within ninety (90) days after Borrower's fiscal year end of each year;

15. Failure of Borrower to maintain the following:

15.1. Tangible Net Worth [plus Subordinated Debt] of not less than $* at all times;

15.2. A ratio of Total Senior Liabilities to Tangible Net Worth *[plus Subordinated Debt*] of not more than * to 1 at all times;

15.3. A ratio of Current Assets to Current Liabilities of not less than * to 1 at all times;

15.4. A ratio of Quick Assets to Current Liabilities of not less than * to 1 at all times; and

15.5. Working Capital of not less than $* at all times.

For purposes of this Note, the following terms have the following meanings:

"Current Assets" shall be determined on a consolidated basis for Borrower and the Subsidiaries in accordance with generally accepted accounting principles, consistently applied, excluding, however, from the determination of Current Assets, loans to shareholders, management or employees, amounts due from Subsidiaries or affiliates, deferred costs, and other intangible assets.

"Current Liabilities" shall be determined on a consolidated basis for Borrower and the Subsidiaries in accordance with generally accepted accounting principles, consistently applied, and shall include without limitation (a) all payments on Subordinated Debt required to be made within one (1) year after the date on which the determination is made; and (b) all indebtedness payable to stockholders, affiliates, Subsidiaries or officers regardless of maturity, unless such indebtedness shall have been subordinated to CNB, on terms satisfactory to CNB.

"Quick Assets" shall mean the sum of cash, plus cash equivalents, plus accounts receivable, plus securities classified as short-term marketable securities according to generally accepted accounting principles, consistently applied, as such items appear on Borrower's consolidated balance sheet, determined in accordance with generally accepted accounting principles consistently applied.

"Subordinated Debt" shall mean indebtedness of Borrower or any Subsidiary the repayment of principal and interest of which is subordinated to CNB, on terms satisfactory to CNB.

"Subsidiary" shall mean any corporation, the majority of whose voting shares are at any time owned, directly or indirectly by Borrower and/or by one or more Subsidiaries.

"Tangible Net Worth" shall mean the total of all assets appearing on a balance sheet prepared in accordance with generally accepted accounting principles consistently applied for Borrower and the Subsidiaries on a consolidated basis, minus (a) all intangible assets, including, without limitation, unamortized debt discount, affiliate, employee and officer receivables or advances, goodwill, research and development costs, patents, trademarks, the excess of purchase price over underlying values of acquired companies, any covenants not to compete, deferred charges, copyrights, franchises and appraisal surplus; minus (b) all obligations which are required by generally accepted accounting principles consistently applied to be reflected as a liability on the consolidated balance sheet of Borrower and the Subsidiaries; minus, (c) the amount, if any, at which shares of stock of a non-wholly owned Subsidiary appear on the asset side of Borrower's consolidated balance sheet, as determined in accordance with generally accepted accounting principles consistently applied; minus (d) minority interests; and minus (e) deferred income and reserves not otherwise reflected as a liability on the consolidated balance sheet of Borrower and the Subsidiaries.

"Total Senior Liabilities" shall mean, as of any date of determination, the amount of all obligations that should be reflected as a liability on a consolidated balance sheet of Borrower and the Subsidiaries prepared in accordance with generally accepted accounting principles, consistently applied, less Subordinated Debt.

"Working Capital" shall mean Current Assets minus Current Liabilities.

Upon the occurrence of any Event of Default, CNB, at its option, may declare all sums of principal and interest outstanding hereunder to be immediately due and payable without presentment, demand, protest or notice of dishonor all of which are expressly waived by Borrower, and CNB shall have no obligation to make any further advances hereunder. Borrower agrees to pay all costs and expenses, including reasonable attorneys' fees (which counsel may be CNB employees), expended or incurred by CNB (or allocable to CNB's in-house counsel) in connection with the enforcement of this Note or the collection of any sums due hereunder and irrespective of whether suit is filed. Any principal or interest not paid when due hereunder shall thereafter bear additional interest from its due date at a rate of five percent (5.0%) per year higher than the interest rate as determined and computed above, and continuing thereafter until paid.

Should more than one person or entity execute this Note as Borrower, the liability and obligations of each Borrower shall be joint and several.

This Note and all matters relating thereto, shall be governed by the laws of the State of California.

Index

CASHIER'S CHECKS